GOOD AND EVIL

Writer: MICHAEL PEARL

Pencils: DANNY BULANADI   **Colors:** CLINT CEARLEY

Inks: DANNY BULANADI   **Letters:** CLINT CEARLEY

Good and Evil®
Copyright © 2006 by Michael and Debi Pearl
ISBN-13: 978-1-892112-38-5
ISBN-10: 1-892112-38-8
First printing: June 2006 – 20,000

Visit www.NoGreaterJoy.org for information on other products produced by No Greater Joy Ministries.

Requests for information should be addressed to:
No Greater Joy Ministries Inc. *1000 Pearl Road, Pleasantville, TN 37033 USA*

The King James Holy Bible is the written word of God to English-speaking people. This product is a story form of God's word. We encourage you to look up the reference verses at the bottom of the pages for an in depth study of God's word corresponding with this book.

Printed in the United States of America

INTRODUCTION

This book is the product of seven years. It began as the answer to a need. The greatest endeavor on the earth is to take the message of Jesus Christ to those who have never heard. Michael and Debi Pearl, founders and directors of No Greater Joy Ministries, have participated in and supported missionaries for over forty years. When their daughter Rebekah was a missionary to a primitive tribe on a remote mountain in the highlands of Papua New Guinea, they sought to acquire simple Bible story art that could be translated into the language of the Kumboi tribe. Art was available, but it was either poorly done or expensive to purchase. So Michael put out an APB for a first class professional artist.

Several years earlier, Danny Bulanadi, an artist for Marvel Comics, heard the gospel of Jesus Christ and became a born again Christian. He was not comfortable with the work he was doing and so quit to become a night watchman in San Francisco. Danny and Michael got together and developed a plan. Michael, somewhat of an artist himself, wrote the script and did rough sketches of each frame, and then turned them over to Danny. Danny developed it into the best-drawn Bible comic of all times. It was a long tedious process of sometimes drawing and redrawing. The finished ink drawings were then put into the computer and Clint Cearley did the shading in Photoshop. Next came the addition of balloons and text, another time-consuming process. Finally the editing and proofing.

It was our intention from the beginning that the art not look like the typical religious art. We wanted the traditional comic that is so familiar all over the world. We have created a product that will sell itself on any roadside stand in Thailand or India. It will find acceptance in countries otherwise closed to Christians. A box of them can be given to a Moslem or Hindu vendor, and he will put them on his stand for sale. They will go where no Bible is allowed, but they will carry the same message.

You will not find the story of David and Goliath or of Daniel in the Lions' den. It is impossible to cover the entire Bible in just three hundred pages. But the stories are not arbitrarily chosen. This is a chronological presentation of the Bible message, providing just that Old Testament background that is pertinent to one's understanding of who Jehovah God is and of the gospel of Jesus Christ.

As this first printing goes to press, the text is already being translated into over 11 languages. Proceeds from the sale of this book in English make it possible for us to provide it free to missionaries in many foreign languages.

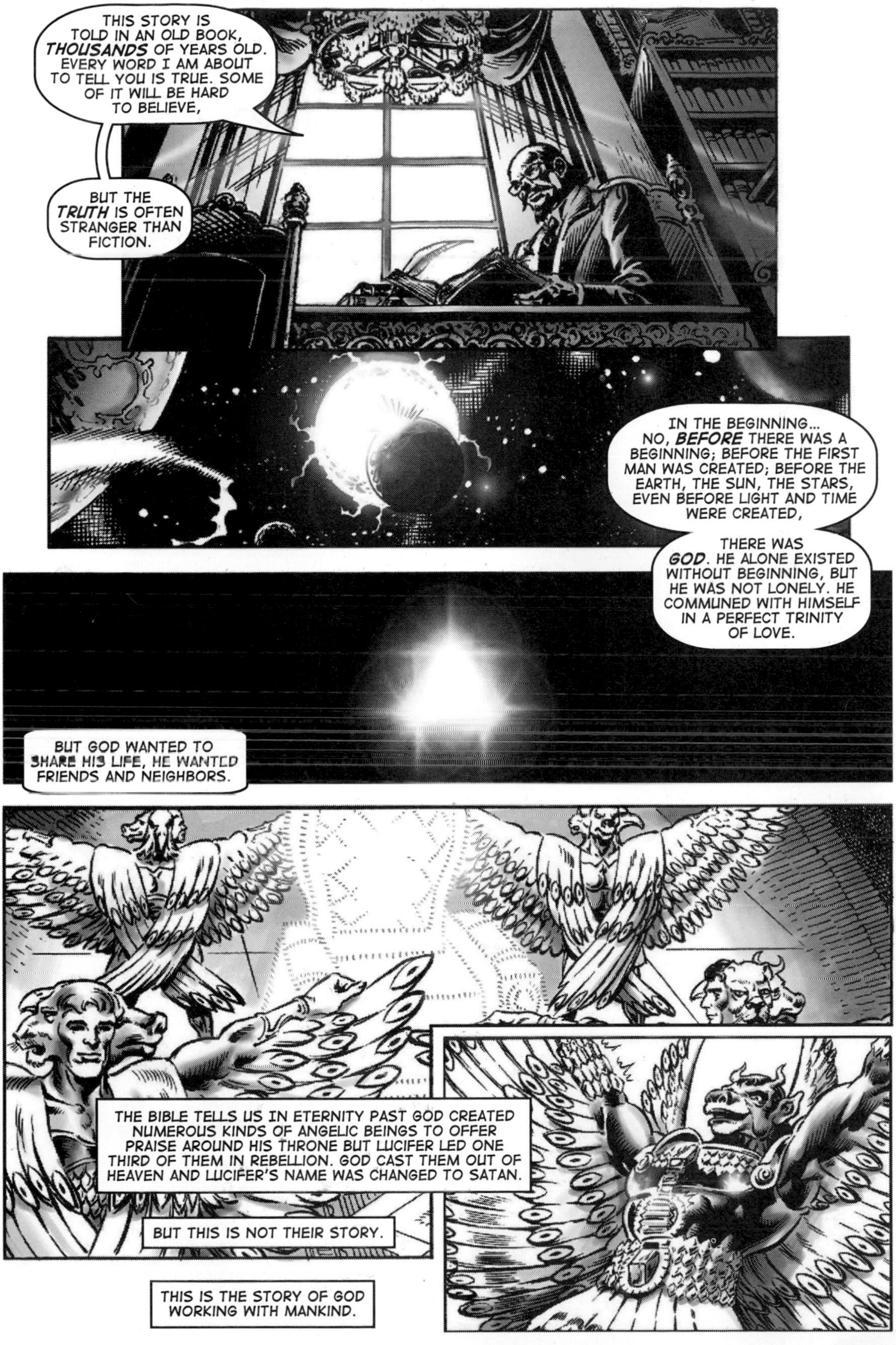
THIS STORY IS TOLD IN AN OLD BOOK, THOUSANDS OF YEARS OLD. EVERY WORD I AM ABOUT TO TELL YOU IS TRUE. SOME OF IT WILL BE HARD TO BELIEVE,
BUT THE TRUTH IS OFTEN STRANGER THAN FICTION.
IN THE BEGINNING... NO, BEFORE THERE WAS A BEGINNING; BEFORE THE FIRST MAN WAS CREATED; BEFORE THE EARTH, THE SUN, THE STARS, EVEN BEFORE LIGHT AND TIME WERE CREATED,
THERE WAS GOD. HE ALONE EXISTED WITHOUT BEGINNING, BUT HE WAS NOT LONELY. HE COMMUNED WITH HIMSELF IN A PERFECT TRINITY OF LOVE.
BUT GOD WANTED TO SHARE HIS LIFE, HE WANTED FRIENDS AND NEIGHBORS.
THE BIBLE TELLS US IN ETERNITY PAST GOD CREATED NUMEROUS KINDS OF ANGELIC BEINGS TO OFFER PRAISE AROUND HIS THRONE BUT LUCIFER LED ONE THIRD OF THEM IN REBELLION. GOD CAST THEM OUT OF HEAVEN AND LUCIFER'S NAME WAS CHANGED TO SATAN.
BUT THIS IS NOT THEIR STORY.
THIS IS THE STORY OF GOD WORKING WITH MANKIND.

SATAN'S HISTORY AND FUTURE CAN BE FOUND IN: ISAIAH 14:12-14; EZEKIEL 28:13-19; MATTHEW 25:41; LUKE 10:18; REVELATION 12:4, 20:2. ISA 45:18

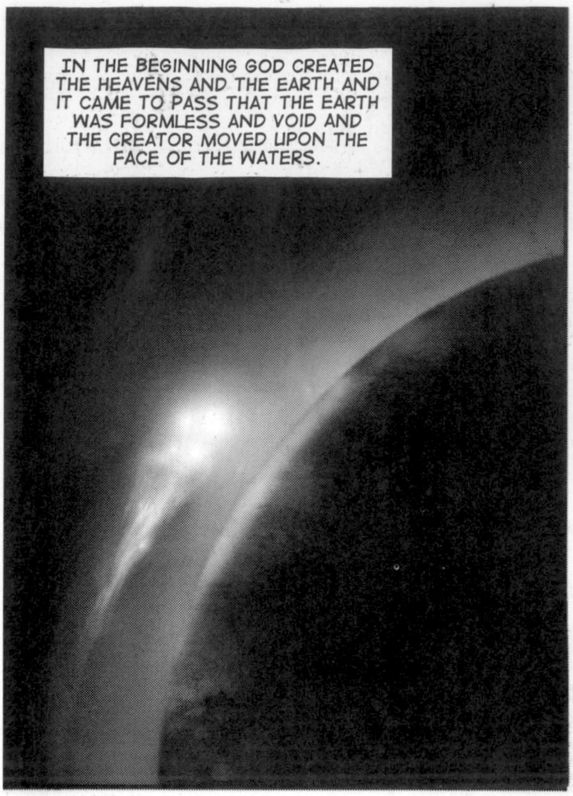
IN THE BEGINNING GOD CREATED THE HEAVENS AND THE EARTH AND IT CAME TO PASS THAT THE EARTH WAS FORMLESS AND VOID AND THE CREATOR MOVED UPON THE FACE OF THE WATERS.

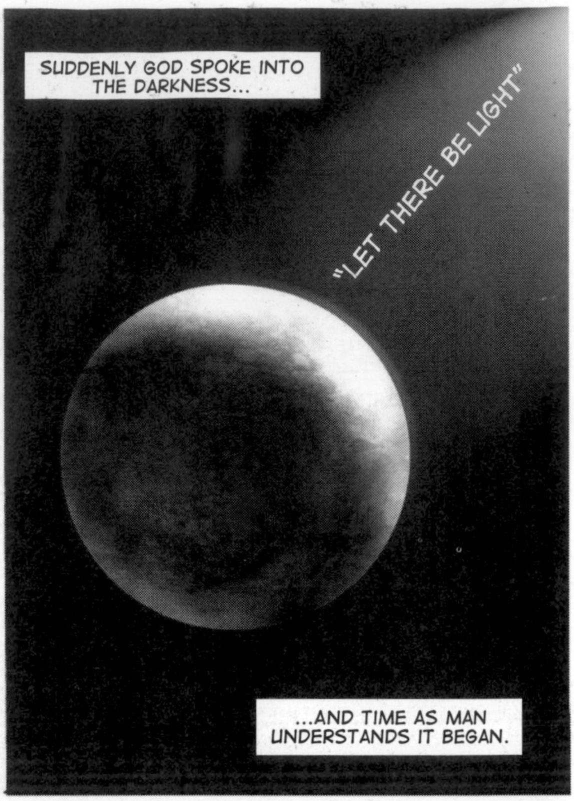
SUDDENLY GOD SPOKE INTO THE DARKNESS...
"LET THERE BE LIGHT"
...AND TIME AS MAN UNDERSTANDS IT BEGAN.

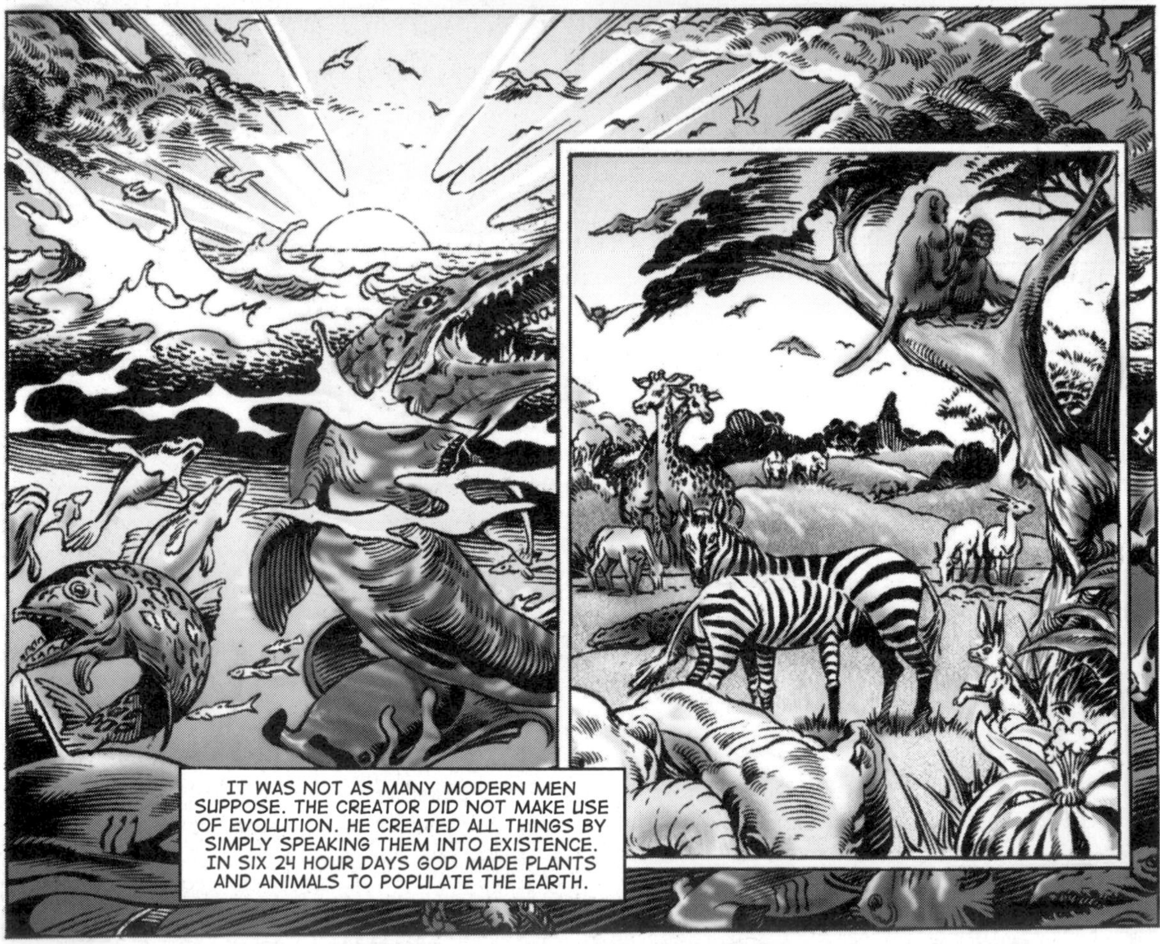
IT WAS NOT AS MANY MODERN MEN SUPPOSE. THE CREATOR DID NOT MAKE USE OF EVOLUTION. HE CREATED ALL THINGS BY SIMPLY SPEAKING THEM INTO EXISTENCE. IN SIX 24 HOUR DAYS GOD MADE PLANTS AND ANIMALS TO POPULATE THE EARTH.

APPROXIMATELY 4004 B.C. - GENESIS 1:2-3

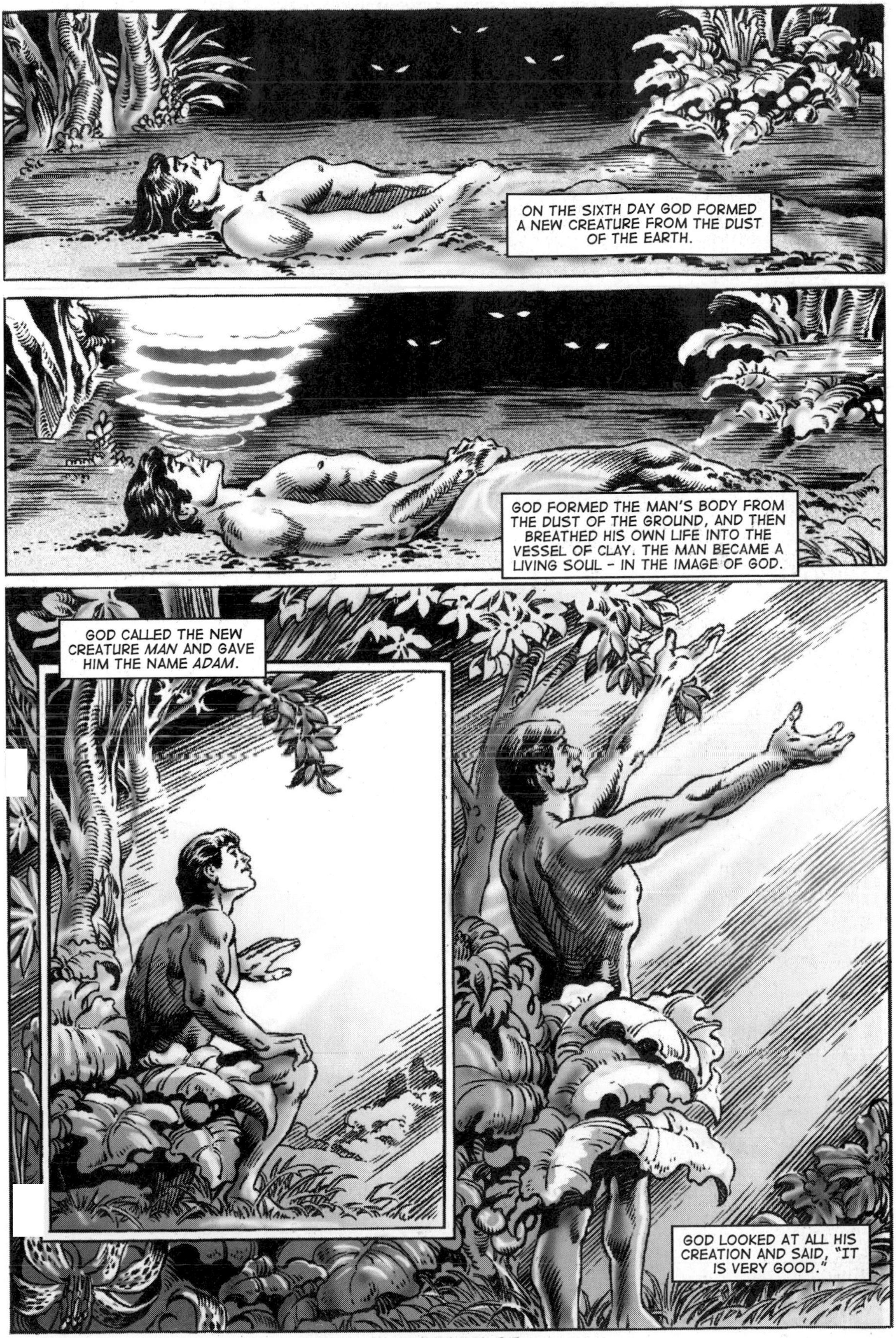
ON THE SIXTH DAY GOD FORMED A NEW CREATURE FROM THE DUST OF THE EARTH.
GOD FORMED THE MAN'S BODY FROM THE DUST OF THE GROUND, AND THEN BREATHED HIS OWN LIFE INTO THE VESSEL OF CLAY. THE MAN BECAME A LIVING SOUL - IN THE IMAGE OF GOD.
GOD CALLED THE NEW CREATURE *MAN* AND GAVE HIM THE NAME *ADAM*.
GOD LOOKED AT ALL HIS CREATION AND SAID, "IT IS VERY GOOD."

GENESIS 1:31, 2:7

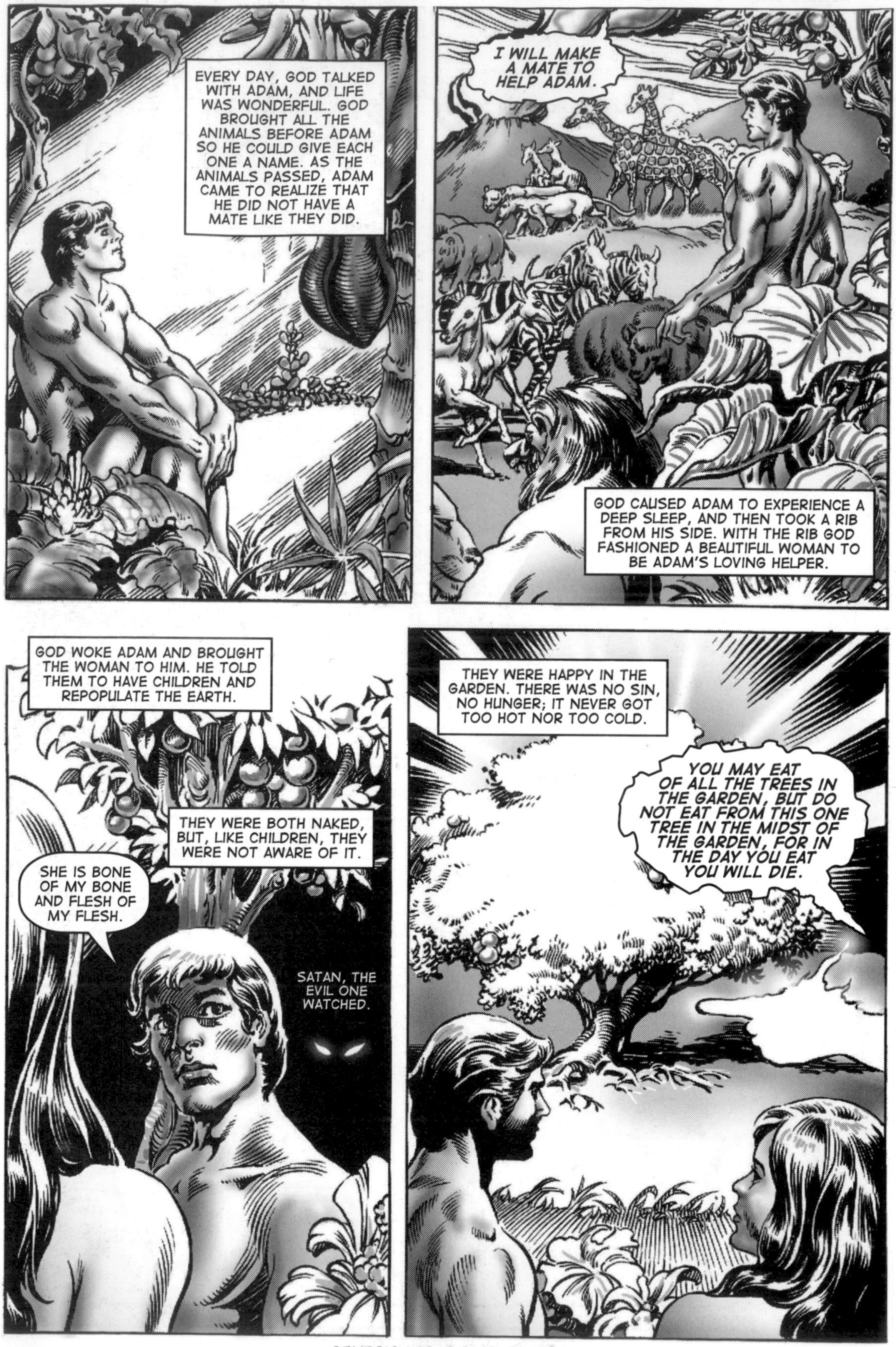
EVERY DAY, GOD TALKED WITH ADAM, AND LIFE WAS WONDERFUL. GOD BROUGHT ALL THE ANIMALS BEFORE ADAM SO HE COULD GIVE EACH ONE A NAME. AS THE ANIMALS PASSED, ADAM CAME TO REALIZE THAT HE DID NOT HAVE A MATE LIKE THEY DID.
I WILL MAKE A MATE TO HELP ADAM.
GOD CAUSED ADAM TO EXPERIENCE A DEEP SLEEP, AND THEN TOOK A RIB FROM HIS SIDE. WITH THE RIB GOD FASHIONED A BEAUTIFUL WOMAN TO BE ADAM'S LOVING HELPER.
GOD WOKE ADAM AND BROUGHT THE WOMAN TO HIM. HE TOLD THEM TO HAVE CHILDREN AND REPOPULATE THE EARTH.
THEY WERE BOTH NAKED, BUT, LIKE CHILDREN, THEY WERE NOT AWARE OF IT.
SHE IS BONE OF MY BONE AND FLESH OF MY FLESH.
SATAN, THE EVIL ONE WATCHED.
THEY WERE HAPPY IN THE GARDEN. THERE WAS NO SIN, NO HUNGER; IT NEVER GOT TOO HOT NOR TOO COLD.
YOU MAY EAT OF ALL THE TREES IN THE GARDEN, BUT DO NOT EAT FROM THIS ONE TREE IN THE MIDST OF THE GARDEN, FOR IN THE DAY YOU EAT YOU WILL DIE.

GENESIS 1:28, 2:2, 16-22, 25

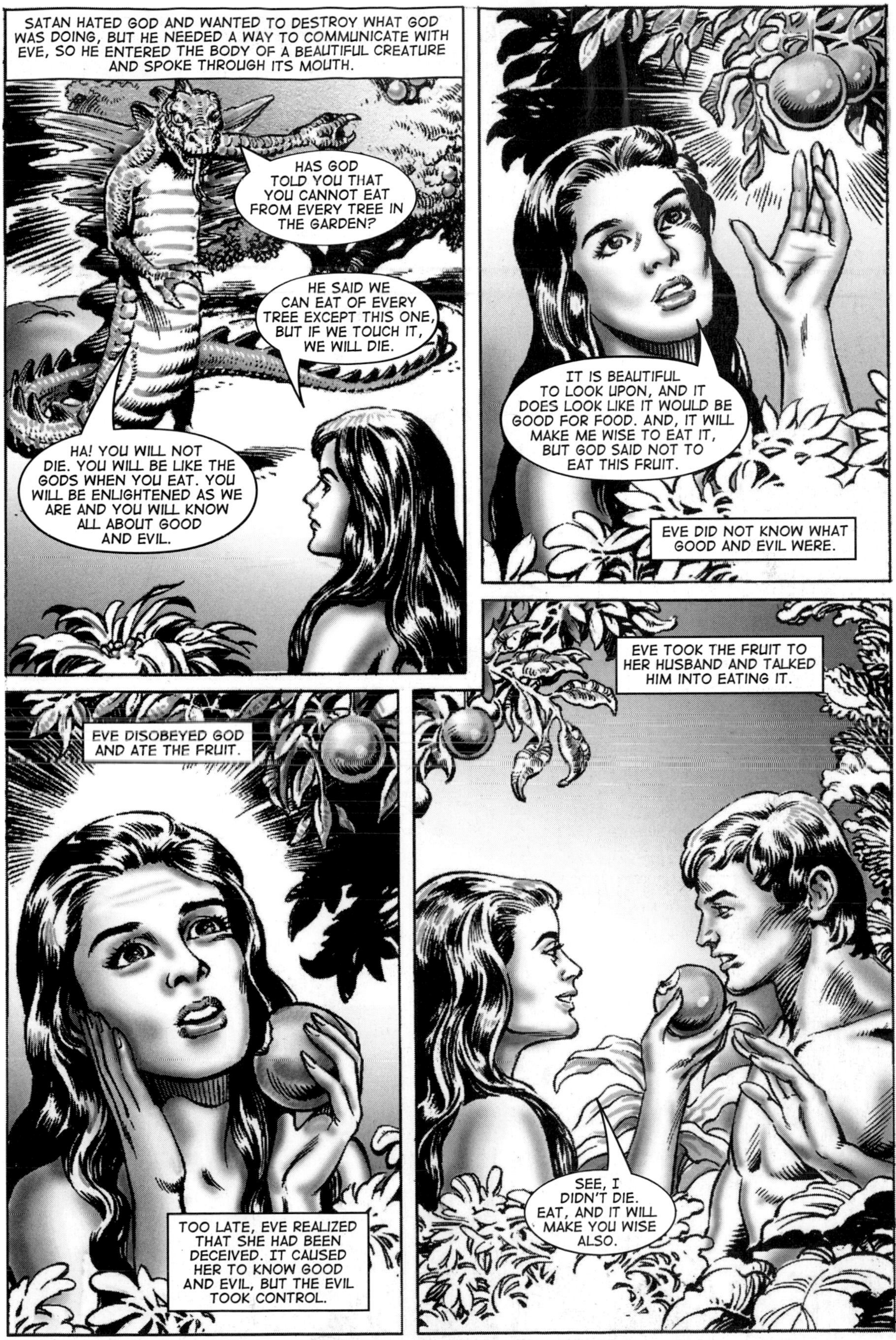
SATAN HATED GOD AND WANTED TO DESTROY WHAT GOD WAS DOING, BUT HE NEEDED A WAY TO COMMUNICATE WITH EVE, SO HE ENTERED THE BODY OF A BEAUTIFUL CREATURE AND SPOKE THROUGH ITS MOUTH.
HAS GOD TOLD YOU THAT YOU CANNOT EAT FROM EVERY TREE IN THE GARDEN?
HE SAID WE CAN EAT OF EVERY TREE EXCEPT THIS ONE, BUT IF WE TOUCH IT, WE WILL DIE.
HA! YOU WILL NOT DIE. YOU WILL BE LIKE THE GODS WHEN YOU EAT. YOU WILL BE ENLIGHTENED AS WE ARE AND YOU WILL KNOW ALL ABOUT GOOD AND EVIL.
IT IS BEAUTIFUL TO LOOK UPON, AND IT DOES LOOK LIKE IT WOULD BE GOOD FOR FOOD. AND, IT WILL MAKE ME WISE TO EAT IT, BUT GOD SAID NOT TO EAT THIS FRUIT.
EVE DID NOT KNOW WHAT GOOD AND EVIL WERE.
EVE DISOBEYED GOD AND ATE THE FRUIT.
TOO LATE, EVE REALIZED THAT SHE HAD BEEN DECEIVED. IT CAUSED HER TO KNOW GOOD AND EVIL, BUT THE EVIL TOOK CONTROL.
EVE TOOK THE FRUIT TO HER HUSBAND AND TALKED HIM INTO EATING IT.
SEE, I DIDN'T DIE. EAT, AND IT WILL MAKE YOU WISE ALSO.

GENESIS 3:1-6; REVELATION 20:2

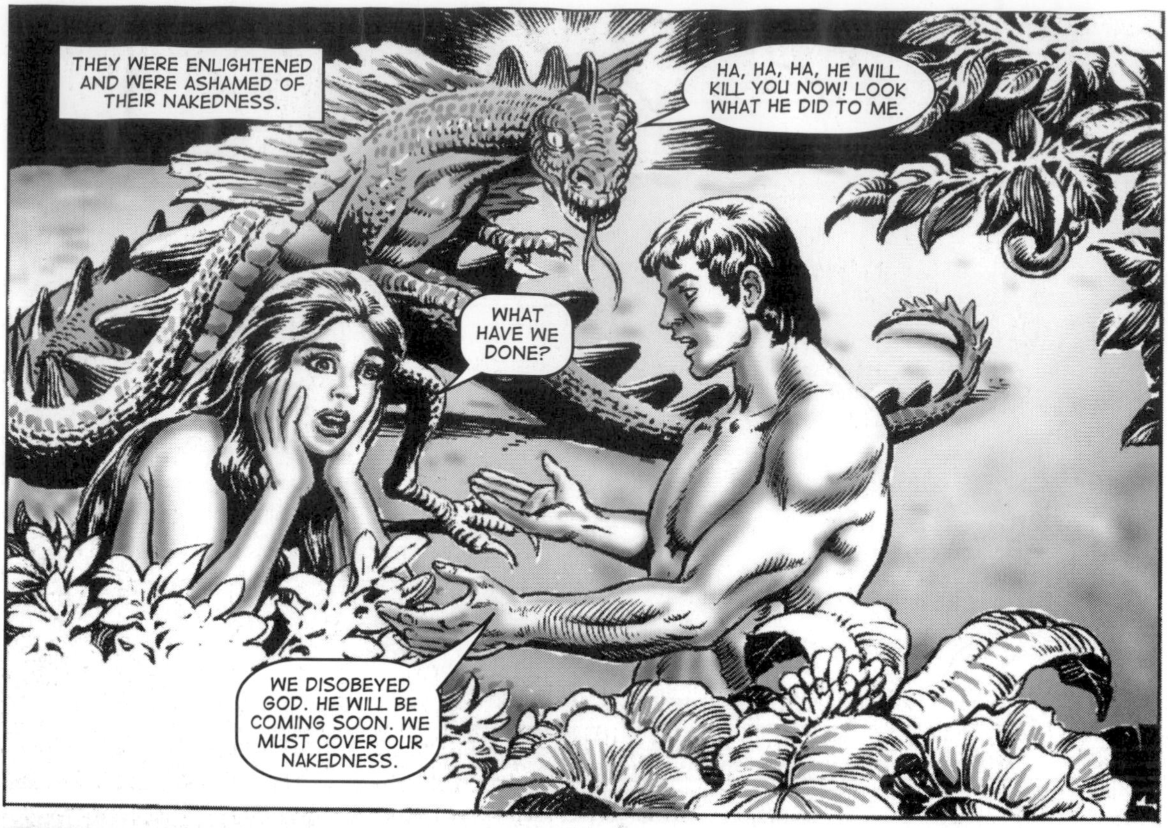
THEY WERE ENLIGHTENED AND WERE ASHAMED OF THEIR NAKEDNESS.
HA, HA, HA, HE WILL KILL YOU NOW! LOOK WHAT HE DID TO ME.
WHAT HAVE WE DONE?
WE DISOBEYED GOD. HE WILL BE COMING SOON. WE MUST COVER OUR NAKEDNESS.

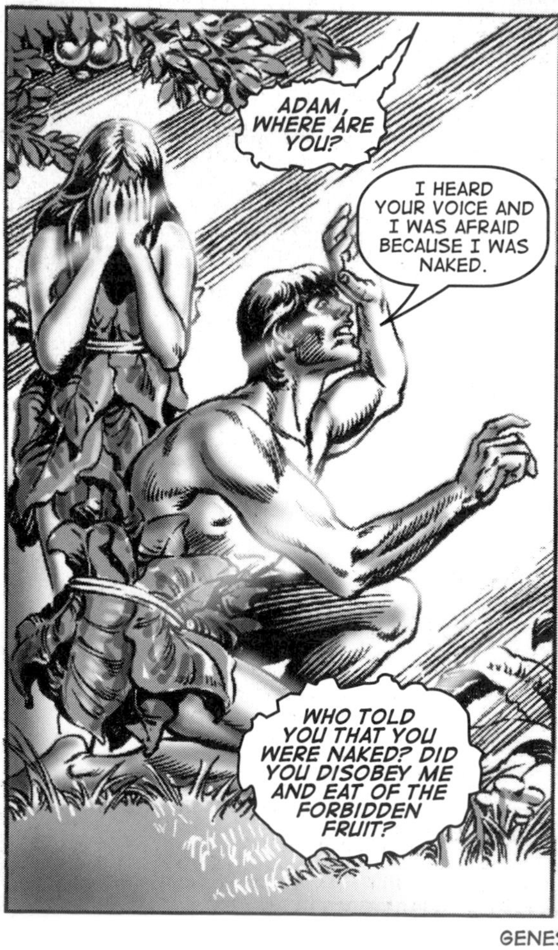
ADAM, WHERE ARE YOU?
I HEARD YOUR VOICE AND I WAS AFRAID BECAUSE I WAS NAKED.
WHO TOLD YOU THAT YOU WERE NAKED? DID YOU DISOBEY ME AND EAT OF THE FORBIDDEN FRUIT?

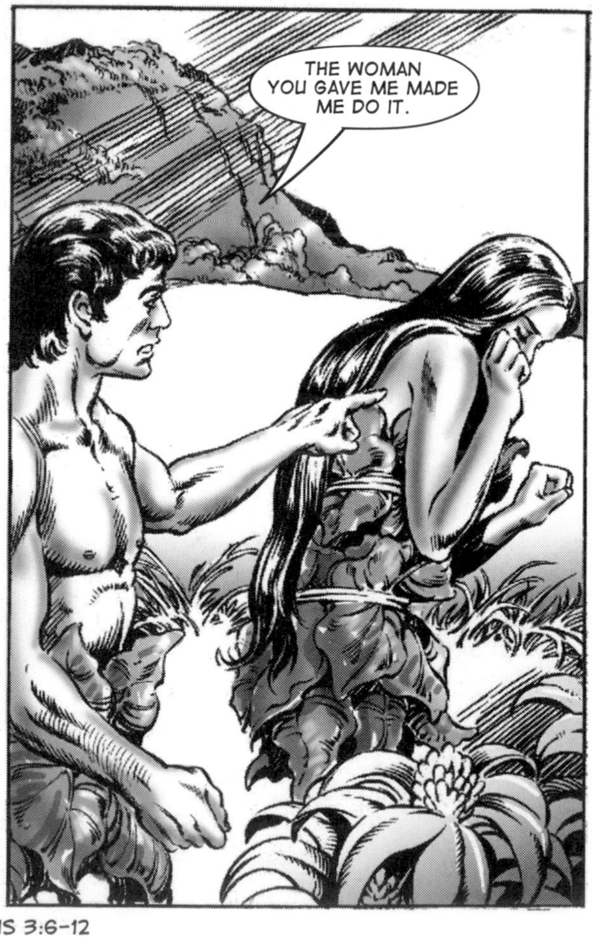
THE WOMAN YOU GAVE ME MADE ME DO IT.

GENESIS 3:6-12

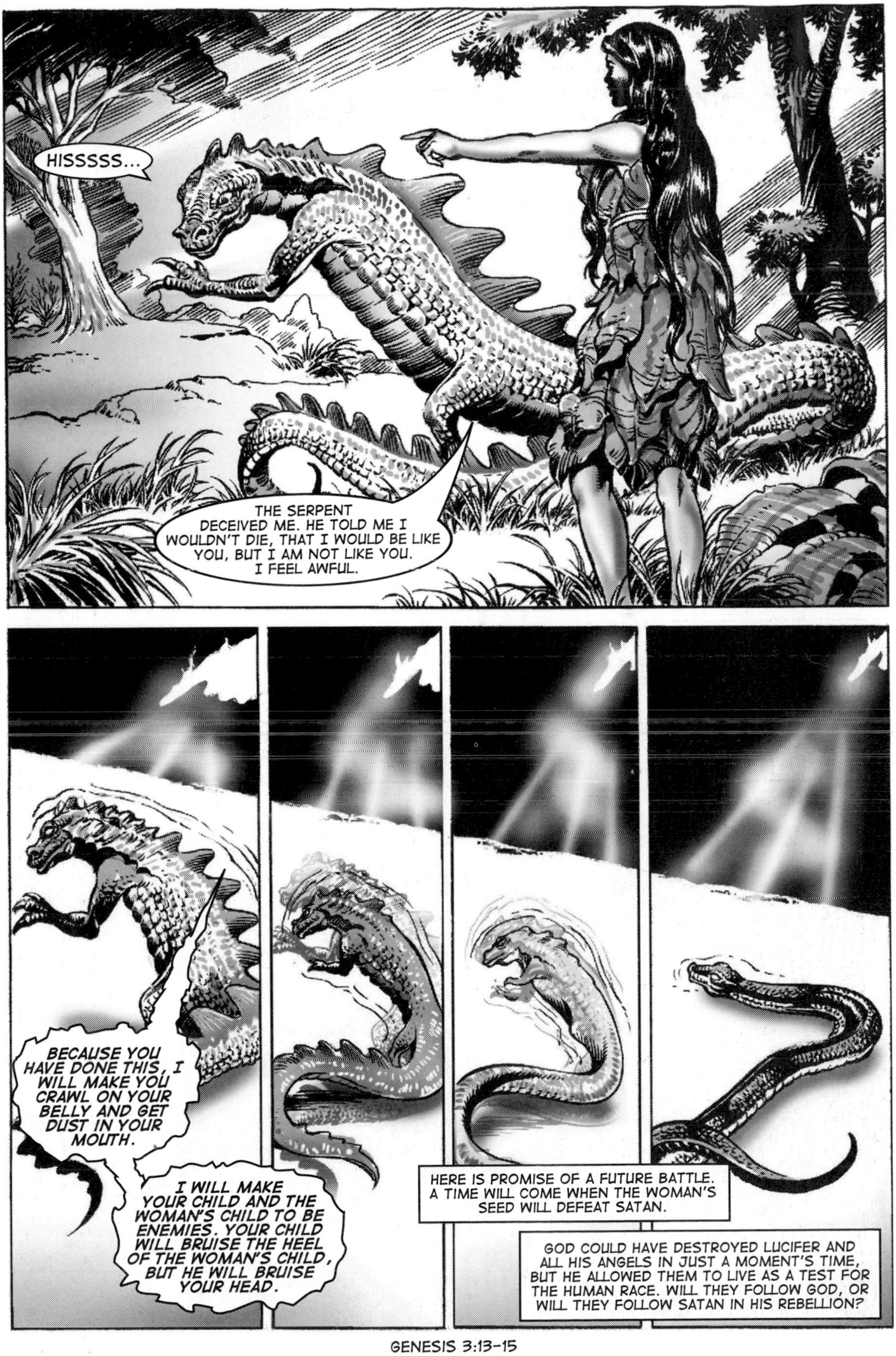
HISSSSS...
THE SERPENT DECEIVED ME. HE TOLD ME I WOULDN'T DIE, THAT I WOULD BE LIKE YOU, BUT I AM NOT LIKE YOU. I FEEL AWFUL.
BECAUSE YOU HAVE DONE THIS, I WILL MAKE YOU CRAWL ON YOUR BELLY AND GET DUST IN YOUR MOUTH.
I WILL MAKE YOUR CHILD AND THE WOMAN'S CHILD TO BE ENEMIES. YOUR CHILD WILL BRUISE THE HEEL OF THE WOMAN'S CHILD, BUT HE WILL BRUISE YOUR HEAD.
HERE IS PROMISE OF A FUTURE BATTLE. A TIME WILL COME WHEN THE WOMAN'S SEED WILL DEFEAT SATAN.
GOD COULD HAVE DESTROYED LUCIFER AND ALL HIS ANGELS IN JUST A MOMENT'S TIME, BUT HE ALLOWED THEM TO LIVE AS A TEST FOR THE HUMAN RACE. WILL THEY FOLLOW GOD, OR WILL THEY FOLLOW SATAN IN HIS REBELLION?

GENESIS 3:13–15

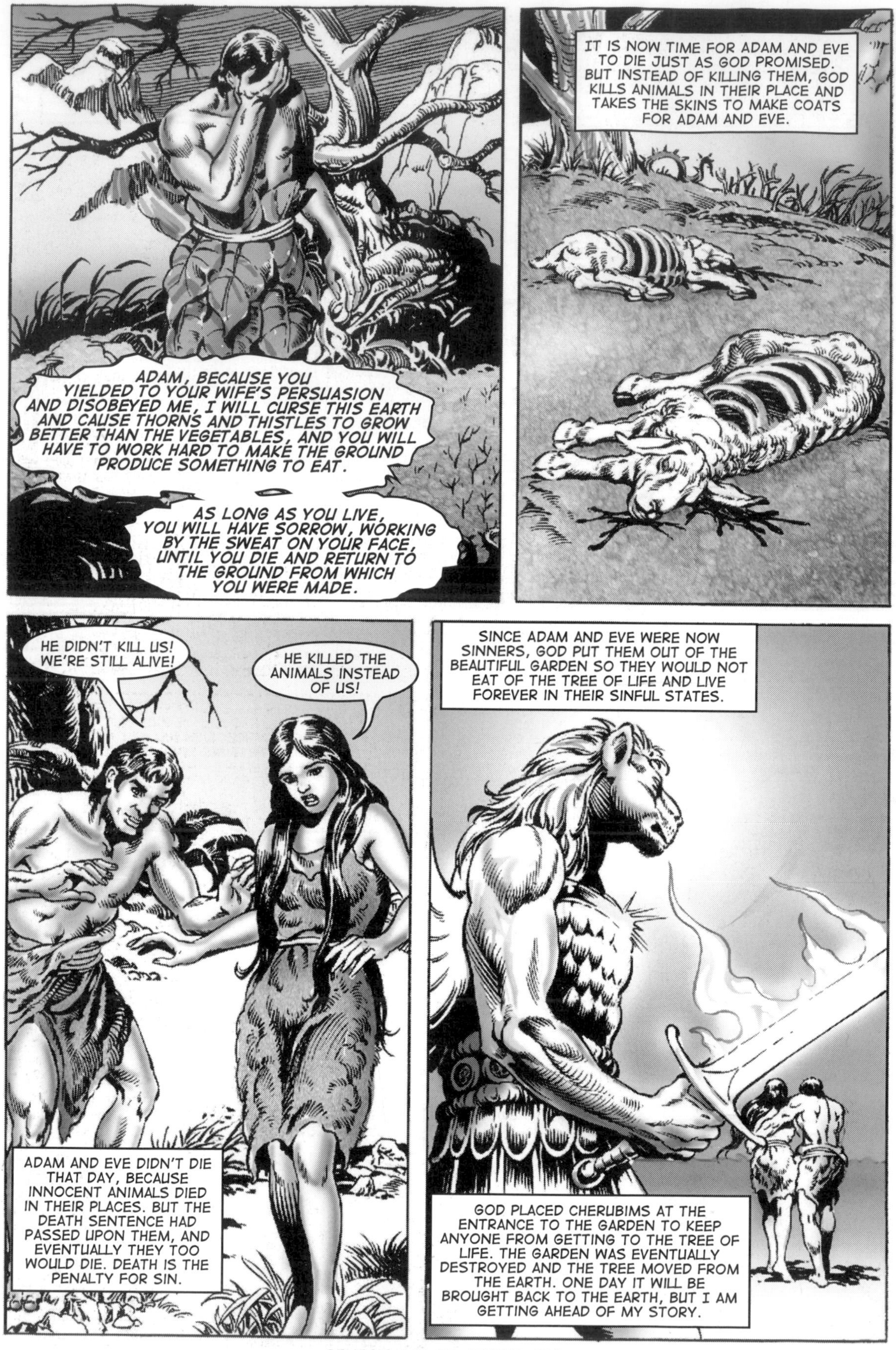
ADAM, BECAUSE YOU YIELDED TO YOUR WIFE'S PERSUASION AND DISOBEYED ME, I WILL CURSE THIS EARTH AND CAUSE THORNS AND THISTLES TO GROW BETTER THAN THE VEGETABLES, AND YOU WILL HAVE TO WORK HARD TO MAKE THE GROUND PRODUCE SOMETHING TO EAT.
AS LONG AS YOU LIVE, YOU WILL HAVE SORROW, WORKING BY THE SWEAT ON YOUR FACE, UNTIL YOU DIE AND RETURN TO THE GROUND FROM WHICH YOU WERE MADE.
IT IS NOW TIME FOR ADAM AND EVE TO DIE JUST AS GOD PROMISED. BUT INSTEAD OF KILLING THEM, GOD KILLS ANIMALS IN THEIR PLACE AND TAKES THE SKINS TO MAKE COATS FOR ADAM AND EVE.
HE DIDN'T KILL US! WE'RE STILL ALIVE!
HE KILLED THE ANIMALS INSTEAD OF US!
ADAM AND EVE DIDN'T DIE THAT DAY, BECAUSE INNOCENT ANIMALS DIED IN THEIR PLACES. BUT THE DEATH SENTENCE HAD PASSED UPON THEM, AND EVENTUALLY THEY TOO WOULD DIE. DEATH IS THE PENALTY FOR SIN.
SINCE ADAM AND EVE WERE NOW SINNERS, GOD PUT THEM OUT OF THE BEAUTIFUL GARDEN SO THEY WOULD NOT EAT OF THE TREE OF LIFE AND LIVE FOREVER IN THEIR SINFUL STATES.
GOD PLACED CHERUBIMS AT THE ENTRANCE TO THE GARDEN TO KEEP ANYONE FROM GETTING TO THE TREE OF LIFE. THE GARDEN WAS EVENTUALLY DESTROYED AND THE TREE MOVED FROM THE EARTH. ONE DAY IT WILL BE BROUGHT BACK TO THE EARTH, BUT I AM GETTING AHEAD OF MY STORY.

GENESIS 3:17-24; EZEKIEL 18:4

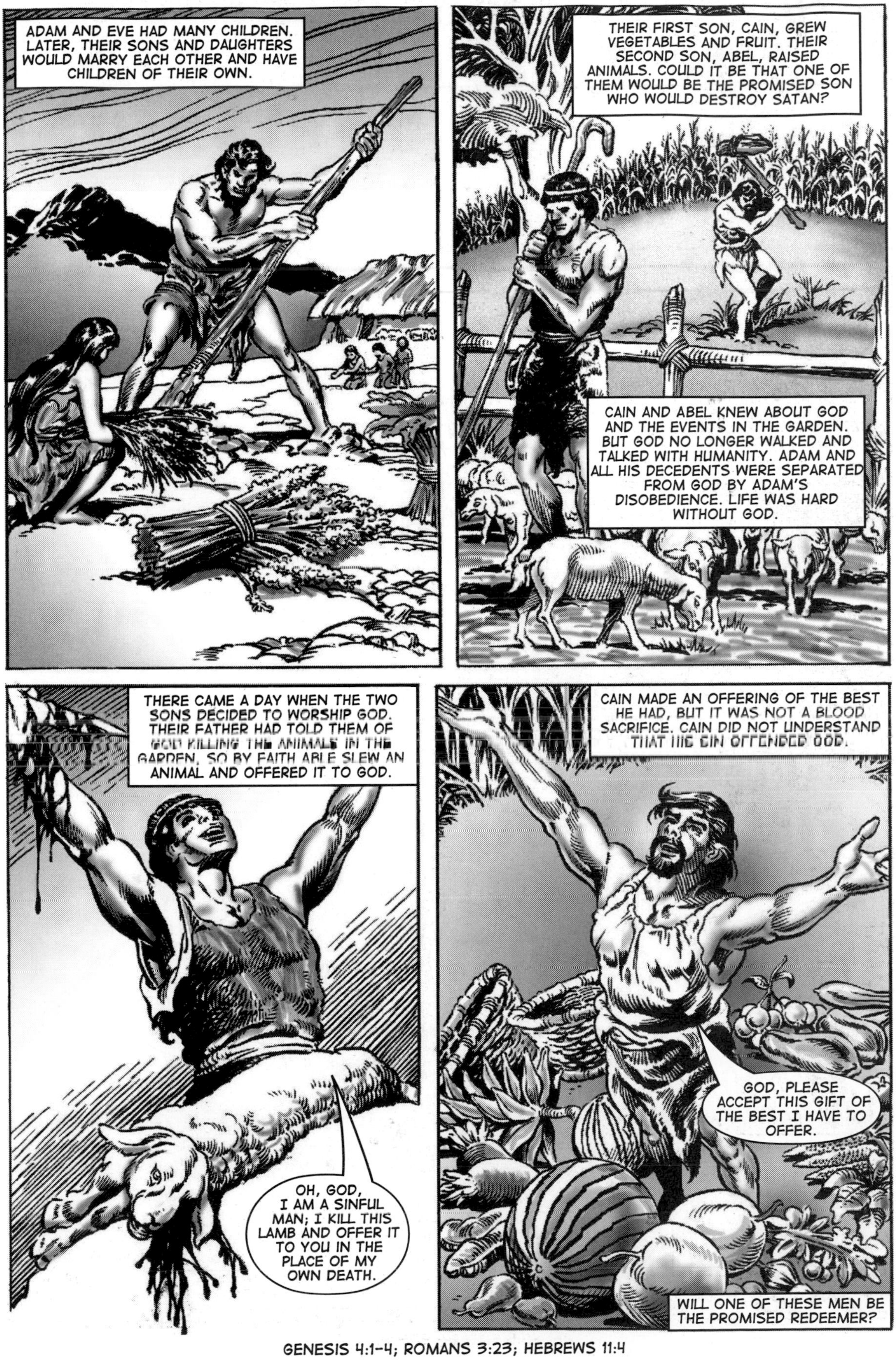
ADAM AND EVE HAD MANY CHILDREN. LATER, THEIR SONS AND DAUGHTERS WOULD MARRY EACH OTHER AND HAVE CHILDREN OF THEIR OWN.
THEIR FIRST SON, CAIN, GREW VEGETABLES AND FRUIT. THEIR SECOND SON, ABEL, RAISED ANIMALS. COULD IT BE THAT ONE OF THEM WOULD BE THE PROMISED SON WHO WOULD DESTROY SATAN?
CAIN AND ABEL KNEW ABOUT GOD AND THE EVENTS IN THE GARDEN. BUT GOD NO LONGER WALKED AND TALKED WITH HUMANITY. ADAM AND ALL HIS DECEDENTS WERE SEPARATED FROM GOD BY ADAM'S DISOBEDIENCE. LIFE WAS HARD WITHOUT GOD.
THERE CAME A DAY WHEN THE TWO SONS DECIDED TO WORSHIP GOD. THEIR FATHER HAD TOLD THEM OF GOD KILLING THE ANIMALS IN THE GARDEN, SO BY FAITH ABLE SLEW AN ANIMAL AND OFFERED IT TO GOD.
OH, GOD, I AM A SINFUL MAN; I KILL THIS LAMB AND OFFER IT TO YOU IN THE PLACE OF MY OWN DEATH.
CAIN MADE AN OFFERING OF THE BEST HE HAD, BUT IT WAS NOT A BLOOD SACRIFICE. CAIN DID NOT UNDERSTAND THAT HIS SIN OFFENDED GOD.
GOD, PLEASE ACCEPT THIS GIFT OF THE BEST I HAVE TO OFFER.
WILL ONE OF THESE MEN BE THE PROMISED REDEEMER?

GENESIS 4:1-4; ROMANS 3:23; HEBREWS 11:4

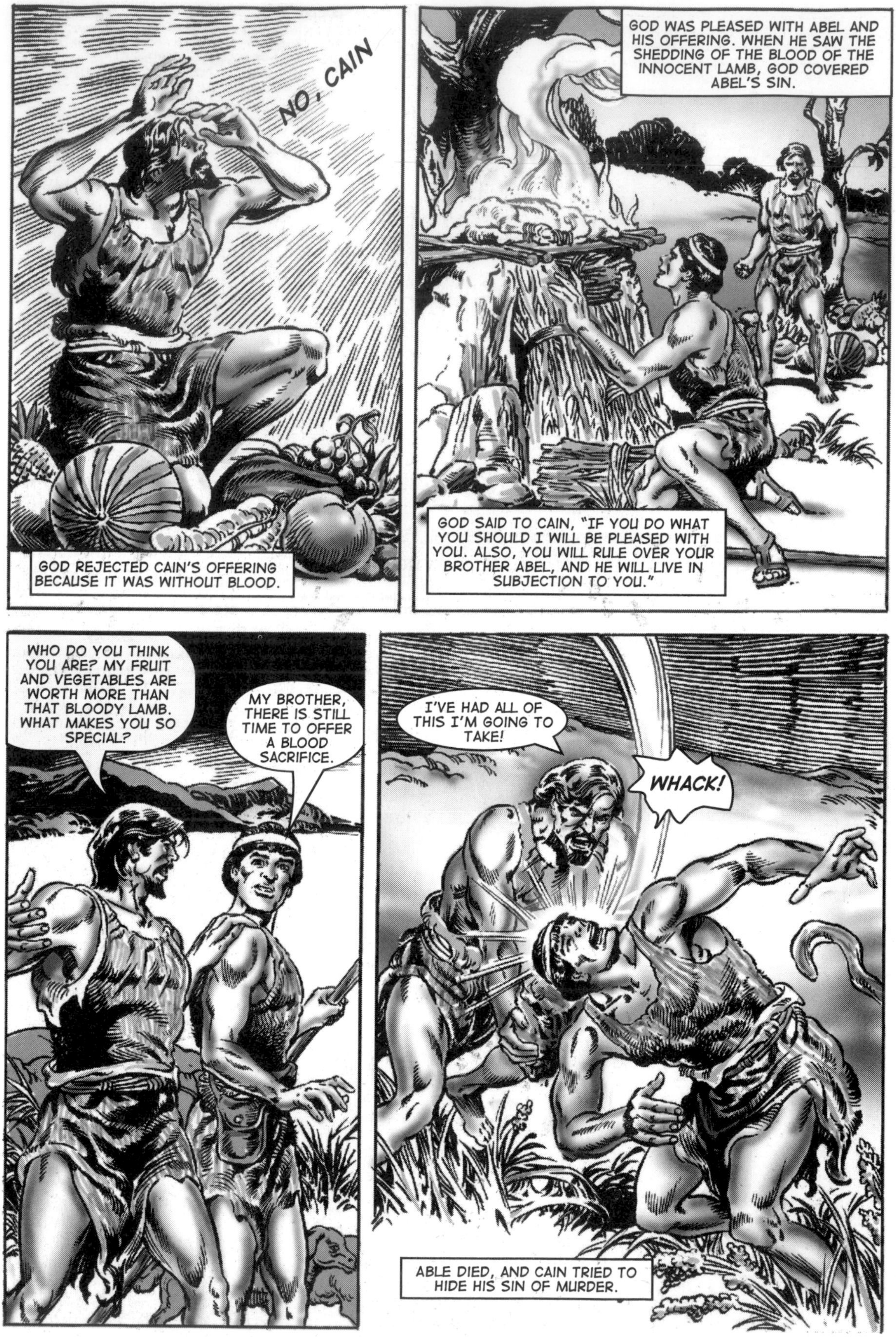
NO, CAIN
GOD REJECTED CAIN'S OFFERING BECAUSE IT WAS WITHOUT BLOOD.
GOD WAS PLEASED WITH ABEL AND HIS OFFERING. WHEN HE SAW THE SHEDDING OF THE BLOOD OF THE INNOCENT LAMB, GOD COVERED ABEL'S SIN.
GOD SAID TO CAIN, "IF YOU DO WHAT YOU SHOULD I WILL BE PLEASED WITH YOU. ALSO, YOU WILL RULE OVER YOUR BROTHER ABEL, AND HE WILL LIVE IN SUBJECTION TO YOU."
WHO DO YOU THINK YOU ARE? MY FRUIT AND VEGETABLES ARE WORTH MORE THAN THAT BLOODY LAMB. WHAT MAKES YOU SO SPECIAL?
MY BROTHER, THERE IS STILL TIME TO OFFER A BLOOD SACRIFICE.
I'VE HAD ALL OF THIS I'M GOING TO TAKE!
WHACK!
ABLE DIED, AND CAIN TRIED TO HIDE HIS SIN OF MURDER.

GENESIS 4:5-8

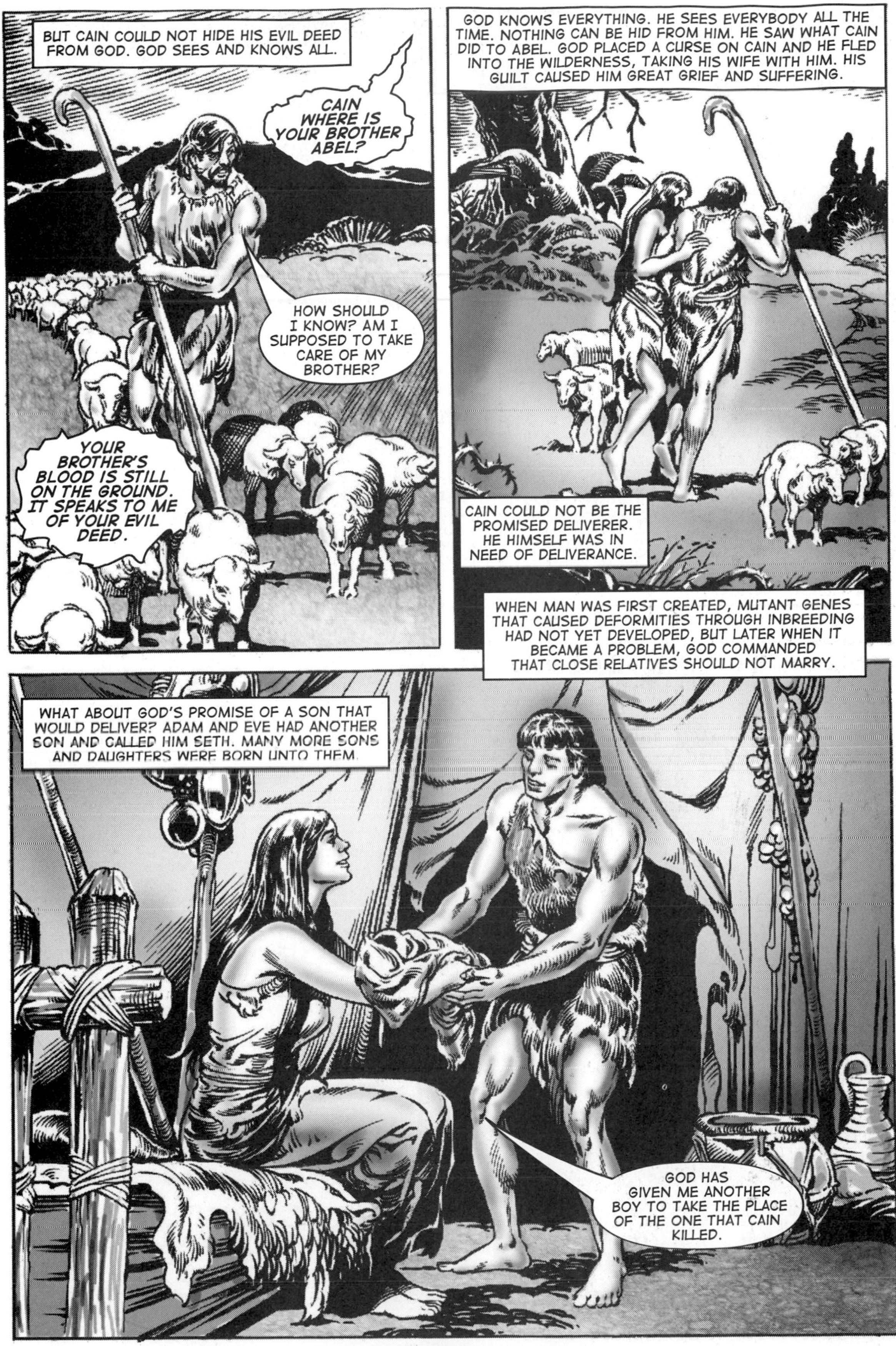
BUT CAIN COULD NOT HIDE HIS EVIL DEED FROM GOD. GOD SEES AND KNOWS ALL.
CAIN WHERE IS YOUR BROTHER ABEL?
HOW SHOULD I KNOW? AM I SUPPOSED TO TAKE CARE OF MY BROTHER?
YOUR BROTHER'S BLOOD IS STILL ON THE GROUND. IT SPEAKS TO ME OF YOUR EVIL DEED.
GOD KNOWS EVERYTHING. HE SEES EVERYBODY ALL THE TIME. NOTHING CAN BE HID FROM HIM. HE SAW WHAT CAIN DID TO ABEL. GOD PLACED A CURSE ON CAIN AND HE FLED INTO THE WILDERNESS, TAKING HIS WIFE WITH HIM. HIS GUILT CAUSED HIM GREAT GRIEF AND SUFFERING.
CAIN COULD NOT BE THE PROMISED DELIVERER. HE HIMSELF WAS IN NEED OF DELIVERANCE.
WHEN MAN WAS FIRST CREATED, MUTANT GENES THAT CAUSED DEFORMITIES THROUGH INBREEDING HAD NOT YET DEVELOPED, BUT LATER WHEN IT BECAME A PROBLEM, GOD COMMANDED THAT CLOSE RELATIVES SHOULD NOT MARRY.
WHAT ABOUT GOD'S PROMISE OF A SON THAT WOULD DELIVER? ADAM AND EVE HAD ANOTHER SON AND CALLED HIM SETH. MANY MORE SONS AND DAUGHTERS WERE BORN UNTO THEM.
GOD HAS GIVEN ME ANOTHER BOY TO TAKE THE PLACE OF THE ONE THAT CAIN KILLED.

GENESIS 4:9-16, 5:4; ACTS 17:24-26

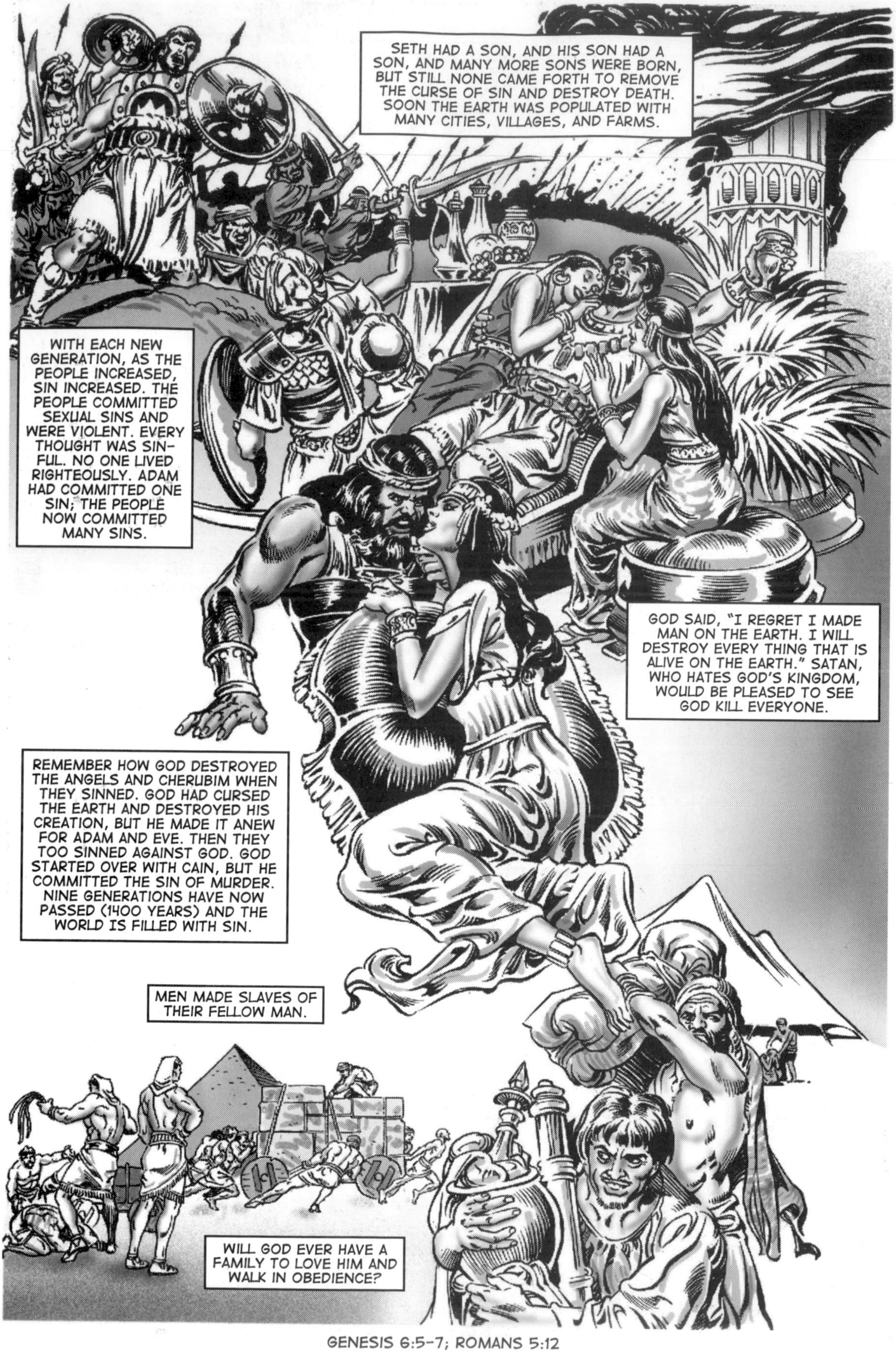
SETH HAD A SON, AND HIS SON HAD A SON, AND MANY MORE SONS WERE BORN, BUT STILL NONE CAME FORTH TO REMOVE THE CURSE OF SIN AND DESTROY DEATH. SOON THE EARTH WAS POPULATED WITH MANY CITIES, VILLAGES, AND FARMS.
WITH EACH NEW GENERATION, AS THE PEOPLE INCREASED, SIN INCREASED. THE PEOPLE COMMITTED SEXUAL SINS AND WERE VIOLENT. EVERY THOUGHT WAS SIN-FUL. NO ONE LIVED RIGHTEOUSLY. ADAM HAD COMMITTED ONE SIN; THE PEOPLE NOW COMMITTED MANY SINS.
GOD SAID, "I REGRET I MADE MAN ON THE EARTH. I WILL DESTROY EVERY THING THAT IS ALIVE ON THE EARTH." SATAN, WHO HATES GOD'S KINGDOM, WOULD BE PLEASED TO SEE GOD KILL EVERYONE.
REMEMBER HOW GOD DESTROYED THE ANGELS AND CHERUBIM WHEN THEY SINNED. GOD HAD CURSED THE EARTH AND DESTROYED HIS CREATION, BUT HE MADE IT ANEW FOR ADAM AND EVE. THEN THEY TOO SINNED AGAINST GOD. GOD STARTED OVER WITH CAIN, BUT HE COMMITTED THE SIN OF MURDER. NINE GENERATIONS HAVE NOW PASSED (1400 YEARS) AND THE WORLD IS FILLED WITH SIN.
MEN MADE SLAVES OF THEIR FELLOW MAN.
WILL GOD EVER HAVE A FAMILY TO LOVE HIM AND WALK IN OBEDIENCE?

GENESIS 6:5-7; ROMANS 5:12

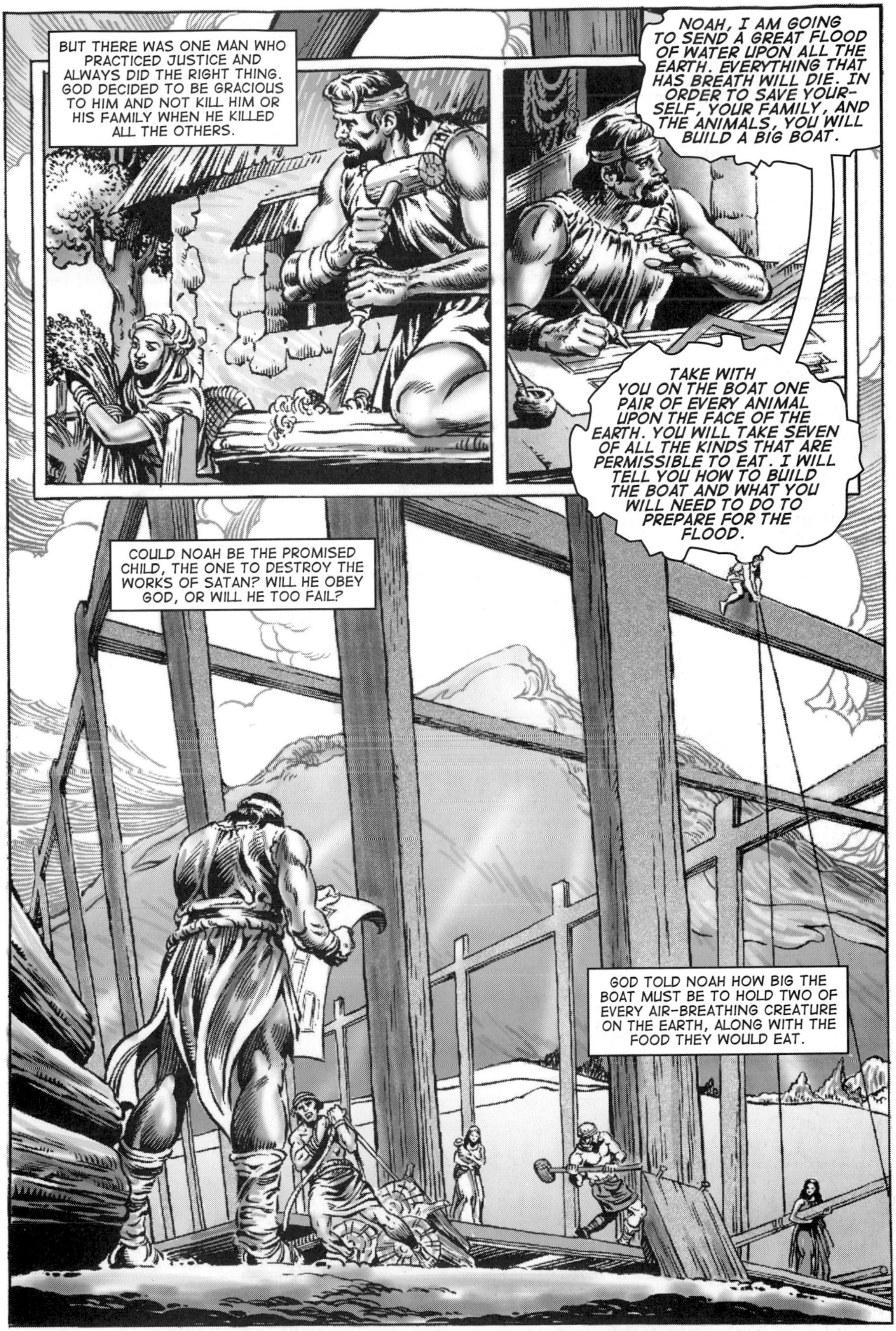
BUT THERE WAS ONE MAN WHO PRACTICED JUSTICE AND ALWAYS DID THE RIGHT THING. GOD DECIDED TO BE GRACIOUS TO HIM AND NOT KILL HIM OR HIS FAMILY WHEN HE KILLED ALL THE OTHERS.
NOAH, I AM GOING TO SEND A GREAT FLOOD OF WATER UPON ALL THE EARTH. EVERYTHING THAT HAS BREATH WILL DIE. IN ORDER TO SAVE YOURSELF, YOUR FAMILY, AND THE ANIMALS, YOU WILL BUILD A BIG BOAT.
TAKE WITH YOU ON THE BOAT ONE PAIR OF EVERY ANIMAL UPON THE FACE OF THE EARTH. YOU WILL TAKE SEVEN OF ALL THE KINDS THAT ARE PERMISSIBLE TO EAT. I WILL TELL YOU HOW TO BUILD THE BOAT AND WHAT YOU WILL NEED TO DO TO PREPARE FOR THE FLOOD.
COULD NOAH BE THE PROMISED CHILD, THE ONE TO DESTROY THE WORKS OF SATAN? WILL HE OBEY GOD, OR WILL HE TOO FAIL?
GOD TOLD NOAH HOW BIG THE BOAT MUST BE TO HOLD TWO OF EVERY AIR-BREATHING CREATURE ON THE EARTH, ALONG WITH THE FOOD THEY WOULD EAT.

APPROXIMATELY 2500 B.C. - GENESIS 6:8-9, 17-22, 7:2

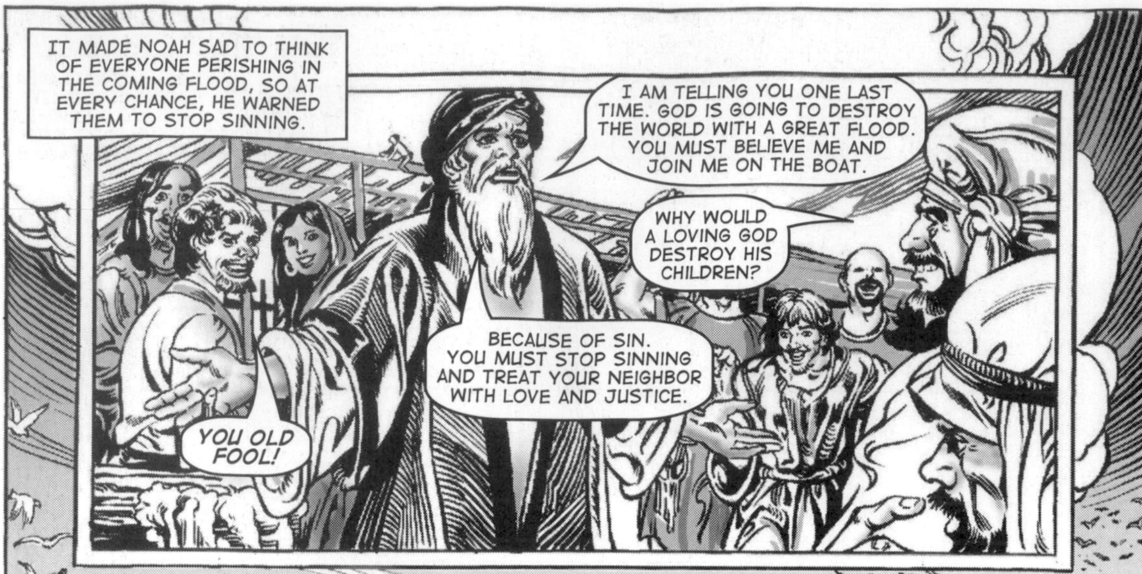
IT MADE NOAH SAD TO THINK OF EVERYONE PERISHING IN THE COMING FLOOD, SO AT EVERY CHANCE, HE WARNED THEM TO STOP SINNING.
I AM TELLING YOU ONE LAST TIME. GOD IS GOING TO DESTROY THE WORLD WITH A GREAT FLOOD. YOU MUST BELIEVE ME AND JOIN ME ON THE BOAT.
WHY WOULD A LOVING GOD DESTROY HIS CHILDREN?
BECAUSE OF SIN. YOU MUST STOP SINNING AND TREAT YOUR NEIGHBOR WITH LOVE AND JUSTICE.
YOU OLD FOOL!

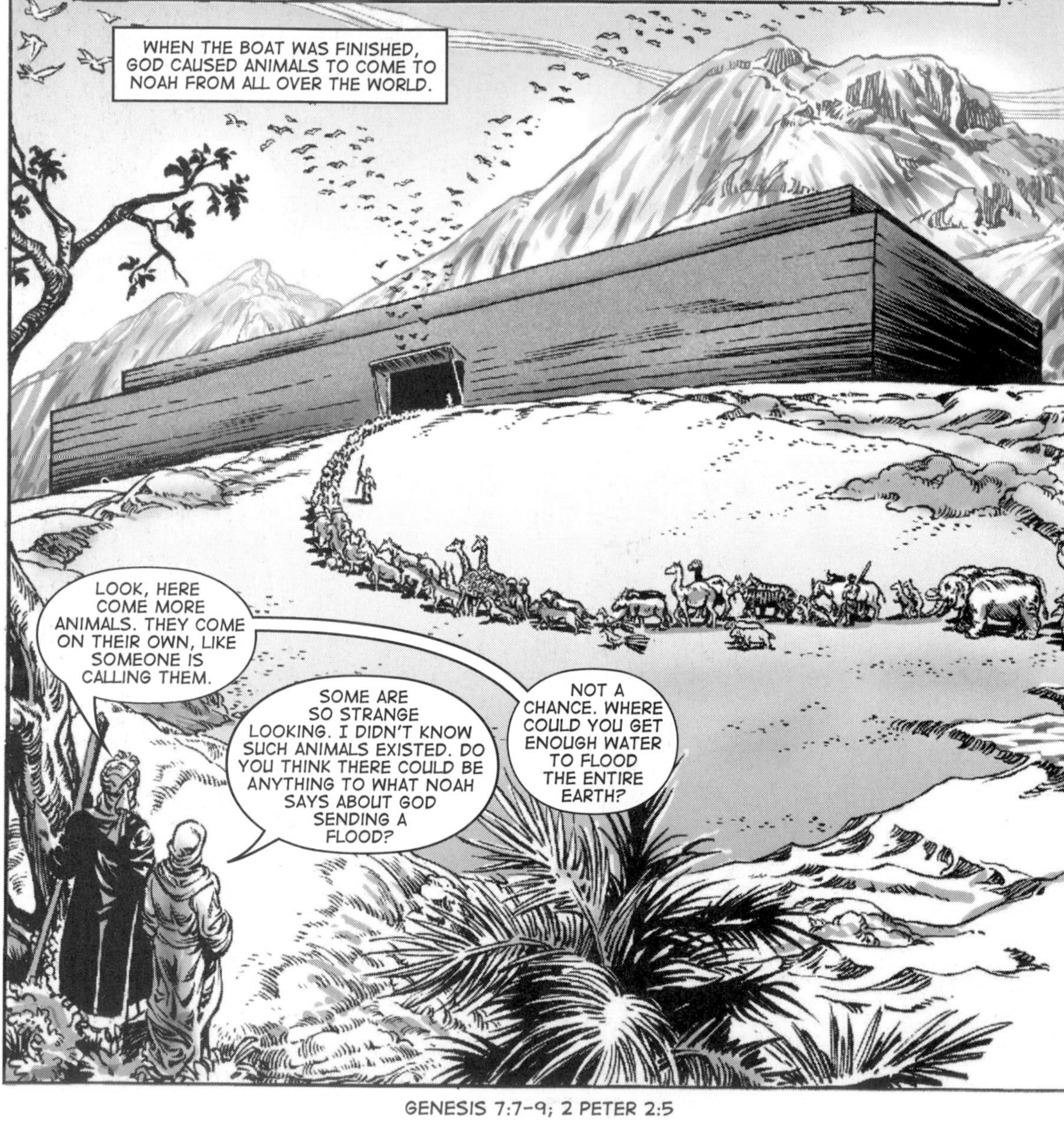
WHEN THE BOAT WAS FINISHED, GOD CAUSED ANIMALS TO COME TO NOAH FROM ALL OVER THE WORLD.
LOOK, HERE COME MORE ANIMALS. THEY COME ON THEIR OWN, LIKE SOMEONE IS CALLING THEM.
SOME ARE SO STRANGE LOOKING. I DIDN'T KNOW SUCH ANIMALS EXISTED. DO YOU THINK THERE COULD BE ANYTHING TO WHAT NOAH SAYS ABOUT GOD SENDING A FLOOD?
NOT A CHANCE. WHERE COULD YOU GET ENOUGH WATER TO FLOOD THE ENTIRE EARTH?

GENESIS 7:7–9; 2 PETER 2:5

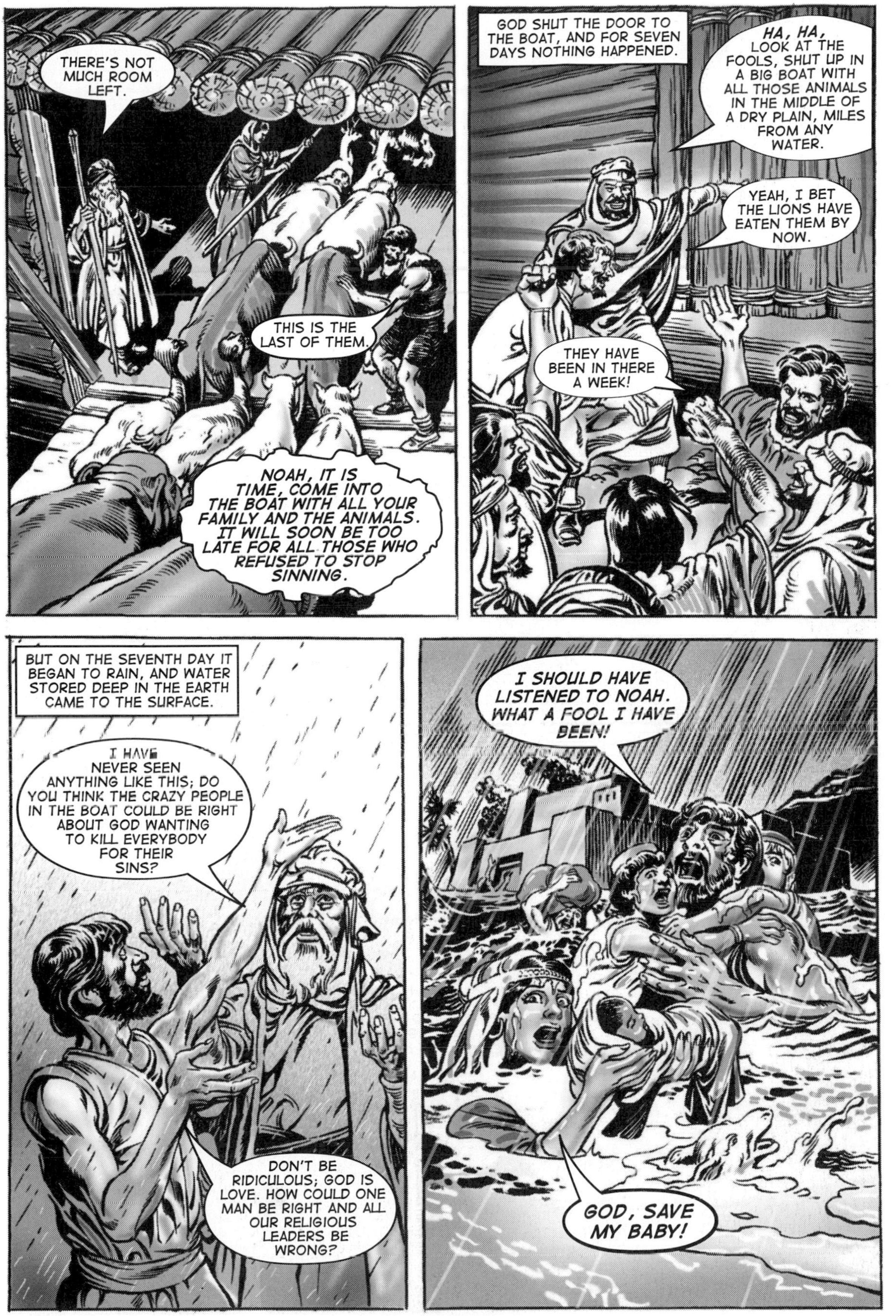
THERE'S NOT MUCH ROOM LEFT.
THIS IS THE LAST OF THEM.
NOAH, IT IS TIME, COME INTO THE BOAT WITH ALL YOUR FAMILY AND THE ANIMALS. IT WILL SOON BE TOO LATE FOR ALL THOSE WHO REFUSED TO STOP SINNING.
GOD SHUT THE DOOR TO THE BOAT, AND FOR SEVEN DAYS NOTHING HAPPENED.
HA, HA, LOOK AT THE FOOLS, SHUT UP IN A BIG BOAT WITH ALL THOSE ANIMALS IN THE MIDDLE OF A DRY PLAIN, MILES FROM ANY WATER.
YEAH, I BET THE LIONS HAVE EATEN THEM BY NOW.
THEY HAVE BEEN IN THERE A WEEK!
BUT ON THE SEVENTH DAY IT BEGAN TO RAIN, AND WATER STORED DEEP IN THE EARTH CAME TO THE SURFACE.
I HAVE NEVER SEEN ANYTHING LIKE THIS; DO YOU THINK THE CRAZY PEOPLE IN THE BOAT COULD BE RIGHT ABOUT GOD WANTING TO KILL EVERYBODY FOR THEIR SINS?
DON'T BE RIDICULOUS; GOD IS LOVE. HOW COULD ONE MAN BE RIGHT AND ALL OUR RELIGIOUS LEADERS BE WRONG?
I SHOULD HAVE LISTENED TO NOAH. WHAT A FOOL I HAVE BEEN!
GOD, SAVE MY BABY!

GENESIS 7:9-11, 16

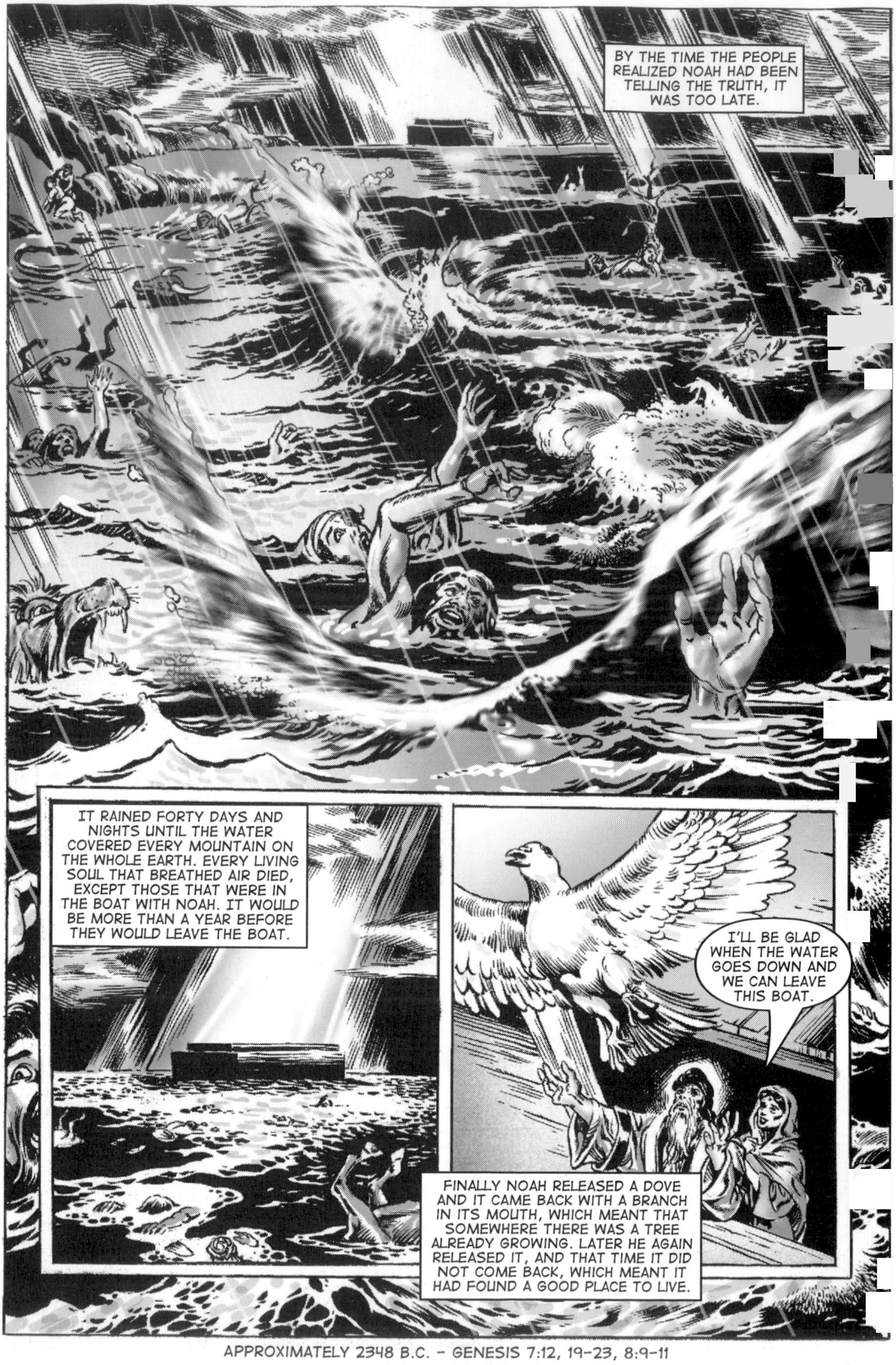
BY THE TIME THE PEOPLE REALIZED NOAH HAD BEEN TELLING THE TRUTH, IT WAS TOO LATE.
IT RAINED FORTY DAYS AND NIGHTS UNTIL THE WATER COVERED EVERY MOUNTAIN ON THE WHOLE EARTH. EVERY LIVING SOUL THAT BREATHED AIR DIED, EXCEPT THOSE THAT WERE IN THE BOAT WITH NOAH. IT WOULD BE MORE THAN A YEAR BEFORE THEY WOULD LEAVE THE BOAT.
I'LL BE GLAD WHEN THE WATER GOES DOWN AND WE CAN LEAVE THIS BOAT.
FINALLY NOAH RELEASED A DOVE AND IT CAME BACK WITH A BRANCH IN ITS MOUTH, WHICH MEANT THAT SOMEWHERE THERE WAS A TREE ALREADY GROWING. LATER HE AGAIN RELEASED IT, AND THAT TIME IT DID NOT COME BACK, WHICH MEANT IT HAD FOUND A GOOD PLACE TO LIVE.

APPROXIMATELY 2348 B.C. - GENESIS 7:12, 19-23, 8:9-11

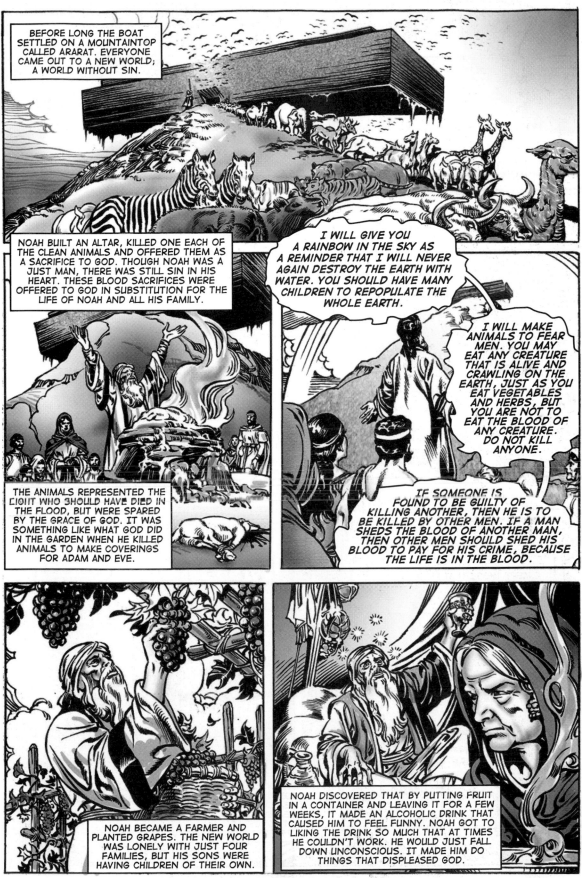

BEFORE LONG THE BOAT SETTLED ON A MOUNTAINTOP CALLED ARARAT. EVERYONE CAME OUT TO A NEW WORLD; A WORLD WITHOUT SIN.

NOAH BUILT AN ALTAR, KILLED ONE EACH OF THE CLEAN ANIMALS AND OFFERED THEM AS A SACRIFICE TO GOD. THOUGH NOAH WAS A JUST MAN, THERE WAS STILL SIN IN HIS HEART. THESE BLOOD SACRIFICES WERE OFFERED TO GOD IN SUBSTITUTION FOR THE LIFE OF NOAH AND ALL HIS FAMILY.

I WILL GIVE YOU A RAINBOW IN THE SKY AS A REMINDER THAT I WILL NEVER AGAIN DESTROY THE EARTH WITH WATER. YOU SHOULD HAVE MANY CHILDREN TO REPOPULATE THE WHOLE EARTH.

I WILL MAKE ANIMALS TO FEAR MEN. YOU MAY EAT ANY CREATURE THAT IS ALIVE AND CRAWLING ON THE EARTH, JUST AS YOU EAT VEGETABLES AND HERBS, BUT YOU ARE NOT TO EAT THE BLOOD OF ANY CREATURE. DO NOT KILL ANYONE.

THE ANIMALS REPRESENTED THE LIGHT WHO SHOULD HAVE DIED IN THE FLOOD, BUT WERE SPARED BY THE GRACE OF GOD. IT WAS SOMETHING LIKE WHAT GOD DID IN THE GARDEN WHEN HE KILLED ANIMALS TO MAKE COVERINGS FOR ADAM AND EVE.

IF SOMEONE IS FOUND TO BE GUILTY OF KILLING ANOTHER, THEN HE IS TO BE KILLED BY OTHER MEN. IF A MAN SHEDS THE BLOOD OF ANOTHER MAN, THEN OTHER MEN SHOULD SHED HIS BLOOD TO PAY FOR HIS CRIME, BECAUSE THE LIFE IS IN THE BLOOD.

NOAH BECAME A FARMER AND PLANTED GRAPES. THE NEW WORLD WAS LONELY WITH JUST FOUR FAMILIES, BUT HIS SONS WERE HAVING CHILDREN OF THEIR OWN.

NOAH DISCOVERED THAT BY PUTTING FRUIT IN A CONTAINER AND LEAVING IT FOR A FEW WEEKS, IT MADE AN ALCOHOLIC DRINK THAT CAUSED HIM TO FEEL FUNNY. NOAH GOT TO LIKING THE DRINK SO MUCH THAT AT TIMES HE COULDN'T WORK. HE WOULD JUST FALL DOWN UNCONSCIOUS. IT MADE HIM DO THINGS THAT DISPLEASED GOD.

GENESIS 8:4, 20, 9:1-29

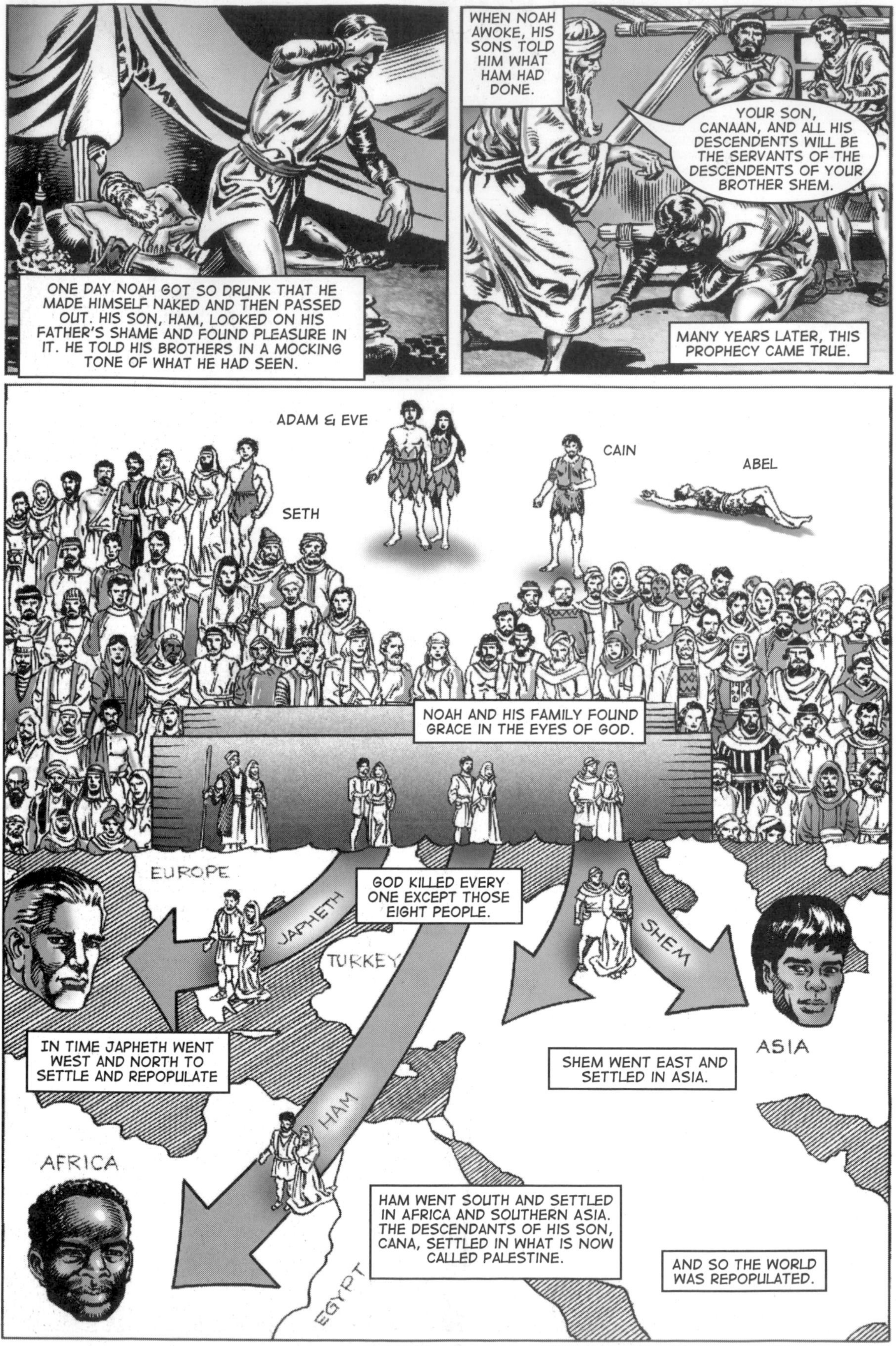
ONE DAY NOAH GOT SO DRUNK THAT HE MADE HIMSELF NAKED AND THEN PASSED OUT. HIS SON, HAM, LOOKED ON HIS FATHER'S SHAME AND FOUND PLEASURE IN IT. HE TOLD HIS BROTHERS IN A MOCKING TONE OF WHAT HE HAD SEEN.
WHEN NOAH AWOKE, HIS SONS TOLD HIM WHAT HAM HAD DONE.
YOUR SON, CANAAN, AND ALL HIS DESCENDENTS WILL BE THE SERVANTS OF THE DESCENDENTS OF YOUR BROTHER SHEM.
MANY YEARS LATER, THIS PROPHECY CAME TRUE.
ADAM & EVE
CAIN
ABEL
SETH
NOAH AND HIS FAMILY FOUND GRACE IN THE EYES OF GOD.
EUROPE
GOD KILLED EVERY ONE EXCEPT THOSE EIGHT PEOPLE.
JAPHETH
SHEM
TURKEY
IN TIME JAPHETH WENT WEST AND NORTH TO SETTLE AND REPOPULATE
SHEM WENT EAST AND SETTLED IN ASIA.
ASIA
HAM
AFRICA
HAM WENT SOUTH AND SETTLED IN AFRICA AND SOUTHERN ASIA. THE DESCENDANTS OF HIS SON, CANA, SETTLED IN WHAT IS NOW CALLED PALESTINE.
AND SO THE WORLD WAS REPOPULATED.
EGYPT

GENESIS 9:21-27; 1 CHRONICLES 4:40: PSALMS 78:51, 105:23,27, 106:22

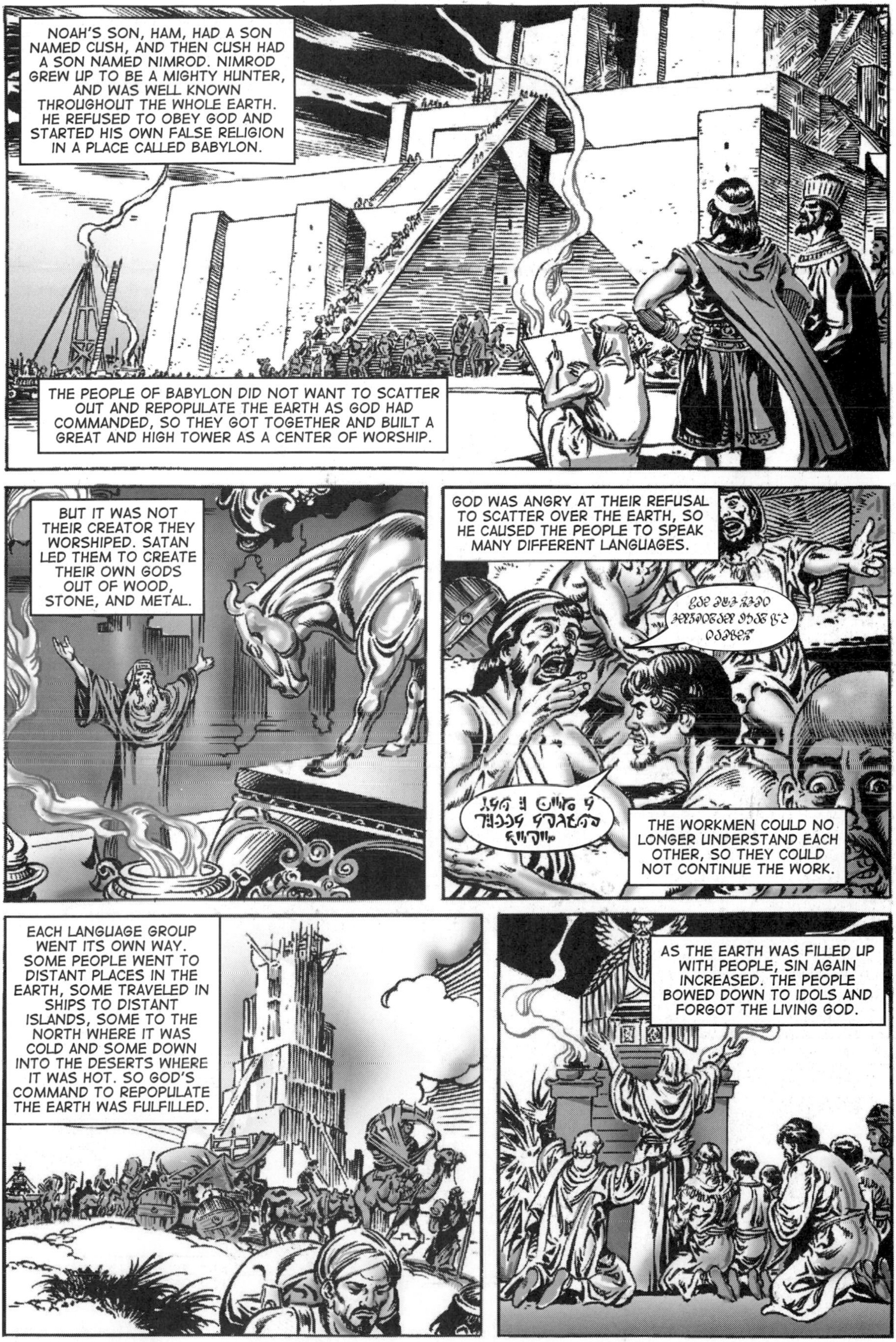
NOAH'S SON, HAM, HAD A SON NAMED CUSH, AND THEN CUSH HAD A SON NAMED NIMROD. NIMROD GREW UP TO BE A MIGHTY HUNTER, AND WAS WELL KNOWN THROUGHOUT THE WHOLE EARTH. HE REFUSED TO OBEY GOD AND STARTED HIS OWN FALSE RELIGION IN A PLACE CALLED BABYLON.
THE PEOPLE OF BABYLON DID NOT WANT TO SCATTER OUT AND REPOPULATE THE EARTH AS GOD HAD COMMANDED, SO THEY GOT TOGETHER AND BUILT A GREAT AND HIGH TOWER AS A CENTER OF WORSHIP.
BUT IT WAS NOT THEIR CREATOR THEY WORSHIPED. SATAN LED THEM TO CREATE THEIR OWN GODS OUT OF WOOD, STONE, AND METAL.
GOD WAS ANGRY AT THEIR REFUSAL TO SCATTER OVER THE EARTH, SO HE CAUSED THE PEOPLE TO SPEAK MANY DIFFERENT LANGUAGES.
THE WORKMEN COULD NO LONGER UNDERSTAND EACH OTHER, SO THEY COULD NOT CONTINUE THE WORK.
EACH LANGUAGE GROUP WENT ITS OWN WAY. SOME PEOPLE WENT TO DISTANT PLACES IN THE EARTH, SOME TRAVELED IN SHIPS TO DISTANT ISLANDS, SOME TO THE NORTH WHERE IT WAS COLD AND SOME DOWN INTO THE DESERTS WHERE IT WAS HOT. SO GOD'S COMMAND TO REPOPULATE THE EARTH WAS FULFILLED.
AS THE EARTH WAS FILLED UP WITH PEOPLE, SIN AGAIN INCREASED. THE PEOPLE BOWED DOWN TO IDOLS AND FORGOT THE LIVING GOD.

APPROXIMATELY 2247 B.C. - GENESIS 10:6-10, 11:1-9

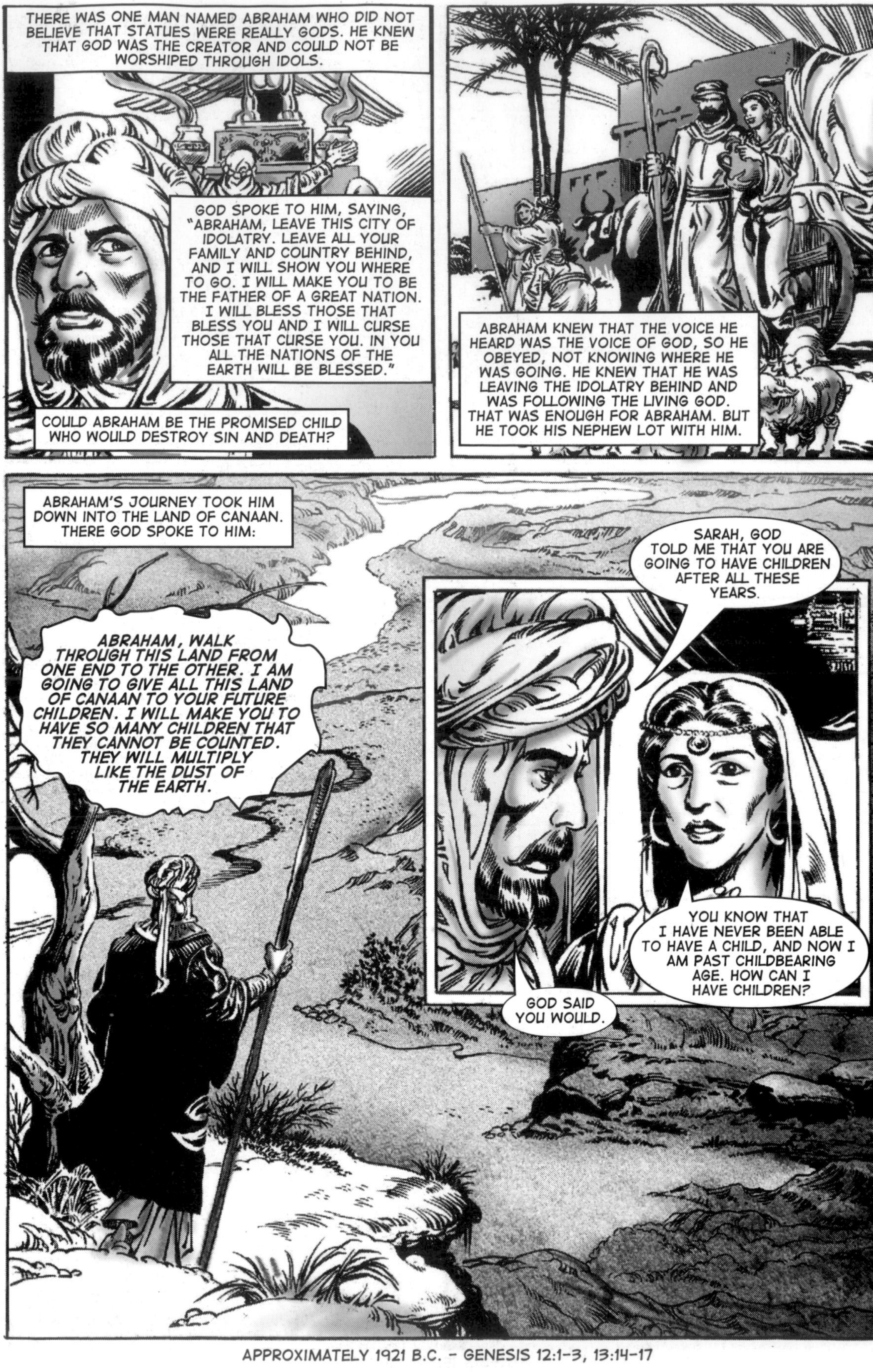
THERE WAS ONE MAN NAMED ABRAHAM WHO DID NOT BELIEVE THAT STATUES WERE REALLY GODS. HE KNEW THAT GOD WAS THE CREATOR AND COULD NOT BE WORSHIPED THROUGH IDOLS.
GOD SPOKE TO HIM, SAYING, "ABRAHAM, LEAVE THIS CITY OF IDOLATRY. LEAVE ALL YOUR FAMILY AND COUNTRY BEHIND, AND I WILL SHOW YOU WHERE TO GO. I WILL MAKE YOU TO BE THE FATHER OF A GREAT NATION. I WILL BLESS THOSE THAT BLESS YOU AND I WILL CURSE THOSE THAT CURSE YOU. IN YOU ALL THE NATIONS OF THE EARTH WILL BE BLESSED."
COULD ABRAHAM BE THE PROMISED CHILD WHO WOULD DESTROY SIN AND DEATH?
ABRAHAM KNEW THAT THE VOICE HE HEARD WAS THE VOICE OF GOD, SO HE OBEYED, NOT KNOWING WHERE HE WAS GOING. HE KNEW THAT HE WAS LEAVING THE IDOLATRY BEHIND AND WAS FOLLOWING THE LIVING GOD. THAT WAS ENOUGH FOR ABRAHAM. BUT HE TOOK HIS NEPHEW LOT WITH HIM.
ABRAHAM'S JOURNEY TOOK HIM DOWN INTO THE LAND OF CANAAN. THERE GOD SPOKE TO HIM:
ABRAHAM, WALK THROUGH THIS LAND FROM ONE END TO THE OTHER. I AM GOING TO GIVE ALL THIS LAND OF CANAAN TO YOUR FUTURE CHILDREN. I WILL MAKE YOU TO HAVE SO MANY CHILDREN THAT THEY CANNOT BE COUNTED. THEY WILL MULTIPLY LIKE THE DUST OF THE EARTH.
SARAH, GOD TOLD ME THAT YOU ARE GOING TO HAVE CHILDREN AFTER ALL THESE YEARS.
YOU KNOW THAT I HAVE NEVER BEEN ABLE TO HAVE A CHILD, AND NOW I AM PAST CHILDBEARING AGE. HOW CAN I HAVE CHILDREN?
GOD SAID YOU WOULD.

APPROXIMATELY 1921 B.C. - GENESIS 12:1-3, 13:14-17

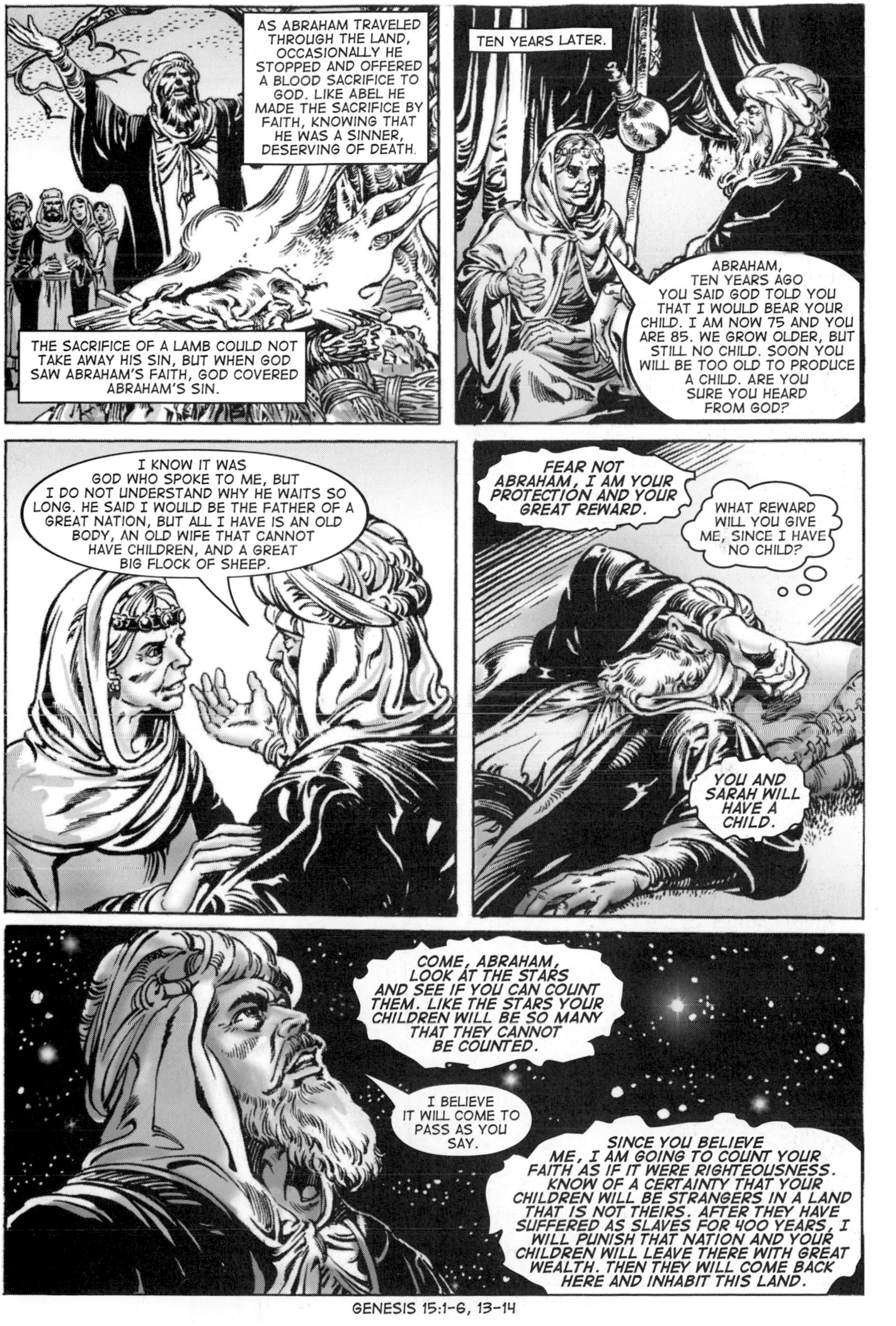
AS ABRAHAM TRAVELED THROUGH THE LAND, OCCASIONALLY HE STOPPED AND OFFERED A BLOOD SACRIFICE TO GOD. LIKE ABEL HE MADE THE SACRIFICE BY FAITH, KNOWING THAT HE WAS A SINNER, DESERVING OF DEATH.
THE SACRIFICE OF A LAMB COULD NOT TAKE AWAY HIS SIN, BUT WHEN GOD SAW ABRAHAM'S FAITH, GOD COVERED ABRAHAM'S SIN.
TEN YEARS LATER.
ABRAHAM, TEN YEARS AGO YOU SAID GOD TOLD YOU THAT I WOULD BEAR YOUR CHILD. I AM NOW 75 AND YOU ARE 85. WE GROW OLDER, BUT STILL NO CHILD. SOON YOU WILL BE TOO OLD TO PRODUCE A CHILD. ARE YOU SURE YOU HEARD FROM GOD?
I KNOW IT WAS GOD WHO SPOKE TO ME, BUT I DO NOT UNDERSTAND WHY HE WAITS SO LONG. HE SAID I WOULD BE THE FATHER OF A GREAT NATION, BUT ALL I HAVE IS AN OLD BODY, AN OLD WIFE THAT CANNOT HAVE CHILDREN, AND A GREAT BIG FLOCK OF SHEEP.
FEAR NOT ABRAHAM, I AM YOUR PROTECTION AND YOUR GREAT REWARD.
WHAT REWARD WILL YOU GIVE ME, SINCE I HAVE NO CHILD?
YOU AND SARAH WILL HAVE A CHILD.
COME, ABRAHAM, LOOK AT THE STARS AND SEE IF YOU CAN COUNT THEM. LIKE THE STARS YOUR CHILDREN WILL BE SO MANY THAT THEY CANNOT BE COUNTED.
I BELIEVE IT WILL COME TO PASS AS YOU SAY.
SINCE YOU BELIEVE ME, I AM GOING TO COUNT YOUR FAITH AS IF IT WERE RIGHTEOUSNESS. KNOW OF A CERTAINTY THAT YOUR CHILDREN WILL BE STRANGERS IN A LAND THAT IS NOT THEIRS. AFTER THEY HAVE SUFFERED AS SLAVES FOR 400 YEARS, I WILL PUNISH THAT NATION AND YOUR CHILDREN WILL LEAVE THERE WITH GREAT WEALTH. THEN THEY WILL COME BACK HERE AND INHABIT THIS LAND.

GENESIS 15:1-6, 13-14

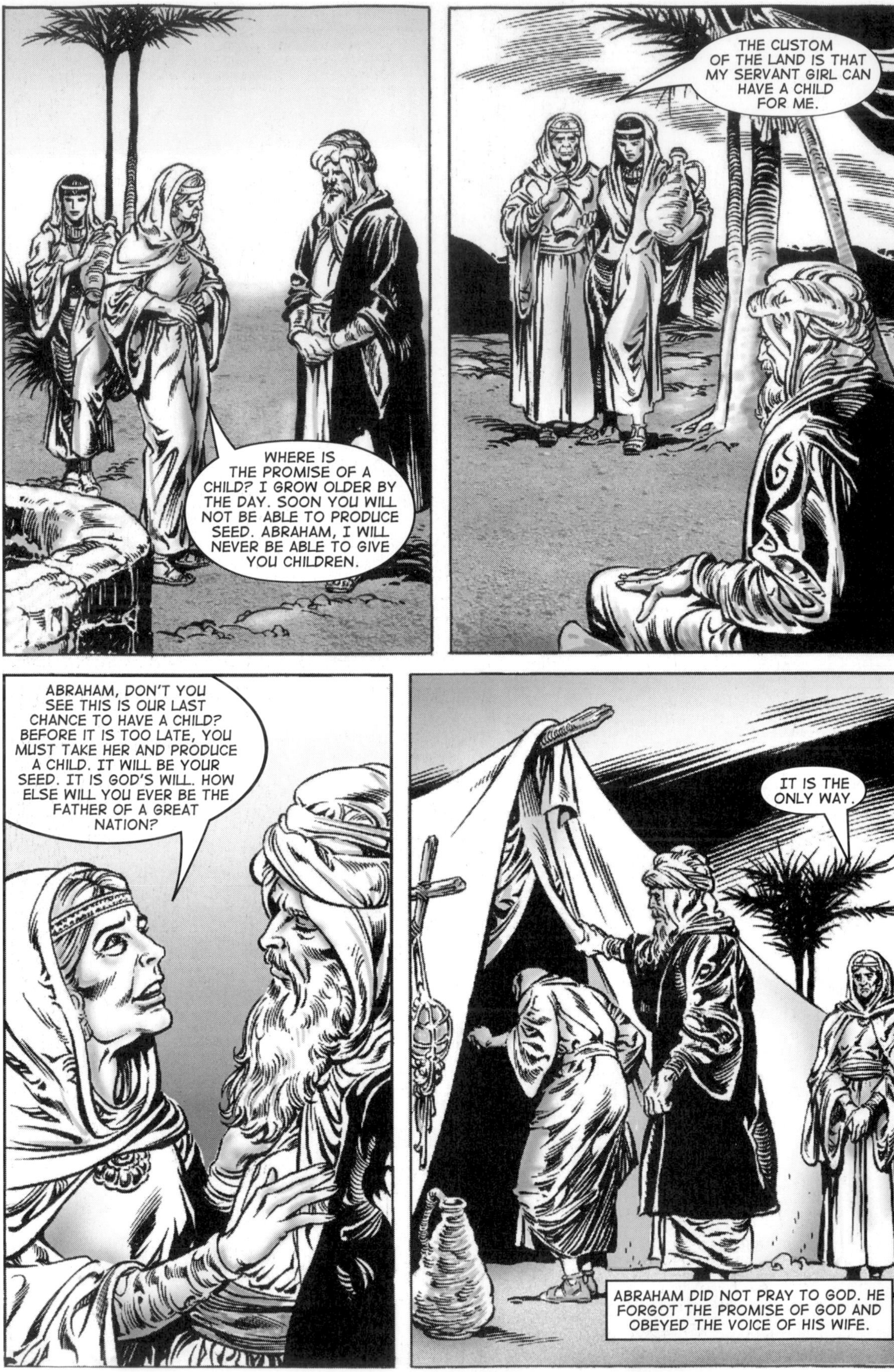
WHERE IS THE PROMISE OF A CHILD? I GROW OLDER BY THE DAY. SOON YOU WILL NOT BE ABLE TO PRODUCE SEED. ABRAHAM, I WILL NEVER BE ABLE TO GIVE YOU CHILDREN.
THE CUSTOM OF THE LAND IS THAT MY SERVANT GIRL CAN HAVE A CHILD FOR ME.
ABRAHAM, DON'T YOU SEE THIS IS OUR LAST CHANCE TO HAVE A CHILD? BEFORE IT IS TOO LATE, YOU MUST TAKE HER AND PRODUCE A CHILD. IT WILL BE YOUR SEED. IT IS GOD'S WILL. HOW ELSE WILL YOU EVER BE THE FATHER OF A GREAT NATION?
IT IS THE ONLY WAY.
ABRAHAM DID NOT PRAY TO GOD. HE FORGOT THE PROMISE OF GOD AND OBEYED THE VOICE OF HIS WIFE.

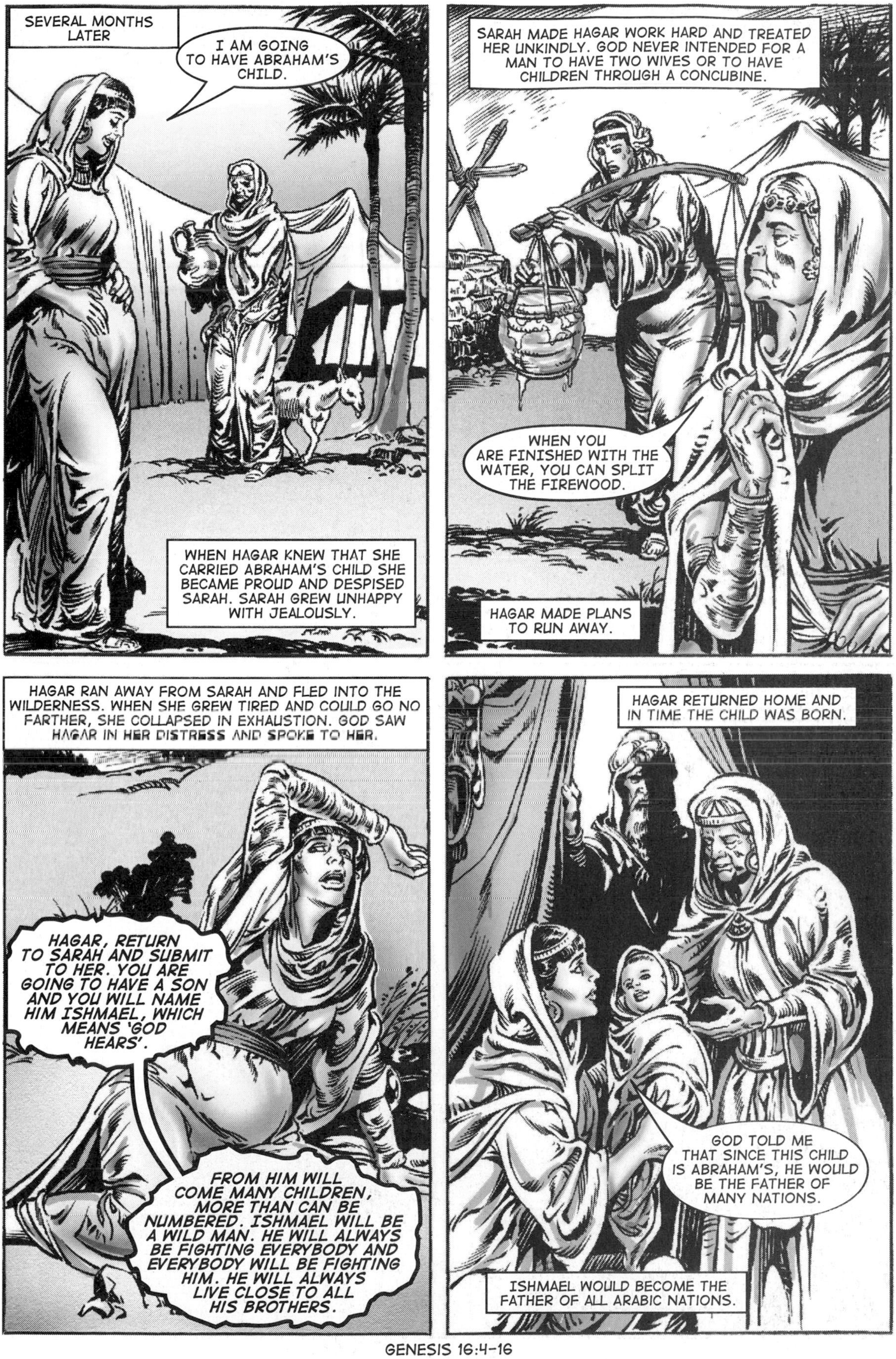
SEVERAL MONTHS LATER
I AM GOING TO HAVE ABRAHAM'S CHILD.
WHEN HAGAR KNEW THAT SHE CARRIED ABRAHAM'S CHILD SHE BECAME PROUD AND DESPISED SARAH. SARAH GREW UNHAPPY WITH JEALOUSLY.
SARAH MADE HAGAR WORK HARD AND TREATED HER UNKINDLY. GOD NEVER INTENDED FOR A MAN TO HAVE TWO WIVES OR TO HAVE CHILDREN THROUGH A CONCUBINE.
WHEN YOU ARE FINISHED WITH THE WATER, YOU CAN SPLIT THE FIREWOOD.
HAGAR MADE PLANS TO RUN AWAY.
HAGAR RAN AWAY FROM SARAH AND FLED INTO THE WILDERNESS. WHEN SHE GREW TIRED AND COULD GO NO FARTHER, SHE COLLAPSED IN EXHAUSTION. GOD SAW HAGAR IN HER DISTRESS AND SPOKE TO HER.
HAGAR, RETURN TO SARAH AND SUBMIT TO HER. YOU ARE GOING TO HAVE A SON AND YOU WILL NAME HIM ISHMAEL, WHICH MEANS 'GOD HEARS'.
FROM HIM WILL COME MANY CHILDREN, MORE THAN CAN BE NUMBERED. ISHMAEL WILL BE A WILD MAN. HE WILL ALWAYS BE FIGHTING EVERYBODY AND EVERYBODY WILL BE FIGHTING HIM. HE WILL ALWAYS LIVE CLOSE TO ALL HIS BROTHERS.
HAGAR RETURNED HOME AND IN TIME THE CHILD WAS BORN.
GOD TOLD ME THAT SINCE THIS CHILD IS ABRAHAM'S, HE WOULD BE THE FATHER OF MANY NATIONS.
ISHMAEL WOULD BECOME THE FATHER OF ALL ARABIC NATIONS.

GENESIS 16:4-16

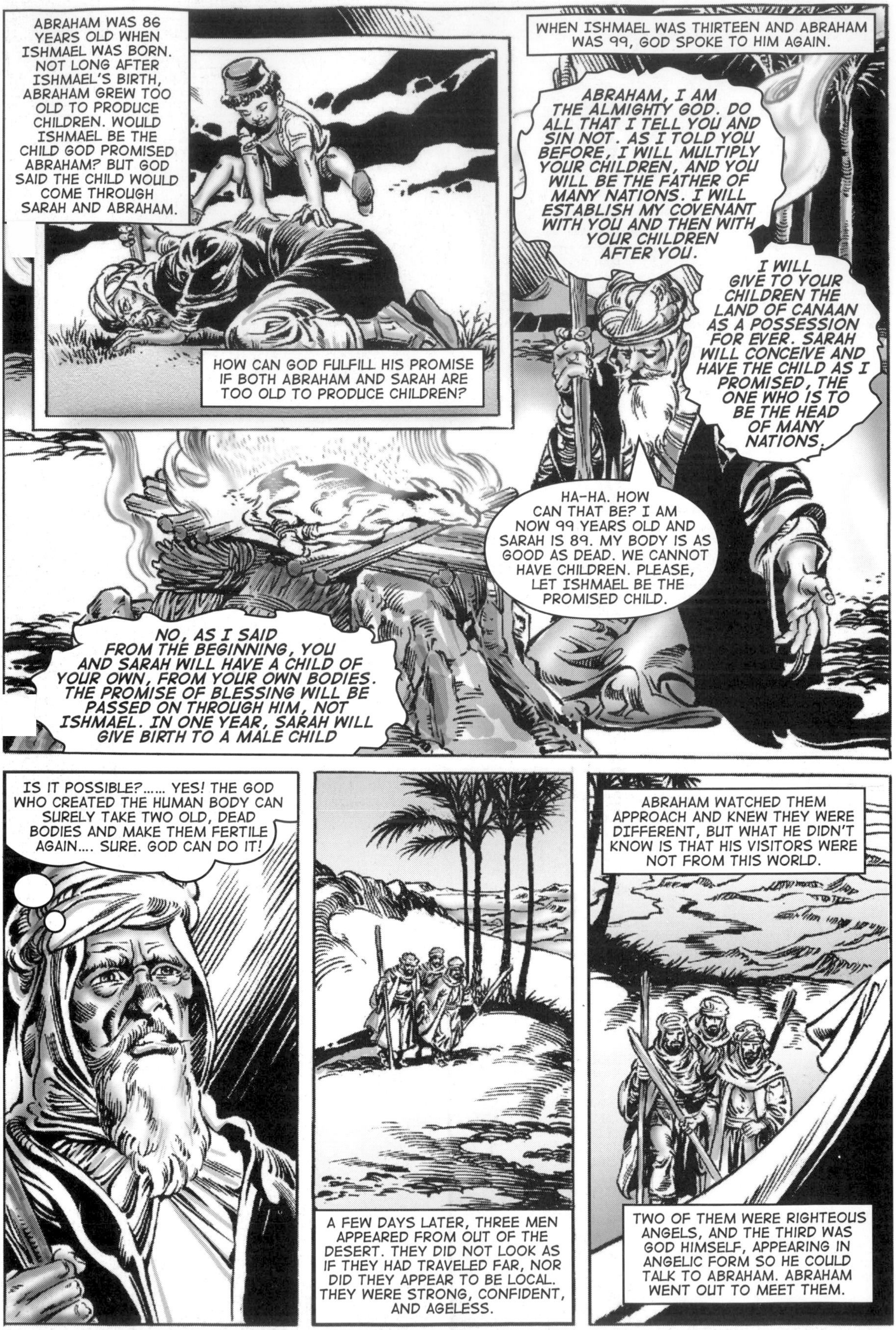
ABRAHAM WAS 86 YEARS OLD WHEN ISHMAEL WAS BORN. NOT LONG AFTER ISHMAEL'S BIRTH, ABRAHAM GREW TOO OLD TO PRODUCE CHILDREN. WOULD ISHMAEL BE THE CHILD GOD PROMISED ABRAHAM? BUT GOD SAID THE CHILD WOULD COME THROUGH SARAH AND ABRAHAM.
HOW CAN GOD FULFILL HIS PROMISE IF BOTH ABRAHAM AND SARAH ARE TOO OLD TO PRODUCE CHILDREN?
WHEN ISHMAEL WAS THIRTEEN AND ABRAHAM WAS 99, GOD SPOKE TO HIM AGAIN.
ABRAHAM, I AM THE ALMIGHTY GOD. DO ALL THAT I TELL YOU AND SIN NOT. AS I TOLD YOU BEFORE, I WILL MULTIPLY YOUR CHILDREN, AND YOU WILL BE THE FATHER OF MANY NATIONS. I WILL ESTABLISH MY COVENANT WITH YOU AND THEN WITH YOUR CHILDREN AFTER YOU.
I WILL GIVE TO YOUR CHILDREN THE LAND OF CANAAN AS A POSSESSION FOR EVER. SARAH WILL CONCEIVE AND HAVE THE CHILD AS I PROMISED, THE ONE WHO IS TO BE THE HEAD OF MANY NATIONS.
HA-HA. HOW CAN THAT BE? I AM NOW 99 YEARS OLD AND SARAH IS 89. MY BODY IS AS GOOD AS DEAD. WE CANNOT HAVE CHILDREN. PLEASE, LET ISHMAEL BE THE PROMISED CHILD.
NO, AS I SAID FROM THE BEGINNING, YOU AND SARAH WILL HAVE A CHILD OF YOUR OWN, FROM YOUR OWN BODIES. THE PROMISE OF BLESSING WILL BE PASSED ON THROUGH HIM, NOT ISHMAEL. IN ONE YEAR, SARAH WILL GIVE BIRTH TO A MALE CHILD
IS IT POSSIBLE?...... YES! THE GOD WHO CREATED THE HUMAN BODY CAN SURELY TAKE TWO OLD, DEAD BODIES AND MAKE THEM FERTILE AGAIN.... SURE. GOD CAN DO IT!
A FEW DAYS LATER, THREE MEN APPEARED FROM OUT OF THE DESERT. THEY DID NOT LOOK AS IF THEY HAD TRAVELED FAR, NOR DID THEY APPEAR TO BE LOCAL. THEY WERE STRONG, CONFIDENT, AND AGELESS.
ABRAHAM WATCHED THEM APPROACH AND KNEW THEY WERE DIFFERENT, BUT WHAT HE DIDN'T KNOW IS THAT HIS VISITORS WERE NOT FROM THIS WORLD.
TWO OF THEM WERE RIGHTEOUS ANGELS, AND THE THIRD WAS GOD HIMSELF, APPEARING IN ANGELIC FORM SO HE COULD TALK TO ABRAHAM. ABRAHAM WENT OUT TO MEET THEM.

GENESIS 17:1-21, 18:1-2

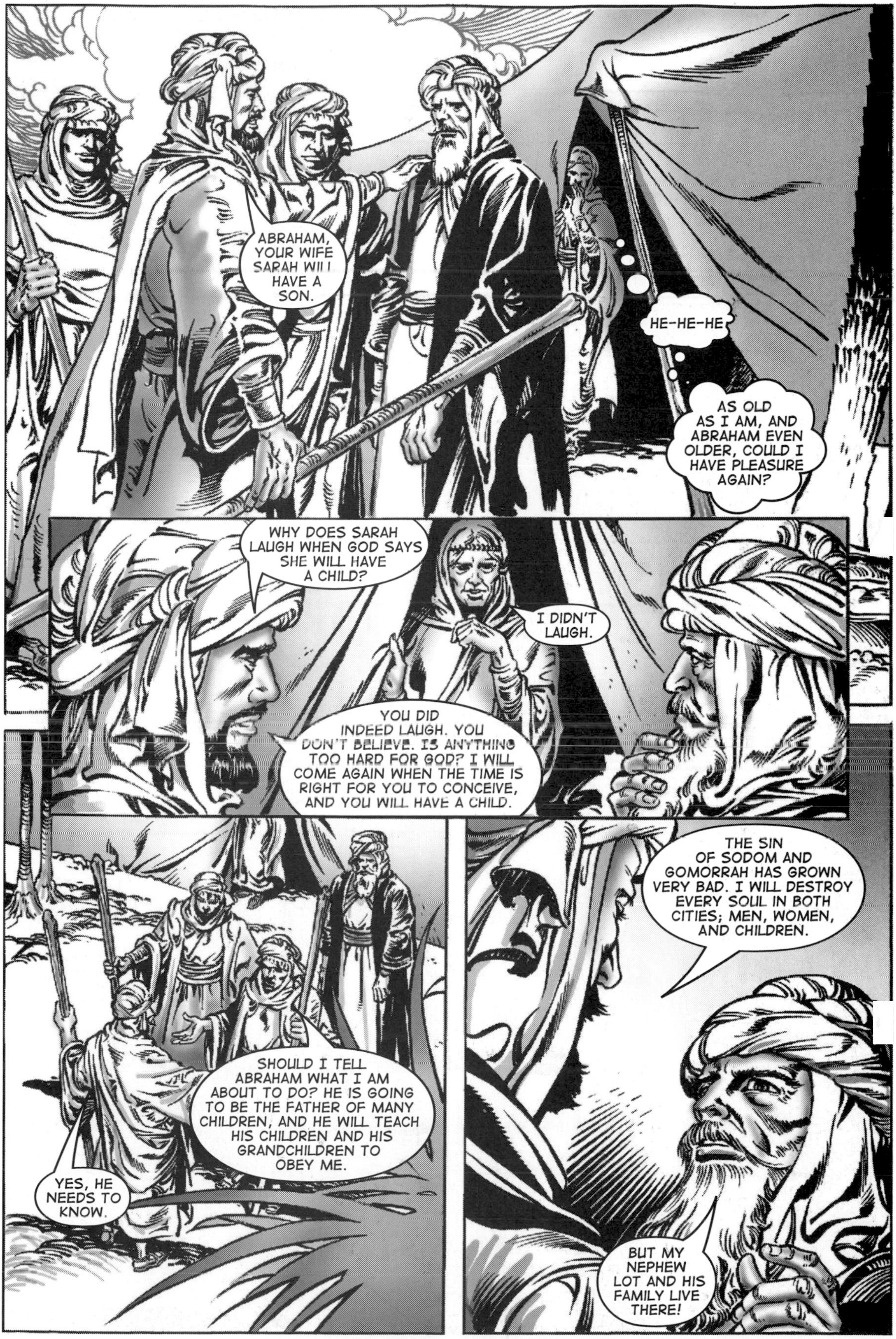
ABRAHAM, YOUR WIFE SARAH WILL HAVE A SON.
HE-HE-HE
AS OLD AS I AM, AND ABRAHAM EVEN OLDER, COULD I HAVE PLEASURE AGAIN?
WHY DOES SARAH LAUGH WHEN GOD SAYS SHE WILL HAVE A CHILD?
I DIDN'T LAUGH.
YOU DID INDEED LAUGH. YOU DON'T BELIEVE. IS ANYTHING TOO HARD FOR GOD? I WILL COME AGAIN WHEN THE TIME IS RIGHT FOR YOU TO CONCEIVE, AND YOU WILL HAVE A CHILD.
SHOULD I TELL ABRAHAM WHAT I AM ABOUT TO DO? HE IS GOING TO BE THE FATHER OF MANY CHILDREN, AND HE WILL TEACH HIS CHILDREN AND HIS GRANDCHILDREN TO OBEY ME.
YES, HE NEEDS TO KNOW.
THE SIN OF SODOM AND GOMORRAH HAS GROWN VERY BAD. I WILL DESTROY EVERY SOUL IN BOTH CITIES; MEN, WOMEN, AND CHILDREN.
BUT MY NEPHEW LOT AND HIS FAMILY LIVE THERE!

GENESIS 18:10-22

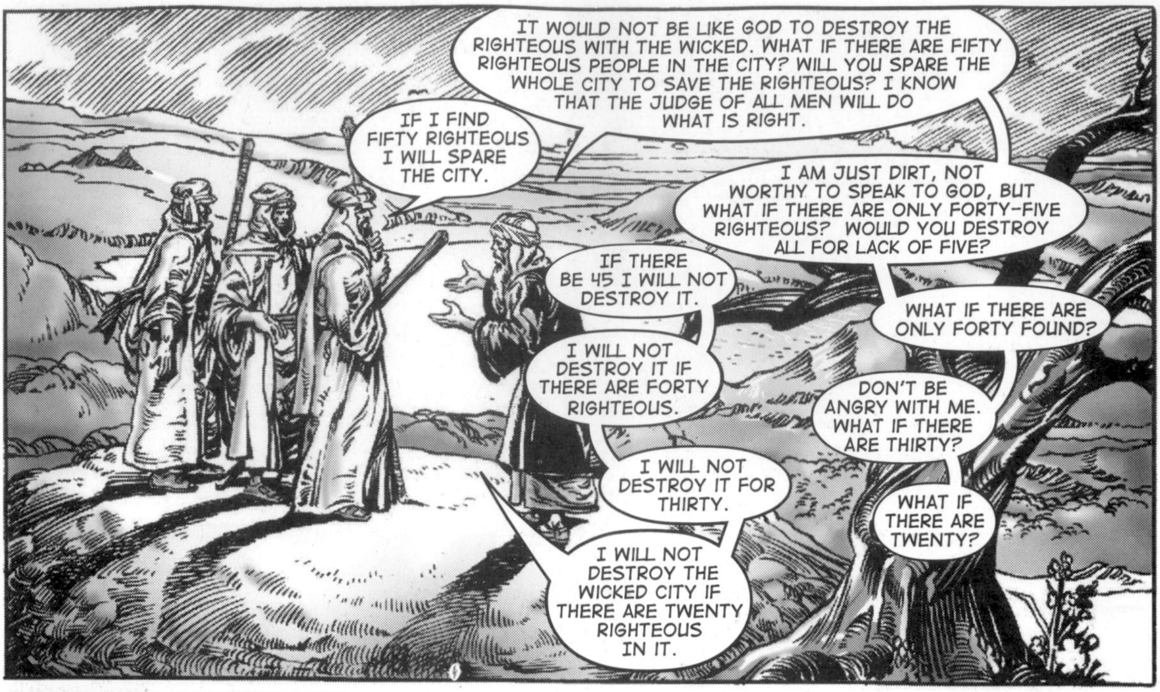
IT WOULD NOT BE LIKE GOD TO DESTROY THE RIGHTEOUS WITH THE WICKED. WHAT IF THERE ARE FIFTY RIGHTEOUS PEOPLE IN THE CITY? WILL YOU SPARE THE WHOLE CITY TO SAVE THE RIGHTEOUS? I KNOW THAT THE JUDGE OF ALL MEN WILL DO WHAT IS RIGHT.
IF I FIND FIFTY RIGHTEOUS I WILL SPARE THE CITY.
I AM JUST DIRT, NOT WORTHY TO SPEAK TO GOD, BUT WHAT IF THERE ARE ONLY FORTY-FIVE RIGHTEOUS? WOULD YOU DESTROY ALL FOR LACK OF FIVE?
IF THERE BE 45 I WILL NOT DESTROY IT.
WHAT IF THERE ARE ONLY FORTY FOUND?
I WILL NOT DESTROY IT IF THERE ARE FORTY RIGHTEOUS.
DON'T BE ANGRY WITH ME. WHAT IF THERE ARE THIRTY?
I WILL NOT DESTROY IT FOR THIRTY.
WHAT IF THERE ARE TWENTY?
I WILL NOT DESTROY THE WICKED CITY IF THERE ARE TWENTY RIGHTEOUS IN IT.

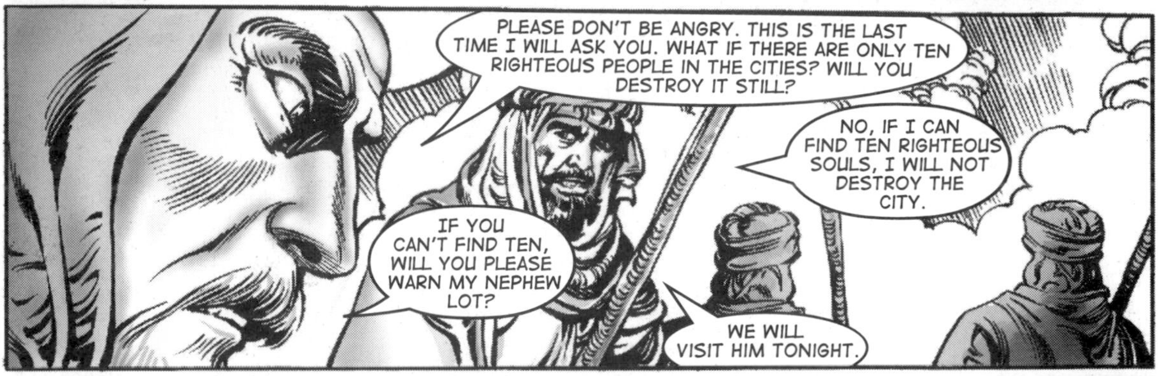
PLEASE DON'T BE ANGRY. THIS IS THE LAST TIME I WILL ASK YOU. WHAT IF THERE ARE ONLY TEN RIGHTEOUS PEOPLE IN THE CITIES? WILL YOU DESTROY IT STILL?
NO, IF I CAN FIND TEN RIGHTEOUS SOULS, I WILL NOT DESTROY THE CITY.
IF YOU CAN'T FIND TEN, WILL YOU PLEASE WARN MY NEPHEW LOT?
WE WILL VISIT HIM TONIGHT.

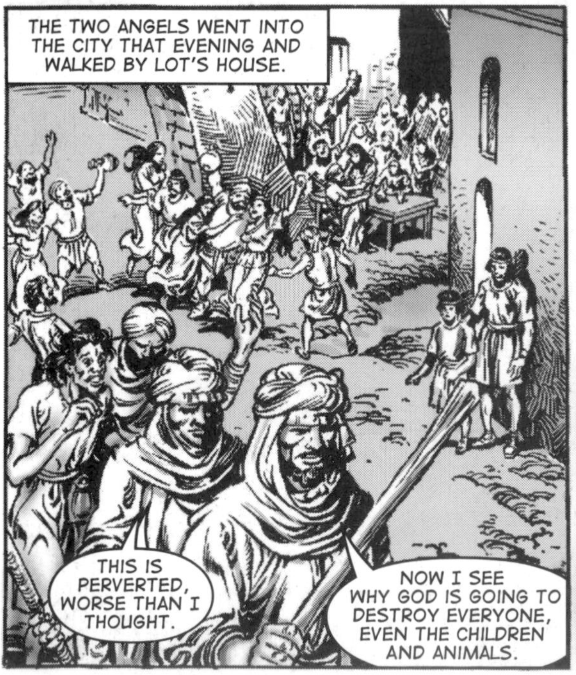
THE TWO ANGELS WENT INTO THE CITY THAT EVENING AND WALKED BY LOT'S HOUSE.
THIS IS PERVERTED, WORSE THAN I THOUGHT.
NOW I SEE WHY GOD IS GOING TO DESTROY EVERYONE, EVEN THE CHILDREN AND ANIMALS.

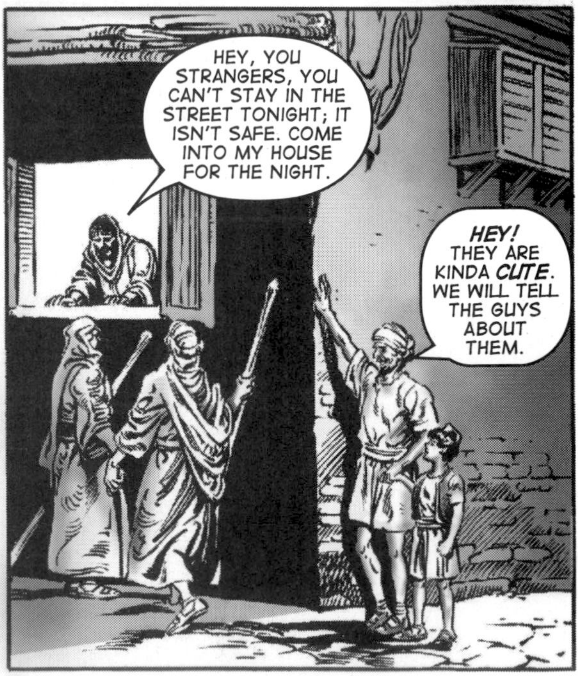
HEY, YOU STRANGERS, YOU CAN'T STAY IN THE STREET TONIGHT; IT ISN'T SAFE. COME INTO MY HOUSE FOR THE NIGHT.
HEY! THEY ARE KINDA CUTE. WE WILL TELL THE GUYS ABOUT THEM.

GENESIS 18:23-19:2

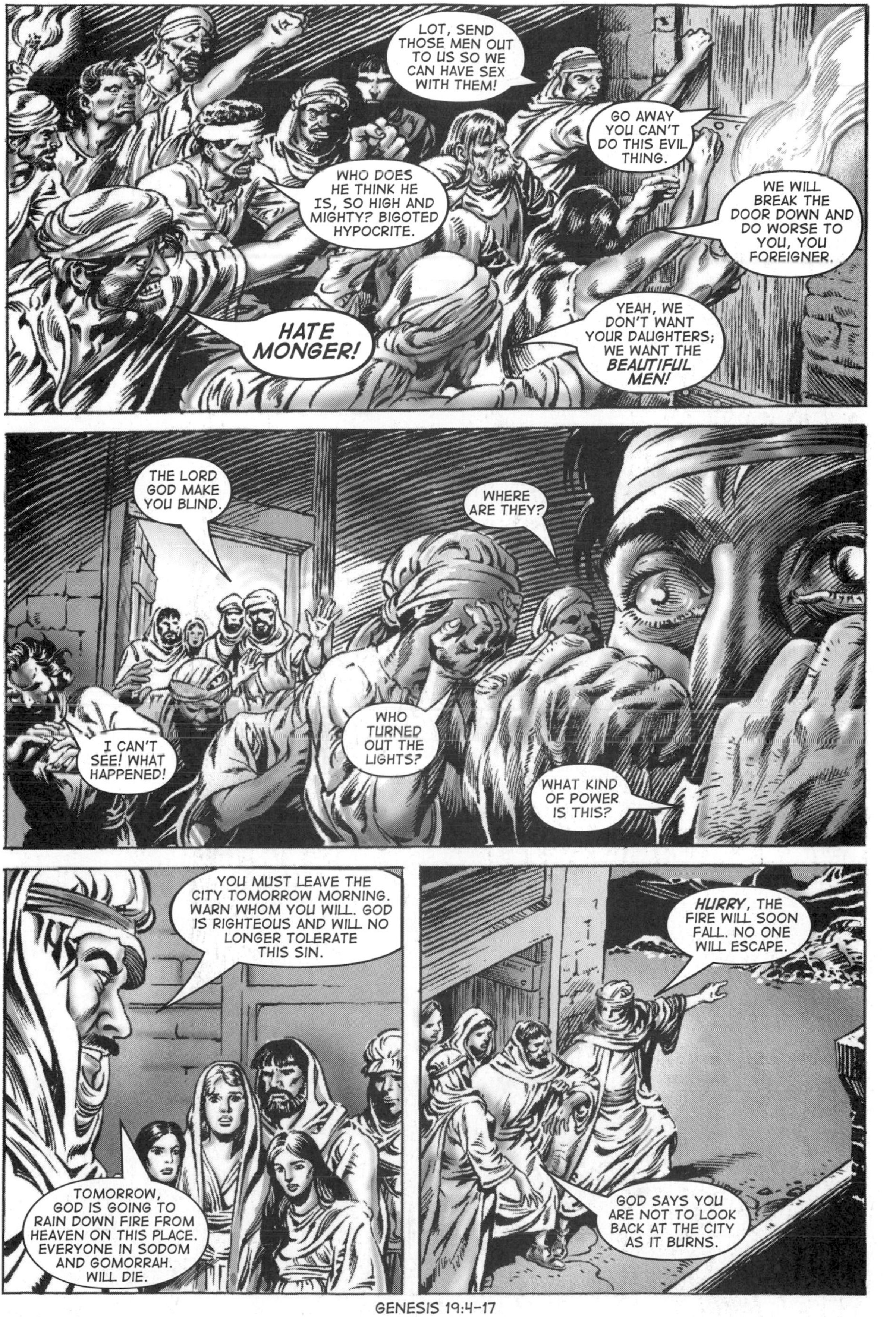
LOT, SEND THOSE MEN OUT TO US SO WE CAN HAVE SEX WITH THEM!
GO AWAY YOU CAN'T DO THIS EVIL THING.
WHO DOES HE THINK HE IS, SO HIGH AND MIGHTY? BIGOTED HYPOCRITE.
WE WILL BREAK THE DOOR DOWN AND DO WORSE TO YOU, YOU FOREIGNER.
HATE MONGER!
YEAH, WE DON'T WANT YOUR DAUGHTERS; WE WANT THE BEAUTIFUL MEN!
THE LORD GOD MAKE YOU BLIND.
WHERE ARE THEY?
I CAN'T SEE! WHAT HAPPENED!
WHO TURNED OUT THE LIGHTS?
WHAT KIND OF POWER IS THIS?
YOU MUST LEAVE THE CITY TOMORROW MORNING. WARN WHOM YOU WILL. GOD IS RIGHTEOUS AND WILL NO LONGER TOLERATE THIS SIN.
TOMORROW, GOD IS GOING TO RAIN DOWN FIRE FROM HEAVEN ON THIS PLACE. EVERYONE IN SODOM AND GOMORRAH. WILL DIE.
HURRY, THE FIRE WILL SOON FALL. NO ONE WILL ESCAPE.
GOD SAYS YOU ARE NOT TO LOOK BACK AT THE CITY AS IT BURNS.

GENESIS 19:4-17

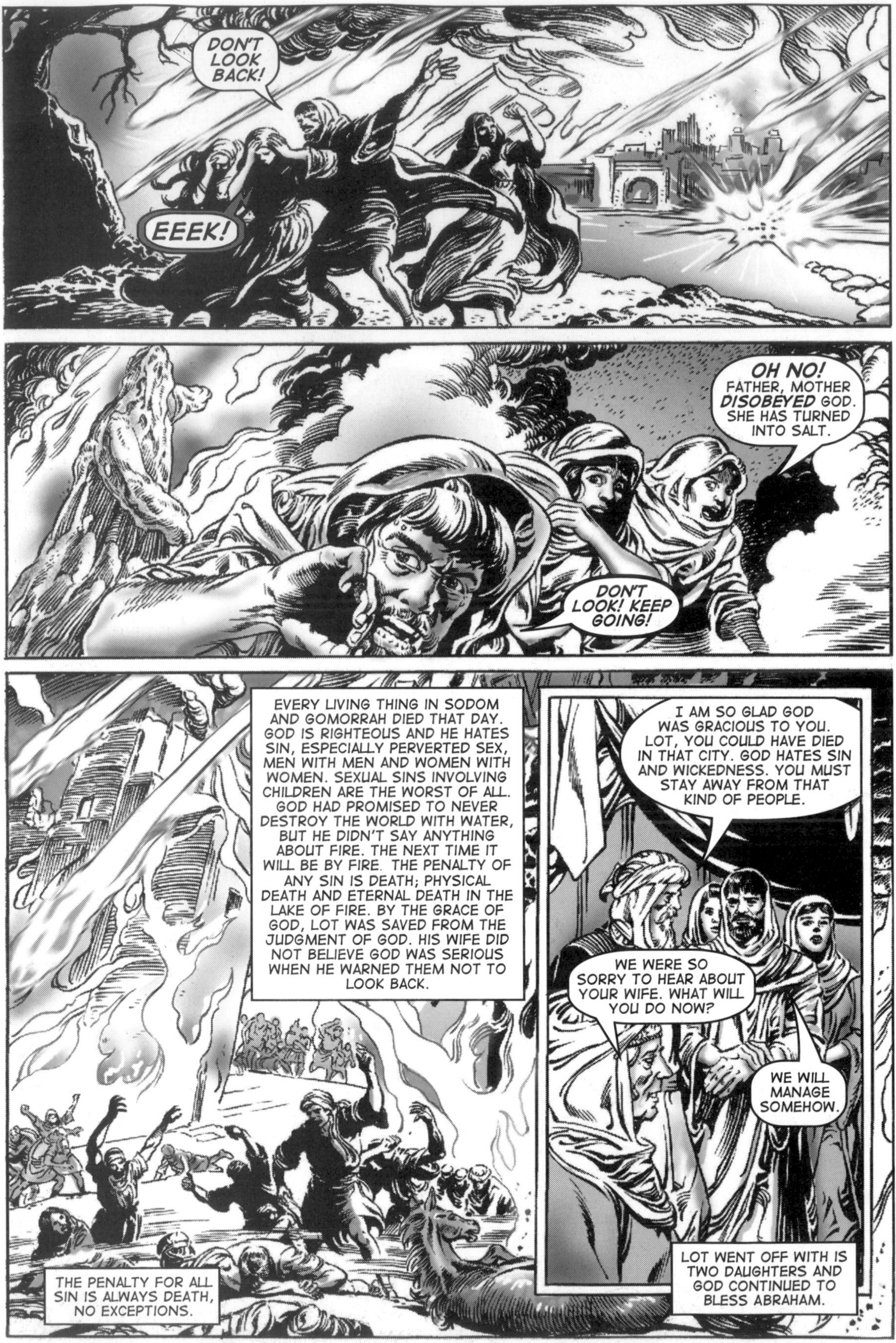
DON'T LOOK BACK!
EEEK!
OH NO! FATHER, MOTHER DISOBEYED GOD. SHE HAS TURNED INTO SALT.
DON'T LOOK! KEEP GOING!
EVERY LIVING THING IN SODOM AND GOMORRAH DIED THAT DAY. GOD IS RIGHTEOUS AND HE HATES SIN, ESPECIALLY PERVERTED SEX, MEN WITH MEN AND WOMEN WITH WOMEN. SEXUAL SINS INVOLVING CHILDREN ARE THE WORST OF ALL. GOD HAD PROMISED TO NEVER DESTROY THE WORLD WITH WATER, BUT HE DIDN'T SAY ANYTHING ABOUT FIRE. THE NEXT TIME IT WILL BE BY FIRE. THE PENALTY OF ANY SIN IS DEATH; PHYSICAL DEATH AND ETERNAL DEATH IN THE LAKE OF FIRE. BY THE GRACE OF GOD, LOT WAS SAVED FROM THE JUDGMENT OF GOD. HIS WIFE DID NOT BELIEVE GOD WAS SERIOUS WHEN HE WARNED THEM NOT TO LOOK BACK.
THE PENALTY FOR ALL SIN IS ALWAYS DEATH, NO EXCEPTIONS.
I AM SO GLAD GOD WAS GRACIOUS TO YOU. LOT, YOU COULD HAVE DIED IN THAT CITY. GOD HATES SIN AND WICKEDNESS. YOU MUST STAY AWAY FROM THAT KIND OF PEOPLE.
WE WERE SO SORRY TO HEAR ABOUT YOUR WIFE. WHAT WILL YOU DO NOW?
WE WILL MANAGE SOMEHOW.
LOT WENT OFF WITH IS TWO DAUGHTERS AND GOD CONTINUED TO BLESS ABRAHAM.

GENESIS 19:24-26; LEVITICUS 18:22; ROMANS 1:23-32, 6:23; 1 CORINTHIANS 6:9-11; REVELATION 21:8

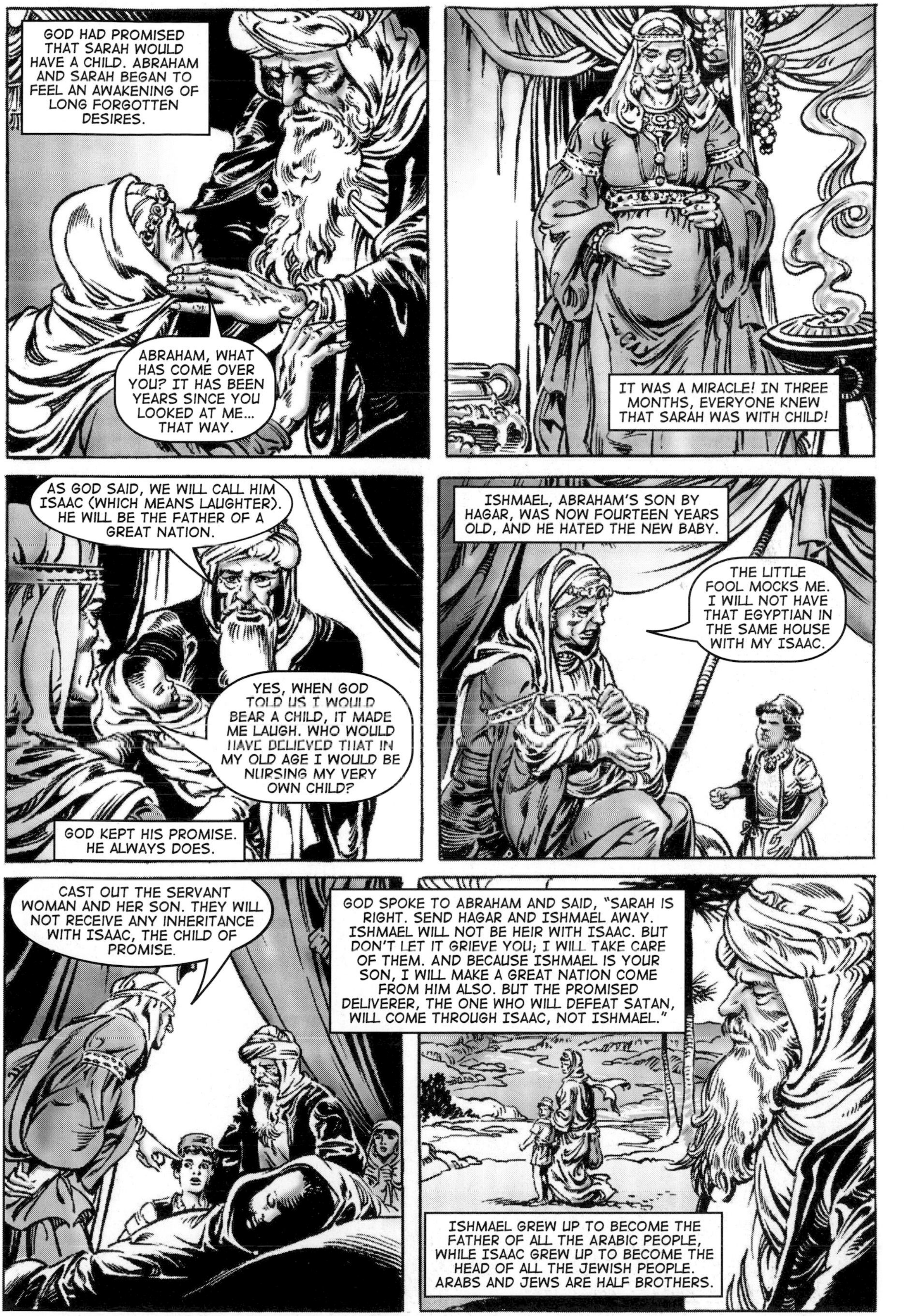
GOD HAD PROMISED THAT SARAH WOULD HAVE A CHILD. ABRAHAM AND SARAH BEGAN TO FEEL AN AWAKENING OF LONG FORGOTTEN DESIRES.
ABRAHAM, WHAT HAS COME OVER YOU? IT HAS BEEN YEARS SINCE YOU LOOKED AT ME... THAT WAY.
IT WAS A MIRACLE! IN THREE MONTHS, EVERYONE KNEW THAT SARAH WAS WITH CHILD!
AS GOD SAID, WE WILL CALL HIM ISAAC (WHICH MEANS LAUGHTER). HE WILL BE THE FATHER OF A GREAT NATION.
YES, WHEN GOD TOLD US I WOULD BEAR A CHILD, IT MADE ME LAUGH. WHO WOULD HAVE BELIEVED THAT IN MY OLD AGE I WOULD BE NURSING MY VERY OWN CHILD?
GOD KEPT HIS PROMISE. HE ALWAYS DOES.
ISHMAEL, ABRAHAM'S SON BY HAGAR, WAS NOW FOURTEEN YEARS OLD, AND HE HATED THE NEW BABY.
THE LITTLE FOOL MOCKS ME. I WILL NOT HAVE THAT EGYPTIAN IN THE SAME HOUSE WITH MY ISAAC.
CAST OUT THE SERVANT WOMAN AND HER SON. THEY WILL NOT RECEIVE ANY INHERITANCE WITH ISAAC, THE CHILD OF PROMISE.
GOD SPOKE TO ABRAHAM AND SAID, "SARAH IS RIGHT. SEND HAGAR AND ISHMAEL AWAY. ISHMAEL WILL NOT BE HEIR WITH ISAAC. BUT DON'T LET IT GRIEVE YOU; I WILL TAKE CARE OF THEM. AND BECAUSE ISHMAEL IS YOUR SON, I WILL MAKE A GREAT NATION COME FROM HIM ALSO. BUT THE PROMISED DELIVERER, THE ONE WHO WILL DEFEAT SATAN, WILL COME THROUGH ISAAC, NOT ISHMAEL."
ISHMAEL GREW UP TO BECOME THE FATHER OF ALL THE ARABIC PEOPLE, WHILE ISAAC GREW UP TO BECOME THE HEAD OF ALL THE JEWISH PEOPLE. ARABS AND JEWS ARE HALF BROTHERS.

GENESIS 21:1-3, 9-14

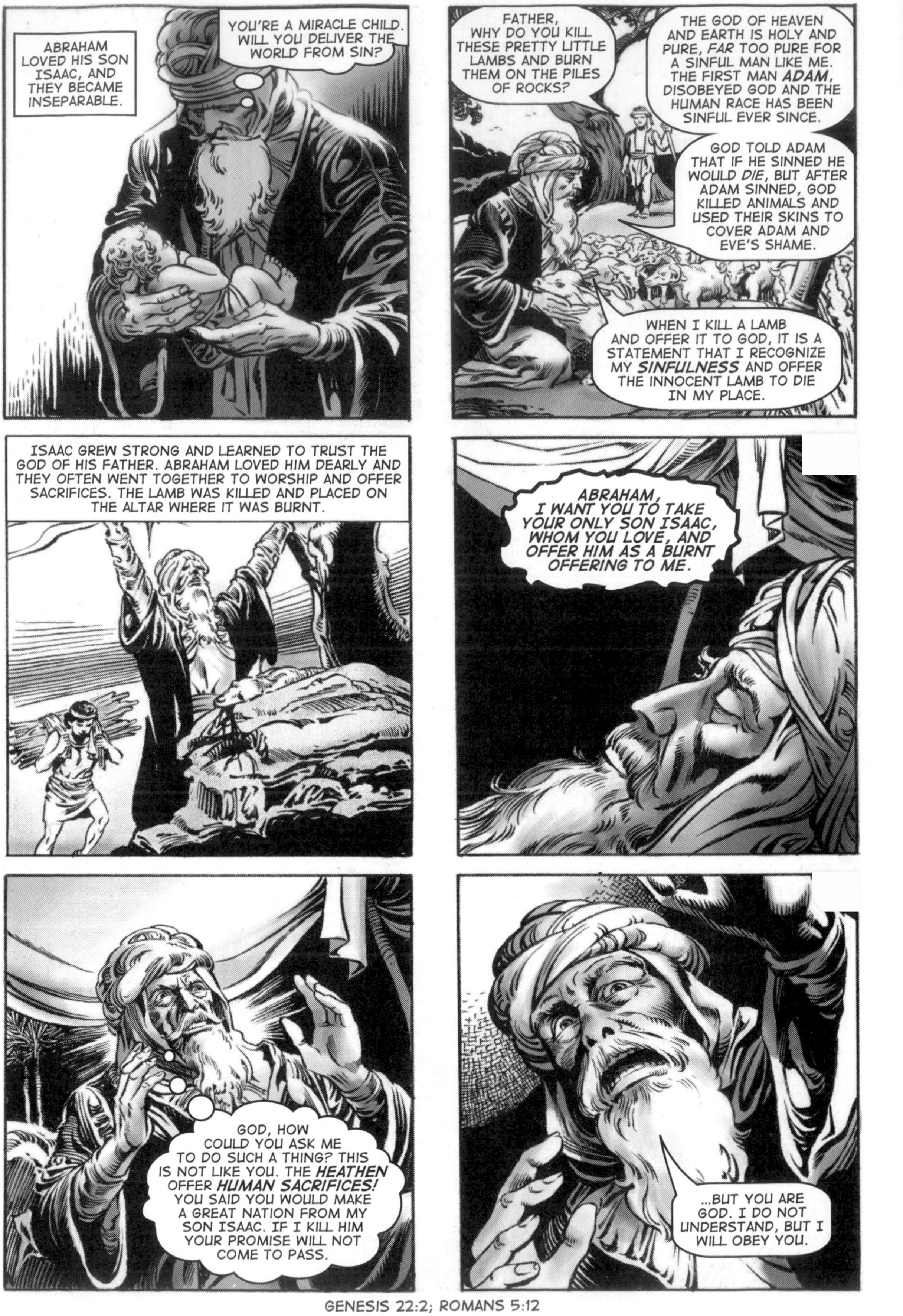
ABRAHAM LOVED HIS SON ISAAC, AND THEY BECAME INSEPARABLE.
YOU'RE A MIRACLE CHILD. WILL YOU DELIVER THE WORLD FROM SIN?
FATHER, WHY DO YOU KILL THESE PRETTY LITTLE LAMBS AND BURN THEM ON THE PILES OF ROCKS?
THE GOD OF HEAVEN AND EARTH IS HOLY AND PURE, FAR TOO PURE FOR A SINFUL MAN LIKE ME. THE FIRST MAN ADAM, DISOBEYED GOD AND THE HUMAN RACE HAS BEEN SINFUL EVER SINCE.
GOD TOLD ADAM THAT IF HE SINNED HE WOULD DIE, BUT AFTER ADAM SINNED, GOD KILLED ANIMALS AND USED THEIR SKINS TO COVER ADAM AND EVE'S SHAME.
WHEN I KILL A LAMB AND OFFER IT TO GOD, IT IS A STATEMENT THAT I RECOGNIZE MY SINFULNESS AND OFFER THE INNOCENT LAMB TO DIE IN MY PLACE.
ISAAC GREW STRONG AND LEARNED TO TRUST THE GOD OF HIS FATHER. ABRAHAM LOVED HIM DEARLY AND THEY OFTEN WENT TOGETHER TO WORSHIP AND OFFER SACRIFICES. THE LAMB WAS KILLED AND PLACED ON THE ALTAR WHERE IT WAS BURNT.
ABRAHAM, I WANT YOU TO TAKE YOUR ONLY SON ISAAC, WHOM YOU LOVE, AND OFFER HIM AS A BURNT OFFERING TO ME.
GOD, HOW COULD YOU ASK ME TO DO SUCH A THING? THIS IS NOT LIKE YOU. THE HEATHEN OFFER HUMAN SACRIFICES! YOU SAID YOU WOULD MAKE A GREAT NATION FROM MY SON ISAAC. IF I KILL HIM YOUR PROMISE WILL NOT COME TO PASS.
...BUT YOU ARE GOD. I DO NOT UNDERSTAND, BUT I WILL OBEY YOU.

GENESIS 22:2; ROMANS 5:12

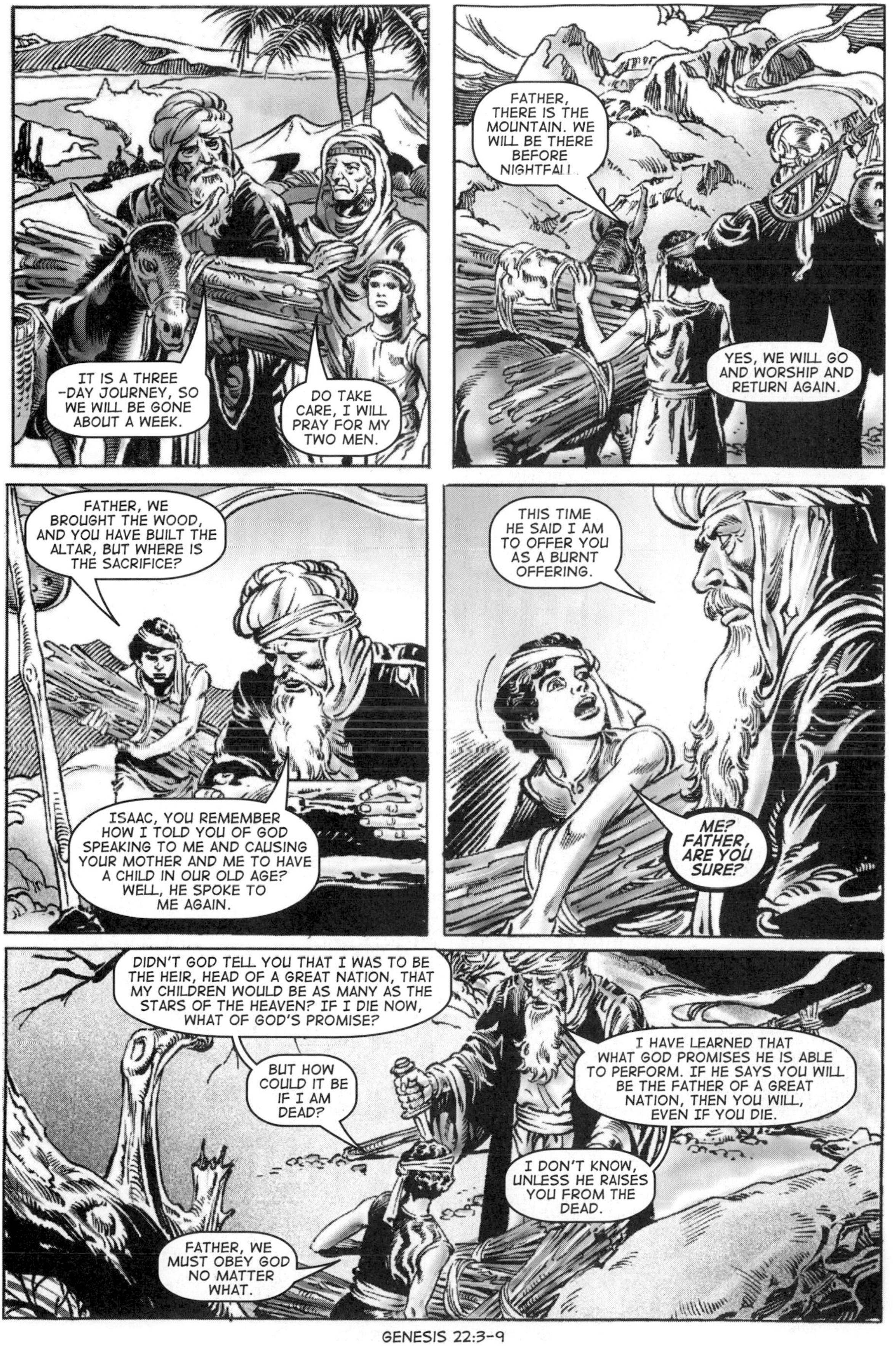
IT IS A THREE -DAY JOURNEY, SO WE WILL BE GONE ABOUT A WEEK.
DO TAKE CARE, I WILL PRAY FOR MY TWO MEN.
FATHER, THERE IS THE MOUNTAIN. WE WILL BE THERE BEFORE NIGHTFALL.
YES, WE WILL GO AND WORSHIP AND RETURN AGAIN.
FATHER, WE BROUGHT THE WOOD, AND YOU HAVE BUILT THE ALTAR, BUT WHERE IS THE SACRIFICE?
ISAAC, YOU REMEMBER HOW I TOLD YOU OF GOD SPEAKING TO ME AND CAUSING YOUR MOTHER AND ME TO HAVE A CHILD IN OUR OLD AGE? WELL, HE SPOKE TO ME AGAIN.
THIS TIME HE SAID I AM TO OFFER YOU AS A BURNT OFFERING.
ME? FATHER, ARE YOU SURE?
DIDN'T GOD TELL YOU THAT I WAS TO BE THE HEIR, HEAD OF A GREAT NATION, THAT MY CHILDREN WOULD BE AS MANY AS THE STARS OF THE HEAVEN? IF I DIE NOW, WHAT OF GOD'S PROMISE?
I HAVE LEARNED THAT WHAT GOD PROMISES HE IS ABLE TO PERFORM. IF HE SAYS YOU WILL BE THE FATHER OF A GREAT NATION, THEN YOU WILL, EVEN IF YOU DIE.
BUT HOW COULD IT BE IF I AM DEAD?
I DON'T KNOW, UNLESS HE RAISES YOU FROM THE DEAD.
FATHER, WE MUST OBEY GOD NO MATTER WHAT.

GENESIS 22:3–9

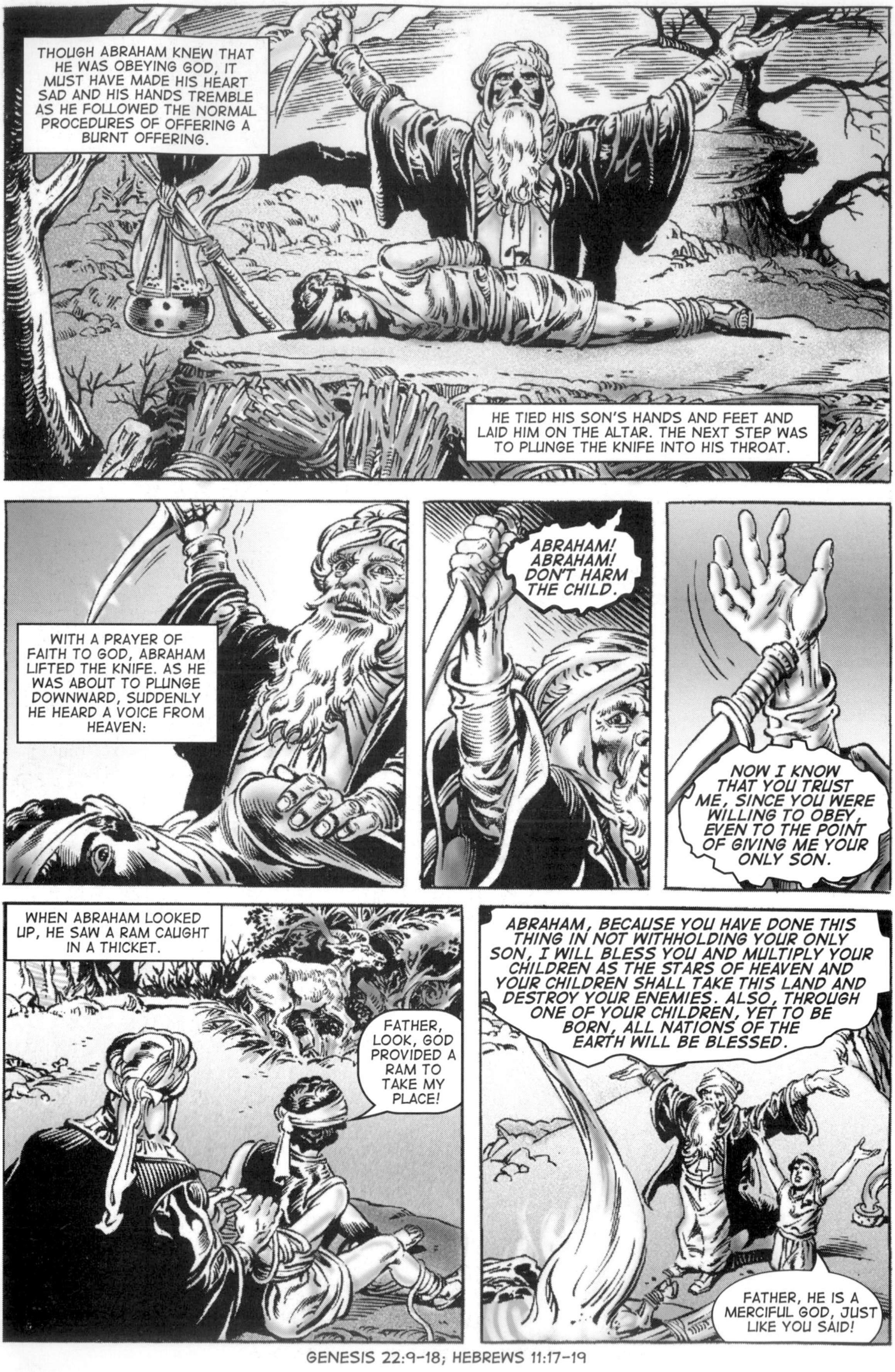
THOUGH ABRAHAM KNEW THAT HE WAS OBEYING GOD, IT MUST HAVE MADE HIS HEART SAD AND HIS HANDS TREMBLE AS HE FOLLOWED THE NORMAL PROCEDURES OF OFFERING A BURNT OFFERING.
HE TIED HIS SON'S HANDS AND FEET AND LAID HIM ON THE ALTAR. THE NEXT STEP WAS TO PLUNGE THE KNIFE INTO HIS THROAT.
WITH A PRAYER OF FAITH TO GOD, ABRAHAM LIFTED THE KNIFE. AS HE WAS ABOUT TO PLUNGE DOWNWARD, SUDDENLY HE HEARD A VOICE FROM HEAVEN:
ABRAHAM! ABRAHAM! DON'T HARM THE CHILD.
NOW I KNOW THAT YOU TRUST ME, SINCE YOU WERE WILLING TO OBEY, EVEN TO THE POINT OF GIVING ME YOUR ONLY SON.
WHEN ABRAHAM LOOKED UP, HE SAW A RAM CAUGHT IN A THICKET.
FATHER, LOOK, GOD PROVIDED A RAM TO TAKE MY PLACE!
ABRAHAM, BECAUSE YOU HAVE DONE THIS THING IN NOT WITHHOLDING YOUR ONLY SON, I WILL BLESS YOU AND MULTIPLY YOUR CHILDREN AS THE STARS OF HEAVEN AND YOUR CHILDREN SHALL TAKE THIS LAND AND DESTROY YOUR ENEMIES. ALSO, THROUGH ONE OF YOUR CHILDREN, YET TO BE BORN, ALL NATIONS OF THE EARTH WILL BE BLESSED.
FATHER, HE IS A MERCIFUL GOD, JUST LIKE YOU SAID!

GENESIS 22:9-18; HEBREWS 11:17-19

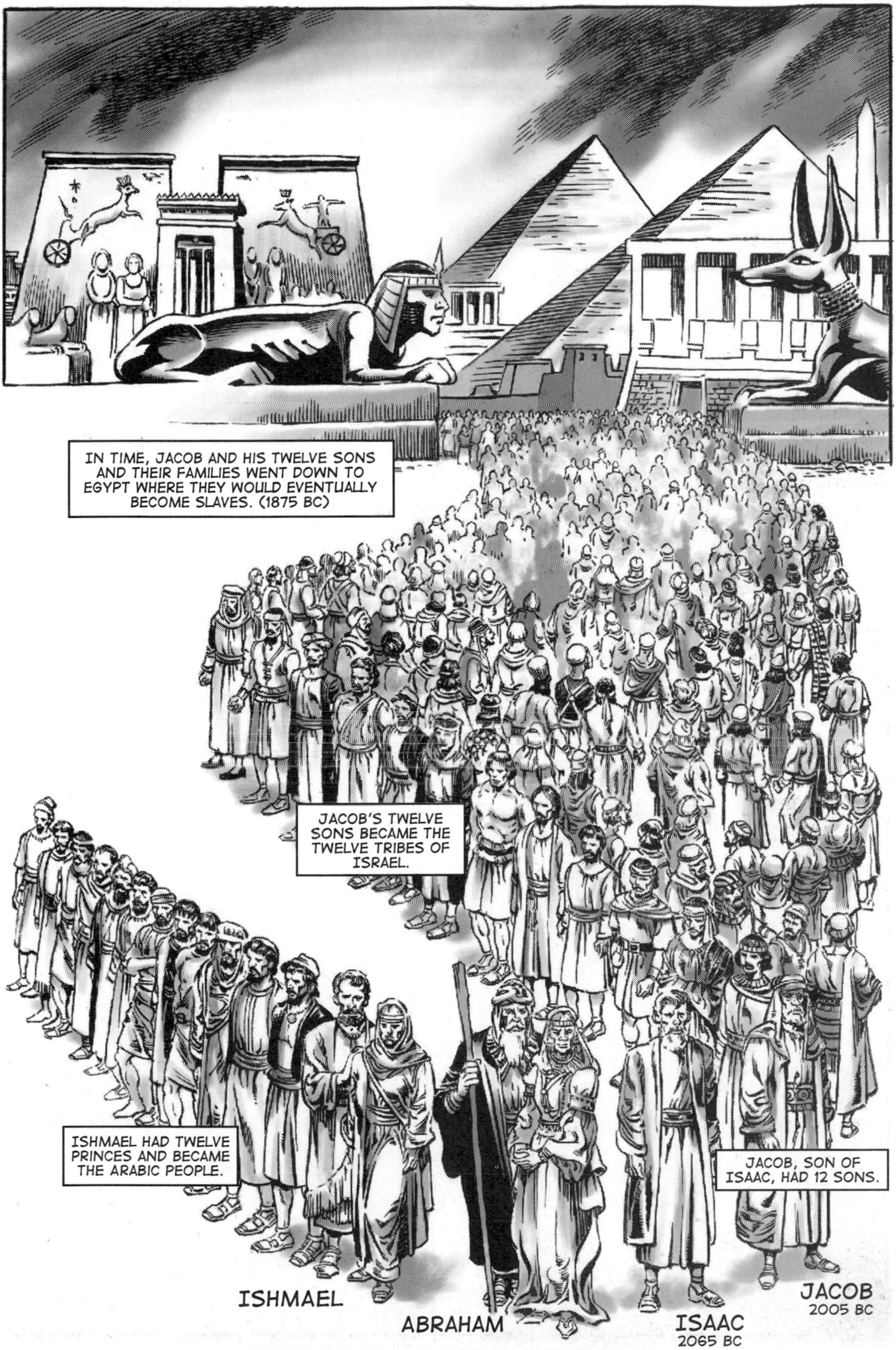
IN TIME, JACOB AND HIS TWELVE SONS AND THEIR FAMILIES WENT DOWN TO EGYPT WHERE THEY WOULD EVENTUALLY BECOME SLAVES. (1875 BC)
JACOB'S TWELVE SONS BECAME THE TWELVE TRIBES OF ISRAEL.
ISHMAEL HAD TWELVE PRINCES AND BECAME THE ARABIC PEOPLE.
JACOB, SON OF ISAAC, HAD 12 SONS.
ISHMAEL
ABRAHAM
ISAAC
2065 BC
JACOB
2005 BC

GENESIS 21:5, 13, 24:67, 25:12-18, 21-26, 29:23-30

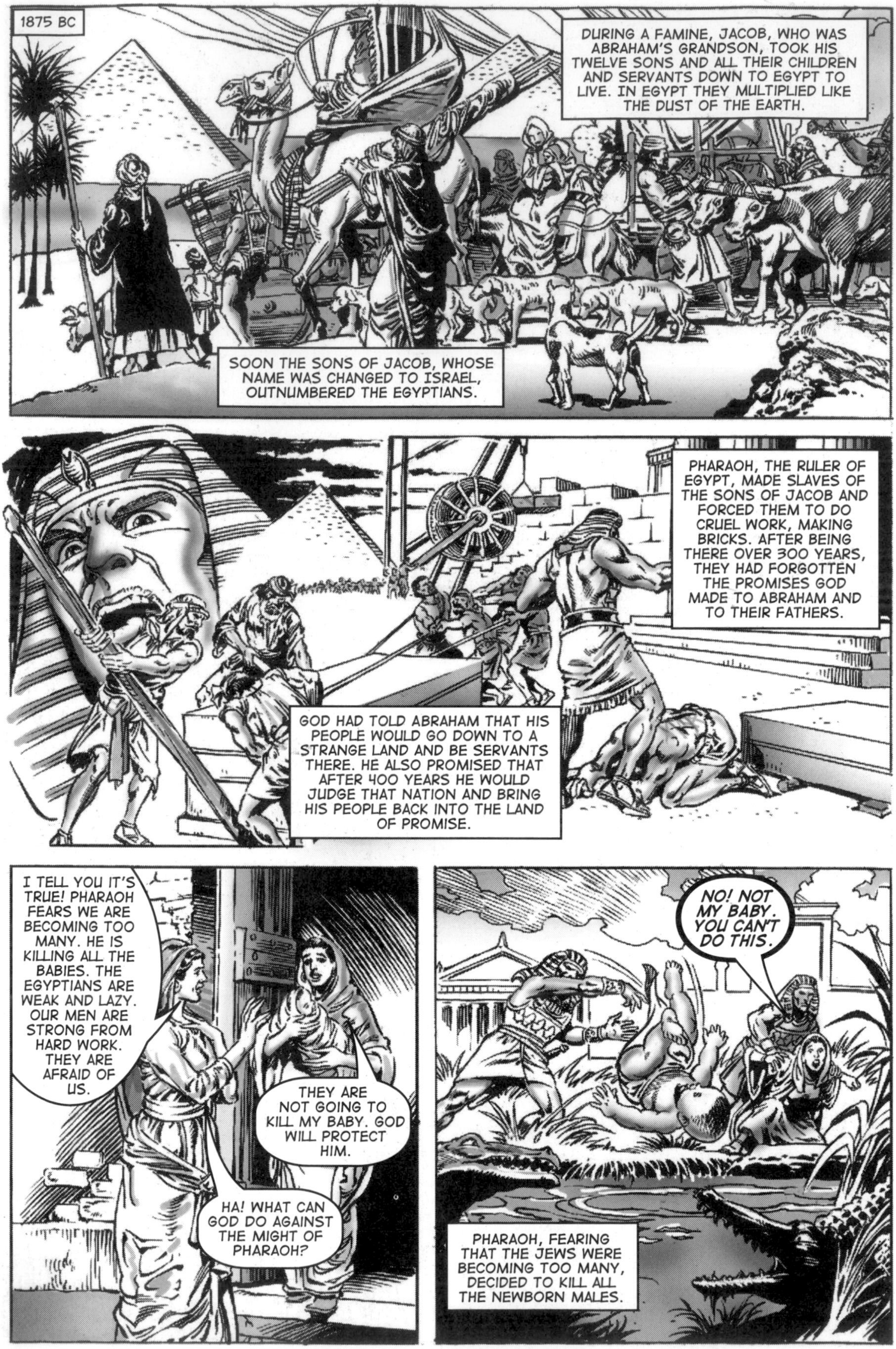
1875 BC
DURING A FAMINE, JACOB, WHO WAS ABRAHAM'S GRANDSON, TOOK HIS TWELVE SONS AND ALL THEIR CHILDREN AND SERVANTS DOWN TO EGYPT TO LIVE. IN EGYPT THEY MULTIPLIED LIKE THE DUST OF THE EARTH.
SOON THE SONS OF JACOB, WHOSE NAME WAS CHANGED TO ISRAEL, OUTNUMBERED THE EGYPTIANS.
PHARAOH, THE RULER OF EGYPT, MADE SLAVES OF THE SONS OF JACOB AND FORCED THEM TO DO CRUEL WORK, MAKING BRICKS. AFTER BEING THERE OVER 300 YEARS, THEY HAD FORGOTTEN THE PROMISES GOD MADE TO ABRAHAM AND TO THEIR FATHERS.
GOD HAD TOLD ABRAHAM THAT HIS PEOPLE WOULD GO DOWN TO A STRANGE LAND AND BE SERVANTS THERE. HE ALSO PROMISED THAT AFTER 400 YEARS HE WOULD JUDGE THAT NATION AND BRING HIS PEOPLE BACK INTO THE LAND OF PROMISE.
I TELL YOU IT'S TRUE! PHARAOH FEARS WE ARE BECOMING TOO MANY. HE IS KILLING ALL THE BABIES. THE EGYPTIANS ARE WEAK AND LAZY. OUR MEN ARE STRONG FROM HARD WORK. THEY ARE AFRAID OF US.
THEY ARE NOT GOING TO KILL MY BABY. GOD WILL PROTECT HIM.
HA! WHAT CAN GOD DO AGAINST THE MIGHT OF PHARAOH?
NO! NOT MY BABY. YOU CAN'T DO THIS.
PHARAOH, FEARING THAT THE JEWS WERE BECOMING TOO MANY, DECIDED TO KILL ALL THE NEWBORN MALES.

GENESIS 46:5-7; EXODUS 1:1-12, 22

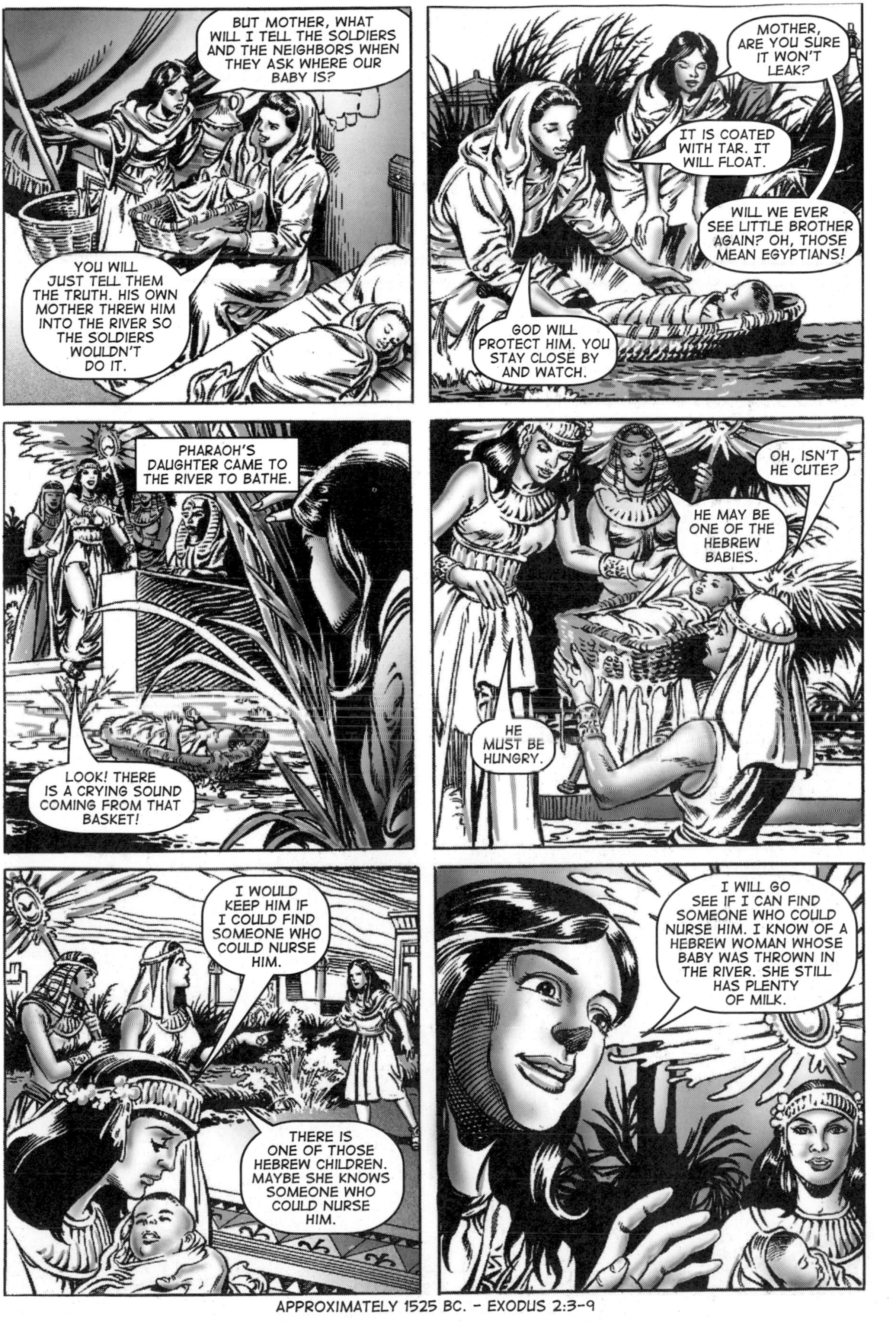

BUT MOTHER, WHAT WILL I TELL THE SOLDIERS AND THE NEIGHBORS WHEN THEY ASK WHERE OUR BABY IS?
YOU WILL JUST TELL THEM THE TRUTH. HIS OWN MOTHER THREW HIM INTO THE RIVER SO THE SOLDIERS WOULDN'T DO IT.
MOTHER, ARE YOU SURE IT WON'T LEAK?
IT IS COATED WITH TAR. IT WILL FLOAT.
WILL WE EVER SEE LITTLE BROTHER AGAIN? OH, THOSE MEAN EGYPTIANS!
GOD WILL PROTECT HIM. YOU STAY CLOSE BY AND WATCH.
PHARAOH'S DAUGHTER CAME TO THE RIVER TO BATHE.
LOOK! THERE IS A CRYING SOUND COMING FROM THAT BASKET!
OH, ISN'T HE CUTE?
HE MAY BE ONE OF THE HEBREW BABIES.
HE MUST BE HUNGRY.
I WOULD KEEP HIM IF I COULD FIND SOMEONE WHO COULD NURSE HIM.
THERE IS ONE OF THOSE HEBREW CHILDREN. MAYBE SHE KNOWS SOMEONE WHO COULD NURSE HIM.
I WILL GO SEE IF I CAN FIND SOMEONE WHO COULD NURSE HIM. I KNOW OF A HEBREW WOMAN WHOSE BABY WAS THROWN IN THE RIVER. SHE STILL HAS PLENTY OF MILK.

APPROXIMATELY 1525 BC. - EXODUS 2:3-9

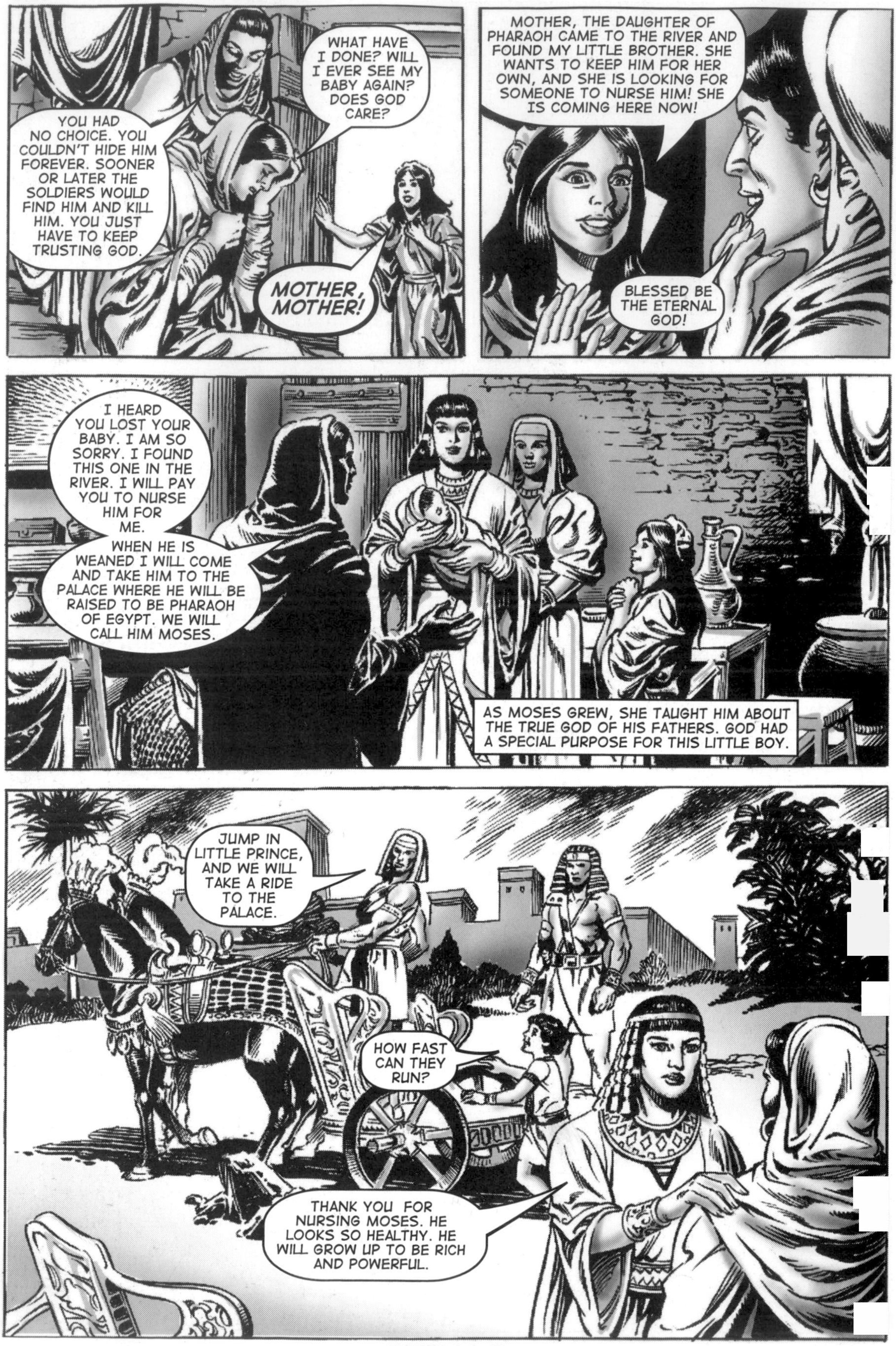
WHAT HAVE I DONE? WILL I EVER SEE MY BABY AGAIN? DOES GOD CARE?
YOU HAD NO CHOICE. YOU COULDN'T HIDE HIM FOREVER. SOONER OR LATER THE SOLDIERS WOULD FIND HIM AND KILL HIM. YOU JUST HAVE TO KEEP TRUSTING GOD.
MOTHER, MOTHER!
MOTHER, THE DAUGHTER OF PHARAOH CAME TO THE RIVER AND FOUND MY LITTLE BROTHER. SHE WANTS TO KEEP HIM FOR HER OWN, AND SHE IS LOOKING FOR SOMEONE TO NURSE HIM! SHE IS COMING HERE NOW!
BLESSED BE THE ETERNAL GOD!
I HEARD YOU LOST YOUR BABY. I AM SO SORRY. I FOUND THIS ONE IN THE RIVER. I WILL PAY YOU TO NURSE HIM FOR ME.
WHEN HE IS WEANED I WILL COME AND TAKE HIM TO THE PALACE WHERE HE WILL BE RAISED TO BE PHARAOH OF EGYPT. WE WILL CALL HIM MOSES.
AS MOSES GREW, SHE TAUGHT HIM ABOUT THE TRUE GOD OF HIS FATHERS. GOD HAD A SPECIAL PURPOSE FOR THIS LITTLE BOY.
JUMP IN LITTLE PRINCE, AND WE WILL TAKE A RIDE TO THE PALACE.
HOW FAST CAN THEY RUN?
THANK YOU FOR NURSING MOSES. HE LOOKS SO HEALTHY. HE WILL GROW UP TO BE RICH AND POWERFUL.

EXODUS 2:8–10

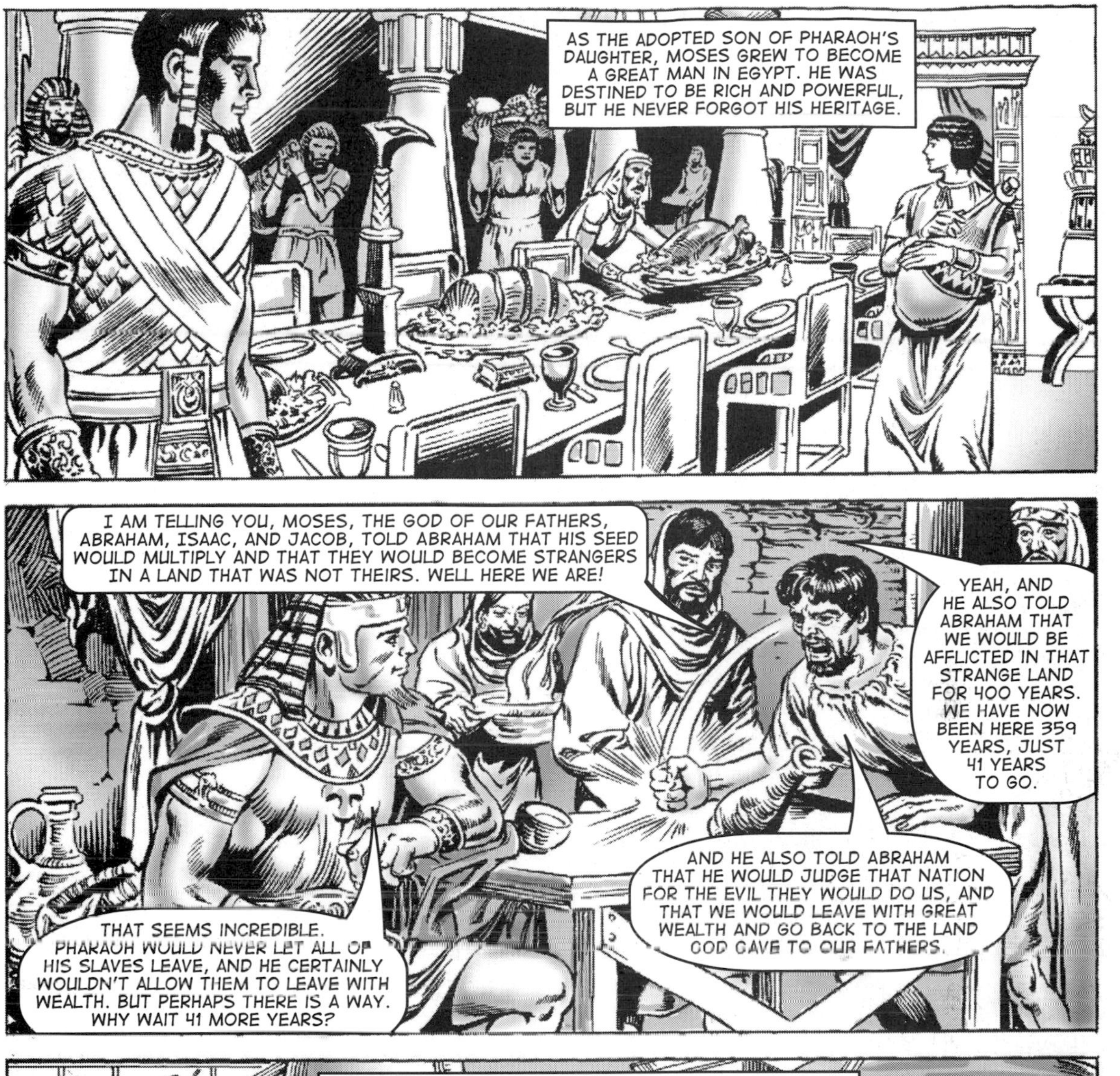
AS THE ADOPTED SON OF PHARAOH'S DAUGHTER, MOSES GREW TO BECOME A GREAT MAN IN EGYPT. HE WAS DESTINED TO BE RICH AND POWERFUL, BUT HE NEVER FORGOT HIS HERITAGE.
I AM TELLING YOU, MOSES, THE GOD OF OUR FATHERS, ABRAHAM, ISAAC, AND JACOB, TOLD ABRAHAM THAT HIS SEED WOULD MULTIPLY AND THAT THEY WOULD BECOME STRANGERS IN A LAND THAT WAS NOT THEIRS. WELL HERE WE ARE!
YEAH, AND HE ALSO TOLD ABRAHAM THAT WE WOULD BE AFFLICTED IN THAT STRANGE LAND FOR 400 YEARS. WE HAVE NOW BEEN HERE 359 YEARS, JUST 41 YEARS TO GO.
AND HE ALSO TOLD ABRAHAM THAT HE WOULD JUDGE THAT NATION FOR THE EVIL THEY WOULD DO US, AND THAT WE WOULD LEAVE WITH GREAT WEALTH AND GO BACK TO THE LAND GOD GAVE TO OUR FATHERS.
THAT SEEMS INCREDIBLE. PHARAOH WOULD NEVER LET ALL OF HIS SLAVES LEAVE, AND HE CERTAINLY WOULDN'T ALLOW THEM TO LEAVE WITH WEALTH. BUT PERHAPS THERE IS A WAY. WHY WAIT 41 MORE YEARS?
THE HEBREW CHILDREN SUFFERED UNDER THE RULE OF THEIR MASTERS. THEY HAD TO WORK IN THE SLIME PITS, MAKING BRICKS. MOSES COULD NOT STAND TO SEE THEM SUFFER, SO HE DECIDED TO DO SOMETHING ABOUT IT.
GET UP, YOU FILTHY SWINE!
GET UP BEFORE HE BEATS YOU TO DEATH!
EBER, GET UP.

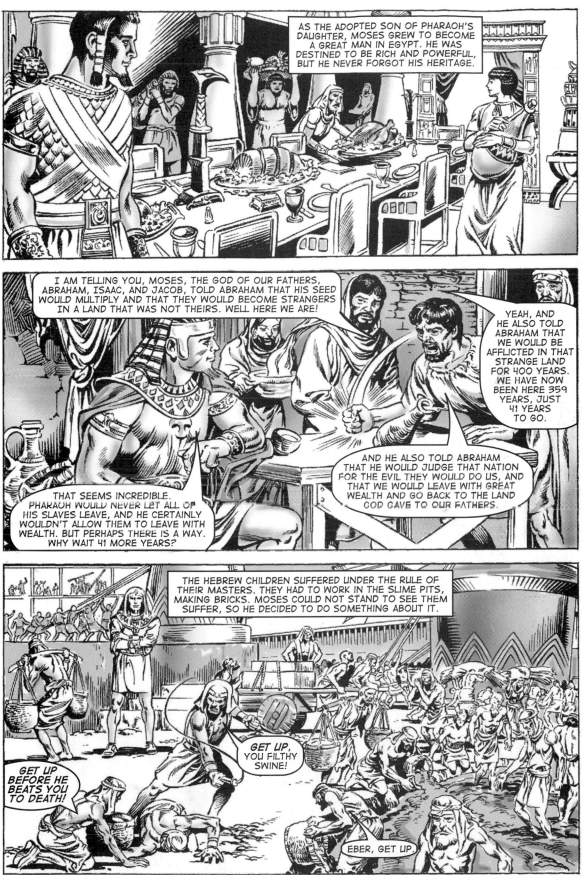

EXODUS 2:10-11

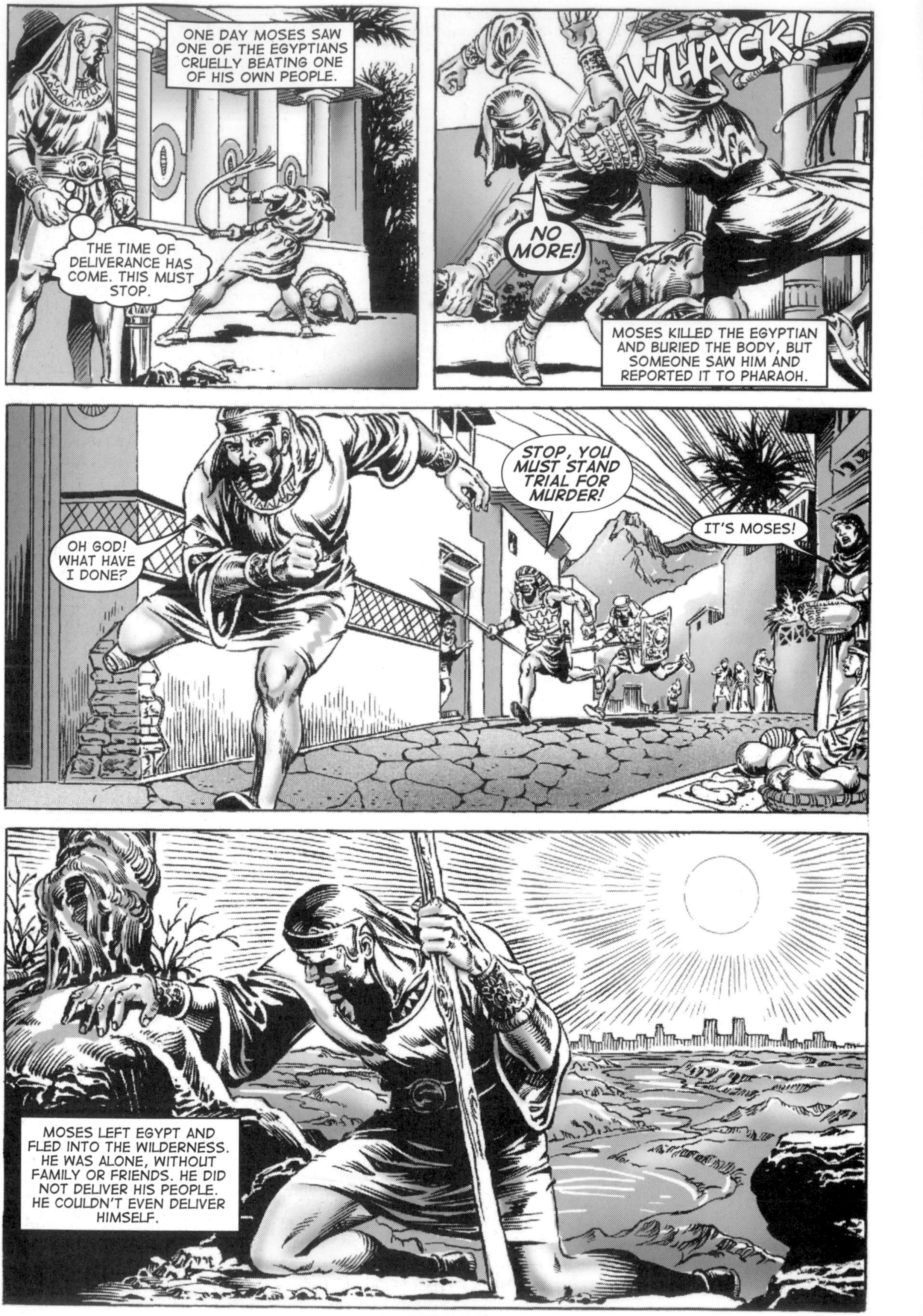
ONE DAY MOSES SAW ONE OF THE EGYPTIANS CRUELLY BEATING ONE OF HIS OWN PEOPLE.
THE TIME OF DELIVERANCE HAS COME. THIS MUST STOP.
WHACK!
NO MORE!
MOSES KILLED THE EGYPTIAN AND BURIED THE BODY, BUT SOMEONE SAW HIM AND REPORTED IT TO PHARAOH.
OH GOD! WHAT HAVE I DONE?
STOP, YOU MUST STAND TRIAL FOR MURDER!
IT'S MOSES!
MOSES LEFT EGYPT AND FLED INTO THE WILDERNESS. HE WAS ALONE, WITHOUT FAMILY OR FRIENDS. HE DID NOT DELIVER HIS PEOPLE. HE COULDN'T EVEN DELIVER HIMSELF.

EXODUS 2:11-15

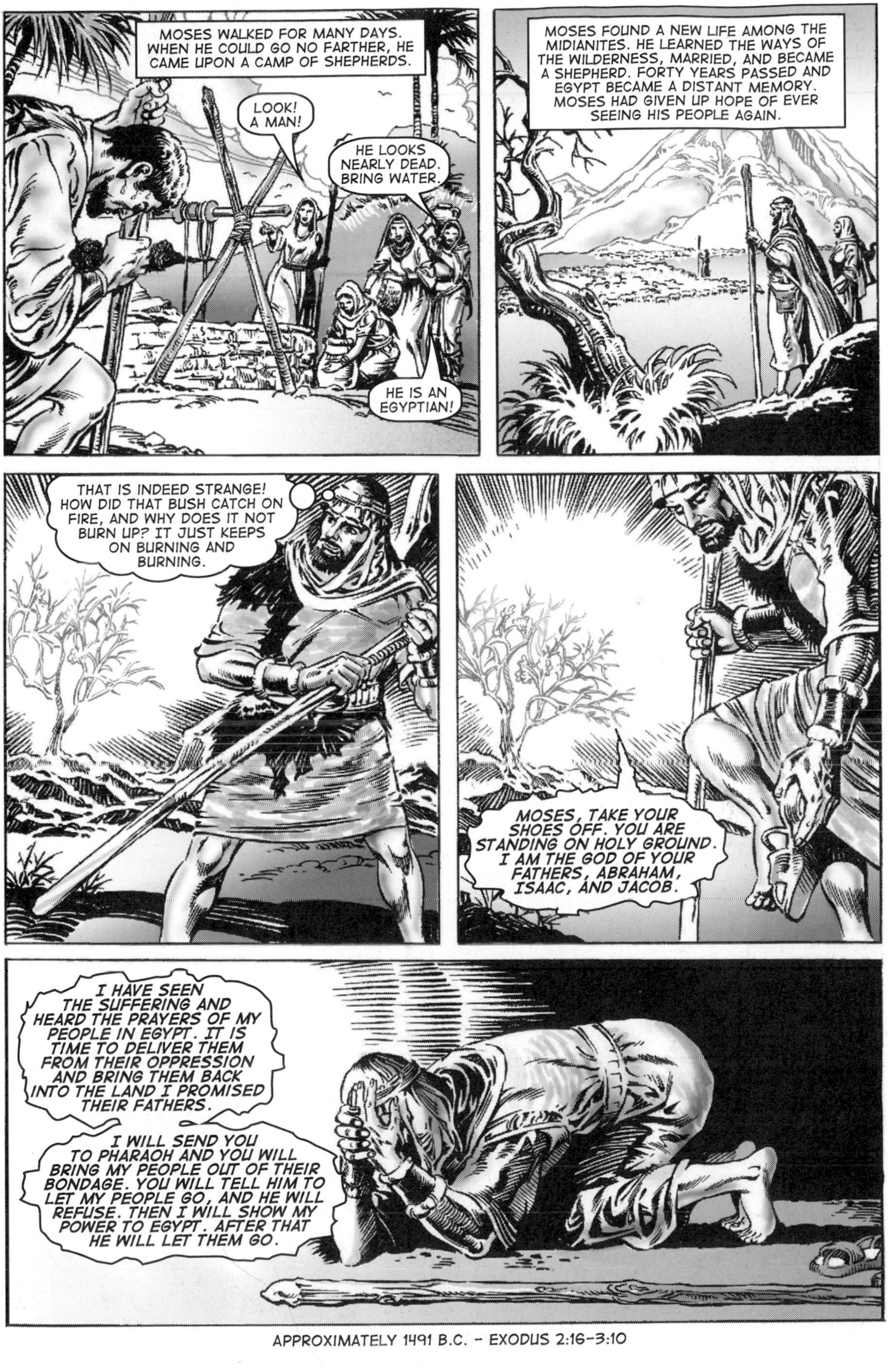
MOSES WALKED FOR MANY DAYS. WHEN HE COULD GO NO FARTHER, HE CAME UPON A CAMP OF SHEPHERDS.
LOOK! A MAN!
HE LOOKS NEARLY DEAD. BRING WATER.
HE IS AN EGYPTIAN!
MOSES FOUND A NEW LIFE AMONG THE MIDIANITES. HE LEARNED THE WAYS OF THE WILDERNESS, MARRIED, AND BECAME A SHEPHERD. FORTY YEARS PASSED AND EGYPT BECAME A DISTANT MEMORY. MOSES HAD GIVEN UP HOPE OF EVER SEEING HIS PEOPLE AGAIN.
THAT IS INDEED STRANGE! HOW DID THAT BUSH CATCH ON FIRE, AND WHY DOES IT NOT BURN UP? IT JUST KEEPS ON BURNING AND BURNING.
MOSES, TAKE YOUR SHOES OFF. YOU ARE STANDING ON HOLY GROUND. I AM THE GOD OF YOUR FATHERS, ABRAHAM, ISAAC, AND JACOB.
I HAVE SEEN THE SUFFERING AND HEARD THE PRAYERS OF MY PEOPLE IN EGYPT. IT IS TIME TO DELIVER THEM FROM THEIR OPPRESSION AND BRING THEM BACK INTO THE LAND I PROMISED THEIR FATHERS.
I WILL SEND YOU TO PHARAOH AND YOU WILL BRING MY PEOPLE OUT OF THEIR BONDAGE. YOU WILL TELL HIM TO LET MY PEOPLE GO, AND HE WILL REFUSE. THEN I WILL SHOW MY POWER TO EGYPT. AFTER THAT HE WILL LET THEM GO.

APPROXIMATELY 1491 B.C. – EXODUS 2:16–3:10

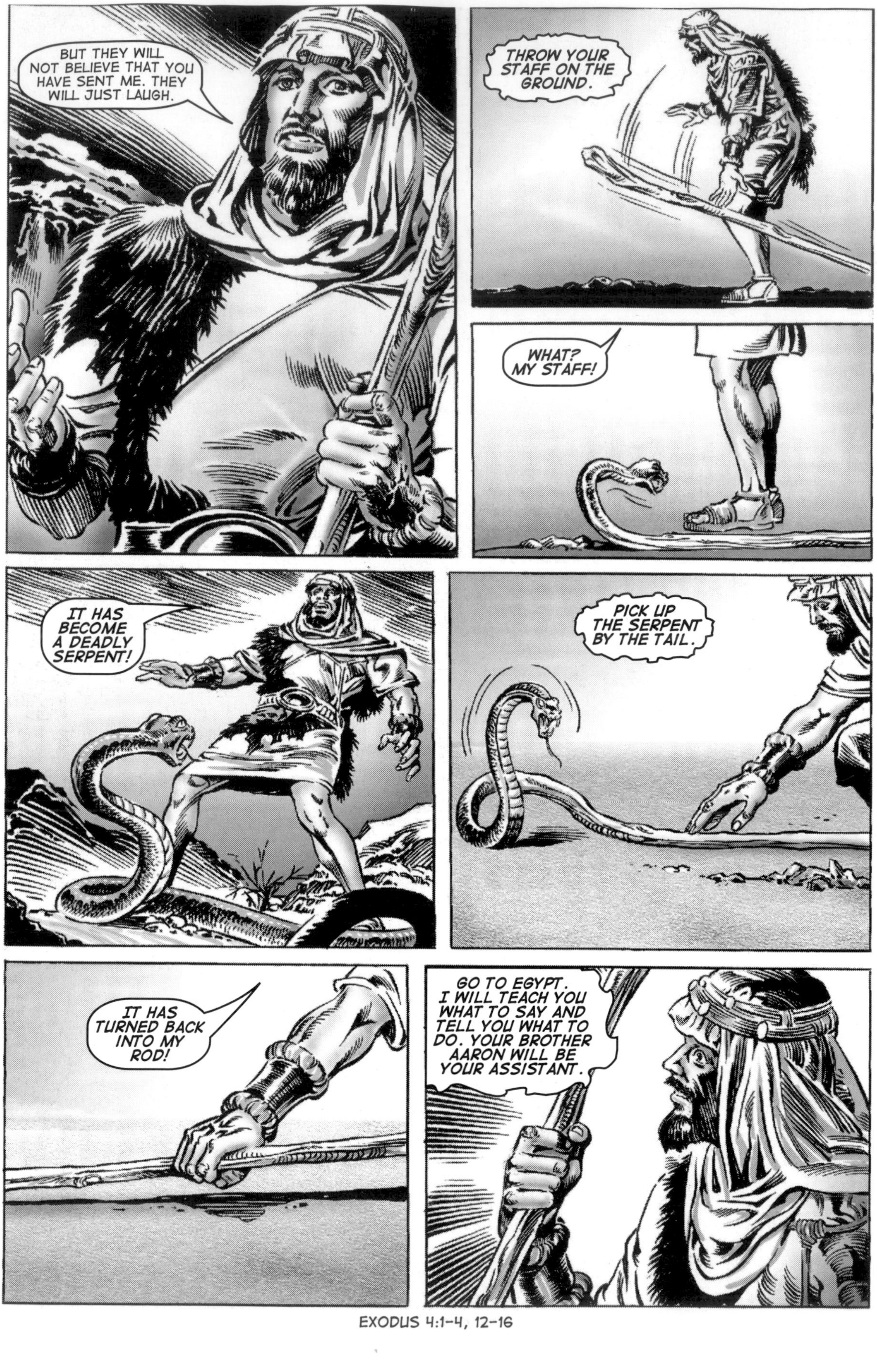
BUT THEY WILL NOT BELIEVE THAT YOU HAVE SENT ME. THEY WILL JUST LAUGH.
THROW YOUR STAFF ON THE GROUND.
WHAT? MY STAFF!
IT HAS BECOME A DEADLY SERPENT!
PICK UP THE SERPENT BY THE TAIL.
IT HAS TURNED BACK INTO MY ROD!
GO TO EGYPT. I WILL TEACH YOU WHAT TO SAY AND TELL YOU WHAT TO DO. YOUR BROTHER AARON WILL BE YOUR ASSISTANT.

EXODUS 4:1-4, 12-16

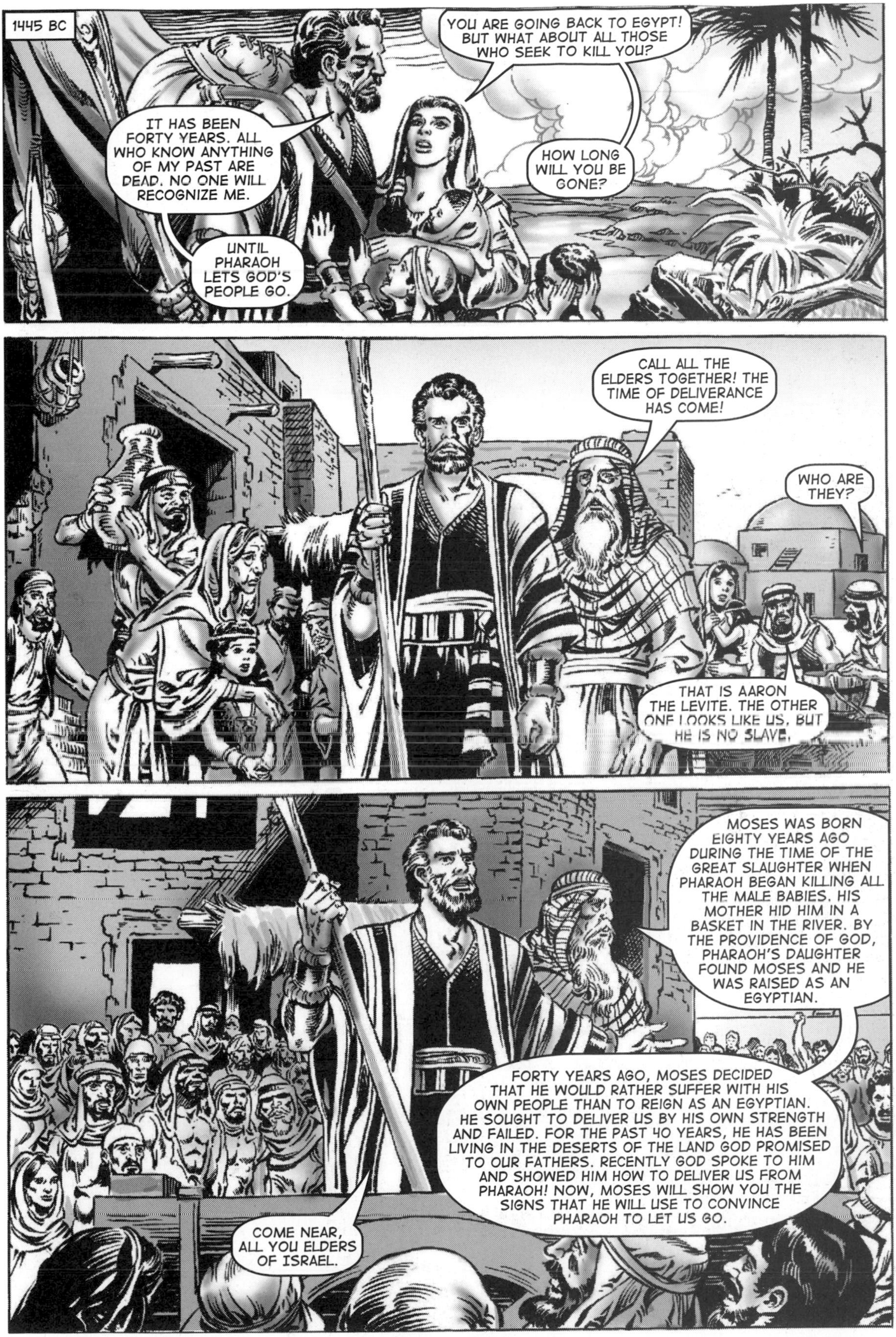
1445 BC
YOU ARE GOING BACK TO EGYPT! BUT WHAT ABOUT ALL THOSE WHO SEEK TO KILL YOU?
IT HAS BEEN FORTY YEARS. ALL WHO KNOW ANYTHING OF MY PAST ARE DEAD. NO ONE WILL RECOGNIZE ME.
HOW LONG WILL YOU BE GONE?
UNTIL PHARAOH LETS GOD'S PEOPLE GO.
CALL ALL THE ELDERS TOGETHER! THE TIME OF DELIVERANCE HAS COME!
WHO ARE THEY?
THAT IS AARON THE LEVITE. THE OTHER ONE LOOKS LIKE US, BUT HE IS NO SLAVE.
MOSES WAS BORN EIGHTY YEARS AGO DURING THE TIME OF THE GREAT SLAUGHTER WHEN PHARAOH BEGAN KILLING ALL THE MALE BABIES. HIS MOTHER HID HIM IN A BASKET IN THE RIVER. BY THE PROVIDENCE OF GOD, PHARAOH'S DAUGHTER FOUND MOSES AND HE WAS RAISED AS AN EGYPTIAN.
FORTY YEARS AGO, MOSES DECIDED THAT HE WOULD RATHER SUFFER WITH HIS OWN PEOPLE THAN TO REIGN AS AN EGYPTIAN. HE SOUGHT TO DELIVER US BY HIS OWN STRENGTH AND FAILED. FOR THE PAST 40 YEARS, HE HAS BEEN LIVING IN THE DESERTS OF THE LAND GOD PROMISED TO OUR FATHERS. RECENTLY GOD SPOKE TO HIM AND SHOWED HIM HOW TO DELIVER US FROM PHARAOH! NOW, MOSES WILL SHOW YOU THE SIGNS THAT HE WILL USE TO CONVINCE PHARAOH TO LET US GO.
COME NEAR, ALL YOU ELDERS OF ISRAEL.

EXODUS 4:29-31

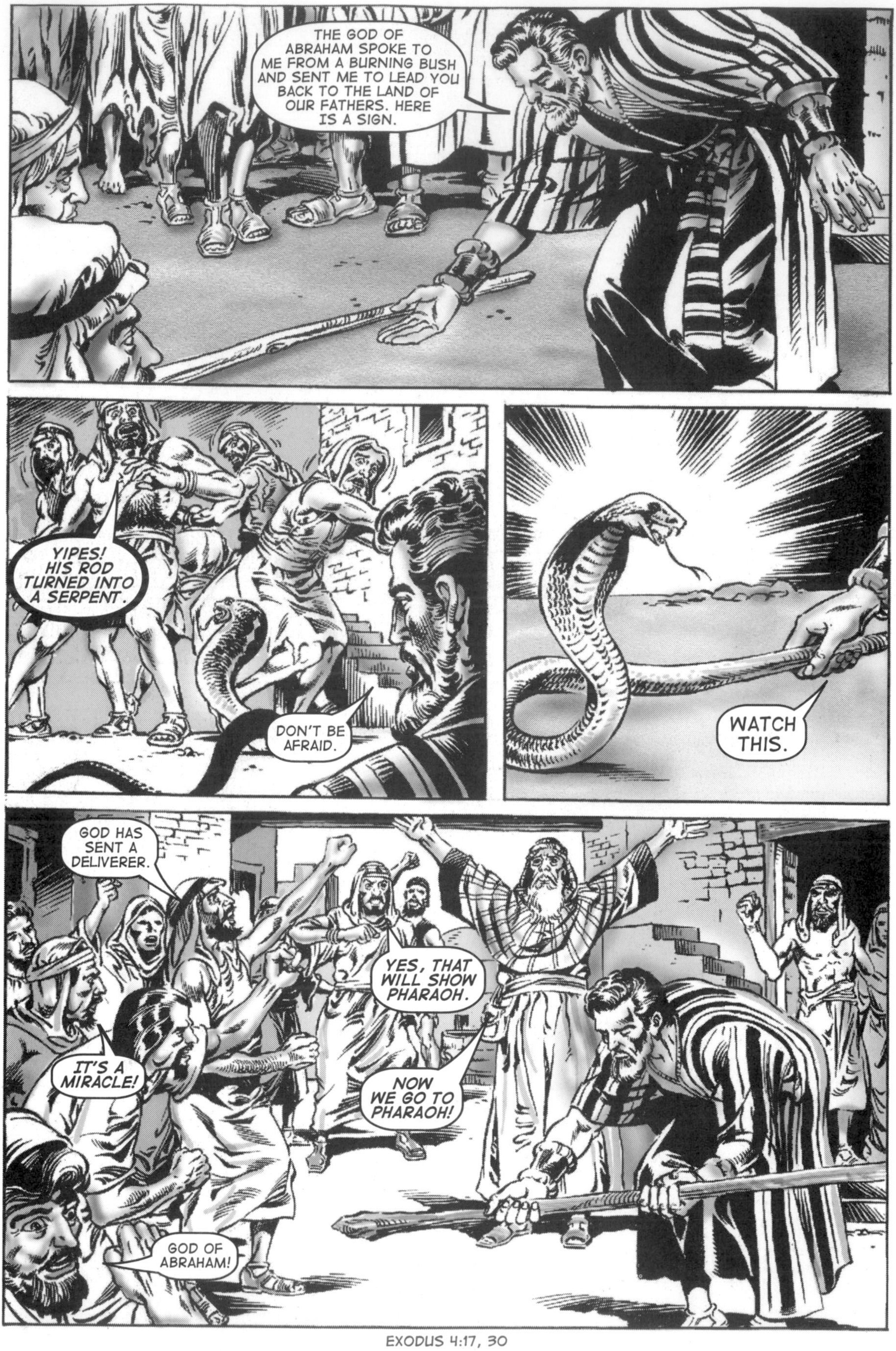
THE GOD OF ABRAHAM SPOKE TO ME FROM A BURNING BUSH AND SENT ME TO LEAD YOU BACK TO THE LAND OF OUR FATHERS. HERE IS A SIGN.
YIPES! HIS ROD TURNED INTO A SERPENT.
DON'T BE AFRAID.
WATCH THIS.
GOD HAS SENT A DELIVERER.
YES, THAT WILL SHOW PHARAOH.
IT'S A MIRACLE!
NOW WE GO TO PHARAOH!
GOD OF ABRAHAM!

EXODUS 4:17, 30

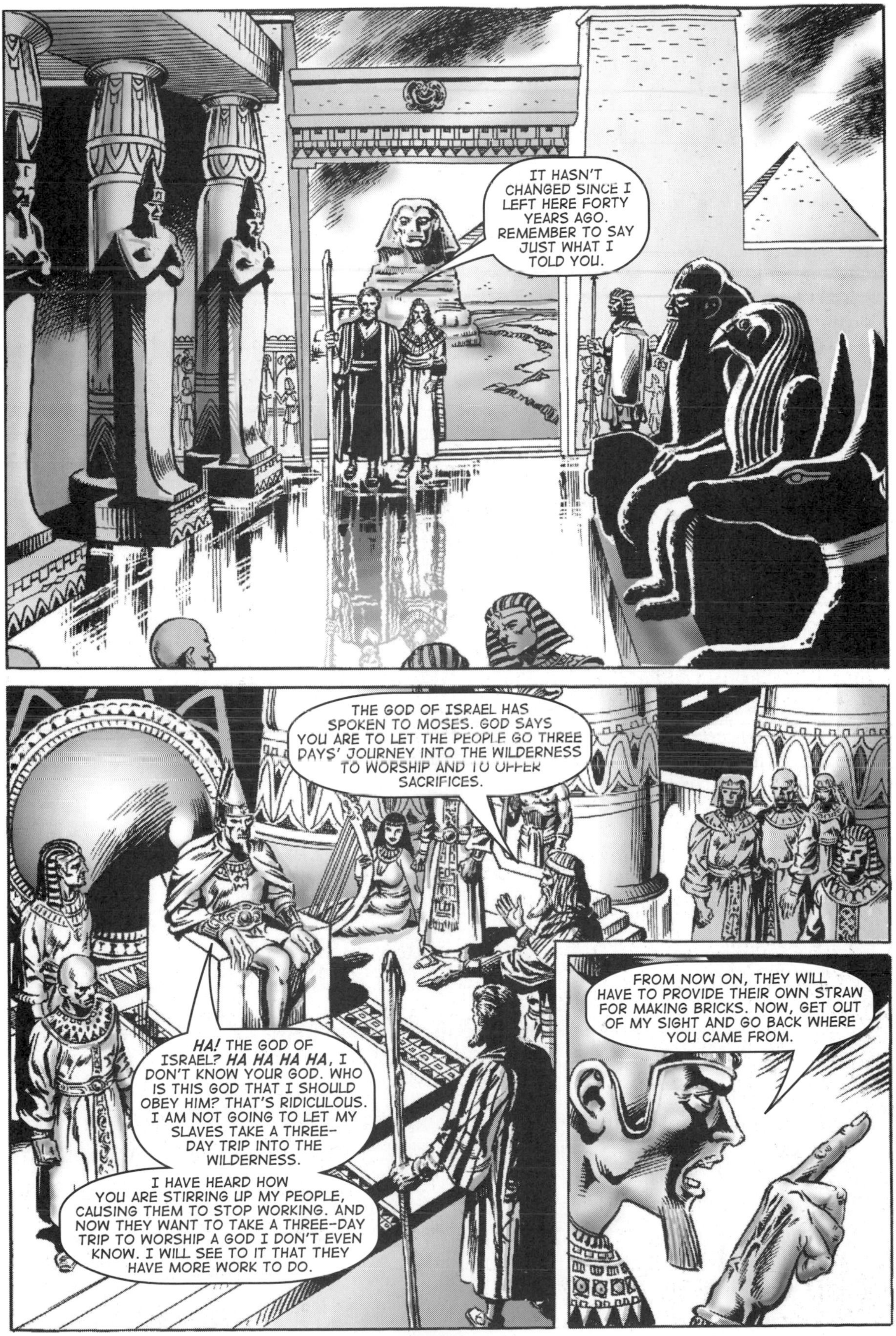
IT HASN'T CHANGED SINCE I LEFT HERE FORTY YEARS AGO. REMEMBER TO SAY JUST WHAT I TOLD YOU.
THE GOD OF ISRAEL HAS SPOKEN TO MOSES. GOD SAYS YOU ARE TO LET THE PEOPLE GO THREE DAYS' JOURNEY INTO THE WILDERNESS TO WORSHIP AND TO OFFER SACRIFICES.
HA! THE GOD OF ISRAEL? HA HA HA HA, I DON'T KNOW YOUR GOD. WHO IS THIS GOD THAT I SHOULD OBEY HIM? THAT'S RIDICULOUS. I AM NOT GOING TO LET MY SLAVES TAKE A THREE-DAY TRIP INTO THE WILDERNESS.
I HAVE HEARD HOW YOU ARE STIRRING UP MY PEOPLE, CAUSING THEM TO STOP WORKING. AND NOW THEY WANT TO TAKE A THREE-DAY TRIP TO WORSHIP A GOD I DON'T EVEN KNOW. I WILL SEE TO IT THAT THEY HAVE MORE WORK TO DO.
FROM NOW ON, THEY WILL HAVE TO PROVIDE THEIR OWN STRAW FOR MAKING BRICKS. NOW, GET OUT OF MY SIGHT AND GO BACK WHERE YOU CAME FROM.

EXODUS 5:1-7

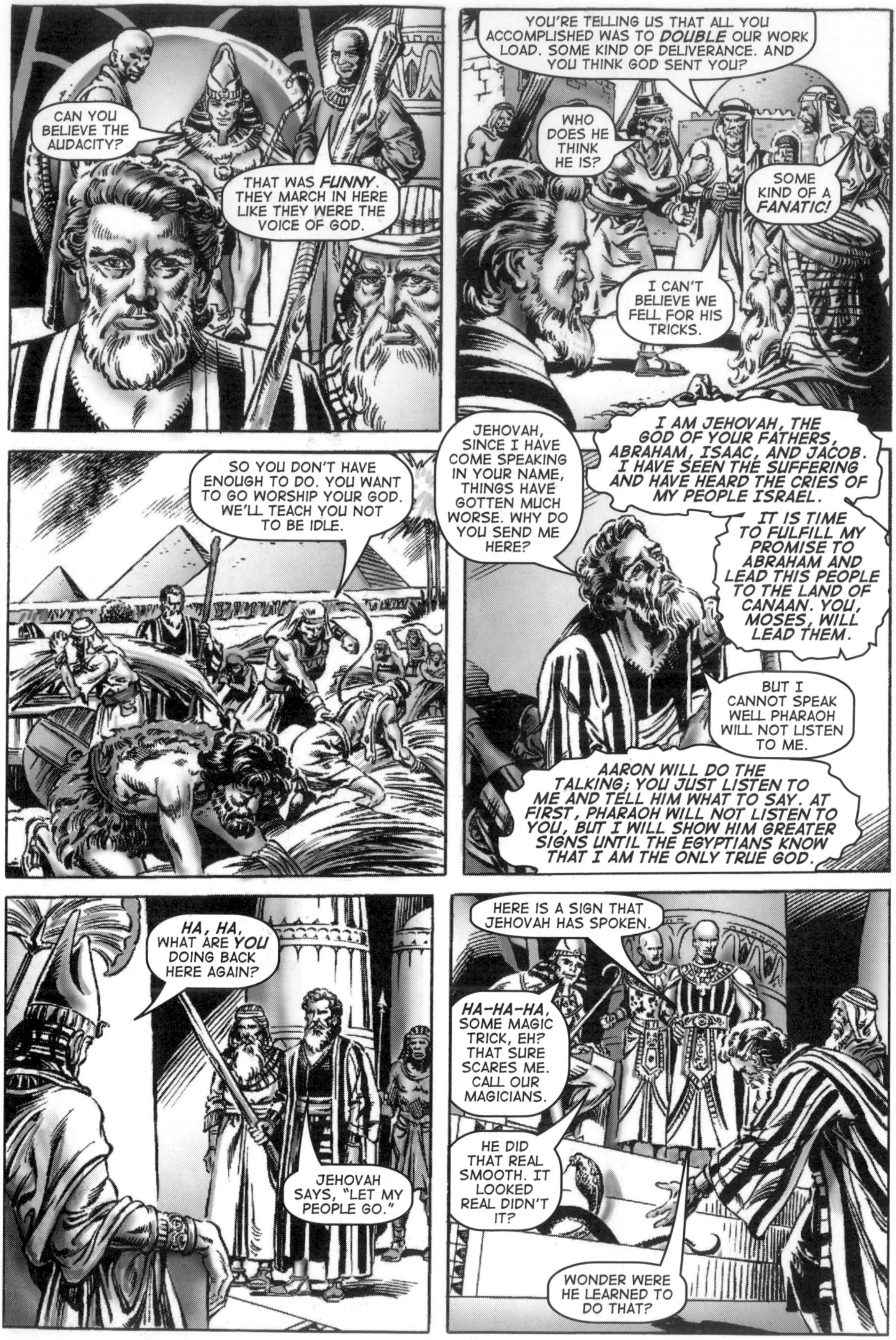
CAN YOU BELIEVE THE AUDACITY?
THAT WAS *FUNNY*. THEY MARCH IN HERE LIKE THEY WERE THE VOICE OF GOD.
YOU'RE TELLING US THAT ALL YOU ACCOMPLISHED WAS TO *DOUBLE* OUR WORK LOAD. SOME KIND OF DELIVERANCE. AND YOU THINK GOD SENT YOU?
WHO DOES HE THINK HE IS?
SOME KIND OF A *FANATIC!*
I CAN'T BELIEVE WE FELL FOR HIS TRICKS.
SO YOU DON'T HAVE ENOUGH TO DO. YOU WANT TO GO WORSHIP YOUR GOD. WE'LL TEACH YOU NOT TO BE IDLE.
JEHOVAH, SINCE I HAVE COME SPEAKING IN YOUR NAME, THINGS HAVE GOTTEN MUCH WORSE. WHY DO YOU SEND ME HERE?
I AM JEHOVAH, THE GOD OF YOUR FATHERS, ABRAHAM, ISAAC, AND JACOB. I HAVE SEEN THE SUFFERING AND HAVE HEARD THE CRIES OF MY PEOPLE ISRAEL.
IT IS TIME TO FULFILL MY PROMISE TO ABRAHAM AND LEAD THIS PEOPLE TO THE LAND OF CANAAN. YOU, MOSES, WILL LEAD THEM.
BUT I CANNOT SPEAK WELL PHARAOH WILL NOT LISTEN TO ME.
AARON WILL DO THE TALKING; YOU JUST LISTEN TO ME AND TELL HIM WHAT TO SAY. AT FIRST, PHARAOH WILL NOT LISTEN TO YOU, BUT I WILL SHOW HIM GREATER SIGNS UNTIL THE EGYPTIANS KNOW THAT I AM THE ONLY TRUE GOD.
HA, HA, WHAT ARE *YOU* DOING BACK HERE AGAIN?
JEHOVAH SAYS, "LET MY PEOPLE GO."
HERE IS A SIGN THAT JEHOVAH HAS SPOKEN.
HA-HA-HA, SOME MAGIC TRICK, EH? THAT SURE SCARES ME. CALL OUR MAGICIANS.
HE DID THAT REAL SMOOTH. IT LOOKED REAL DIDN'T IT?
WONDER WERE HE LEARNED TO DO THAT?

EXODUS 5:10–23, 7:7–11

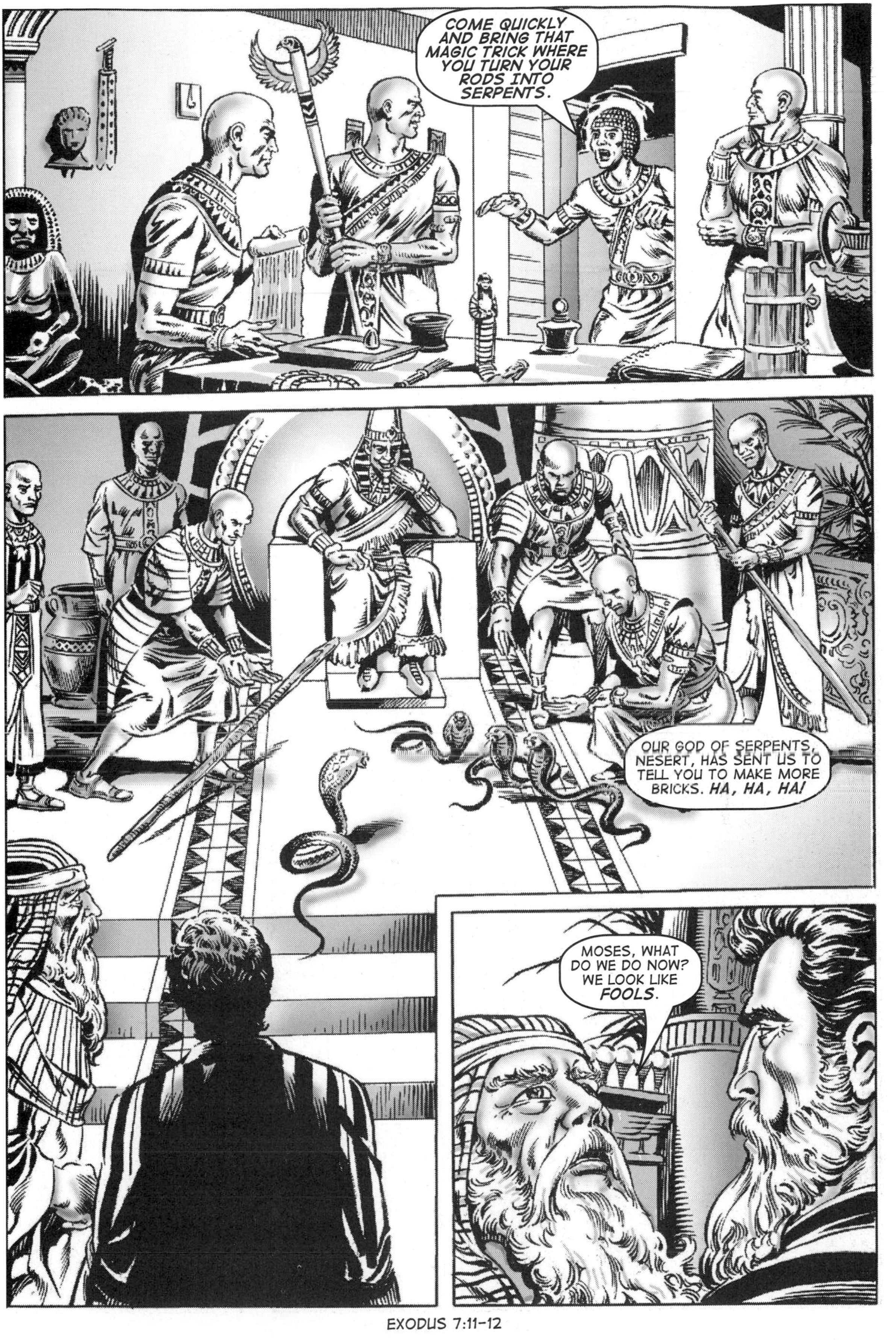
COME QUICKLY AND BRING THAT MAGIC TRICK WHERE YOU TURN YOUR RODS INTO SERPENTS.
OUR GOD OF SERPENTS, NESERT, HAS SENT US TO TELL YOU TO MAKE MORE BRICKS. HA, HA, HA!
MOSES, WHAT DO WE DO NOW? WE LOOK LIKE FOOLS.

EXODUS 7:11-12

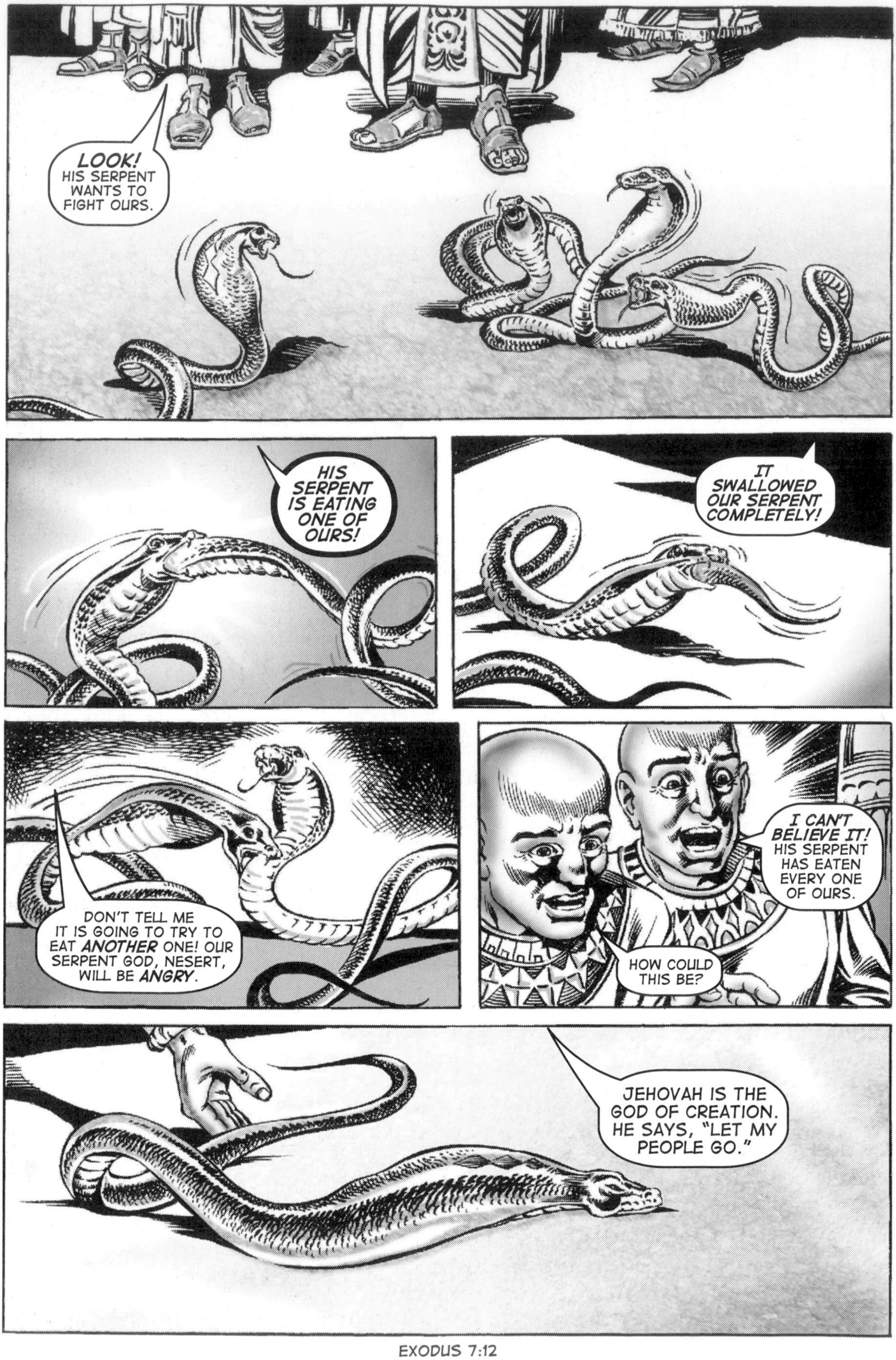
LOOK! HIS SERPENT WANTS TO FIGHT OURS.
HIS SERPENT IS EATING ONE OF OURS!
IT SWALLOWED OUR SERPENT COMPLETELY!
DON'T TELL ME IT IS GOING TO TRY TO EAT ANOTHER ONE! OUR SERPENT GOD, NESERT, WILL BE ANGRY.
I CAN'T BELIEVE IT! HIS SERPENT HAS EATEN EVERY ONE OF OURS.
HOW COULD THIS BE?
JEHOVAH IS THE GOD OF CREATION. HE SAYS, "LET MY PEOPLE GO."

EXODUS 7:12

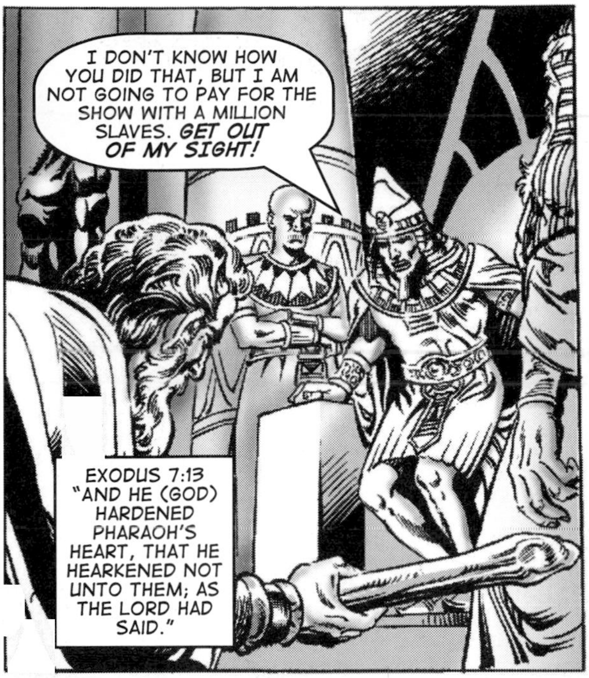
I DON'T KNOW HOW YOU DID THAT, BUT I AM NOT GOING TO PAY FOR THE SHOW WITH A MILLION SLAVES. GET OUT OF MY SIGHT!
EXODUS 7:13 "AND HE (GOD) HARDENED PHARAOH'S HEART, THAT HE HEARKENED NOT UNTO THEM; AS THE LORD HAD SAID."

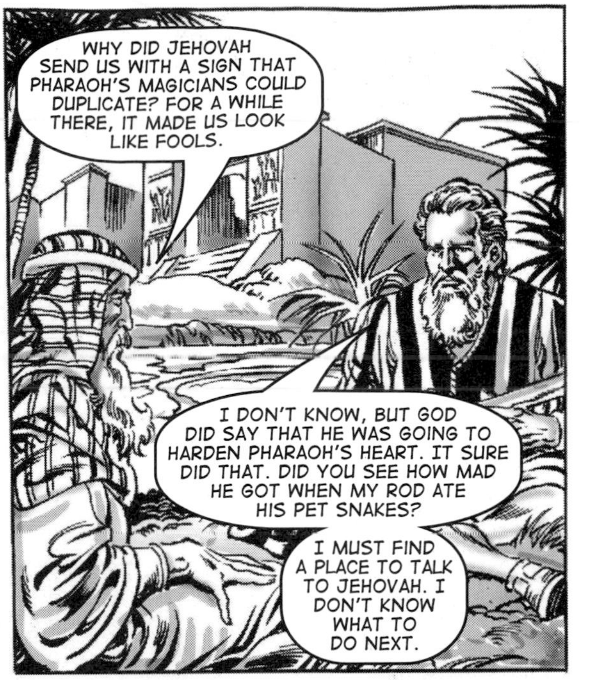
WHY DID JEHOVAH SEND US WITH A SIGN THAT PHARAOH'S MAGICIANS COULD DUPLICATE? FOR A WHILE THERE, IT MADE US LOOK LIKE FOOLS.
I DON'T KNOW, BUT GOD DID SAY THAT HE WAS GOING TO HARDEN PHARAOH'S HEART. IT SURE DID THAT. DID YOU SEE HOW MAD HE GOT WHEN MY ROD ATE HIS PET SNAKES?
I MUST FIND A PLACE TO TALK TO JEHOVAH. I DON'T KNOW WHAT TO DO NEXT.

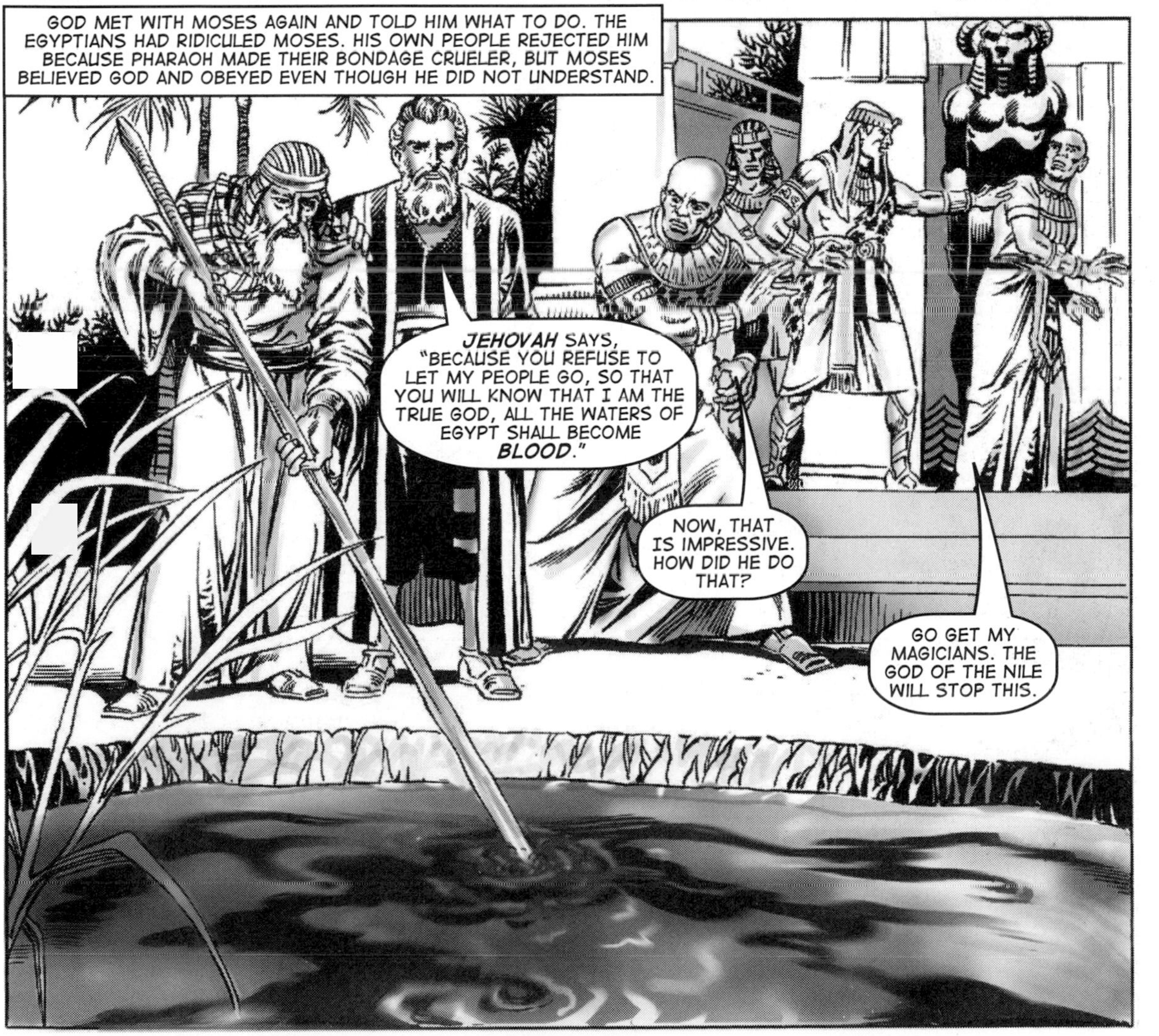
GOD MET WITH MOSES AGAIN AND TOLD HIM WHAT TO DO. THE EGYPTIANS HAD RIDICULED MOSES. HIS OWN PEOPLE REJECTED HIM BECAUSE PHARAOH MADE THEIR BONDAGE CRUELER, BUT MOSES BELIEVED GOD AND OBEYED EVEN THOUGH HE DID NOT UNDERSTAND.
JEHOVAH SAYS, "BECAUSE YOU REFUSE TO LET MY PEOPLE GO, SO THAT YOU WILL KNOW THAT I AM THE TRUE GOD, ALL THE WATERS OF EGYPT SHALL BECOME BLOOD."
NOW, THAT IS IMPRESSIVE. HOW DID HE DO THAT?
GO GET MY MAGICIANS. THE GOD OF THE NILE WILL STOP THIS.

EXODUS 7:15-21

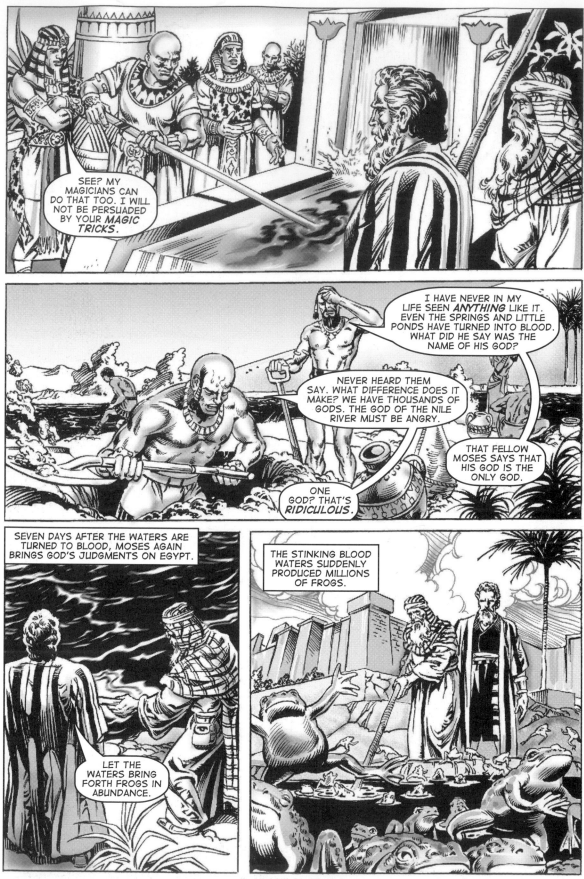

SEE? MY MAGICIANS CAN DO THAT TOO. I WILL NOT BE PERSUADED BY YOUR *MAGIC TRICKS.*

I HAVE NEVER IN MY LIFE SEEN *ANYTHING* LIKE IT. EVEN THE SPRINGS AND LITTLE PONDS HAVE TURNED INTO BLOOD. WHAT DID HE SAY WAS THE NAME OF HIS GOD?

NEVER HEARD THEM SAY. WHAT DIFFERENCE DOES IT MAKE? WE HAVE THOUSANDS OF GODS. THE GOD OF THE NILE RIVER MUST BE ANGRY.

THAT FELLOW MOSES SAYS THAT HIS GOD IS THE ONLY GOD.

ONE GOD? THAT'S *RIDICULOUS.*

SEVEN DAYS AFTER THE WATERS ARE TURNED TO BLOOD, MOSES AGAIN BRINGS GOD'S JUDGMENTS ON EGYPT.

LET THE WATERS BRING FORTH FROGS IN ABUNDANCE.

THE STINKING BLOOD WATERS SUDDENLY PRODUCED MILLIONS OF FROGS.

EXODUS 7:21–25, 8:6

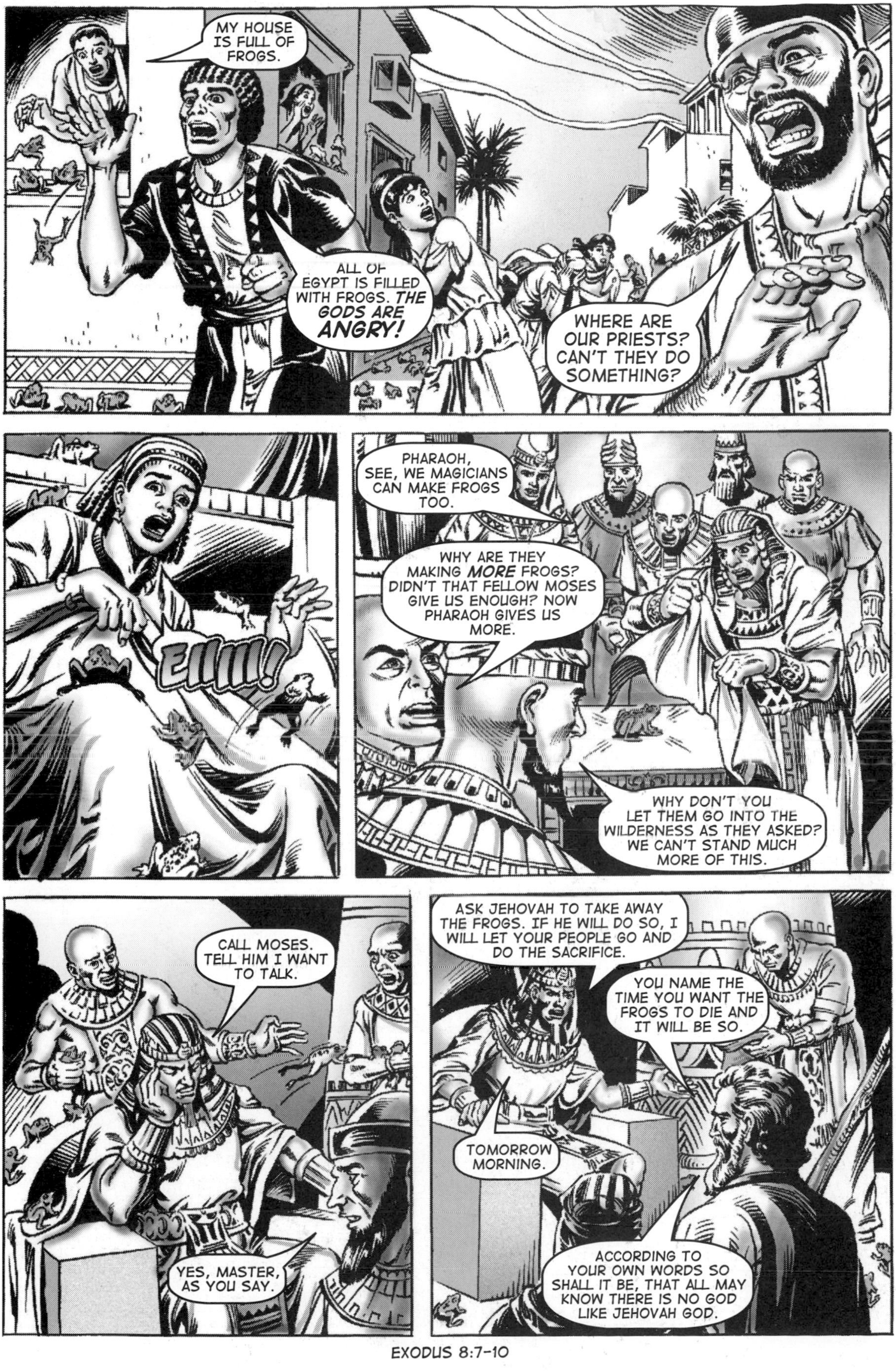
MY HOUSE IS FULL OF FROGS.
ALL OF EGYPT IS FILLED WITH FROGS. THE GODS ARE ANGRY!
WHERE ARE OUR PRIESTS? CAN'T THEY DO SOMETHING?
EIIIII!
PHARAOH, SEE, WE MAGICIANS CAN MAKE FROGS TOO.
WHY ARE THEY MAKING MORE FROGS? DIDN'T THAT FELLOW MOSES GIVE US ENOUGH? NOW PHARAOH GIVES US MORE.
WHY DON'T YOU LET THEM GO INTO THE WILDERNESS AS THEY ASKED? WE CAN'T STAND MUCH MORE OF THIS.
CALL MOSES. TELL HIM I WANT TO TALK.
YES, MASTER, AS YOU SAY.
ASK JEHOVAH TO TAKE AWAY THE FROGS. IF HE WILL DO SO, I WILL LET YOUR PEOPLE GO AND DO THE SACRIFICE.
YOU NAME THE TIME YOU WANT THE FROGS TO DIE AND IT WILL BE SO.
TOMORROW MORNING.
ACCORDING TO YOUR OWN WORDS SO SHALL IT BE, THAT ALL MAY KNOW THERE IS NO GOD LIKE JEHOVAH GOD.

EXODUS 8:7–10

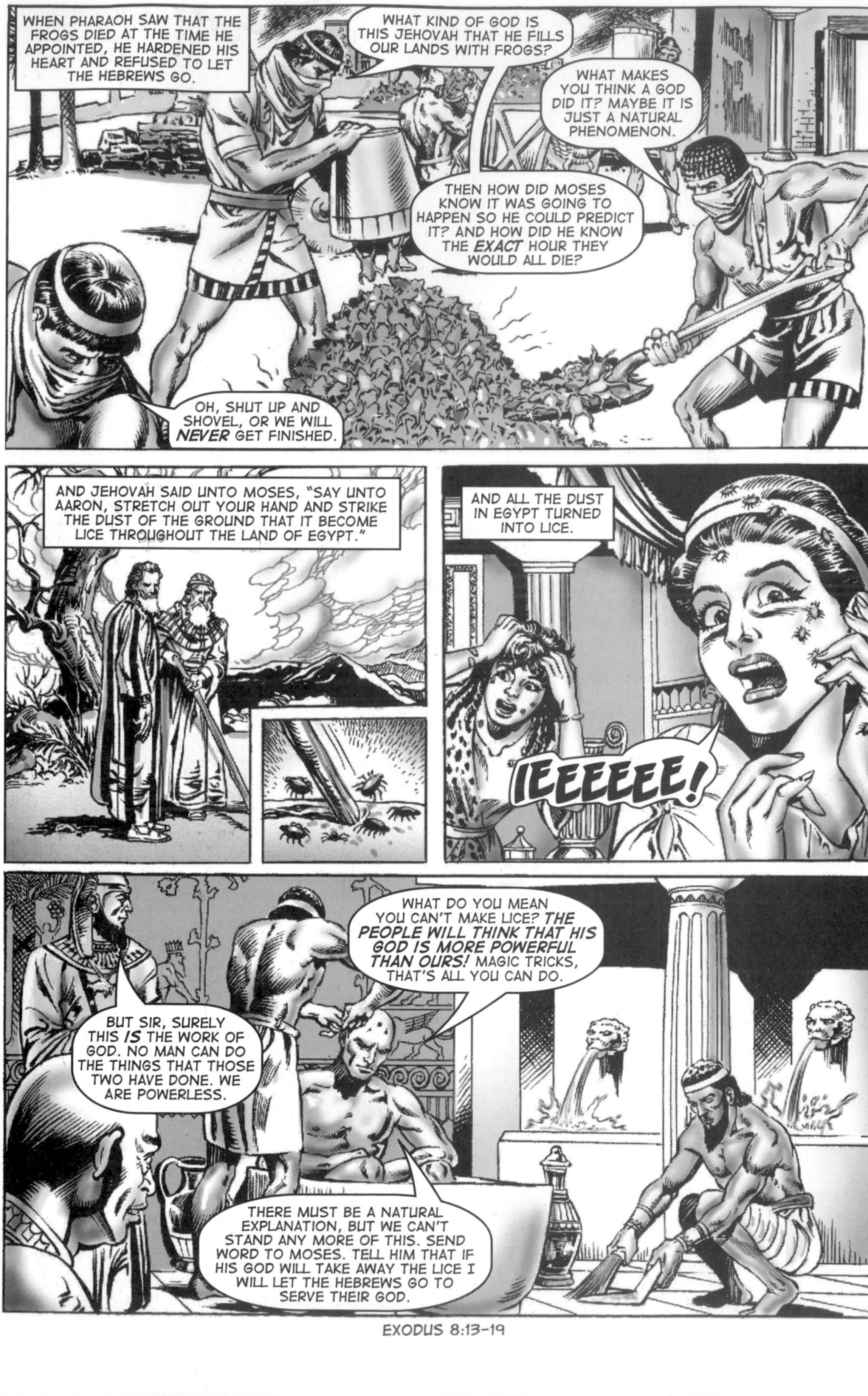
WHEN PHARAOH SAW THAT THE FROGS DIED AT THE TIME HE APPOINTED, HE HARDENED HIS HEART AND REFUSED TO LET THE HEBREWS GO.
WHAT KIND OF GOD IS THIS JEHOVAH THAT HE FILLS OUR LANDS WITH FROGS?
WHAT MAKES YOU THINK A GOD DID IT? MAYBE IT IS JUST A NATURAL PHENOMENON.
THEN HOW DID MOSES KNOW IT WAS GOING TO HAPPEN SO HE COULD PREDICT IT? AND HOW DID HE KNOW THE EXACT HOUR THEY WOULD ALL DIE?
OH, SHUT UP AND SHOVEL, OR WE WILL NEVER GET FINISHED.
AND JEHOVAH SAID UNTO MOSES, "SAY UNTO AARON, STRETCH OUT YOUR HAND AND STRIKE THE DUST OF THE GROUND THAT IT BECOME LICE THROUGHOUT THE LAND OF EGYPT."
AND ALL THE DUST IN EGYPT TURNED INTO LICE.
IEEEEEE!
WHAT DO YOU MEAN YOU CAN'T MAKE LICE? THE PEOPLE WILL THINK THAT HIS GOD IS MORE POWERFUL THAN OURS! MAGIC TRICKS, THAT'S ALL YOU CAN DO.
BUT SIR, SURELY THIS IS THE WORK OF GOD. NO MAN CAN DO THE THINGS THAT THOSE TWO HAVE DONE. WE ARE POWERLESS.
THERE MUST BE A NATURAL EXPLANATION, BUT WE CAN'T STAND ANY MORE OF THIS. SEND WORD TO MOSES. TELL HIM THAT IF HIS GOD WILL TAKE AWAY THE LICE I WILL LET THE HEBREWS GO TO SERVE THEIR GOD.

EXODUS 8:13–19

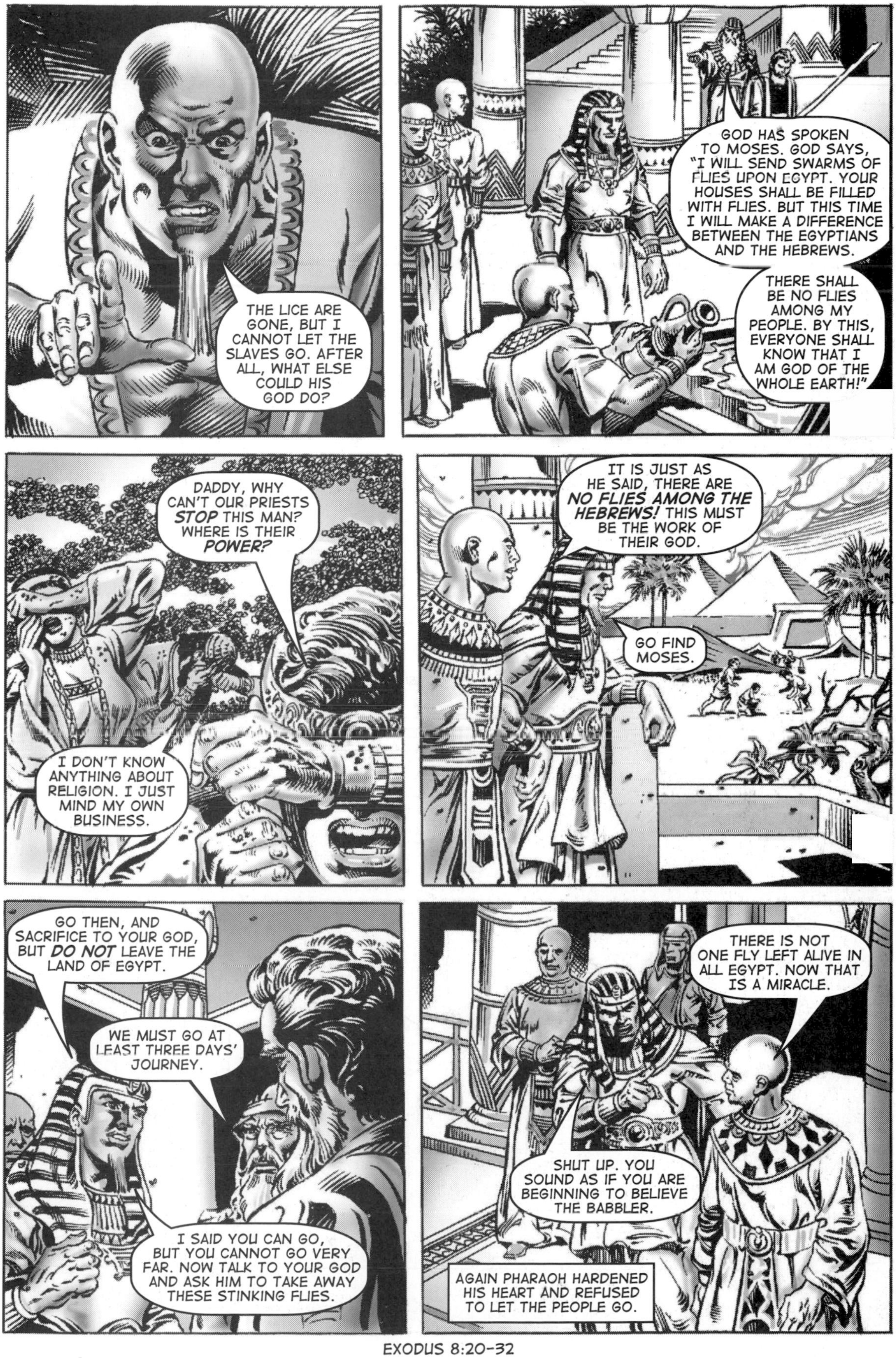
THE LICE ARE GONE, BUT I CANNOT LET THE SLAVES GO. AFTER ALL, WHAT ELSE COULD HIS GOD DO?
GOD HAS SPOKEN TO MOSES. GOD SAYS, "I WILL SEND SWARMS OF FLIES UPON EGYPT. YOUR HOUSES SHALL BE FILLED WITH FLIES. BUT THIS TIME I WILL MAKE A DIFFERENCE BETWEEN THE EGYPTIANS AND THE HEBREWS.
THERE SHALL BE NO FLIES AMONG MY PEOPLE. BY THIS, EVERYONE SHALL KNOW THAT I AM GOD OF THE WHOLE EARTH!"
DADDY, WHY CAN'T OUR PRIESTS STOP THIS MAN? WHERE IS THEIR POWER?
I DON'T KNOW ANYTHING ABOUT RELIGION. I JUST MIND MY OWN BUSINESS.
IT IS JUST AS HE SAID, THERE ARE NO FLIES AMONG THE HEBREWS! THIS MUST BE THE WORK OF THEIR GOD.
GO FIND MOSES.
GO THEN, AND SACRIFICE TO YOUR GOD, BUT DO NOT LEAVE THE LAND OF EGYPT.
WE MUST GO AT LEAST THREE DAYS' JOURNEY.
I SAID YOU CAN GO, BUT YOU CANNOT GO VERY FAR. NOW TALK TO YOUR GOD AND ASK HIM TO TAKE AWAY THESE STINKING FLIES.
THERE IS NOT ONE FLY LEFT ALIVE IN ALL EGYPT. NOW THAT IS A MIRACLE.
SHUT UP. YOU SOUND AS IF YOU ARE BEGINNING TO BELIEVE THE BABBLER.
AGAIN PHARAOH HARDENED HIS HEART AND REFUSED TO LET THE PEOPLE GO.

EXODUS 8:20-32

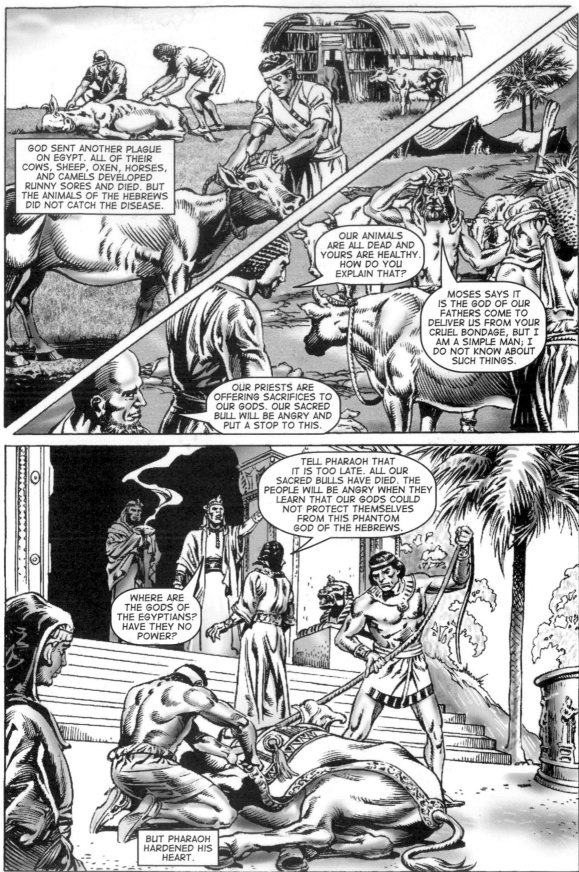

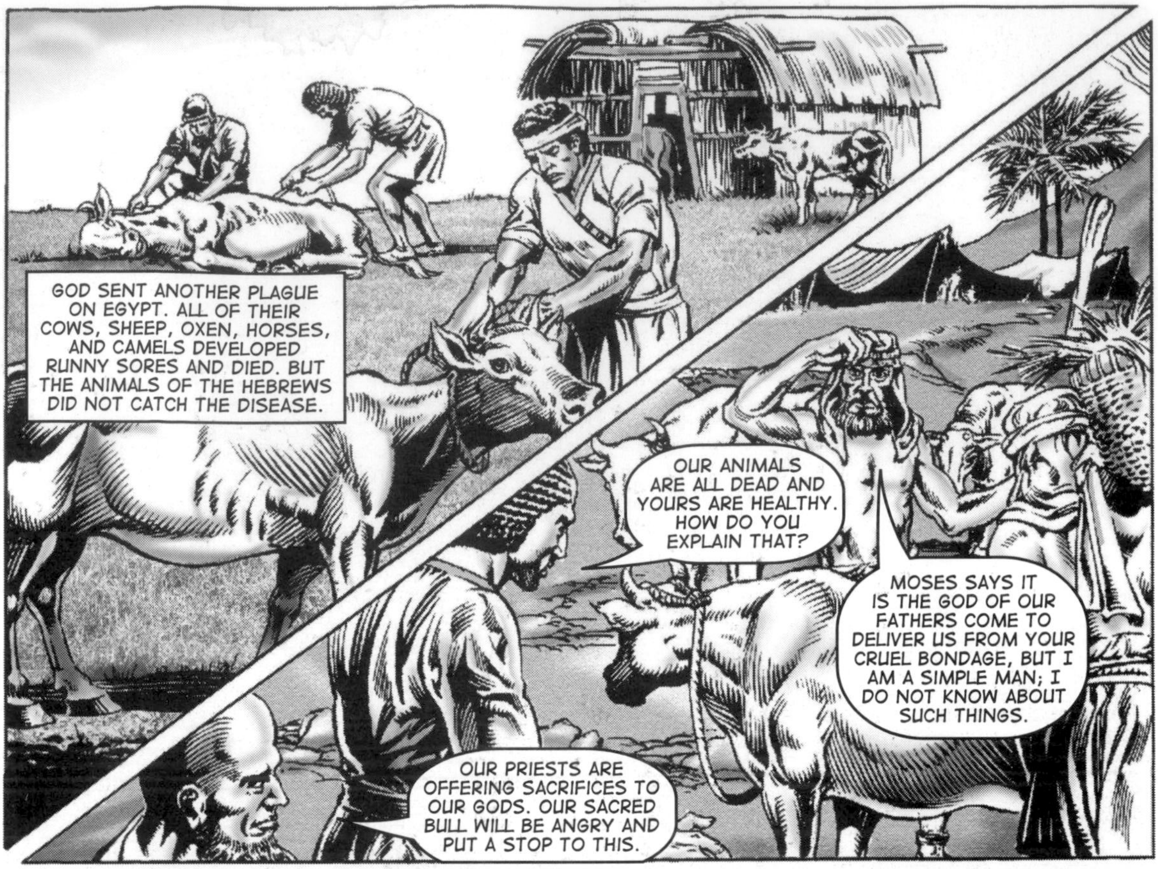
GOD SENT ANOTHER PLAGUE ON EGYPT. ALL OF THEIR COWS, SHEEP, OXEN, HORSES, AND CAMELS DEVELOPED RUNNY SORES AND DIED. BUT THE ANIMALS OF THE HEBREWS DID NOT CATCH THE DISEASE.
OUR ANIMALS ARE ALL DEAD AND YOURS ARE HEALTHY. HOW DO YOU EXPLAIN THAT?
MOSES SAYS IT IS THE GOD OF OUR FATHERS COME TO DELIVER US FROM YOUR CRUEL BONDAGE, BUT I AM A SIMPLE MAN; I DO NOT KNOW ABOUT SUCH THINGS.
OUR PRIESTS ARE OFFERING SACRIFICES TO OUR GODS. OUR SACRED BULL WILL BE ANGRY AND PUT A STOP TO THIS.

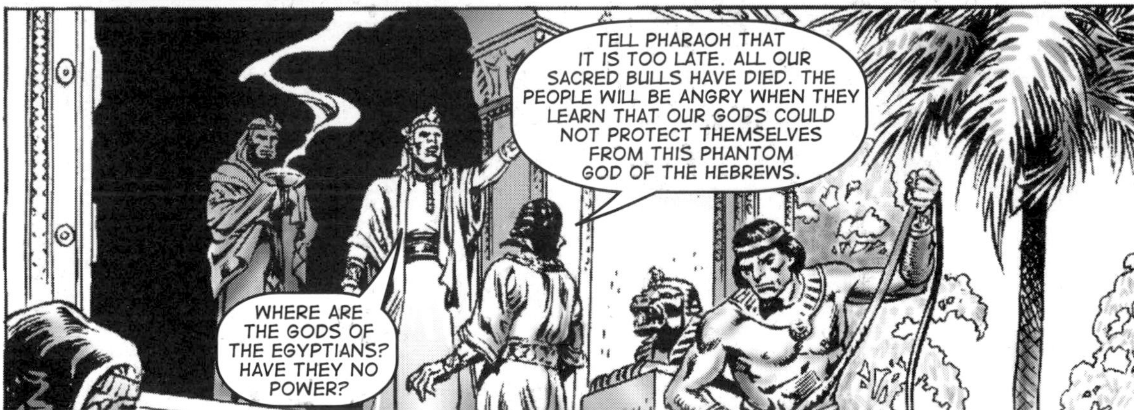
TELL PHARAOH THAT IT IS TOO LATE. ALL OUR SACRED BULLS HAVE DIED. THE PEOPLE WILL BE ANGRY WHEN THEY LEARN THAT OUR GODS COULD NOT PROTECT THEMSELVES FROM THIS PHANTOM GOD OF THE HEBREWS.
WHERE ARE THE GODS OF THE EGYPTIANS? HAVE THEY NO POWER?
BUT PHARAOH HARDENED HIS HEART.

EXODUS 9:6-7

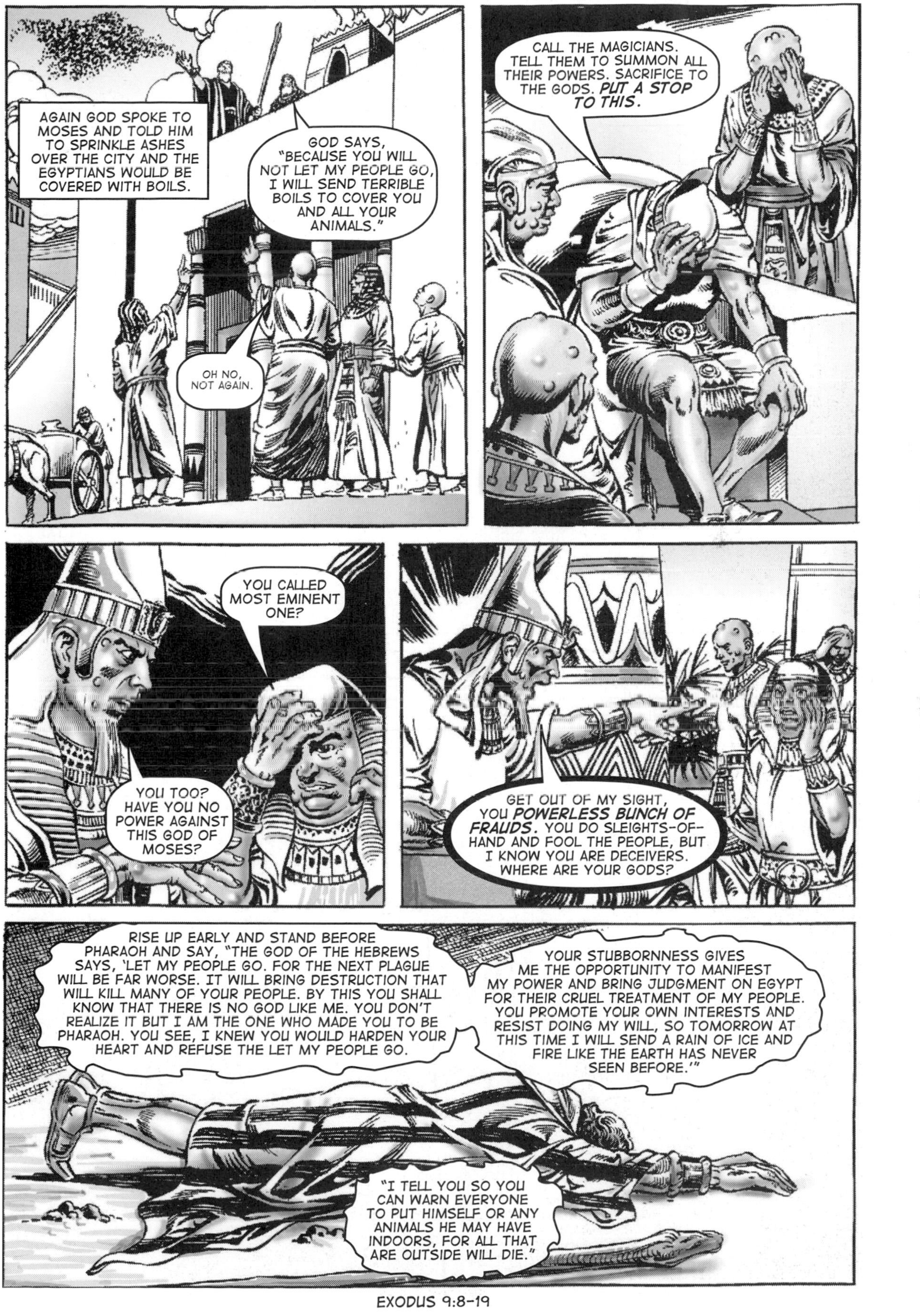
AGAIN GOD SPOKE TO MOSES AND TOLD HIM TO SPRINKLE ASHES OVER THE CITY AND THE EGYPTIANS WOULD BE COVERED WITH BOILS.
GOD SAYS, "BECAUSE YOU WILL NOT LET MY PEOPLE GO, I WILL SEND TERRIBLE BOILS TO COVER YOU AND ALL YOUR ANIMALS."
OH NO, NOT AGAIN.
CALL THE MAGICIANS. TELL THEM TO SUMMON ALL THEIR POWERS. SACRIFICE TO THE GODS. *PUT A STOP TO THIS*.
YOU CALLED MOST EMINENT ONE?
YOU TOO? HAVE YOU NO POWER AGAINST THIS GOD OF MOSES?
GET OUT OF MY SIGHT, YOU *POWERLESS BUNCH OF FRAUDS*. YOU DO SLEIGHTS-OF-HAND AND FOOL THE PEOPLE, BUT I KNOW YOU ARE DECEIVERS. WHERE ARE YOUR GODS?
RISE UP EARLY AND STAND BEFORE PHARAOH AND SAY, "THE GOD OF THE HEBREWS SAYS, 'LET MY PEOPLE GO. FOR THE NEXT PLAGUE WILL BE FAR WORSE. IT WILL BRING DESTRUCTION THAT WILL KILL MANY OF YOUR PEOPLE. BY THIS YOU SHALL KNOW THAT THERE IS NO GOD LIKE ME. YOU DON'T REALIZE IT BUT I AM THE ONE WHO MADE YOU TO BE PHARAOH. YOU SEE, I KNEW YOU WOULD HARDEN YOUR HEART AND REFUSE THE LET MY PEOPLE GO.
YOUR STUBBORNNESS GIVES ME THE OPPORTUNITY TO MANIFEST MY POWER AND BRING JUDGMENT ON EGYPT FOR THEIR CRUEL TREATMENT OF MY PEOPLE. YOU PROMOTE YOUR OWN INTERESTS AND RESIST DOING MY WILL, SO TOMORROW AT THIS TIME I WILL SEND A RAIN OF ICE AND FIRE LIKE THE EARTH HAS NEVER SEEN BEFORE.'"
"I TELL YOU SO YOU CAN WARN EVERYONE TO PUT HIMSELF OR ANY ANIMALS HE MAY HAVE INDOORS, FOR ALL THAT ARE OUTSIDE WILL DIE."

EXODUS 9:8-19

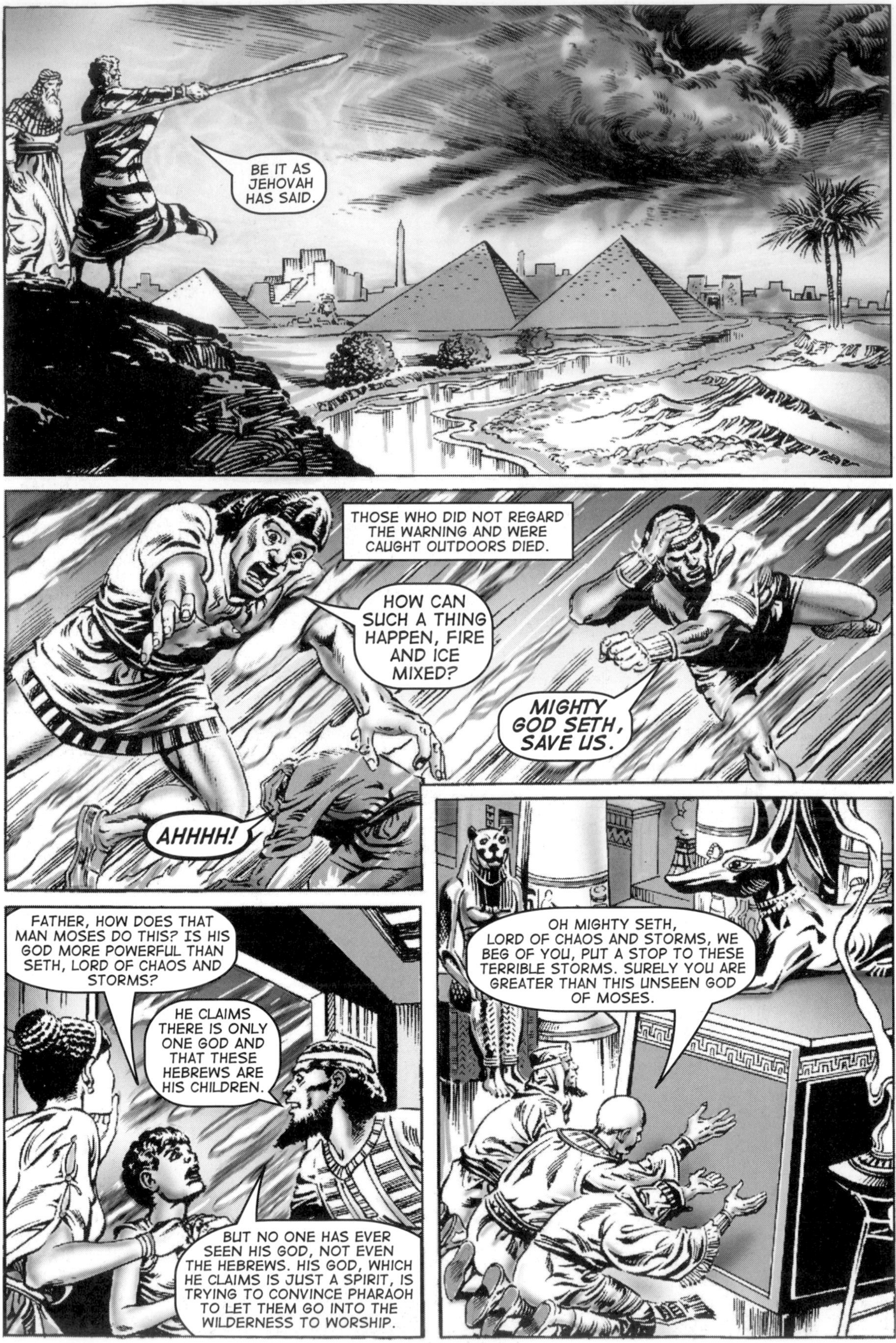
BE IT AS JEHOVAH HAS SAID.
THOSE WHO DID NOT REGARD THE WARNING AND WERE CAUGHT OUTDOORS DIED.
HOW CAN SUCH A THING HAPPEN, FIRE AND ICE MIXED?
MIGHTY GOD SETH, SAVE US.
AHHHH!
FATHER, HOW DOES THAT MAN MOSES DO THIS? IS HIS GOD MORE POWERFUL THAN SETH, LORD OF CHAOS AND STORMS?
HE CLAIMS THERE IS ONLY ONE GOD AND THAT THESE HEBREWS ARE HIS CHILDREN.
BUT NO ONE HAS EVER SEEN HIS GOD, NOT EVEN THE HEBREWS. HIS GOD, WHICH HE CLAIMS IS JUST A SPIRIT, IS TRYING TO CONVINCE PHARAOH TO LET THEM GO INTO THE WILDERNESS TO WORSHIP.
OH MIGHTY SETH, LORD OF CHAOS AND STORMS, WE BEG OF YOU, PUT A STOP TO THESE TERRIBLE STORMS. SURELY YOU ARE GREATER THAN THIS UNSEEN GOD OF MOSES.

EXODUS 9:23-26

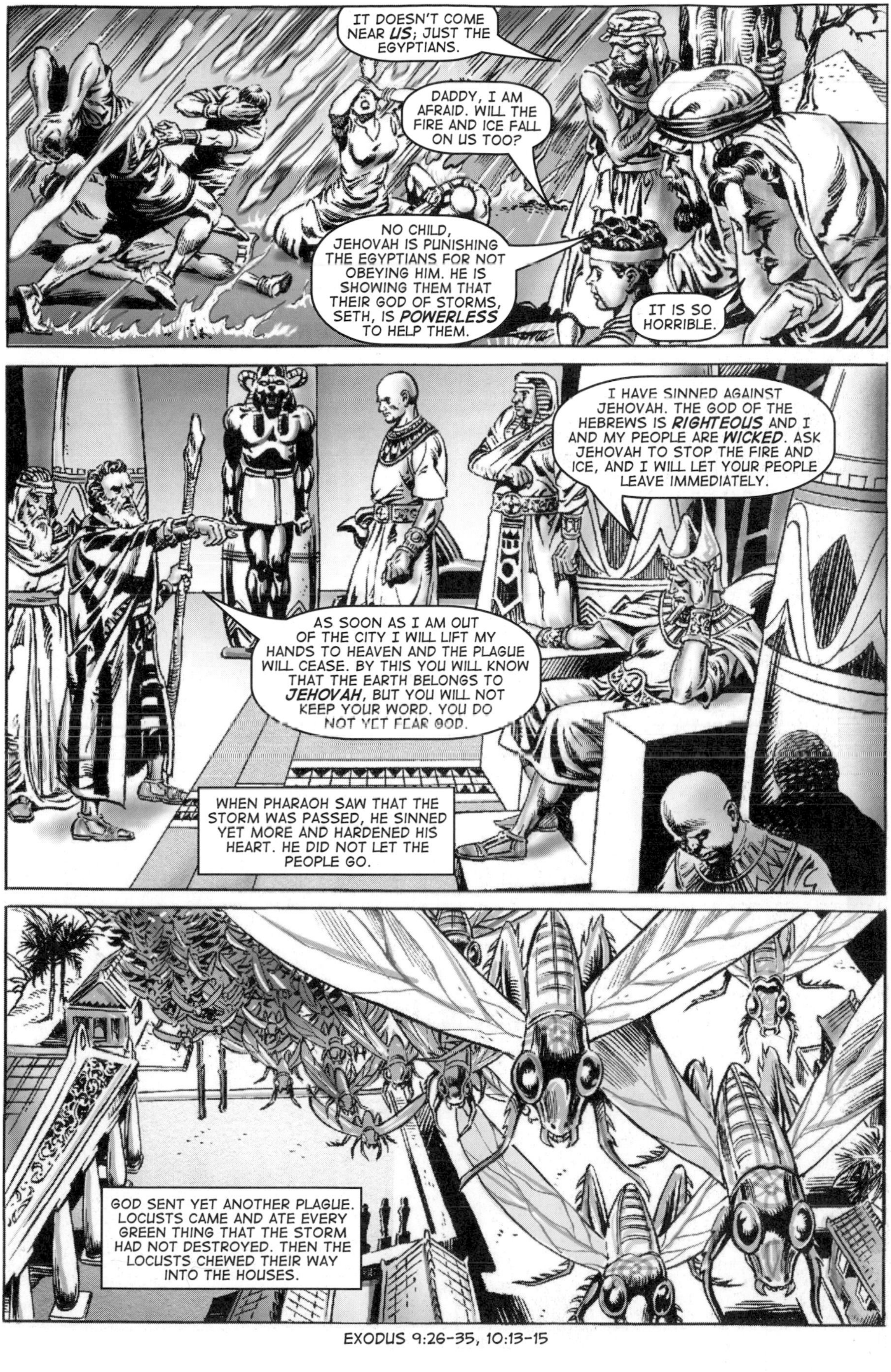
IT DOESN'T COME NEAR US; JUST THE EGYPTIANS.
DADDY, I AM AFRAID. WILL THE FIRE AND ICE FALL ON US TOO?
NO CHILD, JEHOVAH IS PUNISHING THE EGYPTIANS FOR NOT OBEYING HIM. HE IS SHOWING THEM THAT THEIR GOD OF STORMS, SETH, IS POWERLESS TO HELP THEM.
IT IS SO HORRIBLE.
I HAVE SINNED AGAINST JEHOVAH. THE GOD OF THE HEBREWS IS RIGHTEOUS AND I AND MY PEOPLE ARE WICKED. ASK JEHOVAH TO STOP THE FIRE AND ICE, AND I WILL LET YOUR PEOPLE LEAVE IMMEDIATELY.
AS SOON AS I AM OUT OF THE CITY I WILL LIFT MY HANDS TO HEAVEN AND THE PLAGUE WILL CEASE. BY THIS YOU WILL KNOW THAT THE EARTH BELONGS TO JEHOVAH, BUT YOU WILL NOT KEEP YOUR WORD. YOU DO NOT YET FEAR GOD.
WHEN PHARAOH SAW THAT THE STORM WAS PASSED, HE SINNED YET MORE AND HARDENED HIS HEART. HE DID NOT LET THE PEOPLE GO.
GOD SENT YET ANOTHER PLAGUE. LOCUSTS CAME AND ATE EVERY GREEN THING THAT THE STORM HAD NOT DESTROYED. THEN THE LOCUSTS CHEWED THEIR WAY INTO THE HOUSES.

EXODUS 9:26-35, 10:13-15

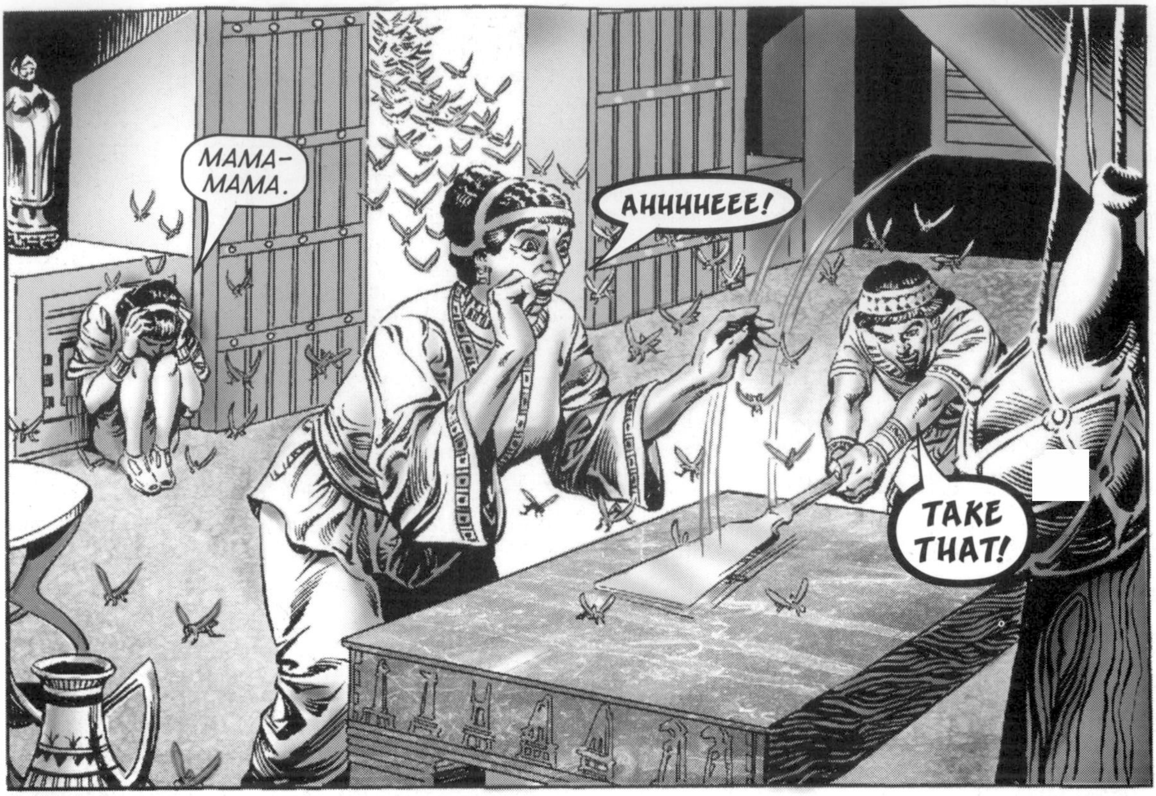
MAMA-
MAMA.
AHHHHEEE!
TAKE
THAT!

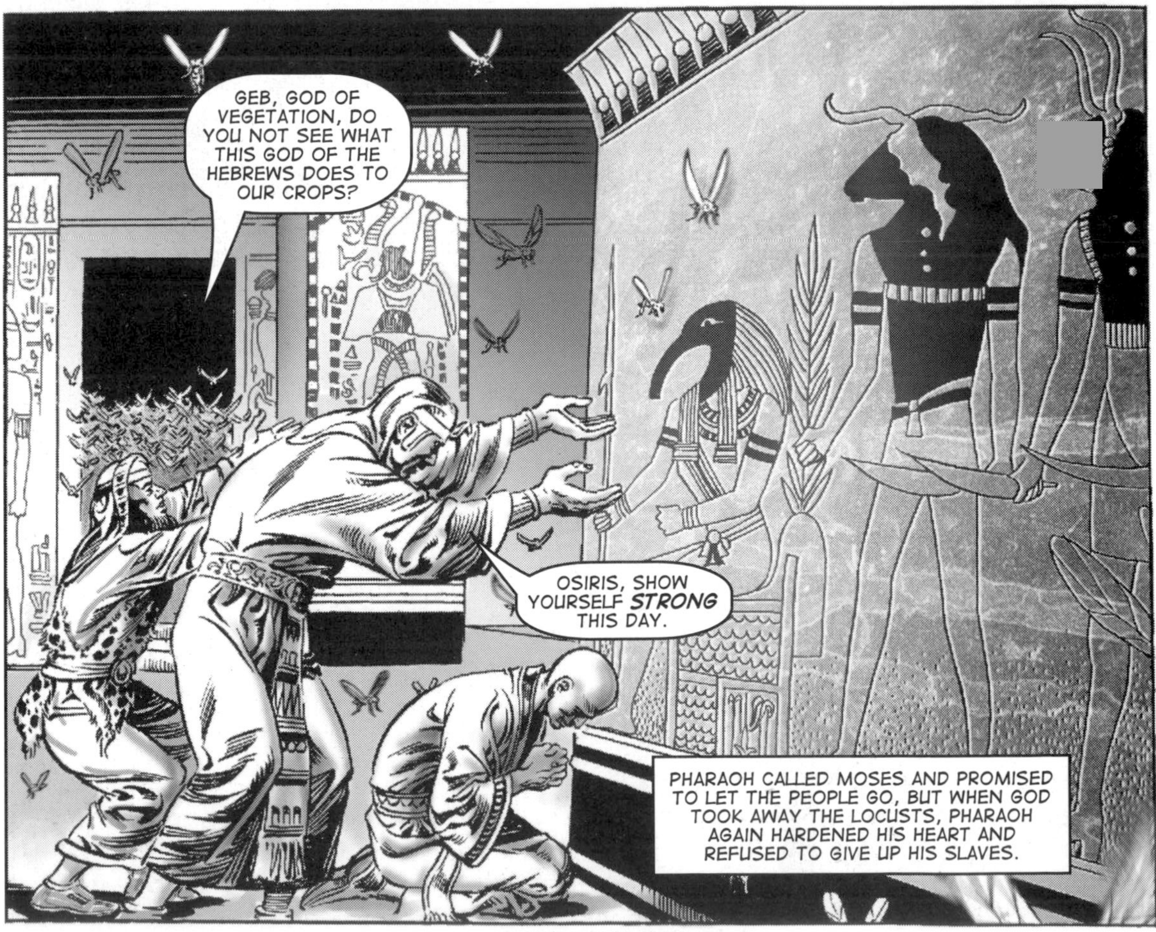
GEB, GOD OF VEGETATION, DO YOU NOT SEE WHAT THIS GOD OF THE HEBREWS DOES TO OUR CROPS?
OSIRIS, SHOW YOURSELF ***STRONG*** THIS DAY.
PHARAOH CALLED MOSES AND PROMISED TO LET THE PEOPLE GO, BUT WHEN GOD TOOK AWAY THE LOCUSTS, PHARAOH AGAIN HARDENED HIS HEART AND REFUSED TO GIVE UP HIS SLAVES.

EXODUS 10:14-20

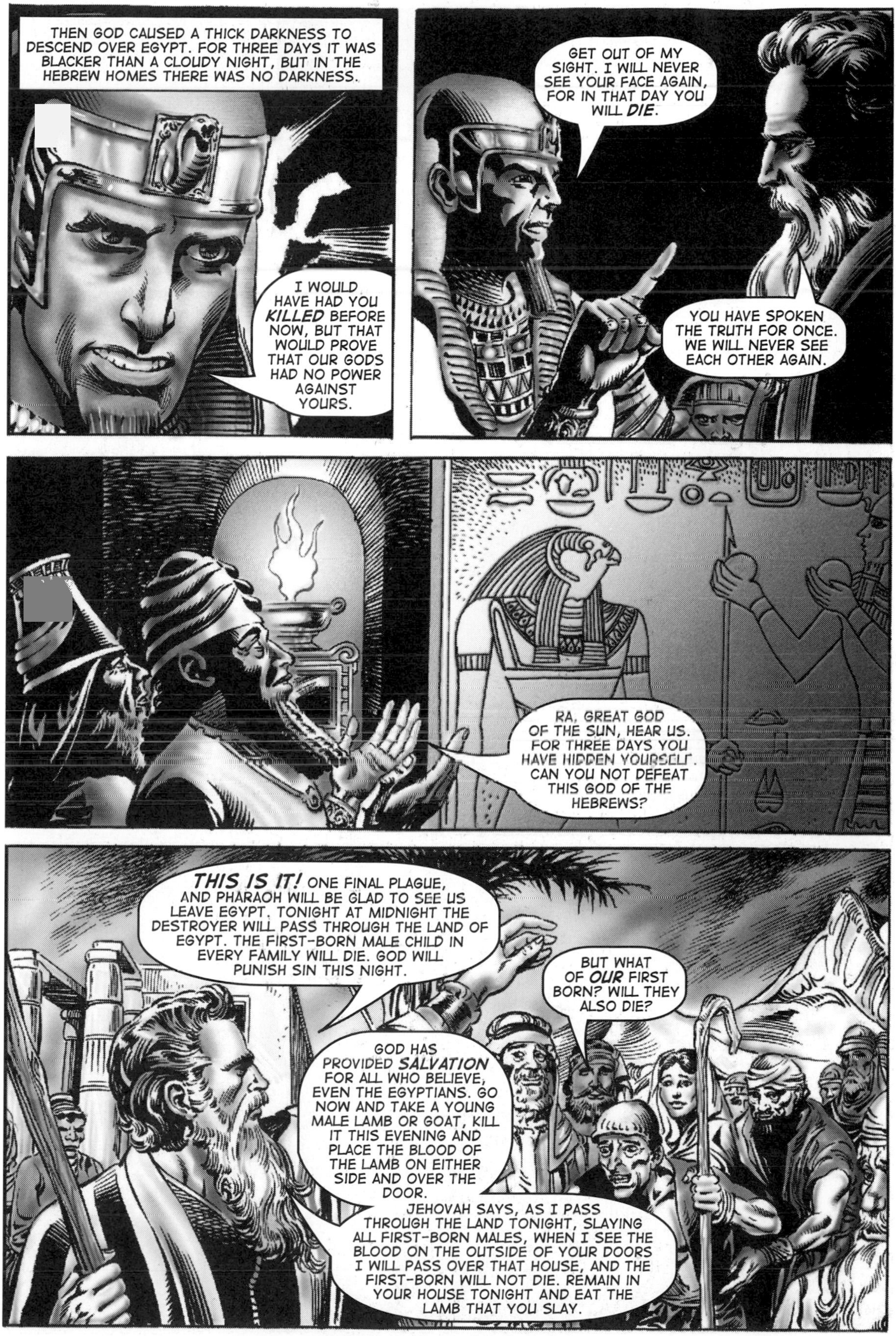
THEN GOD CAUSED A THICK DARKNESS TO DESCEND OVER EGYPT. FOR THREE DAYS IT WAS BLACKER THAN A CLOUDY NIGHT, BUT IN THE HEBREW HOMES THERE WAS NO DARKNESS.
I WOULD HAVE HAD YOU *KILLED* BEFORE NOW, BUT THAT WOULD PROVE THAT OUR GODS HAD NO POWER AGAINST YOURS.
GET OUT OF MY SIGHT. I WILL NEVER SEE YOUR FACE AGAIN, FOR IN THAT DAY YOU WILL *DIE*.
YOU HAVE SPOKEN THE TRUTH FOR ONCE. WE WILL NEVER SEE EACH OTHER AGAIN.
RA, GREAT GOD OF THE SUN, HEAR US. FOR THREE DAYS YOU HAVE HIDDEN YOURSELF. CAN YOU NOT DEFEAT THIS GOD OF THE HEBREWS?
THIS IS IT! ONE FINAL PLAGUE, AND PHARAOH WILL BE GLAD TO SEE US LEAVE EGYPT. TONIGHT AT MIDNIGHT THE DESTROYER WILL PASS THROUGH THE LAND OF EGYPT. THE FIRST-BORN MALE CHILD IN EVERY FAMILY WILL DIE. GOD WILL PUNISH SIN THIS NIGHT.
BUT WHAT OF *OUR* FIRST BORN? WILL THEY ALSO DIE?
GOD HAS PROVIDED *SALVATION* FOR ALL WHO BELIEVE, EVEN THE EGYPTIANS. GO NOW AND TAKE A YOUNG MALE LAMB OR GOAT, KILL IT THIS EVENING AND PLACE THE BLOOD OF THE LAMB ON EITHER SIDE AND OVER THE DOOR.
JEHOVAH SAYS, AS I PASS THROUGH THE LAND TONIGHT, SLAYING ALL FIRST-BORN MALES, WHEN I SEE THE BLOOD ON THE OUTSIDE OF YOUR DOORS I WILL PASS OVER THAT HOUSE, AND THE FIRST-BORN WILL NOT DIE. REMAIN IN YOUR HOUSE TONIGHT AND EAT THE LAMB THAT YOU SLAY.

EXODUS 10:22-29, 11:4-5, 12:3-7

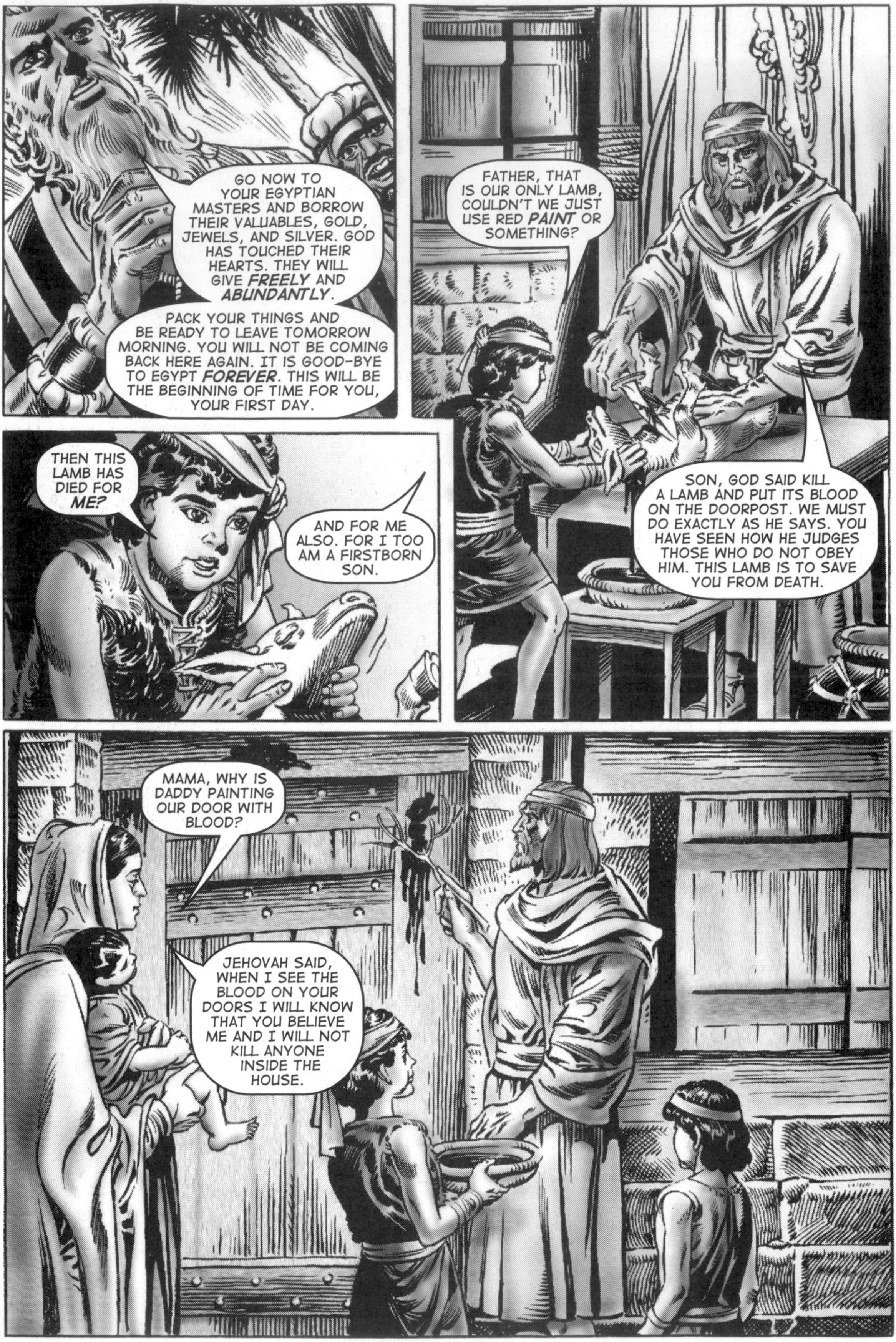
GO NOW TO YOUR EGYPTIAN MASTERS AND BORROW THEIR VALUABLES, GOLD, JEWELS, AND SILVER. GOD HAS TOUCHED THEIR HEARTS. THEY WILL GIVE **FREELY** AND **ABUNDANTLY**.
PACK YOUR THINGS AND BE READY TO LEAVE TOMORROW MORNING. YOU WILL NOT BE COMING BACK HERE AGAIN. IT IS GOOD-BYE TO EGYPT **FOREVER**. THIS WILL BE THE BEGINNING OF TIME FOR YOU, YOUR FIRST DAY.
FATHER, THAT IS OUR ONLY LAMB, COULDN'T WE JUST USE RED **PAINT** OR SOMETHING?
SON, GOD SAID KILL A LAMB AND PUT ITS BLOOD ON THE DOORPOST. WE MUST DO EXACTLY AS HE SAYS. YOU HAVE SEEN HOW HE JUDGES THOSE WHO DO NOT OBEY HIM. THIS LAMB IS TO SAVE YOU FROM DEATH.
THEN THIS LAMB HAS DIED FOR **ME?**
AND FOR ME ALSO. FOR I TOO AM A FIRSTBORN SON.
MAMA, WHY IS DADDY PAINTING OUR DOOR WITH BLOOD?
JEHOVAH SAID, WHEN I SEE THE BLOOD ON YOUR DOORS I WILL KNOW THAT YOU BELIEVE ME AND I WILL NOT KILL ANYONE INSIDE THE HOUSE.

EXODUS 12:26-28, 35-36

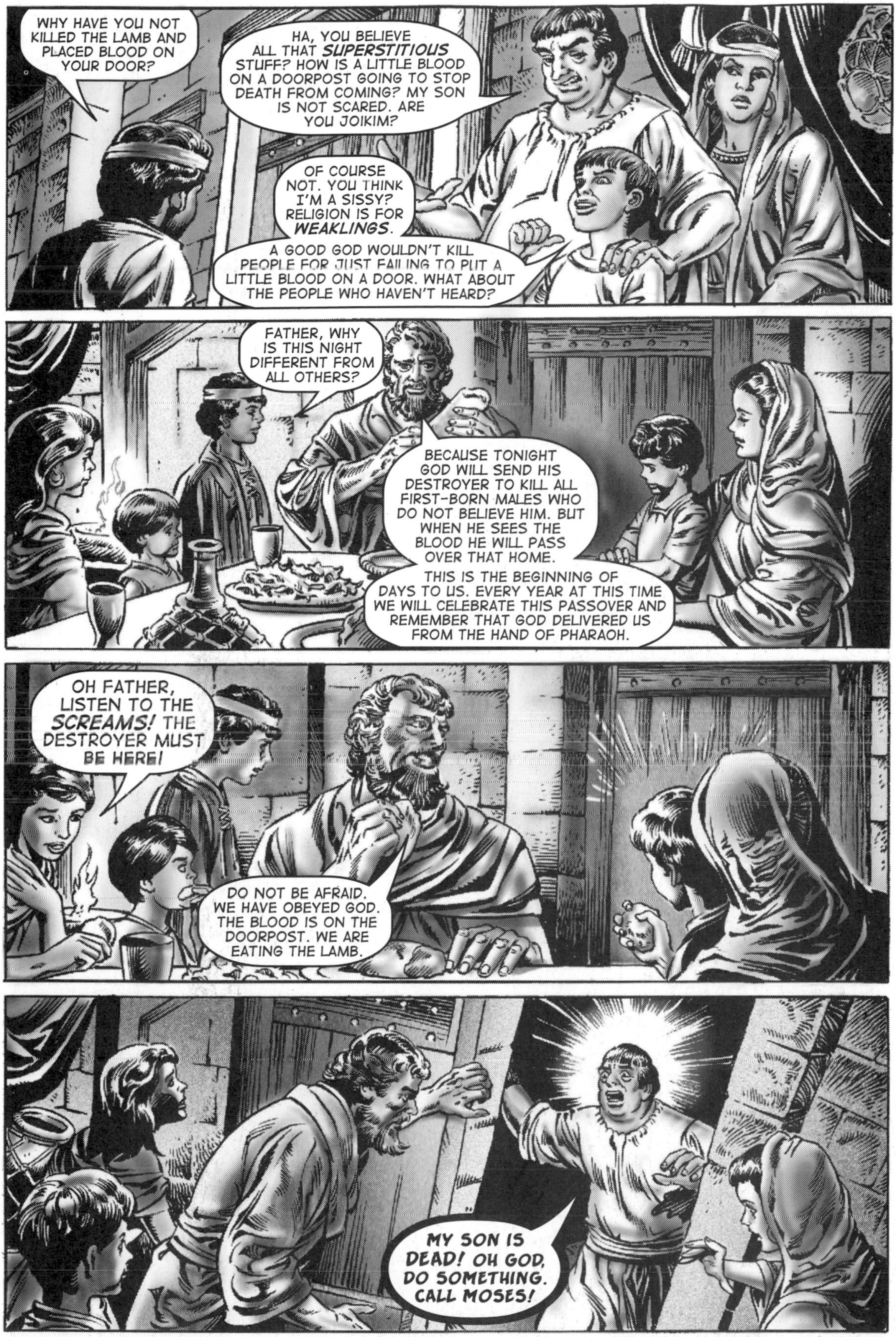
WHY HAVE YOU NOT KILLED THE LAMB AND PLACED BLOOD ON YOUR DOOR?
HA, YOU BELIEVE ALL THAT SUPERSTITIOUS STUFF? HOW IS A LITTLE BLOOD ON A DOORPOST GOING TO STOP DEATH FROM COMING? MY SON IS NOT SCARED. ARE YOU JOIKIM?
OF COURSE NOT. YOU THINK I'M A SISSY? RELIGION IS FOR WEAKLINGS.
A GOOD GOD WOULDN'T KILL PEOPLE FOR JUST FAILING TO PUT A LITTLE BLOOD ON A DOOR. WHAT ABOUT THE PEOPLE WHO HAVEN'T HEARD?
FATHER, WHY IS THIS NIGHT DIFFERENT FROM ALL OTHERS?
BECAUSE TONIGHT GOD WILL SEND HIS DESTROYER TO KILL ALL FIRST-BORN MALES WHO DO NOT BELIEVE HIM. BUT WHEN HE SEES THE BLOOD HE WILL PASS OVER THAT HOME.
THIS IS THE BEGINNING OF DAYS TO US. EVERY YEAR AT THIS TIME WE WILL CELEBRATE THIS PASSOVER AND REMEMBER THAT GOD DELIVERED US FROM THE HAND OF PHARAOH.
OH FATHER, LISTEN TO THE SCREAMS! THE DESTROYER MUST BE HERE!
DO NOT BE AFRAID. WE HAVE OBEYED GOD. THE BLOOD IS ON THE DOORPOST. WE ARE EATING THE LAMB.
MY SON IS DEAD! OH GOD, DO SOMETHING. CALL MOSES!

EXODUS 12:28

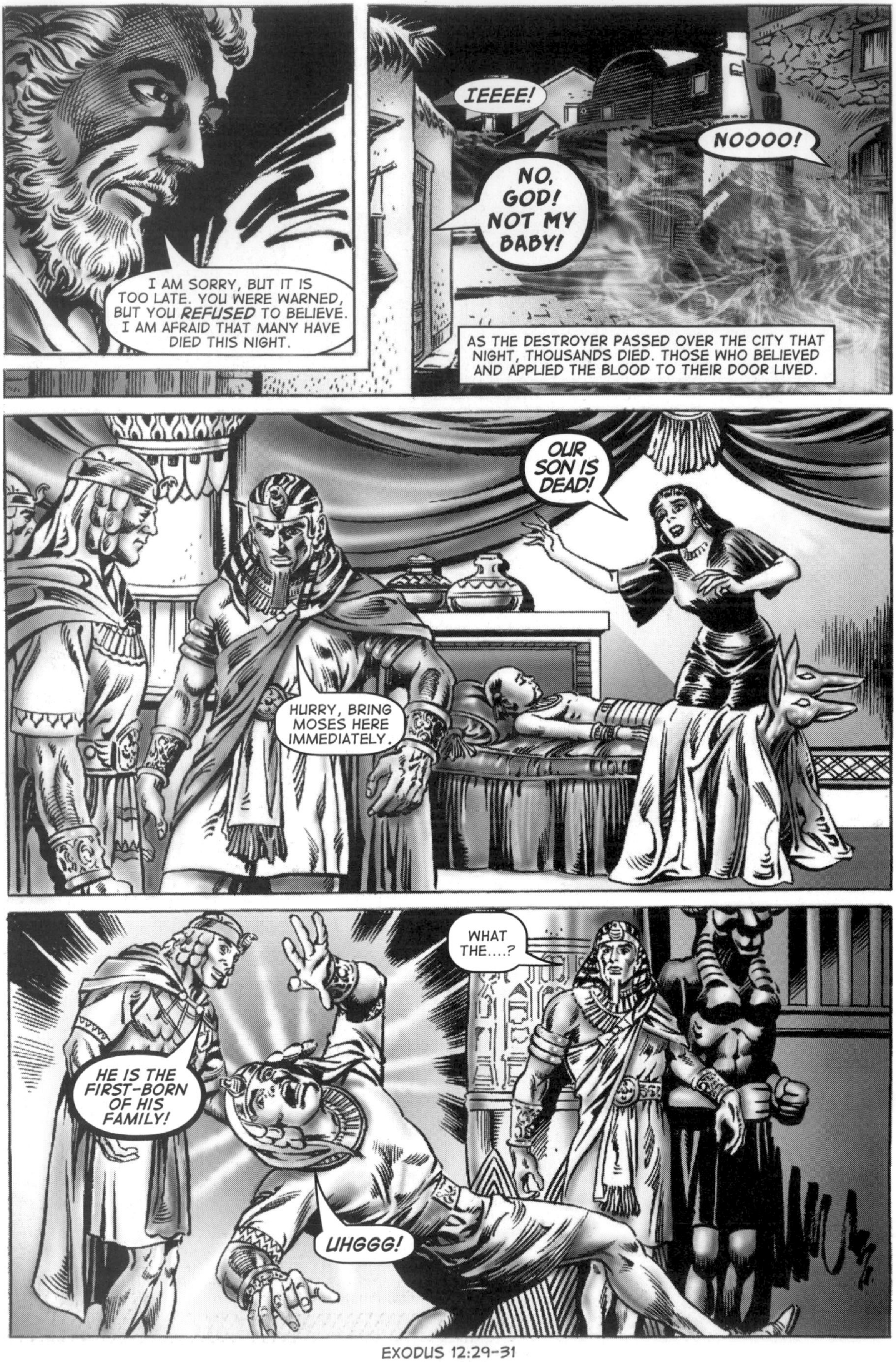
I AM SORRY, BUT IT IS TOO LATE. YOU WERE WARNED, BUT YOU **REFUSED** TO BELIEVE. I AM AFRAID THAT MANY HAVE DIED THIS NIGHT.
IEEEE!
NOOOO!
NO, GOD! NOT MY BABY!
AS THE DESTROYER PASSED OVER THE CITY THAT NIGHT, THOUSANDS DIED. THOSE WHO BELIEVED AND APPLIED THE BLOOD TO THEIR DOOR LIVED.
OUR SON IS DEAD!
HURRY, BRING MOSES HERE IMMEDIATELY.
WHAT THE....?
HE IS THE FIRST-BORN OF HIS FAMILY!
UHGGG!

EXODUS 12:29-31

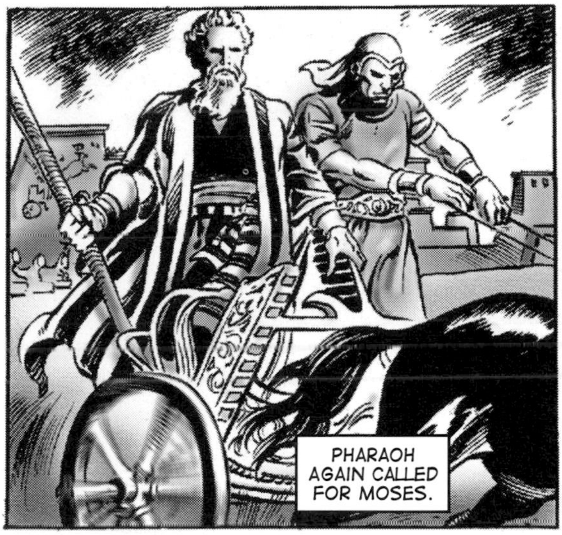
PHARAOH AGAIN CALLED FOR MOSES.

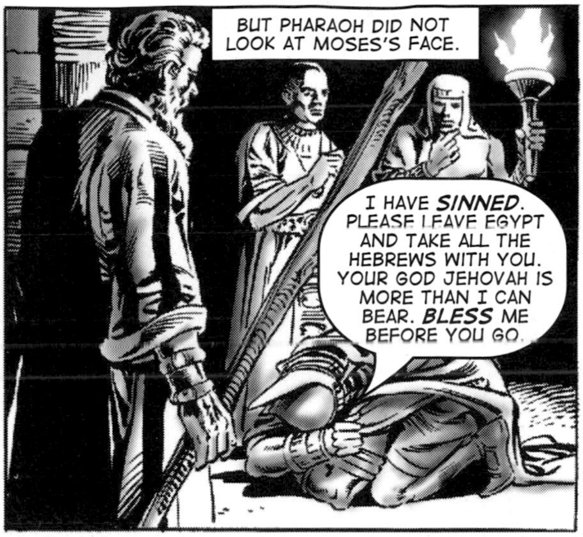
BUT PHARAOH DID NOT LOOK AT MOSES'S FACE.
I HAVE *SINNED*. PLEASE LEAVE EGYPT AND TAKE ALL THE HEBREWS WITH YOU. YOUR GOD JEHOVAH IS MORE THAN I CAN BEAR. *BLESS* ME BEFORE YOU GO.

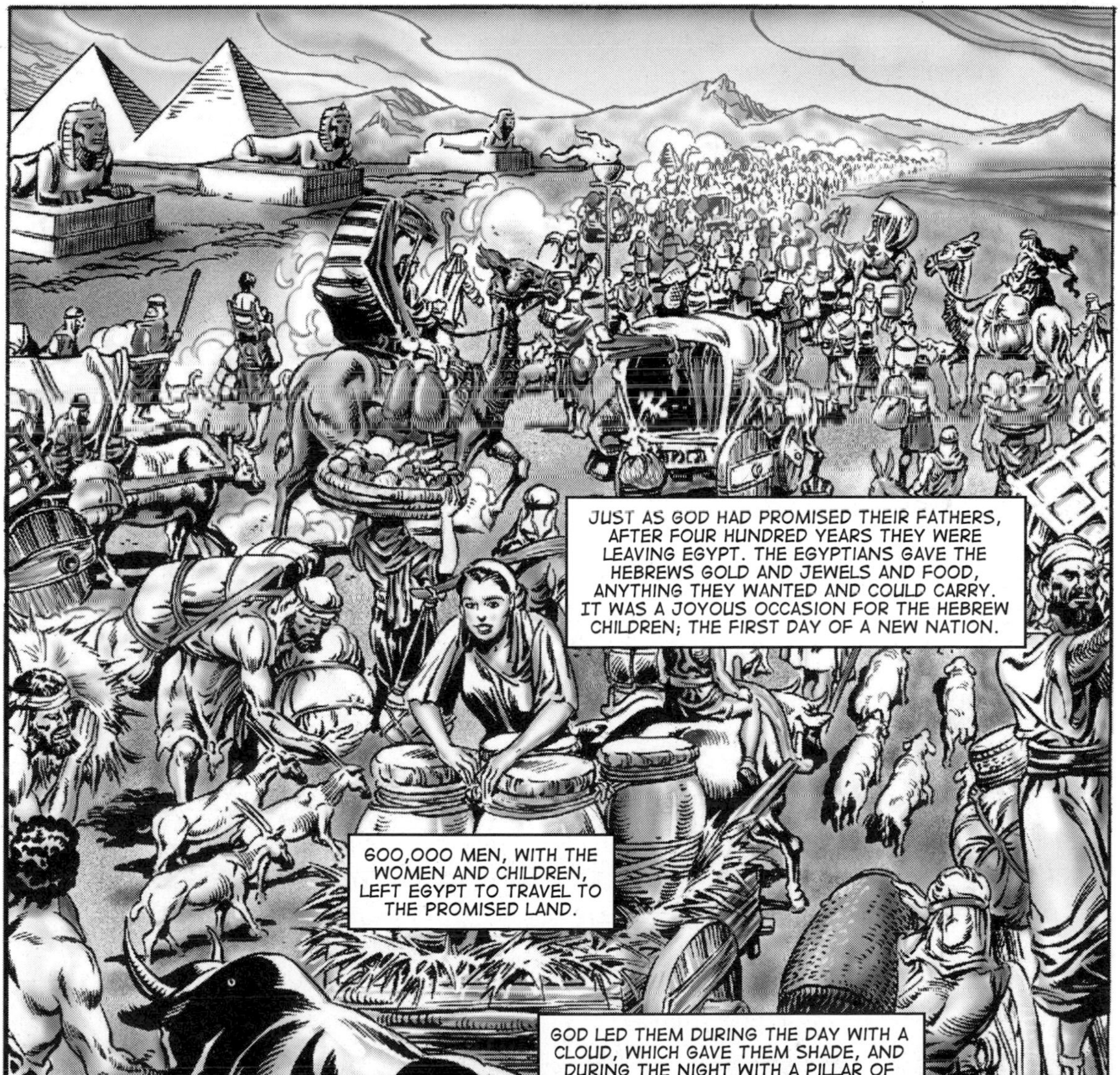
JUST AS GOD HAD PROMISED THEIR FATHERS, AFTER FOUR HUNDRED YEARS THEY WERE LEAVING EGYPT. THE EGYPTIANS GAVE THE HEBREWS GOLD AND JEWELS AND FOOD, ANYTHING THEY WANTED AND COULD CARRY. IT WAS A JOYOUS OCCASION FOR THE HEBREW CHILDREN; THE FIRST DAY OF A NEW NATION.
600,000 MEN, WITH THE WOMEN AND CHILDREN, LEFT EGYPT TO TRAVEL TO THE PROMISED LAND.
GOD LED THEM DURING THE DAY WITH A CLOUD, WHICH GAVE THEM SHADE, AND DURING THE NIGHT WITH A PILLAR OF FIRE, WHICH GAVE THEM LIGHT.

EXODUS 12:21-22, 31-38

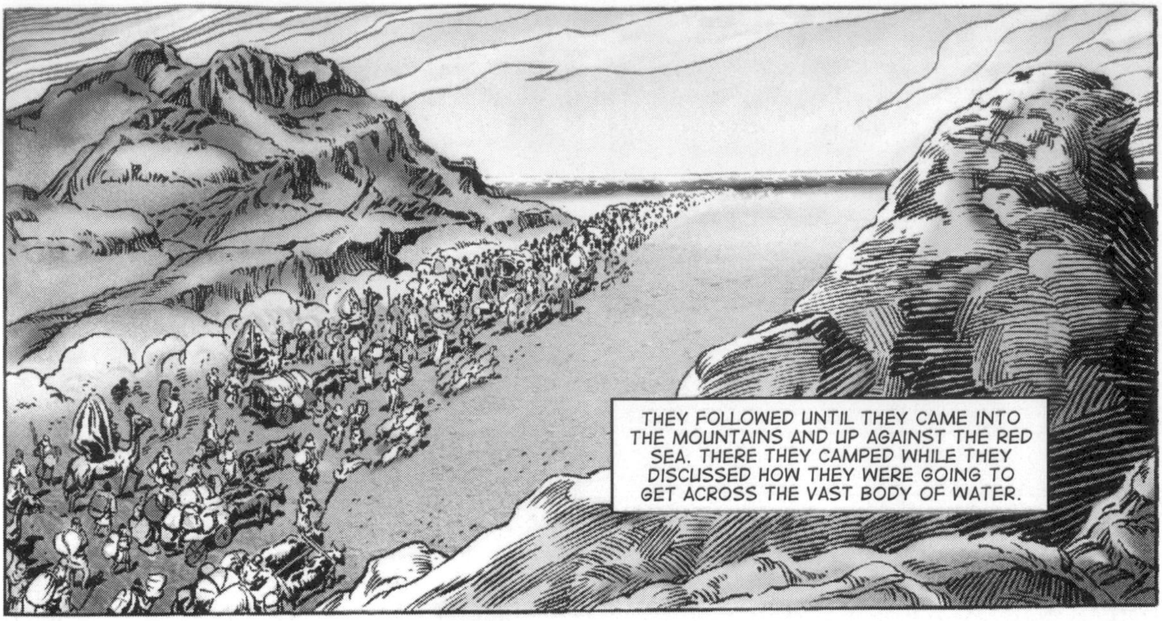
THEY FOLLOWED UNTIL THEY CAME INTO THE MOUNTAINS AND UP AGAINST THE RED SEA. THERE THEY CAMPED WHILE THEY DISCUSSED HOW THEY WERE GOING TO GET ACROSS THE VAST BODY OF WATER.

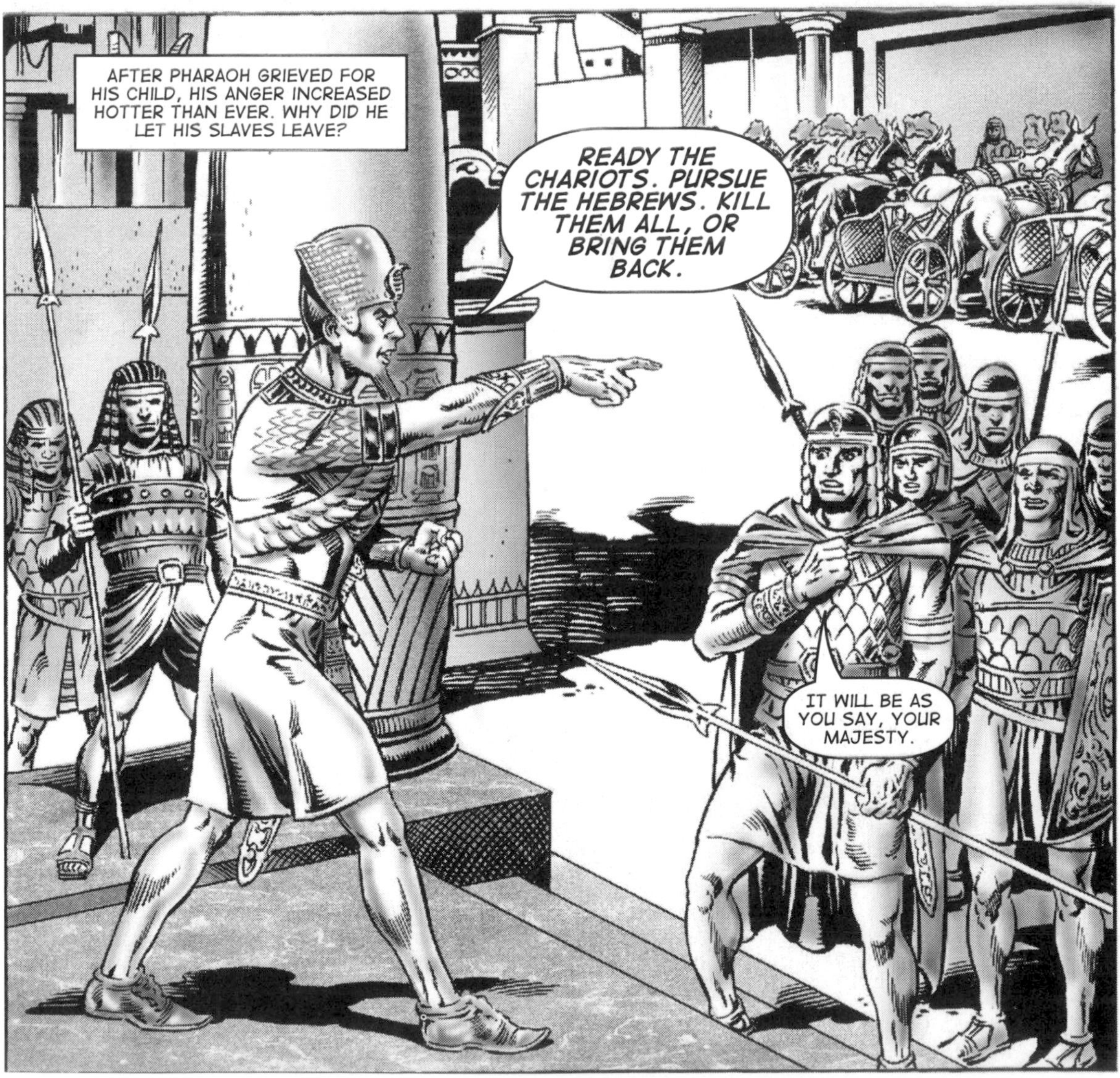
AFTER PHARAOH GRIEVED FOR HIS CHILD, HIS ANGER INCREASED HOTTER THAN EVER. WHY DID HE LET HIS SLAVES LEAVE?
READY THE CHARIOTS. PURSUE THE HEBREWS. KILL THEM ALL, OR BRING THEM BACK.
IT WILL BE AS YOU SAY, YOUR MAJESTY.

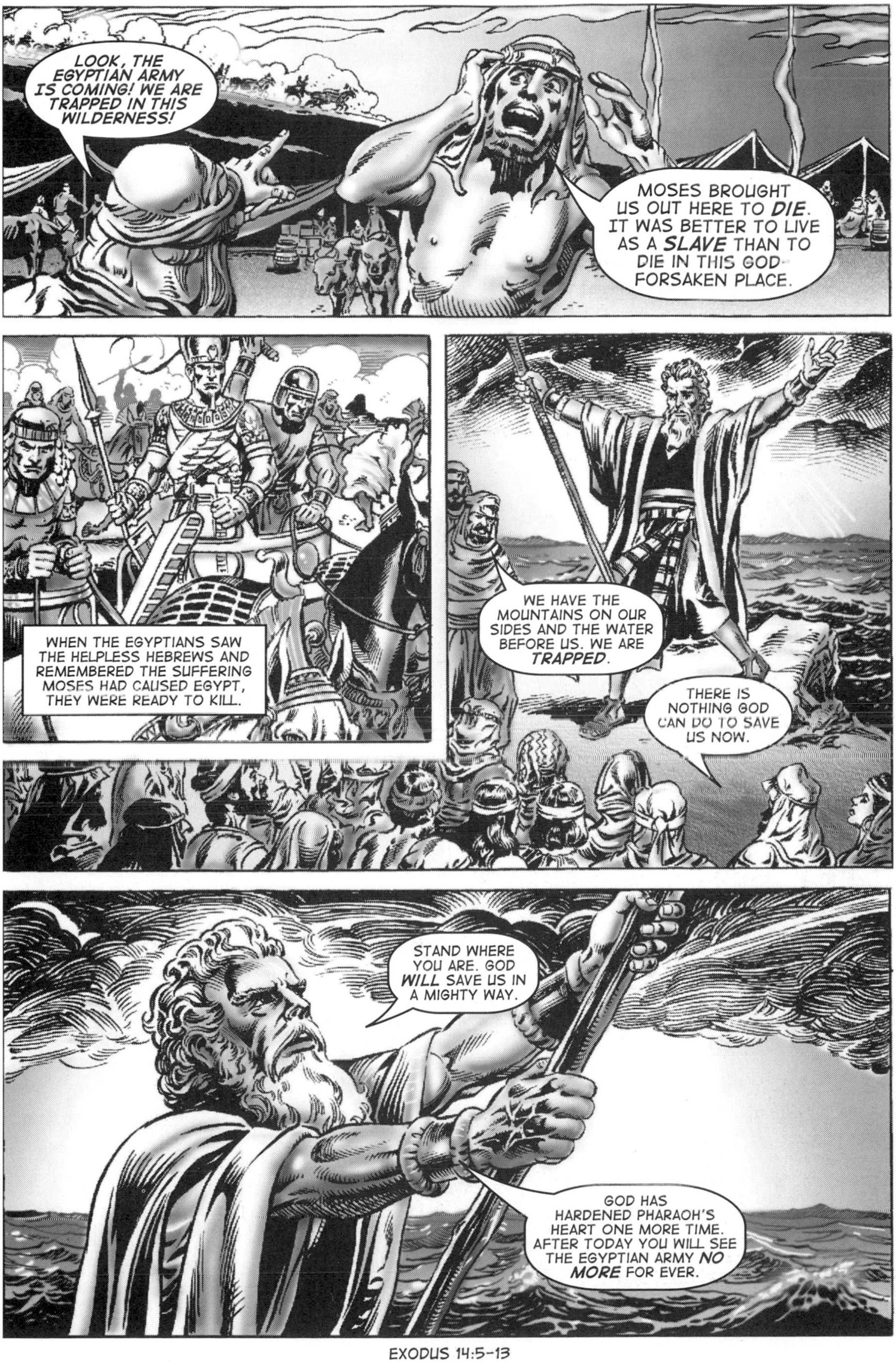
LOOK, THE EGYPTIAN ARMY IS COMING! WE ARE TRAPPED IN THIS WILDERNESS!
MOSES BROUGHT US OUT HERE TO DIE. IT WAS BETTER TO LIVE AS A SLAVE THAN TO DIE IN THIS GOD-FORSAKEN PLACE.
WHEN THE EGYPTIANS SAW THE HELPLESS HEBREWS AND REMEMBERED THE SUFFERING MOSES HAD CAUSED EGYPT, THEY WERE READY TO KILL.
WE HAVE THE MOUNTAINS ON OUR SIDES AND THE WATER BEFORE US. WE ARE TRAPPED.
THERE IS NOTHING GOD CAN DO TO SAVE US NOW.
STAND WHERE YOU ARE. GOD WILL SAVE US IN A MIGHTY WAY.
GOD HAS HARDENED PHARAOH'S HEART ONE MORE TIME. AFTER TODAY YOU WILL SEE THE EGYPTIAN ARMY NO MORE FOR EVER.

EXODUS 14:5–13

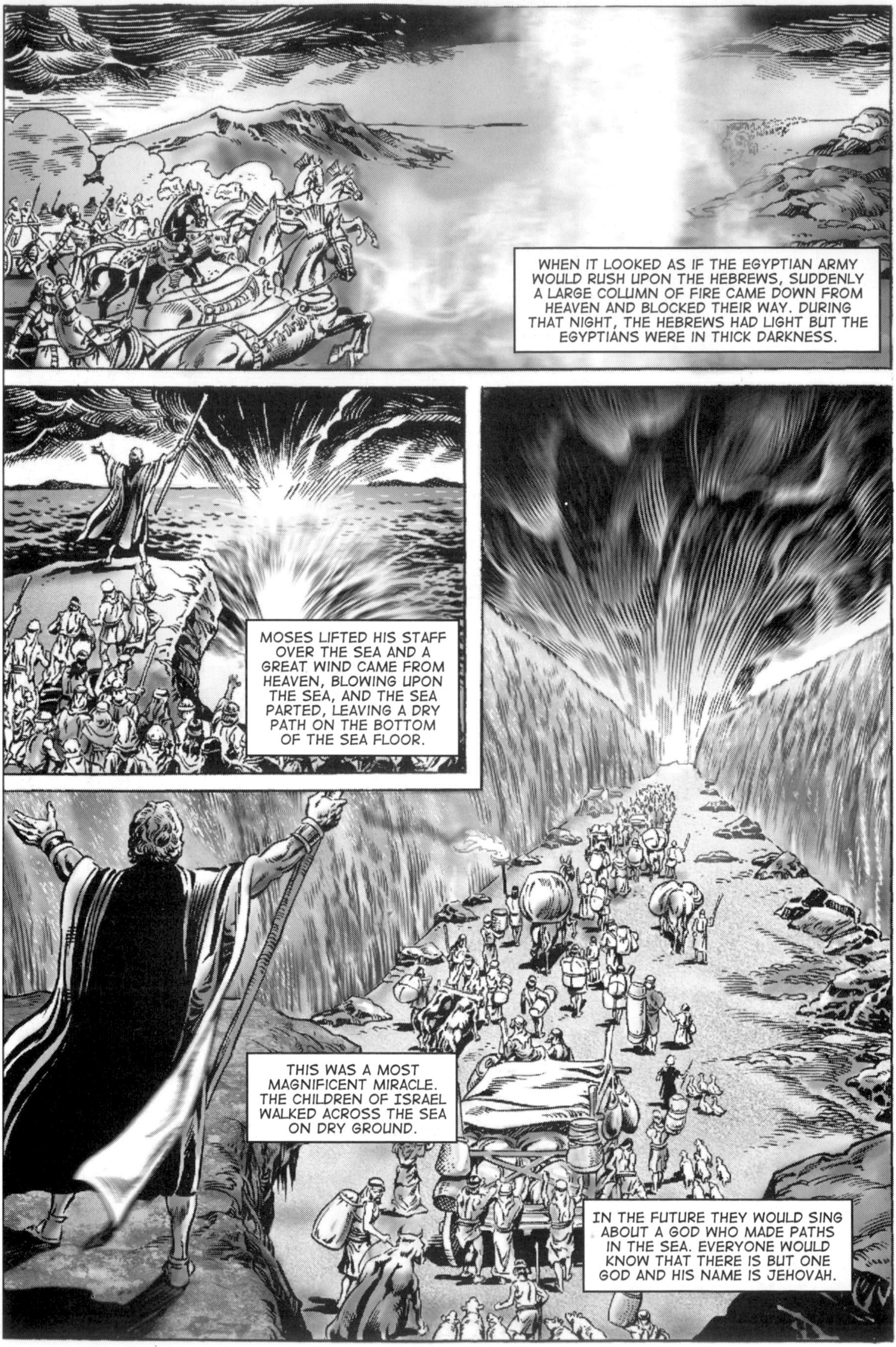
WHEN IT LOOKED AS IF THE EGYPTIAN ARMY WOULD RUSH UPON THE HEBREWS, SUDDENLY A LARGE COLUMN OF FIRE CAME DOWN FROM HEAVEN AND BLOCKED THEIR WAY. DURING THAT NIGHT, THE HEBREWS HAD LIGHT BUT THE EGYPTIANS WERE IN THICK DARKNESS.
MOSES LIFTED HIS STAFF OVER THE SEA AND A GREAT WIND CAME FROM HEAVEN, BLOWING UPON THE SEA, AND THE SEA PARTED, LEAVING A DRY PATH ON THE BOTTOM OF THE SEA FLOOR.
THIS WAS A MOST MAGNIFICENT MIRACLE. THE CHILDREN OF ISRAEL WALKED ACROSS THE SEA ON DRY GROUND.
IN THE FUTURE THEY WOULD SING ABOUT A GOD WHO MADE PATHS IN THE SEA. EVERYONE WOULD KNOW THAT THERE IS BUT ONE GOD AND HIS NAME IS JEHOVAH.

EXODUS 14:15-22

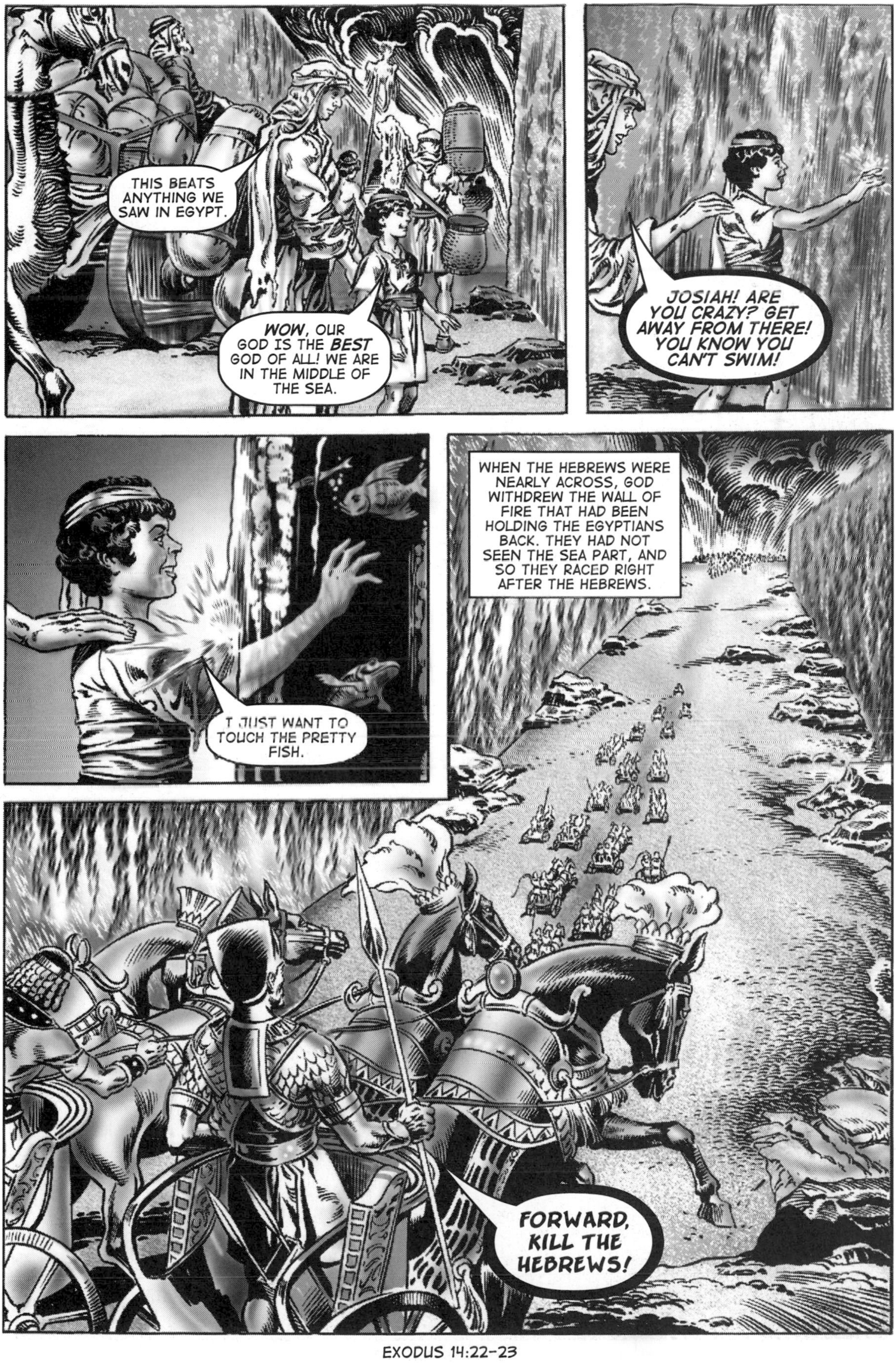
THIS BEATS ANYTHING WE SAW IN EGYPT.
WOW, OUR GOD IS THE BEST GOD OF ALL! WE ARE IN THE MIDDLE OF THE SEA.
JOSIAH! ARE YOU CRAZY? GET AWAY FROM THERE! YOU KNOW YOU CAN'T SWIM!
I JUST WANT TO TOUCH THE PRETTY FISH.
WHEN THE HEBREWS WERE NEARLY ACROSS, GOD WITHDREW THE WALL OF FIRE THAT HAD BEEN HOLDING THE EGYPTIANS BACK. THEY HAD NOT SEEN THE SEA PART, AND SO THEY RACED RIGHT AFTER THE HEBREWS.
FORWARD, KILL THE HEBREWS!

EXODUS 14:22-23

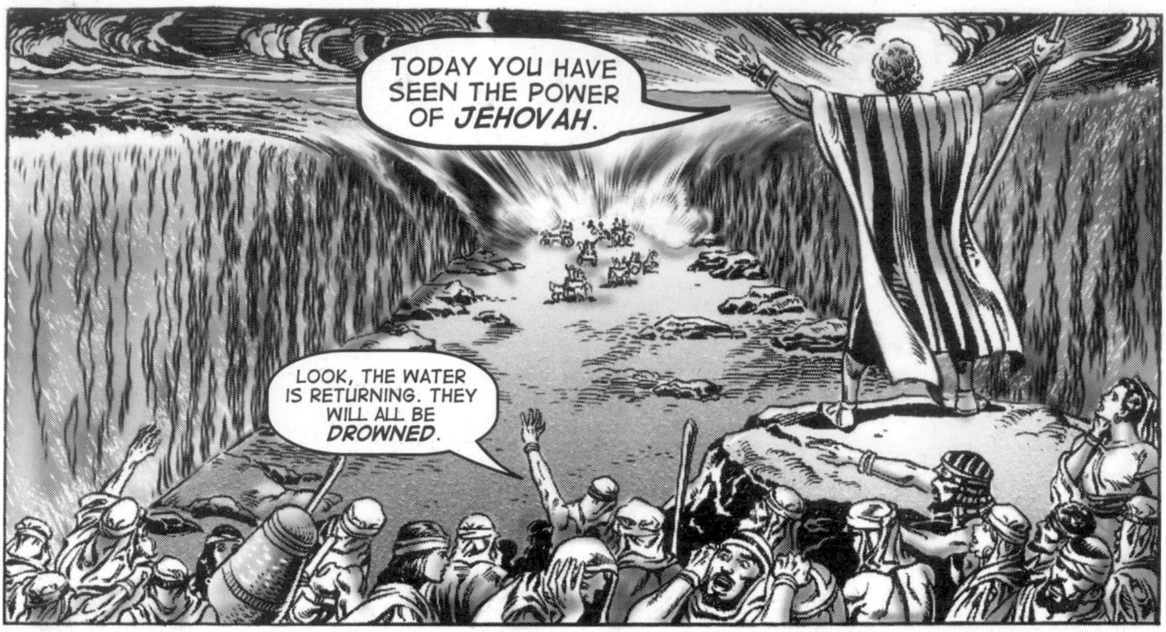
TODAY YOU HAVE SEEN THE POWER OF JEHOVAH.
LOOK, THE WATER IS RETURNING. THEY WILL ALL BE DROWNED.

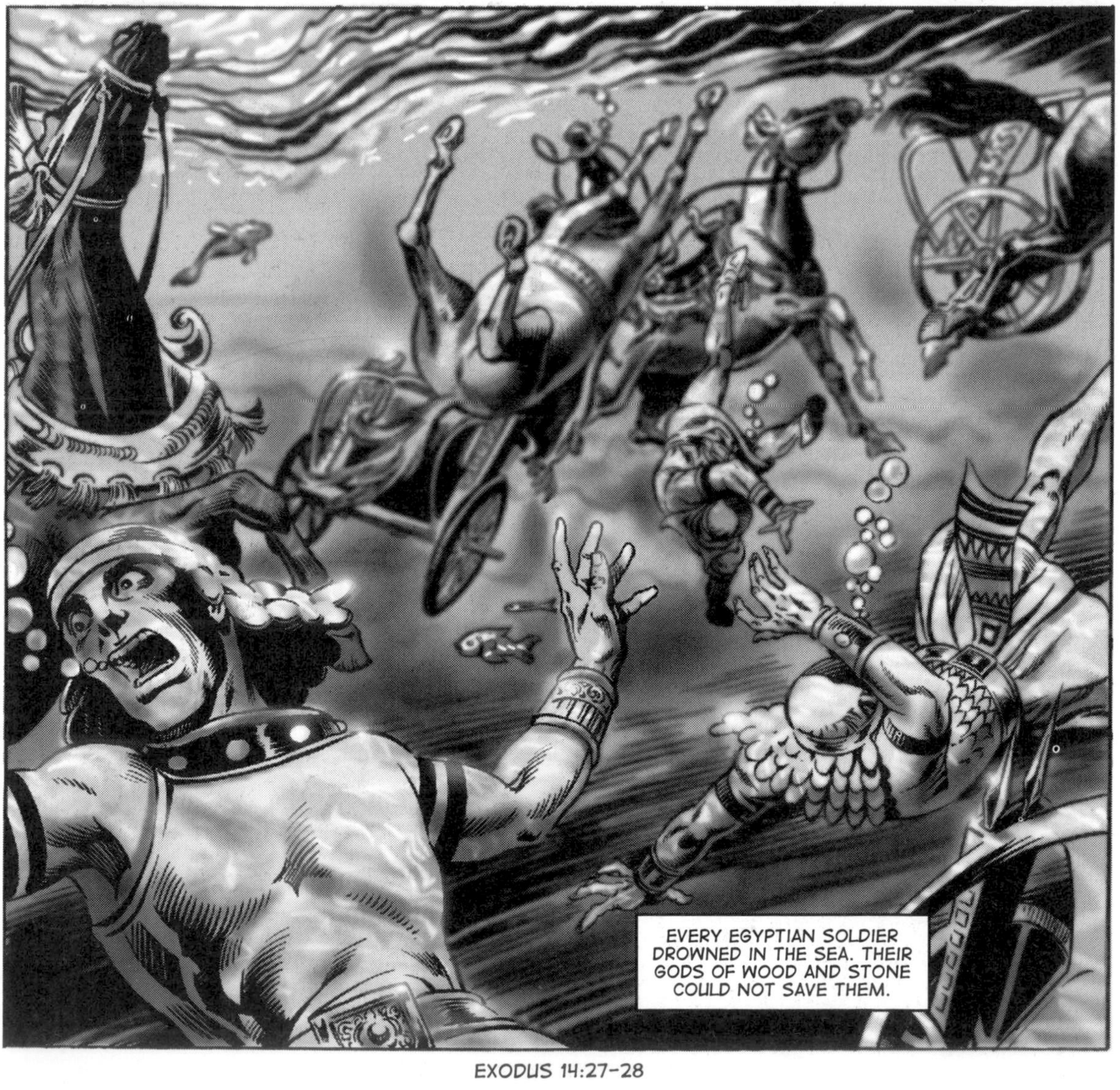
EVERY EGYPTIAN SOLDIER DROWNED IN THE SEA. THEIR GODS OF WOOD AND STONE COULD NOT SAVE THEM.

EXODUS 14:27-28

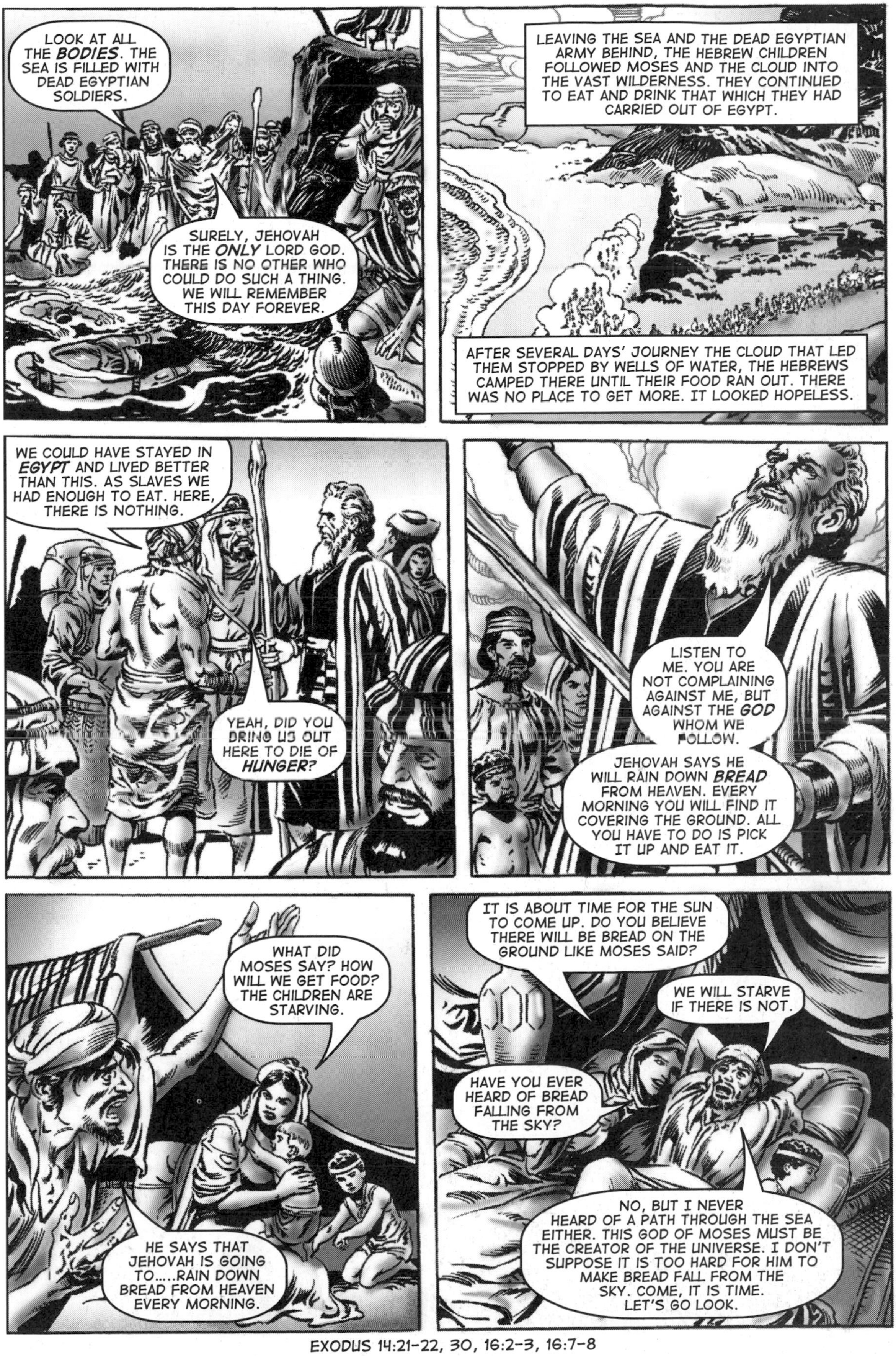
LOOK AT ALL THE BODIES. THE SEA IS FILLED WITH DEAD EGYPTIAN SOLDIERS.
SURELY, JEHOVAH IS THE ONLY LORD GOD. THERE IS NO OTHER WHO COULD DO SUCH A THING. WE WILL REMEMBER THIS DAY FOREVER.
LEAVING THE SEA AND THE DEAD EGYPTIAN ARMY BEHIND, THE HEBREW CHILDREN FOLLOWED MOSES AND THE CLOUD INTO THE VAST WILDERNESS. THEY CONTINUED TO EAT AND DRINK THAT WHICH THEY HAD CARRIED OUT OF EGYPT.
AFTER SEVERAL DAYS' JOURNEY THE CLOUD THAT LED THEM STOPPED BY WELLS OF WATER, THE HEBREWS CAMPED THERE UNTIL THEIR FOOD RAN OUT. THERE WAS NO PLACE TO GET MORE. IT LOOKED HOPELESS.
WE COULD HAVE STAYED IN EGYPT AND LIVED BETTER THAN THIS. AS SLAVES WE HAD ENOUGH TO EAT. HERE, THERE IS NOTHING.
YEAH, DID YOU BRING US OUT HERE TO DIE OF HUNGER?
LISTEN TO ME. YOU ARE NOT COMPLAINING AGAINST ME, BUT AGAINST THE GOD WHOM WE FOLLOW.
JEHOVAH SAYS HE WILL RAIN DOWN BREAD FROM HEAVEN. EVERY MORNING YOU WILL FIND IT COVERING THE GROUND. ALL YOU HAVE TO DO IS PICK IT UP AND EAT IT.
WHAT DID MOSES SAY? HOW WILL WE GET FOOD? THE CHILDREN ARE STARVING.
HE SAYS THAT JEHOVAH IS GOING TO.....RAIN DOWN BREAD FROM HEAVEN EVERY MORNING.
IT IS ABOUT TIME FOR THE SUN TO COME UP. DO YOU BELIEVE THERE WILL BE BREAD ON THE GROUND LIKE MOSES SAID?
WE WILL STARVE IF THERE IS NOT.
HAVE YOU EVER HEARD OF BREAD FALLING FROM THE SKY?
NO, BUT I NEVER HEARD OF A PATH THROUGH THE SEA EITHER. THIS GOD OF MOSES MUST BE THE CREATOR OF THE UNIVERSE. I DON'T SUPPOSE IT IS TOO HARD FOR HIM TO MAKE BREAD FALL FROM THE SKY. COME, IT IS TIME. LET'S GO LOOK.

EXODUS 14:21-22, 30, 16:2-3, 16:7-8

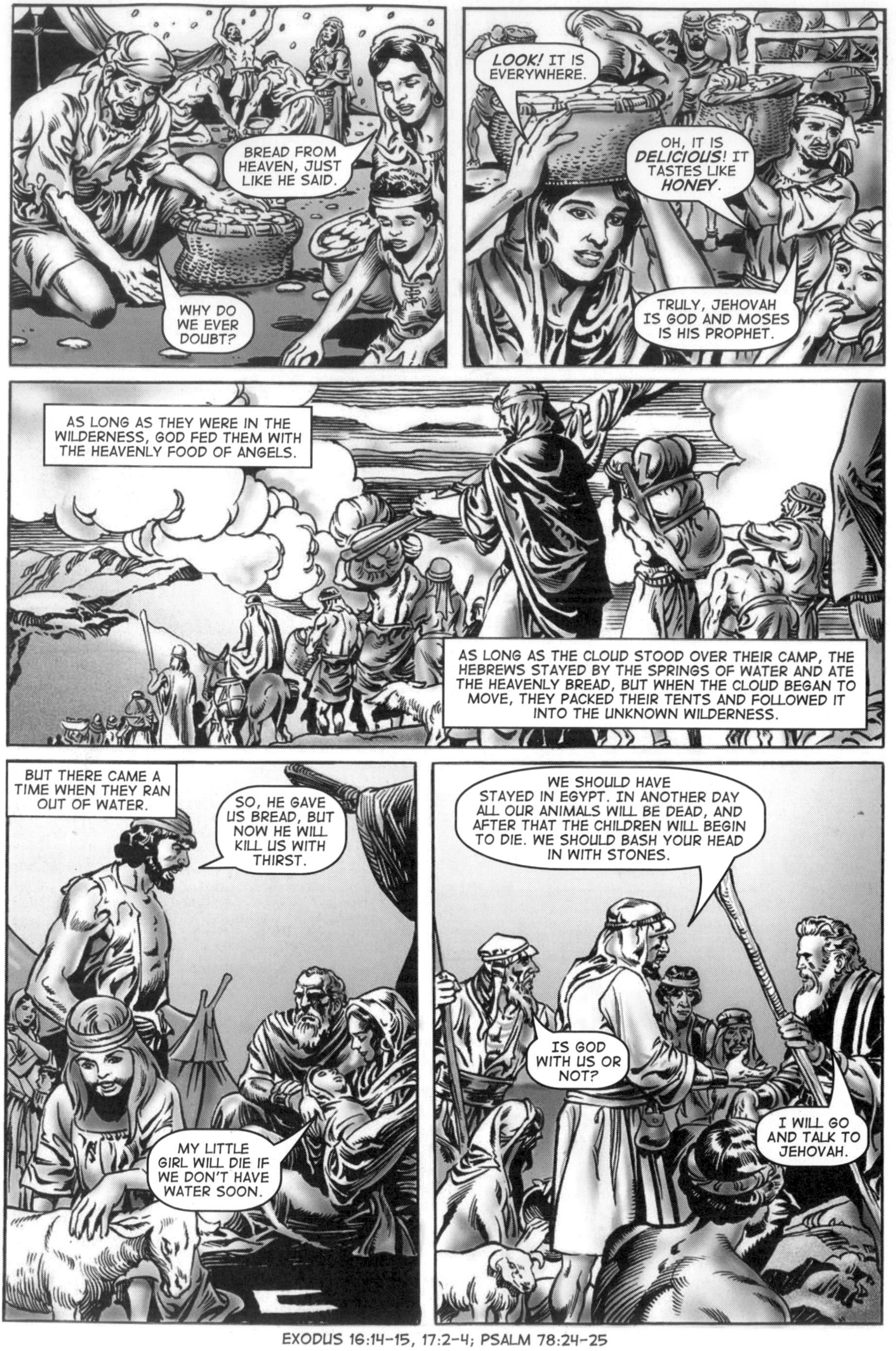
BREAD FROM HEAVEN, JUST LIKE HE SAID.
WHY DO WE EVER DOUBT?
LOOK! IT IS EVERYWHERE.
OH, IT IS DELICIOUS! IT TASTES LIKE HONEY.
TRULY, JEHOVAH IS GOD AND MOSES IS HIS PROPHET.
AS LONG AS THEY WERE IN THE WILDERNESS, GOD FED THEM WITH THE HEAVENLY FOOD OF ANGELS.
AS LONG AS THE CLOUD STOOD OVER THEIR CAMP, THE HEBREWS STAYED BY THE SPRINGS OF WATER AND ATE THE HEAVENLY BREAD, BUT WHEN THE CLOUD BEGAN TO MOVE, THEY PACKED THEIR TENTS AND FOLLOWED IT INTO THE UNKNOWN WILDERNESS.
BUT THERE CAME A TIME WHEN THEY RAN OUT OF WATER.
SO, HE GAVE US BREAD, BUT NOW HE WILL KILL US WITH THIRST.
MY LITTLE GIRL WILL DIE IF WE DON'T HAVE WATER SOON.
WE SHOULD HAVE STAYED IN EGYPT. IN ANOTHER DAY ALL OUR ANIMALS WILL BE DEAD, AND AFTER THAT THE CHILDREN WILL BEGIN TO DIE. WE SHOULD BASH YOUR HEAD IN WITH STONES.
IS GOD WITH US OR NOT?
I WILL GO AND TALK TO JEHOVAH.

EXODUS 16:14-15, 17:2-4; PSALM 78:24-25

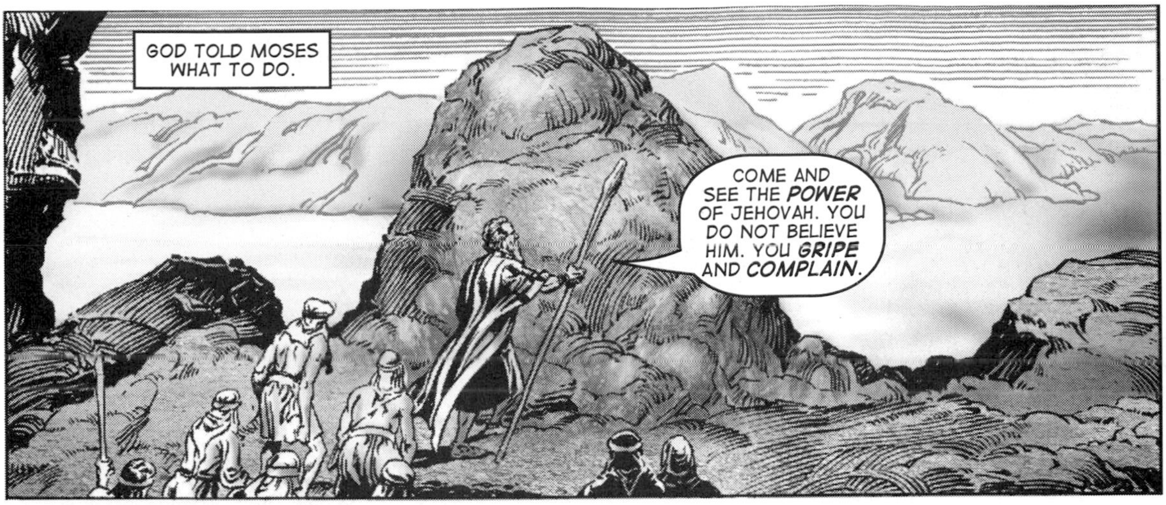
GOD TOLD MOSES WHAT TO DO.
COME AND SEE THE POWER OF JEHOVAH. YOU DO NOT BELIEVE HIM. YOU GRIPE AND COMPLAIN.

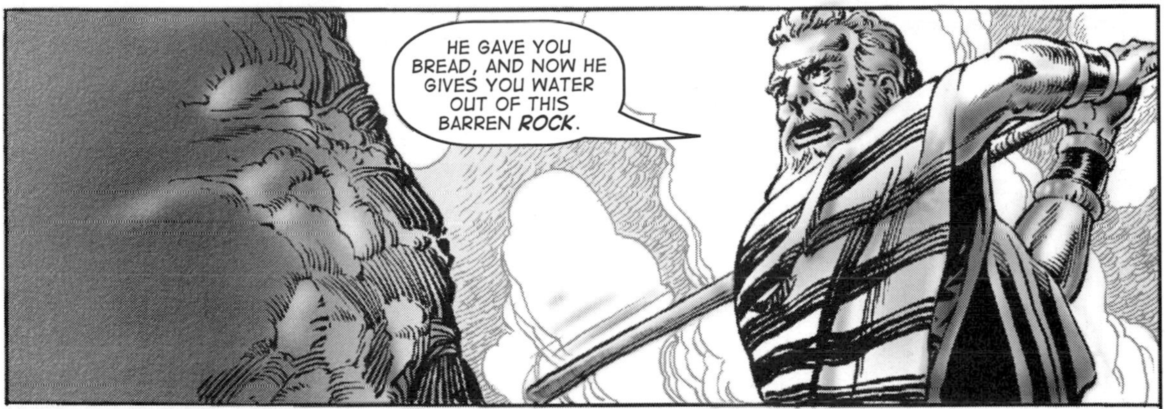
HE GAVE YOU BREAD, AND NOW HE GIVES YOU WATER OUT OF THIS BARREN ROCK.

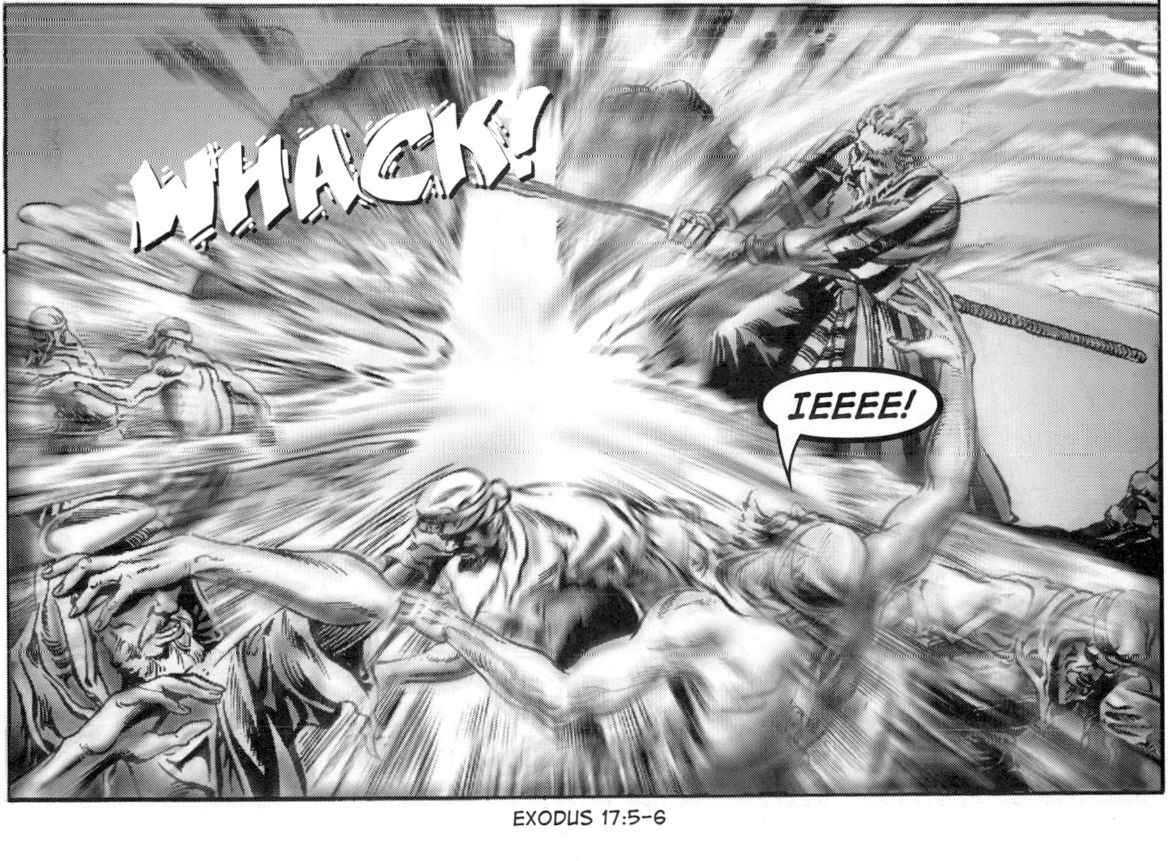
WHACK!
IEEEE!

EXODUS 17:5-6

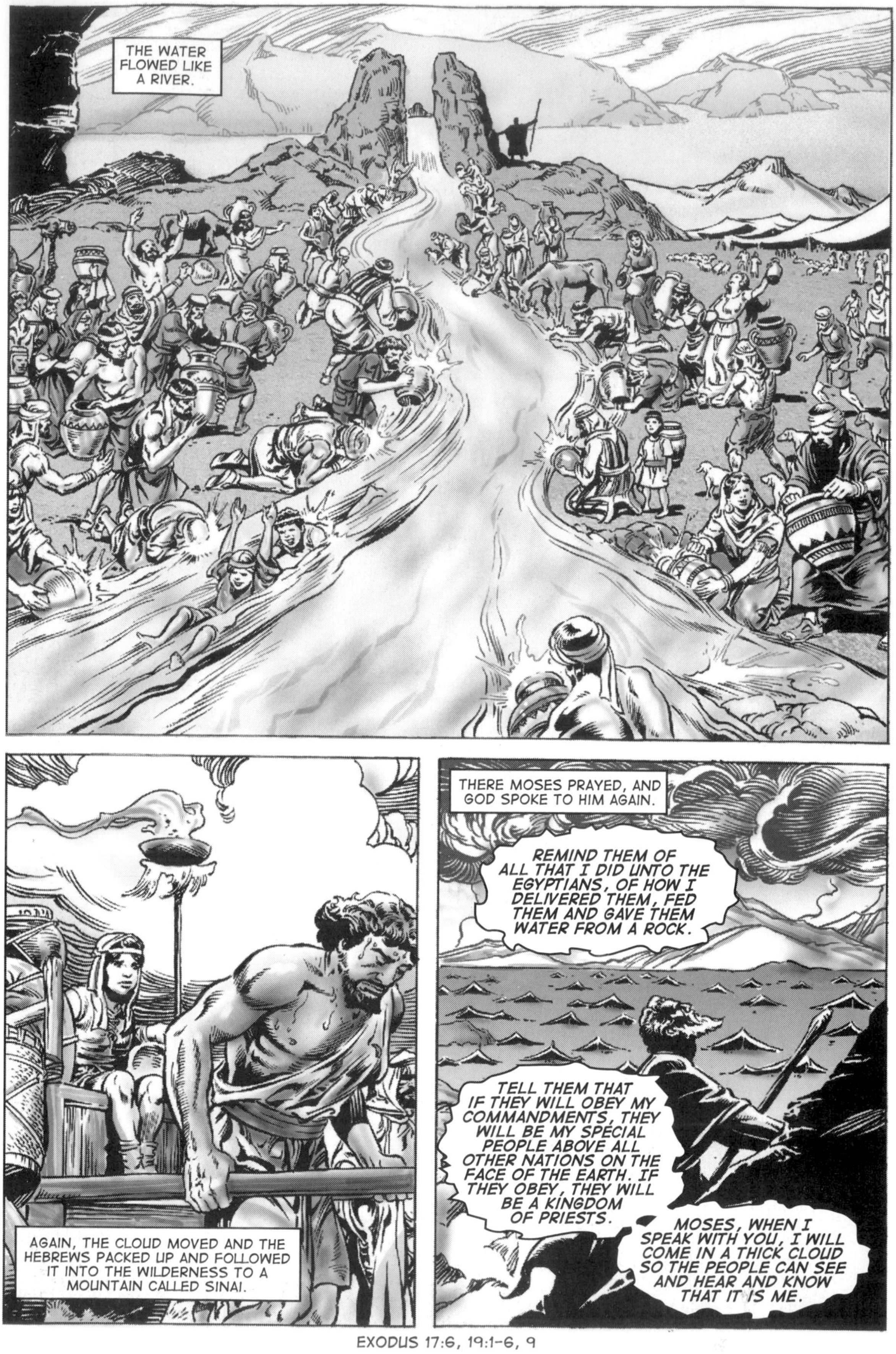
THE WATER FLOWED LIKE A RIVER.
AGAIN, THE CLOUD MOVED AND THE HEBREWS PACKED UP AND FOLLOWED IT INTO THE WILDERNESS TO A MOUNTAIN CALLED SINAI.
THERE MOSES PRAYED, AND GOD SPOKE TO HIM AGAIN.
REMIND THEM OF ALL THAT I DID UNTO THE EGYPTIANS, OF HOW I DELIVERED THEM, FED THEM AND GAVE THEM WATER FROM A ROCK.
TELL THEM THAT IF THEY WILL OBEY MY COMMANDMENTS, THEY WILL BE MY SPECIAL PEOPLE ABOVE ALL OTHER NATIONS ON THE FACE OF THE EARTH. IF THEY OBEY, THEY WILL BE A KINGDOM OF PRIESTS.
MOSES, WHEN I SPEAK WITH YOU, I WILL COME IN A THICK CLOUD SO THE PEOPLE CAN SEE AND HEAR AND KNOW THAT IT IS ME.

EXODUS 17:6, 19:1-6, 9

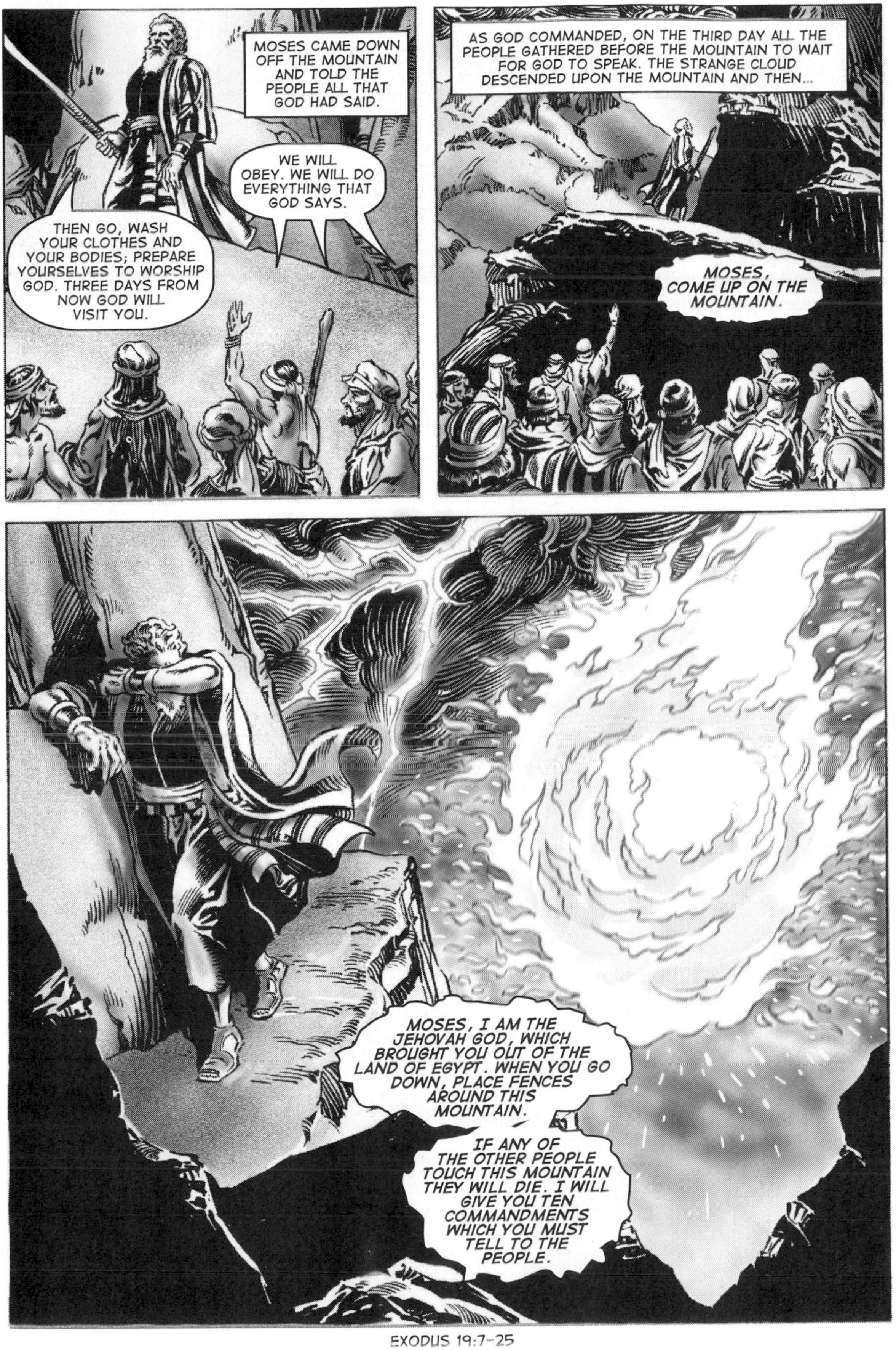
MOSES CAME DOWN OFF THE MOUNTAIN AND TOLD THE PEOPLE ALL THAT GOD HAD SAID.
WE WILL OBEY. WE WILL DO EVERYTHING THAT GOD SAYS.
THEN GO, WASH YOUR CLOTHES AND YOUR BODIES; PREPARE YOURSELVES TO WORSHIP GOD. THREE DAYS FROM NOW GOD WILL VISIT YOU.
AS GOD COMMANDED, ON THE THIRD DAY ALL THE PEOPLE GATHERED BEFORE THE MOUNTAIN TO WAIT FOR GOD TO SPEAK. THE STRANGE CLOUD DESCENDED UPON THE MOUNTAIN AND THEN...
MOSES, COME UP ON THE MOUNTAIN.
MOSES, I AM THE JEHOVAH GOD, WHICH BROUGHT YOU OUT OF THE LAND OF EGYPT. WHEN YOU GO DOWN, PLACE FENCES AROUND THIS MOUNTAIN.
IF ANY OF THE OTHER PEOPLE TOUCH THIS MOUNTAIN THEY WILL DIE. I WILL GIVE YOU TEN COMMANDMENTS WHICH YOU MUST TELL TO THE PEOPLE.

EXODUS 19:7–25

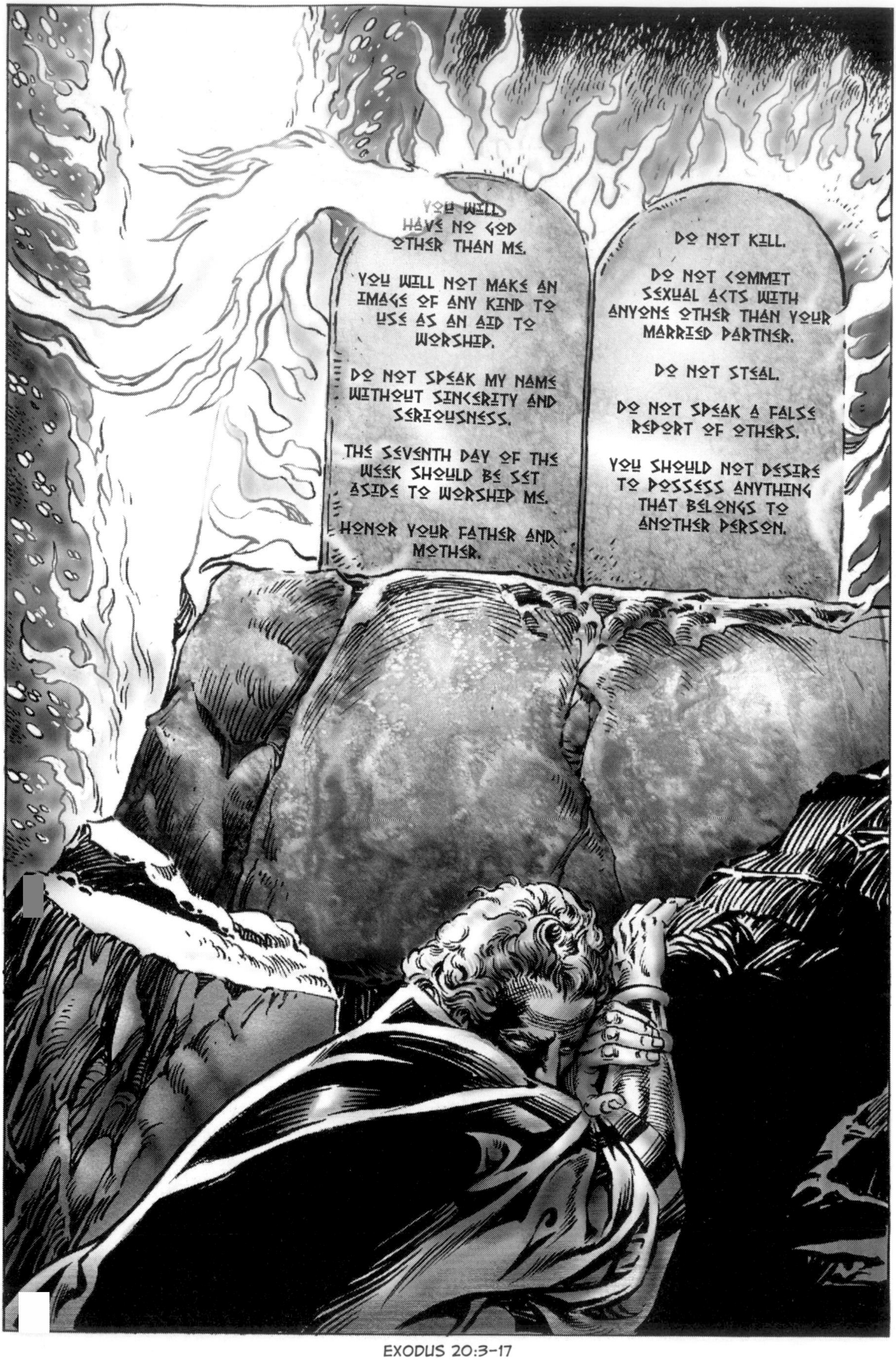
YOU WILL HAVE NO GOD OTHER THAN ME.
YOU WILL NOT MAKE AN IMAGE OF ANY KIND TO USE AS AN AID TO WORSHIP.
DO NOT SPEAK MY NAME WITHOUT SINCERITY AND SERIOUSNESS.
THE SEVENTH DAY OF THE WEEK SHOULD BE SET ASIDE TO WORSHIP ME.
HONOR YOUR FATHER AND MOTHER.
DO NOT KILL.
DO NOT COMMIT SEXUAL ACTS WITH ANYONE OTHER THAN YOUR MARRIED PARTNER.
DO NOT STEAL.
DO NOT SPEAK A FALSE REPORT OF OTHERS.
YOU SHOULD NOT DESIRE TO POSSESS ANYTHING THAT BELONGS TO ANOTHER PERSON.

EXODUS 20:3-17

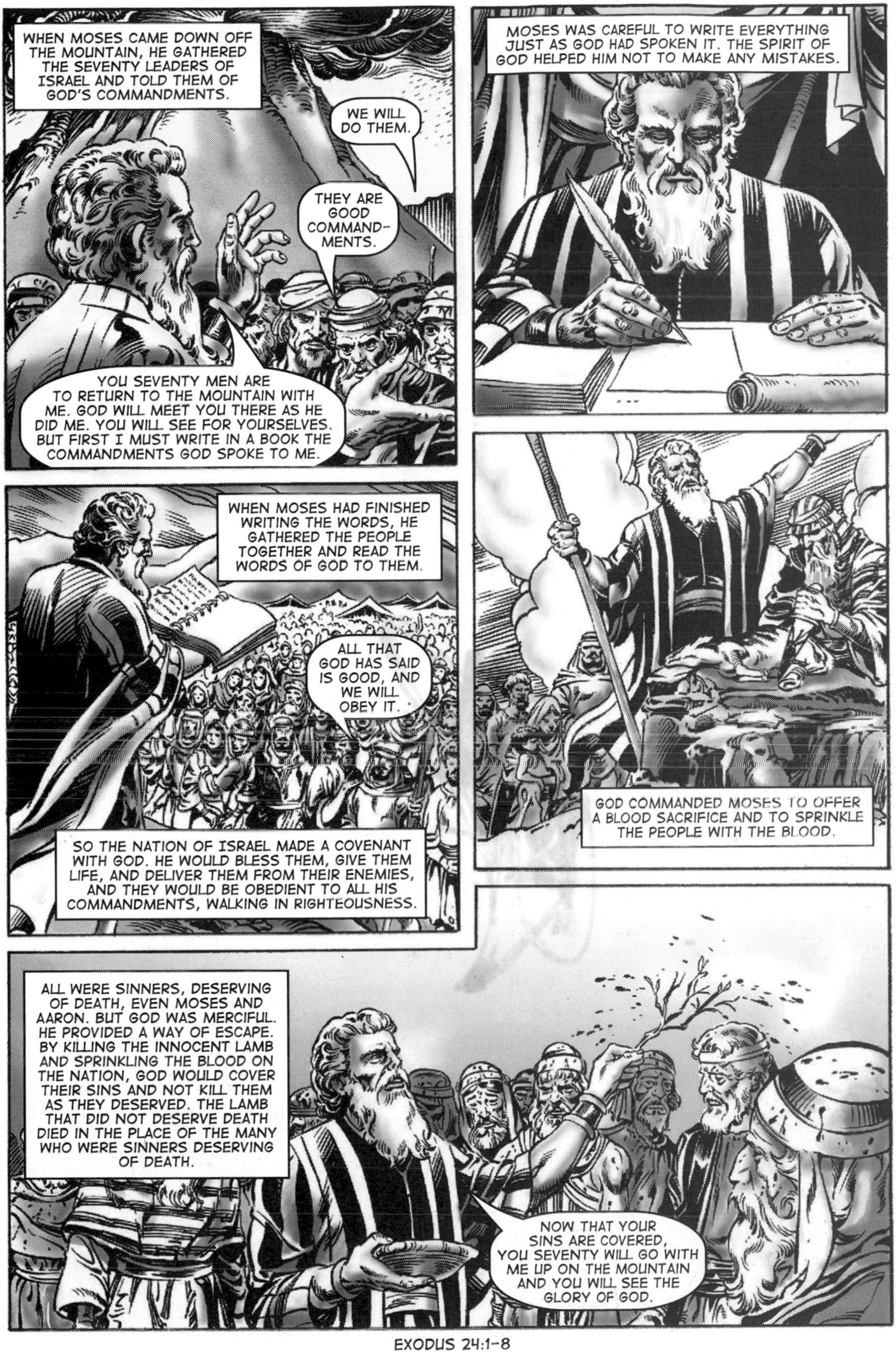
WHEN MOSES CAME DOWN OFF THE MOUNTAIN, HE GATHERED THE SEVENTY LEADERS OF ISRAEL AND TOLD THEM OF GOD'S COMMANDMENTS.
WE WILL DO THEM.
THEY ARE GOOD COMMAND-MENTS.
YOU SEVENTY MEN ARE TO RETURN TO THE MOUNTAIN WITH ME. GOD WILL MEET YOU THERE AS HE DID ME. YOU WILL SEE FOR YOURSELVES. BUT FIRST I MUST WRITE IN A BOOK THE COMMANDMENTS GOD SPOKE TO ME.
MOSES WAS CAREFUL TO WRITE EVERYTHING JUST AS GOD HAD SPOKEN IT. THE SPIRIT OF GOD HELPED HIM NOT TO MAKE ANY MISTAKES.
WHEN MOSES HAD FINISHED WRITING THE WORDS, HE GATHERED THE PEOPLE TOGETHER AND READ THE WORDS OF GOD TO THEM.
ALL THAT GOD HAS SAID IS GOOD, AND WE WILL OBEY IT.
SO THE NATION OF ISRAEL MADE A COVENANT WITH GOD. HE WOULD BLESS THEM, GIVE THEM LIFE, AND DELIVER THEM FROM THEIR ENEMIES, AND THEY WOULD BE OBEDIENT TO ALL HIS COMMANDMENTS, WALKING IN RIGHTEOUSNESS.
GOD COMMANDED MOSES TO OFFER A BLOOD SACRIFICE AND TO SPRINKLE THE PEOPLE WITH THE BLOOD.
ALL WERE SINNERS, DESERVING OF DEATH, EVEN MOSES AND AARON. BUT GOD WAS MERCIFUL. HE PROVIDED A WAY OF ESCAPE. BY KILLING THE INNOCENT LAMB AND SPRINKLING THE BLOOD ON THE NATION, GOD WOULD COVER THEIR SINS AND NOT KILL THEM AS THEY DESERVED. THE LAMB THAT DID NOT DESERVE DEATH DIED IN THE PLACE OF THE MANY WHO WERE SINNERS DESERVING OF DEATH.
NOW THAT YOUR SINS ARE COVERED, YOU SEVENTY WILL GO WITH ME UP ON THE MOUNTAIN AND YOU WILL SEE THE GLORY OF GOD.

EXODUS 24:1-8

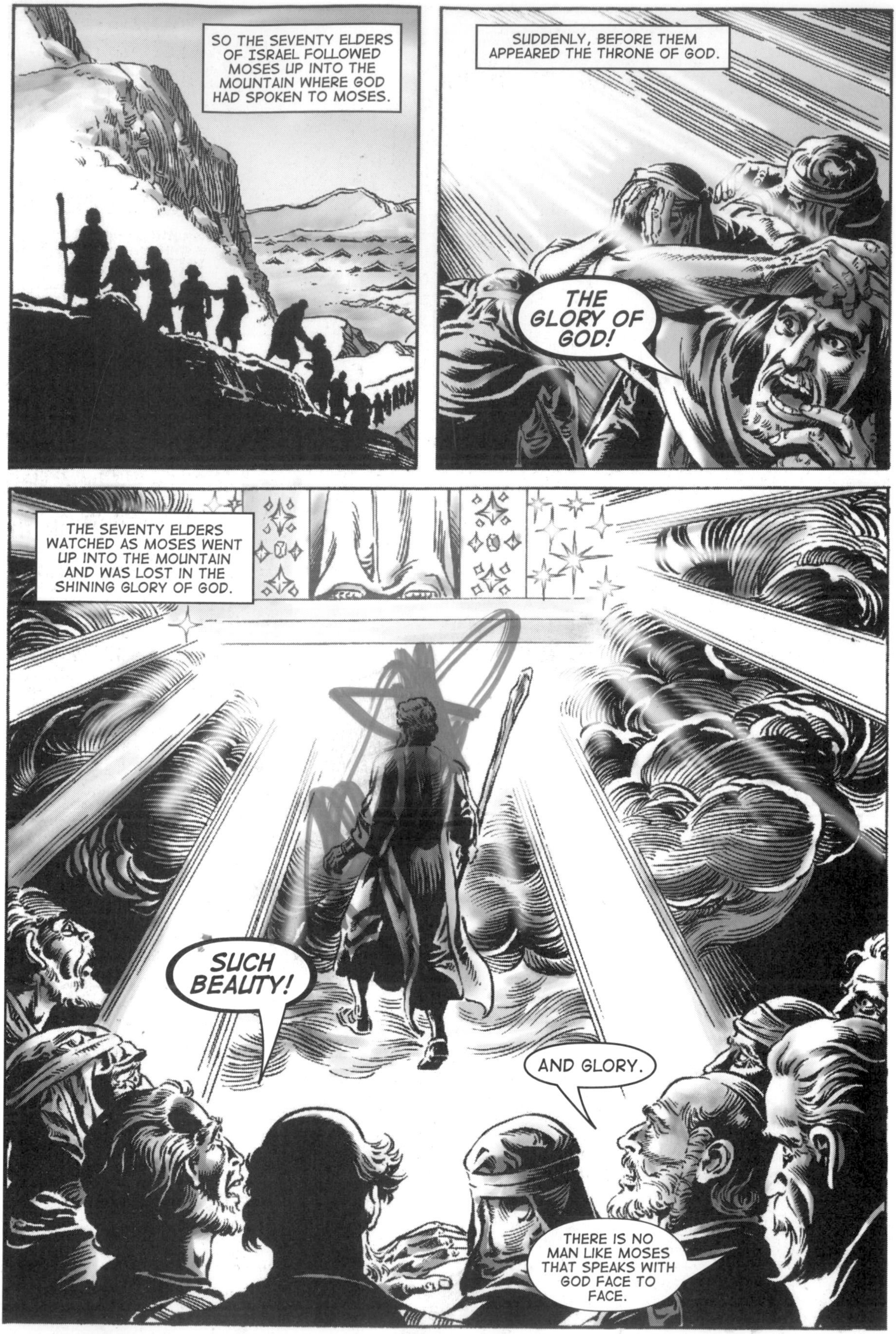
SO THE SEVENTY ELDERS OF ISRAEL FOLLOWED MOSES UP INTO THE MOUNTAIN WHERE GOD HAD SPOKEN TO MOSES.
SUDDENLY, BEFORE THEM APPEARED THE THRONE OF GOD.
THE GLORY OF GOD!
THE SEVENTY ELDERS WATCHED AS MOSES WENT UP INTO THE MOUNTAIN AND WAS LOST IN THE SHINING GLORY OF GOD.
SUCH BEAUTY!
AND GLORY.
THERE IS NO MAN LIKE MOSES THAT SPEAKS WITH GOD FACE TO FACE.

EXODUS 24:9-10

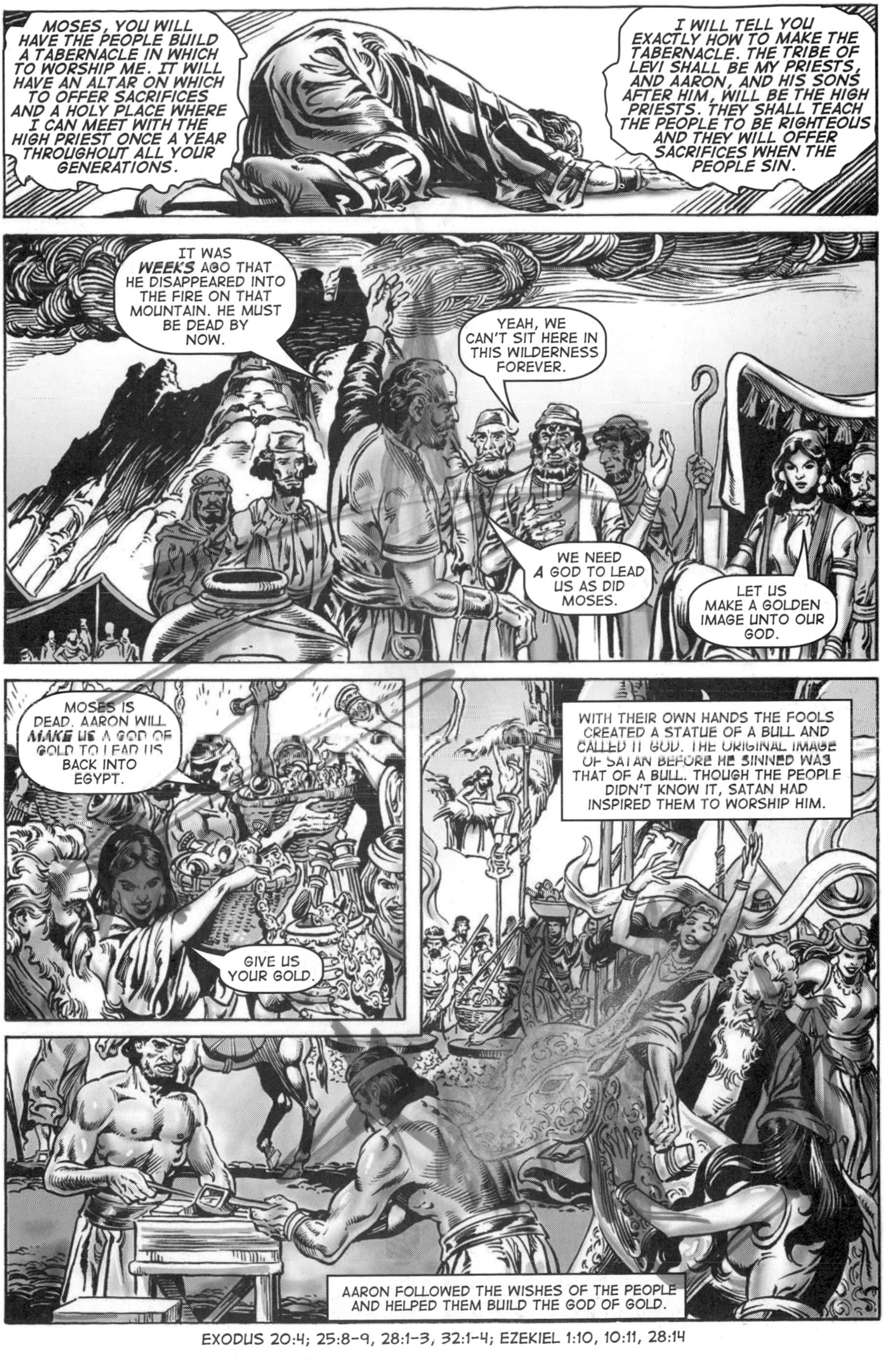
MOSES, YOU WILL HAVE THE PEOPLE BUILD A TABERNACLE IN WHICH TO WORSHIP ME. IT WILL HAVE AN ALTAR ON WHICH TO OFFER SACRIFICES AND A HOLY PLACE WHERE I CAN MEET WITH THE HIGH PRIEST ONCE A YEAR THROUGHOUT ALL YOUR GENERATIONS.
I WILL TELL YOU EXACTLY HOW TO MAKE THE TABERNACLE. THE TRIBE OF LEVI SHALL BE MY PRIESTS, AND AARON, AND HIS SONS AFTER HIM, WILL BE THE HIGH PRIESTS. THEY SHALL TEACH THE PEOPLE TO BE RIGHTEOUS AND THEY WILL OFFER SACRIFICES WHEN THE PEOPLE SIN.
IT WAS WEEKS AGO THAT HE DISAPPEARED INTO THE FIRE ON THAT MOUNTAIN. HE MUST BE DEAD BY NOW.
YEAH, WE CAN'T SIT HERE IN THIS WILDERNESS FOREVER.
WE NEED A GOD TO LEAD US AS DID MOSES.
LET US MAKE A GOLDEN IMAGE UNTO OUR GOD.
MOSES IS DEAD. AARON WILL MAKE US A GOD OF GOLD TO LEAD US BACK INTO EGYPT.
GIVE US YOUR GOLD.
WITH THEIR OWN HANDS THE FOOLS CREATED A STATUE OF A BULL AND CALLED IT GOD. THE ORIGINAL IMAGE OF SATAN BEFORE HE SINNED WAS THAT OF A BULL. THOUGH THE PEOPLE DIDN'T KNOW IT, SATAN HAD INSPIRED THEM TO WORSHIP HIM.
AARON FOLLOWED THE WISHES OF THE PEOPLE AND HELPED THEM BUILD THE GOD OF GOLD.

EXODUS 20:4; 25:8-9, 28:1-3, 32:1-4; EZEKIEL 1:10, 10:11, 28:14

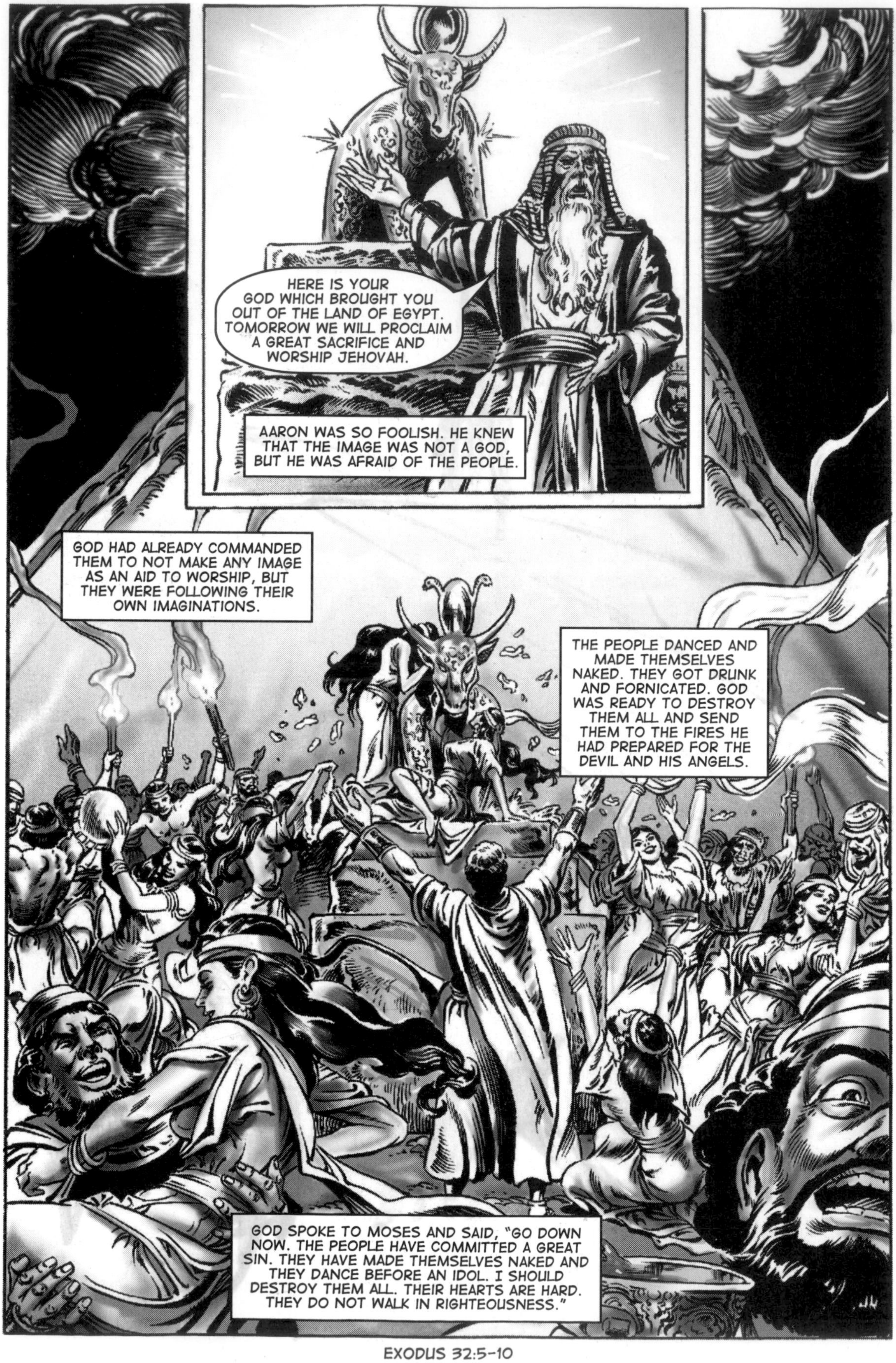
HERE IS YOUR GOD WHICH BROUGHT YOU OUT OF THE LAND OF EGYPT. TOMORROW WE WILL PROCLAIM A GREAT SACRIFICE AND WORSHIP JEHOVAH.
AARON WAS SO FOOLISH. HE KNEW THAT THE IMAGE WAS NOT A GOD, BUT HE WAS AFRAID OF THE PEOPLE.
GOD HAD ALREADY COMMANDED THEM TO NOT MAKE ANY IMAGE AS AN AID TO WORSHIP, BUT THEY WERE FOLLOWING THEIR OWN IMAGINATIONS.
THE PEOPLE DANCED AND MADE THEMSELVES NAKED. THEY GOT DRUNK AND FORNICATED. GOD WAS READY TO DESTROY THEM ALL AND SEND THEM TO THE FIRES HE HAD PREPARED FOR THE DEVIL AND HIS ANGELS.
GOD SPOKE TO MOSES AND SAID, "GO DOWN NOW. THE PEOPLE HAVE COMMITTED A GREAT SIN. THEY HAVE MADE THEMSELVES NAKED AND THEY DANCE BEFORE AN IDOL. I SHOULD DESTROY THEM ALL. THEIR HEARTS ARE HARD. THEY DO NOT WALK IN RIGHTEOUSNESS."

EXODUS 32:5-10

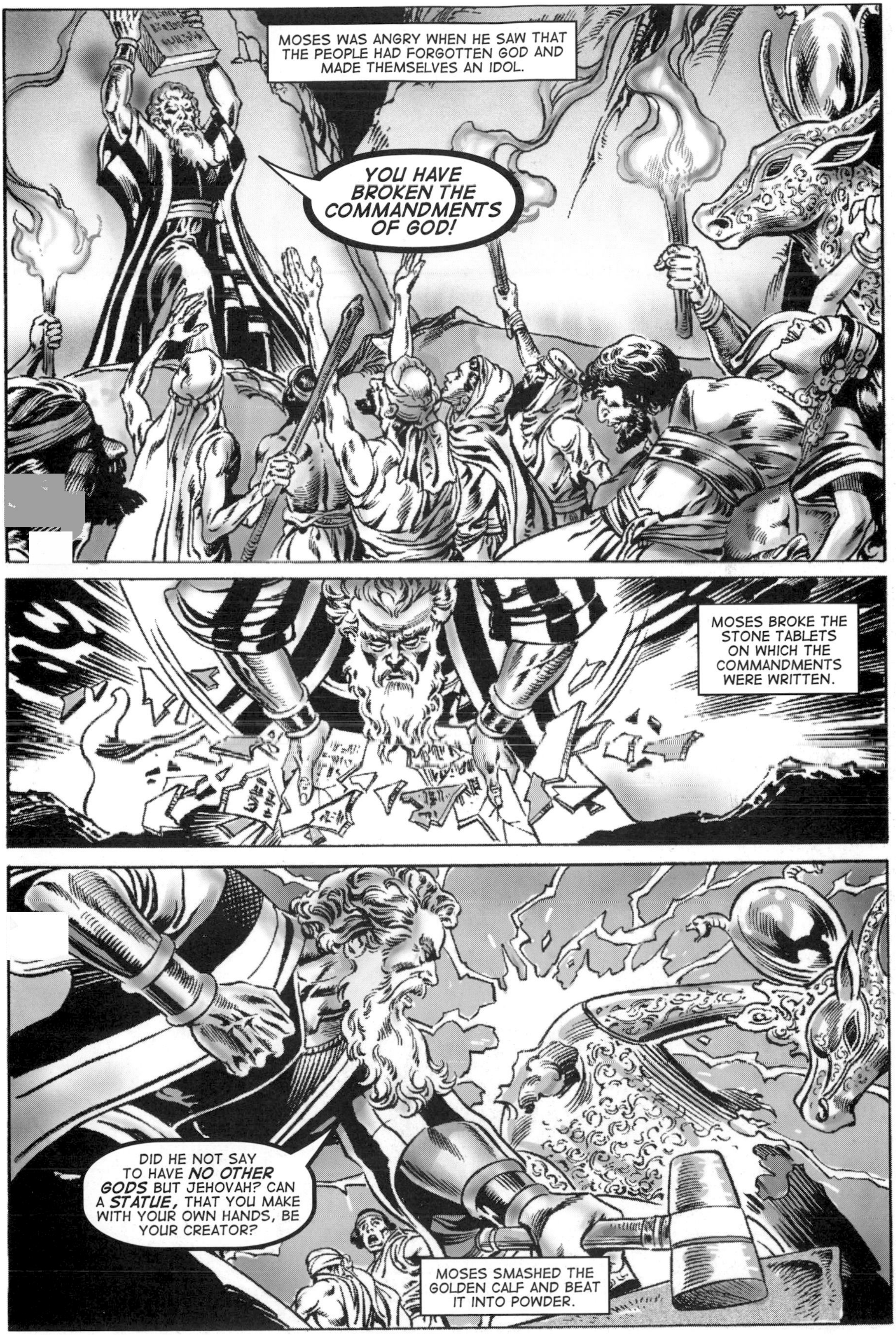
MOSES WAS ANGRY WHEN HE SAW THAT THE PEOPLE HAD FORGOTTEN GOD AND MADE THEMSELVES AN IDOL.
YOU HAVE BROKEN THE COMMANDMENTS OF GOD!
MOSES BROKE THE STONE TABLETS ON WHICH THE COMMANDMENTS WERE WRITTEN.
DID HE NOT SAY TO HAVE NO OTHER GODS BUT JEHOVAH? CAN A STATUE, THAT YOU MAKE WITH YOUR OWN HANDS, BE YOUR CREATOR?
MOSES SMASHED THE GOLDEN CALF AND BEAT IT INTO POWDER.

EXODUS 20:3-4; 32:15-20

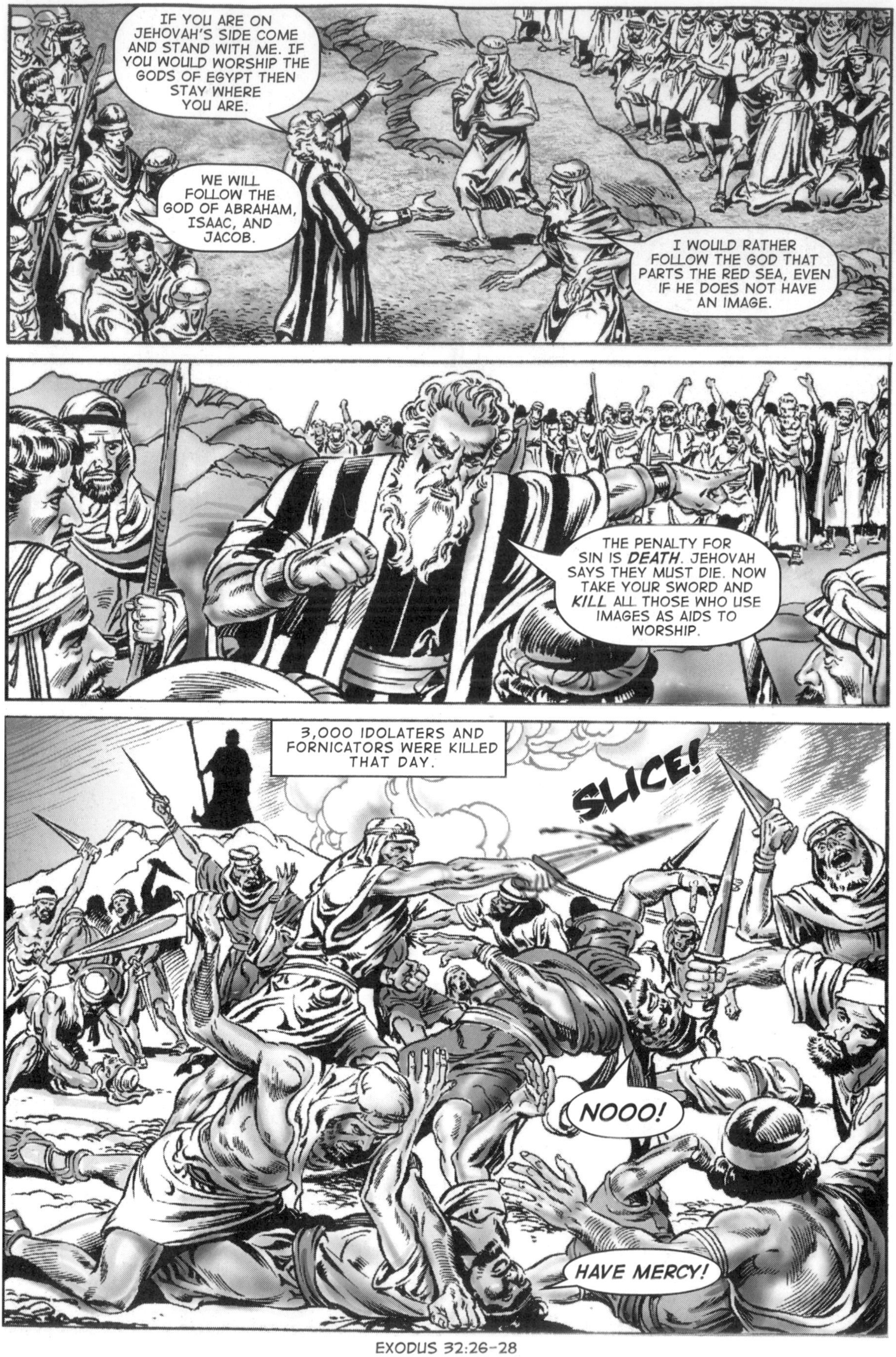
IF YOU ARE ON JEHOVAH'S SIDE COME AND STAND WITH ME. IF YOU WOULD WORSHIP THE GODS OF EGYPT THEN STAY WHERE YOU ARE.
WE WILL FOLLOW THE GOD OF ABRAHAM, ISAAC, AND JACOB.
I WOULD RATHER FOLLOW THE GOD THAT PARTS THE RED SEA, EVEN IF HE DOES NOT HAVE AN IMAGE.
THE PENALTY FOR SIN IS ***DEATH***. JEHOVAH SAYS THEY MUST DIE. NOW TAKE YOUR SWORD AND ***KILL*** ALL THOSE WHO USE IMAGES AS AIDS TO WORSHIP.
3,000 IDOLATERS AND FORNICATORS WERE KILLED THAT DAY.
SLICE!
NOOO!
HAVE MERCY!

EXODUS 32:26-28

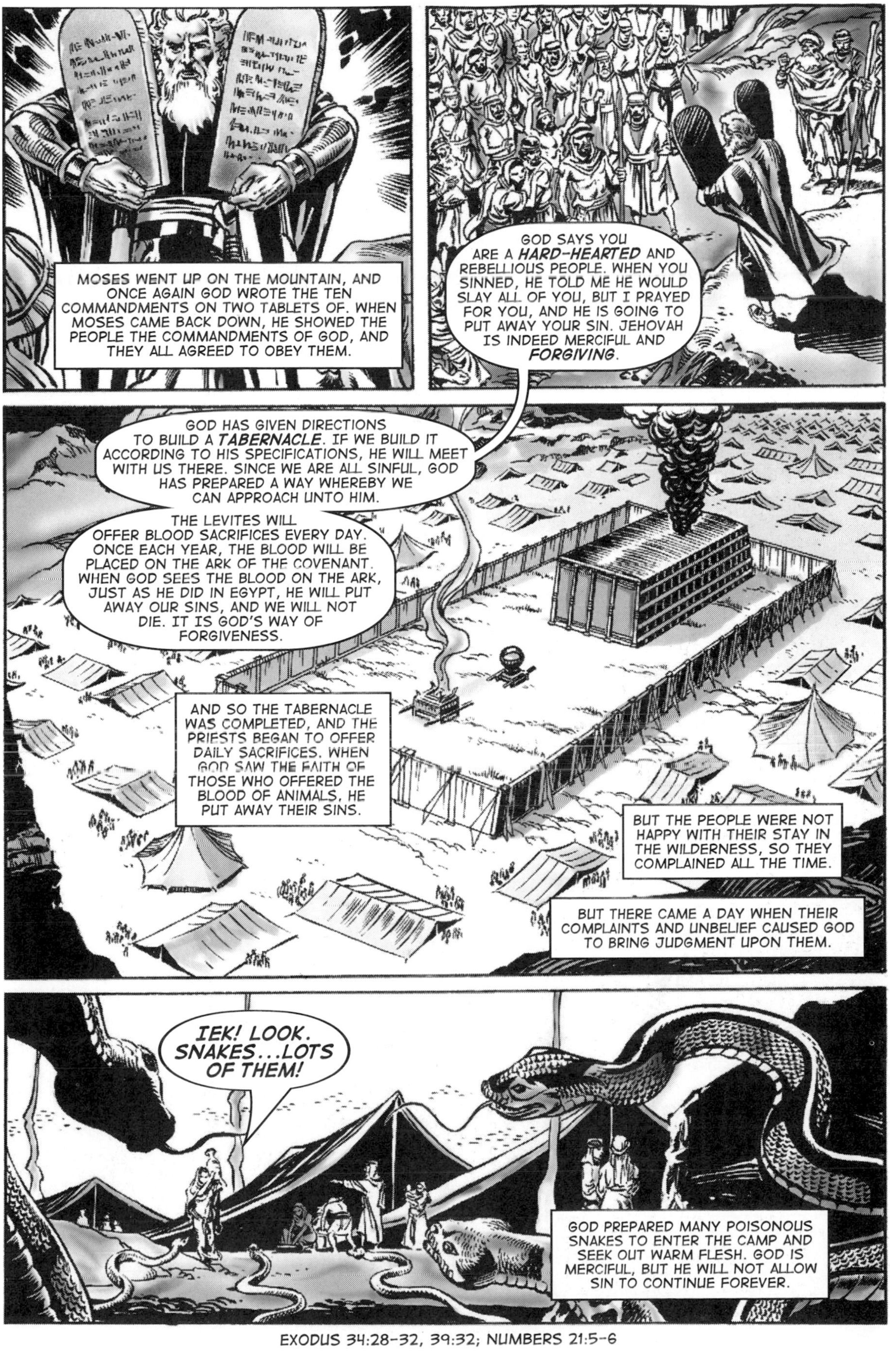
MOSES WENT UP ON THE MOUNTAIN, AND ONCE AGAIN GOD WROTE THE TEN COMMANDMENTS ON TWO TABLETS OF. WHEN MOSES CAME BACK DOWN, HE SHOWED THE PEOPLE THE COMMANDMENTS OF GOD, AND THEY ALL AGREED TO OBEY THEM.
GOD SAYS YOU ARE A HARD-HEARTED AND REBELLIOUS PEOPLE. WHEN YOU SINNED, HE TOLD ME HE WOULD SLAY ALL OF YOU, BUT I PRAYED FOR YOU, AND HE IS GOING TO PUT AWAY YOUR SIN. JEHOVAH IS INDEED MERCIFUL AND FORGIVING.
GOD HAS GIVEN DIRECTIONS TO BUILD A TABERNACLE. IF WE BUILD IT ACCORDING TO HIS SPECIFICATIONS, HE WILL MEET WITH US THERE. SINCE WE ARE ALL SINFUL, GOD HAS PREPARED A WAY WHEREBY WE CAN APPROACH UNTO HIM.
THE LEVITES WILL OFFER BLOOD SACRIFICES EVERY DAY. ONCE EACH YEAR, THE BLOOD WILL BE PLACED ON THE ARK OF THE COVENANT. WHEN GOD SEES THE BLOOD ON THE ARK, JUST AS HE DID IN EGYPT, HE WILL PUT AWAY OUR SINS, AND WE WILL NOT DIE. IT IS GOD'S WAY OF FORGIVENESS.
AND SO THE TABERNACLE WAS COMPLETED, AND THE PRIESTS BEGAN TO OFFER DAILY SACRIFICES. WHEN GOD SAW THE FAITH OF THOSE WHO OFFERED THE BLOOD OF ANIMALS, HE PUT AWAY THEIR SINS.
BUT THE PEOPLE WERE NOT HAPPY WITH THEIR STAY IN THE WILDERNESS, SO THEY COMPLAINED ALL THE TIME.
BUT THERE CAME A DAY WHEN THEIR COMPLAINTS AND UNBELIEF CAUSED GOD TO BRING JUDGMENT UPON THEM.
IEK! LOOK. SNAKES...LOTS OF THEM!
GOD PREPARED MANY POISONOUS SNAKES TO ENTER THE CAMP AND SEEK OUT WARM FLESH. GOD IS MERCIFUL, BUT HE WILL NOT ALLOW SIN TO CONTINUE FOREVER.

EXODUS 34:28-32, 39:32; NUMBERS 21:5-6

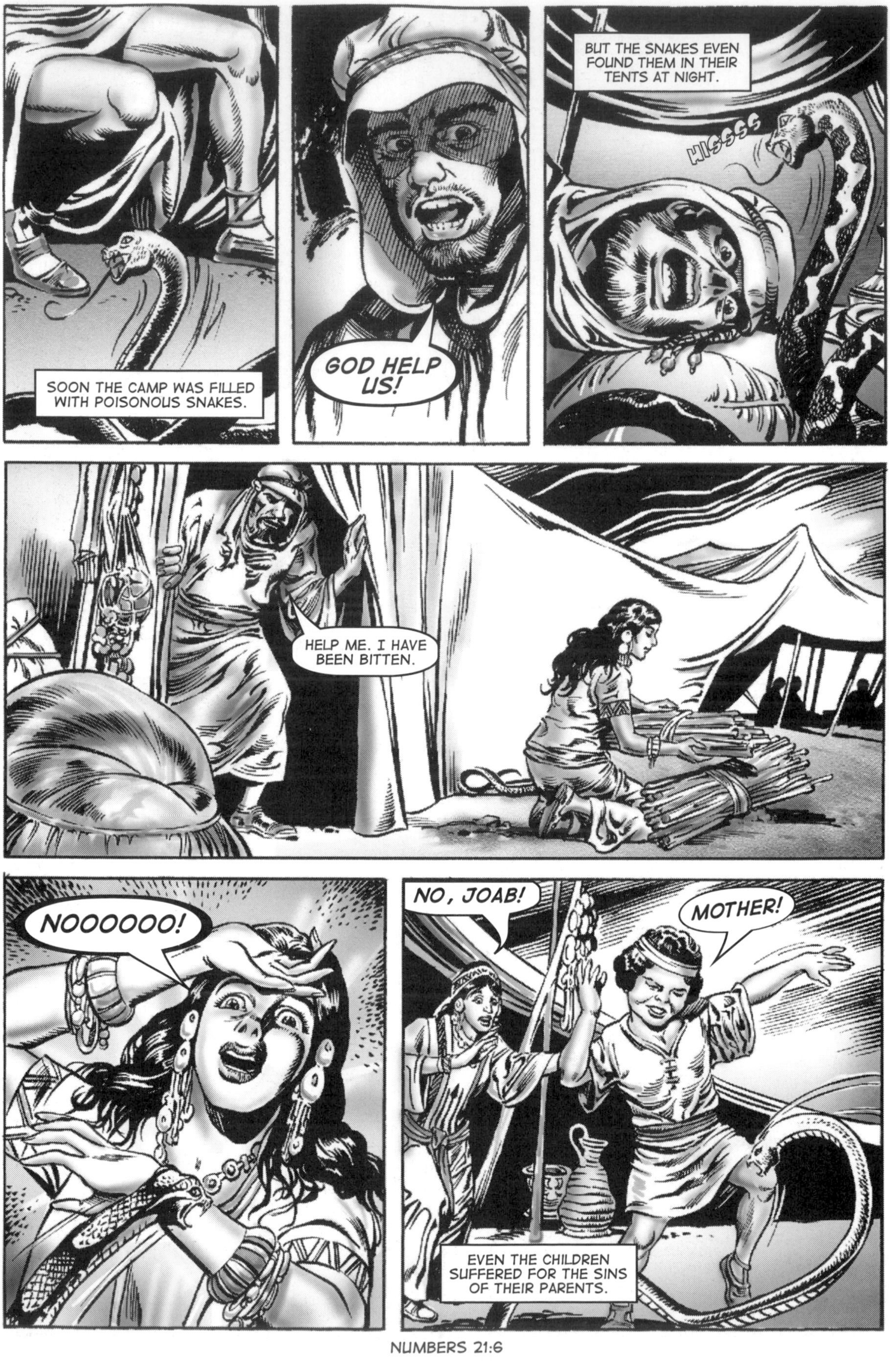
SOON THE CAMP WAS FILLED WITH POISONOUS SNAKES.
GOD HELP US!
BUT THE SNAKES EVEN FOUND THEM IN THEIR TENTS AT NIGHT.
HISSSS
HELP ME. I HAVE BEEN BITTEN.
NOOOOOO!
NO, JOAB!
MOTHER!
EVEN THE CHILDREN SUFFERED FOR THE SINS OF THEIR PARENTS.

NUMBERS 21:6

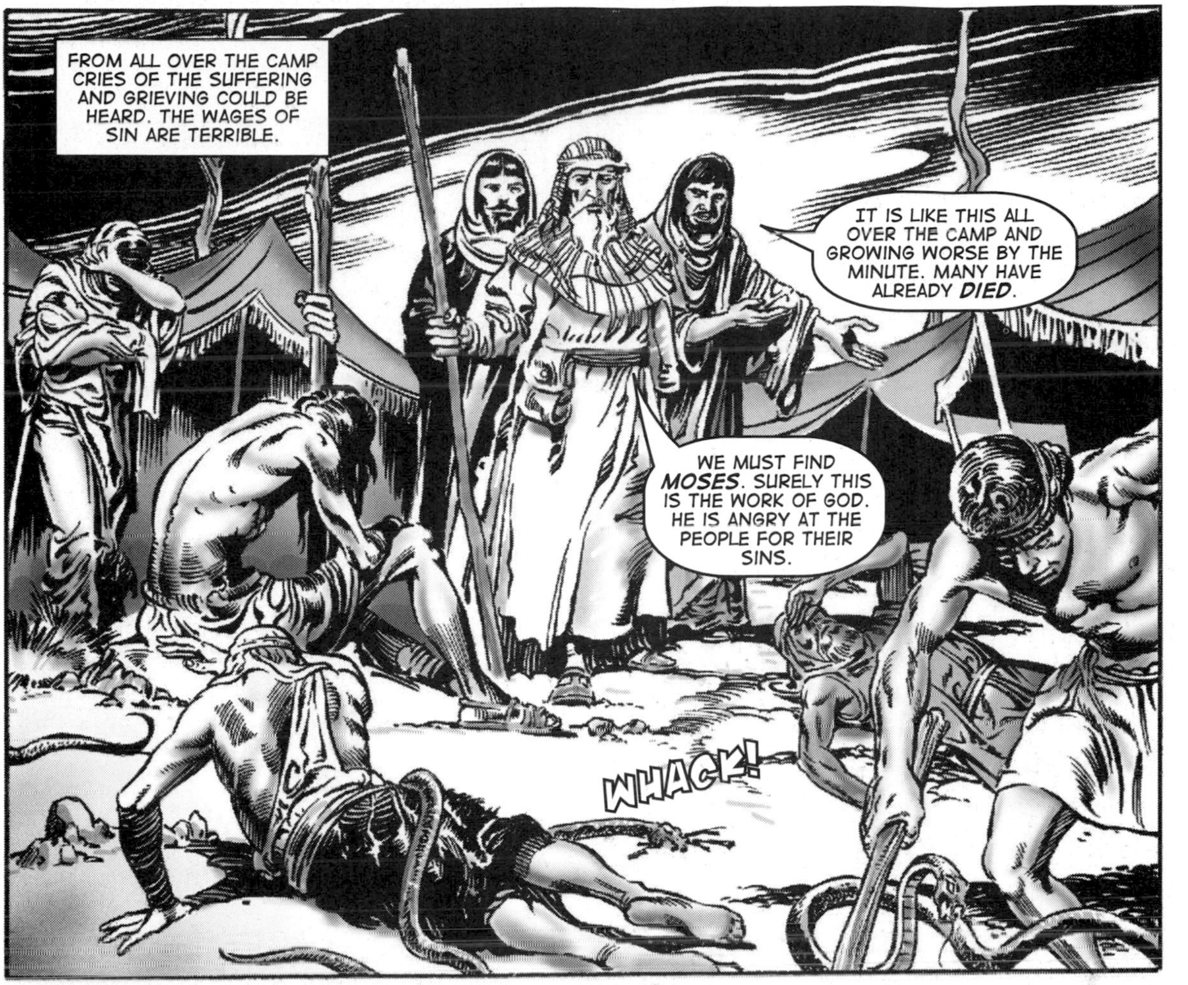
FROM ALL OVER THE CAMP CRIES OF THE SUFFERING AND GRIEVING COULD BE HEARD. THE WAGES OF SIN ARE TERRIBLE.
IT IS LIKE THIS ALL OVER THE CAMP AND GROWING WORSE BY THE MINUTE. MANY HAVE ALREADY DIED.
WE MUST FIND MOSES. SURELY THIS IS THE WORK OF GOD. HE IS ANGRY AT THE PEOPLE FOR THEIR SINS.
WHACK!

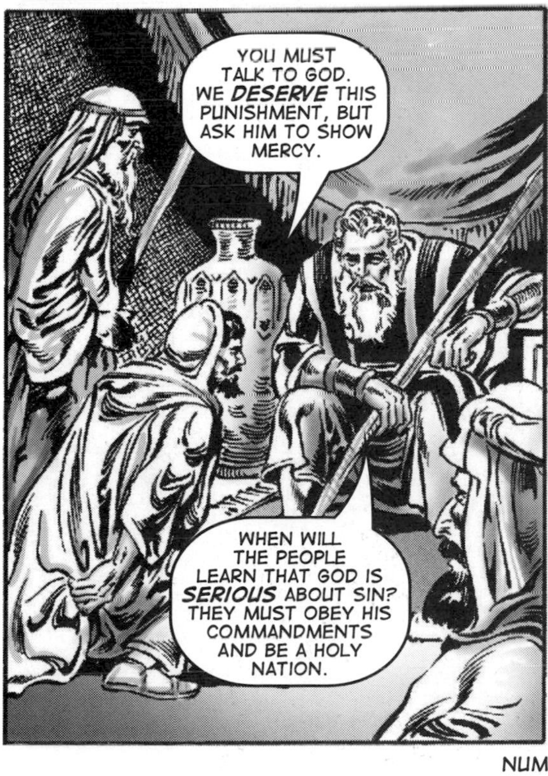
YOU MUST TALK TO GOD. WE DESERVE THIS PUNISHMENT, BUT ASK HIM TO SHOW MERCY.
WHEN WILL THE PEOPLE LEARN THAT GOD IS SERIOUS ABOUT SIN? THEY MUST OBEY HIS COMMANDMENTS AND BE A HOLY NATION.

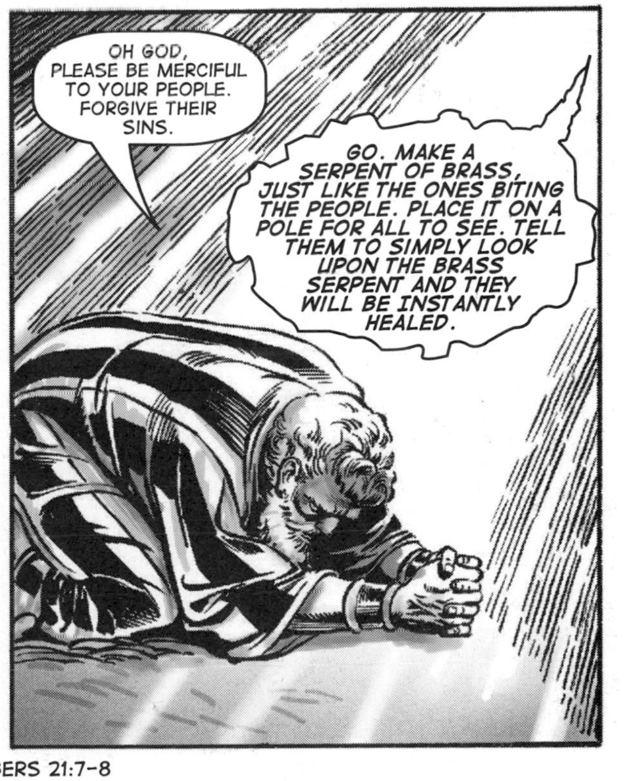
OH GOD, PLEASE BE MERCIFUL TO YOUR PEOPLE. FORGIVE THEIR SINS.
GO. MAKE A SERPENT OF BRASS, JUST LIKE THE ONES BITING THE PEOPLE. PLACE IT ON A POLE FOR ALL TO SEE. TELL THEM TO SIMPLY LOOK UPON THE BRASS SERPENT AND THEY WILL BE INSTANTLY HEALED.

NUMBERS 21:7-8

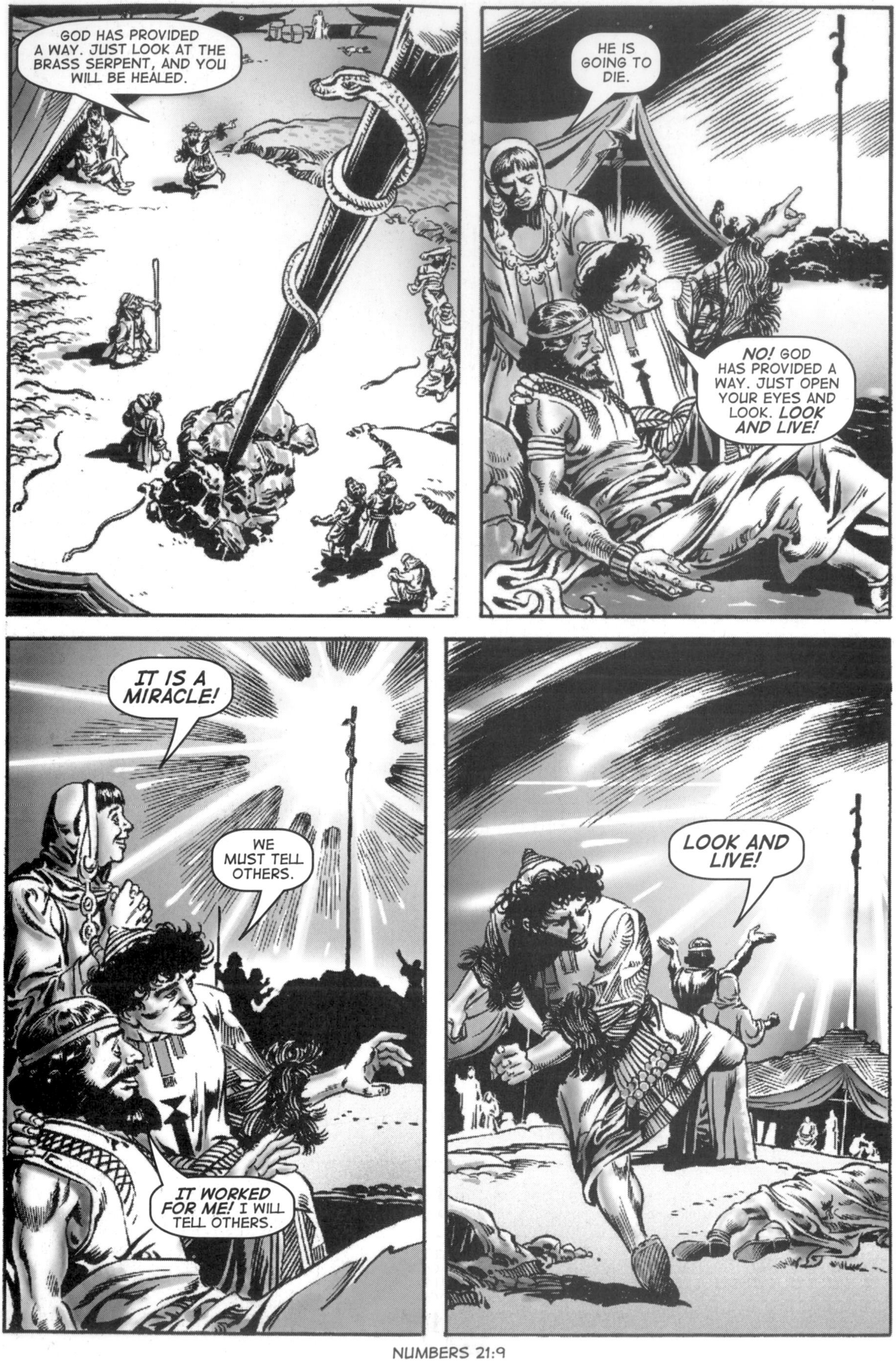
GOD HAS PROVIDED A WAY. JUST LOOK AT THE BRASS SERPENT, AND YOU WILL BE HEALED.
HE IS GOING TO DIE.
NO! GOD HAS PROVIDED A WAY. JUST OPEN YOUR EYES AND LOOK. LOOK AND LIVE!
IT IS A MIRACLE!
WE MUST TELL OTHERS.
IT WORKED FOR ME! I WILL TELL OTHERS.
LOOK AND LIVE!

NUMBERS 21:9

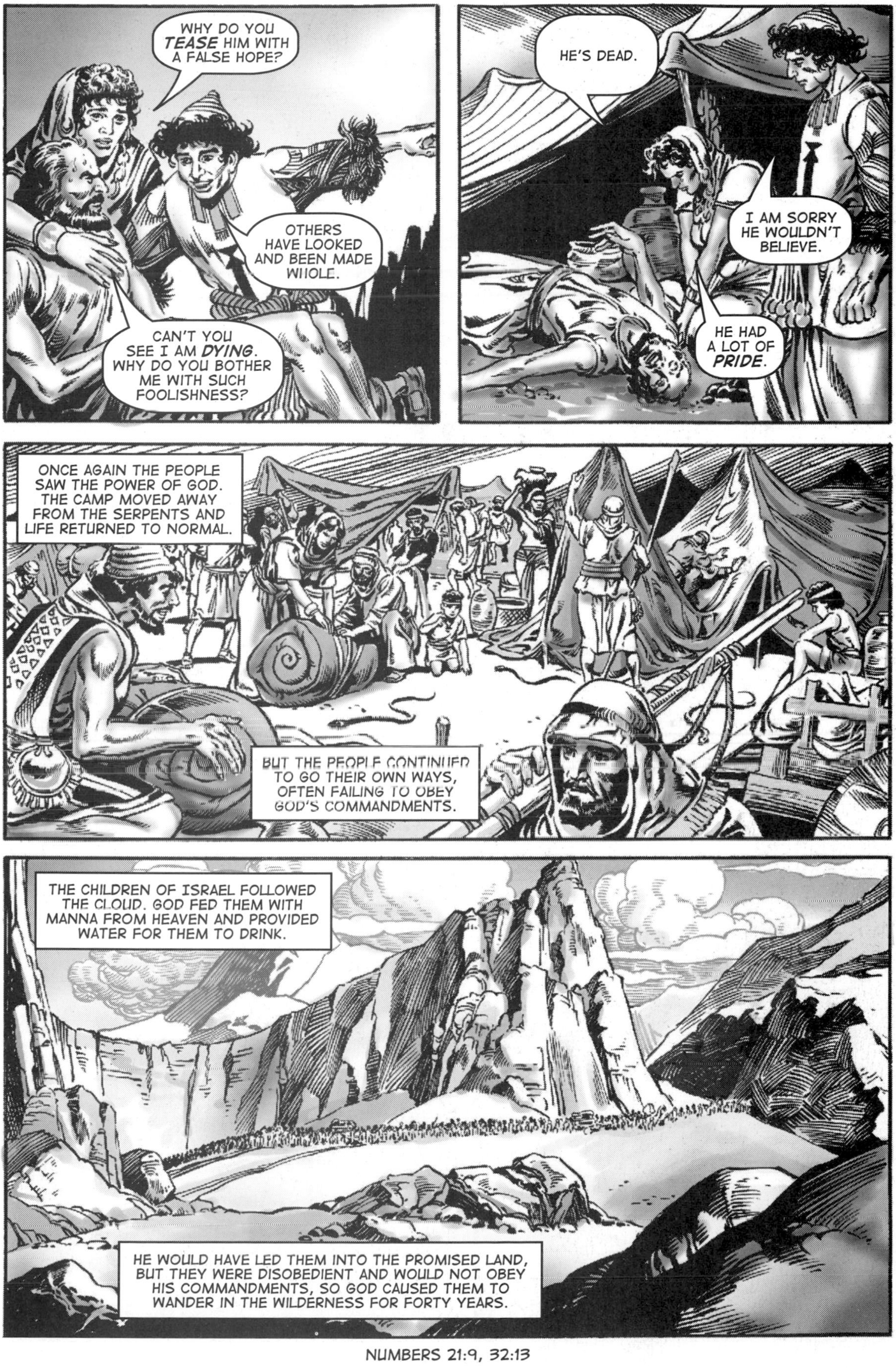
WHY DO YOU TEASE HIM WITH A FALSE HOPE?
OTHERS HAVE LOOKED AND BEEN MADE WHOLE.
CAN'T YOU SEE I AM DYING. WHY DO YOU BOTHER ME WITH SUCH FOOLISHNESS?
HE'S DEAD.
I AM SORRY HE WOULDN'T BELIEVE.
HE HAD A LOT OF PRIDE.
ONCE AGAIN THE PEOPLE SAW THE POWER OF GOD. THE CAMP MOVED AWAY FROM THE SERPENTS AND LIFE RETURNED TO NORMAL.
BUT THE PEOPLE CONTINUED TO GO THEIR OWN WAYS, OFTEN FAILING TO OBEY GOD'S COMMANDMENTS.
THE CHILDREN OF ISRAEL FOLLOWED THE CLOUD. GOD FED THEM WITH MANNA FROM HEAVEN AND PROVIDED WATER FOR THEM TO DRINK.
HE WOULD HAVE LED THEM INTO THE PROMISED LAND, BUT THEY WERE DISOBEDIENT AND WOULD NOT OBEY HIS COMMANDMENTS, SO GOD CAUSED THEM TO WANDER IN THE WILDERNESS FOR FORTY YEARS.

NUMBERS 21:9, 32:13

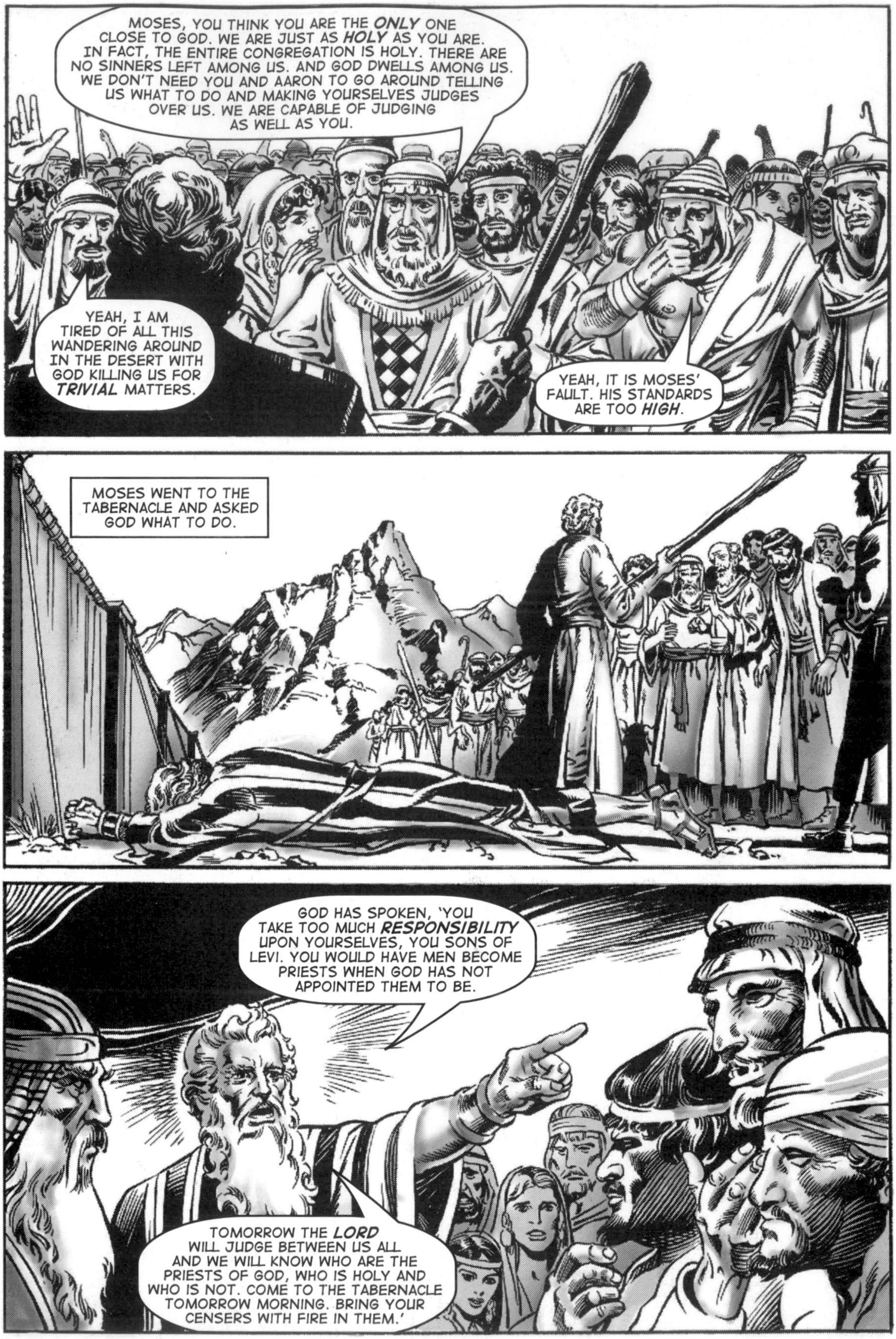
MOSES, YOU THINK YOU ARE THE *ONLY* ONE CLOSE TO GOD. WE ARE JUST AS *HOLY* AS YOU ARE. IN FACT, THE ENTIRE CONGREGATION IS HOLY. THERE ARE NO SINNERS LEFT AMONG US. AND GOD DWELLS AMONG US. WE DON'T NEED YOU AND AARON TO GO AROUND TELLING US WHAT TO DO AND MAKING YOURSELVES JUDGES OVER US. WE ARE CAPABLE OF JUDGING AS WELL AS YOU.
YEAH, I AM TIRED OF ALL THIS WANDERING AROUND IN THE DESERT WITH GOD KILLING US FOR *TRIVIAL* MATTERS.
YEAH, IT IS MOSES' FAULT. HIS STANDARDS ARE TOO *HIGH*.
MOSES WENT TO THE TABERNACLE AND ASKED GOD WHAT TO DO.
GOD HAS SPOKEN, 'YOU TAKE TOO MUCH *RESPONSIBILITY* UPON YOURSELVES, YOU SONS OF LEVI. YOU WOULD HAVE MEN BECOME PRIESTS WHEN GOD HAS NOT APPOINTED THEM TO BE.
TOMORROW THE *LORD* WILL JUDGE BETWEEN US ALL AND WE WILL KNOW WHO ARE THE PRIESTS OF GOD, WHO IS HOLY AND WHO IS NOT. COME TO THE TABERNACLE TOMORROW MORNING. BRING YOUR CENSERS WITH FIRE IN THEM.'

NUMBERS 16:2-6

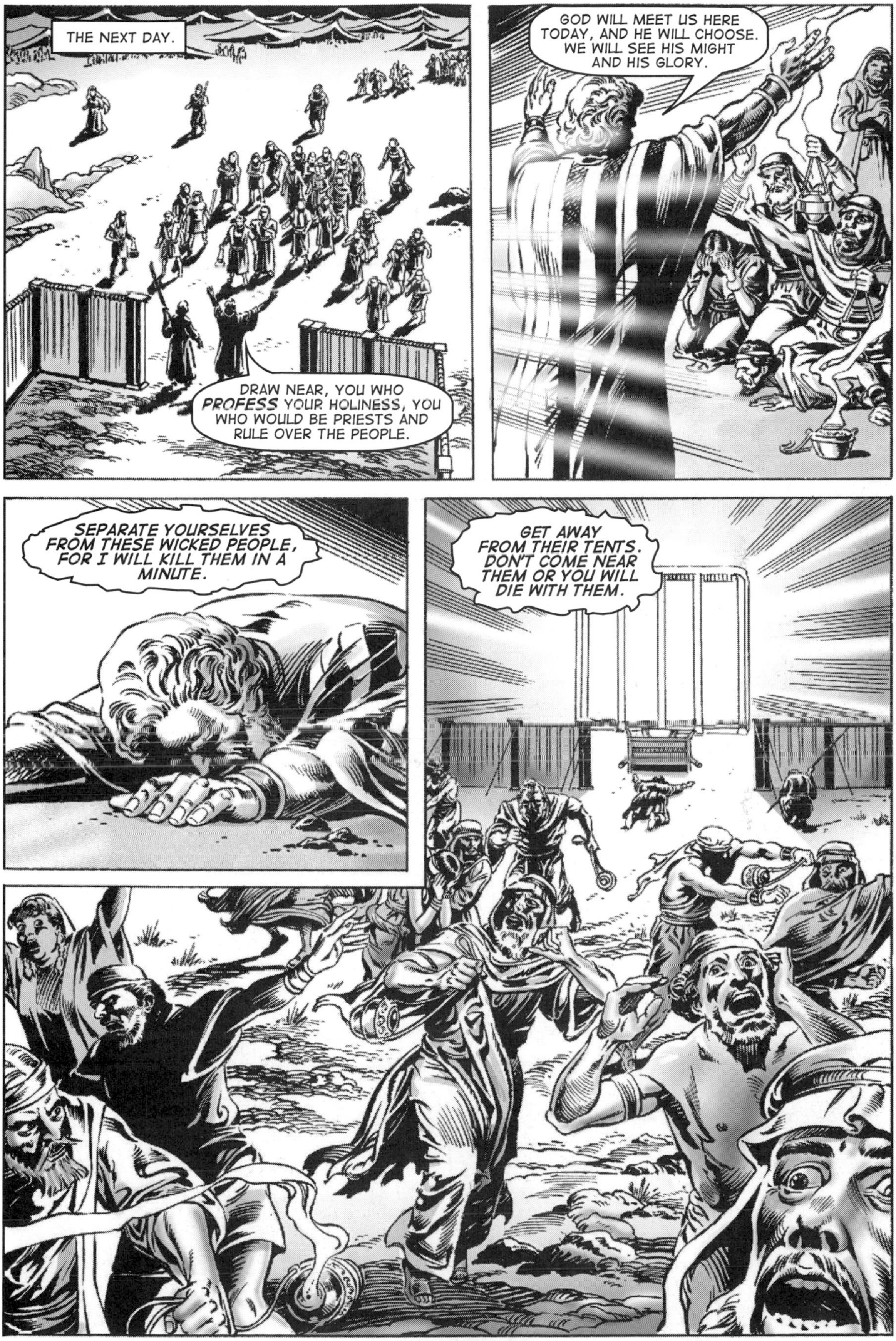
THE NEXT DAY.
DRAW NEAR, YOU WHO PROFESS YOUR HOLINESS, YOU WHO WOULD BE PRIESTS AND RULE OVER THE PEOPLE.
GOD WILL MEET US HERE TODAY, AND HE WILL CHOOSE. WE WILL SEE HIS MIGHT AND HIS GLORY.
SEPARATE YOURSELVES FROM THESE WICKED PEOPLE, FOR I WILL KILL THEM IN A MINUTE.
GET AWAY FROM THEIR TENTS. DON'T COME NEAR THEM OR YOU WILL DIE WITH THEM.

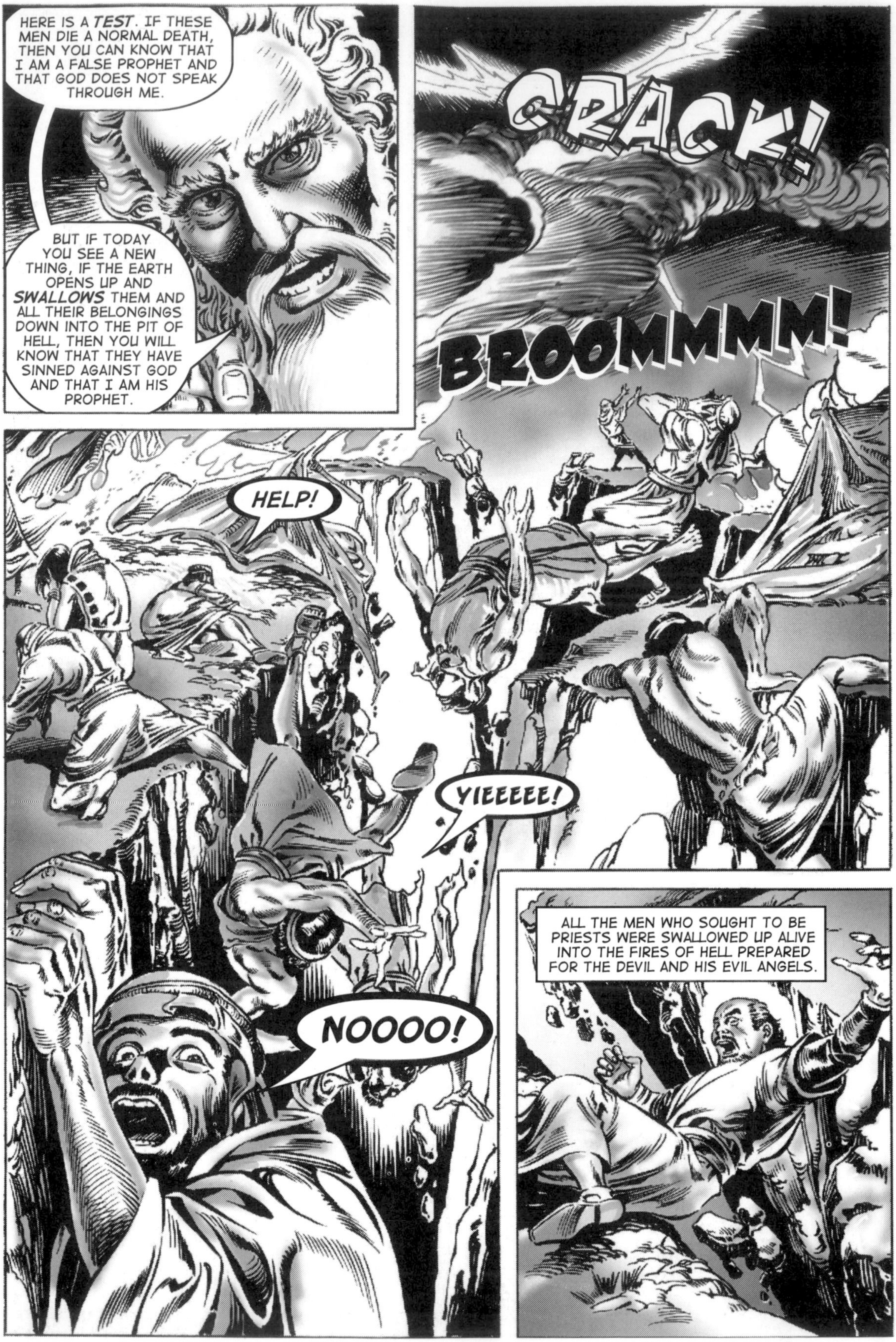
HERE IS A TEST. IF THESE MEN DIE A NORMAL DEATH, THEN YOU CAN KNOW THAT I AM A FALSE PROPHET AND THAT GOD DOES NOT SPEAK THROUGH ME.
BUT IF TODAY YOU SEE A NEW THING, IF THE EARTH OPENS UP AND SWALLOWS THEM AND ALL THEIR BELONGINGS DOWN INTO THE PIT OF HELL, THEN YOU WILL KNOW THAT THEY HAVE SINNED AGAINST GOD AND THAT I AM HIS PROPHET.
CRACK!
BROOMMMM!
HELP!
YIEEEEE!
NOOOO!
ALL THE MEN WHO SOUGHT TO BE PRIESTS WERE SWALLOWED UP ALIVE INTO THE FIRES OF HELL PREPARED FOR THE DEVIL AND HIS EVIL ANGELS.

NUMBERS 16:28-33

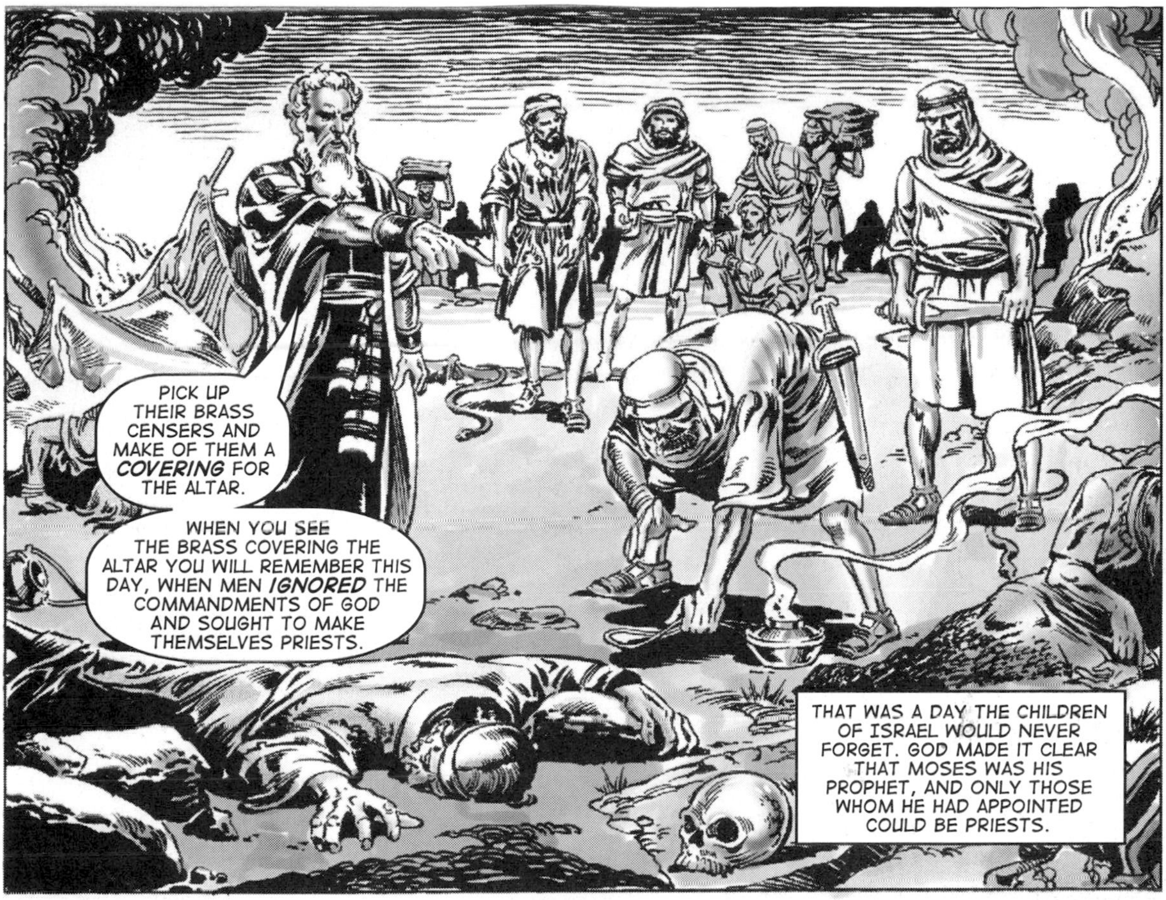
PICK UP THEIR BRASS CENSERS AND MAKE OF THEM A *COVERING* FOR THE ALTAR.
WHEN YOU SEE THE BRASS COVERING THE ALTAR YOU WILL REMEMBER THIS DAY, WHEN MEN *IGNORED* THE COMMANDMENTS OF GOD AND SOUGHT TO MAKE THEMSELVES PRIESTS.
THAT WAS A DAY THE CHILDREN OF ISRAEL WOULD NEVER FORGET. GOD MADE IT CLEAR THAT MOSES WAS HIS PROPHET, AND ONLY THOSE WHOM HE HAD APPOINTED COULD BE PRIESTS.

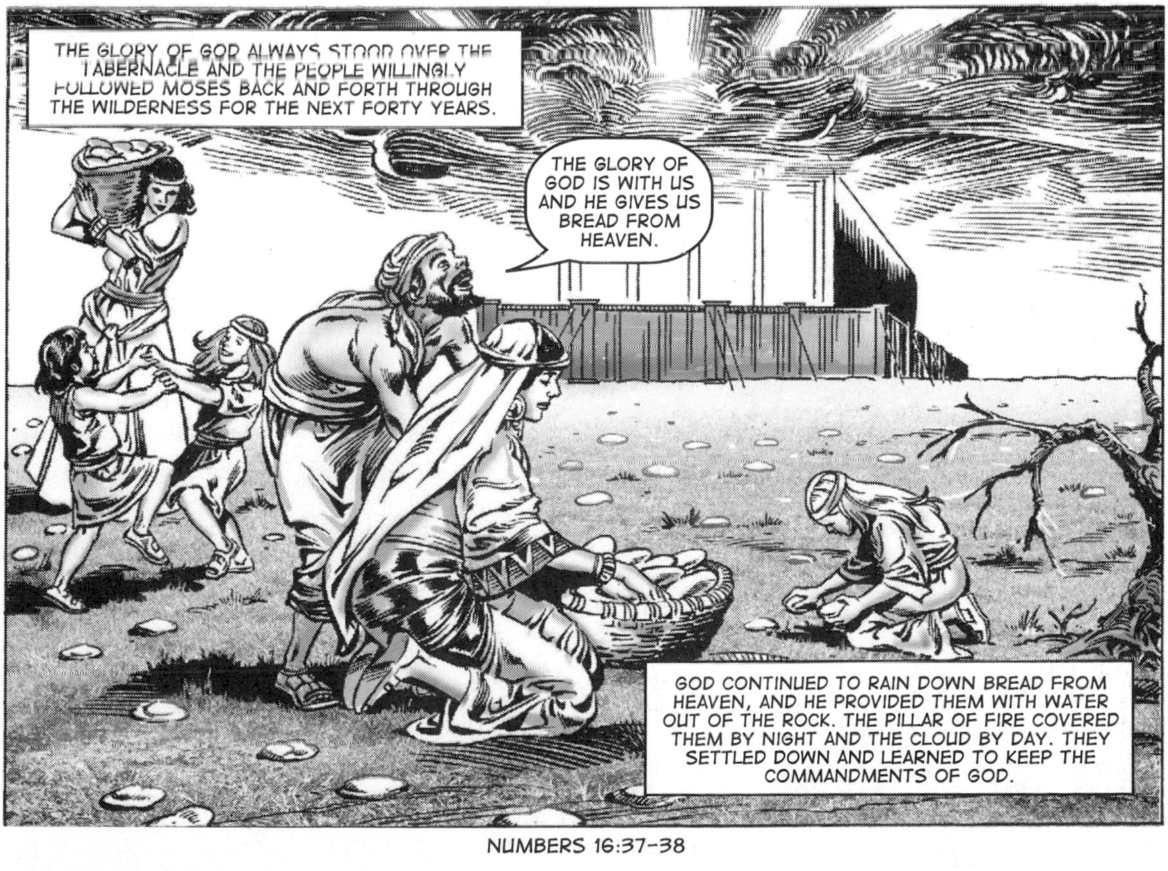
THE GLORY OF GOD ALWAYS STOOD OVER THE TABERNACLE AND THE PEOPLE WILLINGLY FOLLOWED MOSES BACK AND FORTH THROUGH THE WILDERNESS FOR THE NEXT FORTY YEARS.
THE GLORY OF GOD IS WITH US AND HE GIVES US BREAD FROM HEAVEN.
GOD CONTINUED TO RAIN DOWN BREAD FROM HEAVEN, AND HE PROVIDED THEM WITH WATER OUT OF THE ROCK. THE PILLAR OF FIRE COVERED THEM BY NIGHT AND THE CLOUD BY DAY. THEY SETTLED DOWN AND LEARNED TO KEEP THE COMMANDMENTS OF GOD.

NUMBERS 16:37-38

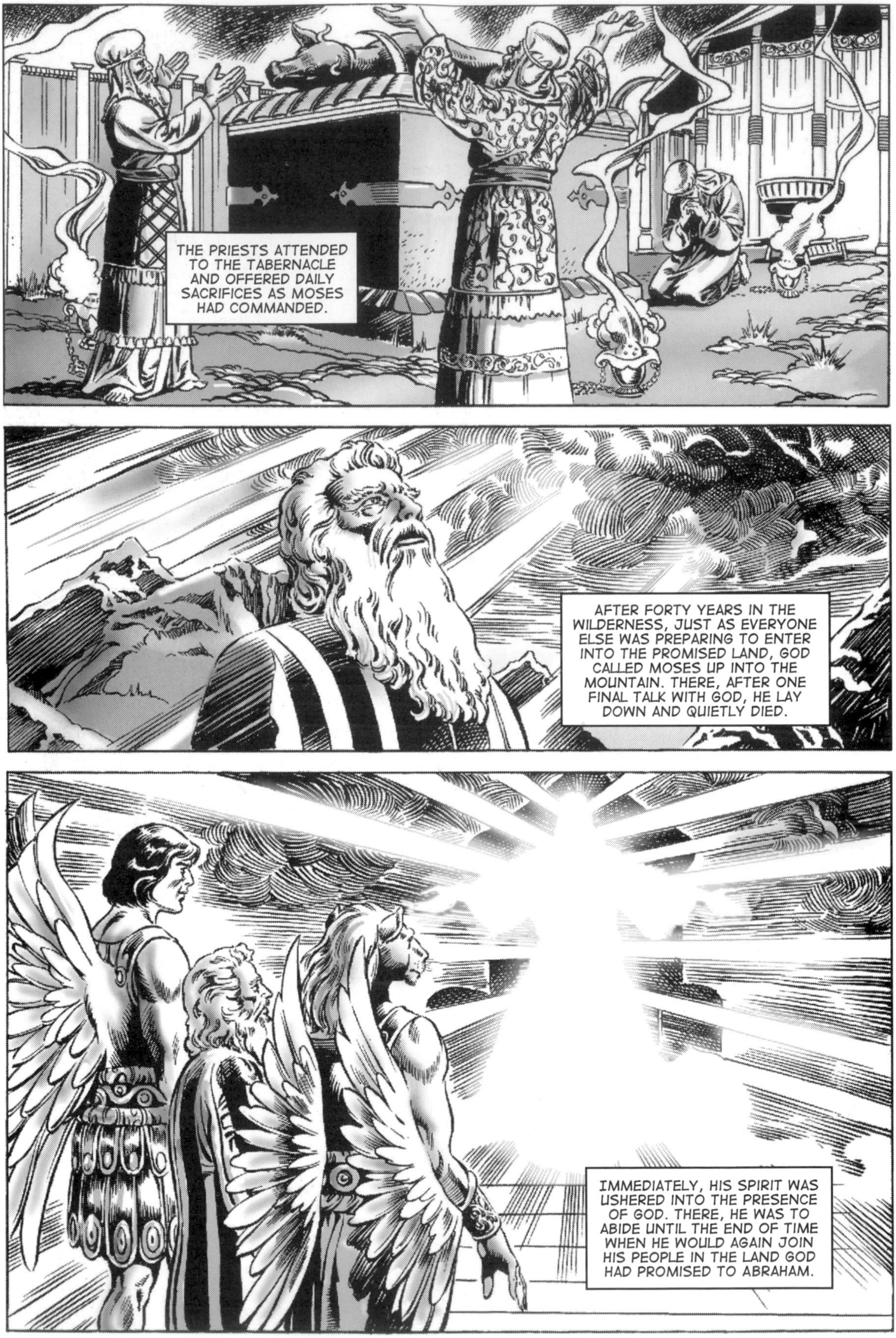
THE PRIESTS ATTENDED TO THE TABERNACLE AND OFFERED DAILY SACRIFICES AS MOSES HAD COMMANDED.
AFTER FORTY YEARS IN THE WILDERNESS, JUST AS EVERYONE ELSE WAS PREPARING TO ENTER INTO THE PROMISED LAND, GOD CALLED MOSES UP INTO THE MOUNTAIN. THERE, AFTER ONE FINAL TALK WITH GOD, HE LAY DOWN AND QUIETLY DIED.
IMMEDIATELY, HIS SPIRIT WAS USHERED INTO THE PRESENCE OF GOD. THERE, HE WAS TO ABIDE UNTIL THE END OF TIME WHEN HE WOULD AGAIN JOIN HIS PEOPLE IN THE LAND GOD HAD PROMISED TO ABRAHAM.

APPROXIMATELY 1451 B.C. - DEUTERONOMY 34:4-5

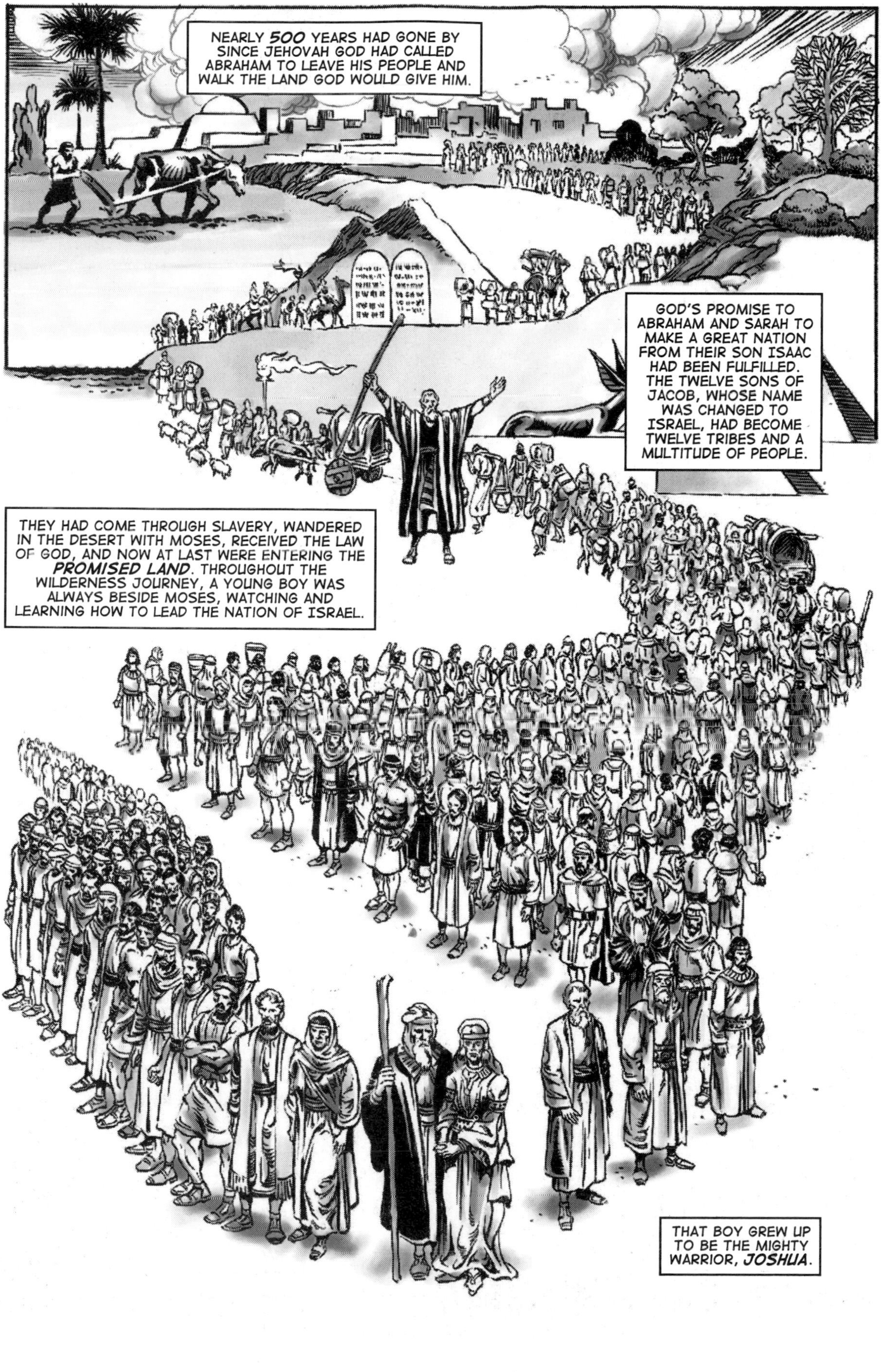
NEARLY 500 YEARS HAD GONE BY SINCE JEHOVAH GOD HAD CALLED ABRAHAM TO LEAVE HIS PEOPLE AND WALK THE LAND GOD WOULD GIVE HIM.
GOD'S PROMISE TO ABRAHAM AND SARAH TO MAKE A GREAT NATION FROM THEIR SON ISAAC HAD BEEN FULFILLED. THE TWELVE SONS OF JACOB, WHOSE NAME WAS CHANGED TO ISRAEL, HAD BECOME TWELVE TRIBES AND A MULTITUDE OF PEOPLE.
THEY HAD COME THROUGH SLAVERY, WANDERED IN THE DESERT WITH MOSES, RECEIVED THE LAW OF GOD, AND NOW AT LAST WERE ENTERING THE PROMISED LAND. THROUGHOUT THE WILDERNESS JOURNEY, A YOUNG BOY WAS ALWAYS BESIDE MOSES, WATCHING AND LEARNING HOW TO LEAD THE NATION OF ISRAEL.
THAT BOY GREW UP TO BE THE MIGHTY WARRIOR, JOSHUA.

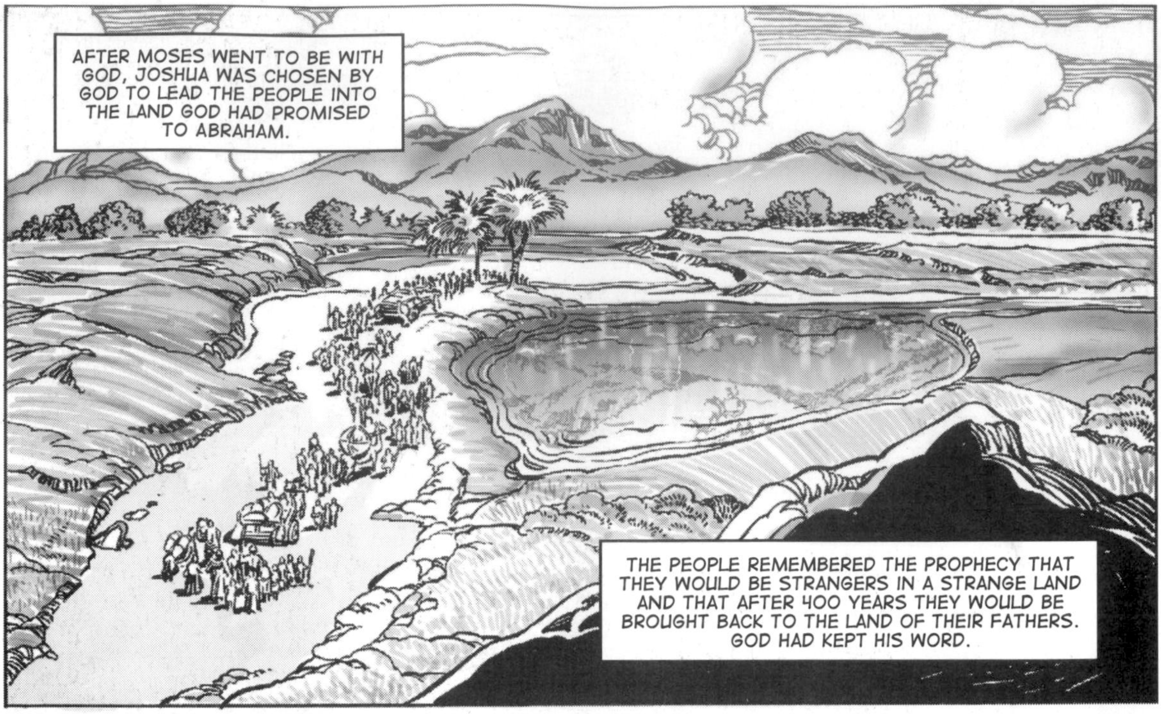
AFTER MOSES WENT TO BE WITH GOD, JOSHUA WAS CHOSEN BY GOD TO LEAD THE PEOPLE INTO THE LAND GOD HAD PROMISED TO ABRAHAM.
THE PEOPLE REMEMBERED THE PROPHECY THAT THEY WOULD BE STRANGERS IN A STRANGE LAND AND THAT AFTER 400 YEARS THEY WOULD BE BROUGHT BACK TO THE LAND OF THEIR FATHERS. GOD HAD KEPT HIS WORD.

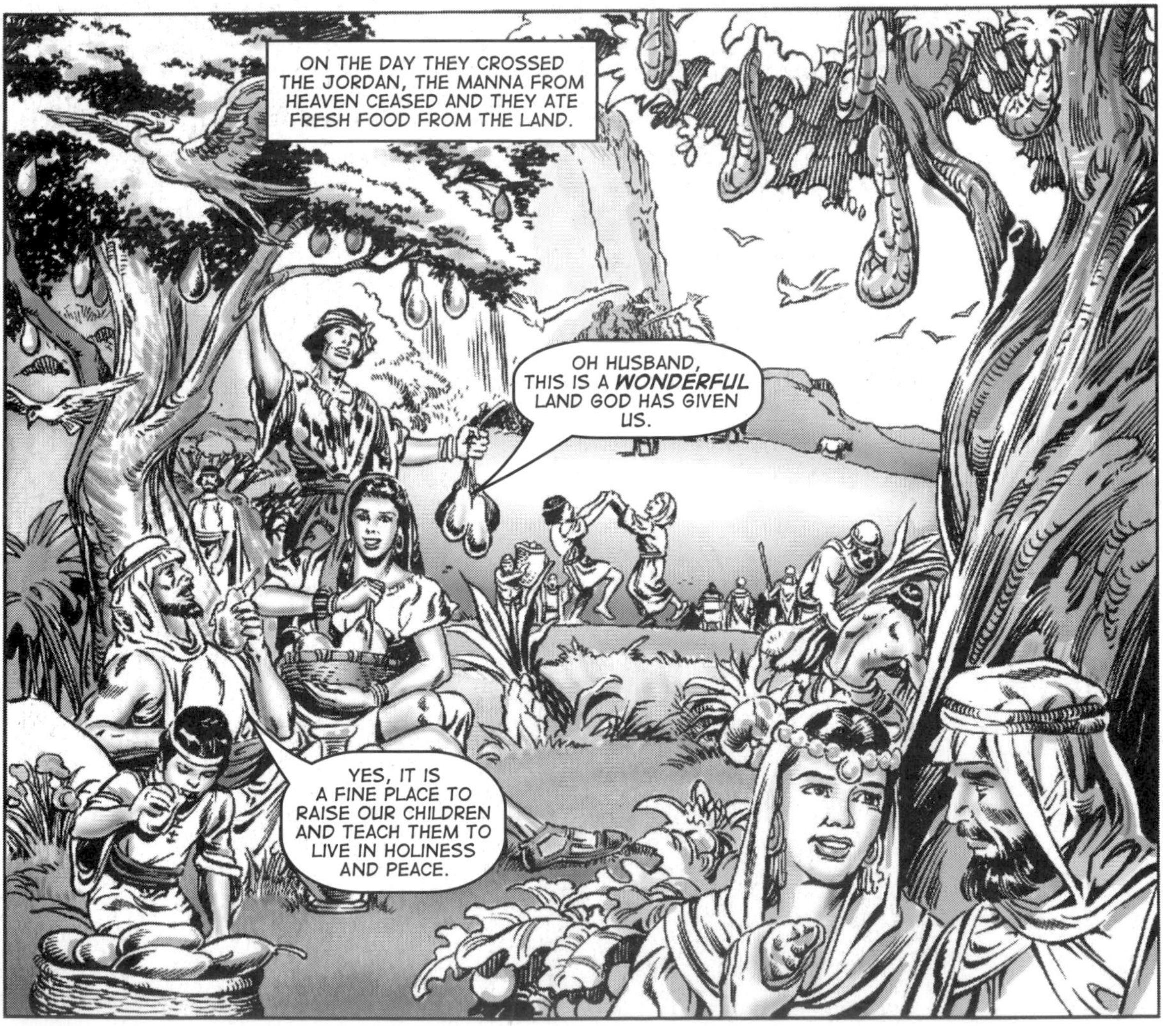
ON THE DAY THEY CROSSED THE JORDAN, THE MANNA FROM HEAVEN CEASED AND THEY ATE FRESH FOOD FROM THE LAND.
OH HUSBAND, THIS IS A ***WONDERFUL*** LAND GOD HAS GIVEN US.
YES, IT IS A FINE PLACE TO RAISE OUR CHILDREN AND TEACH THEM TO LIVE IN HOLINESS AND PEACE.

DEUTERONOMY 34:9; JOSHUA 5:12

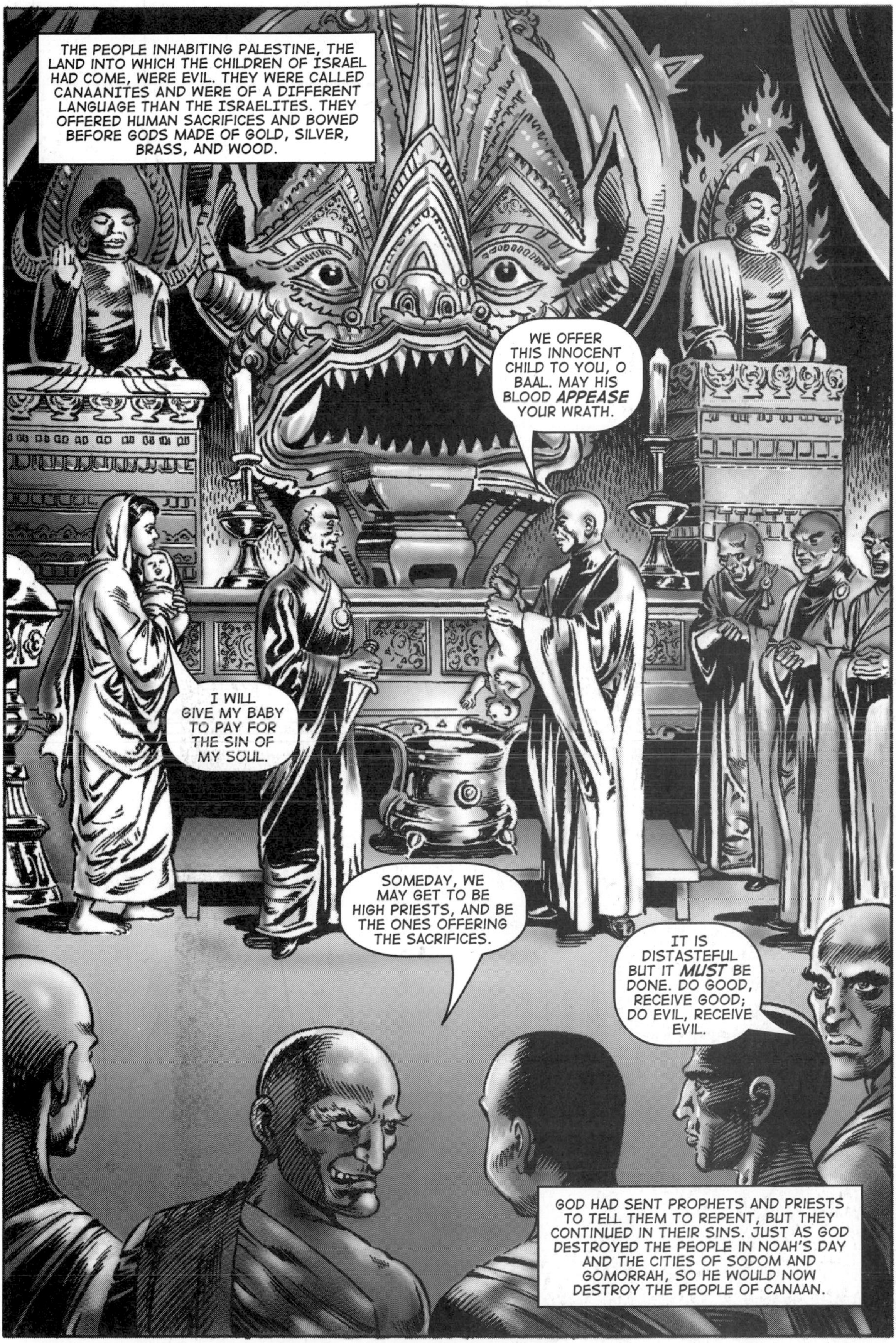
THE PEOPLE INHABITING PALESTINE, THE LAND INTO WHICH THE CHILDREN OF ISRAEL HAD COME, WERE EVIL. THEY WERE CALLED CANAANITES AND WERE OF A DIFFERENT LANGUAGE THAN THE ISRAELITES. THEY OFFERED HUMAN SACRIFICES AND BOWED BEFORE GODS MADE OF GOLD, SILVER, BRASS, AND WOOD.
WE OFFER THIS INNOCENT CHILD TO YOU, O BAAL. MAY HIS BLOOD *APPEASE* YOUR WRATH.
I WILL GIVE MY BABY TO PAY FOR THE SIN OF MY SOUL.
SOMEDAY, WE MAY GET TO BE HIGH PRIESTS, AND BE THE ONES OFFERING THE SACRIFICES.
IT IS DISTASTEFUL BUT IT *MUST* BE DONE. DO GOOD, RECEIVE GOOD; DO EVIL, RECEIVE EVIL.
GOD HAD SENT PROPHETS AND PRIESTS TO TELL THEM TO REPENT, BUT THEY CONTINUED IN THEIR SINS. JUST AS GOD DESTROYED THE PEOPLE IN NOAH'S DAY AND THE CITIES OF SODOM AND GOMORRAH, SO HE WOULD NOW DESTROY THE PEOPLE OF CANAAN.

DEUTERONOMY 18:9–11

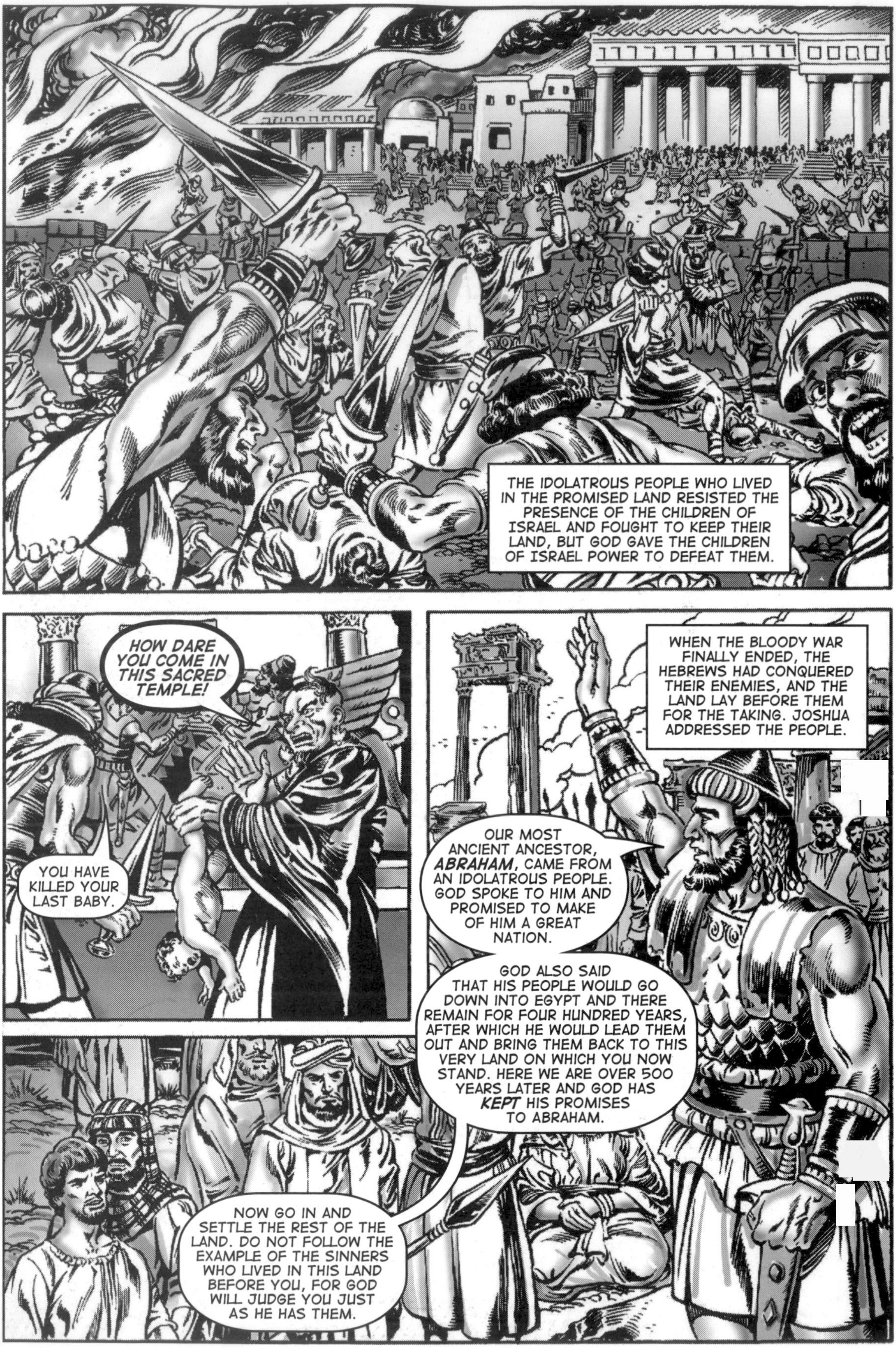
THE IDOLATROUS PEOPLE WHO LIVED IN THE PROMISED LAND RESISTED THE PRESENCE OF THE CHILDREN OF ISRAEL AND FOUGHT TO KEEP THEIR LAND, BUT GOD GAVE THE CHILDREN OF ISRAEL POWER TO DEFEAT THEM.
HOW DARE YOU COME IN THIS SACRED TEMPLE!
YOU HAVE KILLED YOUR LAST BABY.
WHEN THE BLOODY WAR FINALLY ENDED, THE HEBREWS HAD CONQUERED THEIR ENEMIES, AND THE LAND LAY BEFORE THEM FOR THE TAKING. JOSHUA ADDRESSED THE PEOPLE.
OUR MOST ANCIENT ANCESTOR, ABRAHAM, CAME FROM AN IDOLATROUS PEOPLE. GOD SPOKE TO HIM AND PROMISED TO MAKE OF HIM A GREAT NATION.
GOD ALSO SAID THAT HIS PEOPLE WOULD GO DOWN INTO EGYPT AND THERE REMAIN FOR FOUR HUNDRED YEARS, AFTER WHICH HE WOULD LEAD THEM OUT AND BRING THEM BACK TO THIS VERY LAND ON WHICH YOU NOW STAND. HERE WE ARE OVER 500 YEARS LATER AND GOD HAS KEPT HIS PROMISES TO ABRAHAM.
NOW GO IN AND SETTLE THE REST OF THE LAND. DO NOT FOLLOW THE EXAMPLE OF THE SINNERS WHO LIVED IN THIS LAND BEFORE YOU, FOR GOD WILL JUDGE YOU JUST AS HE HAS THEM.

JOSHUA 24:2-14

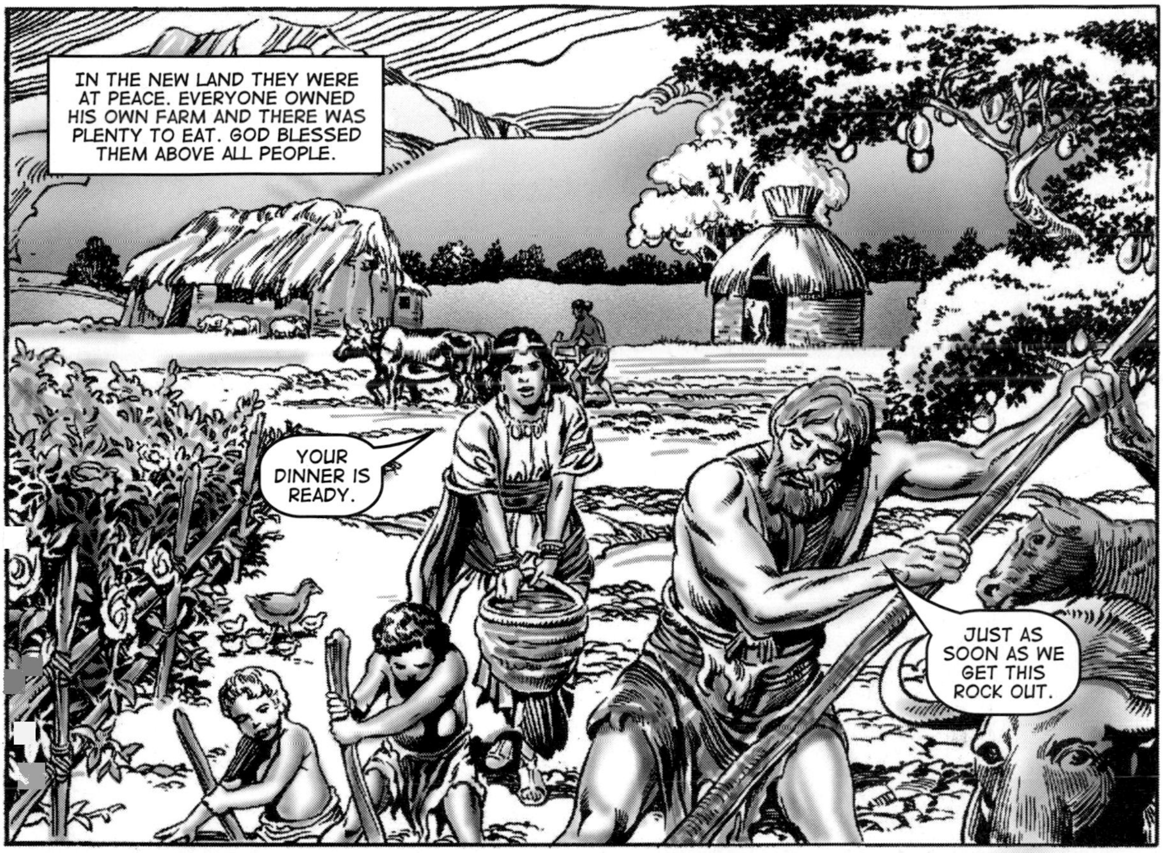
IN THE NEW LAND THEY WERE AT PEACE. EVERYONE OWNED HIS OWN FARM AND THERE WAS PLENTY TO EAT. GOD BLESSED THEM ABOVE ALL PEOPLE.
YOUR DINNER IS READY.
JUST AS SOON AS WE GET THIS ROCK OUT.

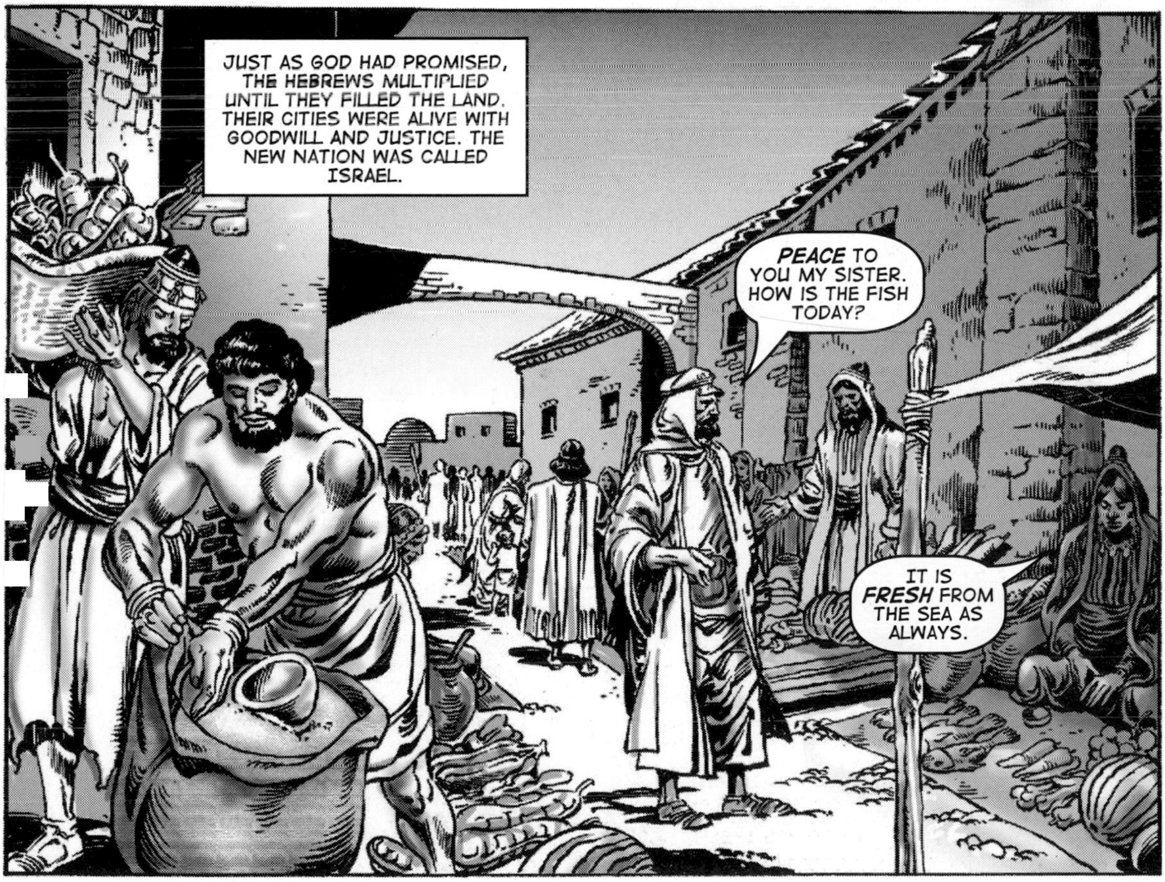
JUST AS GOD HAD PROMISED, THE HEBREWS MULTIPLIED UNTIL THEY FILLED THE LAND. THEIR CITIES WERE ALIVE WITH GOODWILL AND JUSTICE. THE NEW NATION WAS CALLED ISRAEL.
PEACE TO YOU MY SISTER. HOW IS THE FISH TODAY?
IT IS FRESH FROM THE SEA AS ALWAYS.

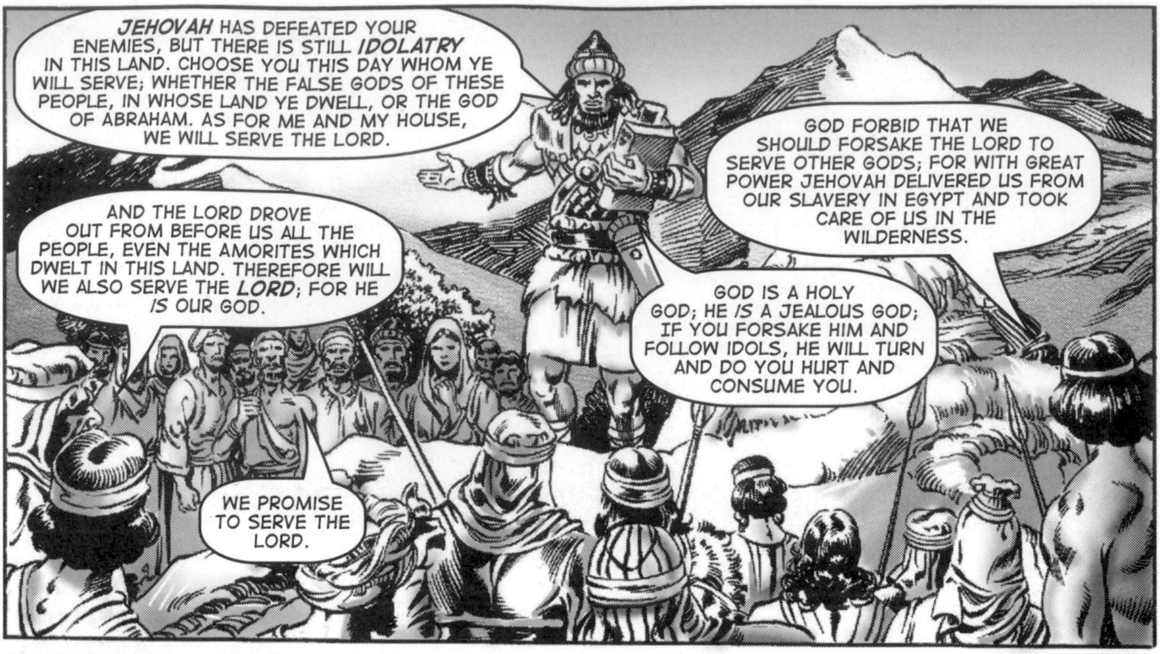
JEHOVAH HAS DEFEATED YOUR ENEMIES, BUT THERE IS STILL IDOLATRY IN THIS LAND. CHOOSE YOU THIS DAY WHOM YE WILL SERVE; WHETHER THE FALSE GODS OF THESE PEOPLE, IN WHOSE LAND YE DWELL, OR THE GOD OF ABRAHAM. AS FOR ME AND MY HOUSE, WE WILL SERVE THE LORD.
GOD FORBID THAT WE SHOULD FORSAKE THE LORD TO SERVE OTHER GODS; FOR WITH GREAT POWER JEHOVAH DELIVERED US FROM OUR SLAVERY IN EGYPT AND TOOK CARE OF US IN THE WILDERNESS.
AND THE LORD DROVE OUT FROM BEFORE US ALL THE PEOPLE, EVEN THE AMORITES WHICH DWELT IN THIS LAND. THEREFORE WILL WE ALSO SERVE THE LORD; FOR HE IS OUR GOD.
GOD IS A HOLY GOD; HE IS A JEALOUS GOD; IF YOU FORSAKE HIM AND FOLLOW IDOLS, HE WILL TURN AND DO YOU HURT AND CONSUME YOU.
WE PROMISE TO SERVE THE LORD.

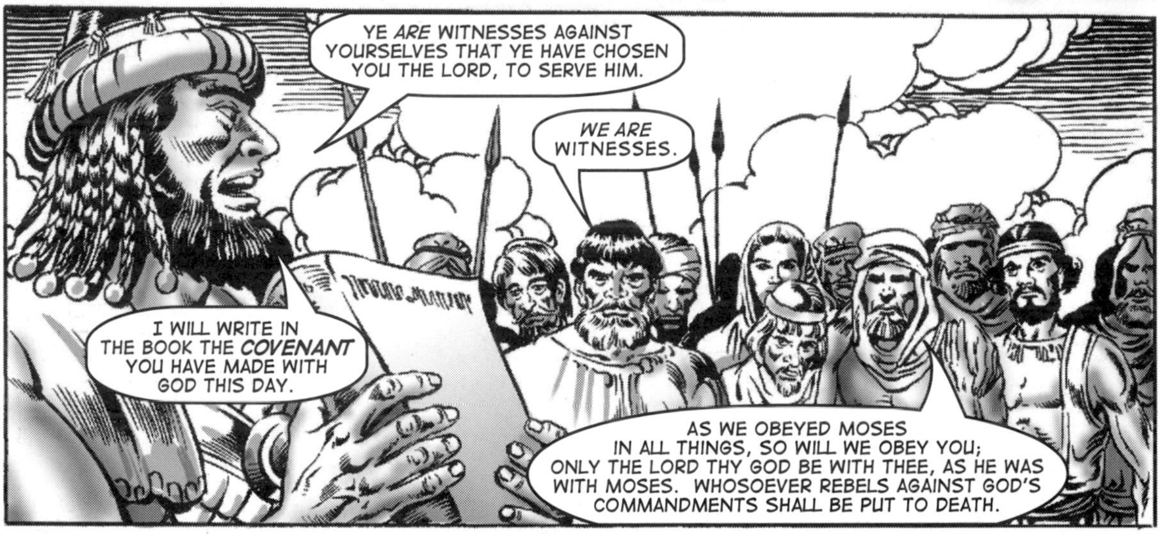
YE ARE WITNESSES AGAINST YOURSELVES THAT YE HAVE CHOSEN YOU THE LORD, TO SERVE HIM.
WE ARE WITNESSES.
I WILL WRITE IN THE BOOK THE COVENANT YOU HAVE MADE WITH GOD THIS DAY.
AS WE OBEYED MOSES IN ALL THINGS, SO WILL WE OBEY YOU; ONLY THE LORD THY GOD BE WITH THEE, AS HE WAS WITH MOSES. WHOSOEVER REBELS AGAINST GOD'S COMMANDMENTS SHALL BE PUT TO DEATH.

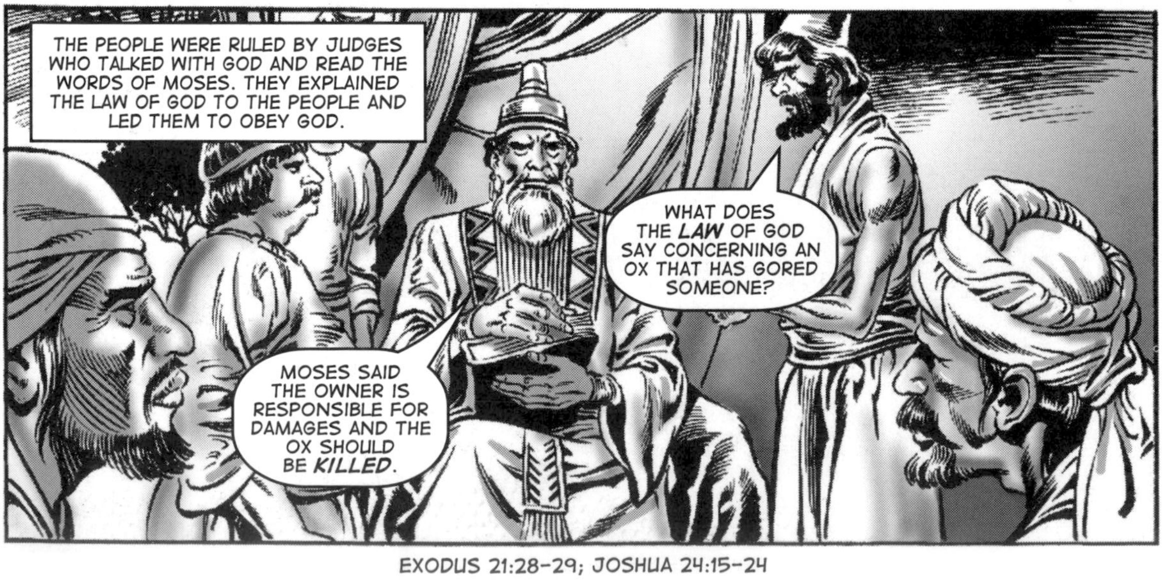
THE PEOPLE WERE RULED BY JUDGES WHO TALKED WITH GOD AND READ THE WORDS OF MOSES. THEY EXPLAINED THE LAW OF GOD TO THE PEOPLE AND LED THEM TO OBEY GOD.
WHAT DOES THE LAW OF GOD SAY CONCERNING AN OX THAT HAS GORED SOMEONE?
MOSES SAID THE OWNER IS RESPONSIBLE FOR DAMAGES AND THE OX SHOULD BE KILLED.

EXODUS 21:28-29; JOSHUA 24:15-24

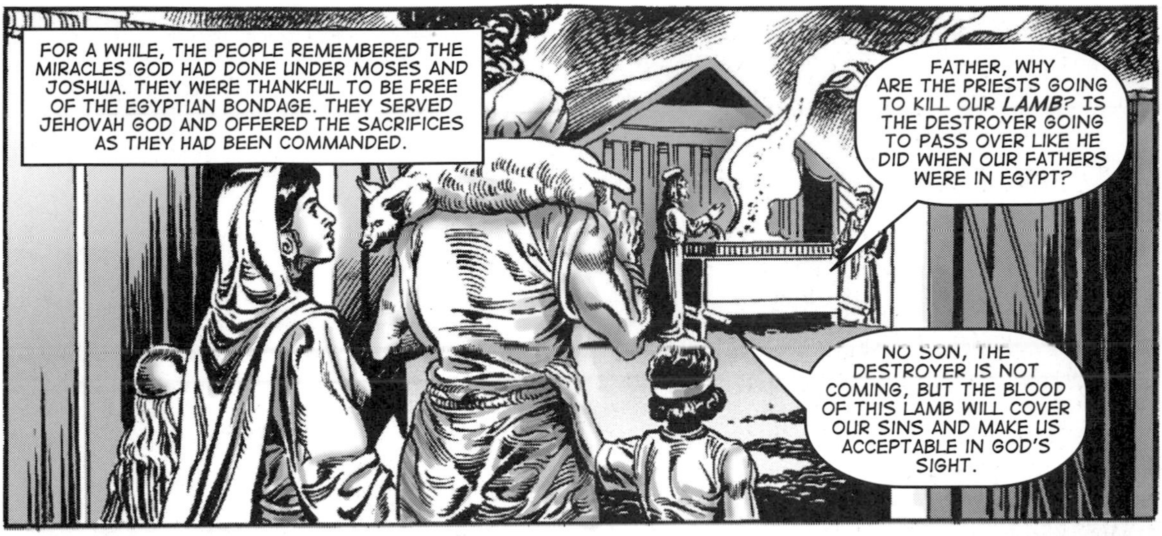
FOR A WHILE, THE PEOPLE REMEMBERED THE MIRACLES GOD HAD DONE UNDER MOSES AND JOSHUA. THEY WERE THANKFUL TO BE FREE OF THE EGYPTIAN BONDAGE. THEY SERVED JEHOVAH GOD AND OFFERED THE SACRIFICES AS THEY HAD BEEN COMMANDED.
FATHER, WHY ARE THE PRIESTS GOING TO KILL OUR *LAMB*? IS THE DESTROYER GOING TO PASS OVER LIKE HE DID WHEN OUR FATHERS WERE IN EGYPT?
NO SON, THE DESTROYER IS NOT COMING, BUT THE BLOOD OF THIS LAMB WILL COVER OUR SINS AND MAKE US ACCEPTABLE IN GOD'S SIGHT.

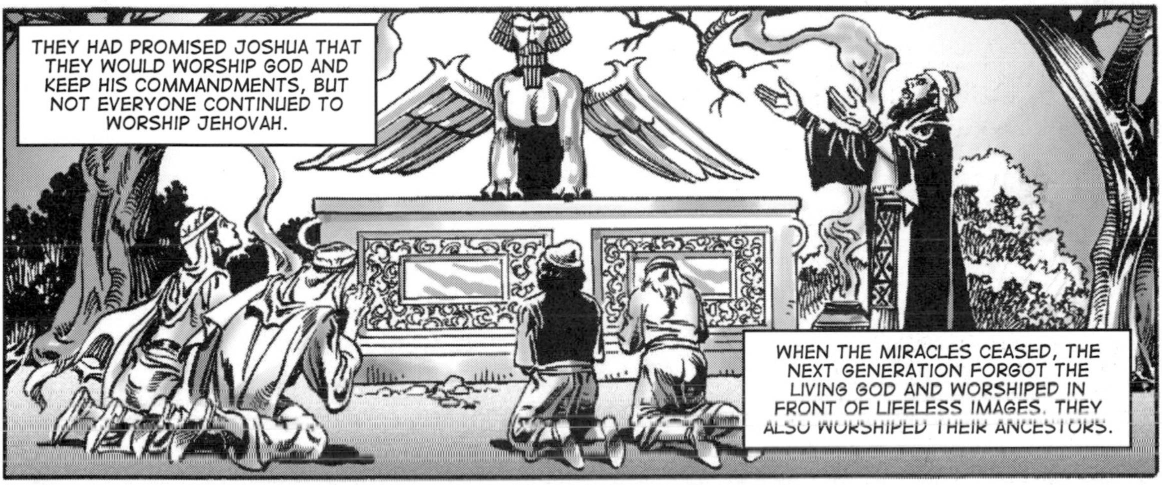
THEY HAD PROMISED JOSHUA THAT THEY WOULD WORSHIP GOD AND KEEP HIS COMMANDMENTS, BUT NOT EVERYONE CONTINUED TO WORSHIP JEHOVAH.
WHEN THE MIRACLES CEASED, THE NEXT GENERATION FORGOT THE LIVING GOD AND WORSHIPED IN FRONT OF LIFELESS IMAGES. THEY ALSO WORSHIPED THEIR ANCESTORS.

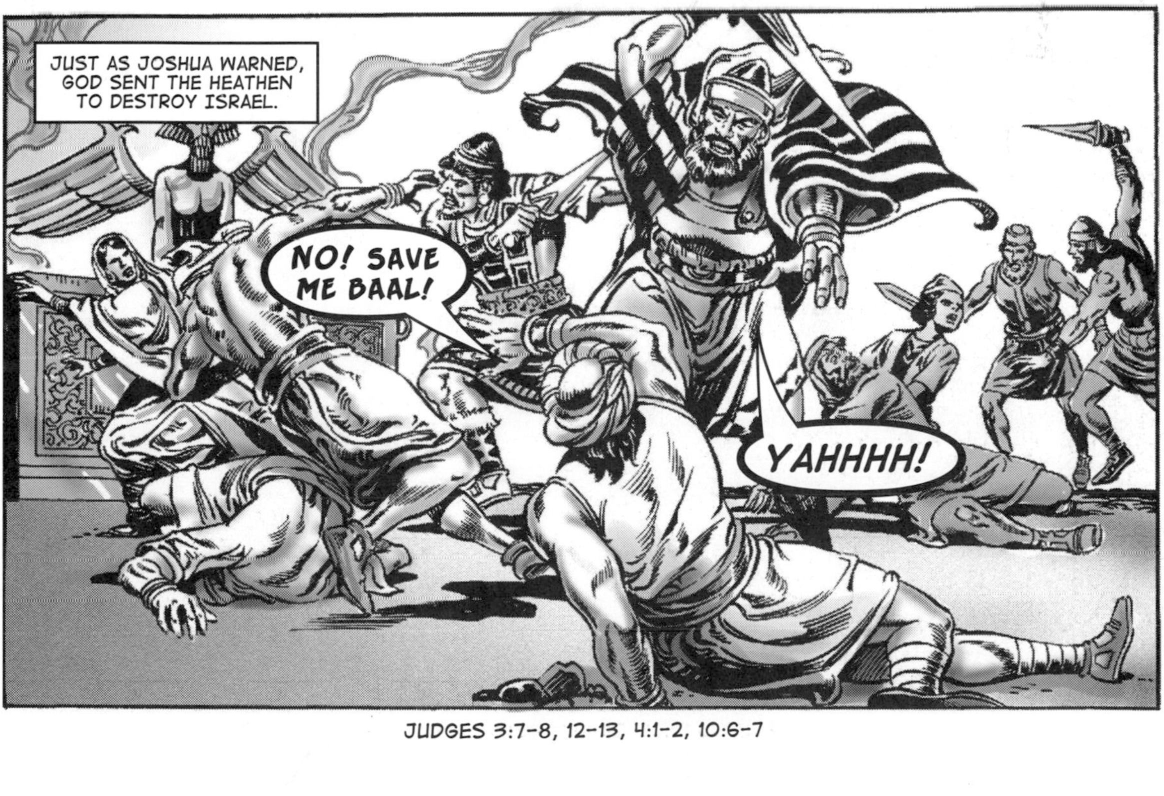
JUST AS JOSHUA WARNED, GOD SENT THE HEATHEN TO DESTROY ISRAEL.
NO! SAVE ME BAAL!
YAHHHH!

JUDGES 3:7-8, 12-13, 4:1-2, 10:6-7

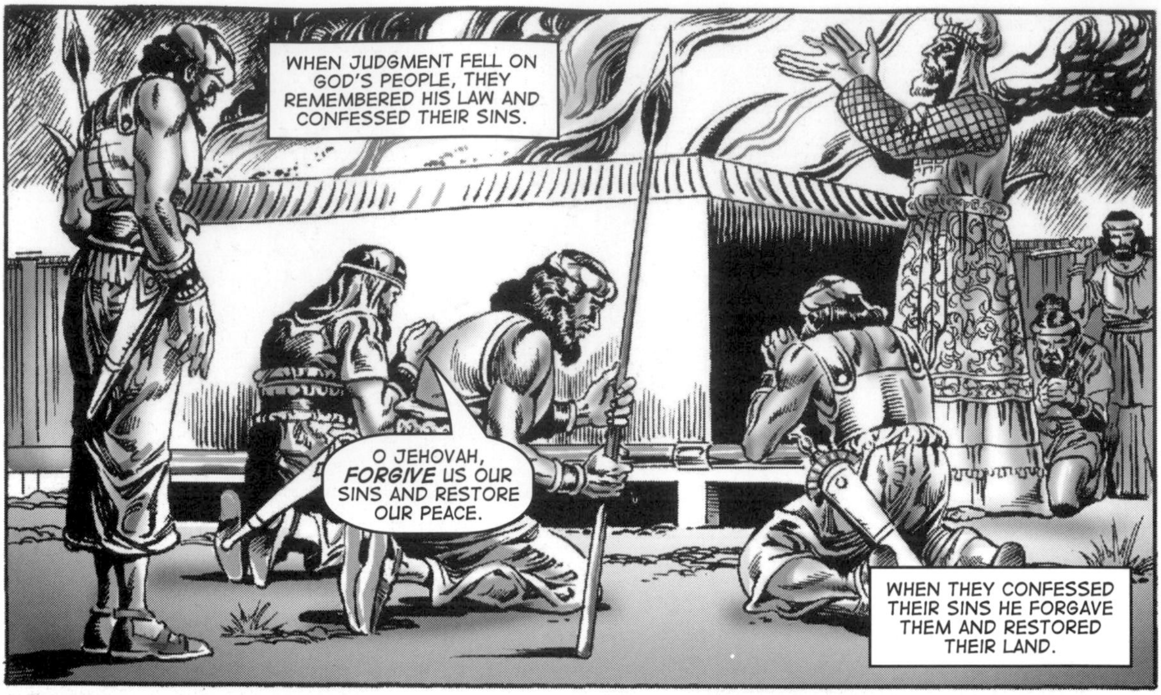
WHEN JUDGMENT FELL ON GOD'S PEOPLE, THEY REMEMBERED HIS LAW AND CONFESSED THEIR SINS.
O JEHOVAH, FORGIVE US OUR SINS AND RESTORE OUR PEACE.
WHEN THEY CONFESSED THEIR SINS HE FORGAVE THEM AND RESTORED THEIR LAND.

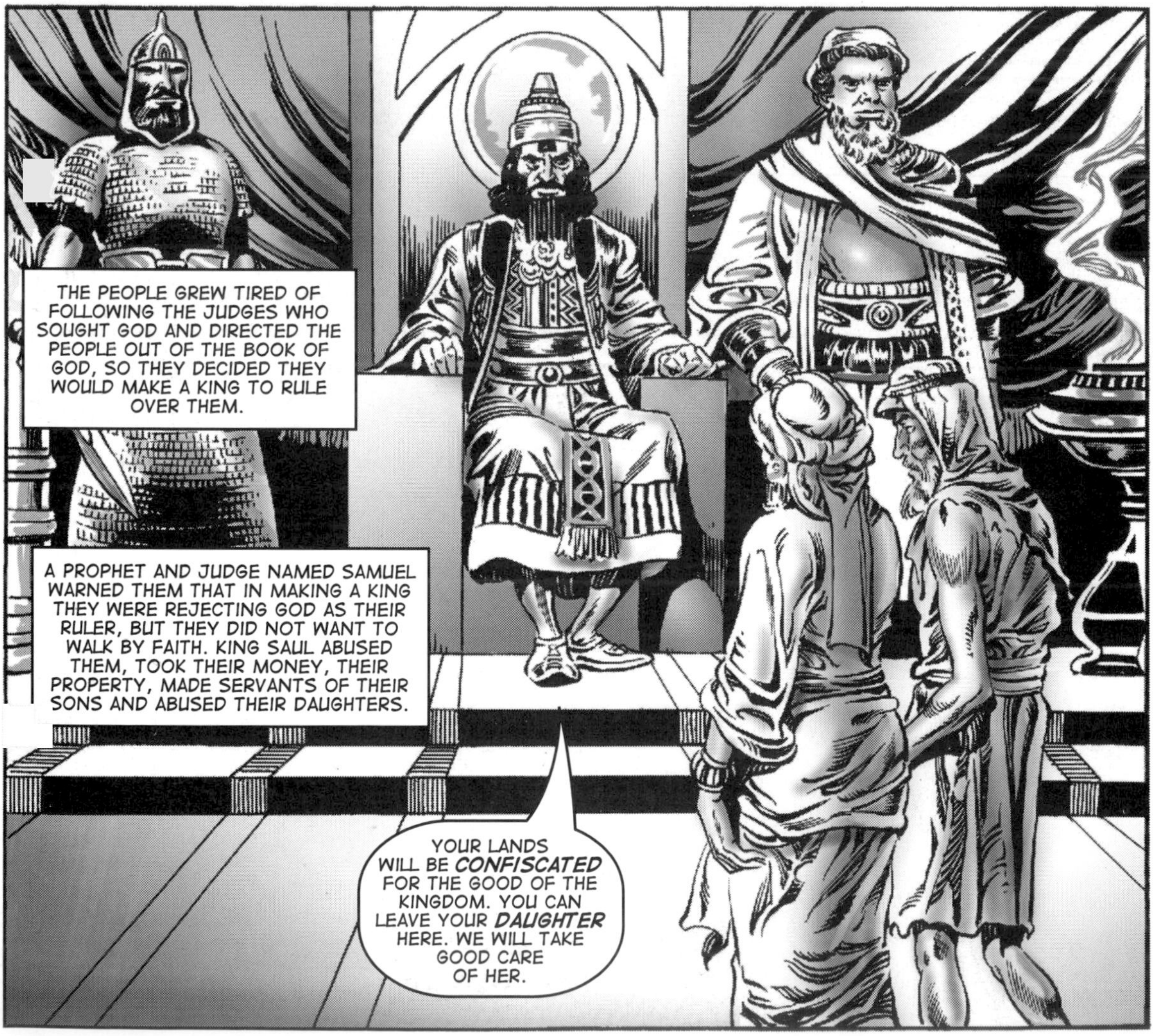
THE PEOPLE GREW TIRED OF FOLLOWING THE JUDGES WHO SOUGHT GOD AND DIRECTED THE PEOPLE OUT OF THE BOOK OF GOD, SO THEY DECIDED THEY WOULD MAKE A KING TO RULE OVER THEM.
A PROPHET AND JUDGE NAMED SAMUEL WARNED THEM THAT IN MAKING A KING THEY WERE REJECTING GOD AS THEIR RULER, BUT THEY DID NOT WANT TO WALK BY FAITH. KING SAUL ABUSED THEM, TOOK THEIR MONEY, THEIR PROPERTY, MADE SERVANTS OF THEIR SONS AND ABUSED THEIR DAUGHTERS.
YOUR LANDS WILL BE CONFISCATED FOR THE GOOD OF THE KINGDOM. YOU CAN LEAVE YOUR DAUGHTER HERE. WE WILL TAKE GOOD CARE OF HER.

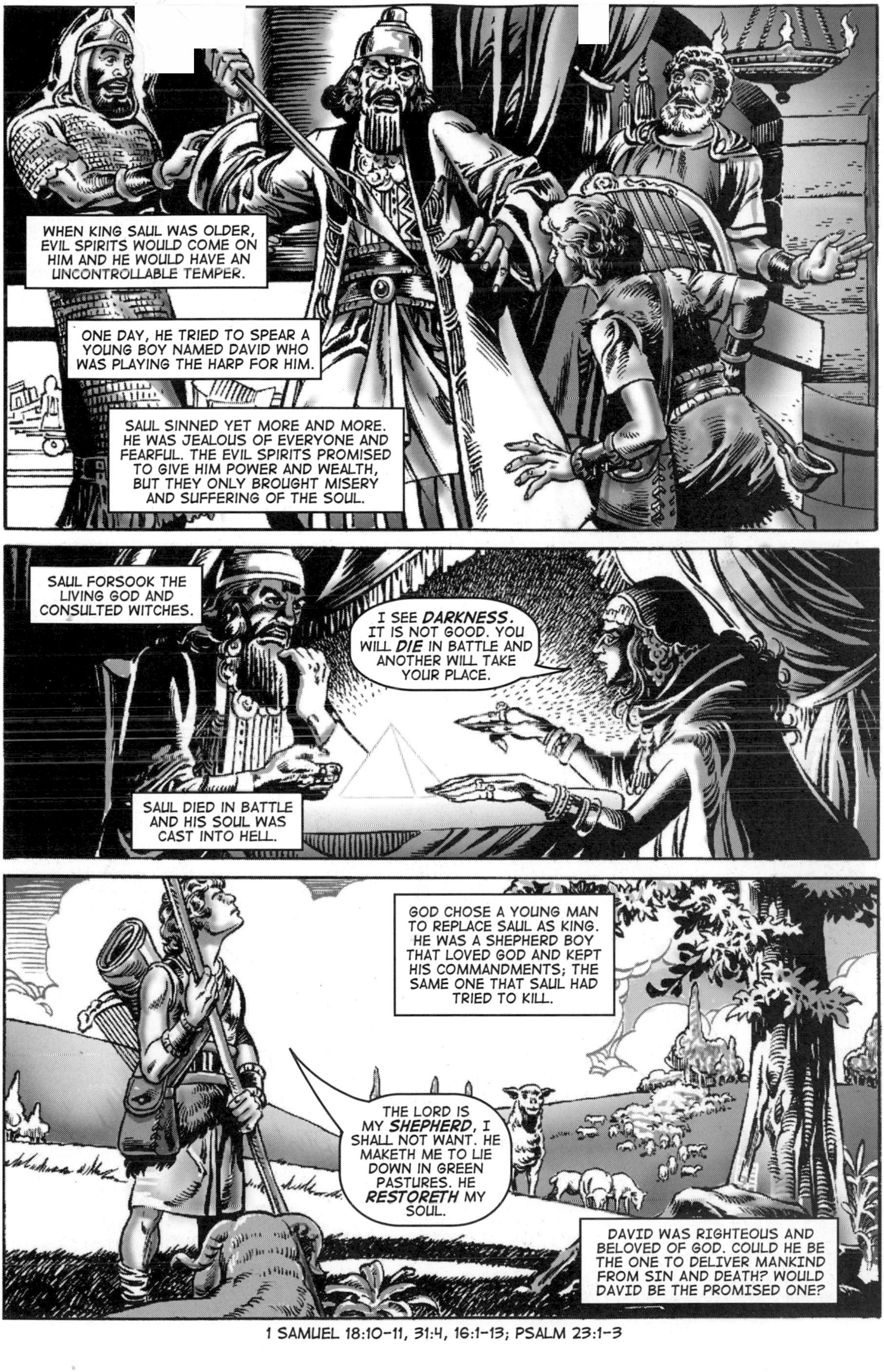
WHEN KING SAUL WAS OLDER, EVIL SPIRITS WOULD COME ON HIM AND HE WOULD HAVE AN UNCONTROLLABLE TEMPER.
ONE DAY, HE TRIED TO SPEAR A YOUNG BOY NAMED DAVID WHO WAS PLAYING THE HARP FOR HIM.
SAUL SINNED YET MORE AND MORE. HE WAS JEALOUS OF EVERYONE AND FEARFUL. THE EVIL SPIRITS PROMISED TO GIVE HIM POWER AND WEALTH, BUT THEY ONLY BROUGHT MISERY AND SUFFERING OF THE SOUL.
SAUL FORSOOK THE LIVING GOD AND CONSULTED WITCHES.
I SEE ***DARKNESS.*** IT IS NOT GOOD. YOU WILL ***DIE*** IN BATTLE AND ANOTHER WILL TAKE YOUR PLACE.
SAUL DIED IN BATTLE AND HIS SOUL WAS CAST INTO HELL.
GOD CHOSE A YOUNG MAN TO REPLACE SAUL AS KING. HE WAS A SHEPHERD BOY THAT LOVED GOD AND KEPT HIS COMMANDMENTS; THE SAME ONE THAT SAUL HAD TRIED TO KILL.
THE LORD IS MY ***SHEPHERD***, I SHALL NOT WANT. HE MAKETH ME TO LIE DOWN IN GREEN PASTURES. HE ***RESTORETH*** MY SOUL.
DAVID WAS RIGHTEOUS AND BELOVED OF GOD. COULD HE BE THE ONE TO DELIVER MANKIND FROM SIN AND DEATH? WOULD DAVID BE THE PROMISED ONE?

1 SAMUEL 18:10-11, 31:4, 16:1-13; PSALM 23:1-3

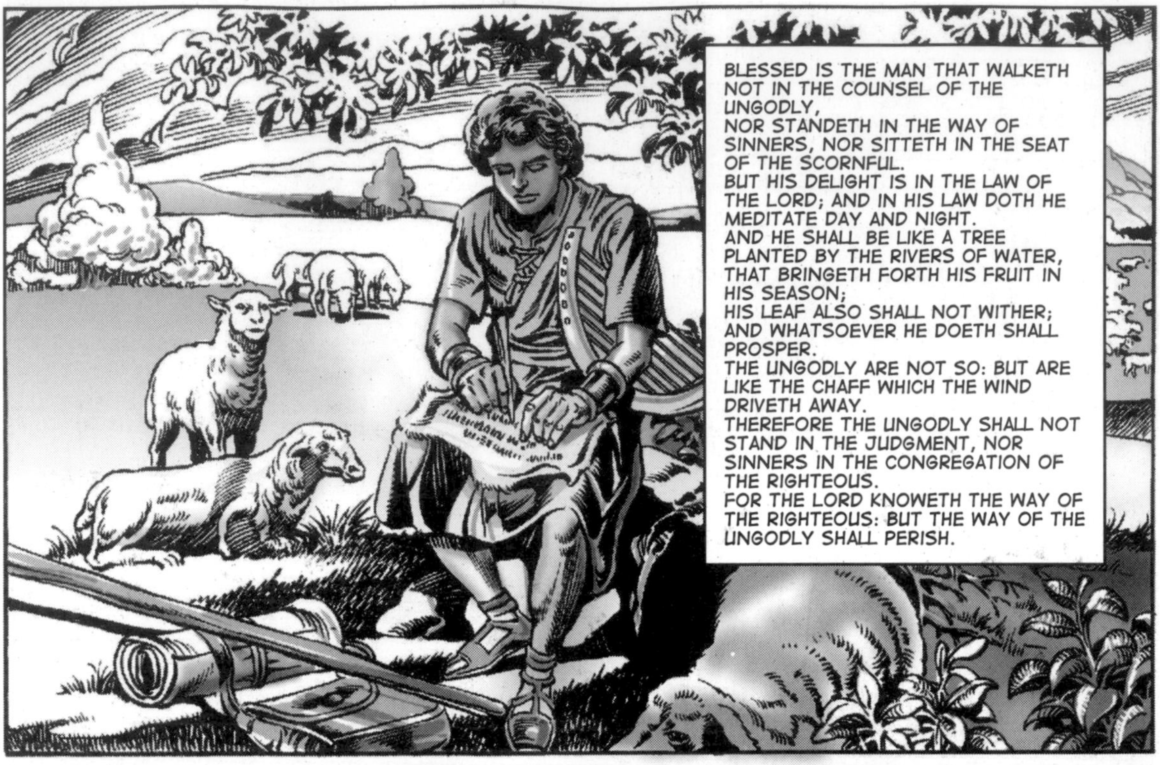
BLESSED IS THE MAN THAT WALKETH NOT IN THE COUNSEL OF THE UNGODLY,
NOR STANDETH IN THE WAY OF SINNERS, NOR SITTETH IN THE SEAT OF THE SCORNFUL.
BUT HIS DELIGHT IS IN THE LAW OF THE LORD; AND IN HIS LAW DOTH HE MEDITATE DAY AND NIGHT.
AND HE SHALL BE LIKE A TREE PLANTED BY THE RIVERS OF WATER, THAT BRINGETH FORTH HIS FRUIT IN HIS SEASON;
HIS LEAF ALSO SHALL NOT WITHER; AND WHATSOEVER HE DOETH SHALL PROSPER.
THE UNGODLY ARE NOT SO: BUT ARE LIKE THE CHAFF WHICH THE WIND DRIVETH AWAY.
THEREFORE THE UNGODLY SHALL NOT STAND IN THE JUDGMENT, NOR SINNERS IN THE CONGREGATION OF THE RIGHTEOUS.
FOR THE LORD KNOWETH THE WAY OF THE RIGHTEOUS: BUT THE WAY OF THE UNGODLY SHALL PERISH.

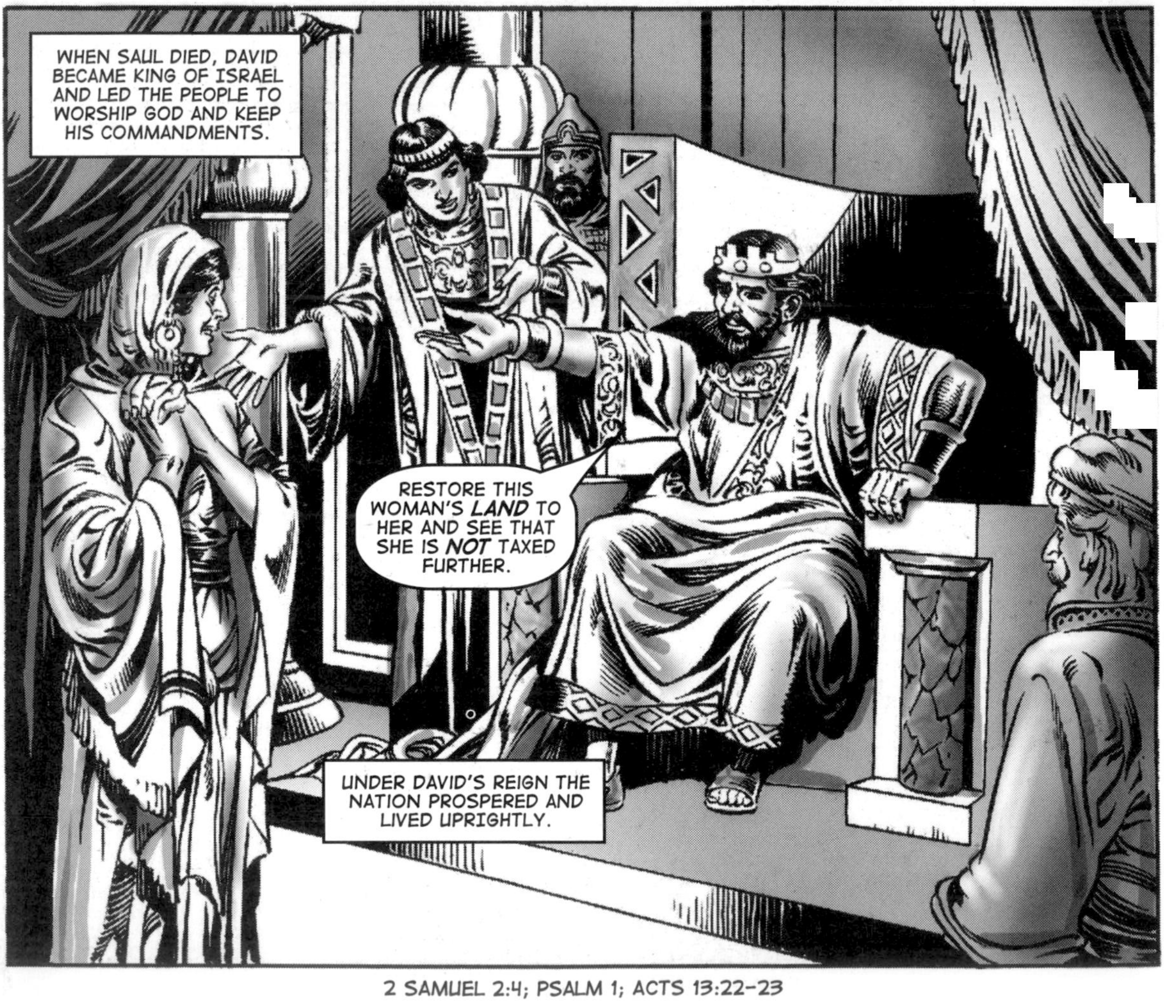
WHEN SAUL DIED, DAVID BECAME KING OF ISRAEL AND LED THE PEOPLE TO WORSHIP GOD AND KEEP HIS COMMANDMENTS.
RESTORE THIS WOMAN'S *LAND* TO HER AND SEE THAT SHE IS *NOT* TAXED FURTHER.
UNDER DAVID'S REIGN THE NATION PROSPERED AND LIVED UPRIGHTLY.

2 SAMUEL 2:4; PSALM 1; ACTS 13:22-23

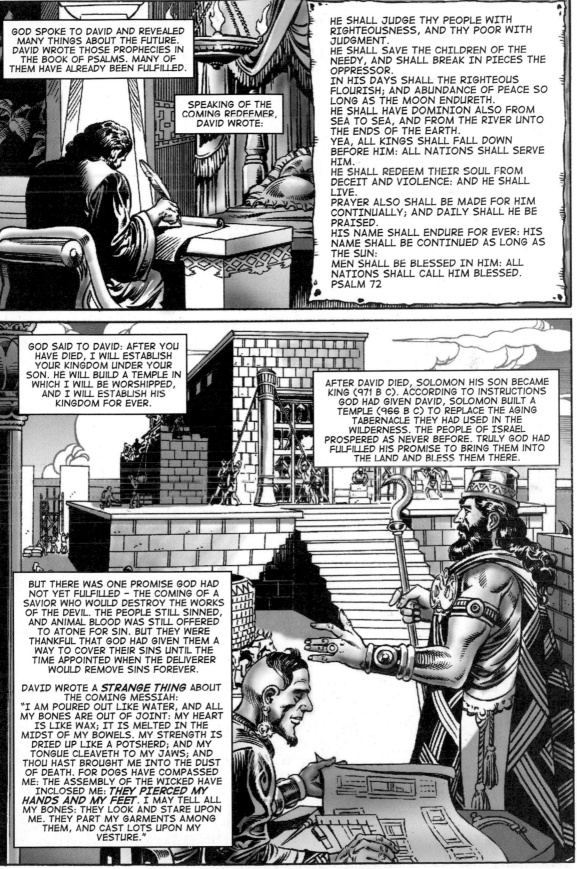

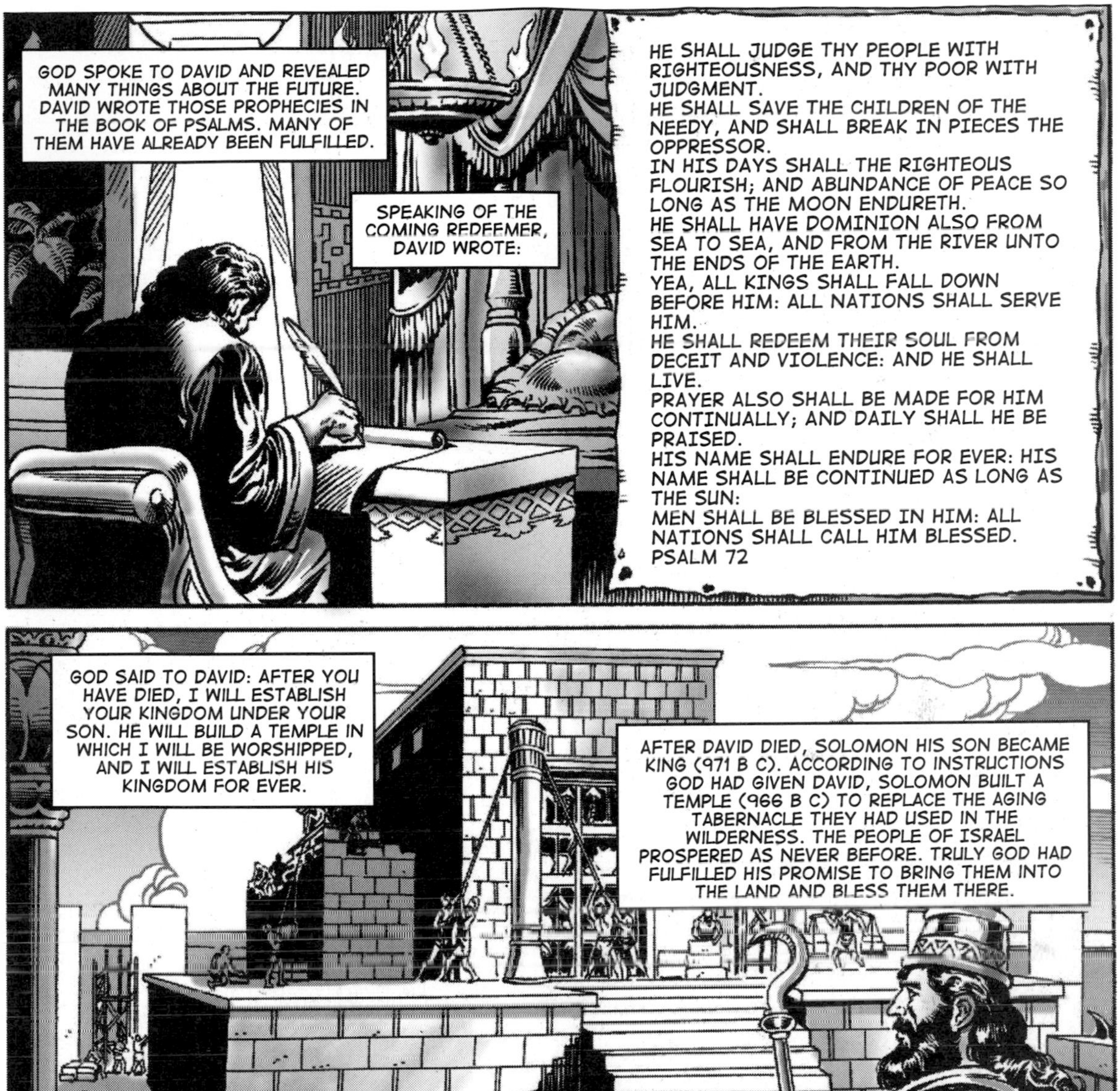
GOD SPOKE TO DAVID AND REVEALED MANY THINGS ABOUT THE FUTURE. DAVID WROTE THOSE PROPHECIES IN THE BOOK OF PSALMS. MANY OF THEM HAVE ALREADY BEEN FULFILLED.
SPEAKING OF THE COMING REDEEMER, DAVID WROTE:
HE SHALL JUDGE THY PEOPLE WITH RIGHTEOUSNESS, AND THY POOR WITH JUDGMENT.
HE SHALL SAVE THE CHILDREN OF THE NEEDY, AND SHALL BREAK IN PIECES THE OPPRESSOR.
IN HIS DAYS SHALL THE RIGHTEOUS FLOURISH; AND ABUNDANCE OF PEACE SO LONG AS THE MOON ENDURETH.
HE SHALL HAVE DOMINION ALSO FROM SEA TO SEA, AND FROM THE RIVER UNTO THE ENDS OF THE EARTH.
YEA, ALL KINGS SHALL FALL DOWN BEFORE HIM: ALL NATIONS SHALL SERVE HIM.
HE SHALL REDEEM THEIR SOUL FROM DECEIT AND VIOLENCE: AND HE SHALL LIVE.
PRAYER ALSO SHALL BE MADE FOR HIM CONTINUALLY; AND DAILY SHALL HE BE PRAISED.
HIS NAME SHALL ENDURE FOR EVER: HIS NAME SHALL BE CONTINUED AS LONG AS THE SUN:
MEN SHALL BE BLESSED IN HIM: ALL NATIONS SHALL CALL HIM BLESSED.
PSALM 72
GOD SAID TO DAVID: AFTER YOU HAVE DIED, I WILL ESTABLISH YOUR KINGDOM UNDER YOUR SON. HE WILL BUILD A TEMPLE IN WHICH I WILL BE WORSHIPPED, AND I WILL ESTABLISH HIS KINGDOM FOR EVER.
AFTER DAVID DIED, SOLOMON HIS SON BECAME KING (971 B C). ACCORDING TO INSTRUCTIONS GOD HAD GIVEN DAVID, SOLOMON BUILT A TEMPLE (966 B C) TO REPLACE THE AGING TABERNACLE THEY HAD USED IN THE WILDERNESS. THE PEOPLE OF ISRAEL PROSPERED AS NEVER BEFORE. TRULY GOD HAD FULFILLED HIS PROMISE TO BRING THEM INTO THE LAND AND BLESS THEM THERE.
BUT THERE WAS ONE PROMISE GOD HAD NOT YET FULFILLED - THE COMING OF A SAVIOR WHO WOULD DESTROY THE WORKS OF THE DEVIL. THE PEOPLE STILL SINNED, AND ANIMAL BLOOD WAS STILL OFFERED TO ATONE FOR SIN. BUT THEY WERE THANKFUL THAT GOD HAD GIVEN THEM A WAY TO COVER THEIR SINS UNTIL THE TIME APPOINTED WHEN THE DELIVERER WOULD REMOVE SINS FOREVER.
DAVID WROTE A ***STRANGE THING*** ABOUT THE COMING MESSIAH:
"I AM POURED OUT LIKE WATER, AND ALL MY BONES ARE OUT OF JOINT: MY HEART IS LIKE WAX; IT IS MELTED IN THE MIDST OF MY BOWELS. MY STRENGTH IS DRIED UP LIKE A POTSHERD; AND MY TONGUE CLEAVETH TO MY JAWS; AND THOU HAST BROUGHT ME INTO THE DUST OF DEATH. FOR DOGS HAVE COMPASSED ME: THE ASSEMBLY OF THE WICKED HAVE INCLOSED ME: ***THEY PIERCED MY HANDS AND MY FEET***. I MAY TELL ALL MY BONES: THEY LOOK AND STARE UPON ME. THEY PART MY GARMENTS AMONG THEM, AND CAST LOTS UPON MY VESTURE."

2 SAMUEL 7:12-16; PSALM 22:14-18, 72:1-20

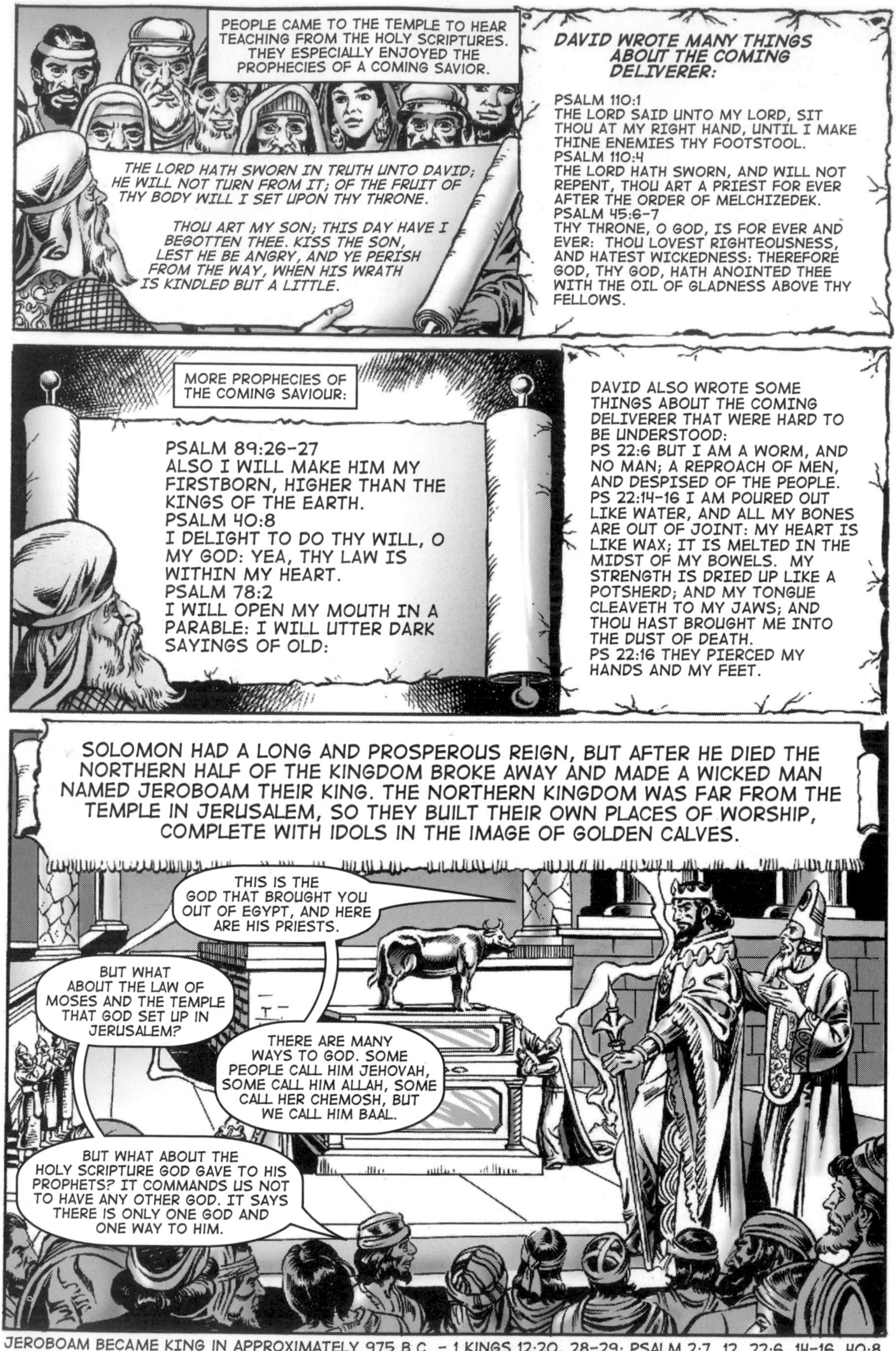
PEOPLE CAME TO THE TEMPLE TO HEAR TEACHING FROM THE HOLY SCRIPTURES. THEY ESPECIALLY ENJOYED THE PROPHECIES OF A COMING SAVIOR.
THE LORD HATH SWORN IN TRUTH UNTO DAVID; HE WILL NOT TURN FROM IT; OF THE FRUIT OF THY BODY WILL I SET UPON THY THRONE.
THOU ART MY SON; THIS DAY HAVE I BEGOTTEN THEE. KISS THE SON, LEST HE BE ANGRY, AND YE PERISH FROM THE WAY, WHEN HIS WRATH IS KINDLED BUT A LITTLE.
DAVID WROTE MANY THINGS ABOUT THE COMING DELIVERER:
PSALM 110:1
THE LORD SAID UNTO MY LORD, SIT THOU AT MY RIGHT HAND, UNTIL I MAKE THINE ENEMIES THY FOOTSTOOL.
PSALM 110:4
THE LORD HATH SWORN, AND WILL NOT REPENT, THOU ART A PRIEST FOR EVER AFTER THE ORDER OF MELCHIZEDEK.
PSALM 45:6-7
THY THRONE, O GOD, IS FOR EVER AND EVER: THOU LOVEST RIGHTEOUSNESS, AND HATEST WICKEDNESS: THEREFORE GOD, THY GOD, HATH ANOINTED THEE WITH THE OIL OF GLADNESS ABOVE THY FELLOWS.
MORE PROPHECIES OF THE COMING SAVIOUR:
PSALM 89:26-27
ALSO I WILL MAKE HIM MY FIRSTBORN, HIGHER THAN THE KINGS OF THE EARTH.
PSALM 40:8
I DELIGHT TO DO THY WILL, O MY GOD: YEA, THY LAW IS WITHIN MY HEART.
PSALM 78:2
I WILL OPEN MY MOUTH IN A PARABLE: I WILL UTTER DARK SAYINGS OF OLD:
DAVID ALSO WROTE SOME THINGS ABOUT THE COMING DELIVERER THAT WERE HARD TO BE UNDERSTOOD:
PS 22:6 BUT I AM A WORM, AND NO MAN; A REPROACH OF MEN, AND DESPISED OF THE PEOPLE.
PS 22:14-16 I AM POURED OUT LIKE WATER, AND ALL MY BONES ARE OUT OF JOINT: MY HEART IS LIKE WAX; IT IS MELTED IN THE MIDST OF MY BOWELS. MY STRENGTH IS DRIED UP LIKE A POTSHERD; AND MY TONGUE CLEAVETH TO MY JAWS; AND THOU HAST BROUGHT ME INTO THE DUST OF DEATH.
PS 22:16 THEY PIERCED MY HANDS AND MY FEET.
SOLOMON HAD A LONG AND PROSPEROUS REIGN, BUT AFTER HE DIED THE NORTHERN HALF OF THE KINGDOM BROKE AWAY AND MADE A WICKED MAN NAMED JEROBOAM THEIR KING. THE NORTHERN KINGDOM WAS FAR FROM THE TEMPLE IN JERUSALEM, SO THEY BUILT THEIR OWN PLACES OF WORSHIP, COMPLETE WITH IDOLS IN THE IMAGE OF GOLDEN CALVES.
THIS IS THE GOD THAT BROUGHT YOU OUT OF EGYPT, AND HERE ARE HIS PRIESTS.
BUT WHAT ABOUT THE LAW OF MOSES AND THE TEMPLE THAT GOD SET UP IN JERUSALEM?
THERE ARE MANY WAYS TO GOD. SOME PEOPLE CALL HIM JEHOVAH, SOME CALL HIM ALLAH, SOME CALL HER CHEMOSH, BUT WE CALL HIM BAAL.
BUT WHAT ABOUT THE HOLY SCRIPTURE GOD GAVE TO HIS PROPHETS? IT COMMANDS US NOT TO HAVE ANY OTHER GOD. IT SAYS THERE IS ONLY ONE GOD AND ONE WAY TO HIM.

JEROBOAM BECAME KING IN APPROXIMATELY 975 B.C. - 1 KINGS 12:20, 28-29; PSALM 2:7, 12, 22:6, 14-16, 40:8, 78:2, 45:6-7, 89:26-27, 110:1, 4, 132:11

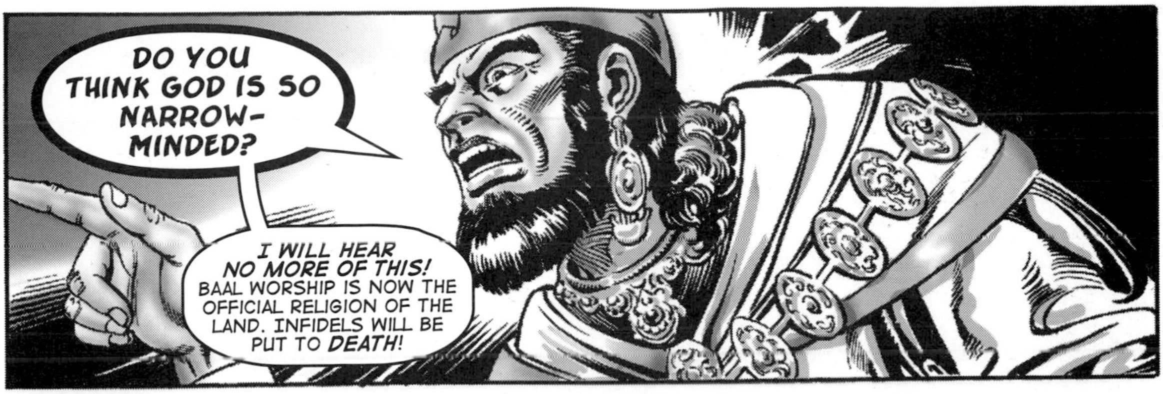
DO YOU THINK GOD IS SO NARROW-MINDED?
I WILL HEAR NO MORE OF THIS! BAAL WORSHIP IS NOW THE OFFICIAL RELIGION OF THE LAND. INFIDELS WILL BE PUT TO DEATH!

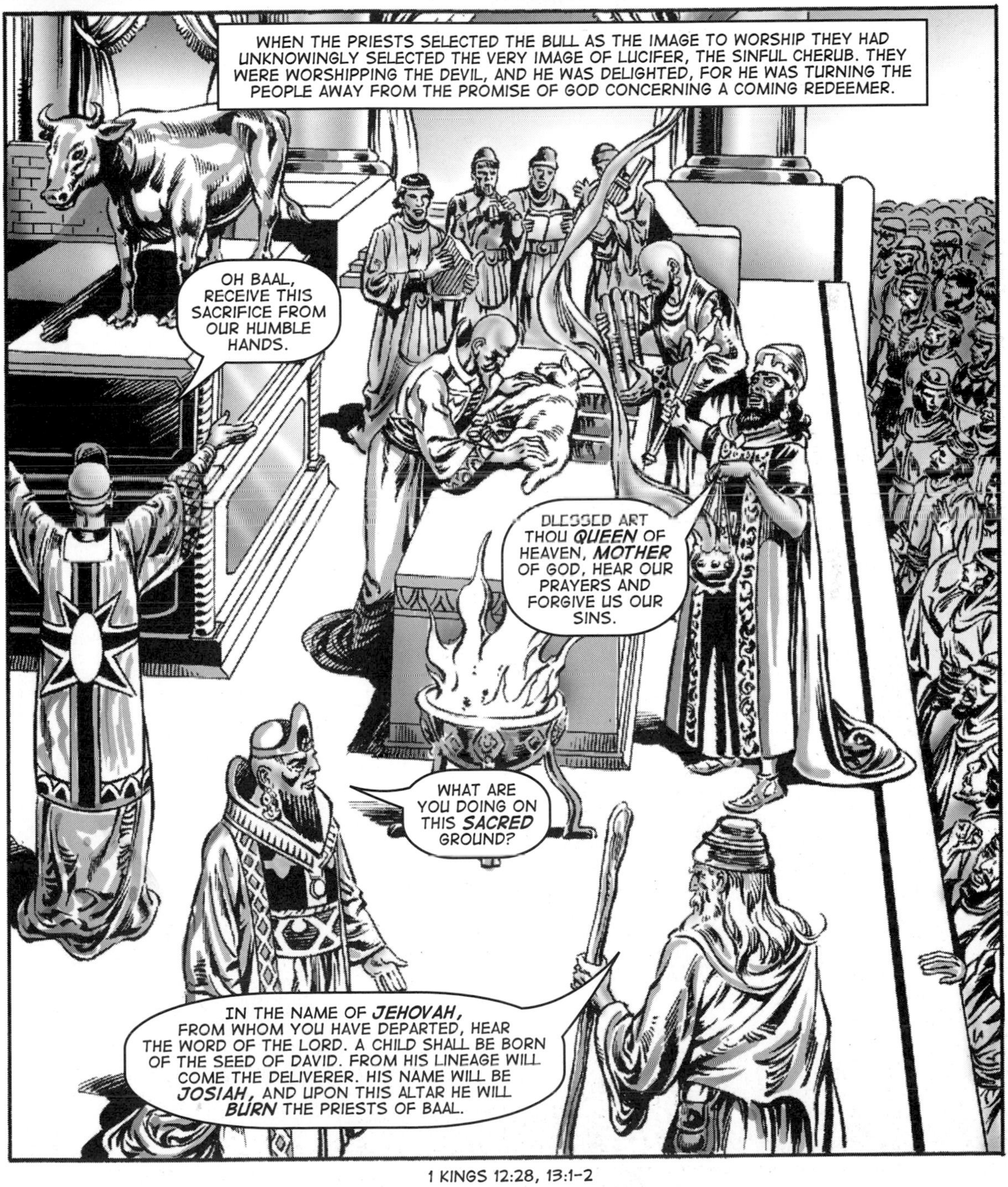
WHEN THE PRIESTS SELECTED THE BULL AS THE IMAGE TO WORSHIP THEY HAD UNKNOWINGLY SELECTED THE VERY IMAGE OF LUCIFER, THE SINFUL CHERUB. THEY WERE WORSHIPPING THE DEVIL, AND HE WAS DELIGHTED, FOR HE WAS TURNING THE PEOPLE AWAY FROM THE PROMISE OF GOD CONCERNING A COMING REDEEMER.
OH BAAL, RECEIVE THIS SACRIFICE FROM OUR HUMBLE HANDS.
BLESSED ART THOU QUEEN OF HEAVEN, MOTHER OF GOD, HEAR OUR PRAYERS AND FORGIVE US OUR SINS.
WHAT ARE YOU DOING ON THIS SACRED GROUND?
IN THE NAME OF JEHOVAH, FROM WHOM YOU HAVE DEPARTED, HEAR THE WORD OF THE LORD. A CHILD SHALL BE BORN OF THE SEED OF DAVID. FROM HIS LINEAGE WILL COME THE DELIVERER. HIS NAME WILL BE JOSIAH, AND UPON THIS ALTAR HE WILL BURN THE PRIESTS OF BAAL.

1 KINGS 12:28, 13:1-2

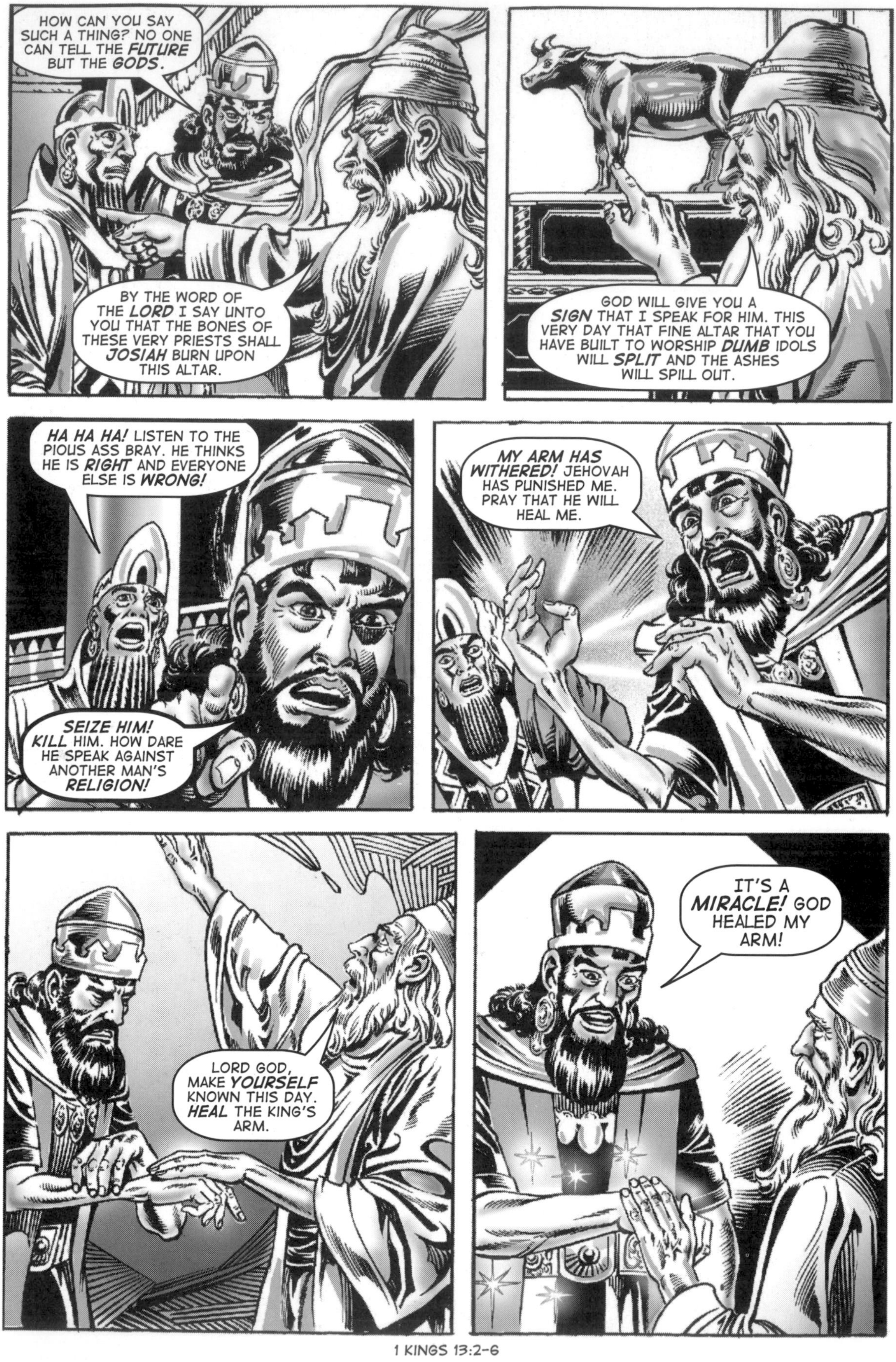
HOW CAN YOU SAY SUCH A THING? NO ONE CAN TELL THE FUTURE BUT THE GODS.
BY THE WORD OF THE LORD I SAY UNTO YOU THAT THE BONES OF THESE VERY PRIESTS SHALL JOSIAH BURN UPON THIS ALTAR.
GOD WILL GIVE YOU A SIGN THAT I SPEAK FOR HIM. THIS VERY DAY THAT FINE ALTAR THAT YOU HAVE BUILT TO WORSHIP DUMB IDOLS WILL SPLIT AND THE ASHES WILL SPILL OUT.
HA HA HA! LISTEN TO THE PIOUS ASS BRAY. HE THINKS HE IS RIGHT AND EVERYONE ELSE IS WRONG!
SEIZE HIM! KILL HIM. HOW DARE HE SPEAK AGAINST ANOTHER MAN'S RELIGION!
MY ARM HAS WITHERED! JEHOVAH HAS PUNISHED ME. PRAY THAT HE WILL HEAL ME.
LORD GOD, MAKE YOURSELF KNOWN THIS DAY. HEAL THE KING'S ARM.
IT'S A MIRACLE! GOD HEALED MY ARM!

1 KINGS 13:2-6

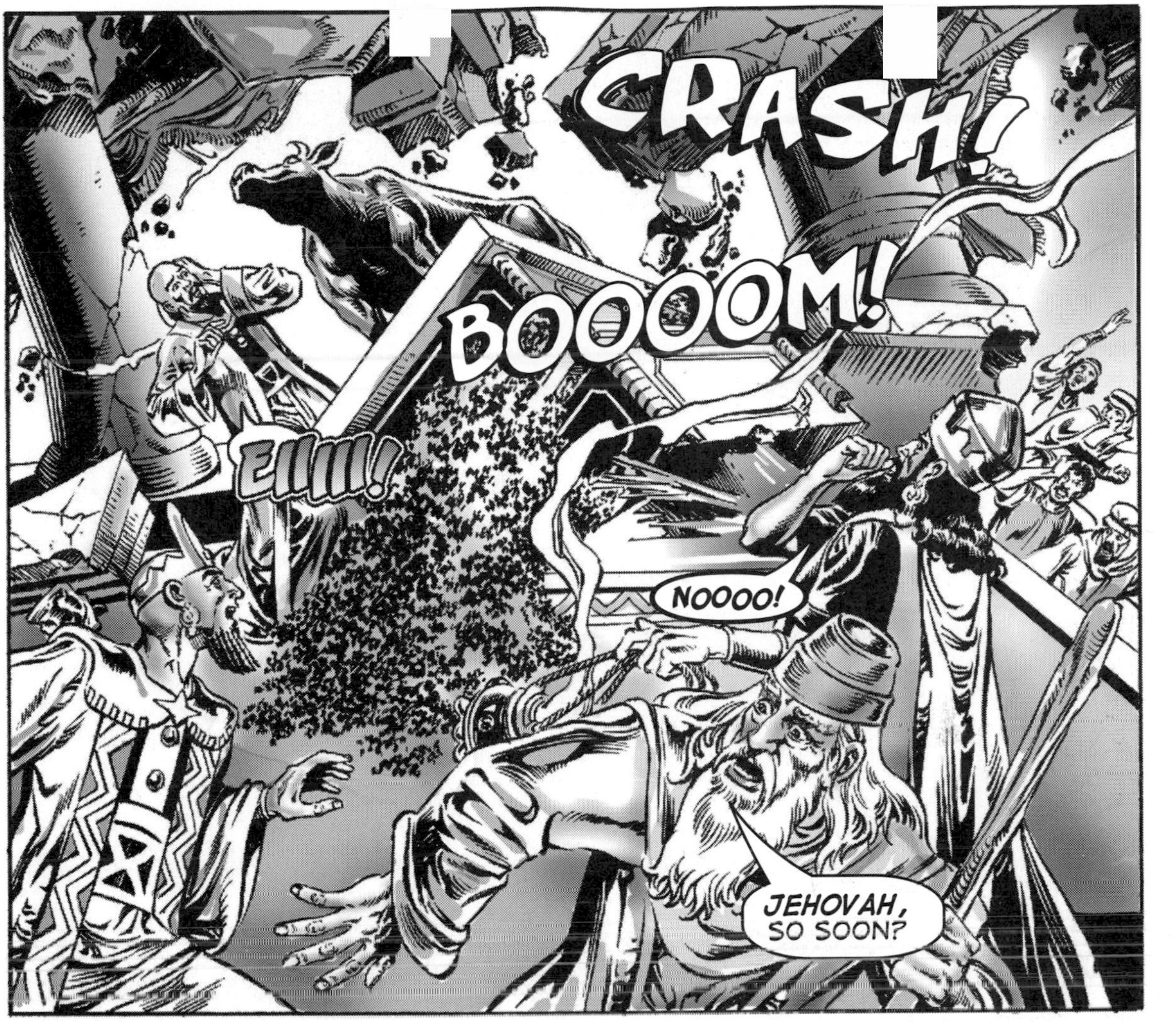
CRASH!
BOOOOM!
EIIIII!
NOOOO!
JEHOVAH, SO SOON?

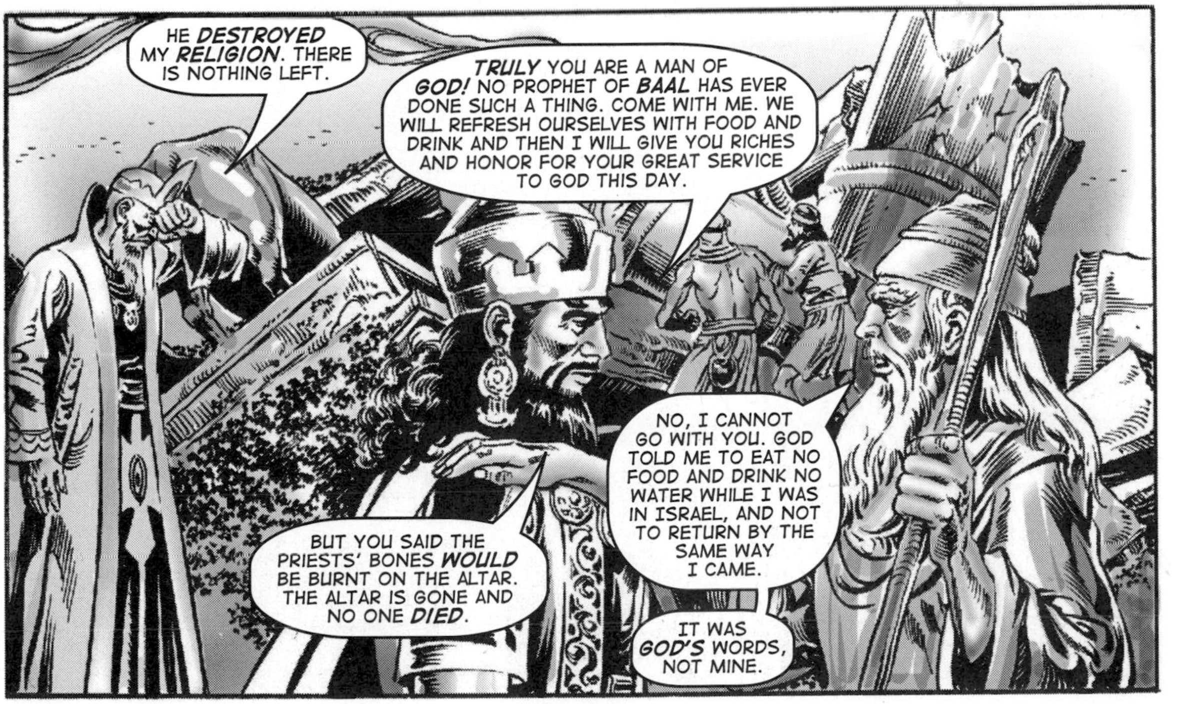
HE DESTROYED MY RELIGION. THERE IS NOTHING LEFT.
TRULY YOU ARE A MAN OF GOD! NO PROPHET OF BAAL HAS EVER DONE SUCH A THING. COME WITH ME. WE WILL REFRESH OURSELVES WITH FOOD AND DRINK AND THEN I WILL GIVE YOU RICHES AND HONOR FOR YOUR GREAT SERVICE TO GOD THIS DAY.
NO, I CANNOT GO WITH YOU. GOD TOLD ME TO EAT NO FOOD AND DRINK NO WATER WHILE I WAS IN ISRAEL, AND NOT TO RETURN BY THE SAME WAY I CAME.
BUT YOU SAID THE PRIESTS' BONES WOULD BE BURNT ON THE ALTAR. THE ALTAR IS GONE AND NO ONE DIED.
IT WAS GOD'S WORDS, NOT MINE.

1 KINGS 13:5, 7–9

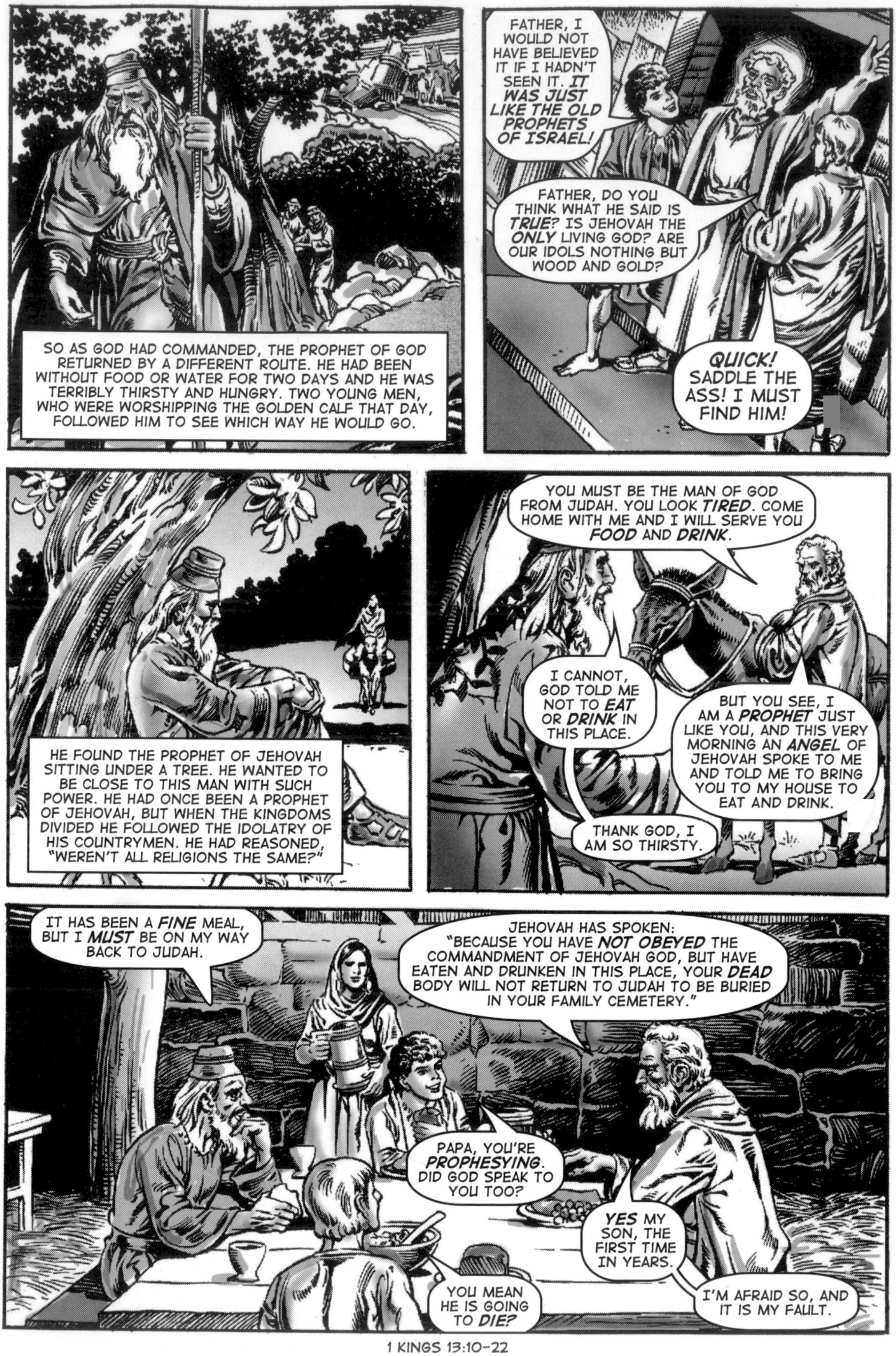
SO AS GOD HAD COMMANDED, THE PROPHET OF GOD RETURNED BY A DIFFERENT ROUTE. HE HAD BEEN WITHOUT FOOD OR WATER FOR TWO DAYS AND HE WAS TERRIBLY THIRSTY AND HUNGRY. TWO YOUNG MEN, WHO WERE WORSHIPPING THE GOLDEN CALF THAT DAY, FOLLOWED HIM TO SEE WHICH WAY HE WOULD GO.
FATHER, I WOULD NOT HAVE BELIEVED IT IF I HADN'T SEEN IT. IT WAS JUST LIKE THE OLD PROPHETS OF ISRAEL!
FATHER, DO YOU THINK WHAT HE SAID IS TRUE? IS JEHOVAH THE ONLY LIVING GOD? ARE OUR IDOLS NOTHING BUT WOOD AND GOLD?
QUICK! SADDLE THE ASS! I MUST FIND HIM!
HE FOUND THE PROPHET OF JEHOVAH SITTING UNDER A TREE. HE WANTED TO BE CLOSE TO THIS MAN WITH SUCH POWER. HE HAD ONCE BEEN A PROPHET OF JEHOVAH, BUT WHEN THE KINGDOMS DIVIDED HE FOLLOWED THE IDOLATRY OF HIS COUNTRYMEN. HE HAD REASONED, "WEREN'T ALL RELIGIONS THE SAME?"
YOU MUST BE THE MAN OF GOD FROM JUDAH. YOU LOOK TIRED. COME HOME WITH ME AND I WILL SERVE YOU FOOD AND DRINK.
I CANNOT, GOD TOLD ME NOT TO EAT OR DRINK IN THIS PLACE.
BUT YOU SEE, I AM A PROPHET JUST LIKE YOU, AND THIS VERY MORNING AN ANGEL OF JEHOVAH SPOKE TO ME AND TOLD ME TO BRING YOU TO MY HOUSE TO EAT AND DRINK.
THANK GOD, I AM SO THIRSTY.
IT HAS BEEN A FINE MEAL, BUT I MUST BE ON MY WAY BACK TO JUDAH.
JEHOVAH HAS SPOKEN: "BECAUSE YOU HAVE NOT OBEYED THE COMMANDMENT OF JEHOVAH GOD, BUT HAVE EATEN AND DRUNKEN IN THIS PLACE, YOUR DEAD BODY WILL NOT RETURN TO JUDAH TO BE BURIED IN YOUR FAMILY CEMETERY."
PAPA, YOU'RE PROPHESYING. DID GOD SPEAK TO YOU TOO?
YES MY SON, THE FIRST TIME IN YEARS.
YOU MEAN HE IS GOING TO DIE?
I'M AFRAID SO, AND IT IS MY FAULT.

1 KINGS 13:10-22

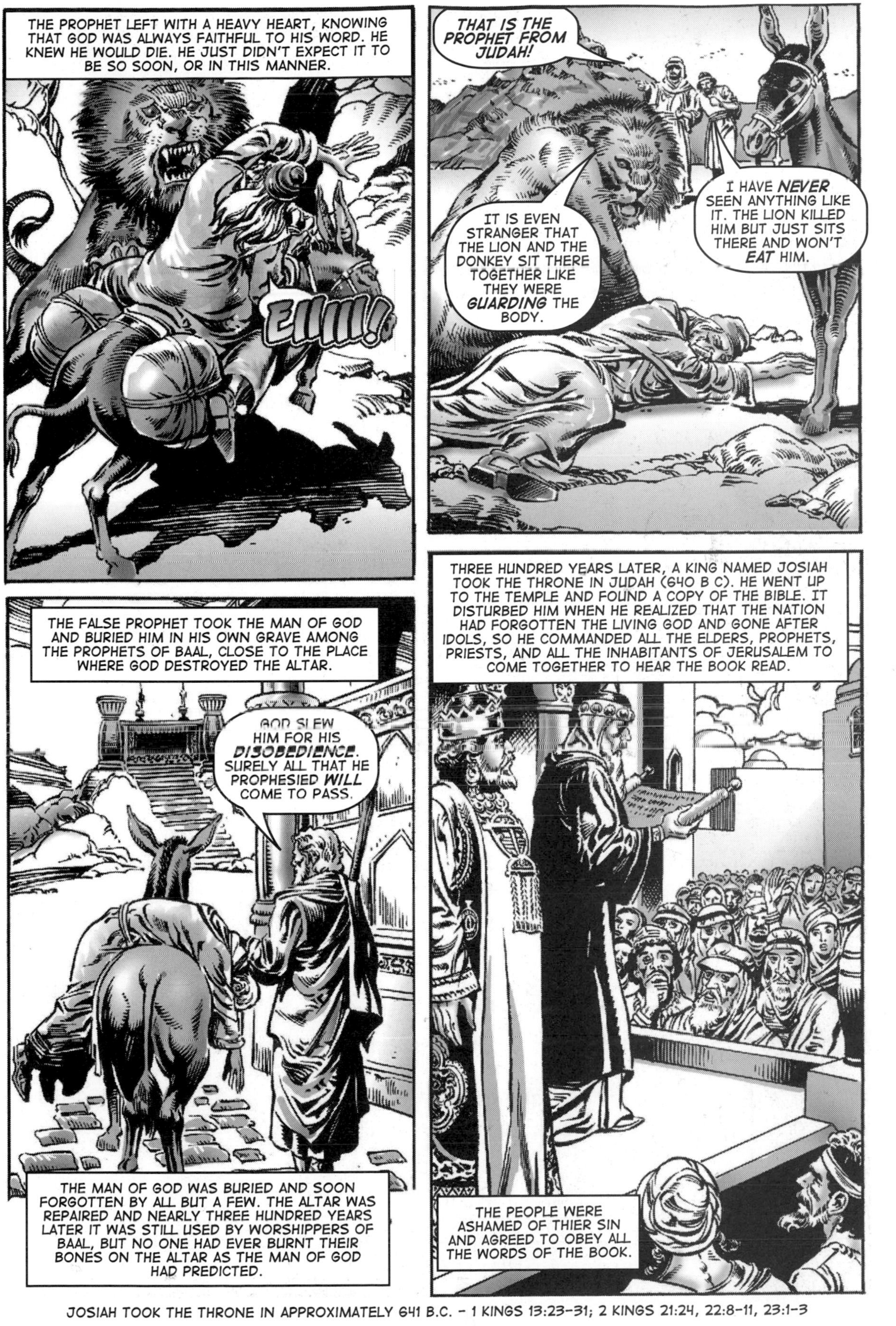
THE PROPHET LEFT WITH A HEAVY HEART, KNOWING THAT GOD WAS ALWAYS FAITHFUL TO HIS WORD. HE KNEW HE WOULD DIE. HE JUST DIDN'T EXPECT IT TO BE SO SOON, OR IN THIS MANNER.
EIIIII!
THAT IS THE PROPHET FROM JUDAH!
IT IS EVEN STRANGER THAT THE LION AND THE DONKEY SIT THERE TOGETHER LIKE THEY WERE GUARDING THE BODY.
I HAVE NEVER SEEN ANYTHING LIKE IT. THE LION KILLED HIM BUT JUST SITS THERE AND WON'T EAT HIM.
THE FALSE PROPHET TOOK THE MAN OF GOD AND BURIED HIM IN HIS OWN GRAVE AMONG THE PROPHETS OF BAAL, CLOSE TO THE PLACE WHERE GOD DESTROYED THE ALTAR.
GOD SLEW HIM FOR HIS DISOBEDIENCE. SURELY ALL THAT HE PROPHESIED WILL COME TO PASS.
THE MAN OF GOD WAS BURIED AND SOON FORGOTTEN BY ALL BUT A FEW. THE ALTAR WAS REPAIRED AND NEARLY THREE HUNDRED YEARS LATER IT WAS STILL USED BY WORSHIPPERS OF BAAL, BUT NO ONE HAD EVER BURNT THEIR BONES ON THE ALTAR AS THE MAN OF GOD HAD PREDICTED.
THREE HUNDRED YEARS LATER, A KING NAMED JOSIAH TOOK THE THRONE IN JUDAH (640 B C). HE WENT UP TO THE TEMPLE AND FOUND A COPY OF THE BIBLE. IT DISTURBED HIM WHEN HE REALIZED THAT THE NATION HAD FORGOTTEN THE LIVING GOD AND GONE AFTER IDOLS, SO HE COMMANDED ALL THE ELDERS, PROPHETS, PRIESTS, AND ALL THE INHABITANTS OF JERUSALEM TO COME TOGETHER TO HEAR THE BOOK READ.
THE PEOPLE WERE ASHAMED OF THIER SIN AND AGREED TO OBEY ALL THE WORDS OF THE BOOK.

JOSIAH TOOK THE THRONE IN APPROXIMATELY 641 B.C. - 1 KINGS 13:23-31; 2 KINGS 21:24, 22:8-11, 23:1-3

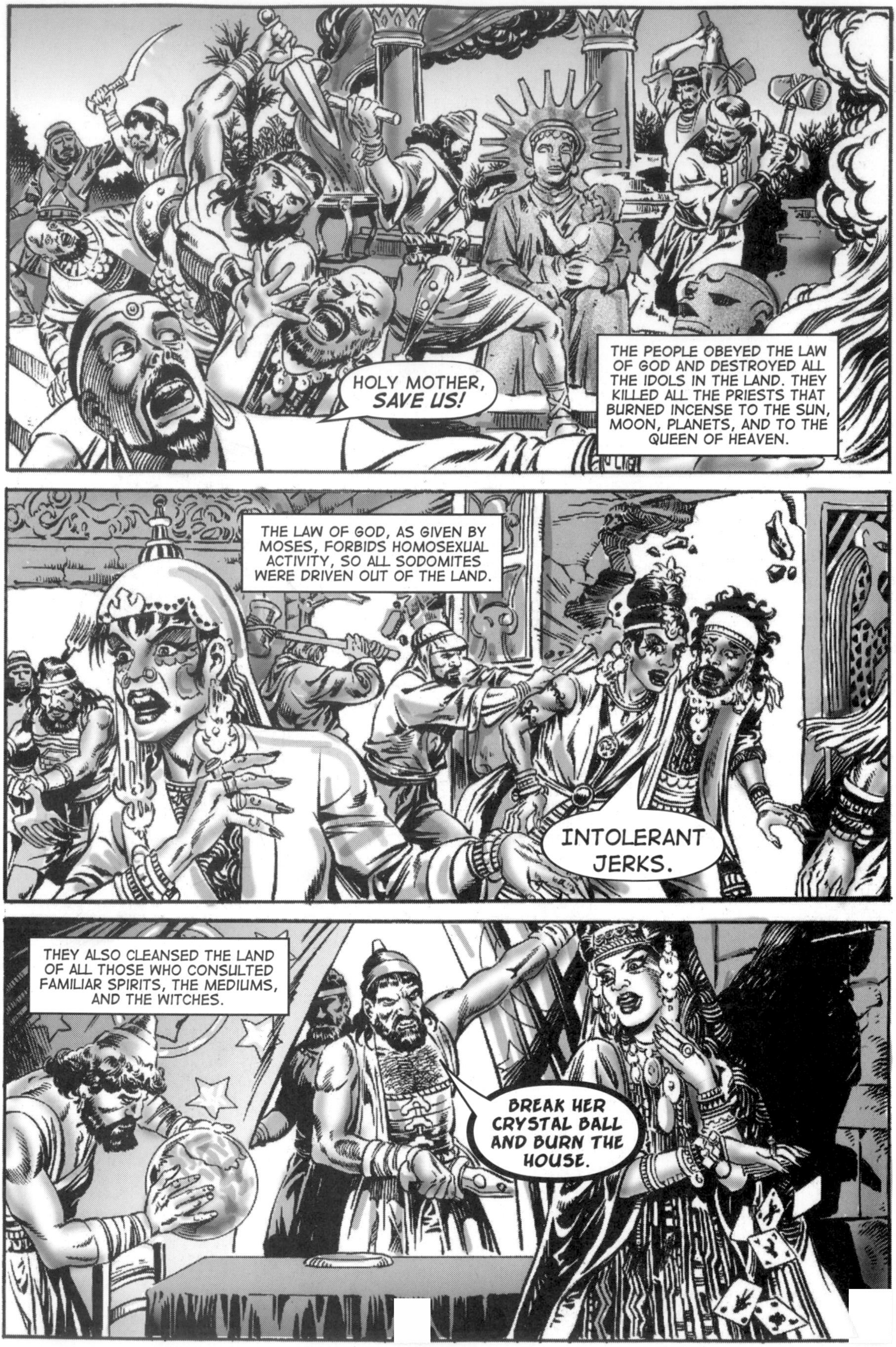
HOLY MOTHER, SAVE US!
THE PEOPLE OBEYED THE LAW OF GOD AND DESTROYED ALL THE IDOLS IN THE LAND. THEY KILLED ALL THE PRIESTS THAT BURNED INCENSE TO THE SUN, MOON, PLANETS, AND TO THE QUEEN OF HEAVEN.
THE LAW OF GOD, AS GIVEN BY MOSES, FORBIDS HOMOSEXUAL ACTIVITY, SO ALL SODOMITES WERE DRIVEN OUT OF THE LAND.
INTOLERANT JERKS.
THEY ALSO CLEANSED THE LAND OF ALL THOSE WHO CONSULTED FAMILIAR SPIRITS, THE MEDIUMS, AND THE WITCHES.
BREAK HER CRYSTAL BALL AND BURN THE HOUSE.

2 KINGS 23:5, 7, 10

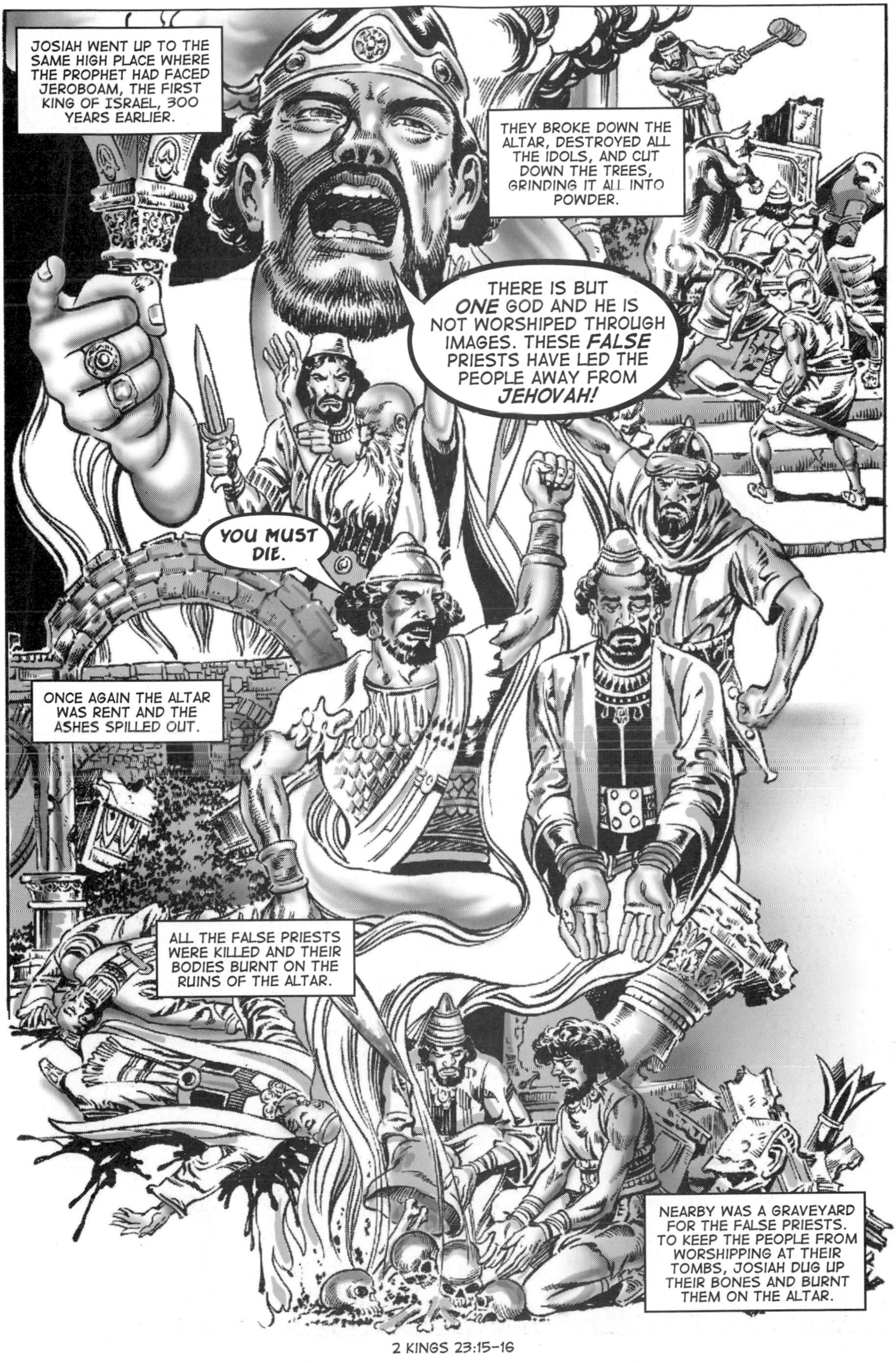
JOSIAH WENT UP TO THE SAME HIGH PLACE WHERE THE PROPHET HAD FACED JEROBOAM, THE FIRST KING OF ISRAEL, 300 YEARS EARLIER.
THEY BROKE DOWN THE ALTAR, DESTROYED ALL THE IDOLS, AND CUT DOWN THE TREES, GRINDING IT ALL INTO POWDER.
THERE IS BUT ONE GOD AND HE IS NOT WORSHIPED THROUGH IMAGES. THESE FALSE PRIESTS HAVE LED THE PEOPLE AWAY FROM JEHOVAH!
YOU MUST DIE.
ONCE AGAIN THE ALTAR WAS RENT AND THE ASHES SPILLED OUT.
ALL THE FALSE PRIESTS WERE KILLED AND THEIR BODIES BURNT ON THE RUINS OF THE ALTAR.
NEARBY WAS A GRAVEYARD FOR THE FALSE PRIESTS. TO KEEP THE PEOPLE FROM WORSHIPPING AT THEIR TOMBS, JOSIAH DUG UP THEIR BONES AND BURNT THEM ON THE ALTAR.

2 KINGS 23:15-16

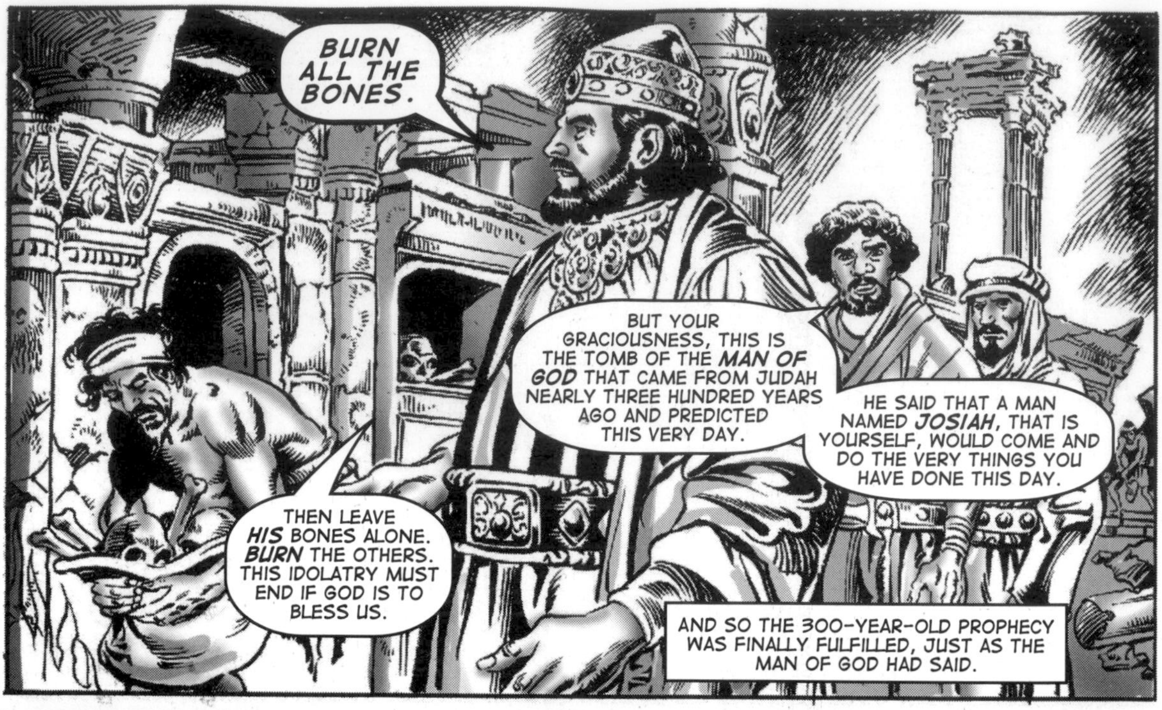
BURN ALL THE BONES.
BUT YOUR GRACIOUSNESS, THIS IS THE TOMB OF THE MAN OF GOD THAT CAME FROM JUDAH NEARLY THREE HUNDRED YEARS AGO AND PREDICTED THIS VERY DAY.
HE SAID THAT A MAN NAMED JOSIAH, THAT IS YOURSELF, WOULD COME AND DO THE VERY THINGS YOU HAVE DONE THIS DAY.
THEN LEAVE HIS BONES ALONE. BURN THE OTHERS. THIS IDOLATRY MUST END IF GOD IS TO BLESS US.
AND SO THE 300-YEAR-OLD PROPHECY WAS FINALLY FULFILLED, JUST AS THE MAN OF GOD HAD SAID.

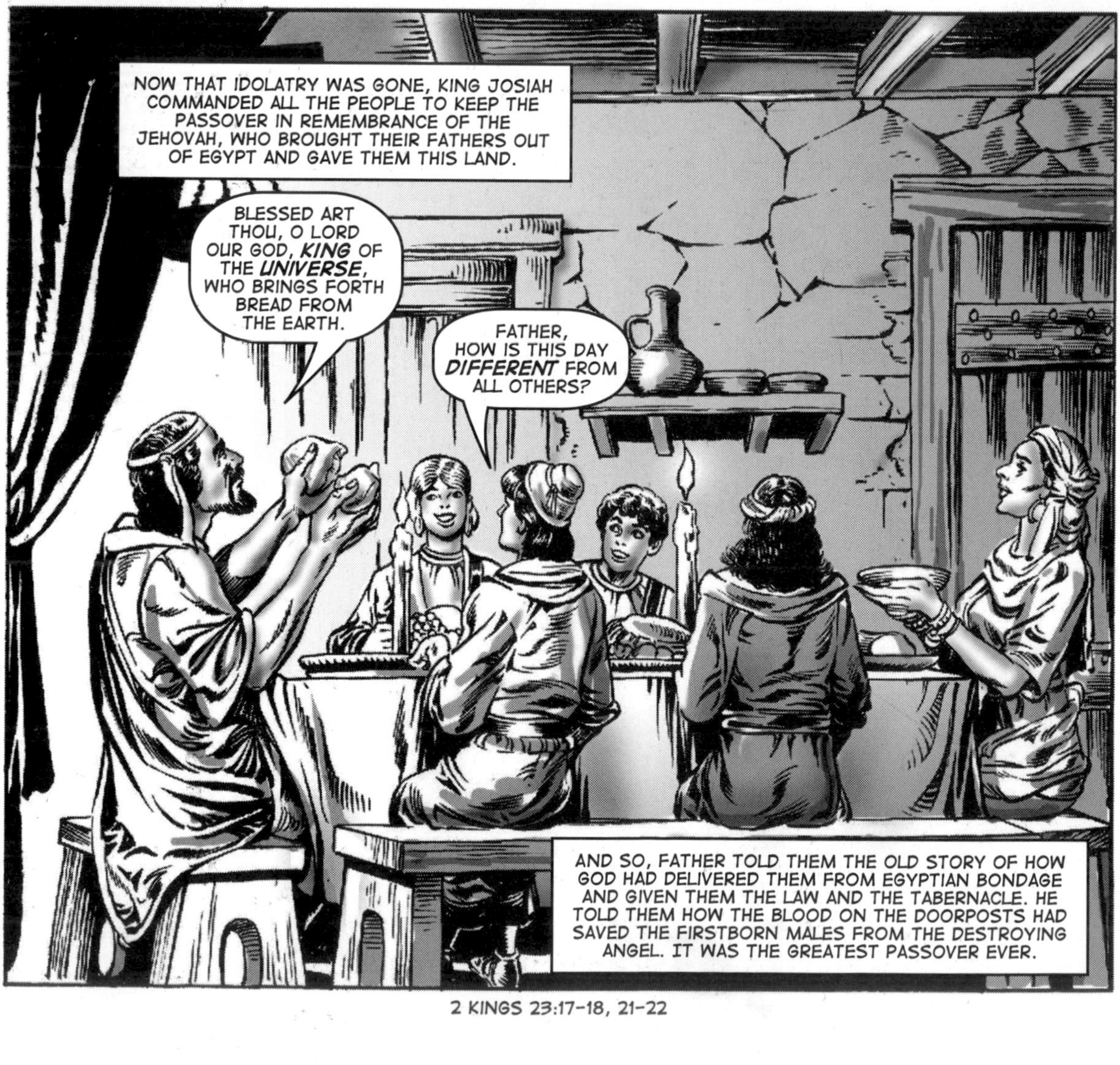
NOW THAT IDOLATRY WAS GONE, KING JOSIAH COMMANDED ALL THE PEOPLE TO KEEP THE PASSOVER IN REMEMBRANCE OF THE JEHOVAH, WHO BROUGHT THEIR FATHERS OUT OF EGYPT AND GAVE THEM THIS LAND.
BLESSED ART THOU, O LORD OUR GOD, KING OF THE UNIVERSE, WHO BRINGS FORTH BREAD FROM THE EARTH.
FATHER, HOW IS THIS DAY DIFFERENT FROM ALL OTHERS?
AND SO, FATHER TOLD THEM THE OLD STORY OF HOW GOD HAD DELIVERED THEM FROM EGYPTIAN BONDAGE AND GIVEN THEM THE LAW AND THE TABERNACLE. HE TOLD THEM HOW THE BLOOD ON THE DOORPOSTS HAD SAVED THE FIRSTBORN MALES FROM THE DESTROYING ANGEL. IT WAS THE GREATEST PASSOVER EVER.

2 KINGS 23:17-18, 21-22

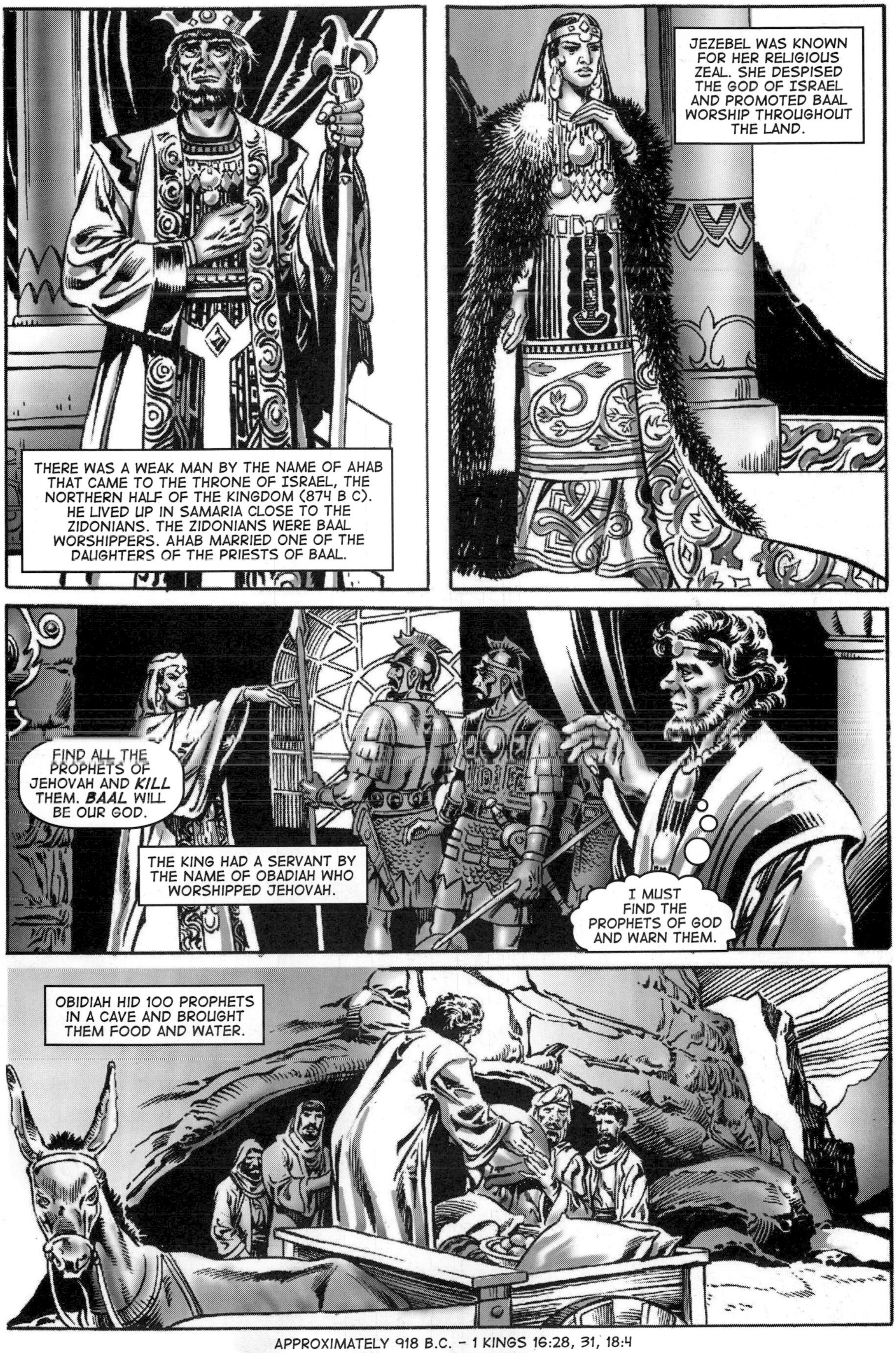
THERE WAS A WEAK MAN BY THE NAME OF AHAB THAT CAME TO THE THRONE OF ISRAEL, THE NORTHERN HALF OF THE KINGDOM (874 B C). HE LIVED UP IN SAMARIA CLOSE TO THE ZIDONIANS. THE ZIDONIANS WERE BAAL WORSHIPPERS. AHAB MARRIED ONE OF THE DAUGHTERS OF THE PRIESTS OF BAAL.
JEZEBEL WAS KNOWN FOR HER RELIGIOUS ZEAL. SHE DESPISED THE GOD OF ISRAEL AND PROMOTED BAAL WORSHIP THROUGHOUT THE LAND.
FIND ALL THE PROPHETS OF JEHOVAH AND *KILL* THEM. *BAAL* WILL BE OUR GOD.
THE KING HAD A SERVANT BY THE NAME OF OBADIAH WHO WORSHIPPED JEHOVAH.
I MUST FIND THE PROPHETS OF GOD AND WARN THEM.
OBIDIAH HID 100 PROPHETS IN A CAVE AND BROUGHT THEM FOOD AND WATER.

APPROXIMATELY 918 B.C. - 1 KINGS 16:28, 31, 18:4

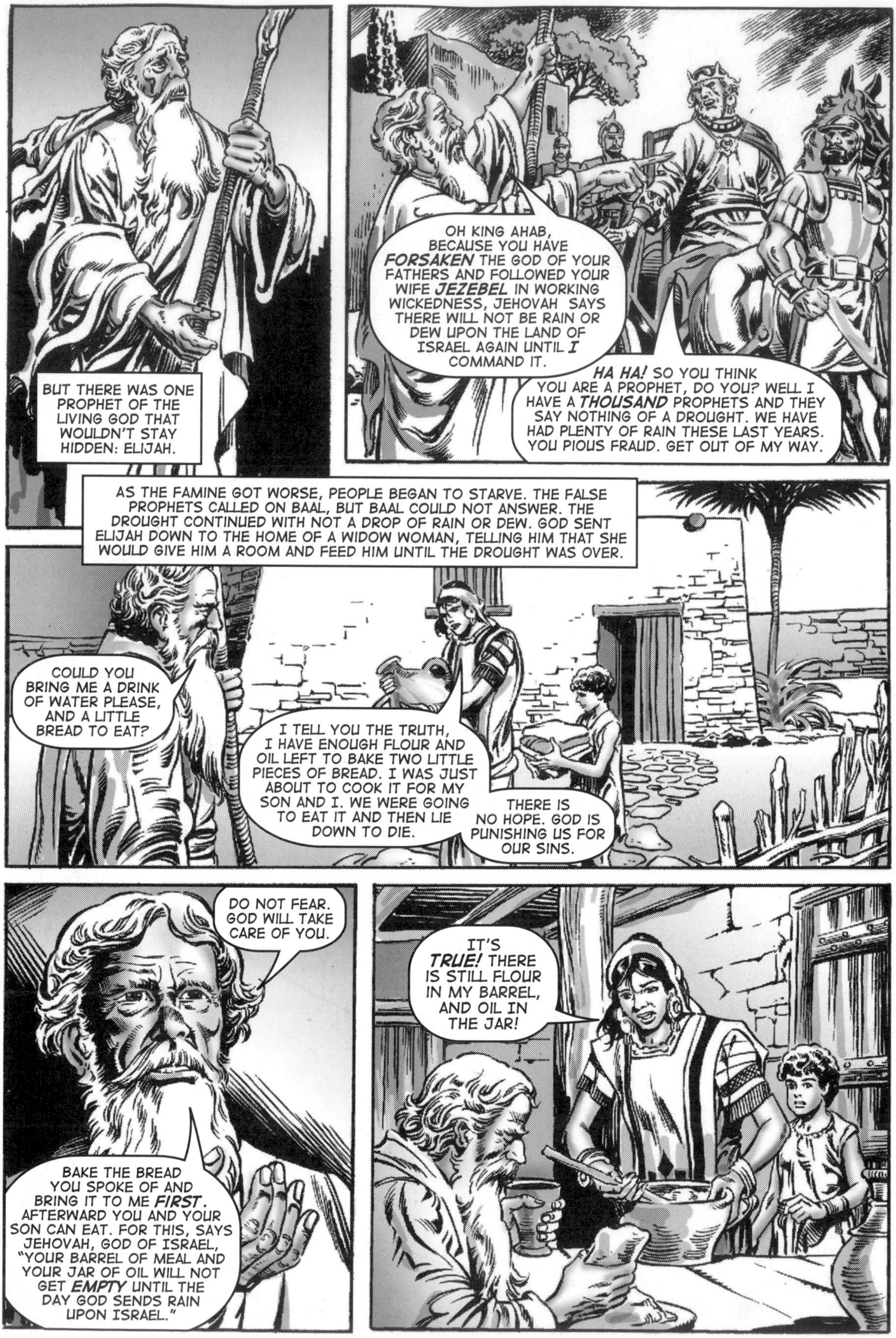
BUT THERE WAS ONE PROPHET OF THE LIVING GOD THAT WOULDN'T STAY HIDDEN: ELIJAH.
OH KING AHAB, BECAUSE YOU HAVE FORSAKEN THE GOD OF YOUR FATHERS AND FOLLOWED YOUR WIFE JEZEBEL IN WORKING WICKEDNESS, JEHOVAH SAYS THERE WILL NOT BE RAIN OR DEW UPON THE LAND OF ISRAEL AGAIN UNTIL I COMMAND IT.
HA HA! SO YOU THINK YOU ARE A PROPHET, DO YOU? WELL I HAVE A THOUSAND PROPHETS AND THEY SAY NOTHING OF A DROUGHT. WE HAVE HAD PLENTY OF RAIN THESE LAST YEARS. YOU PIOUS FRAUD. GET OUT OF MY WAY.
AS THE FAMINE GOT WORSE, PEOPLE BEGAN TO STARVE. THE FALSE PROPHETS CALLED ON BAAL, BUT BAAL COULD NOT ANSWER. THE DROUGHT CONTINUED WITH NOT A DROP OF RAIN OR DEW. GOD SENT ELIJAH DOWN TO THE HOME OF A WIDOW WOMAN, TELLING HIM THAT SHE WOULD GIVE HIM A ROOM AND FEED HIM UNTIL THE DROUGHT WAS OVER.
COULD YOU BRING ME A DRINK OF WATER PLEASE, AND A LITTLE BREAD TO EAT?
I TELL YOU THE TRUTH, I HAVE ENOUGH FLOUR AND OIL LEFT TO BAKE TWO LITTLE PIECES OF BREAD. I WAS JUST ABOUT TO COOK IT FOR MY SON AND I. WE WERE GOING TO EAT IT AND THEN LIE DOWN TO DIE.
THERE IS NO HOPE. GOD IS PUNISHING US FOR OUR SINS.
DO NOT FEAR. GOD WILL TAKE CARE OF YOU.
BAKE THE BREAD YOU SPOKE OF AND BRING IT TO ME FIRST. AFTERWARD YOU AND YOUR SON CAN EAT. FOR THIS, SAYS JEHOVAH, GOD OF ISRAEL, "YOUR BARREL OF MEAL AND YOUR JAR OF OIL WILL NOT GET EMPTY UNTIL THE DAY GOD SENDS RAIN UPON ISRAEL."
IT'S TRUE! THERE IS STILL FLOUR IN MY BARREL, AND OIL IN THE JAR!

1 KINGS 17:1, 10–16

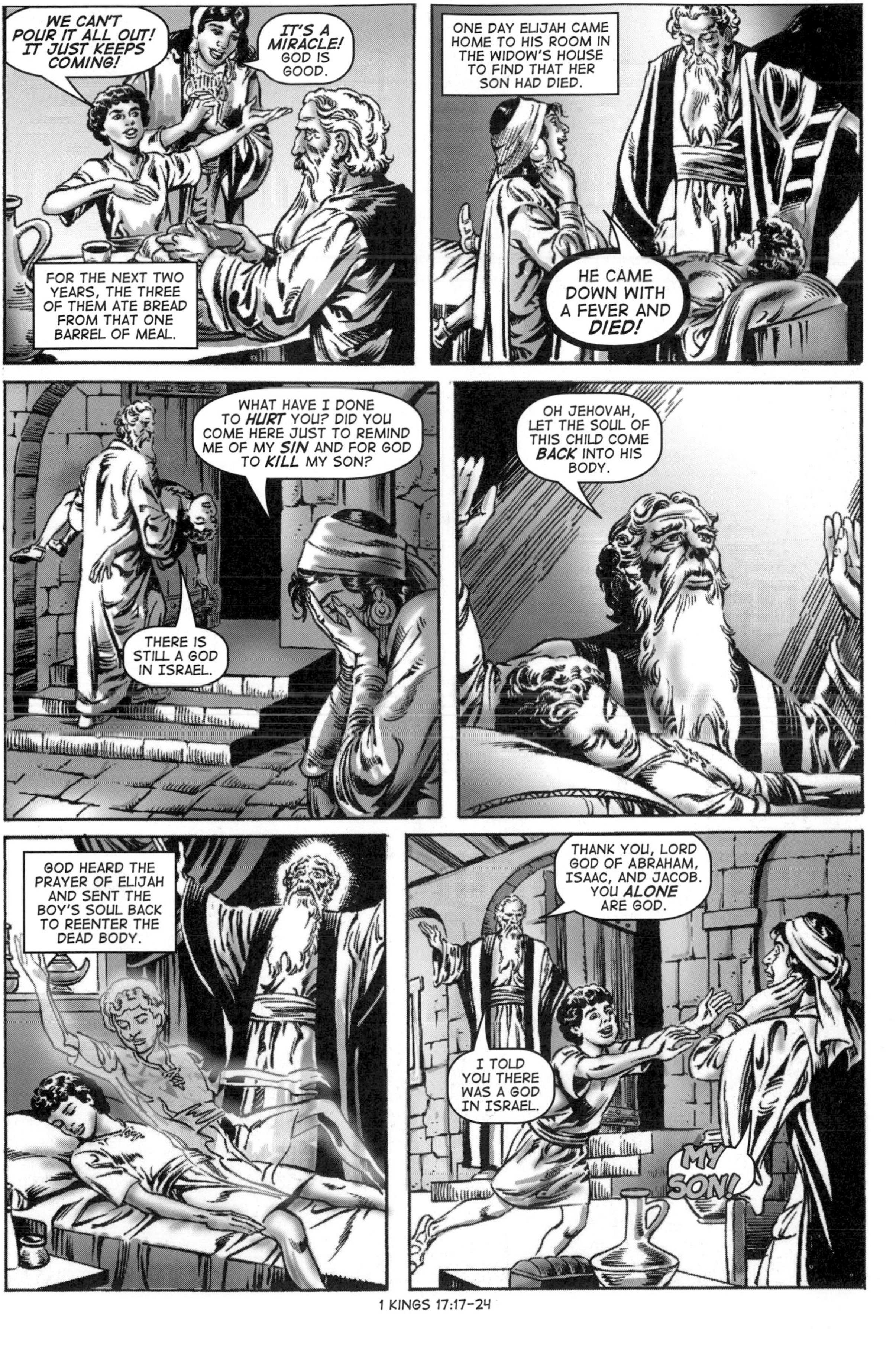
WE CAN'T POUR IT ALL OUT! IT JUST KEEPS COMING!
IT'S A MIRACLE! GOD IS GOOD.
FOR THE NEXT TWO YEARS, THE THREE OF THEM ATE BREAD FROM THAT ONE BARREL OF MEAL.
ONE DAY ELIJAH CAME HOME TO HIS ROOM IN THE WIDOW'S HOUSE TO FIND THAT HER SON HAD DIED.
HE CAME DOWN WITH A FEVER AND DIED!
WHAT HAVE I DONE TO HURT YOU? DID YOU COME HERE JUST TO REMIND ME OF MY SIN AND FOR GOD TO KILL MY SON?
THERE IS STILL A GOD IN ISRAEL.
OH JEHOVAH, LET THE SOUL OF THIS CHILD COME BACK INTO HIS BODY.
GOD HEARD THE PRAYER OF ELIJAH AND SENT THE BOY'S SOUL BACK TO REENTER THE DEAD BODY.
THANK YOU, LORD GOD OF ABRAHAM, ISAAC, AND JACOB. YOU ALONE ARE GOD.
I TOLD YOU THERE WAS A GOD IN ISRAEL.
MY SON!

1 KINGS 17:17–24

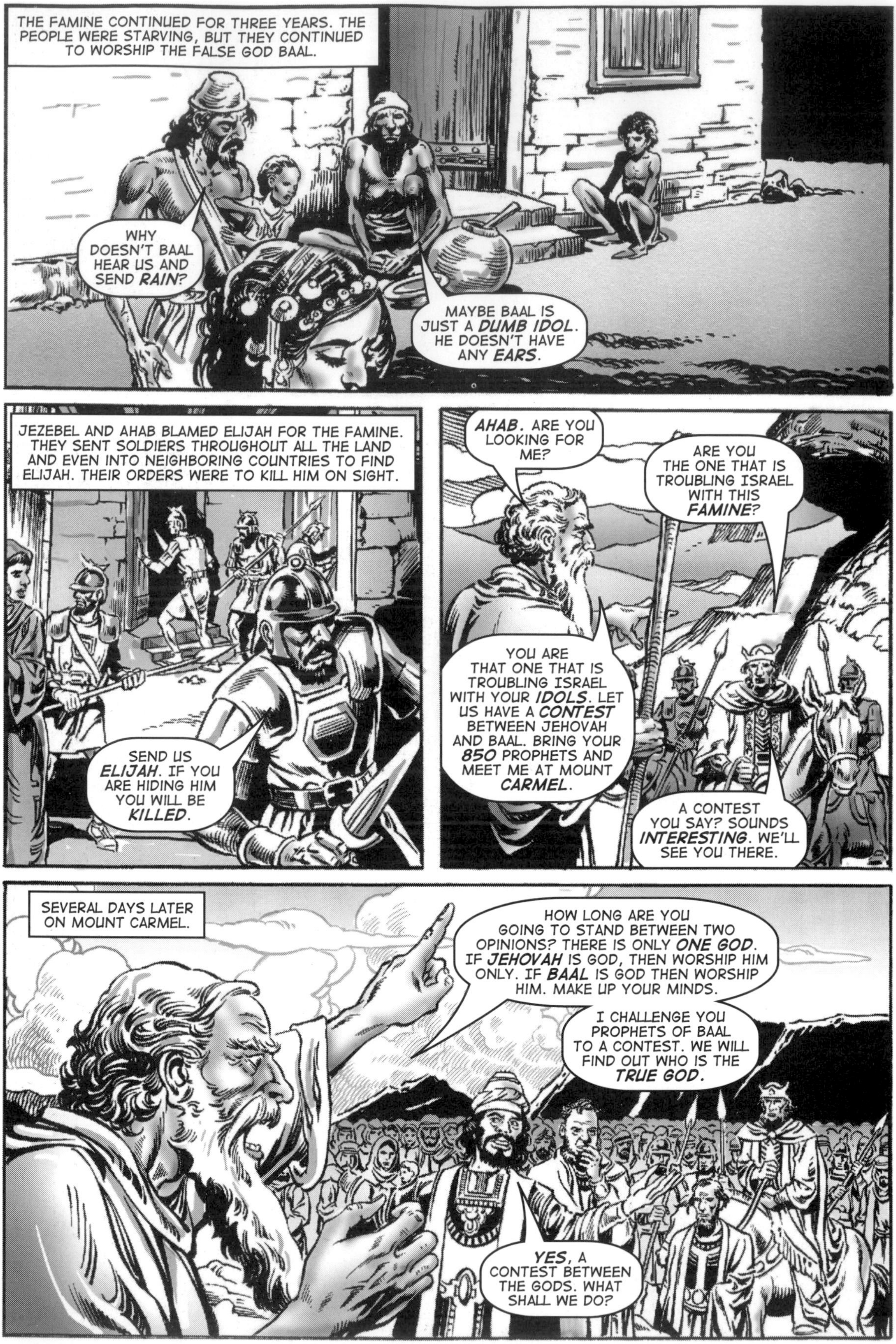
THE FAMINE CONTINUED FOR THREE YEARS. THE PEOPLE WERE STARVING, BUT THEY CONTINUED TO WORSHIP THE FALSE GOD BAAL.
WHY DOESN'T BAAL HEAR US AND SEND RAIN?
MAYBE BAAL IS JUST A DUMB IDOL. HE DOESN'T HAVE ANY EARS.
JEZEBEL AND AHAB BLAMED ELIJAH FOR THE FAMINE. THEY SENT SOLDIERS THROUGHOUT ALL THE LAND AND EVEN INTO NEIGHBORING COUNTRIES TO FIND ELIJAH. THEIR ORDERS WERE TO KILL HIM ON SIGHT.
SEND US ELIJAH. IF YOU ARE HIDING HIM YOU WILL BE KILLED.
AHAB. ARE YOU LOOKING FOR ME?
ARE YOU THE ONE THAT IS TROUBLING ISRAEL WITH THIS FAMINE?
YOU ARE THAT ONE THAT IS TROUBLING ISRAEL WITH YOUR IDOLS. LET US HAVE A CONTEST BETWEEN JEHOVAH AND BAAL. BRING YOUR 850 PROPHETS AND MEET ME AT MOUNT CARMEL.
A CONTEST YOU SAY? SOUNDS INTERESTING. WE'LL SEE YOU THERE.
SEVERAL DAYS LATER ON MOUNT CARMEL.
HOW LONG ARE YOU GOING TO STAND BETWEEN TWO OPINIONS? THERE IS ONLY ONE GOD. IF JEHOVAH IS GOD, THEN WORSHIP HIM ONLY. IF BAAL IS GOD THEN WORSHIP HIM. MAKE UP YOUR MINDS.
I CHALLENGE YOU PROPHETS OF BAAL TO A CONTEST. WE WILL FIND OUT WHO IS THE TRUE GOD.
YES, A CONTEST BETWEEN THE GODS. WHAT SHALL WE DO?

1 KINGS 18:1, 4 17-21

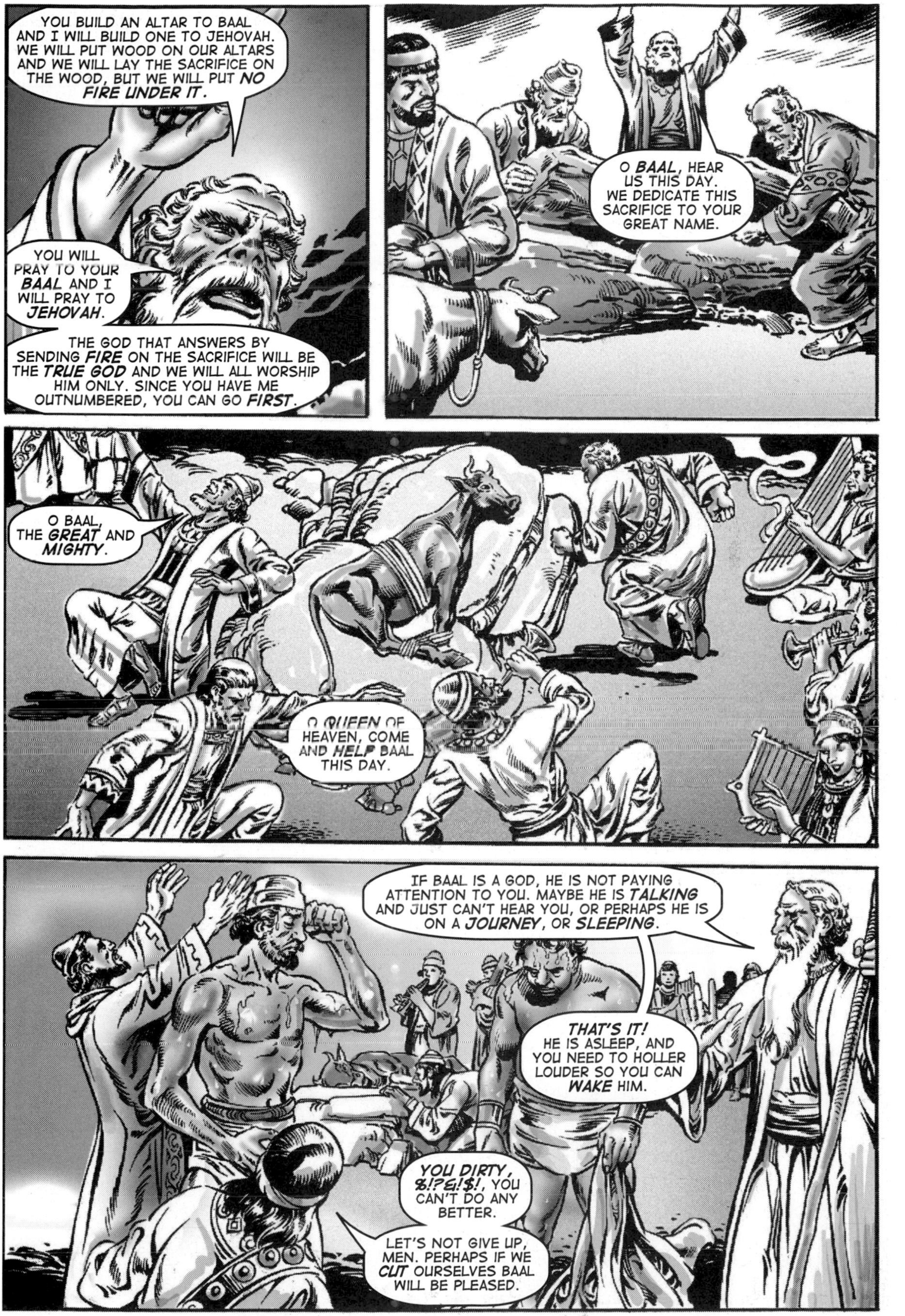
YOU BUILD AN ALTAR TO BAAL AND I WILL BUILD ONE TO JEHOVAH. WE WILL PUT WOOD ON OUR ALTARS AND WE WILL LAY THE SACRIFICE ON THE WOOD, BUT WE WILL PUT NO FIRE UNDER IT.
YOU WILL PRAY TO YOUR BAAL AND I WILL PRAY TO JEHOVAH.
THE GOD THAT ANSWERS BY SENDING FIRE ON THE SACRIFICE WILL BE THE TRUE GOD AND WE WILL ALL WORSHIP HIM ONLY. SINCE YOU HAVE ME OUTNUMBERED, YOU CAN GO FIRST.
O BAAL, HEAR US THIS DAY. WE DEDICATE THIS SACRIFICE TO YOUR GREAT NAME.
O BAAL, THE GREAT AND MIGHTY.
O QUEEN OF HEAVEN, COME AND HELP BAAL THIS DAY.
IF BAAL IS A GOD, HE IS NOT PAYING ATTENTION TO YOU. MAYBE HE IS TALKING AND JUST CAN'T HEAR YOU, OR PERHAPS HE IS ON A JOURNEY, OR SLEEPING.
THAT'S IT! HE IS ASLEEP, AND YOU NEED TO HOLLER LOUDER SO YOU CAN WAKE HIM.
YOU DIRTY, &!?&!$!, YOU CAN'T DO ANY BETTER.
LET'S NOT GIVE UP, MEN. PERHAPS IF WE CUT OURSELVES BAAL WILL BE PLEASED.

1 KINGS 18:22-27

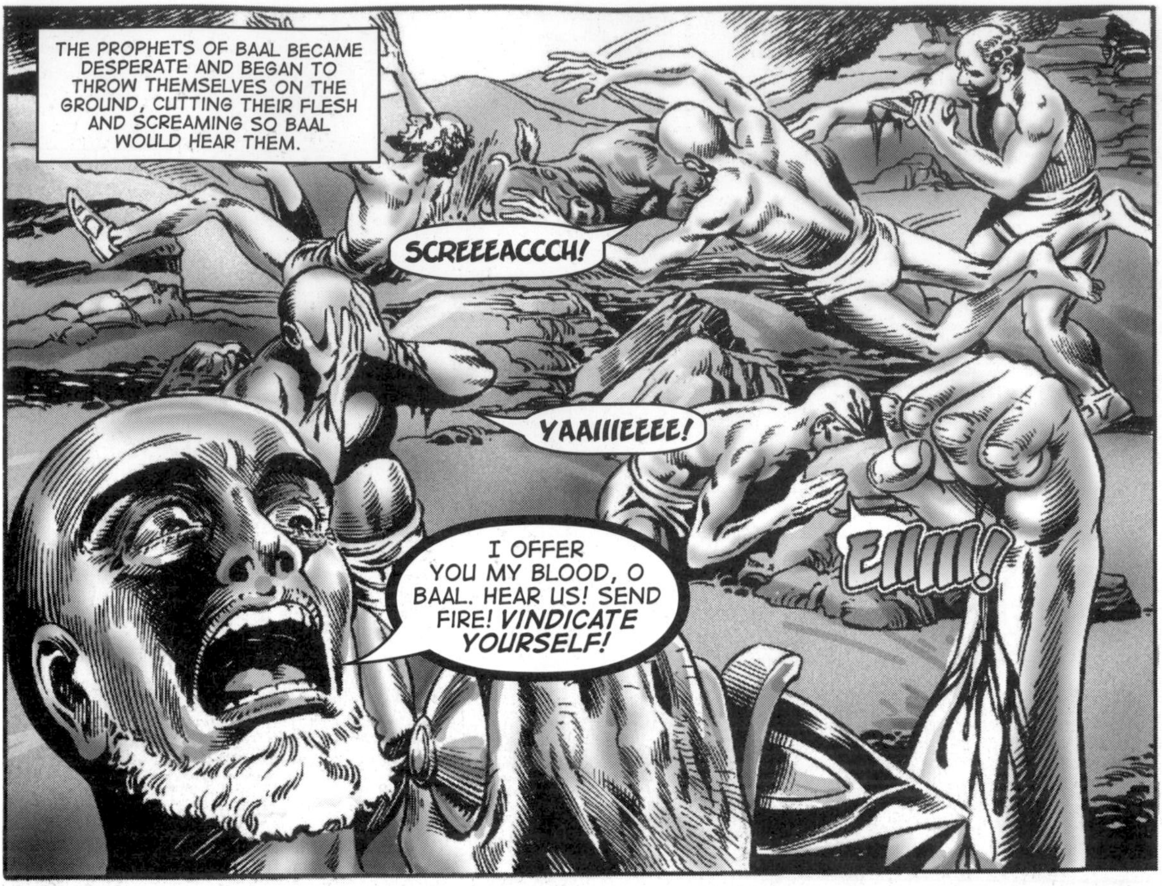
THE PROPHETS OF BAAL BECAME DESPERATE AND BEGAN TO THROW THEMSELVES ON THE GROUND, CUTTING THEIR FLESH AND SCREAMING SO BAAL WOULD HEAR THEM.
SCREEEACCCH!
YAAIIIEEEE!
I OFFER YOU MY BLOOD, O BAAL. HEAR US! SEND FIRE! VINDICATE YOURSELF!
EIIIII!

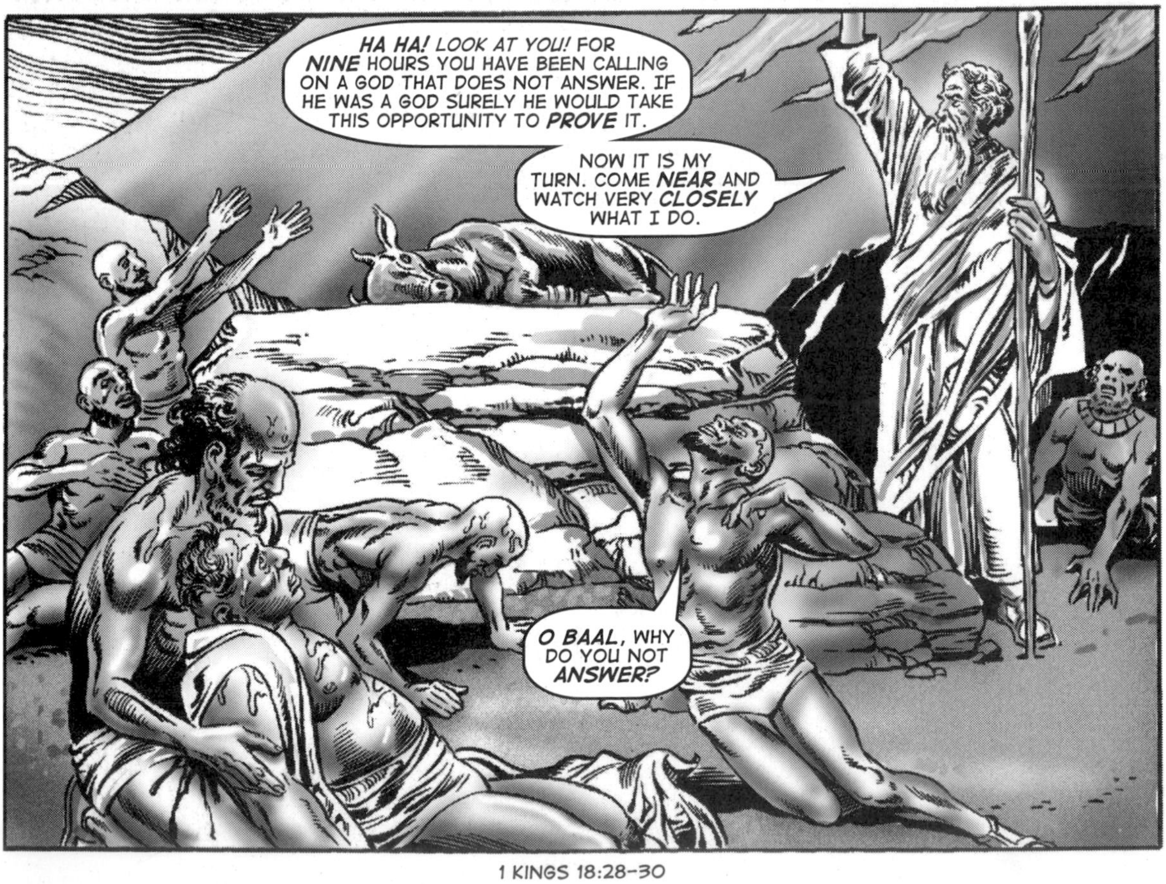
HA HA! LOOK AT YOU! FOR NINE HOURS YOU HAVE BEEN CALLING ON A GOD THAT DOES NOT ANSWER. IF HE WAS A GOD SURELY HE WOULD TAKE THIS OPPORTUNITY TO PROVE IT.
NOW IT IS MY TURN. COME NEAR AND WATCH VERY CLOSELY WHAT I DO.
O BAAL, WHY DO YOU NOT ANSWER?

1 KINGS 18:28-30

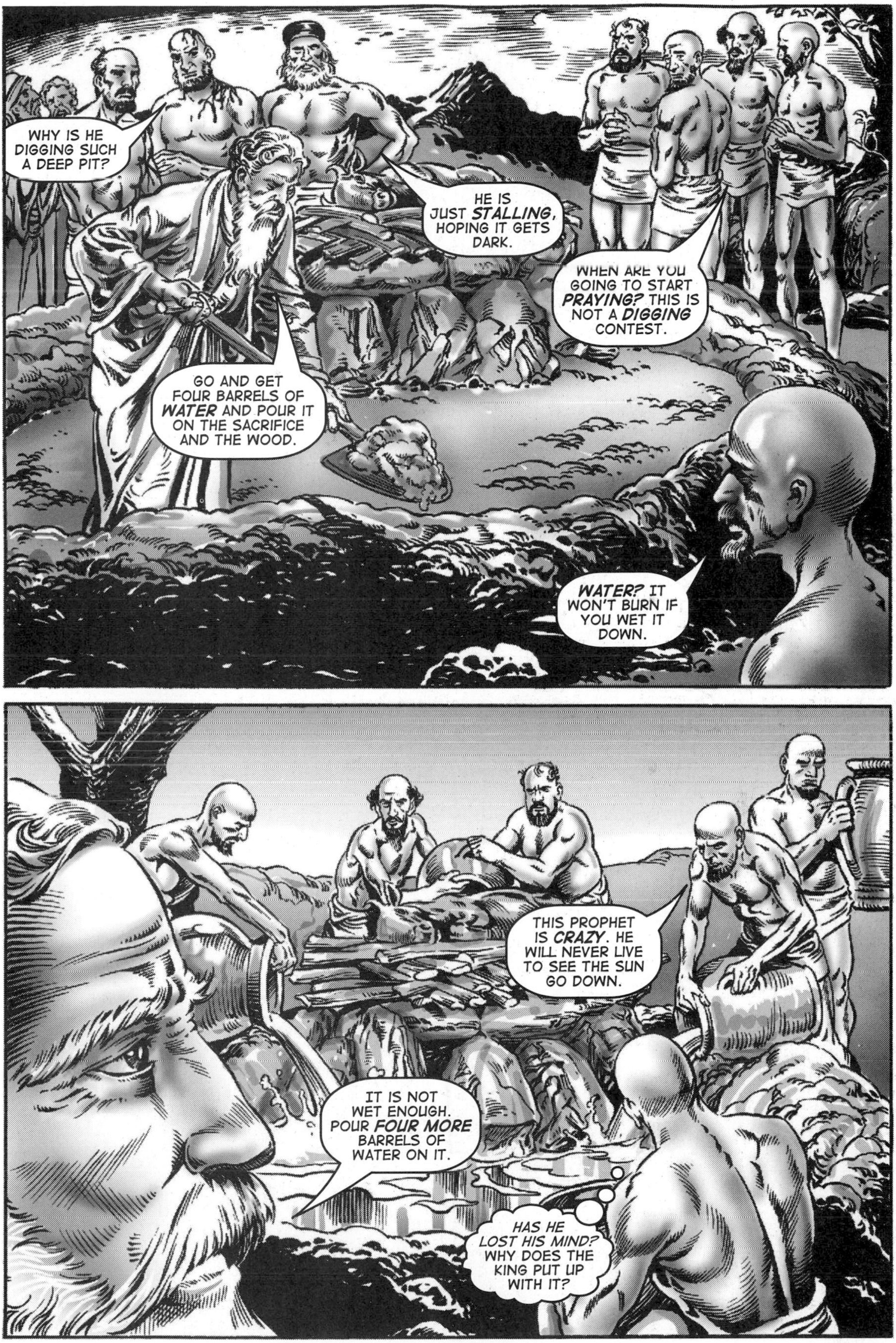
WHY IS HE DIGGING SUCH A DEEP PIT?
HE IS JUST STALLING, HOPING IT GETS DARK.
WHEN ARE YOU GOING TO START PRAYING? THIS IS NOT A DIGGING CONTEST.
GO AND GET FOUR BARRELS OF WATER AND POUR IT ON THE SACRIFICE AND THE WOOD.
WATER? IT WON'T BURN IF YOU WET IT DOWN.
THIS PROPHET IS CRAZY. HE WILL NEVER LIVE TO SEE THE SUN GO DOWN.
IT IS NOT WET ENOUGH. POUR FOUR MORE BARRELS OF WATER ON IT.
HAS HE LOST HIS MIND? WHY DOES THE KING PUT UP WITH IT?

1 KINGS 18:32-34

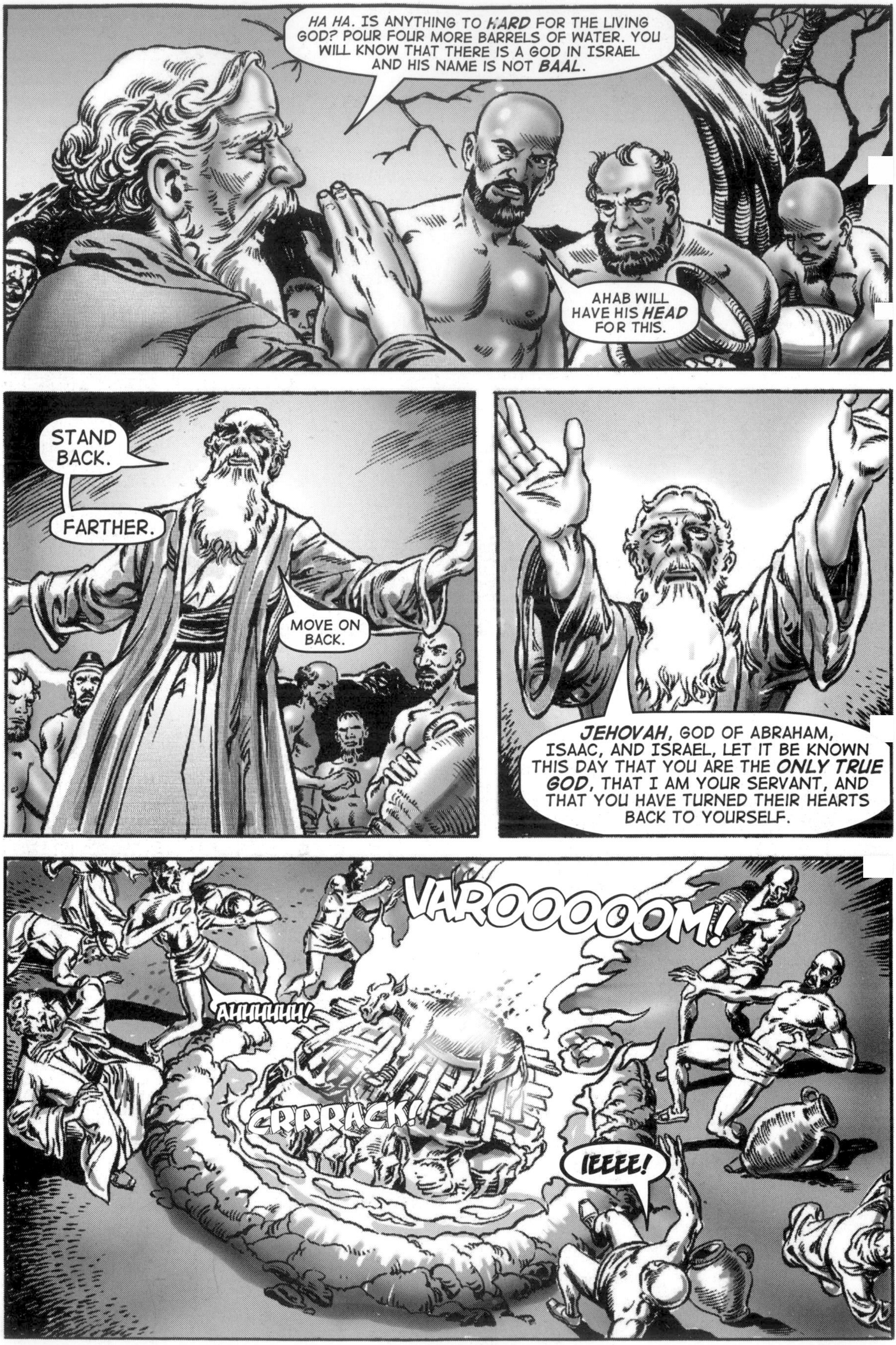
HA HA. IS ANYTHING TO HARD FOR THE LIVING GOD? POUR FOUR MORE BARRELS OF WATER. YOU WILL KNOW THAT THERE IS A GOD IN ISRAEL AND HIS NAME IS NOT BAAL.
AHAB WILL HAVE HIS HEAD FOR THIS.
STAND BACK.
FARTHER.
MOVE ON BACK.
JEHOVAH, GOD OF ABRAHAM, ISAAC, AND ISRAEL, LET IT BE KNOWN THIS DAY THAT YOU ARE THE ONLY TRUE GOD, THAT I AM YOUR SERVANT, AND THAT YOU HAVE TURNED THEIR HEARTS BACK TO YOURSELF.
VAROOOOOOM!
AHHHHHH!
CRRRACK!
IEEEE!

1 KINGS 18:35-38

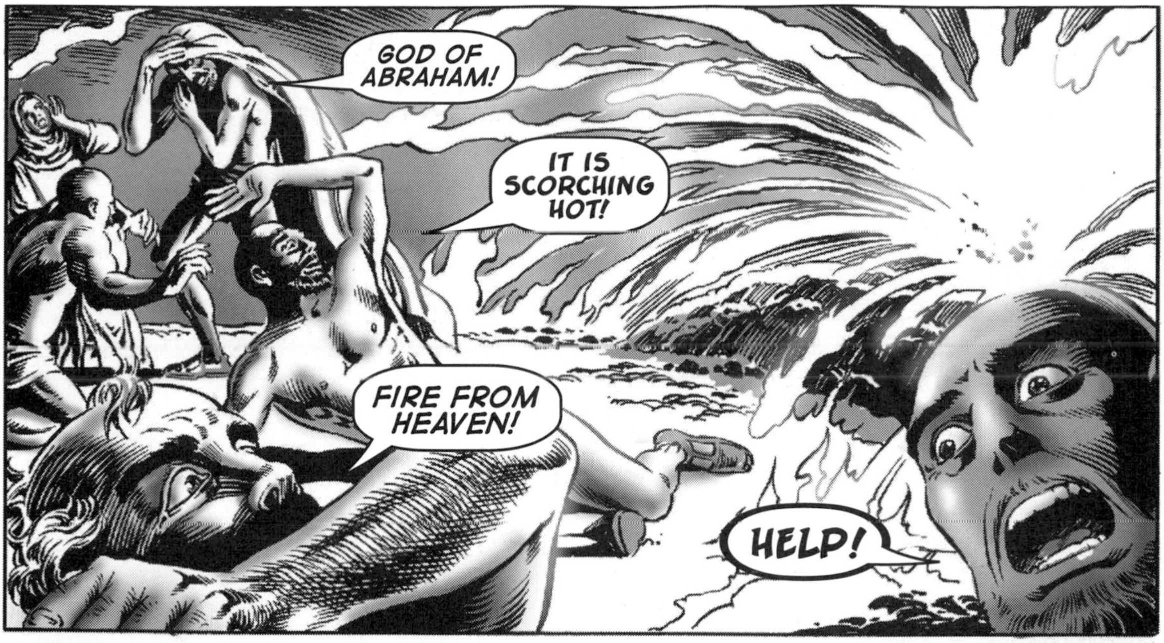
GOD OF ABRAHAM!
IT IS SCORCHING HOT!
FIRE FROM HEAVEN!
HELP!

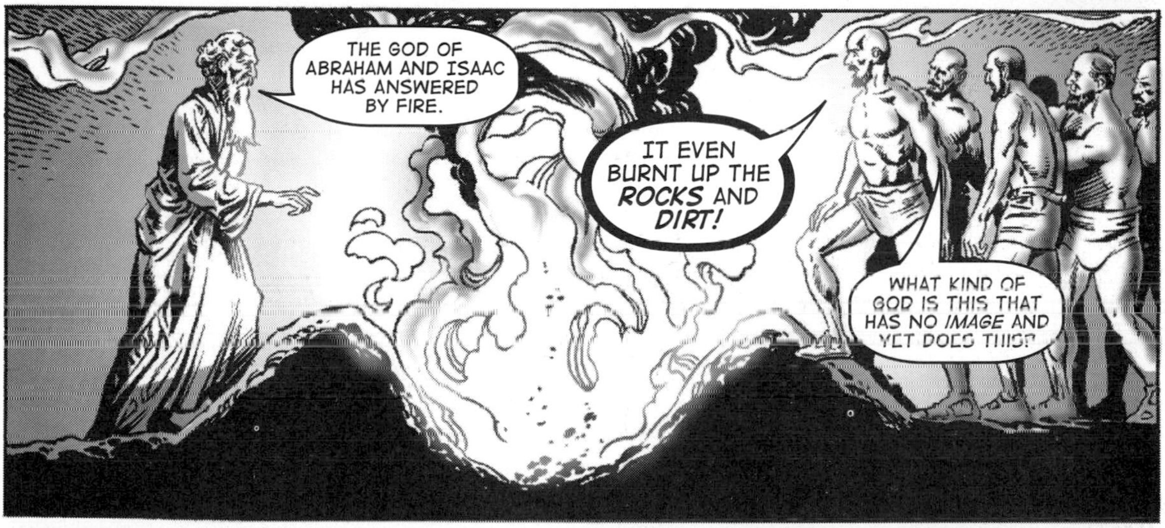
THE GOD OF ABRAHAM AND ISAAC HAS ANSWERED BY FIRE.
IT EVEN BURNT UP THE ROCKS AND DIRT!
WHAT KIND OF GOD IS THIS THAT HAS NO IMAGE AND YET DOES THIS?

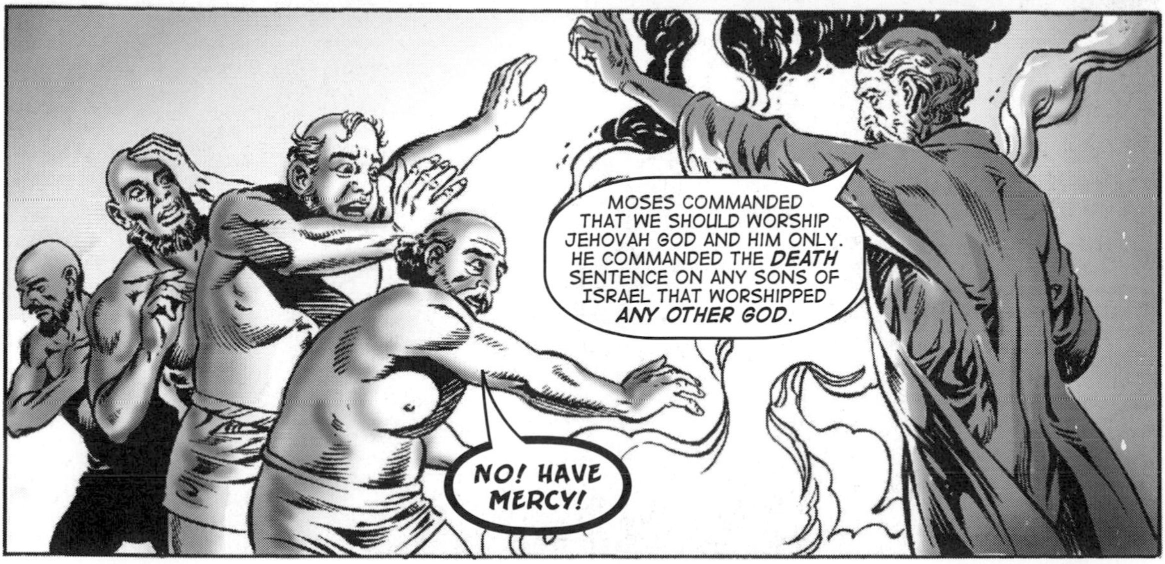
MOSES COMMANDED THAT WE SHOULD WORSHIP JEHOVAH GOD AND HIM ONLY. HE COMMANDED THE DEATH SENTENCE ON ANY SONS OF ISRAEL THAT WORSHIPPED ANY OTHER GOD.
NO! HAVE MERCY!

1 KINGS 18:38-40

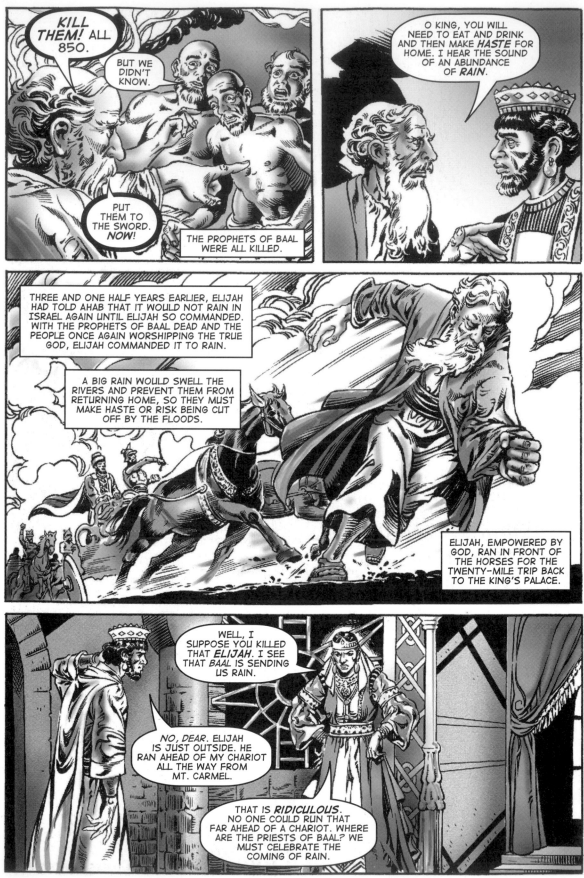

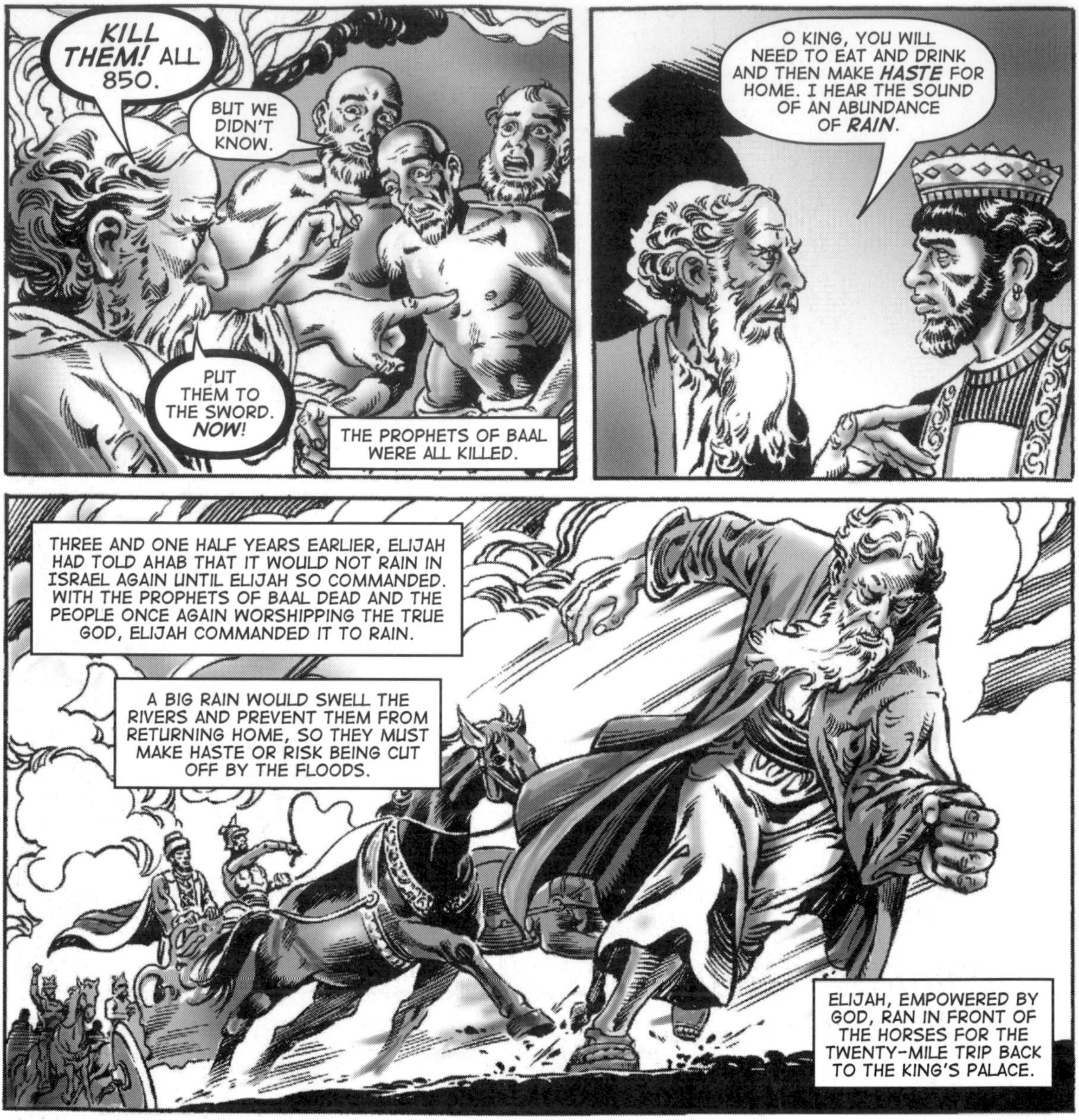
KILL THEM! ALL 850.
BUT WE DIDN'T KNOW.
PUT THEM TO THE SWORD. NOW!
THE PROPHETS OF BAAL WERE ALL KILLED.
O KING, YOU WILL NEED TO EAT AND DRINK AND THEN MAKE HASTE FOR HOME. I HEAR THE SOUND OF AN ABUNDANCE OF RAIN.
THREE AND ONE HALF YEARS EARLIER, ELIJAH HAD TOLD AHAB THAT IT WOULD NOT RAIN IN ISRAEL AGAIN UNTIL ELIJAH SO COMMANDED. WITH THE PROPHETS OF BAAL DEAD AND THE PEOPLE ONCE AGAIN WORSHIPPING THE TRUE GOD, ELIJAH COMMANDED IT TO RAIN.
A BIG RAIN WOULD SWELL THE RIVERS AND PREVENT THEM FROM RETURNING HOME, SO THEY MUST MAKE HASTE OR RISK BEING CUT OFF BY THE FLOODS.
ELIJAH, EMPOWERED BY GOD, RAN IN FRONT OF THE HORSES FOR THE TWENTY-MILE TRIP BACK TO THE KING'S PALACE.
WELL, I SUPPOSE YOU KILLED THAT ELIJAH. I SEE THAT BAAL IS SENDING US RAIN.
NO, DEAR. ELIJAH IS JUST OUTSIDE. HE RAN AHEAD OF MY CHARIOT ALL THE WAY FROM MT. CARMEL.
THAT IS RIDICULOUS. NO ONE COULD RUN THAT FAR AHEAD OF A CHARIOT. WHERE ARE THE PRIESTS OF BAAL? WE MUST CELEBRATE THE COMING OF RAIN.

1 KINGS 18:40–41, 44–46, 19:1

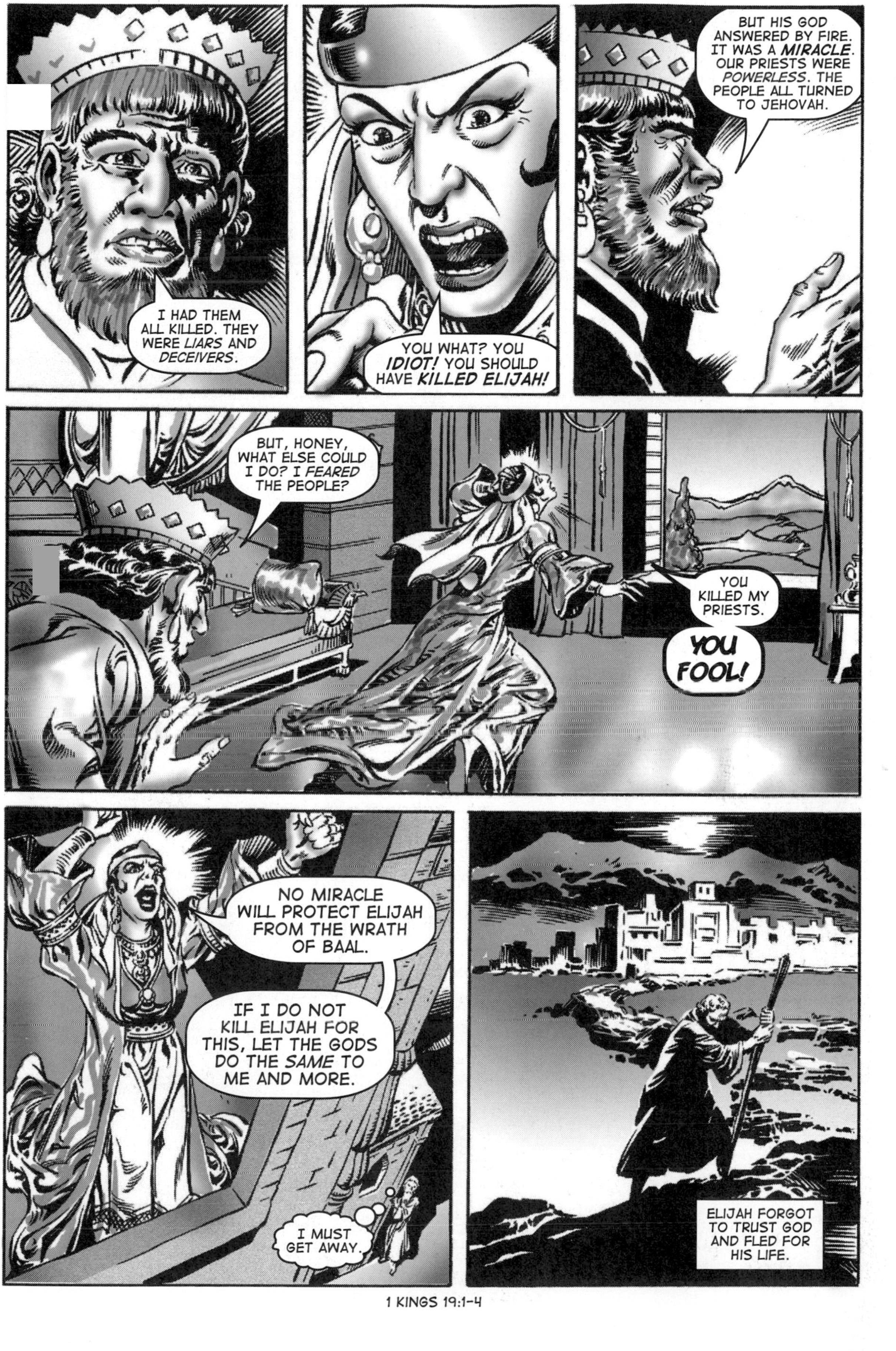
I HAD THEM ALL KILLED. THEY WERE *LIARS* AND *DECEIVERS*.
YOU WHAT? YOU ***IDIOT!*** YOU SHOULD HAVE ***KILLED ELIJAH!***
BUT HIS GOD ANSWERED BY FIRE. IT WAS A ***MIRACLE***. OUR PRIESTS WERE *POWERLESS*. THE PEOPLE ALL TURNED TO JEHOVAH.
BUT, HONEY, WHAT ELSE COULD I DO? I *FEARED* THE PEOPLE?
YOU KILLED MY PRIESTS.
YOU FOOL!
NO MIRACLE WILL PROTECT ELIJAH FROM THE WRATH OF BAAL.
IF I DO NOT KILL ELIJAH FOR THIS, LET THE GODS DO THE *SAME* TO ME AND MORE.
I MUST GET AWAY.
ELIJAH FORGOT TO TRUST GOD AND FLED FOR HIS LIFE.

1 KINGS 19:1-4

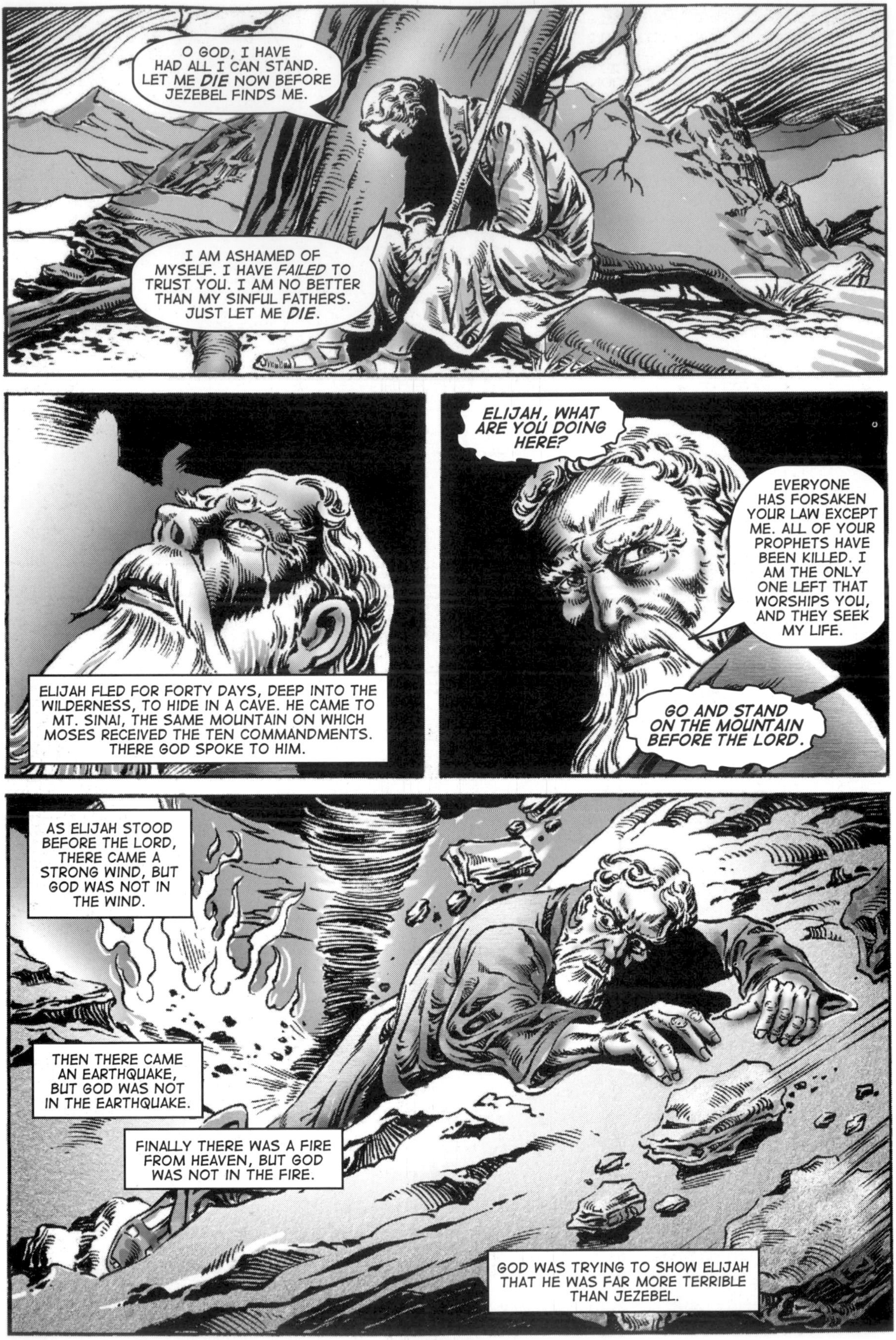
O GOD, I HAVE HAD ALL I CAN STAND. LET ME *DIE* NOW BEFORE JEZEBEL FINDS ME.
I AM ASHAMED OF MYSELF. I HAVE *FAILED* TO TRUST YOU. I AM NO BETTER THAN MY SINFUL FATHERS. JUST LET ME *DIE*.
ELIJAH FLED FOR FORTY DAYS, DEEP INTO THE WILDERNESS, TO HIDE IN A CAVE. HE CAME TO MT. SINAI, THE SAME MOUNTAIN ON WHICH MOSES RECEIVED THE TEN COMMANDMENTS. THERE GOD SPOKE TO HIM.
ELIJAH, WHAT ARE YOU DOING HERE?
EVERYONE HAS FORSAKEN YOUR LAW EXCEPT ME. ALL OF YOUR PROPHETS HAVE BEEN KILLED. I AM THE ONLY ONE LEFT THAT WORSHIPS YOU, AND THEY SEEK MY LIFE.
GO AND STAND ON THE MOUNTAIN BEFORE THE LORD.
AS ELIJAH STOOD BEFORE THE LORD, THERE CAME A STRONG WIND, BUT GOD WAS NOT IN THE WIND.
THEN THERE CAME AN EARTHQUAKE, BUT GOD WAS NOT IN THE EARTHQUAKE.
FINALLY THERE WAS A FIRE FROM HEAVEN, BUT GOD WAS NOT IN THE FIRE.
GOD WAS TRYING TO SHOW ELIJAH THAT HE WAS FAR MORE TERRIBLE THAN JEZEBEL.

1 KINGS 19:4, 8–12

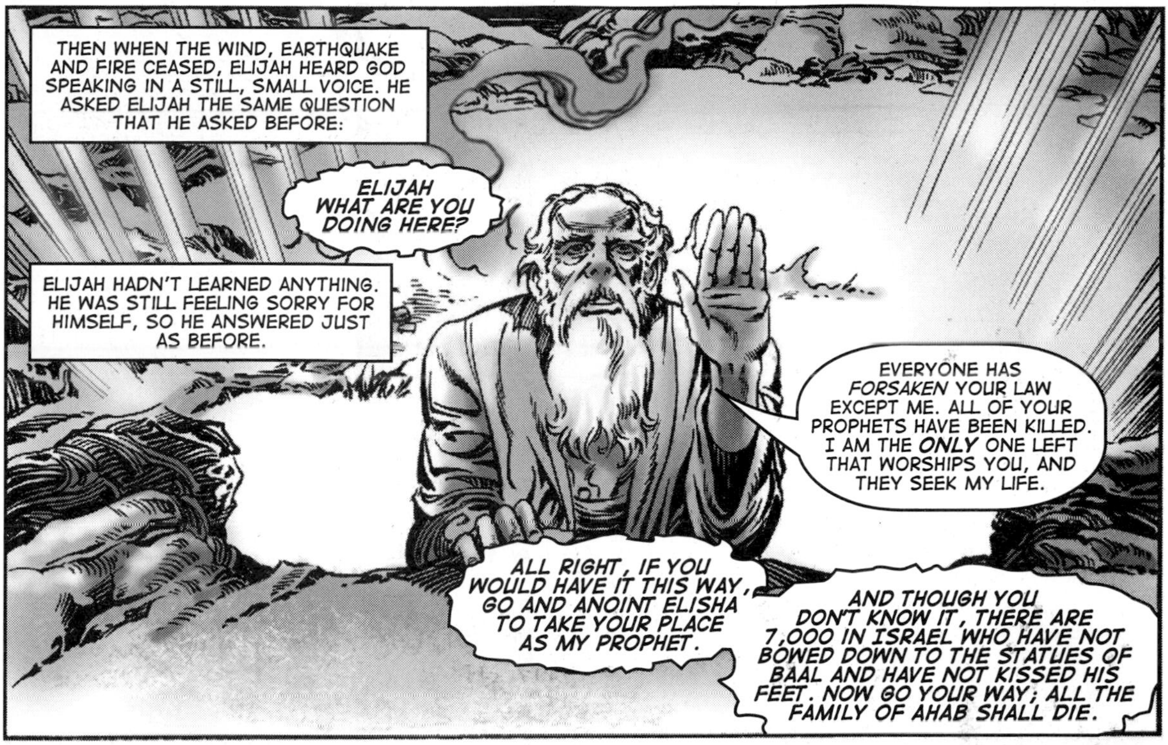
THEN WHEN THE WIND, EARTHQUAKE AND FIRE CEASED, ELIJAH HEARD GOD SPEAKING IN A STILL, SMALL VOICE. HE ASKED ELIJAH THE SAME QUESTION THAT HE ASKED BEFORE:
ELIJAH WHAT ARE YOU DOING HERE?
ELIJAH HADN'T LEARNED ANYTHING. HE WAS STILL FEELING SORRY FOR HIMSELF, SO HE ANSWERED JUST AS BEFORE.
EVERYONE HAS FORSAKEN YOUR LAW EXCEPT ME. ALL OF YOUR PROPHETS HAVE BEEN KILLED. I AM THE ONLY ONE LEFT THAT WORSHIPS YOU, AND THEY SEEK MY LIFE.
ALL RIGHT, IF YOU WOULD HAVE IT THIS WAY, GO AND ANOINT ELISHA TO TAKE YOUR PLACE AS MY PROPHET.
AND THOUGH YOU DON'T KNOW IT, THERE ARE 7,000 IN ISRAEL WHO HAVE NOT BOWED DOWN TO THE STATUES OF BAAL AND HAVE NOT KISSED HIS FEET. NOW GO YOUR WAY; ALL THE FAMILY OF AHAB SHALL DIE.

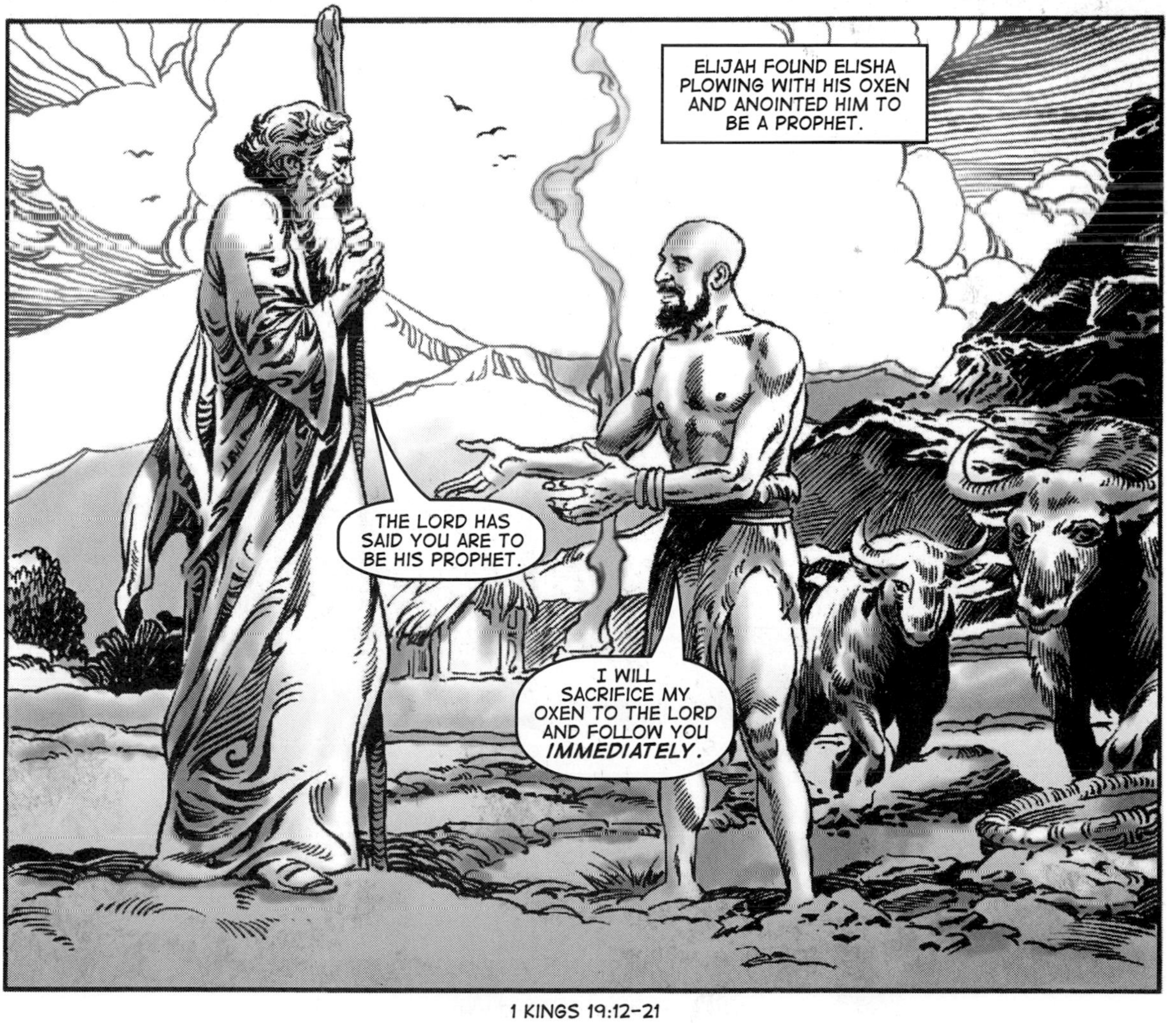
ELIJAH FOUND ELISHA PLOWING WITH HIS OXEN AND ANOINTED HIM TO BE A PROPHET.
THE LORD HAS SAID YOU ARE TO BE HIS PROPHET.
I WILL SACRIFICE MY OXEN TO THE LORD AND FOLLOW YOU IMMEDIATELY.

1 KINGS 19:12–21

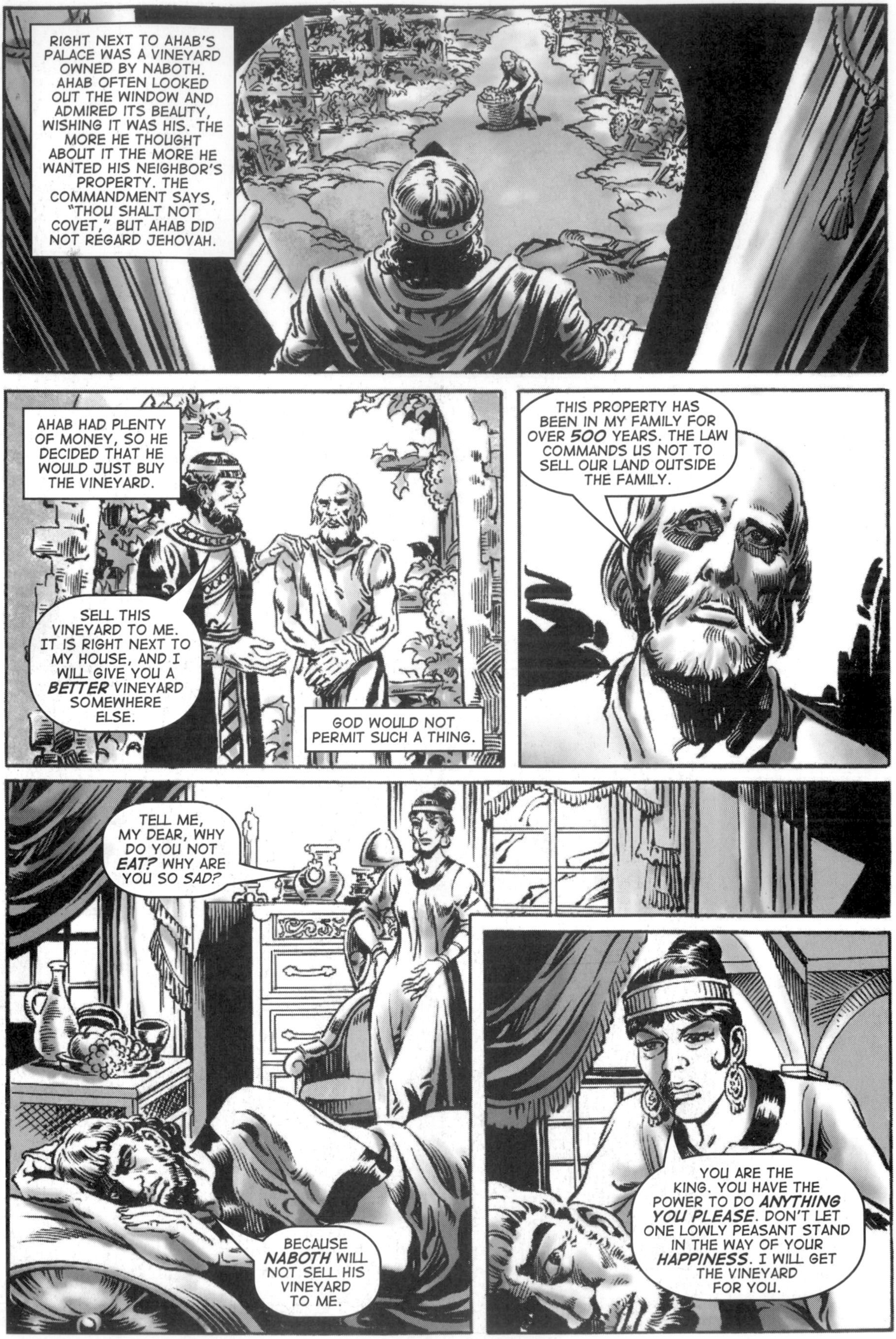
RIGHT NEXT TO AHAB'S PALACE WAS A VINEYARD OWNED BY NABOTH. AHAB OFTEN LOOKED OUT THE WINDOW AND ADMIRED ITS BEAUTY, WISHING IT WAS HIS. THE MORE HE THOUGHT ABOUT IT THE MORE HE WANTED HIS NEIGHBOR'S PROPERTY. THE COMMANDMENT SAYS, "THOU SHALT NOT COVET," BUT AHAB DID NOT REGARD JEHOVAH.
AHAB HAD PLENTY OF MONEY, SO HE DECIDED THAT HE WOULD JUST BUY THE VINEYARD.
SELL THIS VINEYARD TO ME. IT IS RIGHT NEXT TO MY HOUSE, AND I WILL GIVE YOU A **BETTER** VINEYARD SOMEWHERE ELSE.
GOD WOULD NOT PERMIT SUCH A THING.
THIS PROPERTY HAS BEEN IN MY FAMILY FOR OVER **500** YEARS. THE LAW COMMANDS US NOT TO SELL OUR LAND OUTSIDE THE FAMILY.
TELL ME, MY DEAR, WHY DO YOU NOT ***EAT?*** WHY ARE YOU SO *SAD?*
BECAUSE ***NABOTH*** WILL NOT SELL HIS VINEYARD TO ME.
YOU ARE THE KING. YOU HAVE THE POWER TO DO ***ANYTHING YOU PLEASE***. DON'T LET ONE LOWLY PEASANT STAND IN THE WAY OF YOUR ***HAPPINESS***. I WILL GET THE VINEYARD FOR YOU.

EXODUS 20:17; 1 KINGS 21:1–7

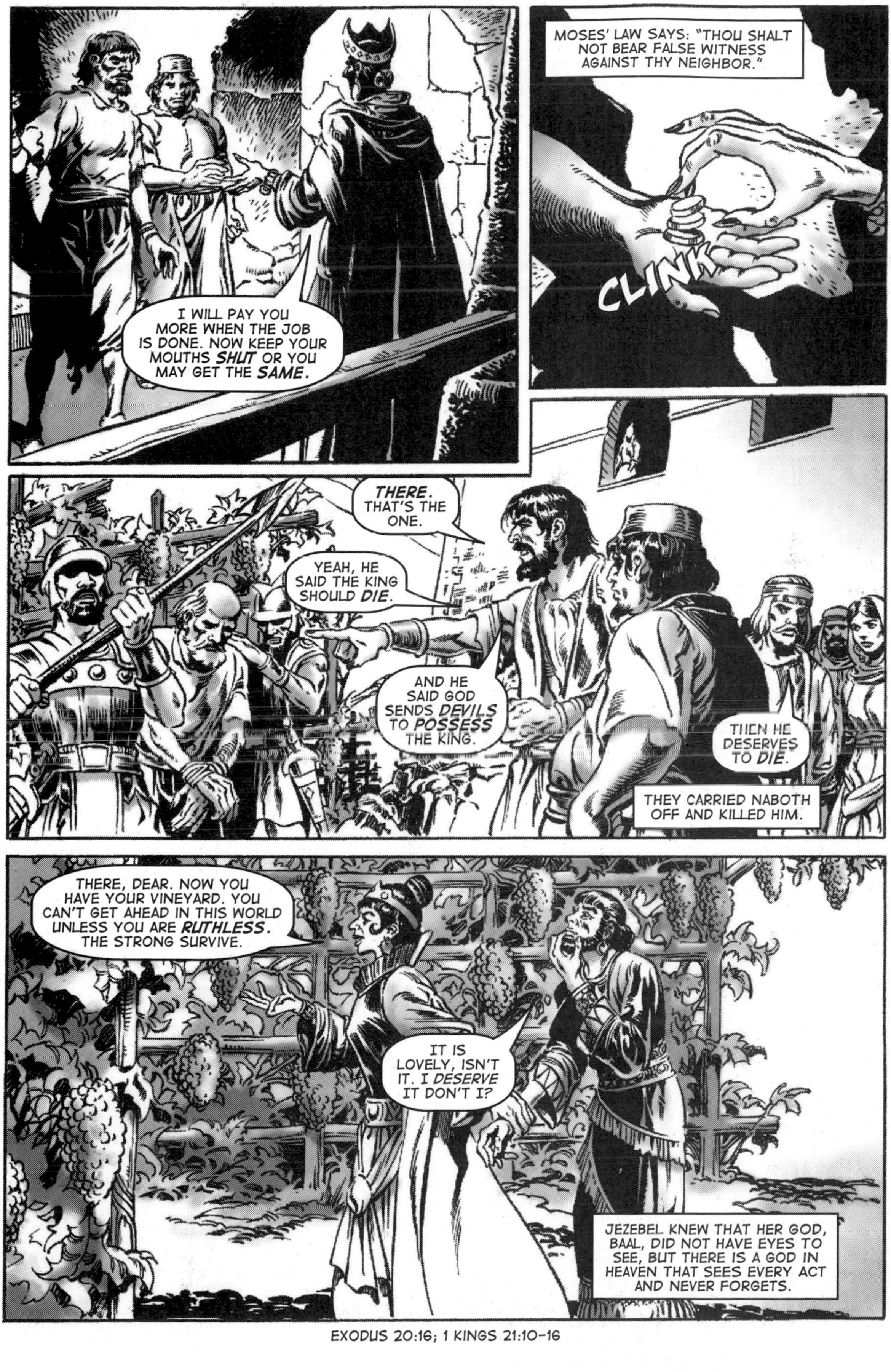
I WILL PAY YOU MORE WHEN THE JOB IS DONE. NOW KEEP YOUR MOUTHS *SHUT* OR YOU MAY GET THE *SAME*.
MOSES' LAW SAYS: "THOU SHALT NOT BEAR FALSE WITNESS AGAINST THY NEIGHBOR."
CLINK
THERE. THAT'S THE ONE.
YEAH, HE SAID THE KING SHOULD *DIE*.
AND HE SAID GOD SENDS *DEVILS* TO *POSSESS* THE KING.
THEN HE DESERVES TO *DIE*.
THEY CARRIED NABOTH OFF AND KILLED HIM.
THERE, DEAR. NOW YOU HAVE YOUR VINEYARD. YOU CAN'T GET AHEAD IN THIS WORLD UNLESS YOU ARE *RUTHLESS*. THE STRONG SURVIVE.
IT IS LOVELY, ISN'T IT. I *DESERVE* IT DON'T I?
JEZEBEL KNEW THAT HER GOD, BAAL, DID NOT HAVE EYES TO SEE, BUT THERE IS A GOD IN HEAVEN THAT SEES EVERY ACT AND NEVER FORGETS.

EXODUS 20:16; 1 KINGS 21:10-16

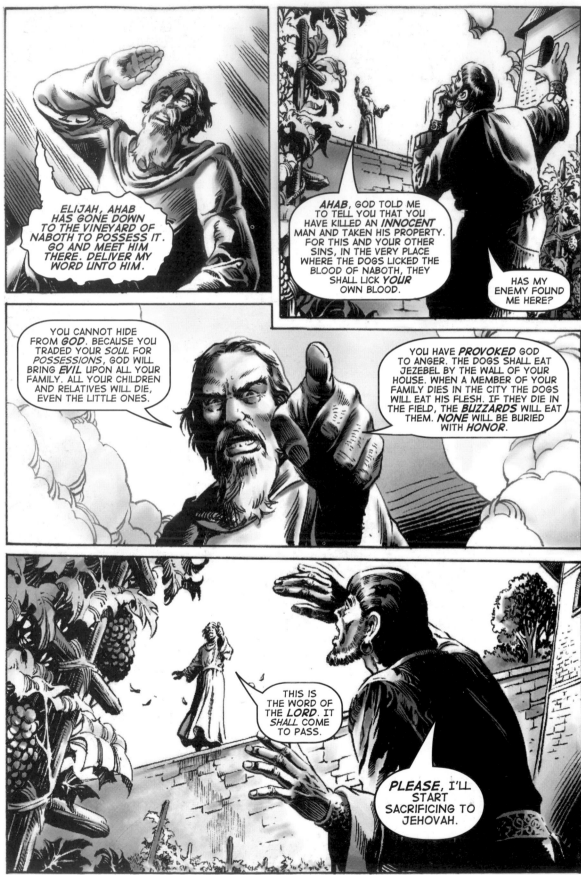

ELIJAH, AHAB HAS GONE DOWN TO THE VINEYARD OF NABOTH TO POSSESS IT. GO AND MEET HIM THERE. DELIVER MY WORD UNTO HIM.

AHAB, GOD TOLD ME TO TELL YOU THAT YOU HAVE KILLED AN *INNOCENT* MAN AND TAKEN HIS PROPERTY. FOR THIS AND YOUR OTHER SINS, IN THE VERY PLACE WHERE THE DOGS LICKED THE BLOOD OF NABOTH, THEY SHALL LICK *YOUR* OWN BLOOD.

HAS MY ENEMY FOUND ME HERE?

YOU CANNOT HIDE FROM *GOD*. BECAUSE YOU TRADED YOUR *SOUL* FOR *POSSESSIONS*, GOD WILL BRING *EVIL* UPON ALL YOUR FAMILY. ALL YOUR CHILDREN AND RELATIVES WILL DIE, EVEN THE LITTLE ONES.

YOU HAVE *PROVOKED* GOD TO ANGER. THE DOGS SHALL EAT JEZEBEL BY THE WALL OF YOUR HOUSE. WHEN A MEMBER OF YOUR FAMILY DIES IN THE CITY THE DOGS WILL EAT HIS FLESH. IF THEY DIE IN THE FIELD, THE *BUZZARDS* WILL EAT THEM. *NONE* WILL BE BURIED WITH *HONOR*.

THIS IS THE WORD OF THE *LORD*. IT *SHALL* COME TO PASS.

PLEASE, I'LL START SACRIFICING TO JEHOVAH.

1 KINGS 21:17-26

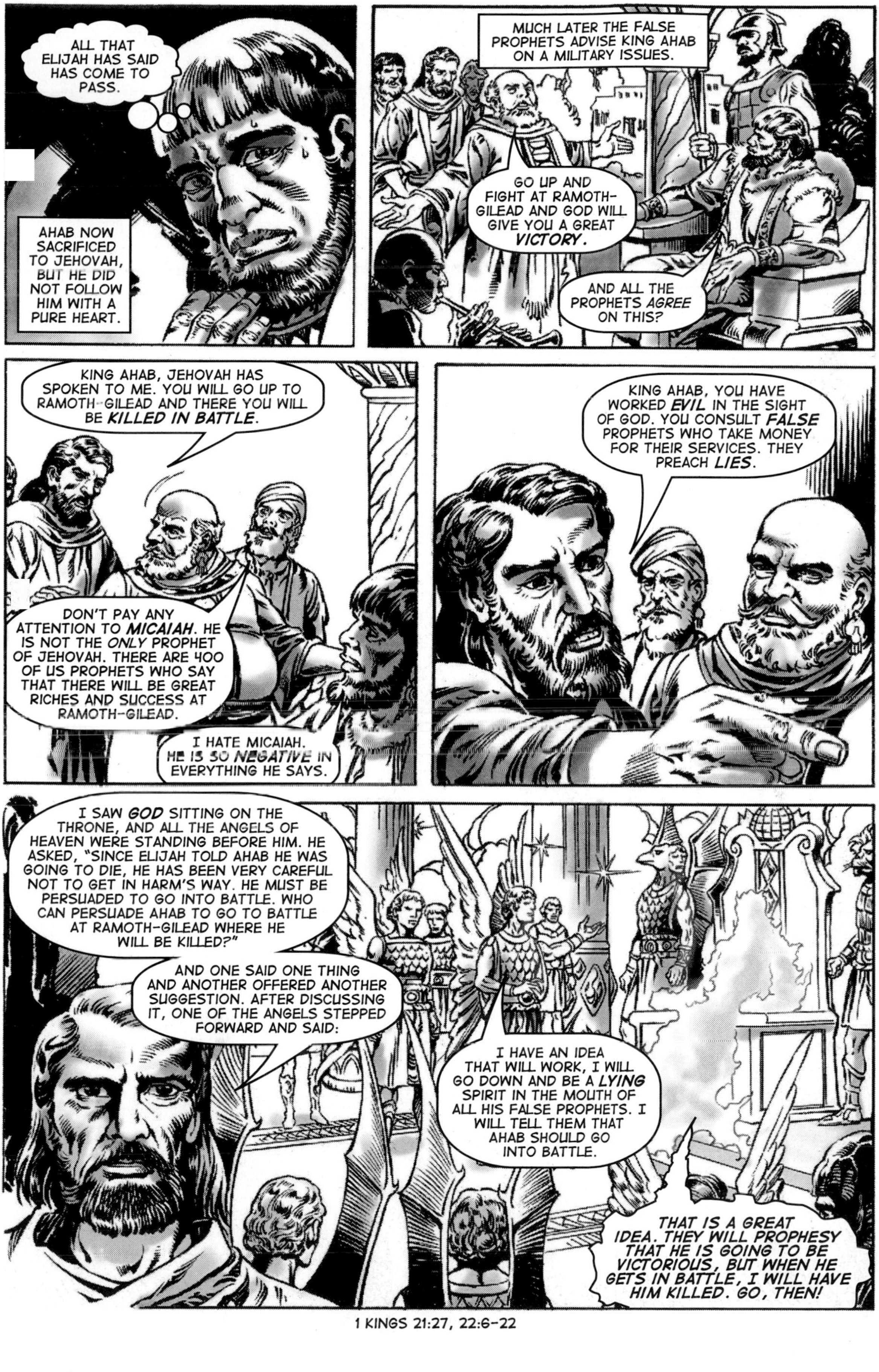
ALL THAT ELIJAH HAS SAID HAS COME TO PASS.
AHAB NOW SACRIFICED TO JEHOVAH, BUT HE DID NOT FOLLOW HIM WITH A PURE HEART.
MUCH LATER THE FALSE PROPHETS ADVISE KING AHAB ON A MILITARY ISSUES.
GO UP AND FIGHT AT RAMOTH-GILEAD AND GOD WILL GIVE YOU A GREAT VICTORY.
AND ALL THE PROPHETS AGREE ON THIS?
KING AHAB, JEHOVAH HAS SPOKEN TO ME. YOU WILL GO UP TO RAMOTH-GILEAD AND THERE YOU WILL BE KILLED IN BATTLE.
DON'T PAY ANY ATTENTION TO MICAIAH. HE IS NOT THE ONLY PROPHET OF JEHOVAH. THERE ARE 400 OF US PROPHETS WHO SAY THAT THERE WILL BE GREAT RICHES AND SUCCESS AT RAMOTH-GILEAD.
I HATE MICAIAH. HE IS SO NEGATIVE IN EVERYTHING HE SAYS.
KING AHAB, YOU HAVE WORKED EVIL IN THE SIGHT OF GOD. YOU CONSULT FALSE PROPHETS WHO TAKE MONEY FOR THEIR SERVICES. THEY PREACH LIES.
I SAW GOD SITTING ON THE THRONE, AND ALL THE ANGELS OF HEAVEN WERE STANDING BEFORE HIM. HE ASKED, "SINCE ELIJAH TOLD AHAB HE WAS GOING TO DIE, HE HAS BEEN VERY CAREFUL NOT TO GET IN HARM'S WAY. HE MUST BE PERSUADED TO GO INTO BATTLE. WHO CAN PERSUADE AHAB TO GO TO BATTLE AT RAMOTH-GILEAD WHERE HE WILL BE KILLED?"
AND ONE SAID ONE THING AND ANOTHER OFFERED ANOTHER SUGGESTION. AFTER DISCUSSING IT, ONE OF THE ANGELS STEPPED FORWARD AND SAID:
I HAVE AN IDEA THAT WILL WORK, I WILL GO DOWN AND BE A LYING SPIRIT IN THE MOUTH OF ALL HIS FALSE PROPHETS. I WILL TELL THEM THAT AHAB SHOULD GO INTO BATTLE.
THAT IS A GREAT IDEA. THEY WILL PROPHESY THAT HE IS GOING TO BE VICTORIOUS, BUT WHEN HE GETS IN BATTLE, I WILL HAVE HIM KILLED. GO, THEN!

1 KINGS 21:27, 22:6-22

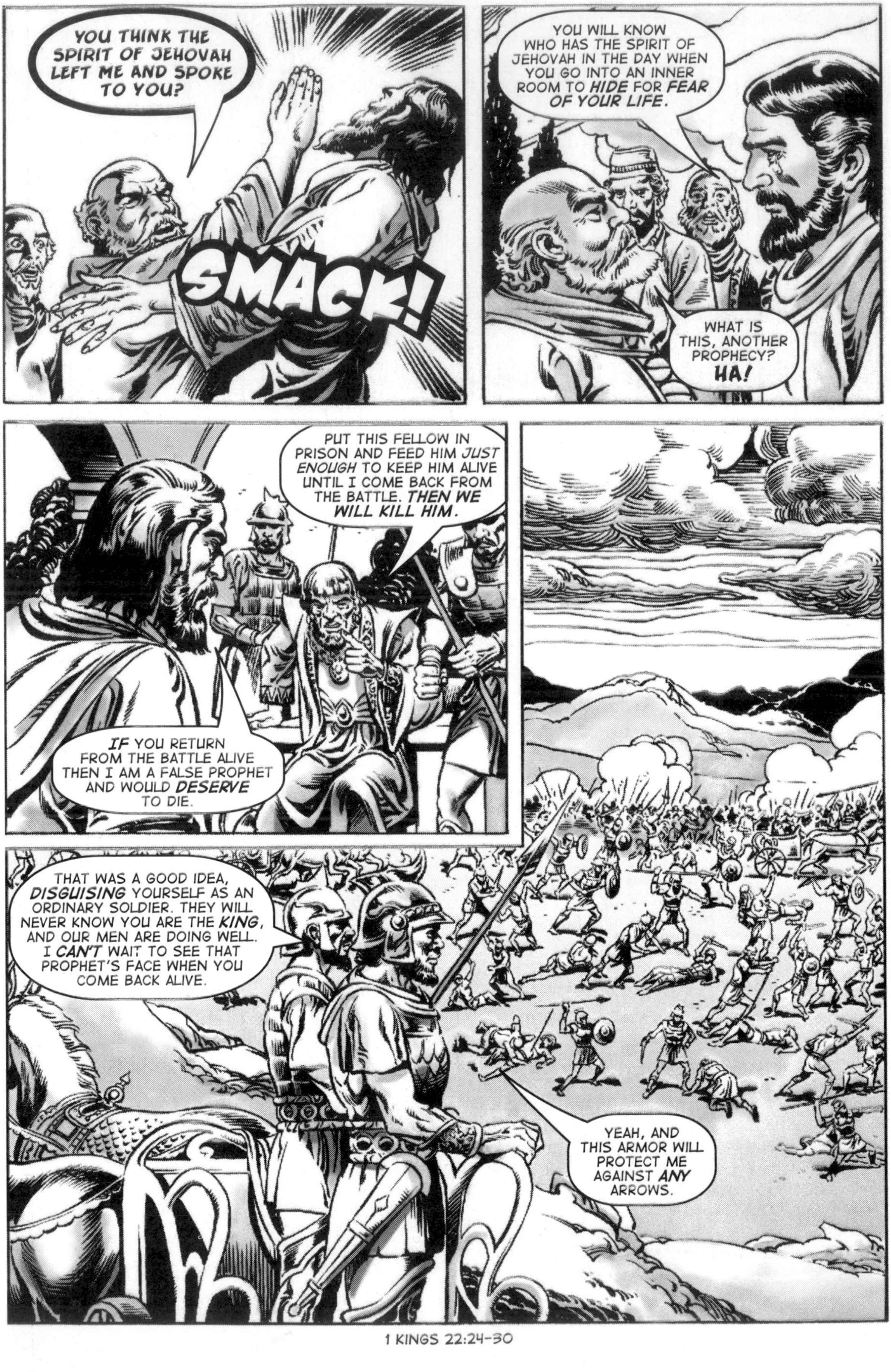
YOU THINK THE SPIRIT OF JEHOVAH LEFT ME AND SPOKE TO YOU?
SMACK!
YOU WILL KNOW WHO HAS THE SPIRIT OF JEHOVAH IN THE DAY WHEN YOU GO INTO AN INNER ROOM TO HIDE FOR FEAR OF YOUR LIFE.
WHAT IS THIS, ANOTHER PROPHECY? HA!
PUT THIS FELLOW IN PRISON AND FEED HIM JUST ENOUGH TO KEEP HIM ALIVE UNTIL I COME BACK FROM THE BATTLE. THEN WE WILL KILL HIM.
IF YOU RETURN FROM THE BATTLE ALIVE THEN I AM A FALSE PROPHET AND WOULD DESERVE TO DIE.
THAT WAS A GOOD IDEA, DISGUISING YOURSELF AS AN ORDINARY SOLDIER. THEY WILL NEVER KNOW YOU ARE THE KING, AND OUR MEN ARE DOING WELL. I CAN'T WAIT TO SEE THAT PROPHET'S FACE WHEN YOU COME BACK ALIVE.
YEAH, AND THIS ARMOR WILL PROTECT ME AGAINST ANY ARROWS.

1 KINGS 22:24-30

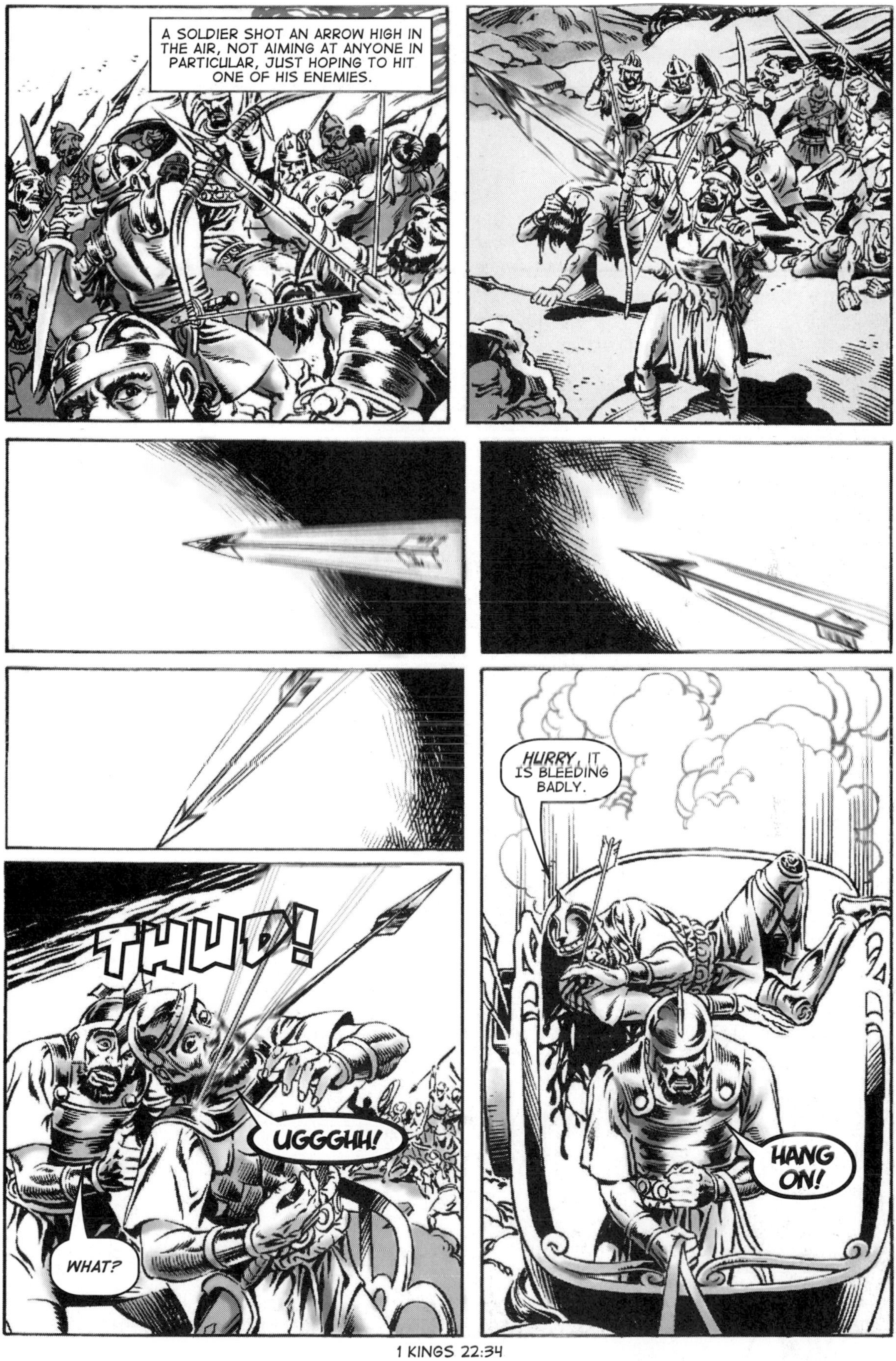
A SOLDIER SHOT AN ARROW HIGH IN THE AIR, NOT AIMING AT ANYONE IN PARTICULAR, JUST HOPING TO HIT ONE OF HIS ENEMIES.
THUD!
UGGGHH!
WHAT?
HURRY, IT IS BLEEDING BADLY.
HANG ON!

1 KINGS 22:34

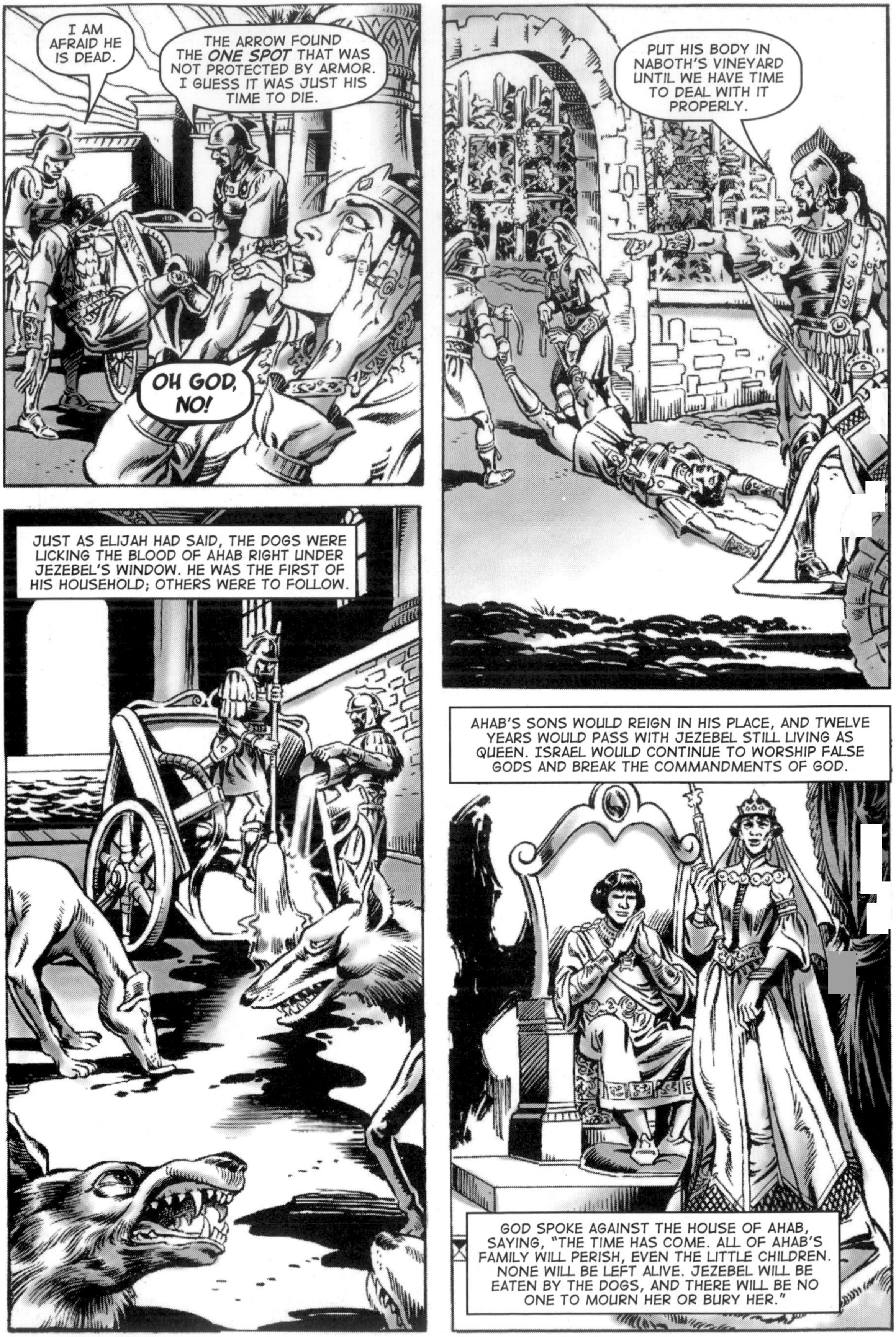
I AM AFRAID HE IS DEAD.
THE ARROW FOUND THE ONE SPOT THAT WAS NOT PROTECTED BY ARMOR. I GUESS IT WAS JUST HIS TIME TO DIE.
OH GOD, NO!
PUT HIS BODY IN NABOTH'S VINEYARD UNTIL WE HAVE TIME TO DEAL WITH IT PROPERLY.
JUST AS ELIJAH HAD SAID, THE DOGS WERE LICKING THE BLOOD OF AHAB RIGHT UNDER JEZEBEL'S WINDOW. HE WAS THE FIRST OF HIS HOUSEHOLD; OTHERS WERE TO FOLLOW.
AHAB'S SONS WOULD REIGN IN HIS PLACE, AND TWELVE YEARS WOULD PASS WITH JEZEBEL STILL LIVING AS QUEEN. ISRAEL WOULD CONTINUE TO WORSHIP FALSE GODS AND BREAK THE COMMANDMENTS OF GOD.
GOD SPOKE AGAINST THE HOUSE OF AHAB, SAYING, "THE TIME HAS COME. ALL OF AHAB'S FAMILY WILL PERISH, EVEN THE LITTLE CHILDREN. NONE WILL BE LEFT ALIVE. JEZEBEL WILL BE EATEN BY THE DOGS, AND THERE WILL BE NO ONE TO MOURN HER OR BURY HER."

1 KINGS 22:37-38; 2 KINGS 9:8-10

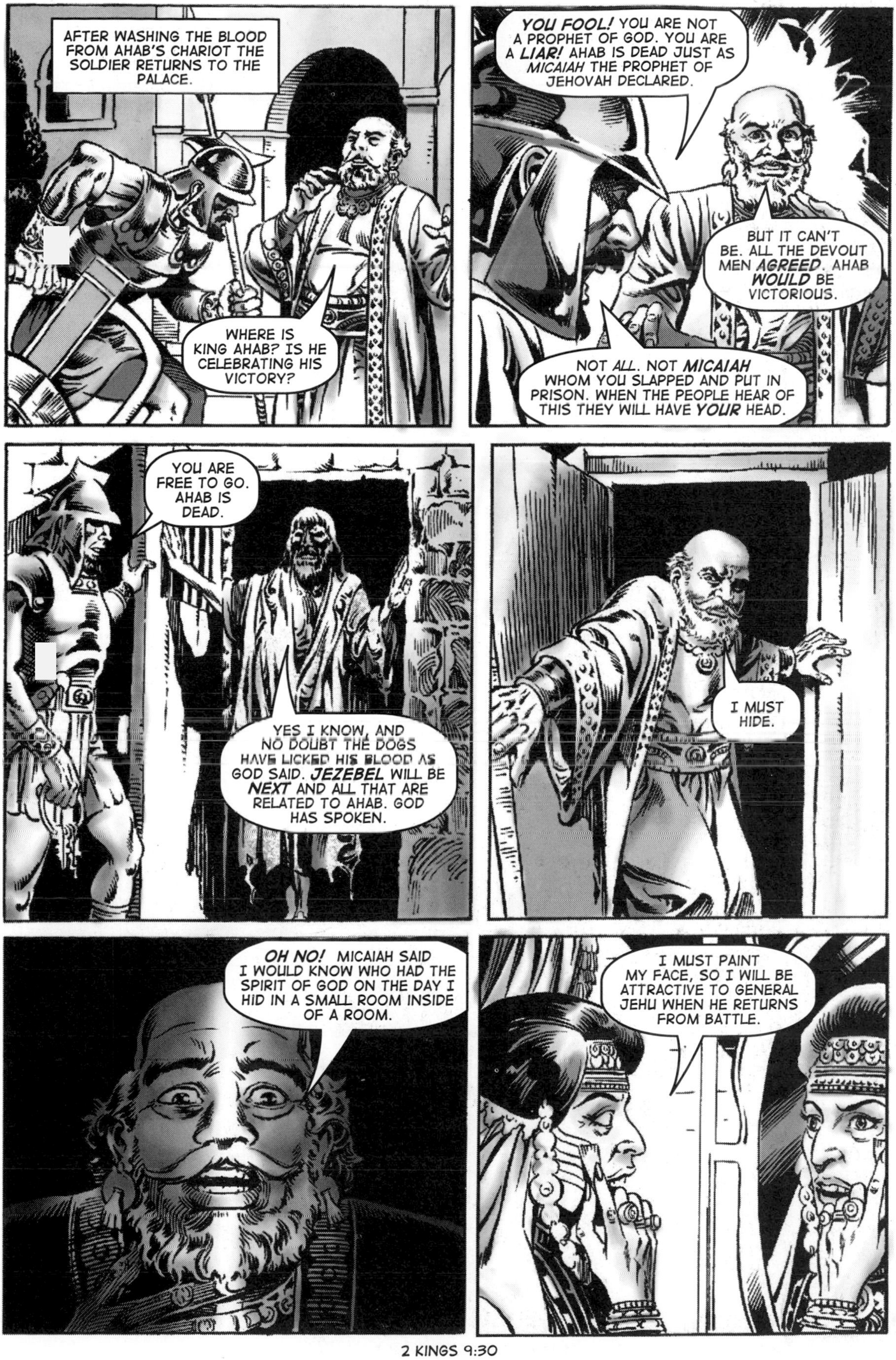
AFTER WASHING THE BLOOD FROM AHAB'S CHARIOT THE SOLDIER RETURNS TO THE PALACE.
WHERE IS KING AHAB? IS HE CELEBRATING HIS VICTORY?
YOU FOOL! YOU ARE NOT A PROPHET OF GOD. YOU ARE A LIAR! AHAB IS DEAD JUST AS MICAIAH THE PROPHET OF JEHOVAH DECLARED.
BUT IT CAN'T BE. ALL THE DEVOUT MEN AGREED. AHAB WOULD BE VICTORIOUS.
NOT ALL. NOT MICAIAH WHOM YOU SLAPPED AND PUT IN PRISON. WHEN THE PEOPLE HEAR OF THIS THEY WILL HAVE YOUR HEAD.
YOU ARE FREE TO GO. AHAB IS DEAD.
YES I KNOW, AND NO DOUBT THE DOGS HAVE LICKED HIS BLOOD AS GOD SAID. JEZEBEL WILL BE NEXT AND ALL THAT ARE RELATED TO AHAB. GOD HAS SPOKEN.
I MUST HIDE.
OH NO! MICAIAH SAID I WOULD KNOW WHO HAD THE SPIRIT OF GOD ON THE DAY I HID IN A SMALL ROOM INSIDE OF A ROOM.
I MUST PAINT MY FACE, SO I WILL BE ATTRACTIVE TO GENERAL JEHU WHEN HE RETURNS FROM BATTLE.

2 KINGS 9:30

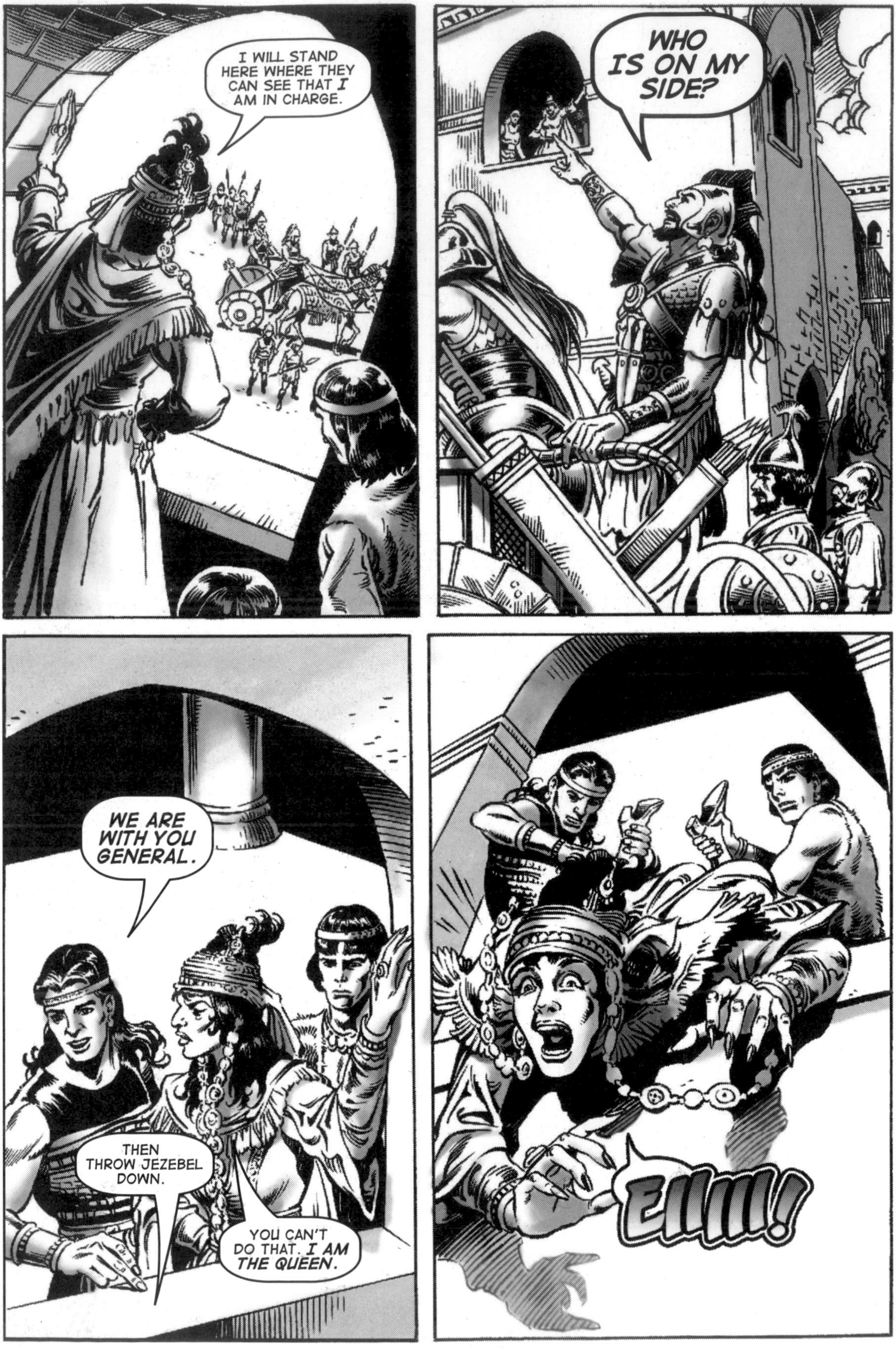
I WILL STAND HERE WHERE THEY CAN SEE THAT I AM IN CHARGE.
WHO IS ON MY SIDE?
WE ARE WITH YOU GENERAL.
THEN THROW JEZEBEL DOWN.
YOU CAN'T DO THAT. I AM THE QUEEN.
EIIIII!

2 KINGS 9:32-33

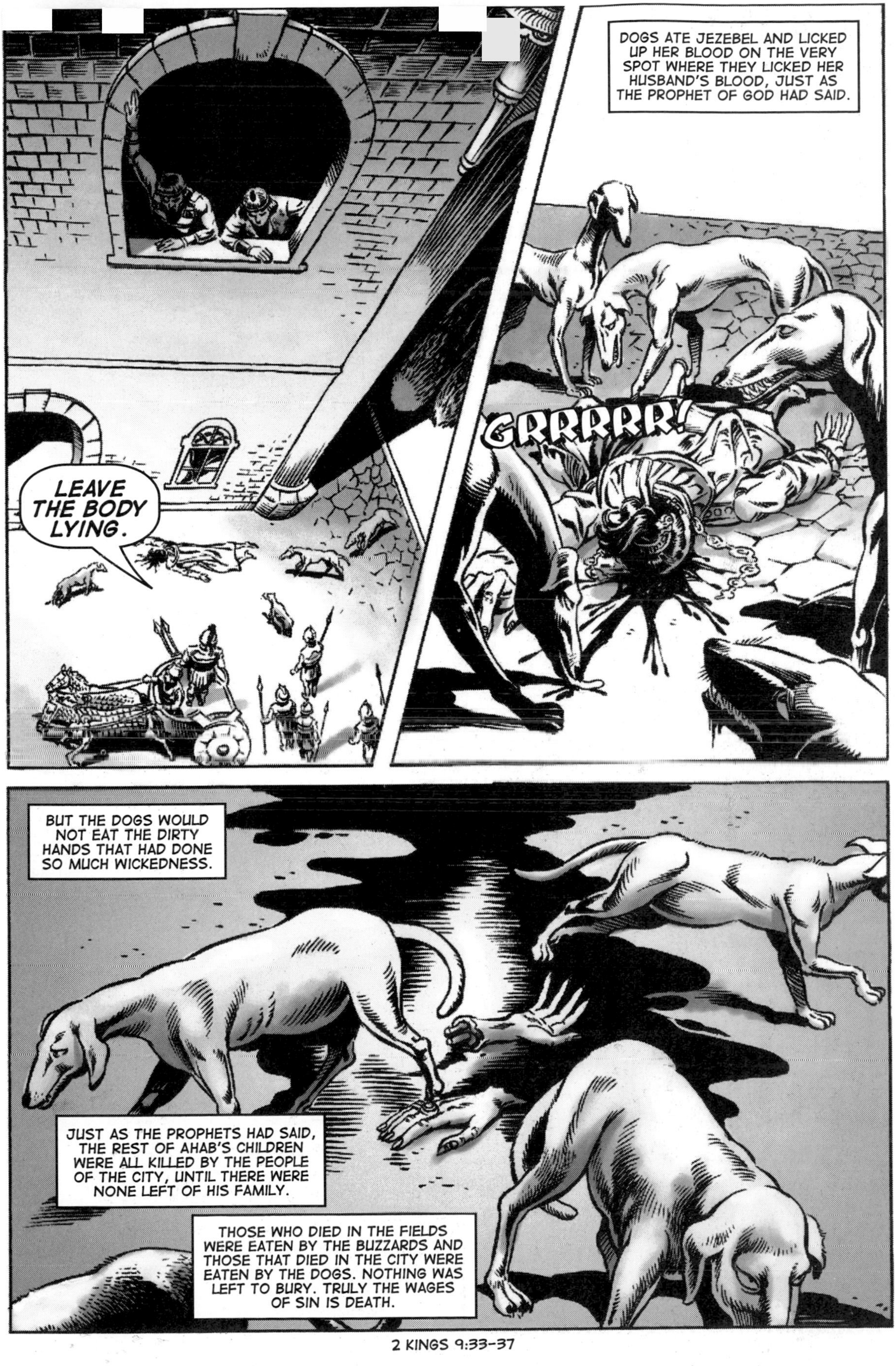
LEAVE THE BODY LYING.
DOGS ATE JEZEBEL AND LICKED UP HER BLOOD ON THE VERY SPOT WHERE THEY LICKED HER HUSBAND'S BLOOD, JUST AS THE PROPHET OF GOD HAD SAID.
GRRRRRR!
BUT THE DOGS WOULD NOT EAT THE DIRTY HANDS THAT HAD DONE SO MUCH WICKEDNESS.
JUST AS THE PROPHETS HAD SAID, THE REST OF AHAB'S CHILDREN WERE ALL KILLED BY THE PEOPLE OF THE CITY, UNTIL THERE WERE NONE LEFT OF HIS FAMILY.
THOSE WHO DIED IN THE FIELDS WERE EATEN BY THE BUZZARDS AND THOSE THAT DIED IN THE CITY WERE EATEN BY THE DOGS. NOTHING WAS LEFT TO BURY. TRULY THE WAGES OF SIN IS DEATH.

2 KINGS 9:33-37

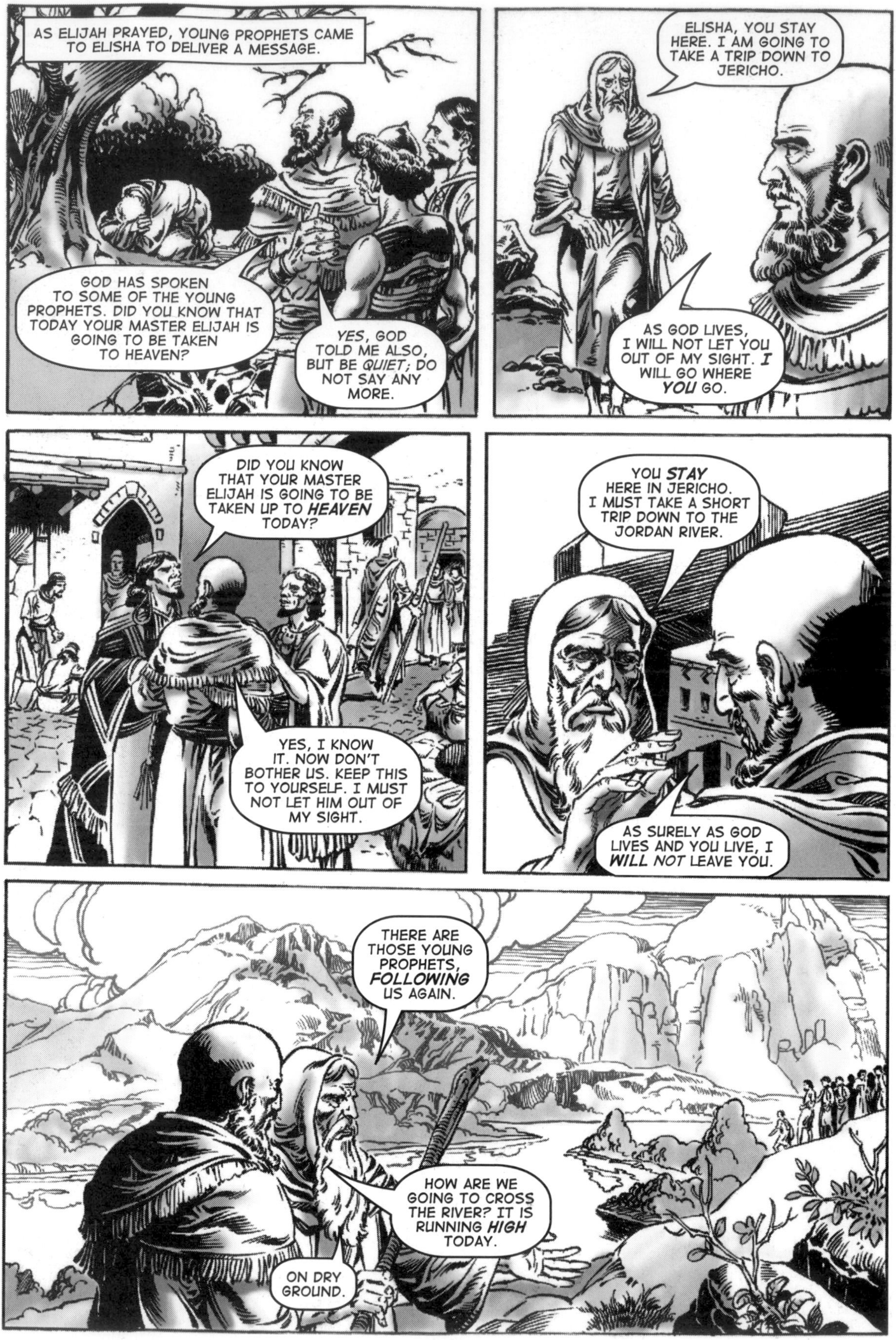
AS ELIJAH PRAYED, YOUNG PROPHETS CAME TO ELISHA TO DELIVER A MESSAGE.
GOD HAS SPOKEN TO SOME OF THE YOUNG PROPHETS. DID YOU KNOW THAT TODAY YOUR MASTER ELIJAH IS GOING TO BE TAKEN TO HEAVEN?
YES, GOD TOLD ME ALSO, BUT BE QUIET; DO NOT SAY ANY MORE.
ELISHA, YOU STAY HERE. I AM GOING TO TAKE A TRIP DOWN TO JERICHO.
AS GOD LIVES, I WILL NOT LET YOU OUT OF MY SIGHT. I WILL GO WHERE YOU GO.
DID YOU KNOW THAT YOUR MASTER ELIJAH IS GOING TO BE TAKEN UP TO HEAVEN TODAY?
YES, I KNOW IT. NOW DON'T BOTHER US. KEEP THIS TO YOURSELF. I MUST NOT LET HIM OUT OF MY SIGHT.
YOU STAY HERE IN JERICHO. I MUST TAKE A SHORT TRIP DOWN TO THE JORDAN RIVER.
AS SURELY AS GOD LIVES AND YOU LIVE, I WILL NOT LEAVE YOU.
THERE ARE THOSE YOUNG PROPHETS, FOLLOWING US AGAIN.
HOW ARE WE GOING TO CROSS THE RIVER? IT IS RUNNING HIGH TODAY.
ON DRY GROUND.

2 KINGS 2:3–7

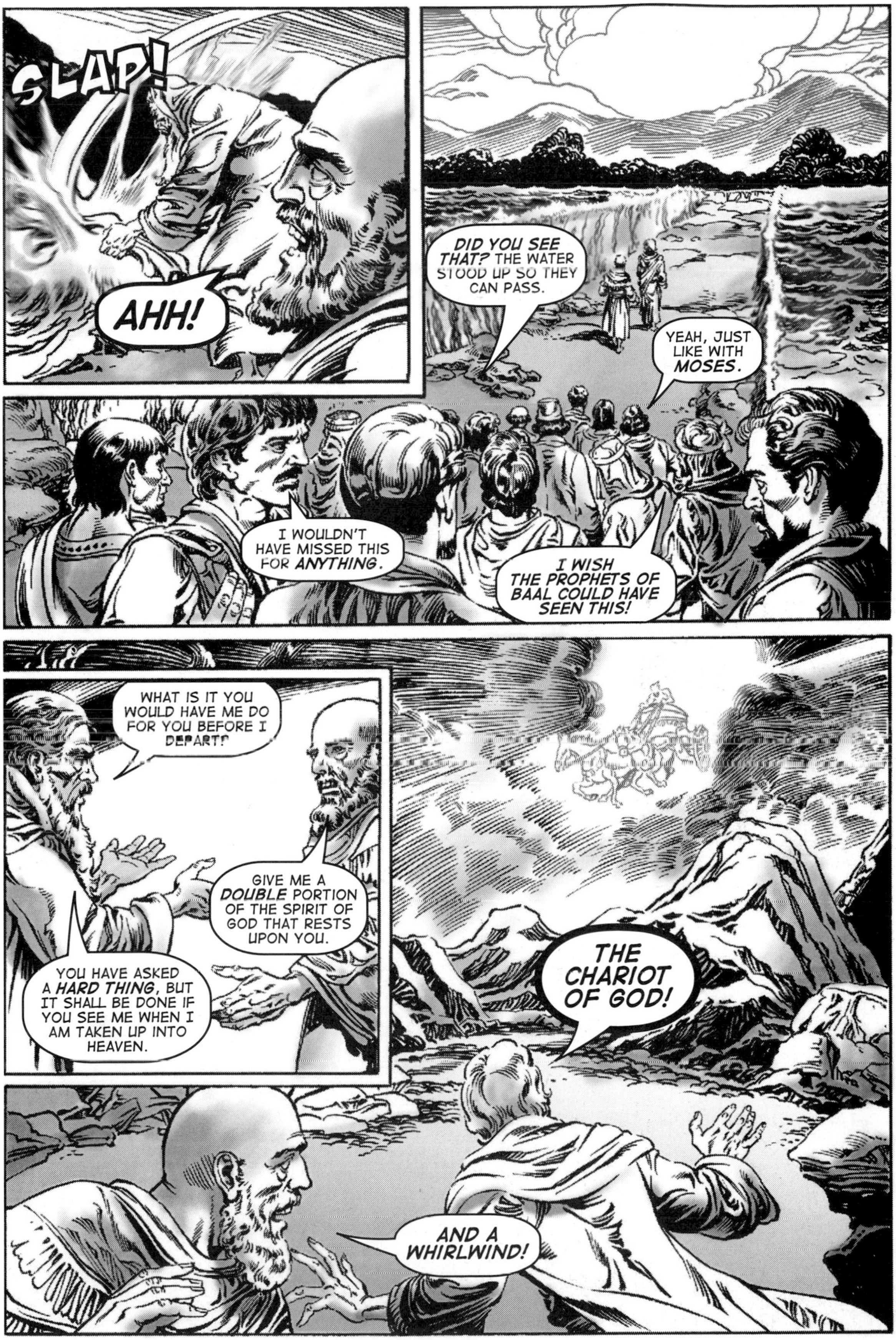
SLAP!
AHH!
DID YOU SEE THAT? THE WATER STOOD UP SO THEY CAN PASS.
YEAH, JUST LIKE WITH MOSES.
I WOULDN'T HAVE MISSED THIS FOR ANYTHING.
I WISH THE PROPHETS OF BAAL COULD HAVE SEEN THIS!
WHAT IS IT YOU WOULD HAVE ME DO FOR YOU BEFORE I DEPART?
GIVE ME A DOUBLE PORTION OF THE SPIRIT OF GOD THAT RESTS UPON YOU.
YOU HAVE ASKED A HARD THING, BUT IT SHALL BE DONE IF YOU SEE ME WHEN I AM TAKEN UP INTO HEAVEN.
THE CHARIOT OF GOD!
AND A WHIRLWIND!

2 KINGS 2:8–11

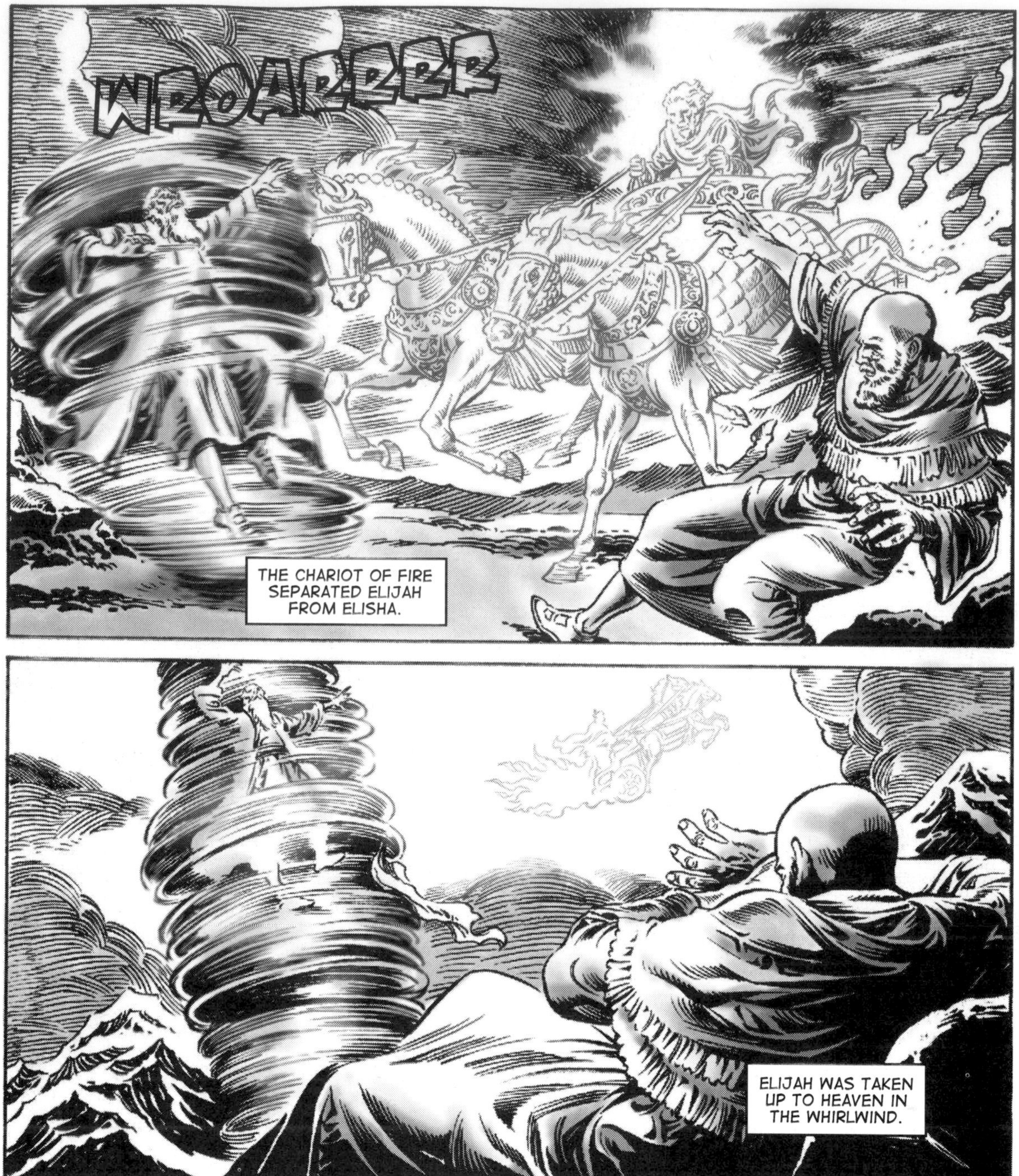
WROARRRR
THE CHARIOT OF FIRE SEPARATED ELIJAH FROM ELISHA.
ELIJAH WAS TAKEN UP TO HEAVEN IN THE WHIRLWIND.
THEN ALL WAS QUIET. ELIJAH WAS NOW IN GOD'S PRESENCE.
ALL THAT IS LEFT IS HIS MANTLE. IT IS WHAT HE USED TO PART THE WATERS.

2 KINGS 2:11–13

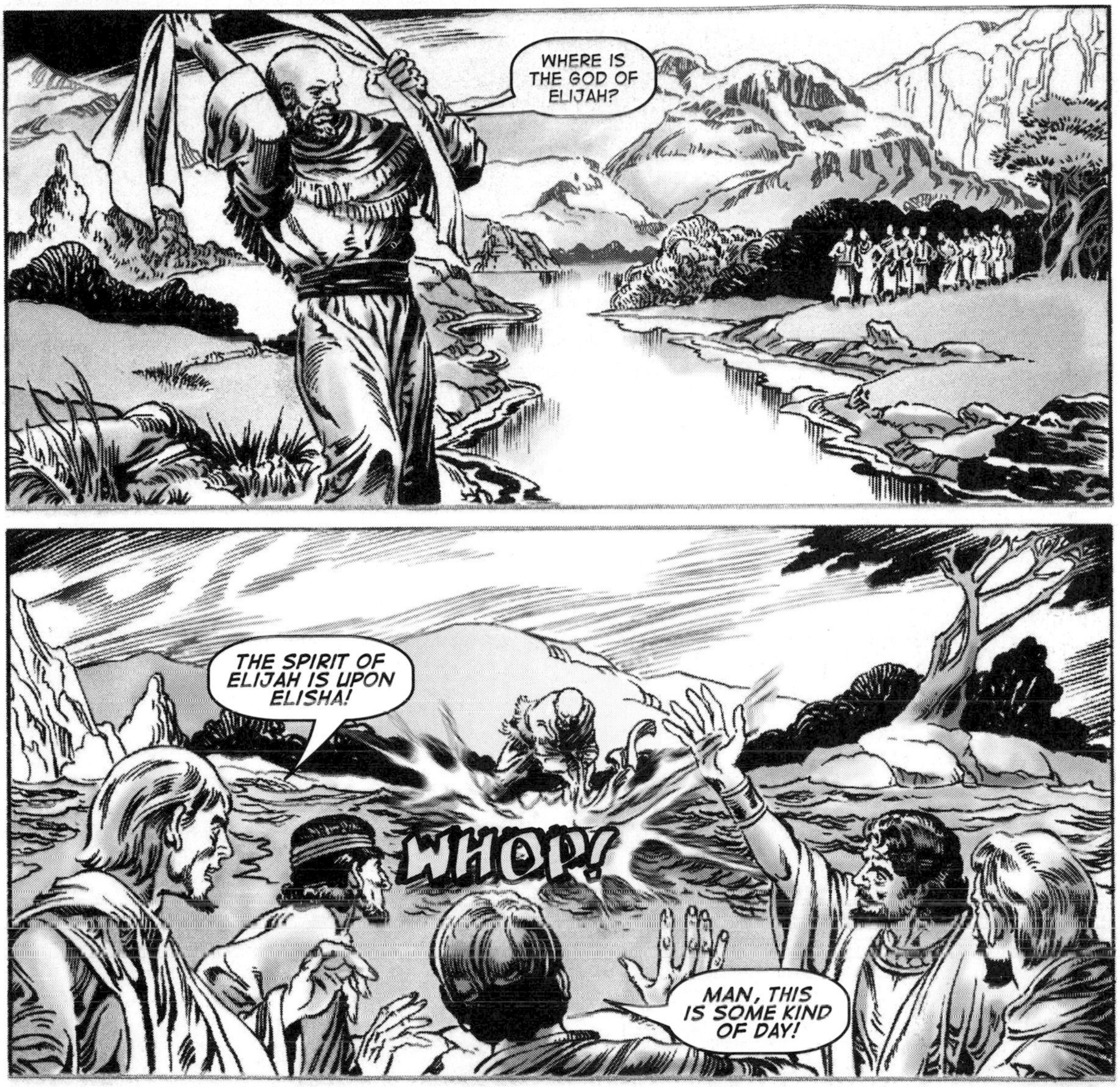
WHERE IS THE GOD OF ELIJAH?
THE SPIRIT OF ELIJAH IS UPON ELISHA!
WHOP!
MAN, THIS IS SOME KIND OF DAY!
ELISHA WENT ON TO PERFORM TWICE AS MANY MIRACLES AS DID ELIJAH. HE WAS FAITHFUL TO GOD, BUT THE PEOPLE WOULD NOT COMPLETELY TURN FROM THEIR IDOLATRY.
WHERE DID ELIJAH GO?
WE MUST GO LOOK FOR HIM!
THERE IS NO USE. HE IS GONE TO HEAVEN.

2 KINGS 2:14-16

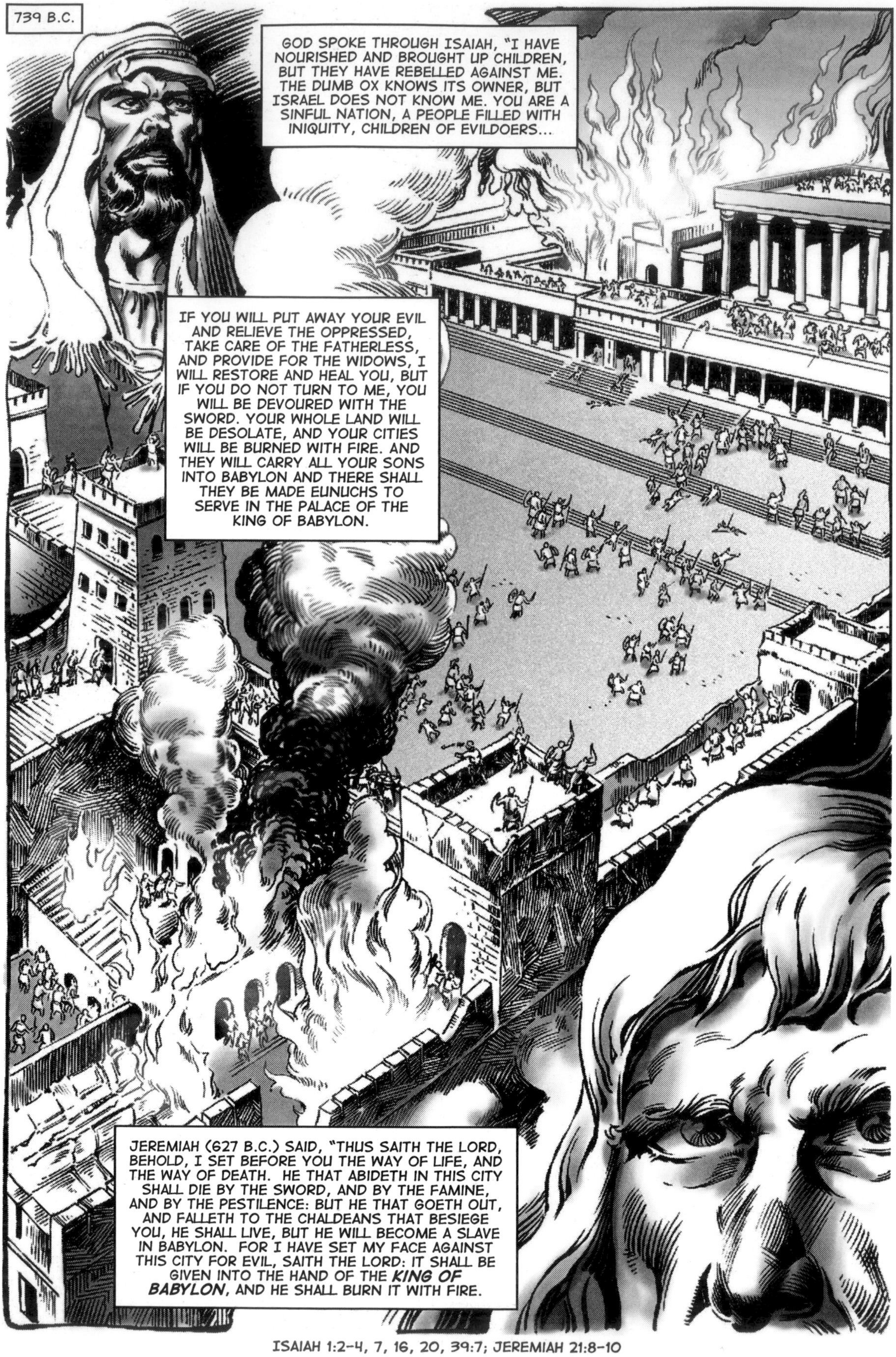
739 B.C.
GOD SPOKE THROUGH ISAIAH, "I HAVE NOURISHED AND BROUGHT UP CHILDREN, BUT THEY HAVE REBELLED AGAINST ME. THE DUMB OX KNOWS ITS OWNER, BUT ISRAEL DOES NOT KNOW ME. YOU ARE A SINFUL NATION, A PEOPLE FILLED WITH INIQUITY, CHILDREN OF EVILDOERS...
IF YOU WILL PUT AWAY YOUR EVIL AND RELIEVE THE OPPRESSED, TAKE CARE OF THE FATHERLESS, AND PROVIDE FOR THE WIDOWS, I WILL RESTORE AND HEAL YOU, BUT IF YOU DO NOT TURN TO ME, YOU WILL BE DEVOURED WITH THE SWORD. YOUR WHOLE LAND WILL BE DESOLATE, AND YOUR CITIES WILL BE BURNED WITH FIRE. AND THEY WILL CARRY ALL YOUR SONS INTO BABYLON AND THERE SHALL THEY BE MADE EUNUCHS TO SERVE IN THE PALACE OF THE KING OF BABYLON.
JEREMIAH (627 B.C.) SAID, "THUS SAITH THE LORD, BEHOLD, I SET BEFORE YOU THE WAY OF LIFE, AND THE WAY OF DEATH. HE THAT ABIDETH IN THIS CITY SHALL DIE BY THE SWORD, AND BY THE FAMINE, AND BY THE PESTILENCE: BUT HE THAT GOETH OUT, AND FALLETH TO THE CHALDEANS THAT BESIEGE YOU, HE SHALL LIVE, BUT HE WILL BECOME A SLAVE IN BABYLON. FOR I HAVE SET MY FACE AGAINST THIS CITY FOR EVIL, SAITH THE LORD: IT SHALL BE GIVEN INTO THE HAND OF THE ***KING OF BABYLON***, AND HE SHALL BURN IT WITH FIRE.

ISAIAH 1:2-4, 7, 16, 20, 39:7; JEREMIAH 21:8-10

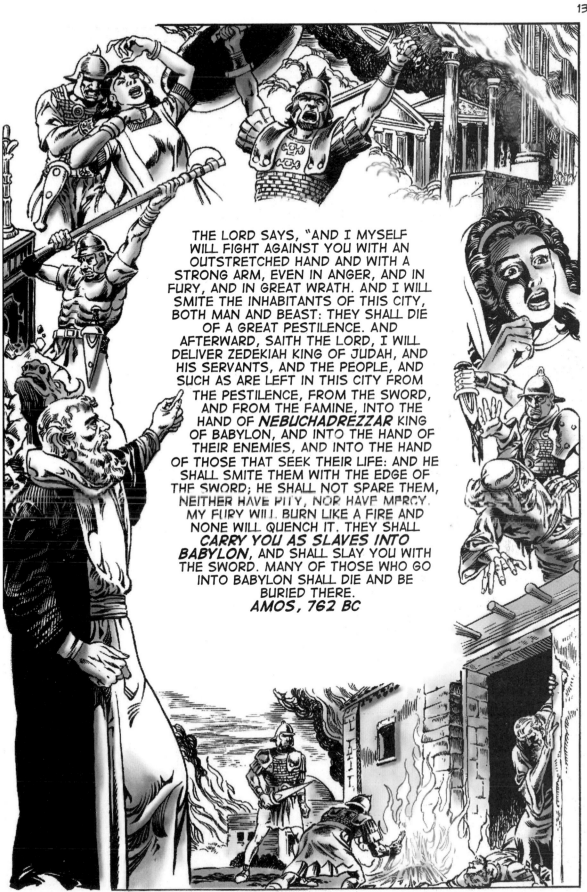

THE LORD SAYS, "AND I MYSELF WILL FIGHT AGAINST YOU WITH AN OUTSTRETCHED HAND AND WITH A STRONG ARM, EVEN IN ANGER, AND IN FURY, AND IN GREAT WRATH. AND I WILL SMITE THE INHABITANTS OF THIS CITY, BOTH MAN AND BEAST: THEY SHALL DIE OF A GREAT PESTILENCE. AND AFTERWARD, SAITH THE LORD, I WILL DELIVER ZEDEKIAH KING OF JUDAH, AND HIS SERVANTS, AND THE PEOPLE, AND SUCH AS ARE LEFT IN THIS CITY FROM THE PESTILENCE, FROM THE SWORD, AND FROM THE FAMINE, INTO THE HAND OF *NEBUCHADREZZAR* KING OF BABYLON, AND INTO THE HAND OF THEIR ENEMIES, AND INTO THE HAND OF THOSE THAT SEEK THEIR LIFE: AND HE SHALL SMITE THEM WITH THE EDGE OF THE SWORD; HE SHALL NOT SPARE THEM, NEITHER HAVE PITY, NOR HAVE MERCY. MY FURY WILL BURN LIKE A FIRE AND NONE WILL QUENCH IT. THEY SHALL *CARRY YOU AS SLAVES INTO BABYLON*, AND SHALL SLAY YOU WITH THE SWORD. MANY OF THOSE WHO GO INTO BABYLON SHALL DIE AND BE BURIED THERE.
AMOS, 762 BC

JEREMIAH 21:5-10; AMOS 1:4-7

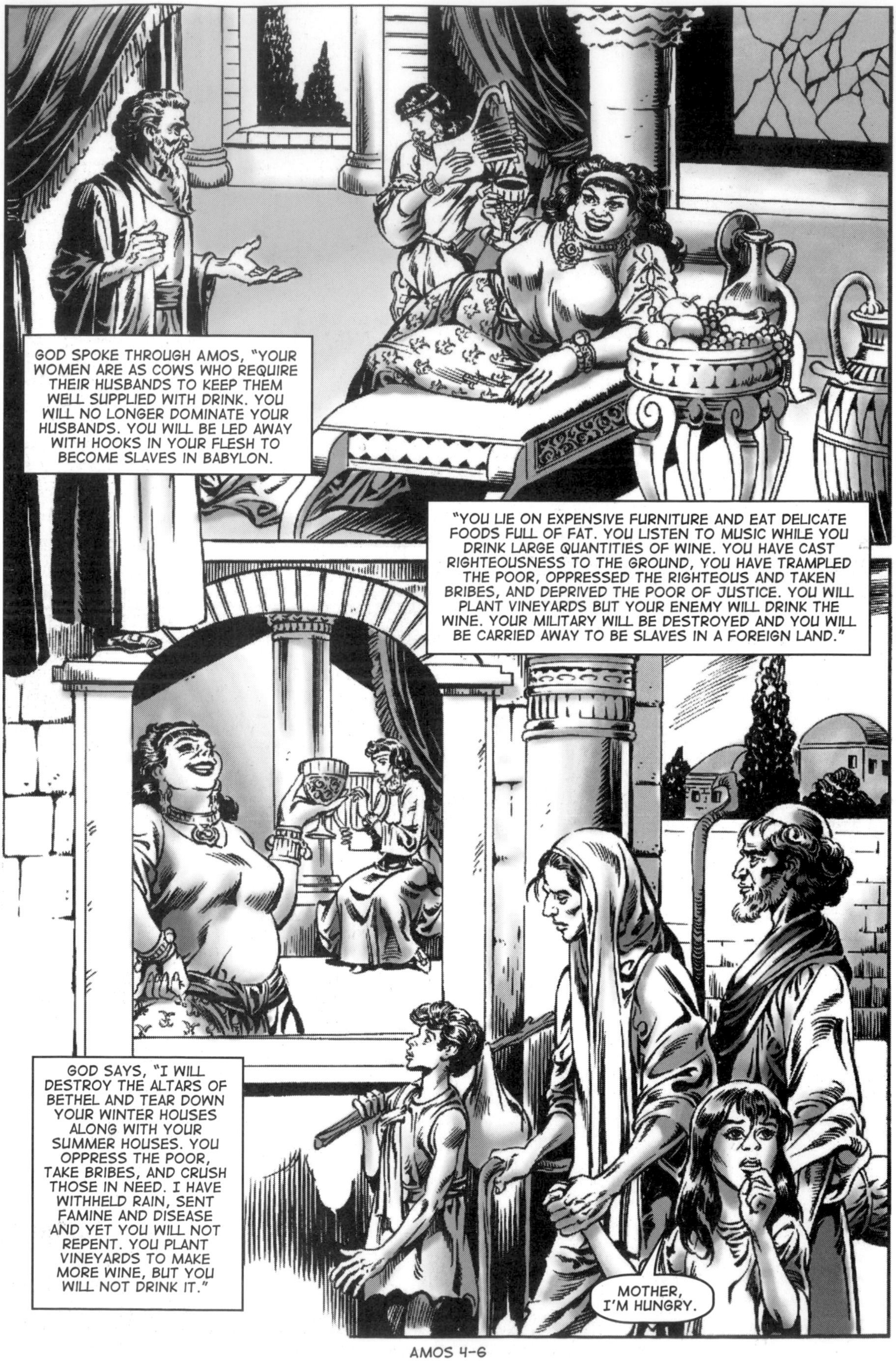
GOD SPOKE THROUGH AMOS, "YOUR WOMEN ARE AS COWS WHO REQUIRE THEIR HUSBANDS TO KEEP THEM WELL SUPPLIED WITH DRINK. YOU WILL NO LONGER DOMINATE YOUR HUSBANDS. YOU WILL BE LED AWAY WITH HOOKS IN YOUR FLESH TO BECOME SLAVES IN BABYLON.
"YOU LIE ON EXPENSIVE FURNITURE AND EAT DELICATE FOODS FULL OF FAT. YOU LISTEN TO MUSIC WHILE YOU DRINK LARGE QUANTITIES OF WINE. YOU HAVE CAST RIGHTEOUSNESS TO THE GROUND, YOU HAVE TRAMPLED THE POOR, OPPRESSED THE RIGHTEOUS AND TAKEN BRIBES, AND DEPRIVED THE POOR OF JUSTICE. YOU WILL PLANT VINEYARDS BUT YOUR ENEMY WILL DRINK THE WINE. YOUR MILITARY WILL BE DESTROYED AND YOU WILL BE CARRIED AWAY TO BE SLAVES IN A FOREIGN LAND."
GOD SAYS, "I WILL DESTROY THE ALTARS OF BETHEL AND TEAR DOWN YOUR WINTER HOUSES ALONG WITH YOUR SUMMER HOUSES. YOU OPPRESS THE POOR, TAKE BRIBES, AND CRUSH THOSE IN NEED. I HAVE WITHHELD RAIN, SENT FAMINE AND DISEASE AND YET YOU WILL NOT REPENT. YOU PLANT VINEYARDS TO MAKE MORE WINE, BUT YOU WILL NOT DRINK IT."
MOTHER, I'M HUNGRY.

AMOS 4-6

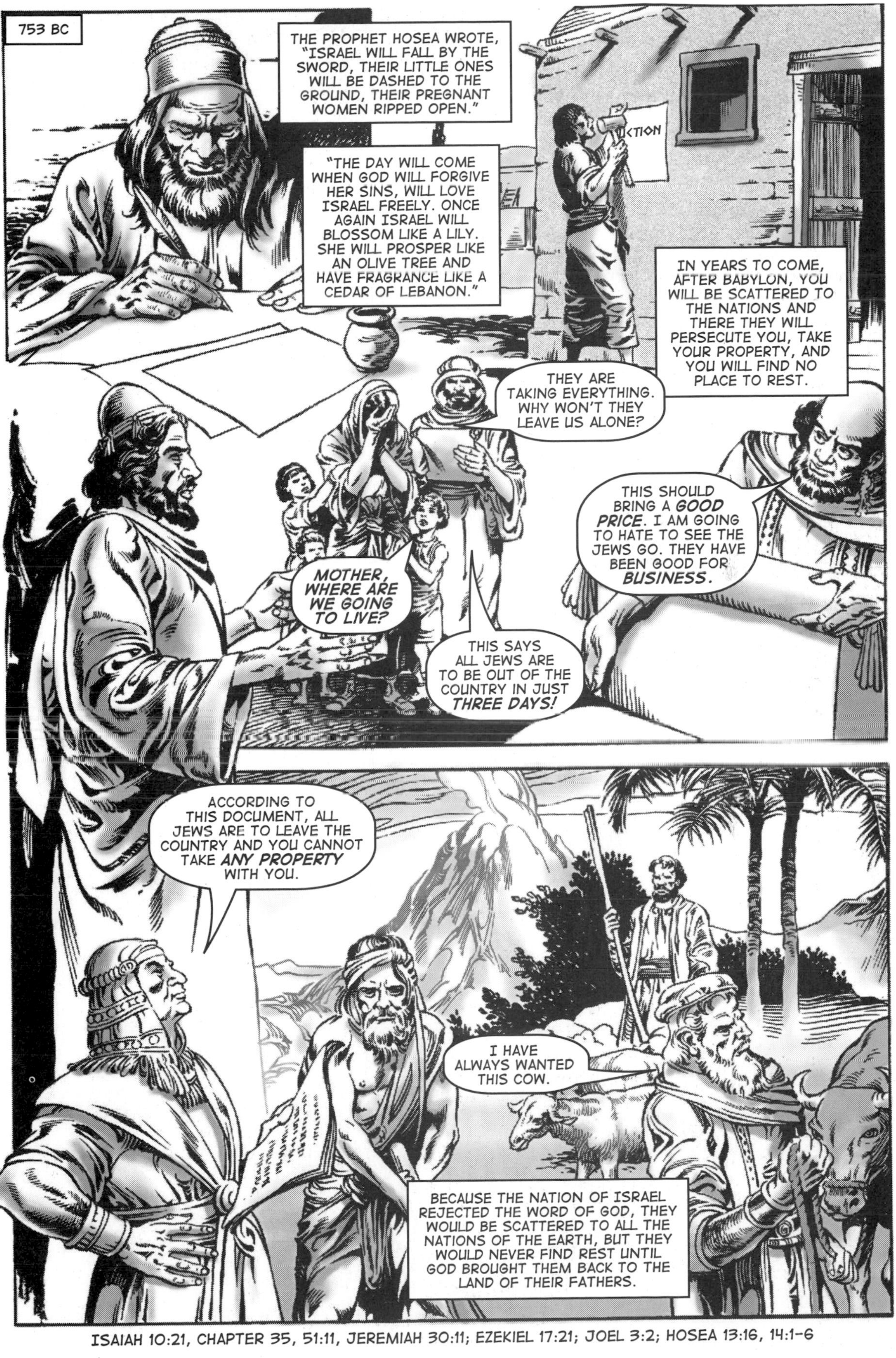
753 BC
THE PROPHET HOSEA WROTE, "ISRAEL WILL FALL BY THE SWORD, THEIR LITTLE ONES WILL BE DASHED TO THE GROUND, THEIR PREGNANT WOMEN RIPPED OPEN."
"THE DAY WILL COME WHEN GOD WILL FORGIVE HER SINS, WILL LOVE ISRAEL FREELY. ONCE AGAIN ISRAEL WILL BLOSSOM LIKE A LILY. SHE WILL PROSPER LIKE AN OLIVE TREE AND HAVE FRAGRANCE LIKE A CEDAR OF LEBANON."
CTION
IN YEARS TO COME, AFTER BABYLON, YOU WILL BE SCATTERED TO THE NATIONS AND THERE THEY WILL PERSECUTE YOU, TAKE YOUR PROPERTY, AND YOU WILL FIND NO PLACE TO REST.
THEY ARE TAKING EVERYTHING. WHY WON'T THEY LEAVE US ALONE?
THIS SHOULD BRING A GOOD PRICE. I AM GOING TO HATE TO SEE THE JEWS GO. THEY HAVE BEEN GOOD FOR BUSINESS.
MOTHER, WHERE ARE WE GOING TO LIVE?
THIS SAYS ALL JEWS ARE TO BE OUT OF THE COUNTRY IN JUST THREE DAYS!
ACCORDING TO THIS DOCUMENT, ALL JEWS ARE TO LEAVE THE COUNTRY AND YOU CANNOT TAKE ANY PROPERTY WITH YOU.
I HAVE ALWAYS WANTED THIS COW.
BECAUSE THE NATION OF ISRAEL REJECTED THE WORD OF GOD, THEY WOULD BE SCATTERED TO ALL THE NATIONS OF THE EARTH, BUT THEY WOULD NEVER FIND REST UNTIL GOD BROUGHT THEM BACK TO THE LAND OF THEIR FATHERS.

ISAIAH 10:21, CHAPTER 35, 51:11, JEREMIAH 30:11; EZEKIEL 17:21; JOEL 3:2; HOSEA 13:16, 14:1-6

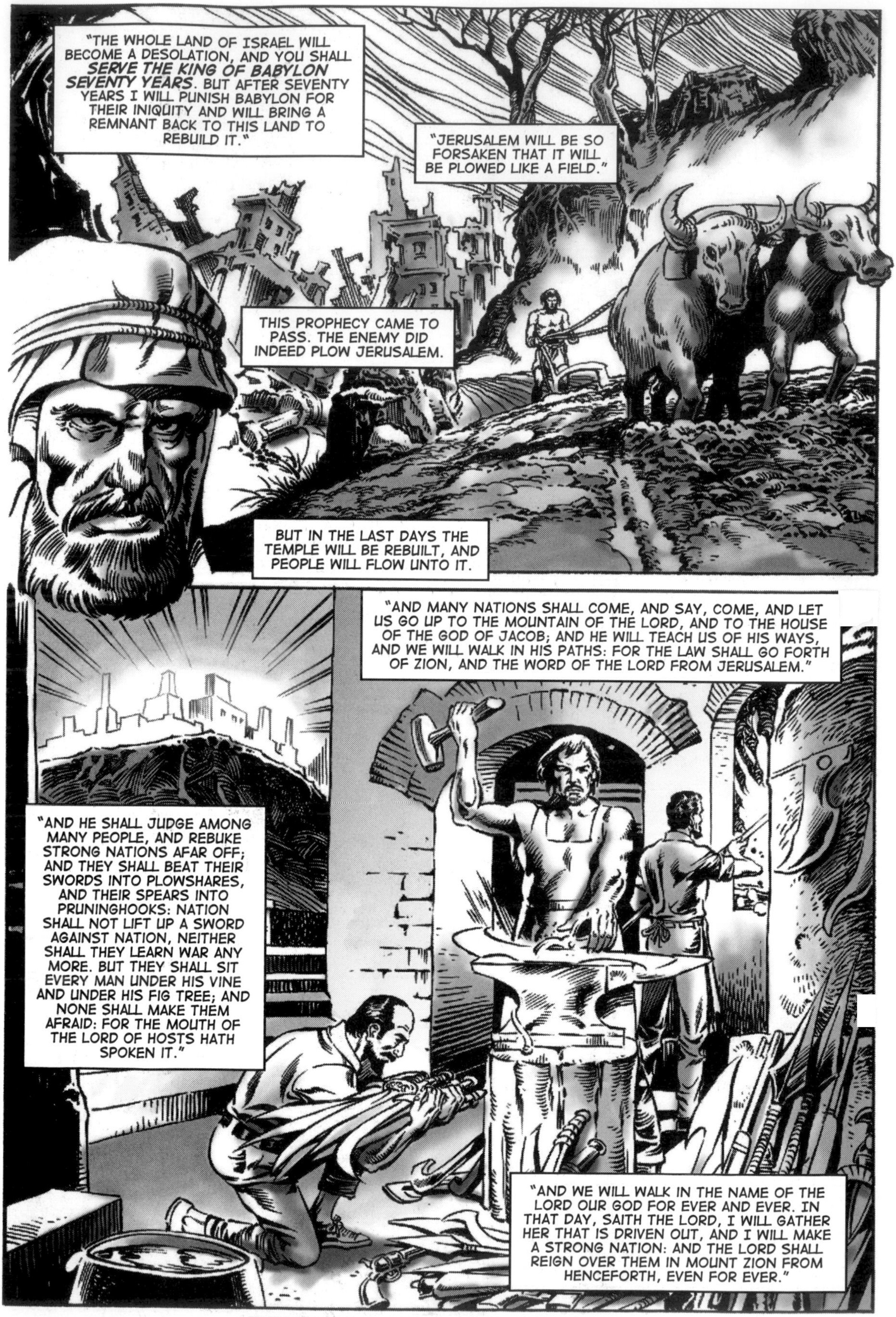
"THE WHOLE LAND OF ISRAEL WILL BECOME A DESOLATION, AND YOU SHALL ***SERVE THE KING OF BABYLON SEVENTY YEARS***. BUT AFTER SEVENTY YEARS I WILL PUNISH BABYLON FOR THEIR INIQUITY AND WILL BRING A REMNANT BACK TO THIS LAND TO REBUILD IT."
"JERUSALEM WILL BE SO FORSAKEN THAT IT WILL BE PLOWED LIKE A FIELD."
THIS PROPHECY CAME TO PASS. THE ENEMY DID INDEED PLOW JERUSALEM.
BUT IN THE LAST DAYS THE TEMPLE WILL BE REBUILT, AND PEOPLE WILL FLOW UNTO IT.
"AND MANY NATIONS SHALL COME, AND SAY, COME, AND LET US GO UP TO THE MOUNTAIN OF THE LORD, AND TO THE HOUSE OF THE GOD OF JACOB; AND HE WILL TEACH US OF HIS WAYS, AND WE WILL WALK IN HIS PATHS: FOR THE LAW SHALL GO FORTH OF ZION, AND THE WORD OF THE LORD FROM JERUSALEM."
"AND HE SHALL JUDGE AMONG MANY PEOPLE, AND REBUKE STRONG NATIONS AFAR OFF; AND THEY SHALL BEAT THEIR SWORDS INTO PLOWSHARES, AND THEIR SPEARS INTO PRUNINGHOOKS: NATION SHALL NOT LIFT UP A SWORD AGAINST NATION, NEITHER SHALL THEY LEARN WAR ANY MORE. BUT THEY SHALL SIT EVERY MAN UNDER HIS VINE AND UNDER HIS FIG TREE; AND NONE SHALL MAKE THEM AFRAID: FOR THE MOUTH OF THE LORD OF HOSTS HATH SPOKEN IT."
"AND WE WILL WALK IN THE NAME OF THE LORD OUR GOD FOR EVER AND EVER. IN THAT DAY, SAITH THE LORD, I WILL GATHER HER THAT IS DRIVEN OUT, AND I WILL MAKE A STRONG NATION: AND THE LORD SHALL REIGN OVER THEM IN MOUNT ZION FROM HENCEFORTH, EVEN FOR EVER."

JEREMIAH 25:11-12; MICAH 3:12 (750-686 B.C.), 4:1-7

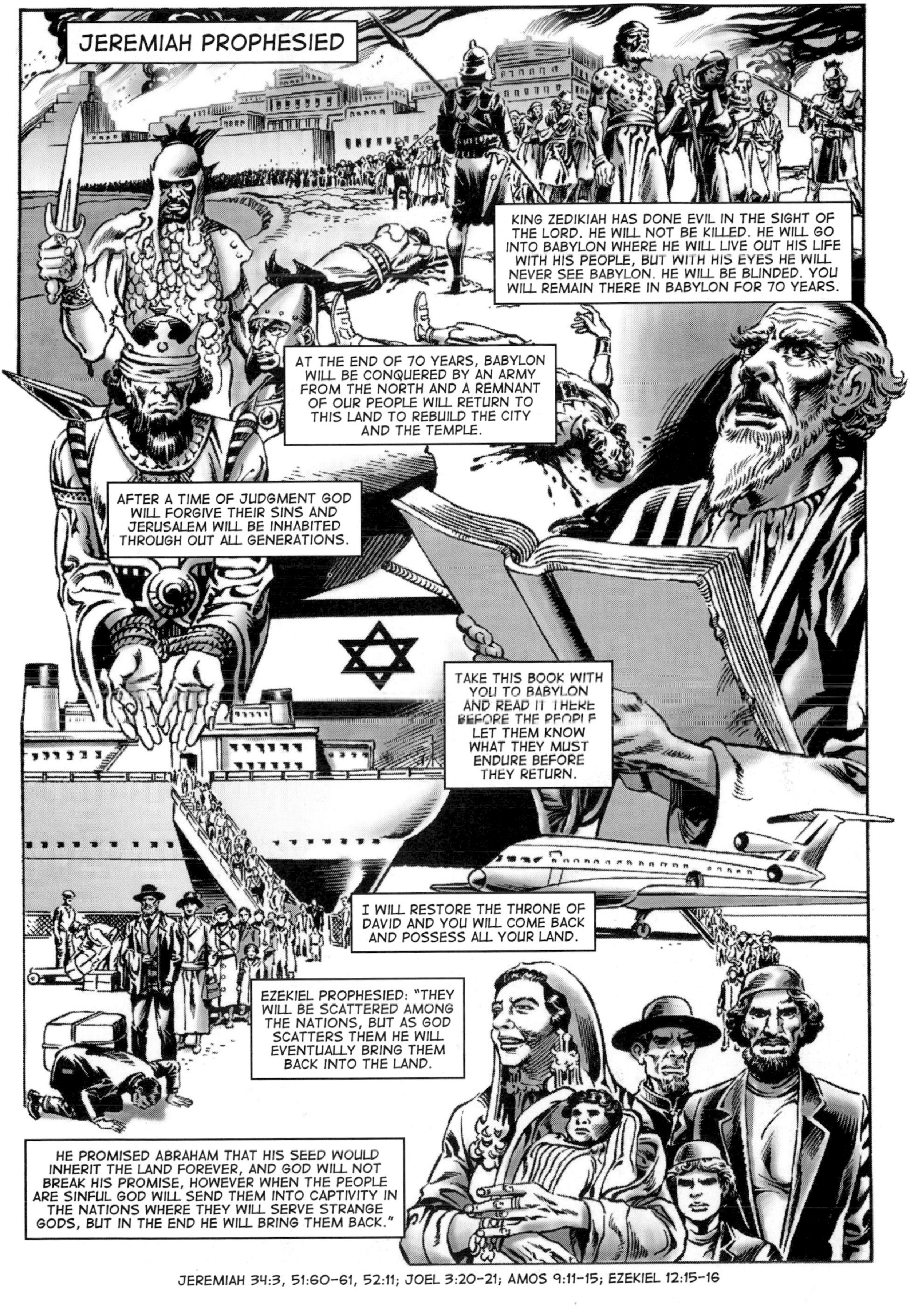
JEREMIAH PROPHESIED
KING ZEDIKIAH HAS DONE EVIL IN THE SIGHT OF THE LORD. HE WILL NOT BE KILLED. HE WILL GO INTO BABYLON WHERE HE WILL LIVE OUT HIS LIFE WITH HIS PEOPLE, BUT WITH HIS EYES HE WILL NEVER SEE BABYLON. HE WILL BE BLINDED. YOU WILL REMAIN THERE IN BABYLON FOR 70 YEARS.
AT THE END OF 70 YEARS, BABYLON WILL BE CONQUERED BY AN ARMY FROM THE NORTH AND A REMNANT OF OUR PEOPLE WILL RETURN TO THIS LAND TO REBUILD THE CITY AND THE TEMPLE.
AFTER A TIME OF JUDGMENT GOD WILL FORGIVE THEIR SINS AND JERUSALEM WILL BE INHABITED THROUGH OUT ALL GENERATIONS.
TAKE THIS BOOK WITH YOU TO BABYLON AND READ IT THERE BEFORE THE PEOPLE LET THEM KNOW WHAT THEY MUST ENDURE BEFORE THEY RETURN.
I WILL RESTORE THE THRONE OF DAVID AND YOU WILL COME BACK AND POSSESS ALL YOUR LAND.
EZEKIEL PROPHESIED: "THEY WILL BE SCATTERED AMONG THE NATIONS, BUT AS GOD SCATTERS THEM HE WILL EVENTUALLY BRING THEM BACK INTO THE LAND.
HE PROMISED ABRAHAM THAT HIS SEED WOULD INHERIT THE LAND FOREVER, AND GOD WILL NOT BREAK HIS PROMISE, HOWEVER WHEN THE PEOPLE ARE SINFUL GOD WILL SEND THEM INTO CAPTIVITY IN THE NATIONS WHERE THEY WILL SERVE STRANGE GODS, BUT IN THE END HE WILL BRING THEM BACK."

JEREMIAH 34:3, 51:60-61, 52:11; JOEL 3:20-21; AMOS 9:11-15; EZEKIEL 12:15-16

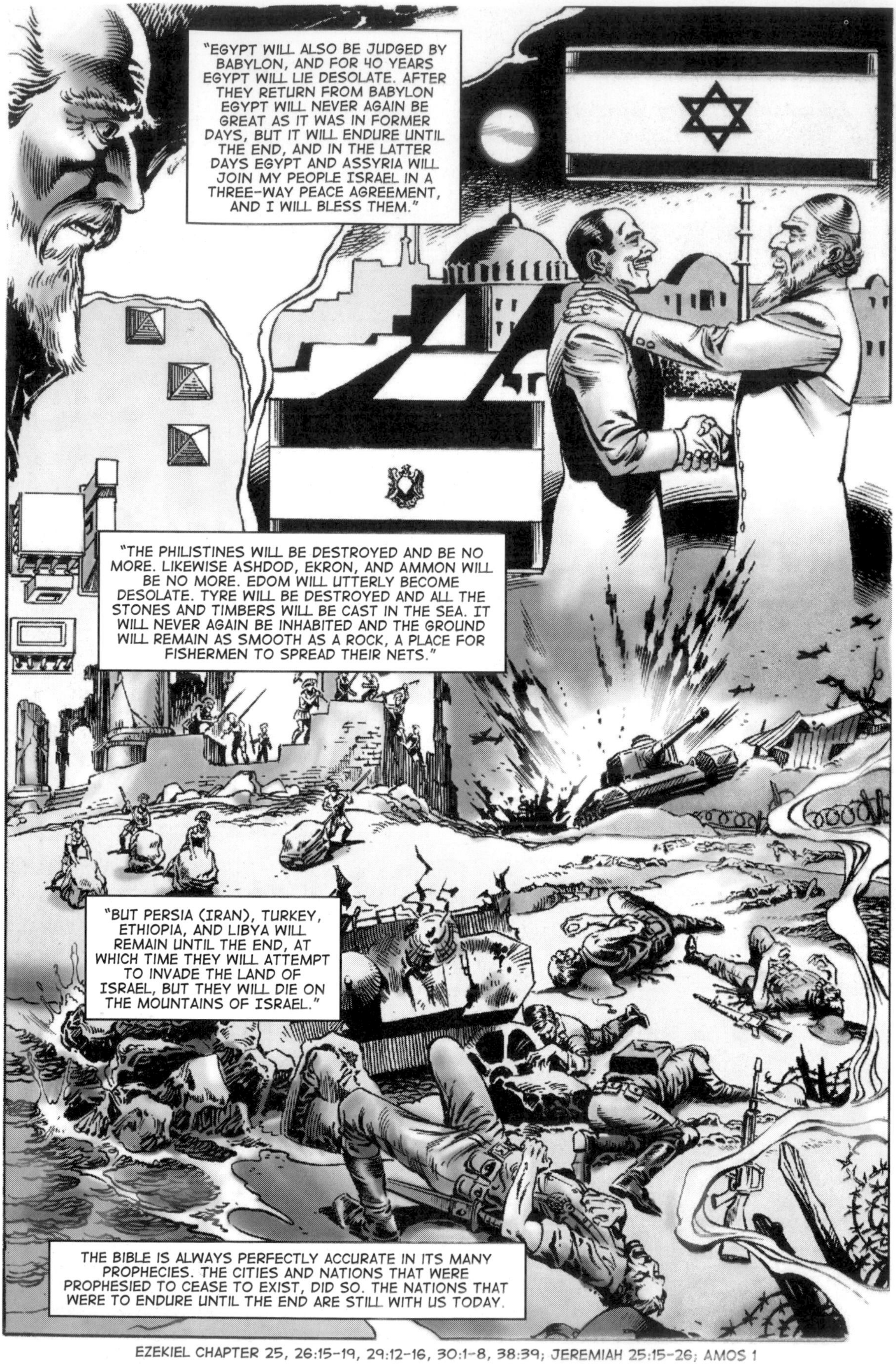
"EGYPT WILL ALSO BE JUDGED BY BABYLON, AND FOR 40 YEARS EGYPT WILL LIE DESOLATE. AFTER THEY RETURN FROM BABYLON EGYPT WILL NEVER AGAIN BE GREAT AS IT WAS IN FORMER DAYS, BUT IT WILL ENDURE UNTIL THE END, AND IN THE LATTER DAYS EGYPT AND ASSYRIA WILL JOIN MY PEOPLE ISRAEL IN A THREE-WAY PEACE AGREEMENT, AND I WILL BLESS THEM."
"THE PHILISTINES WILL BE DESTROYED AND BE NO MORE. LIKEWISE ASHDOD, EKRON, AND AMMON WILL BE NO MORE. EDOM WILL UTTERLY BECOME DESOLATE. TYRE WILL BE DESTROYED AND ALL THE STONES AND TIMBERS WILL BE CAST IN THE SEA. IT WILL NEVER AGAIN BE INHABITED AND THE GROUND WILL REMAIN AS SMOOTH AS A ROCK, A PLACE FOR FISHERMEN TO SPREAD THEIR NETS."
"BUT PERSIA (IRAN), TURKEY, ETHIOPIA, AND LIBYA WILL REMAIN UNTIL THE END, AT WHICH TIME THEY WILL ATTEMPT TO INVADE THE LAND OF ISRAEL, BUT THEY WILL DIE ON THE MOUNTAINS OF ISRAEL."
THE BIBLE IS ALWAYS PERFECTLY ACCURATE IN ITS MANY PROPHECIES. THE CITIES AND NATIONS THAT WERE PROPHESIED TO CEASE TO EXIST, DID SO. THE NATIONS THAT WERE TO ENDURE UNTIL THE END ARE STILL WITH US TODAY.

EZEKIEL CHAPTER 25, 26:15-19, 29:12-16, 30:1-8, 38:39; JEREMIAH 25:15-26; AMOS 1

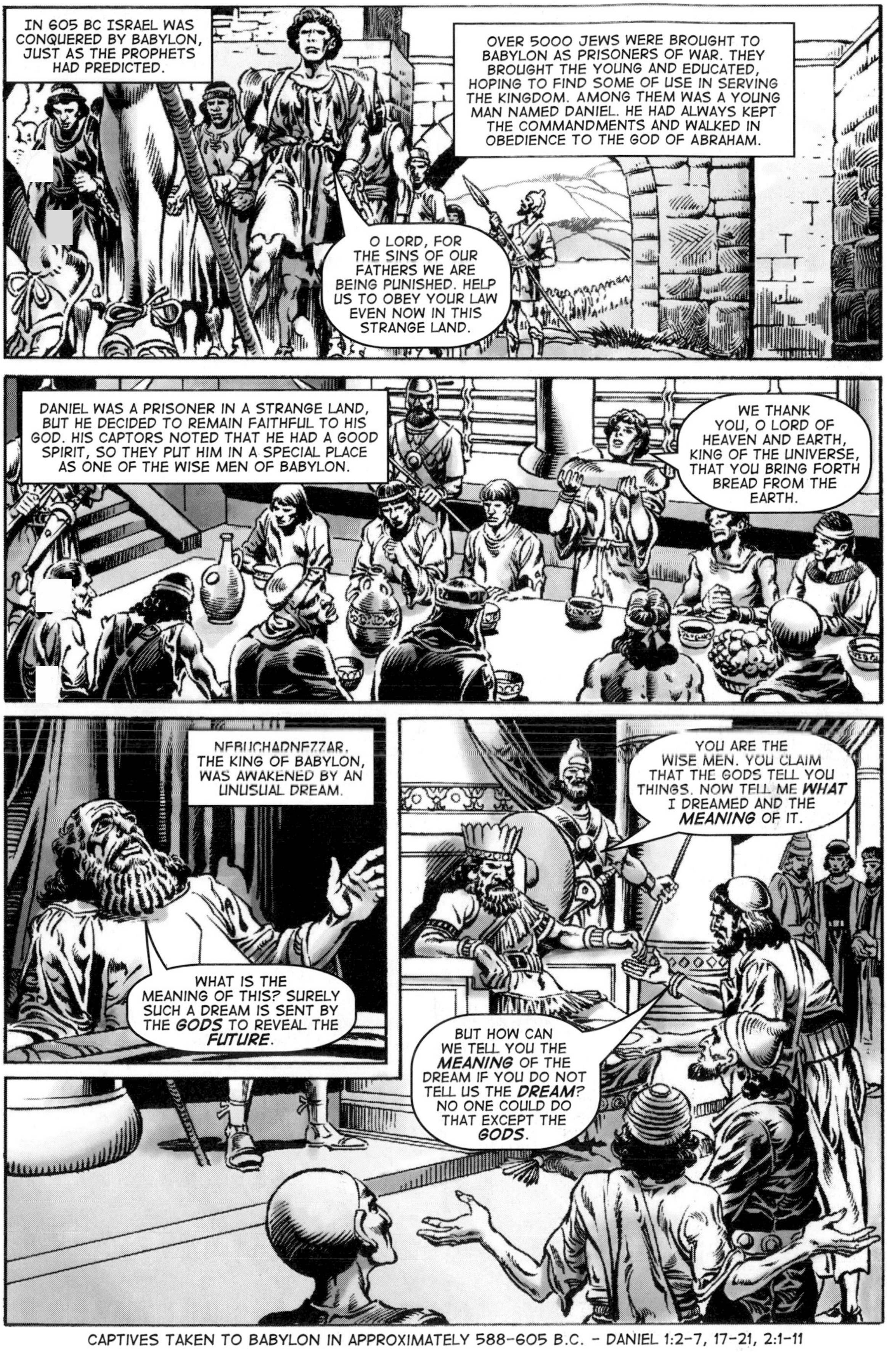
IN 605 BC ISRAEL WAS CONQUERED BY BABYLON, JUST AS THE PROPHETS HAD PREDICTED.
OVER 5000 JEWS WERE BROUGHT TO BABYLON AS PRISONERS OF WAR. THEY BROUGHT THE YOUNG AND EDUCATED, HOPING TO FIND SOME OF USE IN SERVING THE KINGDOM. AMONG THEM WAS A YOUNG MAN NAMED DANIEL. HE HAD ALWAYS KEPT THE COMMANDMENTS AND WALKED IN OBEDIENCE TO THE GOD OF ABRAHAM.
O LORD, FOR THE SINS OF OUR FATHERS WE ARE BEING PUNISHED. HELP US TO OBEY YOUR LAW EVEN NOW IN THIS STRANGE LAND.
DANIEL WAS A PRISONER IN A STRANGE LAND, BUT HE DECIDED TO REMAIN FAITHFUL TO HIS GOD. HIS CAPTORS NOTED THAT HE HAD A GOOD SPIRIT, SO THEY PUT HIM IN A SPECIAL PLACE AS ONE OF THE WISE MEN OF BABYLON.
WE THANK YOU, O LORD OF HEAVEN AND EARTH, KING OF THE UNIVERSE, THAT YOU BRING FORTH BREAD FROM THE EARTH.
NEBUCHADNEZZAR, THE KING OF BABYLON, WAS AWAKENED BY AN UNUSUAL DREAM.
WHAT IS THE MEANING OF THIS? SURELY SUCH A DREAM IS SENT BY THE GODS TO REVEAL THE FUTURE.
YOU ARE THE WISE MEN. YOU CLAIM THAT THE GODS TELL YOU THINGS. NOW TELL ME WHAT I DREAMED AND THE MEANING OF IT.
BUT HOW CAN WE TELL YOU THE MEANING OF THE DREAM IF YOU DO NOT TELL US THE DREAM? NO ONE COULD DO THAT EXCEPT THE GODS.

CAPTIVES TAKEN TO BABYLON IN APPROXIMATELY 588–605 B.C. – DANIEL 1:2–7, 17–21, 2:1–11

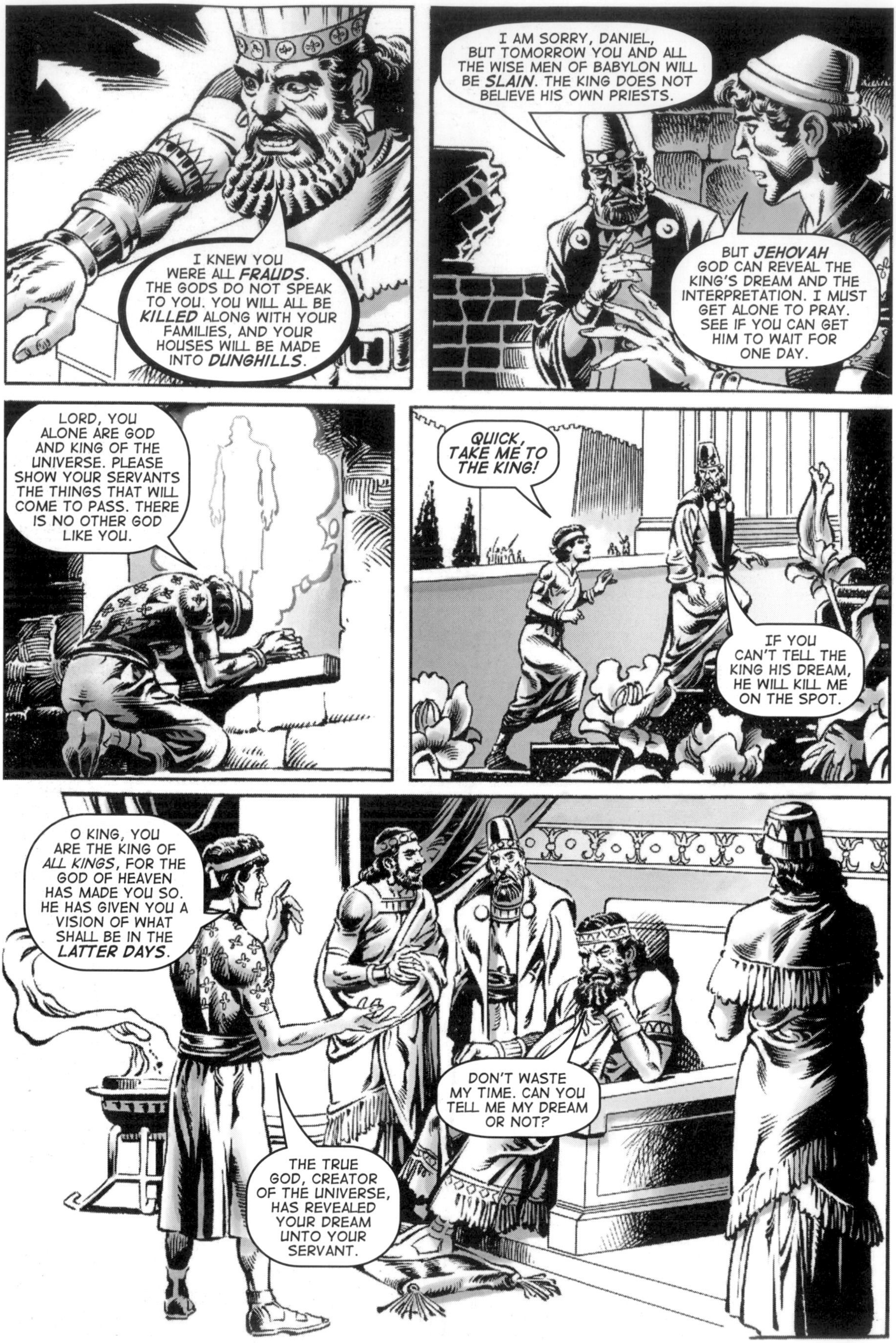
I KNEW YOU WERE ALL ***FRAUDS***. THE GODS DO NOT SPEAK TO YOU. YOU WILL ALL BE ***KILLED*** ALONG WITH YOUR FAMILIES, AND YOUR HOUSES WILL BE MADE INTO ***DUNGHILLS***.
I AM SORRY, DANIEL, BUT TOMORROW YOU AND ALL THE WISE MEN OF BABYLON WILL BE ***SLAIN***. THE KING DOES NOT BELIEVE HIS OWN PRIESTS.
BUT ***JEHOVAH*** GOD CAN REVEAL THE KING'S DREAM AND THE INTERPRETATION. I MUST GET ALONE TO PRAY. SEE IF YOU CAN GET HIM TO WAIT FOR ONE DAY.
LORD, YOU ALONE ARE GOD AND KING OF THE UNIVERSE. PLEASE SHOW YOUR SERVANTS THE THINGS THAT WILL COME TO PASS. THERE IS NO OTHER GOD LIKE YOU.
QUICK, TAKE ME TO THE KING!
IF YOU CAN'T TELL THE KING HIS DREAM, HE WILL KILL ME ON THE SPOT.
O KING, YOU ARE THE KING OF *ALL KINGS*, FOR THE GOD OF HEAVEN HAS MADE YOU SO. HE HAS GIVEN YOU A VISION OF WHAT SHALL BE IN THE ***LATTER DAYS***.
DON'T WASTE MY TIME. CAN YOU TELL ME MY DREAM OR NOT?
THE TRUE GOD, CREATOR OF THE UNIVERSE, HAS REVEALED YOUR DREAM UNTO YOUR SERVANT.

DANIEL 2:12–30

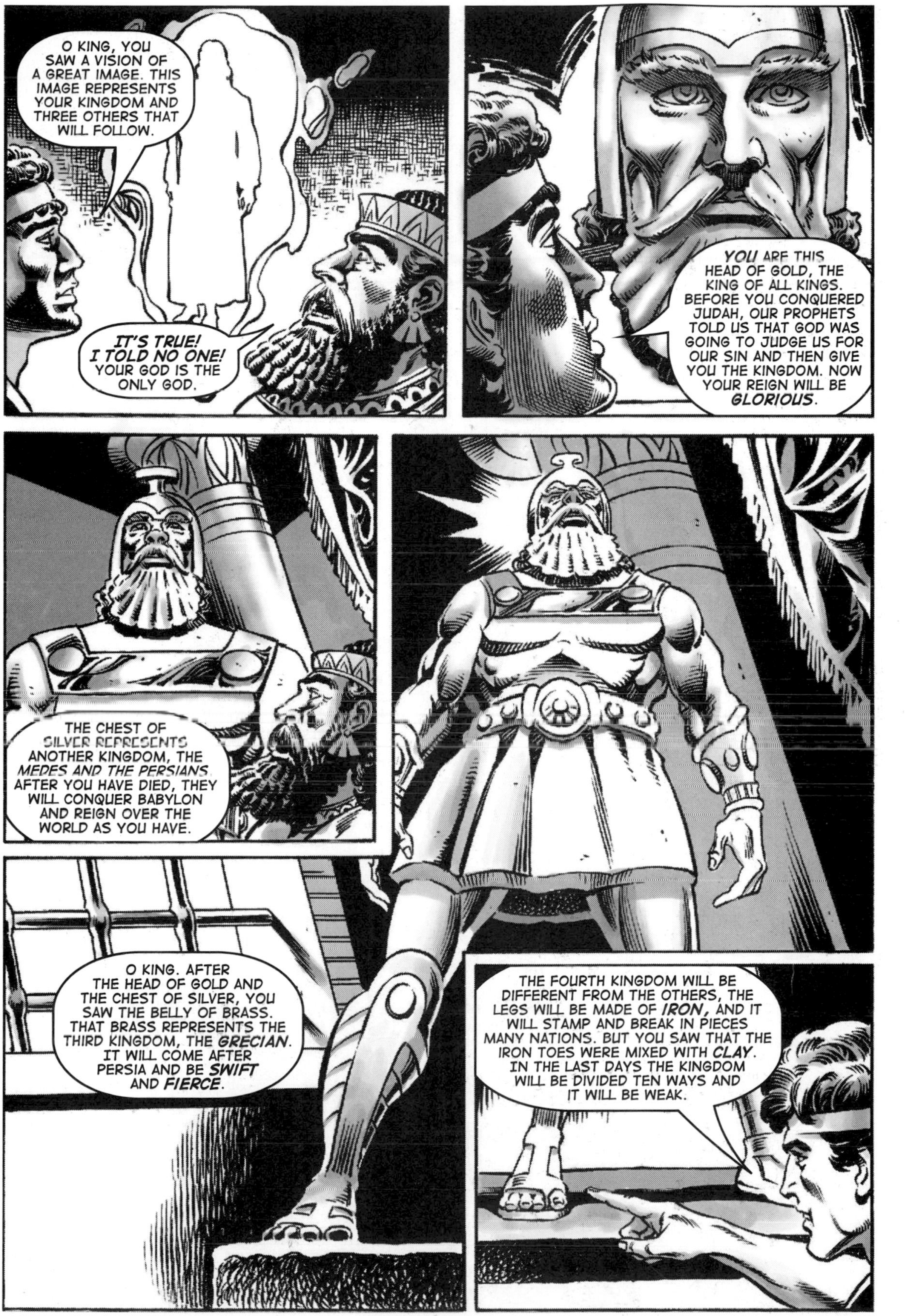
O KING, YOU SAW A VISION OF A GREAT IMAGE. THIS IMAGE REPRESENTS YOUR KINGDOM AND THREE OTHERS THAT WILL FOLLOW.
IT'S TRUE! I TOLD NO ONE! YOUR GOD IS THE ONLY GOD.
YOU ARE THIS HEAD OF GOLD, THE KING OF ALL KINGS. BEFORE YOU CONQUERED JUDAH, OUR PROPHETS TOLD US THAT GOD WAS GOING TO JUDGE US FOR OUR SIN AND THEN GIVE YOU THE KINGDOM. NOW YOUR REIGN WILL BE GLORIOUS.
THE CHEST OF SILVER REPRESENTS ANOTHER KINGDOM, THE MEDES AND THE PERSIANS. AFTER YOU HAVE DIED, THEY WILL CONQUER BABYLON AND REIGN OVER THE WORLD AS YOU HAVE.
O KING. AFTER THE HEAD OF GOLD AND THE CHEST OF SILVER, YOU SAW THE BELLY OF BRASS. THAT BRASS REPRESENTS THE THIRD KINGDOM, THE GRECIAN. IT WILL COME AFTER PERSIA AND BE SWIFT AND FIERCE.
THE FOURTH KINGDOM WILL BE DIFFERENT FROM THE OTHERS, THE LEGS WILL BE MADE OF IRON, AND IT WILL STAMP AND BREAK IN PIECES MANY NATIONS. BUT YOU SAW THAT THE IRON TOES WERE MIXED WITH CLAY. IN THE LAST DAYS THE KINGDOM WILL BE DIVIDED TEN WAYS AND IT WILL BE WEAK.

DANIEL 2:31-33, 39-43

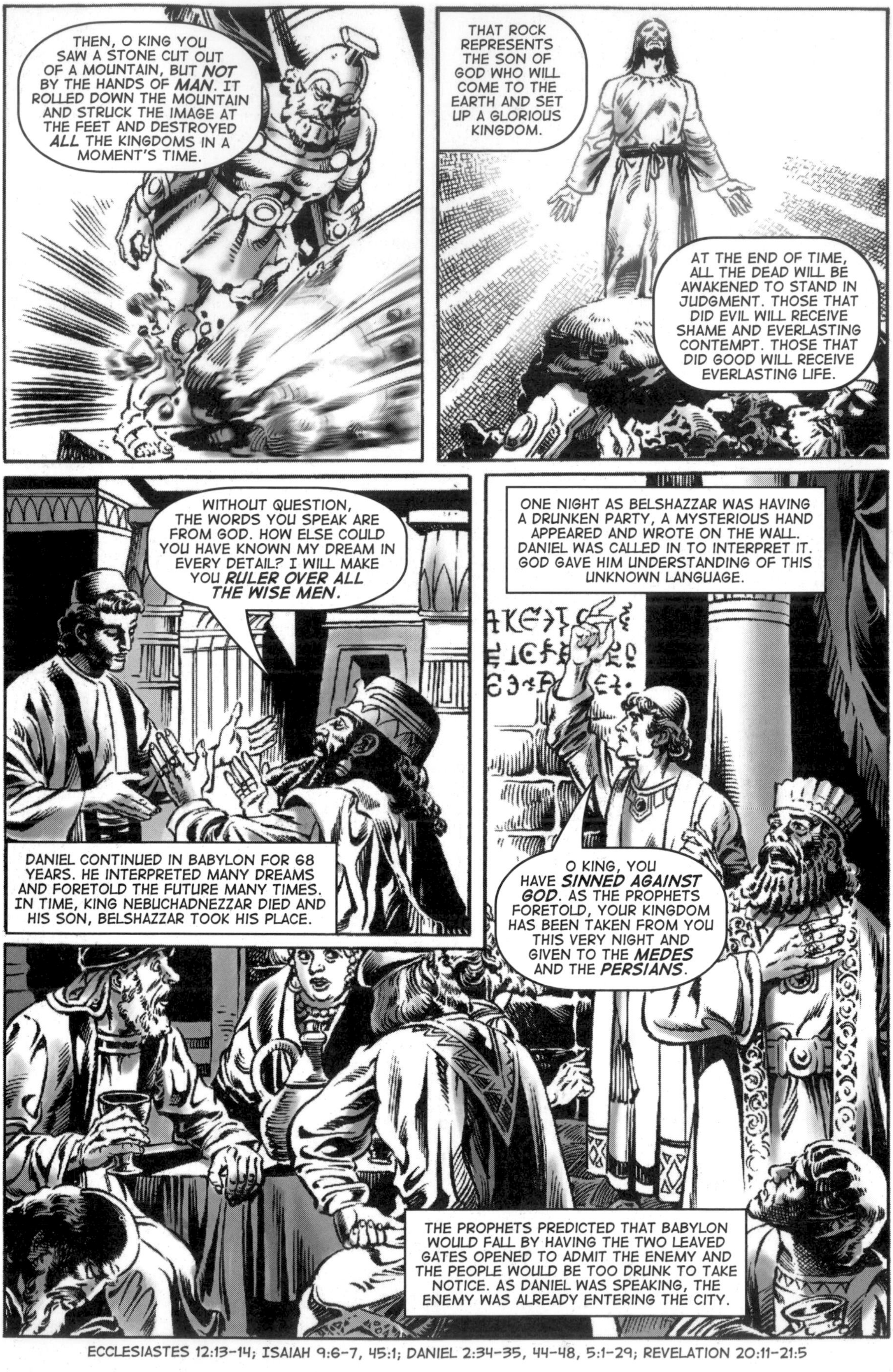
THEN, O KING YOU SAW A STONE CUT OUT OF A MOUNTAIN, BUT NOT BY THE HANDS OF MAN. IT ROLLED DOWN THE MOUNTAIN AND STRUCK THE IMAGE AT THE FEET AND DESTROYED ALL THE KINGDOMS IN A MOMENT'S TIME.
THAT ROCK REPRESENTS THE SON OF GOD WHO WILL COME TO THE EARTH AND SET UP A GLORIOUS KINGDOM.
AT THE END OF TIME, ALL THE DEAD WILL BE AWAKENED TO STAND IN JUDGMENT. THOSE THAT DID EVIL WILL RECEIVE SHAME AND EVERLASTING CONTEMPT. THOSE THAT DID GOOD WILL RECEIVE EVERLASTING LIFE.
WITHOUT QUESTION, THE WORDS YOU SPEAK ARE FROM GOD. HOW ELSE COULD YOU HAVE KNOWN MY DREAM IN EVERY DETAIL? I WILL MAKE YOU RULER OVER ALL THE WISE MEN.
DANIEL CONTINUED IN BABYLON FOR 68 YEARS. HE INTERPRETED MANY DREAMS AND FORETOLD THE FUTURE MANY TIMES. IN TIME, KING NEBUCHADNEZZAR DIED AND HIS SON, BELSHAZZAR TOOK HIS PLACE.
ONE NIGHT AS BELSHAZZAR WAS HAVING A DRUNKEN PARTY, A MYSTERIOUS HAND APPEARED AND WROTE ON THE WALL. DANIEL WAS CALLED IN TO INTERPRET IT. GOD GAVE HIM UNDERSTANDING OF THIS UNKNOWN LANGUAGE.
O KING, YOU HAVE SINNED AGAINST GOD. AS THE PROPHETS FORETOLD, YOUR KINGDOM HAS BEEN TAKEN FROM YOU THIS VERY NIGHT AND GIVEN TO THE MEDES AND THE PERSIANS.
THE PROPHETS PREDICTED THAT BABYLON WOULD FALL BY HAVING THE TWO LEAVED GATES OPENED TO ADMIT THE ENEMY AND THE PEOPLE WOULD BE TOO DRUNK TO TAKE NOTICE. AS DANIEL WAS SPEAKING, THE ENEMY WAS ALREADY ENTERING THE CITY.

ECCLESIASTES 12:13-14; ISAIAH 9:6-7, 45:1; DANIEL 2:34-35, 44-48, 5:1-29; REVELATION 20:11-21:5

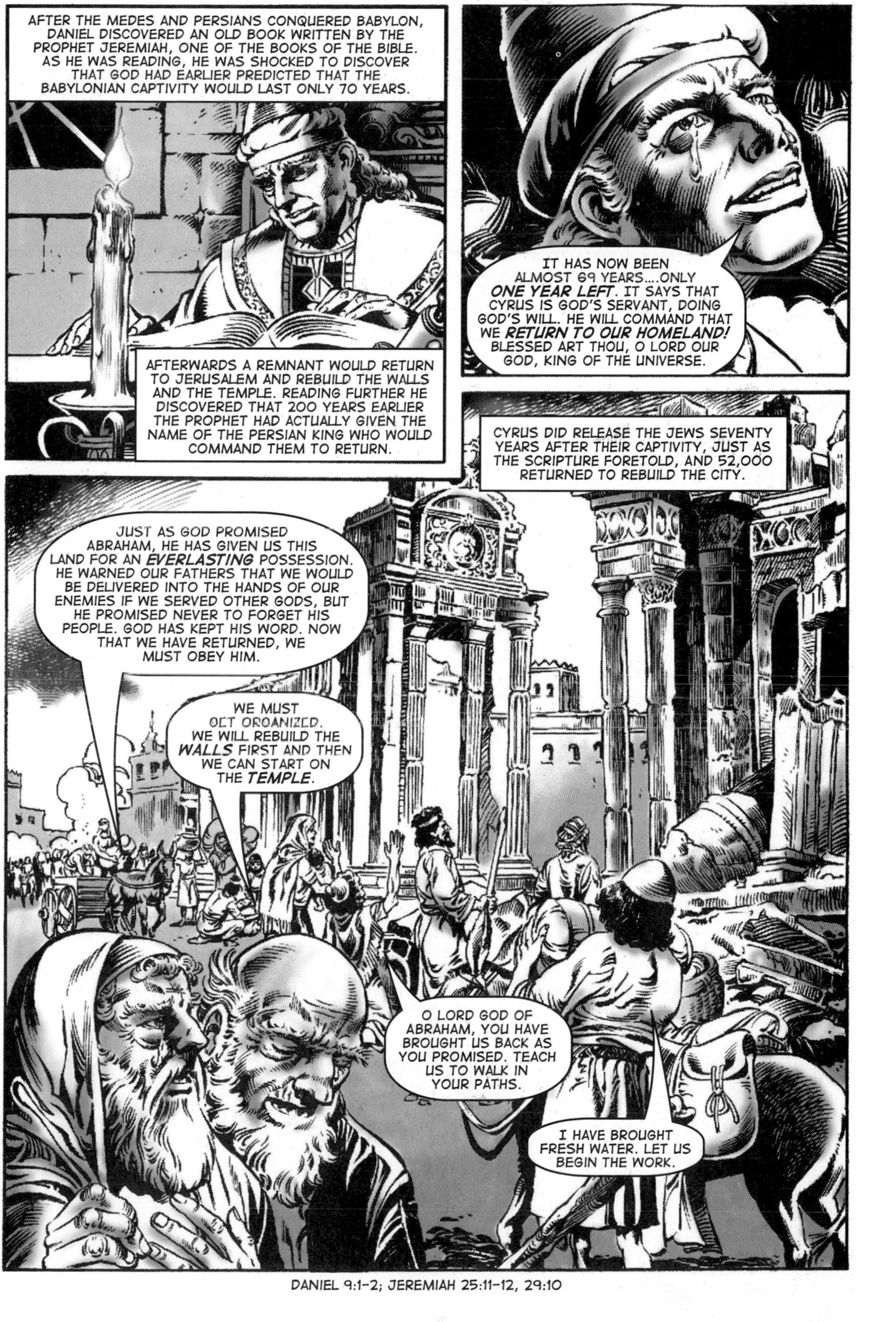
AFTER THE MEDES AND PERSIANS CONQUERED BABYLON, DANIEL DISCOVERED AN OLD BOOK WRITTEN BY THE PROPHET JEREMIAH, ONE OF THE BOOKS OF THE BIBLE. AS HE WAS READING, HE WAS SHOCKED TO DISCOVER THAT GOD HAD EARLIER PREDICTED THAT THE BABYLONIAN CAPTIVITY WOULD LAST ONLY 70 YEARS.
AFTERWARDS A REMNANT WOULD RETURN TO JERUSALEM AND REBUILD THE WALLS AND THE TEMPLE. READING FURTHER HE DISCOVERED THAT 200 YEARS EARLIER THE PROPHET HAD ACTUALLY GIVEN THE NAME OF THE PERSIAN KING WHO WOULD COMMAND THEM TO RETURN.
IT HAS NOW BEEN ALMOST 69 YEARS....ONLY ***ONE YEAR LEFT***. IT SAYS THAT CYRUS IS GOD'S SERVANT, DOING GOD'S WILL. HE WILL COMMAND THAT WE ***RETURN TO OUR HOMELAND!*** BLESSED ART THOU, O LORD OUR GOD, KING OF THE UNIVERSE.
CYRUS DID RELEASE THE JEWS SEVENTY YEARS AFTER THEIR CAPTIVITY, JUST AS THE SCRIPTURE FORETOLD, AND 52,000 RETURNED TO REBUILD THE CITY.
JUST AS GOD PROMISED ABRAHAM, HE HAS GIVEN US THIS LAND FOR AN ***EVERLASTING*** POSSESSION. HE WARNED OUR FATHERS THAT WE WOULD BE DELIVERED INTO THE HANDS OF OUR ENEMIES IF WE SERVED OTHER GODS, BUT HE PROMISED NEVER TO FORGET HIS PEOPLE. GOD HAS KEPT HIS WORD. NOW THAT WE HAVE RETURNED, WE MUST OBEY HIM.
WE MUST GET ORGANIZED. WE WILL REBUILD THE ***WALLS*** FIRST AND THEN WE CAN START ON THE ***TEMPLE***.
O LORD GOD OF ABRAHAM, YOU HAVE BROUGHT US BACK AS YOU PROMISED. TEACH US TO WALK IN YOUR PATHS.
I HAVE BROUGHT FRESH WATER. LET US BEGIN THE WORK.

DANIEL 9:1-2; JEREMIAH 25:11-12, 29:10

DANIEL WAS VERY OLD, SO HE DID NOT GO BACK WITH THE OTHERS. HE STILL PLAYED AN IMPORTANT ROLE AS HE ADVISED THE KINGS OF THE MEDO-PERSIAN EMPIRE NOW LOCATED IN THE CITY OF BABYLON. GOD GAVE HIM SEVERAL MORE VISIONS CONCERNING THE FUTURE, EVEN DOWN TO THE END OF DAYS. IN ONE DREAM HE SAW A METALLIC BEAST. AN ANGEL TOLD HIM WHAT IT MEANT.

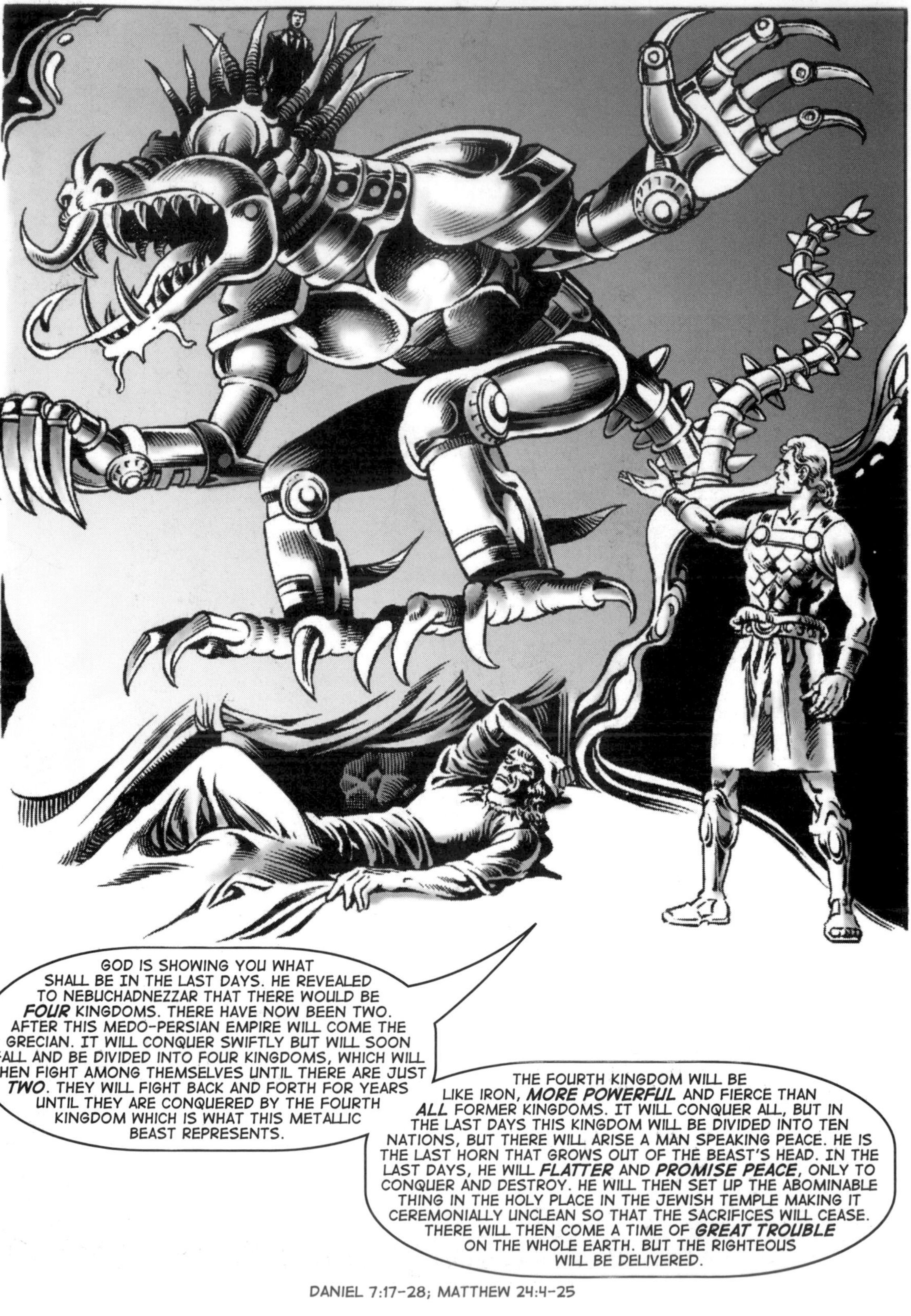
GOD IS SHOWING YOU WHAT SHALL BE IN THE LAST DAYS. HE REVEALED TO NEBUCHADNEZZAR THAT THERE WOULD BE ***FOUR*** KINGDOMS. THERE HAVE NOW BEEN TWO. AFTER THIS MEDO-PERSIAN EMPIRE WILL COME THE GRECIAN. IT WILL CONQUER SWIFTLY BUT WILL SOON FALL AND BE DIVIDED INTO FOUR KINGDOMS, WHICH WILL THEN FIGHT AMONG THEMSELVES UNTIL THERE ARE JUST ***TWO***. THEY WILL FIGHT BACK AND FORTH FOR YEARS UNTIL THEY ARE CONQUERED BY THE FOURTH KINGDOM WHICH IS WHAT THIS METALLIC BEAST REPRESENTS.
THE FOURTH KINGDOM WILL BE LIKE IRON, ***MORE POWERFUL*** AND FIERCE THAN ***ALL*** FORMER KINGDOMS. IT WILL CONQUER ALL, BUT IN THE LAST DAYS THIS KINGDOM WILL BE DIVIDED INTO TEN NATIONS, BUT THERE WILL ARISE A MAN SPEAKING PEACE. HE IS THE LAST HORN THAT GROWS OUT OF THE BEAST'S HEAD. IN THE LAST DAYS, HE WILL ***FLATTER*** AND ***PROMISE PEACE***, ONLY TO CONQUER AND DESTROY. HE WILL THEN SET UP THE ABOMINABLE THING IN THE HOLY PLACE IN THE JEWISH TEMPLE MAKING IT CEREMONIALLY UNCLEAN SO THAT THE SACRIFICES WILL CEASE. THERE WILL THEN COME A TIME OF ***GREAT TROUBLE*** ON THE WHOLE EARTH. BUT THE RIGHTEOUS WILL BE DELIVERED.

DANIEL 7:17-28; MATTHEW 24:4-25

DANIEL, GOD WANTS YOU TO KNOW WHAT IS GOING TO HAPPEN AND WHEN. FROM THE TIME THE COMMANDMENT IS GIVEN TO RESTORE AND REBUILD THE TEMPLE, THERE WILL BE 483 YEARS, AFTER WHICH MESSIAH WILL BE KILLED IN PAYMENT FOR THE SINS OF THE PEOPLE, AND THEN THE TEMPLE WILL AGAIN BE DESTROYED.

THIS PROPHECY WILL BE FULFILLED, AND MESSIAH WILL BE ANOINTED. THERE WILL BE RECONCILIATION MADE FOR SINS, AND EVERLASTING RIGHTEOUSNESS WILL BE BROUGHT TO MAN.

JUST AS DANIEL RECORDED, JESUS MADE HIS TRIUMPHAL ENTRY INTO JERUSALEM ON THE VERY DAY WHEN THE 483 YEARS WERE COMPLETED.

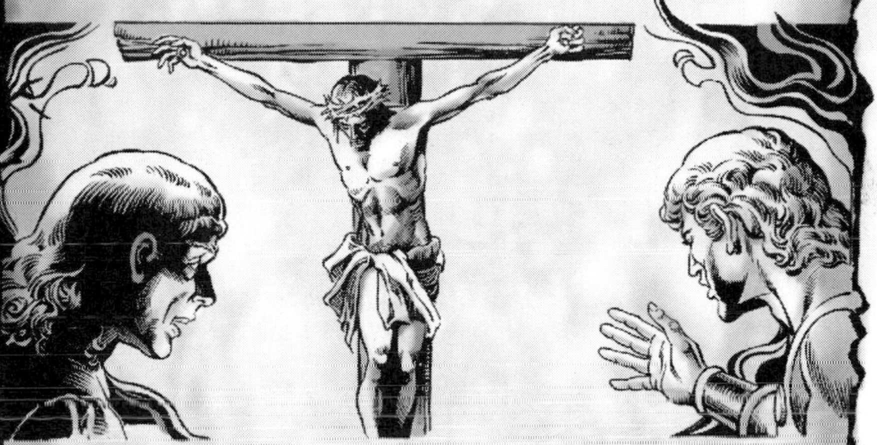

SINCE GOD TOLD ADAM AND EVE OF THE SEED OF THE WOMAN, MANY PROPHECIES HAD BEEN GIVEN ABOUT THE COMING CHRIST:

GOD HAD TOLD ADAM AND EVE THAT THE SEED OF THE WOMAN WOULD COME AND DESTROY THE EVIL ONE. HE TOLD NOAH THAT THE MESSIAH WOULD COME FROM THE FAMILY OF SHEM, NOT JAPHETH AND NOT HAM. GOD TOLD ABRAHAM THAT THE DELIVERER WOULD COME FROM HIS DESCENDENTS THROUGH HIS SON ISAAC. GOD TOLD ISAAC THAT THE PROMISED ONE WOULD COME THROUGH HIS SON JACOB, AND HE TOLD JACOB THAT CHRIST WOULD COME THROUGH JUDAH.

ZECHARIAH 9:9 LOWLY, AND RIDING ON A DONKEY
MICAH 5:2 ***WHOSE GOINGS FORTH HAVE BEEN FROM OF OLD, FROM EVERLASTING.***
GENESIS 49:9–10 SHILOH, A SON OF JUDAH
ISAIAH 7 A VIRGIN
ISAIAH 9:1–2 GALILEE OF THE NATIONS. (IT DID NOT BECOME THIS UNTIL CHRIST'S TIME).
PSALM 22 SUFFERING MESSIAH
ISAIAH 53 HE WILL BE REJECTED BY HIS PEOPLE AND DIE BY HAVING HIS HANDS AND FEET PIERCED. HE WILL HANG NAKED AND WILL THIRST FOR WATER BUT WILL BE GIVEN VINEGAR TO DRINK INSTEAD. HE WILL DIE BETWEEN THIEVES AND BE BURIED IN A RICH MAN'S GRAVE.
ISAIAH 42:1 PUT MY SPIRIT UPON HIM. HE SHALL BRING JUDGMENT TO THE GENTILES
ISAIAH 49:6 HE WILL BE A LIGHT TO THE GENTILES AND WILL TAKE SALVATION TO ALL THAT ARE IN THE EARTH.
ISAIAH 53:2–3 HUMBLE IN APPEARANCE.

DANIEL 9:25–26; MATTHEW 24:1–2; HEBREWS 2:9

150

THE PROPHECIES OF DANIEL CONCERNING THE FOUR KINGDOMS WERE FULFILLED EXACTLY AS HE PREDICTED. IN 330BC, ALEXANDER THE GREAT, FROM GREECE, BEGAN A CAMPAIGN WHICH LASTED SEVEN YEARS, IN WHICH HE CONQUERED THE KNOWN WORLD, INCLUDING THE VAST MEDO-PERSIAN EMPIRE. GREECE HELD POWER UNTIL ABOUT 167BC WHEN THE FOURTH WORLD KINGDOM, ROME, BEGAN TO CONQUER.

ROME, REPRESENTED IN NEBUCHADNEZZAR'S DREAM AS THE FEET AND LEGS OF IRON, AND IN DANIEL'S VISION AS THE METALLIC BEAST, INCREASED ITS POWER AND TERRITORY, JUST AS THE PROPHETS PREDICTED. IN 5 BC, IT RULED ISRAEL WITH AN IRON HAND.

500 YEARS LATER

OVER FIVE HUNDRED YEARS HAD PASSED SINCE DANIEL'S PROPHECIES. IN 4 BC THE ROMANS ALLOWED THE JEWS FREEDOM OF RELIGION, BUT THEY WERE TAXED HEAVILY. THE TEMPLE HAD BEEN REBUILT AND WAS AT THE CENTER OF JEWISH LIFE. MOST HAD FORGOTTEN THE PROPHECIES OF A COMING MESSIAH, BUT SOME STILL KEPT THE LAW AND LOOKED FOR THE CHRIST. AMONG THEM WAS AN OLD MAN NAMED SIMEON. HE WAS A HOLY MAN THAT LONGED TO SEE THE ONE OF WHOM THE PROPHETS SPOKE. FOR YEARS HE HAD READ THE PROPHECIES AND KNEW THAT THE TIME WAS DRAWING NEAR. BUT HE WAS NOW OLD AND WOULD PROBABLY NOT LIVE MUCH LONGER.
IT HAD BEEN 4,000 YEARS SINCE GOD FIRST PROMISED EVE THAT HER SEED WOULD COME AND DESTROY THE WORKS OF THE EVIL ONE.

IT WAS NOW TIME.
OVER 350 PROPHECIES WERE READY TO BE FULFILLED.

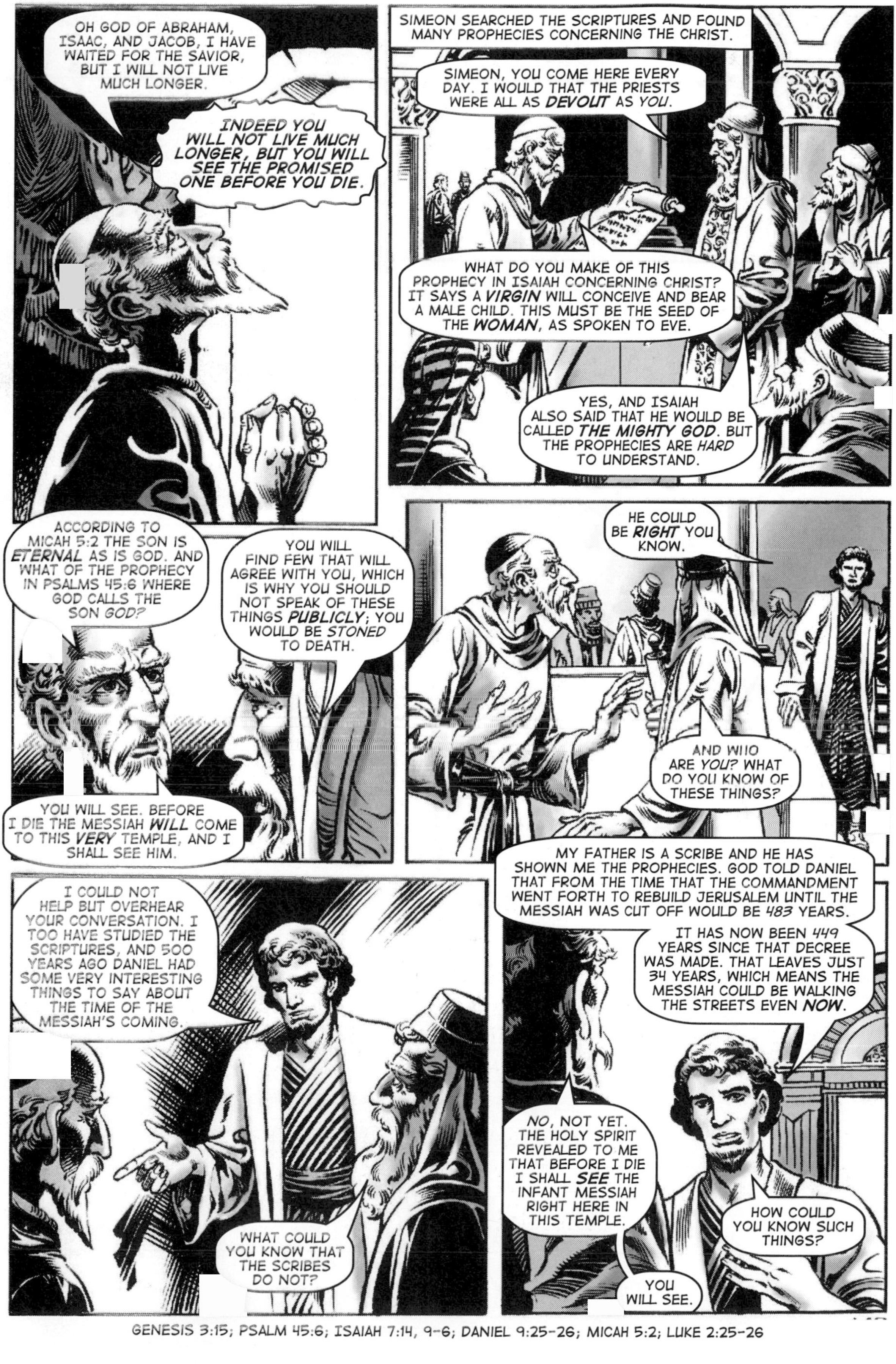
OH GOD OF ABRAHAM, ISAAC, AND JACOB, I HAVE WAITED FOR THE SAVIOR, BUT I WILL NOT LIVE MUCH LONGER.
INDEED YOU WILL NOT LIVE MUCH LONGER, BUT YOU WILL SEE THE PROMISED ONE BEFORE YOU DIE.
SIMEON SEARCHED THE SCRIPTURES AND FOUND MANY PROPHECIES CONCERNING THE CHRIST.
SIMEON, YOU COME HERE EVERY DAY. I WOULD THAT THE PRIESTS WERE ALL AS DEVOUT AS YOU.
WHAT DO YOU MAKE OF THIS PROPHECY IN ISAIAH CONCERNING CHRIST? IT SAYS A VIRGIN WILL CONCEIVE AND BEAR A MALE CHILD. THIS MUST BE THE SEED OF THE WOMAN, AS SPOKEN TO EVE.
YES, AND ISAIAH ALSO SAID THAT HE WOULD BE CALLED THE MIGHTY GOD. BUT THE PROPHECIES ARE HARD TO UNDERSTAND.
ACCORDING TO MICAH 5:2 THE SON IS ETERNAL AS IS GOD. AND WHAT OF THE PROPHECY IN PSALMS 45:6 WHERE GOD CALLS THE SON GOD?
YOU WILL FIND FEW THAT WILL AGREE WITH YOU, WHICH IS WHY YOU SHOULD NOT SPEAK OF THESE THINGS PUBLICLY; YOU WOULD BE STONED TO DEATH.
YOU WILL SEE. BEFORE I DIE THE MESSIAH WILL COME TO THIS VERY TEMPLE, AND I SHALL SEE HIM.
HE COULD BE RIGHT YOU KNOW.
AND WHO ARE YOU? WHAT DO YOU KNOW OF THESE THINGS?
MY FATHER IS A SCRIBE AND HE HAS SHOWN ME THE PROPHECIES. GOD TOLD DANIEL THAT FROM THE TIME THAT THE COMMANDMENT WENT FORTH TO REBUILD JERUSALEM UNTIL THE MESSIAH WAS CUT OFF WOULD BE 483 YEARS.
I COULD NOT HELP BUT OVERHEAR YOUR CONVERSATION. I TOO HAVE STUDIED THE SCRIPTURES, AND 500 YEARS AGO DANIEL HAD SOME VERY INTERESTING THINGS TO SAY ABOUT THE TIME OF THE MESSIAH'S COMING.
WHAT COULD YOU KNOW THAT THE SCRIBES DO NOT?
IT HAS NOW BEEN 449 YEARS SINCE THAT DECREE WAS MADE. THAT LEAVES JUST 34 YEARS, WHICH MEANS THE MESSIAH COULD BE WALKING THE STREETS EVEN NOW.
NO, NOT YET. THE HOLY SPIRIT REVEALED TO ME THAT BEFORE I DIE I SHALL SEE THE INFANT MESSIAH RIGHT HERE IN THIS TEMPLE.
HOW COULD YOU KNOW SUCH THINGS?
YOU WILL SEE.

GENESIS 3:15; PSALM 45:6; ISAIAH 7:14, 9-6; DANIEL 9:25-26; MICAH 5:2; LUKE 2:25-26

AS SIMEON GREW OLDER AND WAITED AT THE TEMPLE, LOOKING FOR THE PROMISED CHRIST, A PRIEST BY THE NAME OF ZACHARIAS WENT INTO THE TEMPLE TO PRAY. HE AND HIS WIFE WERE OLD, BUT THEY HAD NEVER HAD ANY CHILDREN.

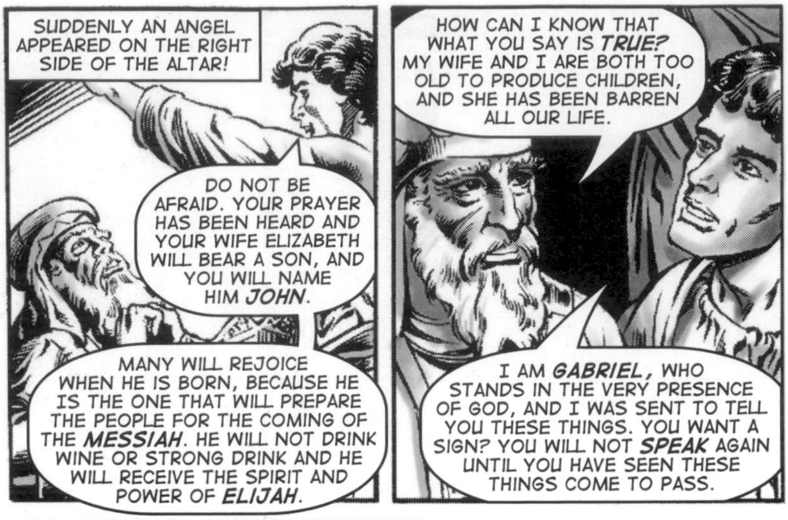
SUDDENLY AN ANGEL APPEARED ON THE RIGHT SIDE OF THE ALTAR!
DO NOT BE AFRAID. YOUR PRAYER HAS BEEN HEARD AND YOUR WIFE ELIZABETH WILL BEAR A SON, AND YOU WILL NAME HIM JOHN.
MANY WILL REJOICE WHEN HE IS BORN, BECAUSE HE IS THE ONE THAT WILL PREPARE THE PEOPLE FOR THE COMING OF THE MESSIAH. HE WILL NOT DRINK WINE OR STRONG DRINK AND HE WILL RECEIVE THE SPIRIT AND POWER OF ELIJAH.
HOW CAN I KNOW THAT WHAT YOU SAY IS TRUE? MY WIFE AND I ARE BOTH TOO OLD TO PRODUCE CHILDREN, AND SHE HAS BEEN BARREN ALL OUR LIFE.
I AM GABRIEL, WHO STANDS IN THE VERY PRESENCE OF GOD, AND I WAS SENT TO TELL YOU THESE THINGS. YOU WANT A SIGN? YOU WILL NOT SPEAK AGAIN UNTIL YOU HAVE SEEN THESE THINGS COME TO PASS.

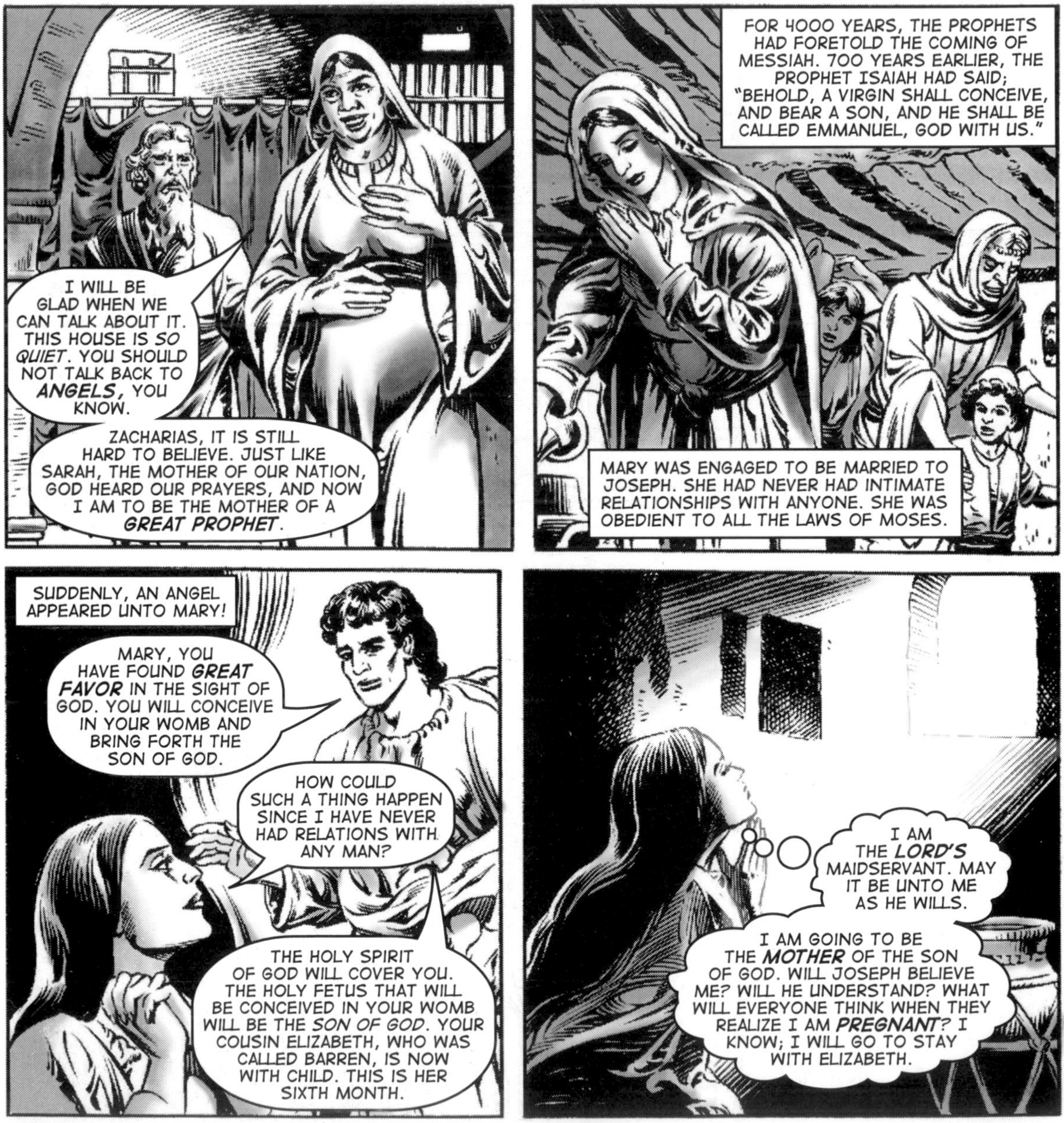
I WILL BE GLAD WHEN WE CAN TALK ABOUT IT. THIS HOUSE IS SO QUIET. YOU SHOULD NOT TALK BACK TO ANGELS, YOU KNOW.
ZACHARIAS, IT IS STILL HARD TO BELIEVE. JUST LIKE SARAH, THE MOTHER OF OUR NATION, GOD HEARD OUR PRAYERS, AND NOW I AM TO BE THE MOTHER OF A GREAT PROPHET.
FOR 4000 YEARS, THE PROPHETS HAD FORETOLD THE COMING OF MESSIAH. 700 YEARS EARLIER, THE PROPHET ISAIAH HAD SAID; "BEHOLD, A VIRGIN SHALL CONCEIVE, AND BEAR A SON, AND HE SHALL BE CALLED EMMANUEL, GOD WITH US."
MARY WAS ENGAGED TO BE MARRIED TO JOSEPH. SHE HAD NEVER HAD INTIMATE RELATIONSHIPS WITH ANYONE. SHE WAS OBEDIENT TO ALL THE LAWS OF MOSES.
SUDDENLY, AN ANGEL APPEARED UNTO MARY!
MARY, YOU HAVE FOUND GREAT FAVOR IN THE SIGHT OF GOD. YOU WILL CONCEIVE IN YOUR WOMB AND BRING FORTH THE SON OF GOD.
HOW COULD SUCH A THING HAPPEN SINCE I HAVE NEVER HAD RELATIONS WITH ANY MAN?
THE HOLY SPIRIT OF GOD WILL COVER YOU. THE HOLY FETUS THAT WILL BE CONCEIVED IN YOUR WOMB WILL BE THE SON OF GOD. YOUR COUSIN ELIZABETH, WHO WAS CALLED BARREN, IS NOW WITH CHILD. THIS IS HER SIXTH MONTH.
I AM THE LORD'S MAIDSERVANT. MAY IT BE UNTO ME AS HE WILLS.
I AM GOING TO BE THE MOTHER OF THE SON OF GOD. WILL JOSEPH BELIEVE ME? WILL HE UNDERSTAND? WHAT WILL EVERYONE THINK WHEN THEY REALIZE I AM PREGNANT? I KNOW; I WILL GO TO STAY WITH ELIZABETH.

LUKE 1:5-20, 26-40

LUKE 1:41-64

GENESIS 3:15; ISAIAH 7:14, 9:7; MATTHEW 1:18-23; LUKE 1:32-33

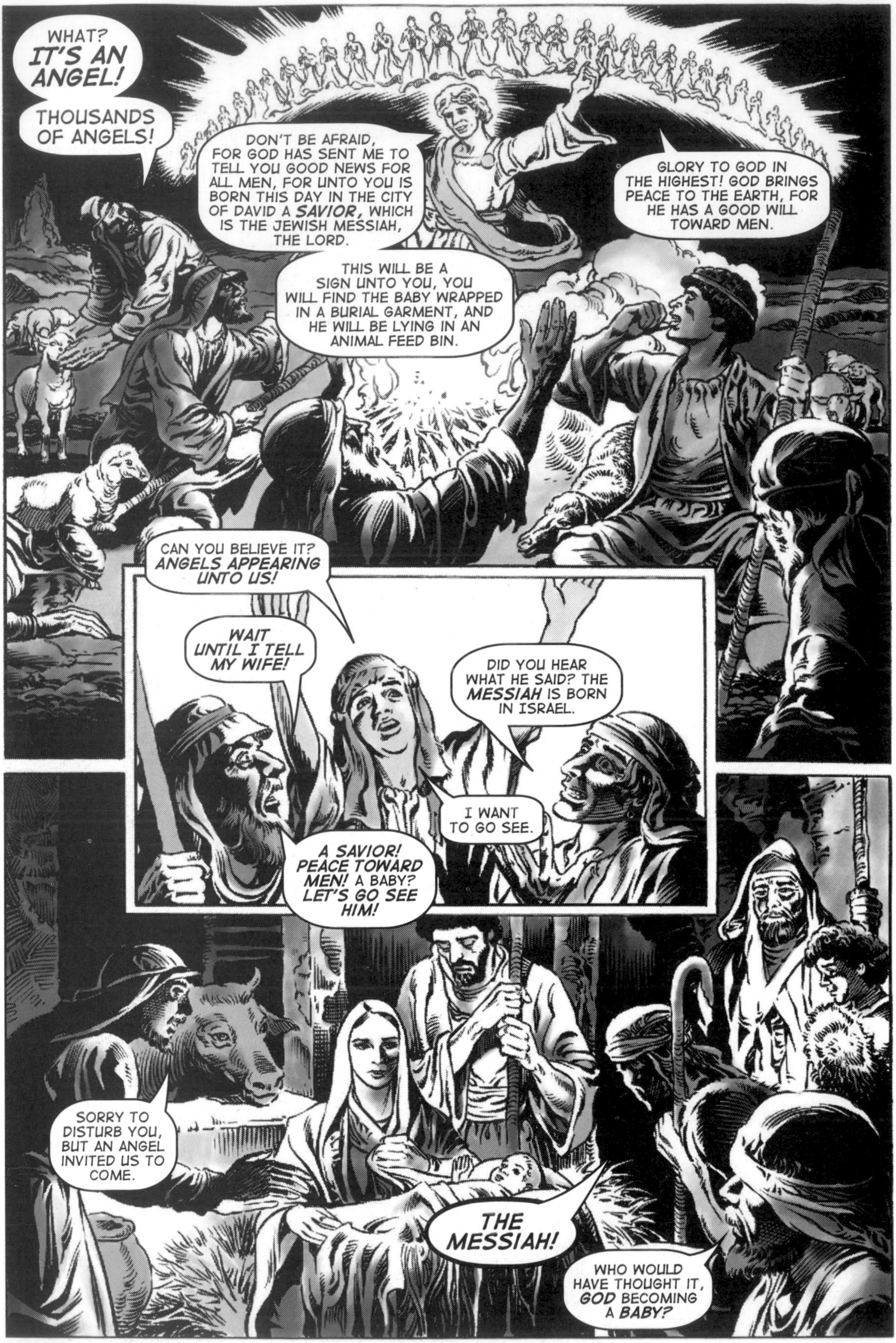

WHAT? IT'S AN ANGEL!
THOUSANDS OF ANGELS!
DON'T BE AFRAID, FOR GOD HAS SENT ME TO TELL YOU GOOD NEWS FOR ALL MEN, FOR UNTO YOU IS BORN THIS DAY IN THE CITY OF DAVID A SAVIOR, WHICH IS THE JEWISH MESSIAH, THE LORD.
GLORY TO GOD IN THE HIGHEST! GOD BRINGS PEACE TO THE EARTH, FOR HE HAS A GOOD WILL TOWARD MEN.
THIS WILL BE A SIGN UNTO YOU, YOU WILL FIND THE BABY WRAPPED IN A BURIAL GARMENT, AND HE WILL BE LYING IN AN ANIMAL FEED BIN.
CAN YOU BELIEVE IT? ANGELS APPEARING UNTO US!
WAIT UNTIL I TELL MY WIFE!
DID YOU HEAR WHAT HE SAID? THE MESSIAH IS BORN IN ISRAEL.
I WANT TO GO SEE.
A SAVIOR! PEACE TOWARD MEN! A BABY? LET'S GO SEE HIM!
SORRY TO DISTURB YOU, BUT AN ANGEL INVITED US TO COME.
THE MESSIAH!
WHO WOULD HAVE THOUGHT IT, GOD BECOMING A BABY?

LUKE 2:8–20

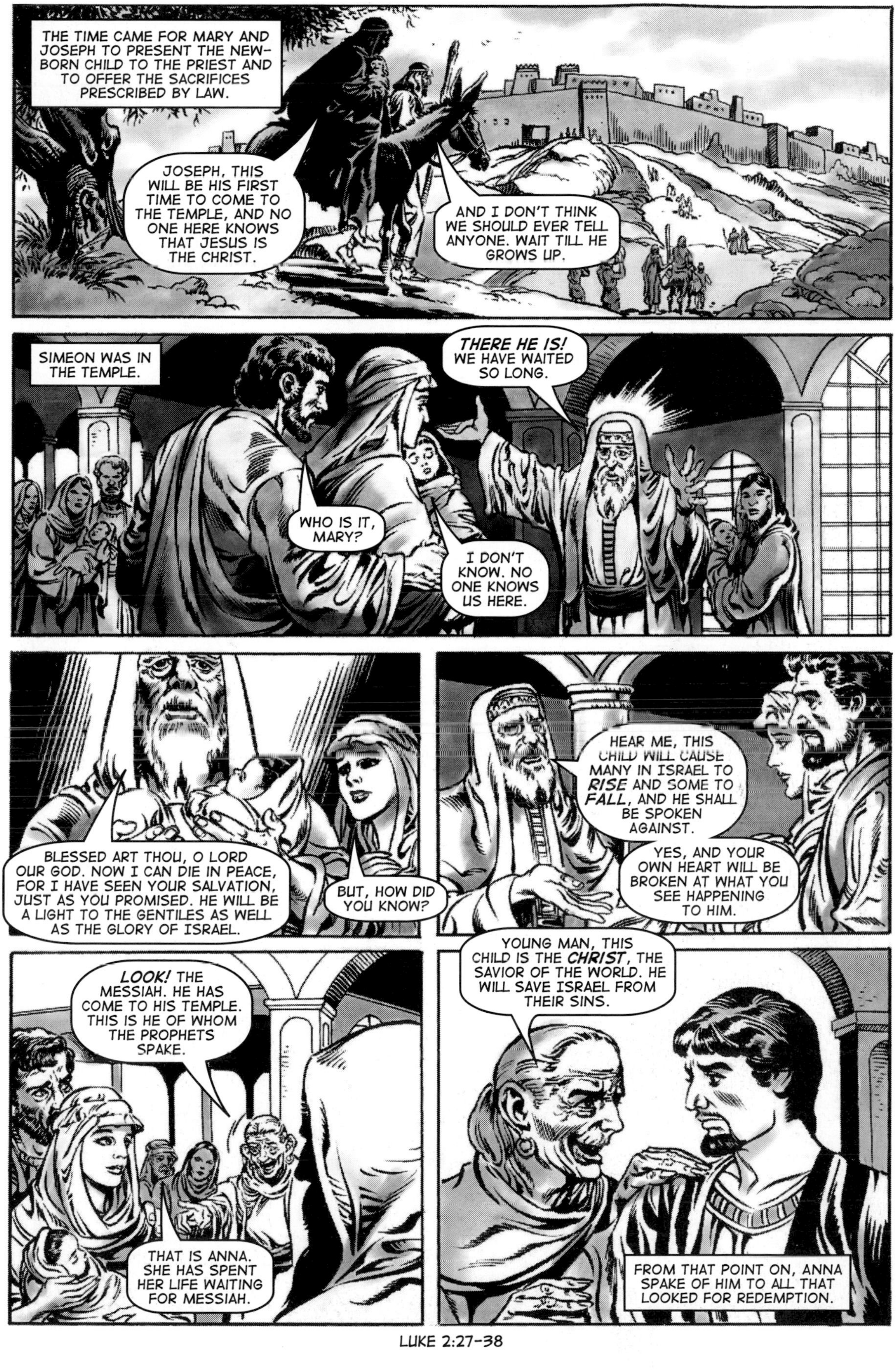
THE TIME CAME FOR MARY AND JOSEPH TO PRESENT THE NEW-BORN CHILD TO THE PRIEST AND TO OFFER THE SACRIFICES PRESCRIBED BY LAW.
JOSEPH, THIS WILL BE HIS FIRST TIME TO COME TO THE TEMPLE, AND NO ONE HERE KNOWS THAT JESUS IS THE CHRIST.
AND I DON'T THINK WE SHOULD EVER TELL ANYONE. WAIT TILL HE GROWS UP.
SIMEON WAS IN THE TEMPLE.
THERE HE IS! WE HAVE WAITED SO LONG.
WHO IS IT, MARY?
I DON'T KNOW. NO ONE KNOWS US HERE.
BLESSED ART THOU, O LORD OUR GOD. NOW I CAN DIE IN PEACE, FOR I HAVE SEEN YOUR SALVATION, JUST AS YOU PROMISED. HE WILL BE A LIGHT TO THE GENTILES AS WELL AS THE GLORY OF ISRAEL.
BUT, HOW DID YOU KNOW?
HEAR ME, THIS CHILD WILL CAUSE MANY IN ISRAEL TO RISE AND SOME TO FALL, AND HE SHALL BE SPOKEN AGAINST.
YES, AND YOUR OWN HEART WILL BE BROKEN AT WHAT YOU SEE HAPPENING TO HIM.
LOOK! THE MESSIAH. HE HAS COME TO HIS TEMPLE. THIS IS HE OF WHOM THE PROPHETS SPAKE.
THAT IS ANNA. SHE HAS SPENT HER LIFE WAITING FOR MESSIAH.
YOUNG MAN, THIS CHILD IS THE CHRIST, THE SAVIOR OF THE WORLD. HE WILL SAVE ISRAEL FROM THEIR SINS.
FROM THAT POINT ON, ANNA SPAKE OF HIM TO ALL THAT LOOKED FOR REDEMPTION.

LUKE 2:27-38

MATTHEW 2:1-8; MICAH 5:2

MATTHEW 2:9-12

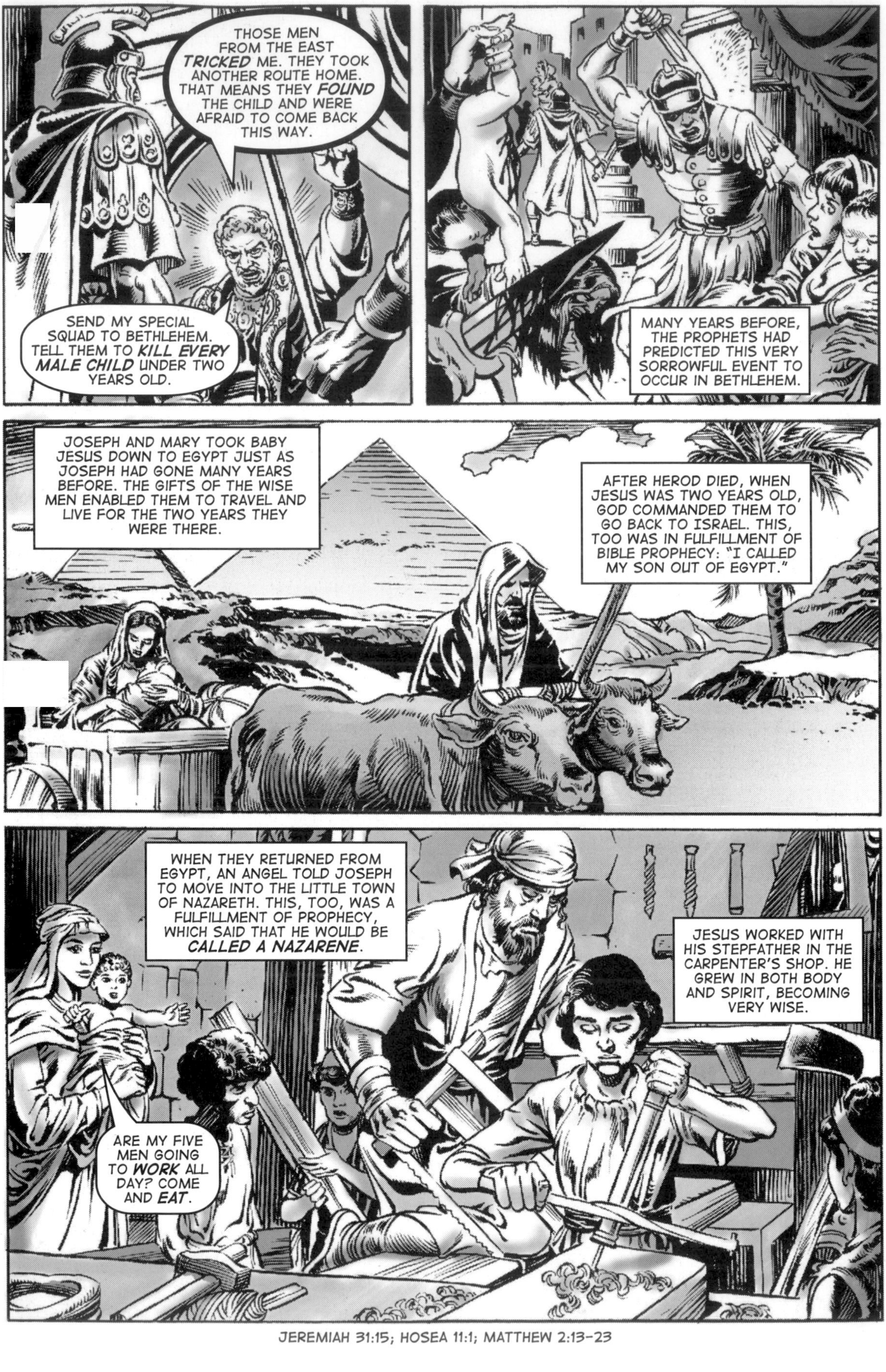
THOSE MEN FROM THE EAST TRICKED ME. THEY TOOK ANOTHER ROUTE HOME. THAT MEANS THEY FOUND THE CHILD AND WERE AFRAID TO COME BACK THIS WAY.
SEND MY SPECIAL SQUAD TO BETHLEHEM. TELL THEM TO KILL EVERY MALE CHILD UNDER TWO YEARS OLD.
MANY YEARS BEFORE, THE PROPHETS HAD PREDICTED THIS VERY SORROWFUL EVENT TO OCCUR IN BETHLEHEM.
JOSEPH AND MARY TOOK BABY JESUS DOWN TO EGYPT JUST AS JOSEPH HAD GONE MANY YEARS BEFORE. THE GIFTS OF THE WISE MEN ENABLED THEM TO TRAVEL AND LIVE FOR THE TWO YEARS THEY WERE THERE.
AFTER HEROD DIED, WHEN JESUS WAS TWO YEARS OLD, GOD COMMANDED THEM TO GO BACK TO ISRAEL. THIS, TOO WAS IN FULFILLMENT OF BIBLE PROPHECY: "I CALLED MY SON OUT OF EGYPT."
WHEN THEY RETURNED FROM EGYPT, AN ANGEL TOLD JOSEPH TO MOVE INTO THE LITTLE TOWN OF NAZARETH. THIS, TOO, WAS A FULFILLMENT OF PROPHECY, WHICH SAID THAT HE WOULD BE CALLED A NAZARENE.
JESUS WORKED WITH HIS STEPFATHER IN THE CARPENTER'S SHOP. HE GREW IN BOTH BODY AND SPIRIT, BECOMING VERY WISE.
ARE MY FIVE MEN GOING TO WORK ALL DAY? COME AND EAT.

JEREMIAH 31:15; HOSEA 11:1; MATTHEW 2:13–23

ISAIAH 9:7; LUKE 2:42-46; 2 TIMOTHY 3:16-17

LUKE 2:46-52

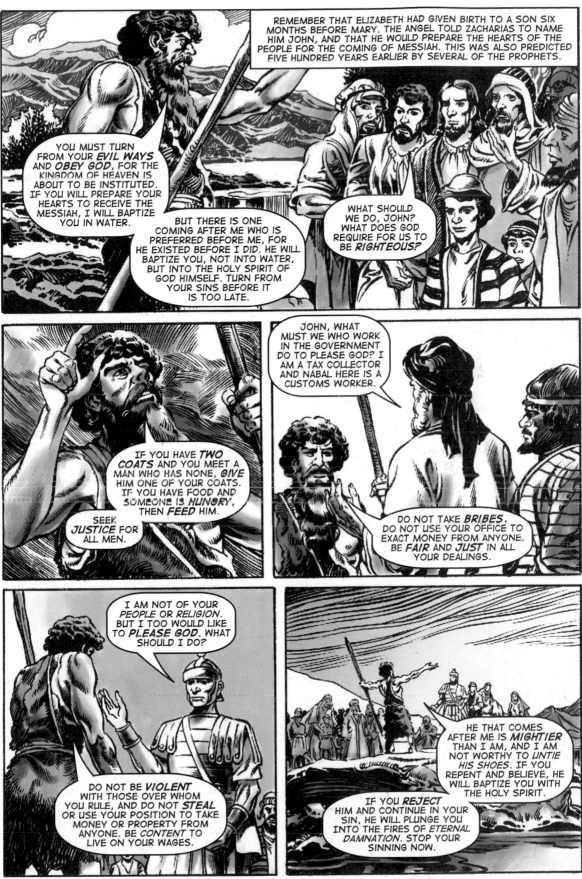

ISAIAH 40:3; MATTHEW 3:1-12; LUKE 3:15-18, 23; JOHN 1:19-27, 33

MATTHEW 3:13-17; LUKE 3:21-22

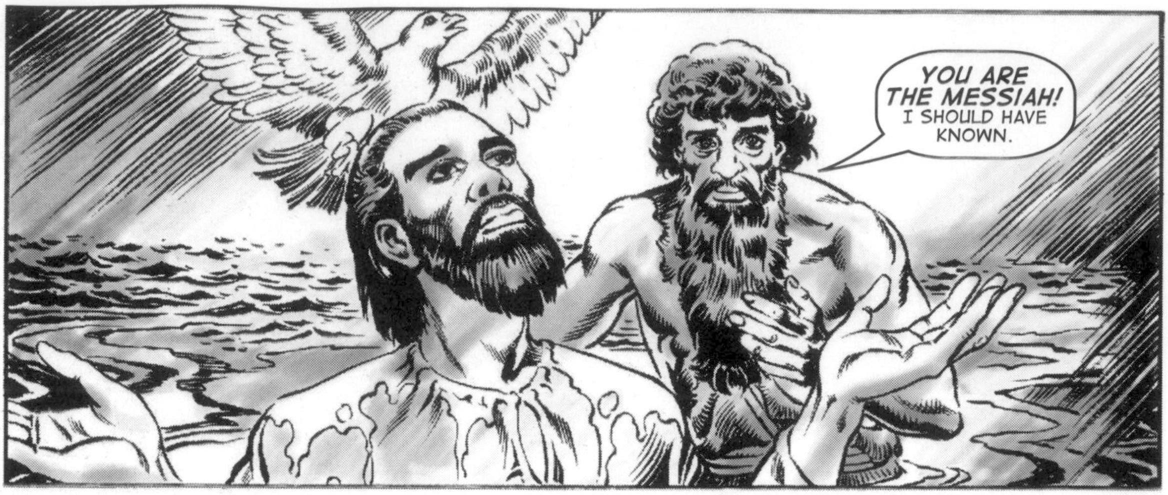
YOU ARE THE MESSIAH! I SHOULD HAVE KNOWN.

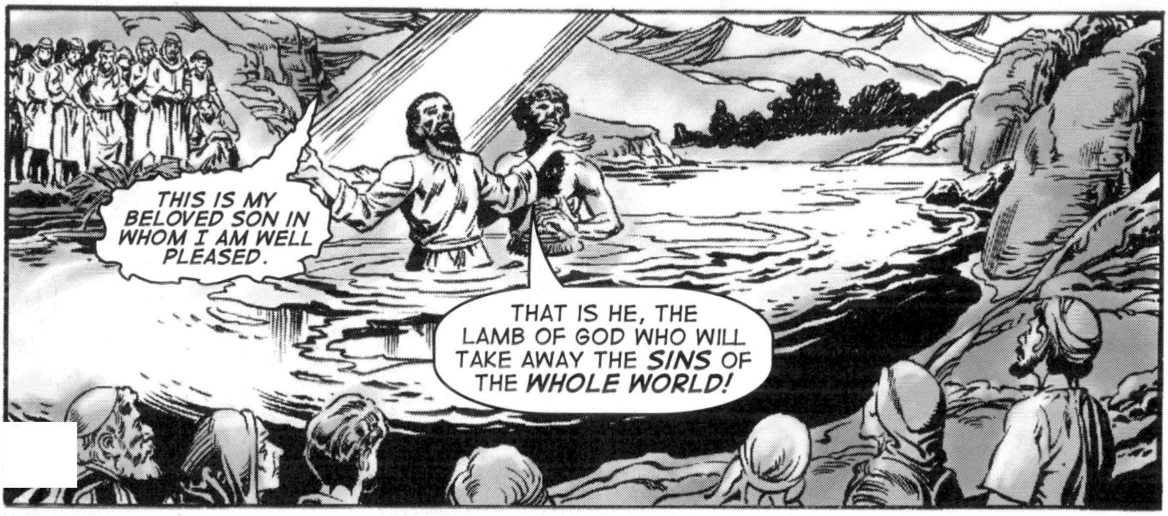
THIS IS MY BELOVED SON IN WHOM I AM WELL PLEASED.
THAT IS HE, THE LAMB OF GOD WHO WILL TAKE AWAY THE SINS OF THE WHOLE WORLD!

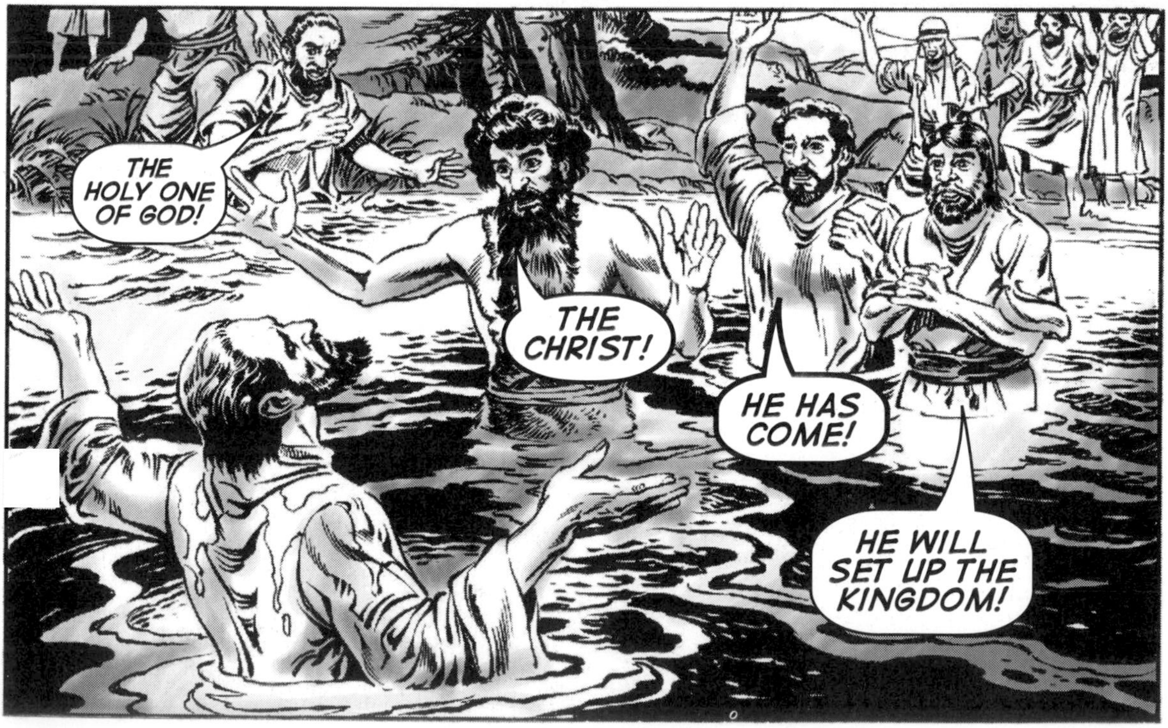
THE HOLY ONE OF GOD!
THE CHRIST!
HE HAS COME!
HE WILL SET UP THE KINGDOM!

LUKE 3:22; JOHN 1:29–34; 1 JOHN 2:1–2

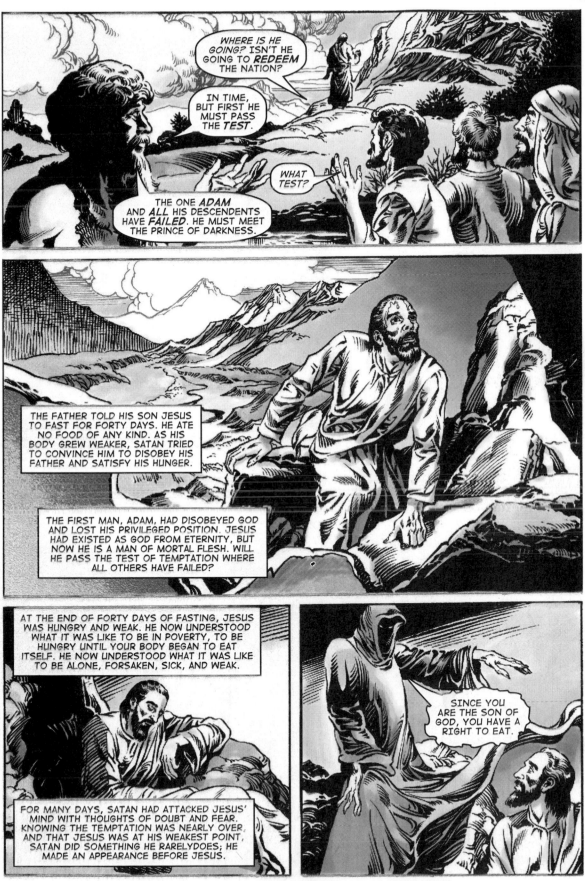

MATTHEW 4:1-3; LUKE 4:1-3; ROMANS 3:23, 5:12-21; HEBREWS 4:15

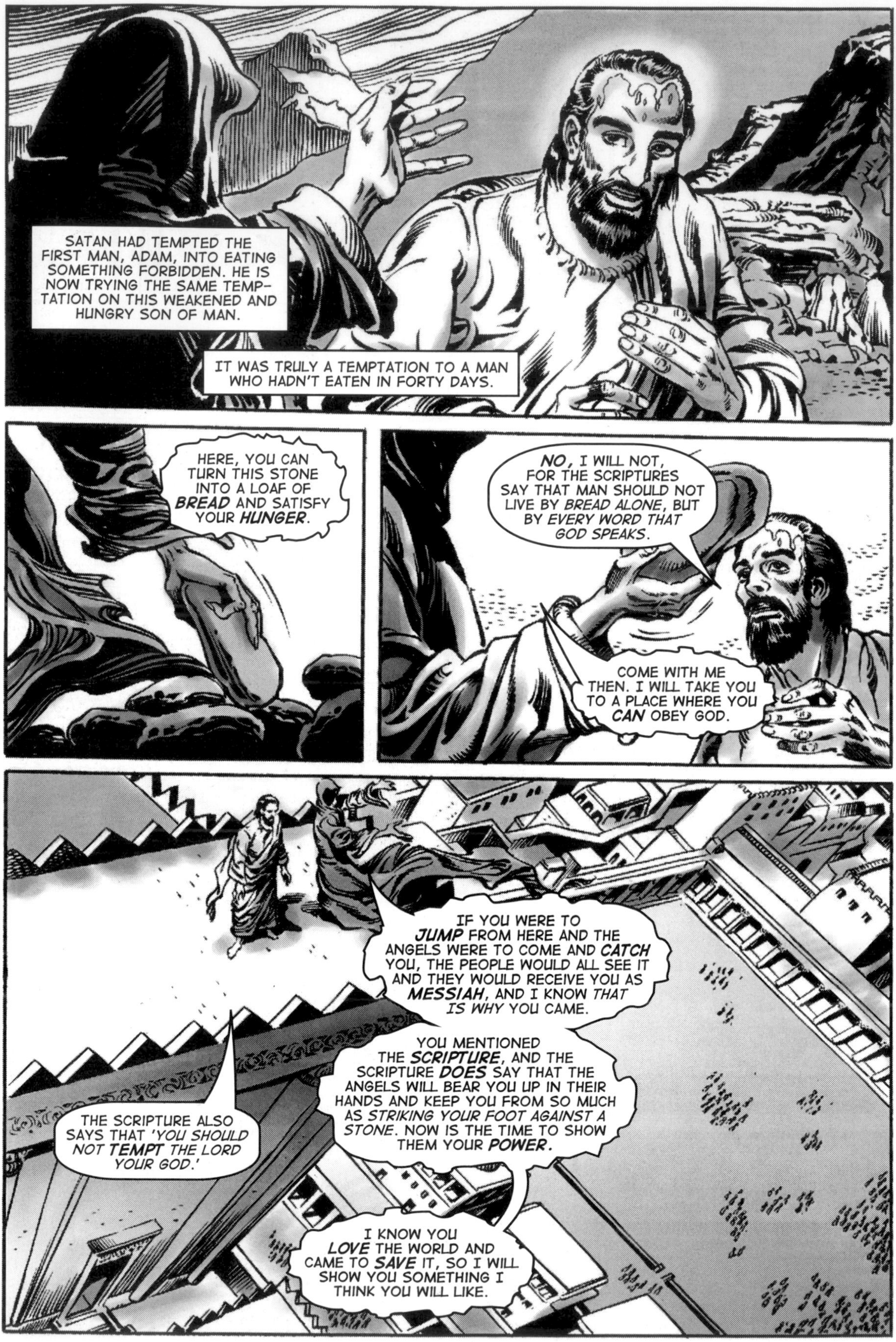
SATAN HAD TEMPTED THE FIRST MAN, ADAM, INTO EATING SOMETHING FORBIDDEN. HE IS NOW TRYING THE SAME TEMPTATION ON THIS WEAKENED AND HUNGRY SON OF MAN.
IT WAS TRULY A TEMPTATION TO A MAN WHO HADN'T EATEN IN FORTY DAYS.
HERE, YOU CAN TURN THIS STONE INTO A LOAF OF **BREAD** AND SATISFY YOUR **HUNGER**.
NO, I WILL NOT, FOR THE SCRIPTURES SAY THAT MAN SHOULD NOT LIVE BY *BREAD ALONE*, BUT BY *EVERY WORD THAT GOD SPEAKS*.
COME WITH ME THEN. I WILL TAKE YOU TO A PLACE WHERE YOU **CAN** OBEY GOD.
IF YOU WERE TO ***JUMP*** FROM HERE AND THE ANGELS WERE TO COME AND ***CATCH*** YOU, THE PEOPLE WOULD ALL SEE IT AND THEY WOULD RECEIVE YOU AS ***MESSIAH***, AND I KNOW *THAT IS WHY* YOU CAME.
YOU MENTIONED THE ***SCRIPTURE***, AND THE SCRIPTURE ***DOES*** SAY THAT THE ANGELS WILL BEAR YOU UP IN THEIR HANDS AND KEEP YOU FROM SO MUCH AS *STRIKING YOUR FOOT AGAINST A STONE*. NOW IS THE TIME TO SHOW THEM YOUR ***POWER***.
THE SCRIPTURE ALSO SAYS THAT *'YOU SHOULD NOT* ***TEMPT*** *THE LORD YOUR GOD.'*
I KNOW YOU ***LOVE*** THE WORLD AND CAME TO ***SAVE*** IT, SO I WILL SHOW YOU SOMETHING I THINK YOU WILL LIKE.

MATTHEW 4:3-7

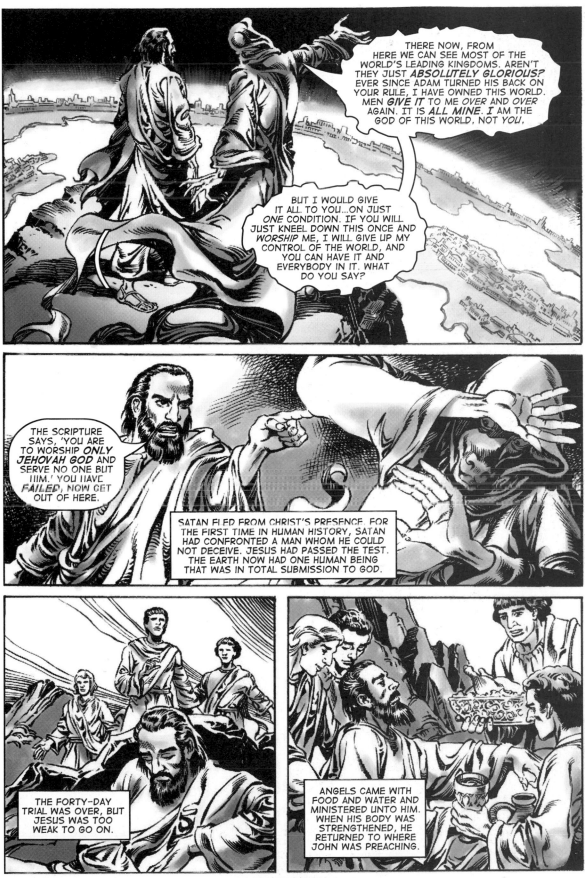

MATTHEW 4:8-11; LUKE 4:14

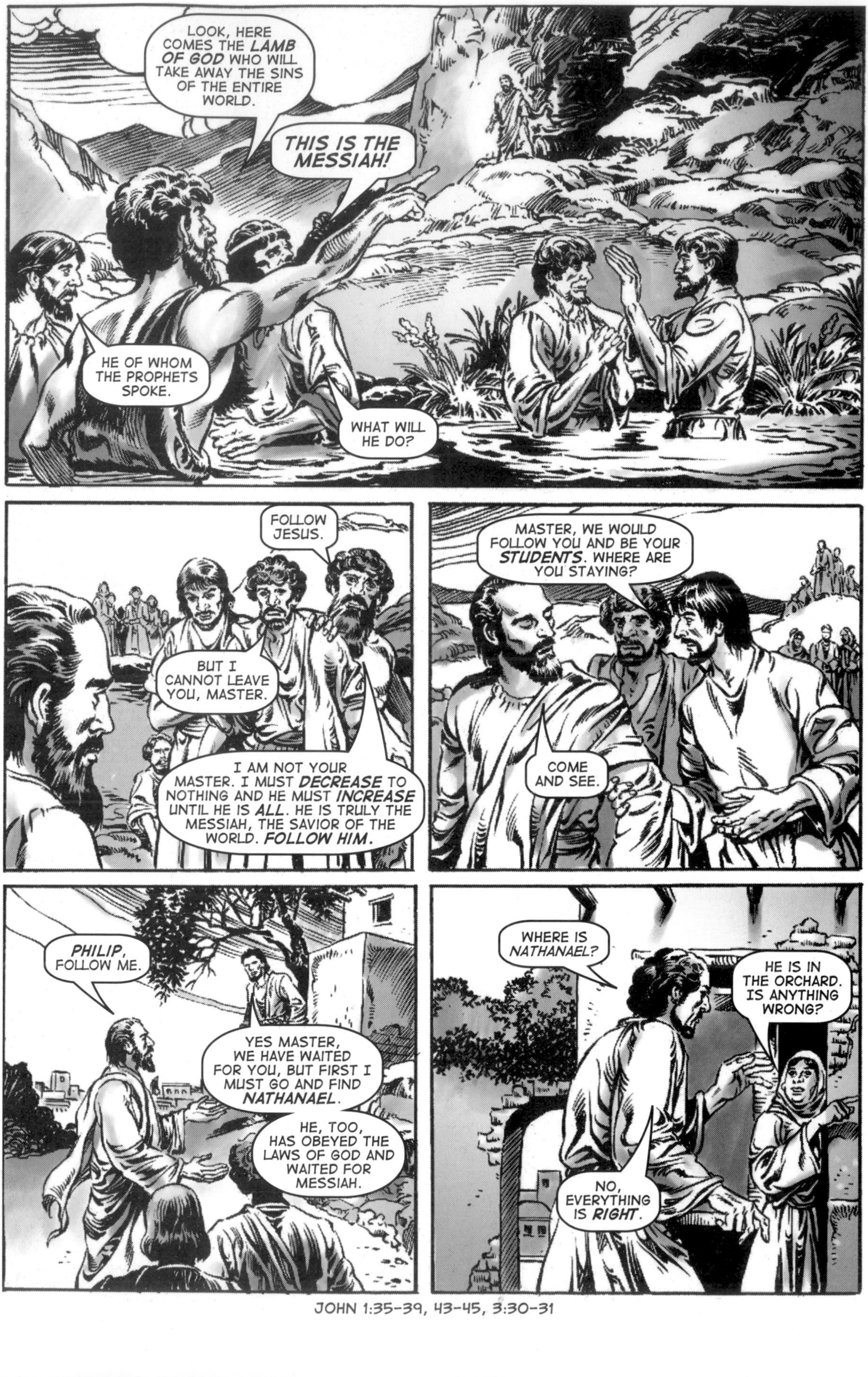
LOOK, HERE COMES THE LAMB OF GOD WHO WILL TAKE AWAY THE SINS OF THE ENTIRE WORLD.
THIS IS THE MESSIAH!
HE OF WHOM THE PROPHETS SPOKE.
WHAT WILL HE DO?
FOLLOW JESUS.
BUT I CANNOT LEAVE YOU, MASTER.
I AM NOT YOUR MASTER. I MUST DECREASE TO NOTHING AND HE MUST INCREASE UNTIL HE IS ALL. HE IS TRULY THE MESSIAH, THE SAVIOR OF THE WORLD. FOLLOW HIM.
MASTER, WE WOULD FOLLOW YOU AND BE YOUR STUDENTS. WHERE ARE YOU STAYING?
COME AND SEE.
PHILIP, FOLLOW ME.
YES MASTER, WE HAVE WAITED FOR YOU, BUT FIRST I MUST GO AND FIND NATHANAEL.
HE, TOO, HAS OBEYED THE LAWS OF GOD AND WAITED FOR MESSIAH.
WHERE IS NATHANAEL?
HE IS IN THE ORCHARD. IS ANYTHING WRONG?
NO, EVERYTHING IS RIGHT.

JOHN 1:35-39, 43-45, 3:30-31

JOHN 1:45-51

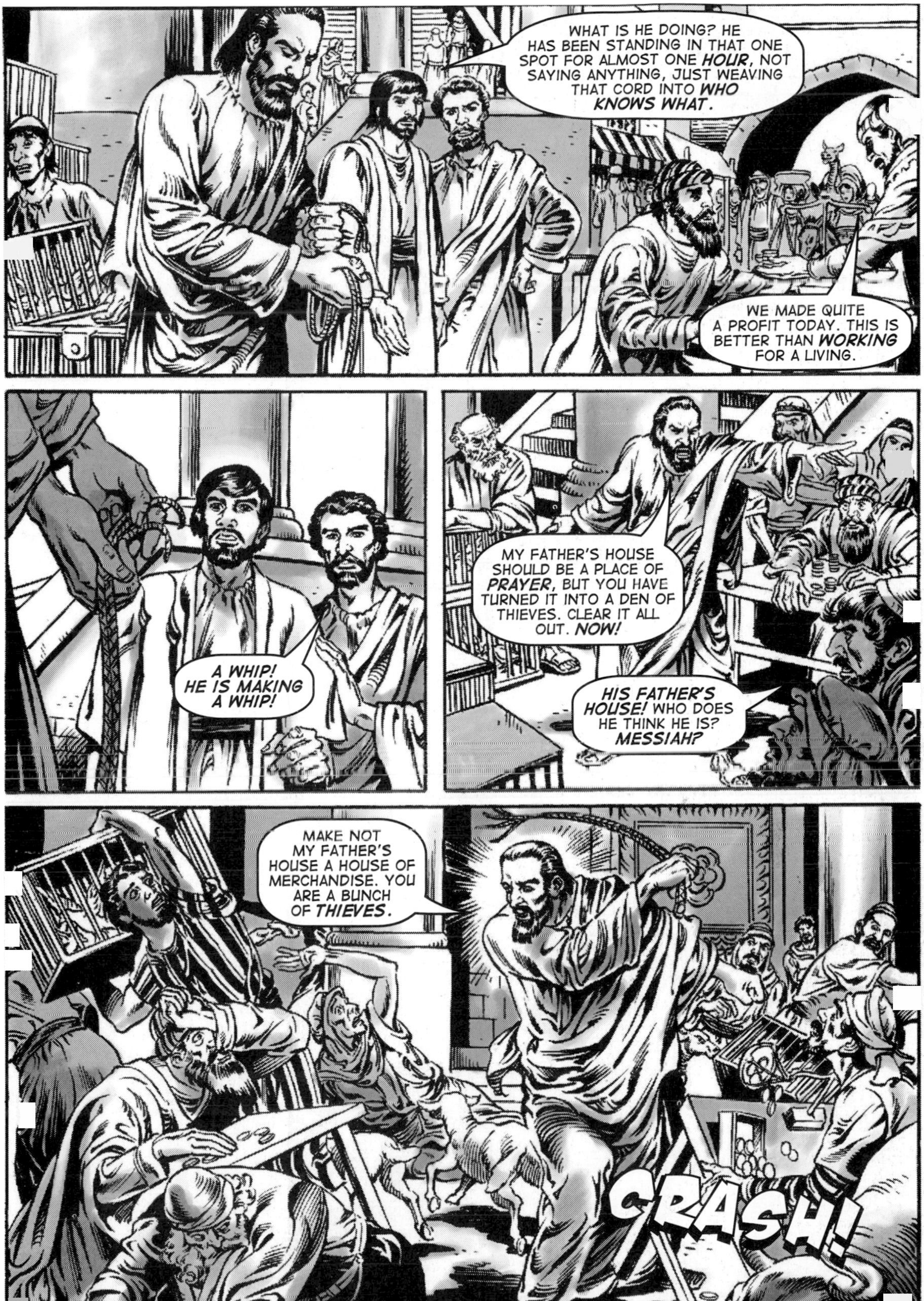
WHAT IS HE DOING? HE HAS BEEN STANDING IN THAT ONE SPOT FOR ALMOST ONE HOUR, NOT SAYING ANYTHING, JUST WEAVING THAT CORD INTO WHO KNOWS WHAT.
WE MADE QUITE A PROFIT TODAY. THIS IS BETTER THAN WORKING FOR A LIVING.
A WHIP! HE IS MAKING A WHIP!
MY FATHER'S HOUSE SHOULD BE A PLACE OF PRAYER, BUT YOU HAVE TURNED IT INTO A DEN OF THIEVES. CLEAR IT ALL OUT. NOW!
HIS FATHER'S HOUSE! WHO DOES HE THINK HE IS? MESSIAH?
MAKE NOT MY FATHER'S HOUSE A HOUSE OF MERCHANDISE. YOU ARE A BUNCH OF THIEVES.
CRASH!

JOHN 2:15-16

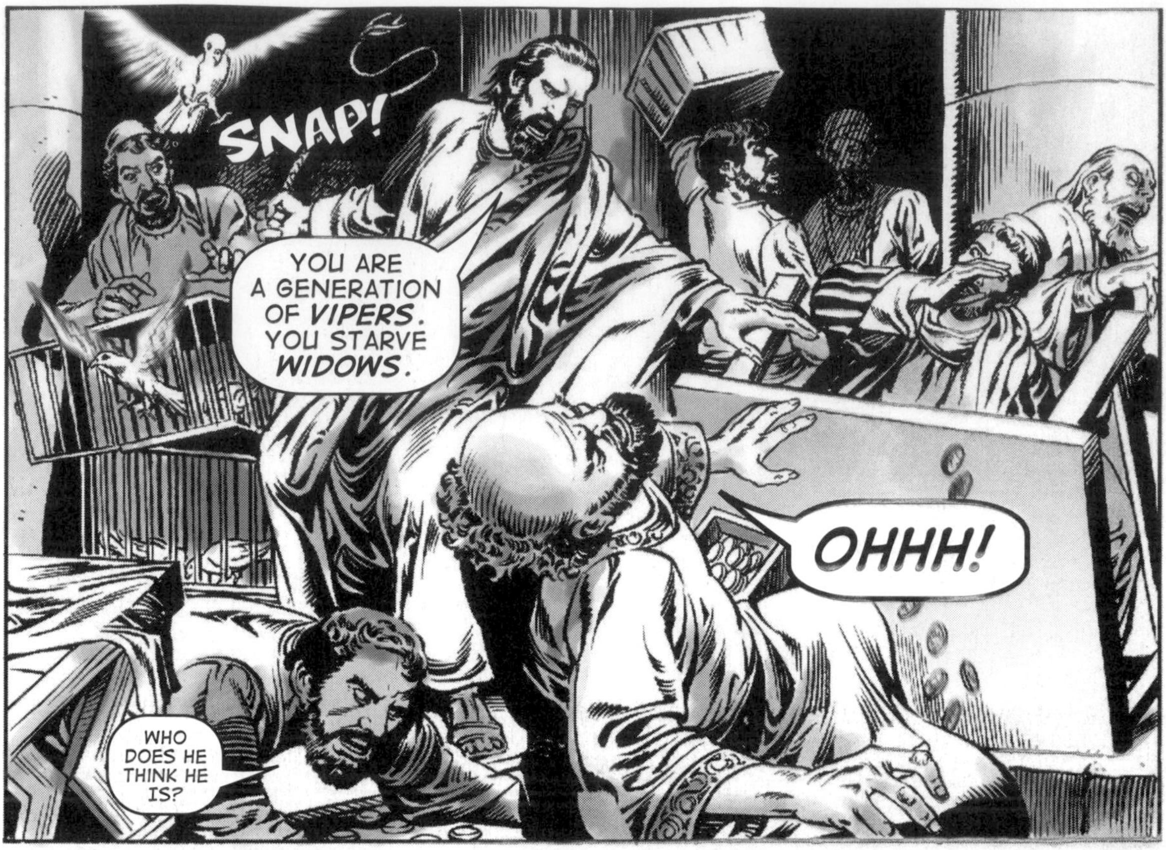
SNAP!
YOU ARE A GENERATION OF VIPERS. YOU STARVE WIDOWS.
OHHH!
WHO DOES HE THINK HE IS?

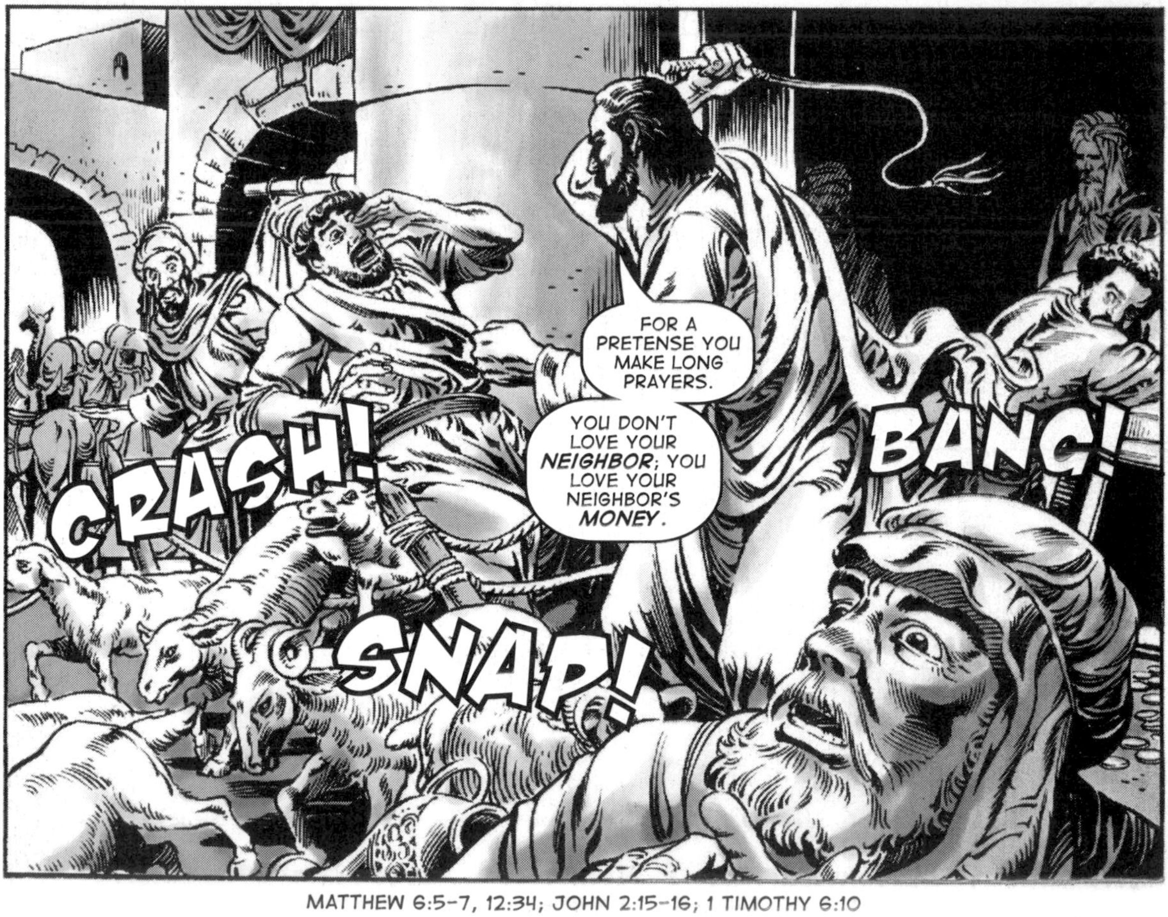
FOR A PRETENSE YOU MAKE LONG PRAYERS.
YOU DON'T LOVE YOUR NEIGHBOR; YOU LOVE YOUR NEIGHBOR'S MONEY.
CRASH!
BANG!
SNAP!

MATTHEW 6:5–7, 12:34; JOHN 2:15–16; 1 TIMOTHY 6:10

PSALM 69:9; JOHN 2:17–22

LUKE 4:16-21

LUKE 4:28-35

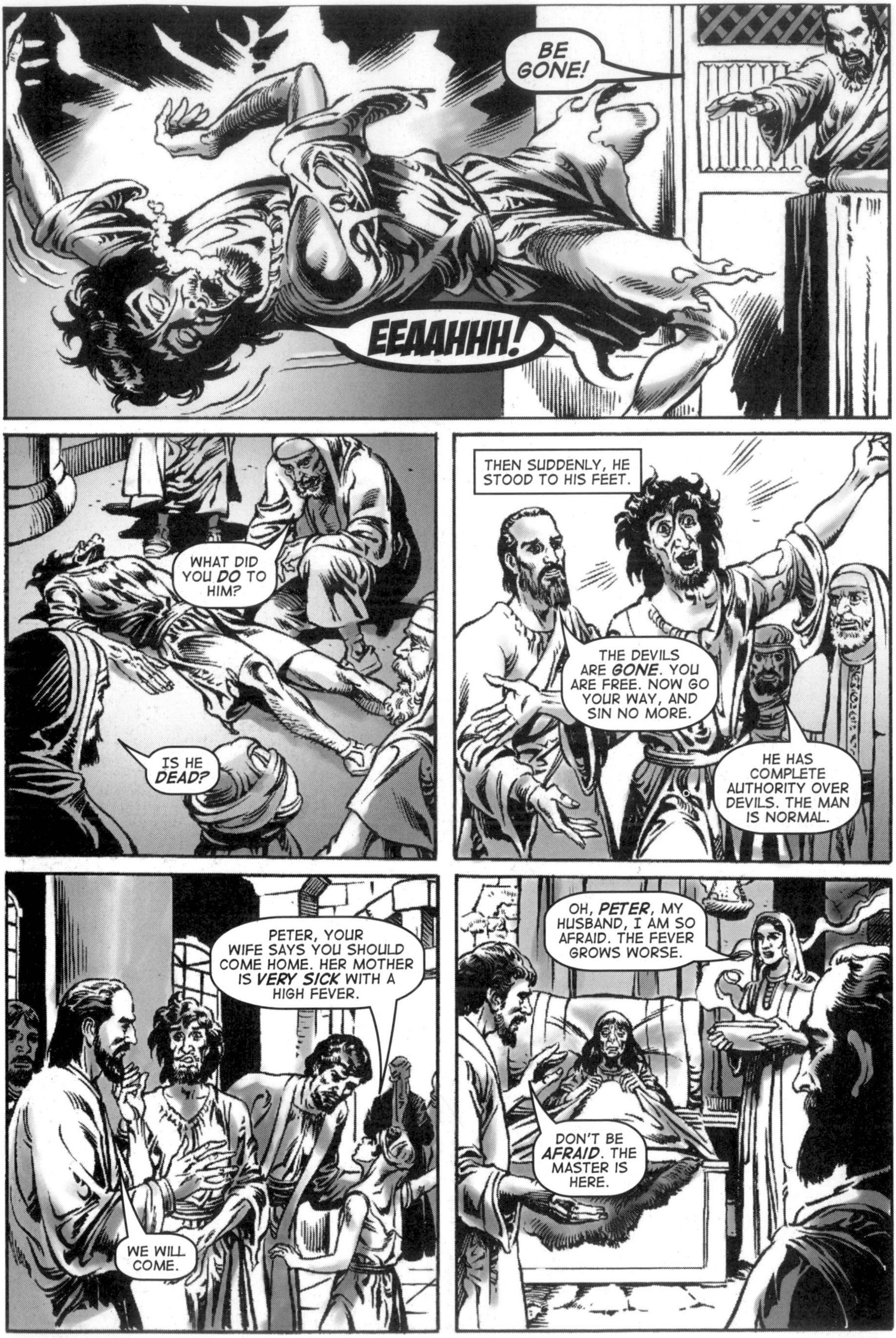
BE GONE!
EEAAHHH!
WHAT DID YOU DO TO HIM?
IS HE DEAD?
THEN SUDDENLY, HE STOOD TO HIS FEET.
THE DEVILS ARE GONE. YOU ARE FREE. NOW GO YOUR WAY, AND SIN NO MORE.
HE HAS COMPLETE AUTHORITY OVER DEVILS. THE MAN IS NORMAL.
PETER, YOUR WIFE SAYS YOU SHOULD COME HOME. HER MOTHER IS VERY SICK WITH A HIGH FEVER.
WE WILL COME.
OH, PETER, MY HUSBAND, I AM SO AFRAID. THE FEVER GROWS WORSE.
DON'T BE AFRAID. THE MASTER IS HERE.

MARK 1:25–28; LUKE 4:35–38

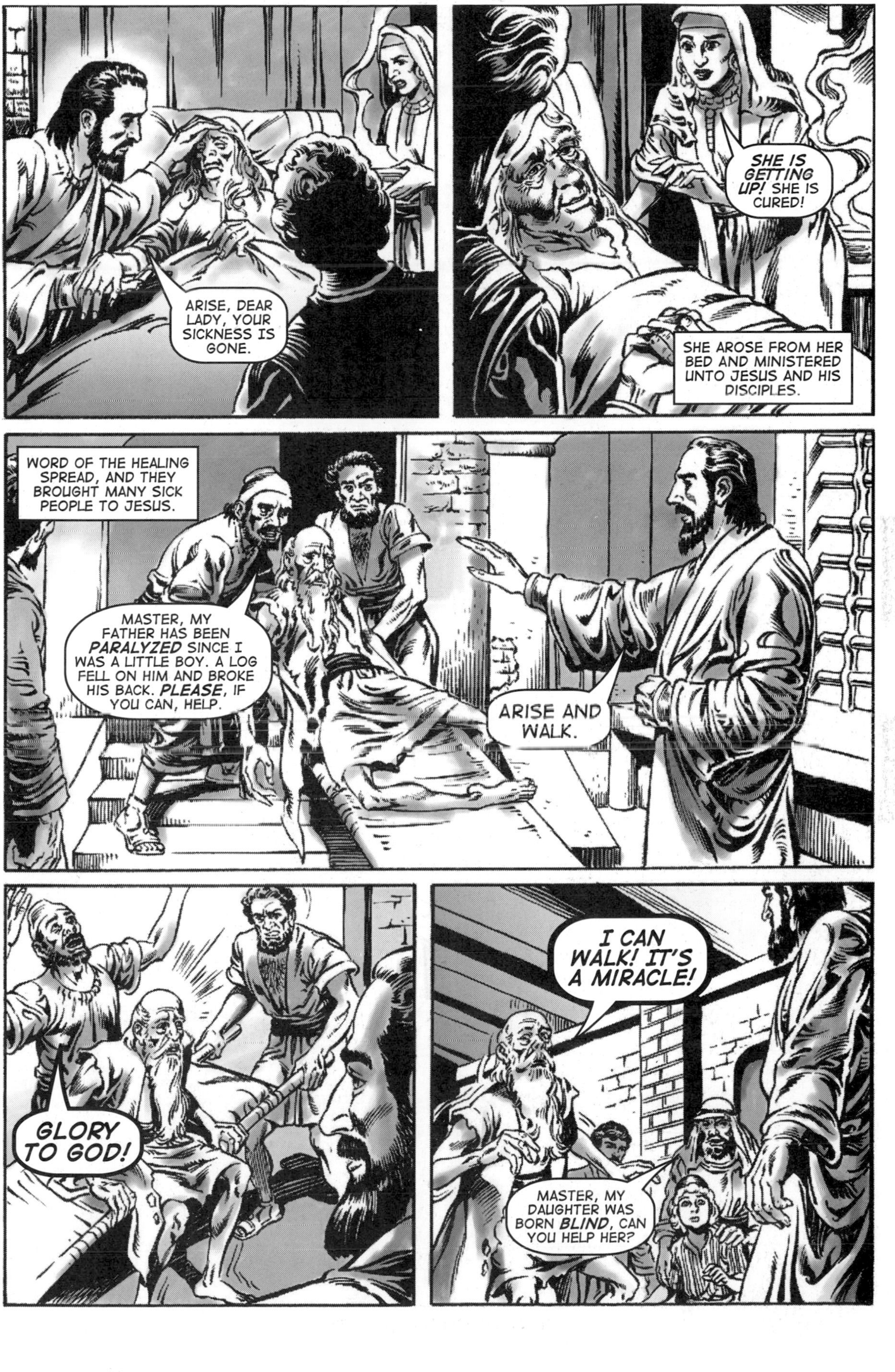
ARISE, DEAR LADY, YOUR SICKNESS IS GONE.
SHE IS GETTING UP! SHE IS CURED!
SHE AROSE FROM HER BED AND MINISTERED UNTO JESUS AND HIS DISCIPLES.
WORD OF THE HEALING SPREAD, AND THEY BROUGHT MANY SICK PEOPLE TO JESUS.
MASTER, MY FATHER HAS BEEN PARALYZED SINCE I WAS A LITTLE BOY. A LOG FELL ON HIM AND BROKE HIS BACK. PLEASE, IF YOU CAN, HELP.
ARISE AND WALK.
GLORY TO GOD!
I CAN WALK! IT'S A MIRACLE!
MASTER, MY DAUGHTER WAS BORN BLIND, CAN YOU HELP HER?

MATTHEW 5:43-44, 6:12, 5:8, 38-42, 5:21-22; MARK 1:34; LUKE 4:39-41

181

MATTHEW 5:27-28, 7:13-14, 28-29, 23:27-28; JOHN 5:18-19, 23, 29-30, 14:6

NUMBERS 21:5–9; JOHN 3:1–14

JOHN 3:14-18

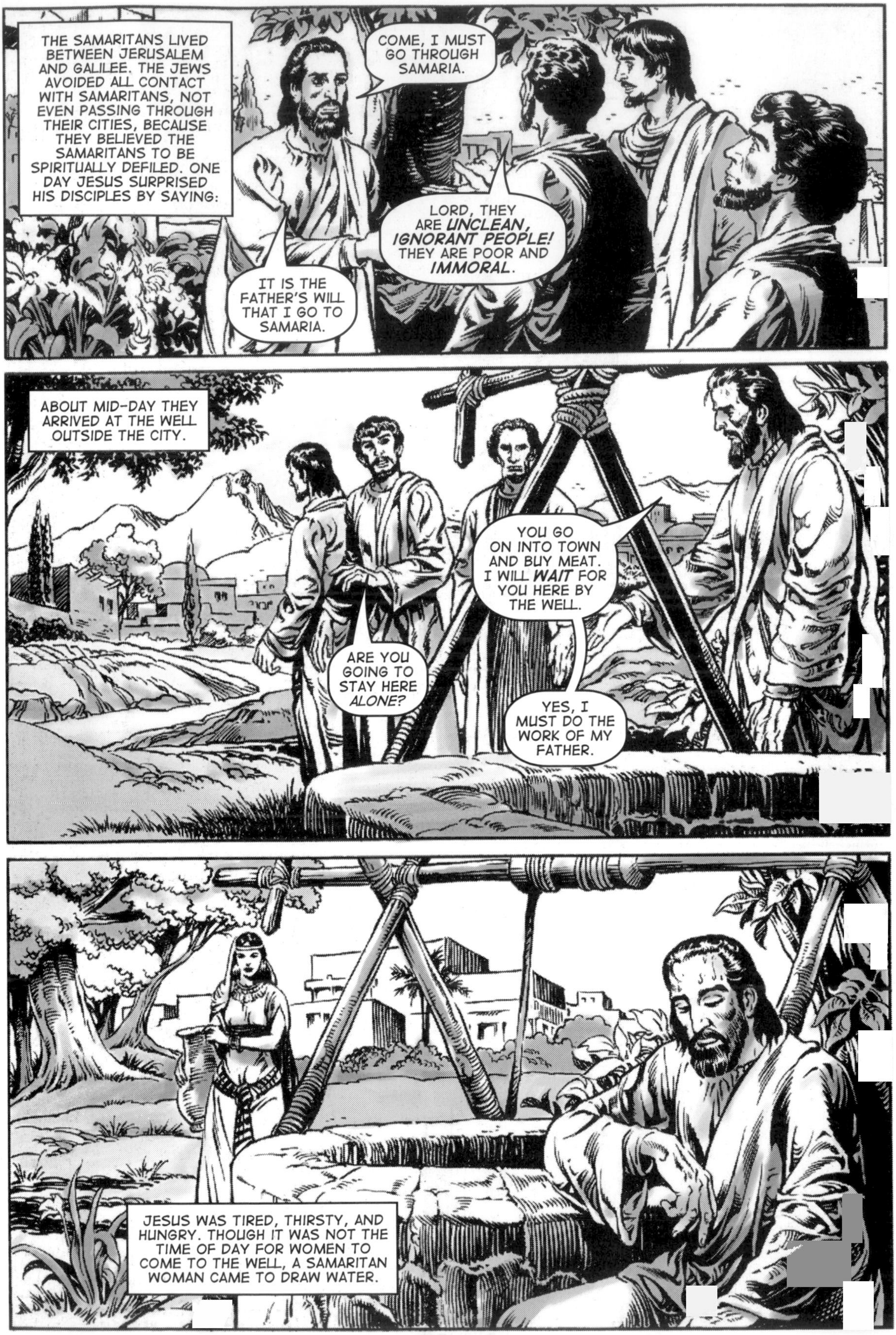
THE SAMARITANS LIVED BETWEEN JERUSALEM AND GALILEE. THE JEWS AVOIDED ALL CONTACT WITH SAMARITANS, NOT EVEN PASSING THROUGH THEIR CITIES, BECAUSE THEY BELIEVED THE SAMARITANS TO BE SPIRITUALLY DEFILED. ONE DAY JESUS SURPRISED HIS DISCIPLES BY SAYING:
COME, I MUST GO THROUGH SAMARIA.
LORD, THEY ARE ***UNCLEAN, IGNORANT PEOPLE!*** THEY ARE POOR AND ***IMMORAL***.
IT IS THE FATHER'S WILL THAT I GO TO SAMARIA.
ABOUT MID-DAY THEY ARRIVED AT THE WELL OUTSIDE THE CITY.
YOU GO ON INTO TOWN AND BUY MEAT. I WILL ***WAIT*** FOR YOU HERE BY THE WELL.
ARE YOU GOING TO STAY HERE *ALONE?*
YES, I MUST DO THE WORK OF MY FATHER.
JESUS WAS TIRED, THIRSTY, AND HUNGRY. THOUGH IT WAS NOT THE TIME OF DAY FOR WOMEN TO COME TO THE WELL, A SAMARITAN WOMAN CAME TO DRAW WATER.

185

JOHN 4:7-29, 40

186

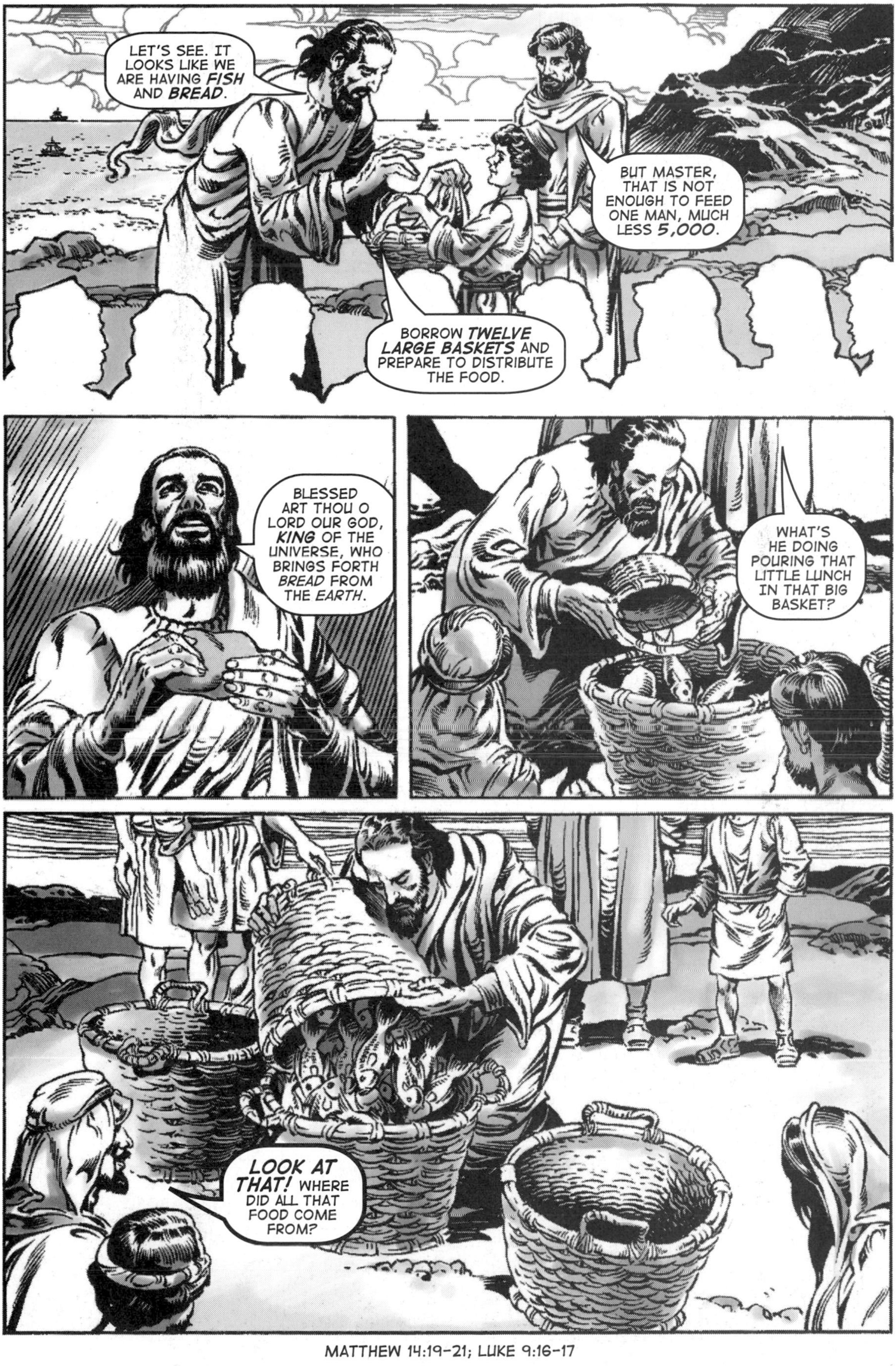
LET'S SEE. IT LOOKS LIKE WE ARE HAVING FISH AND BREAD.
BUT MASTER, THAT IS NOT ENOUGH TO FEED ONE MAN, MUCH LESS 5,000.
BORROW TWELVE LARGE BASKETS AND PREPARE TO DISTRIBUTE THE FOOD.
BLESSED ART THOU O LORD OUR GOD, KING OF THE UNIVERSE, WHO BRINGS FORTH BREAD FROM THE EARTH.
WHAT'S HE DOING POURING THAT LITTLE LUNCH IN THAT BIG BASKET?
LOOK AT THAT! WHERE DID ALL THAT FOOD COME FROM?

MATTHEW 14:19–21; LUKE 9:16–17

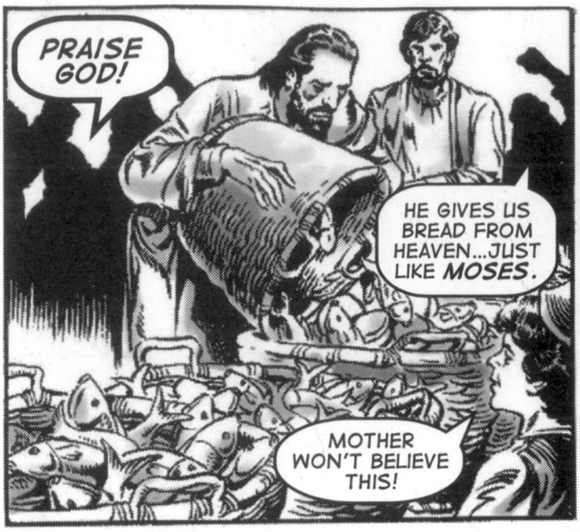
PRAISE GOD!
HE GIVES US BREAD FROM HEAVEN...JUST LIKE **MOSES**.
MOTHER WON'T BELIEVE THIS!

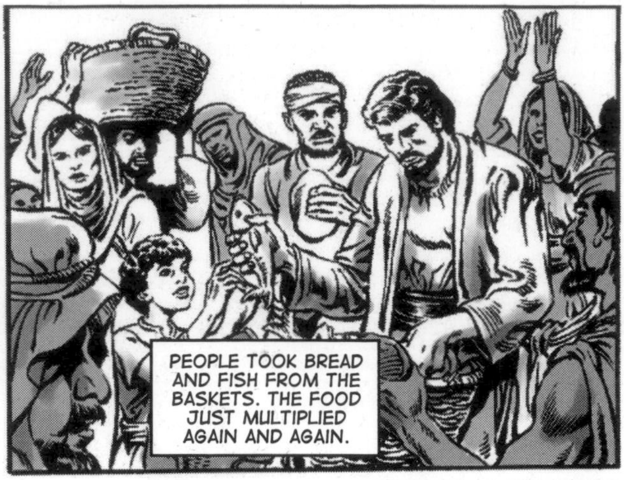
PEOPLE TOOK BREAD AND FISH FROM THE BASKETS. THE FOOD JUST MULTIPLIED AGAIN AND AGAIN.

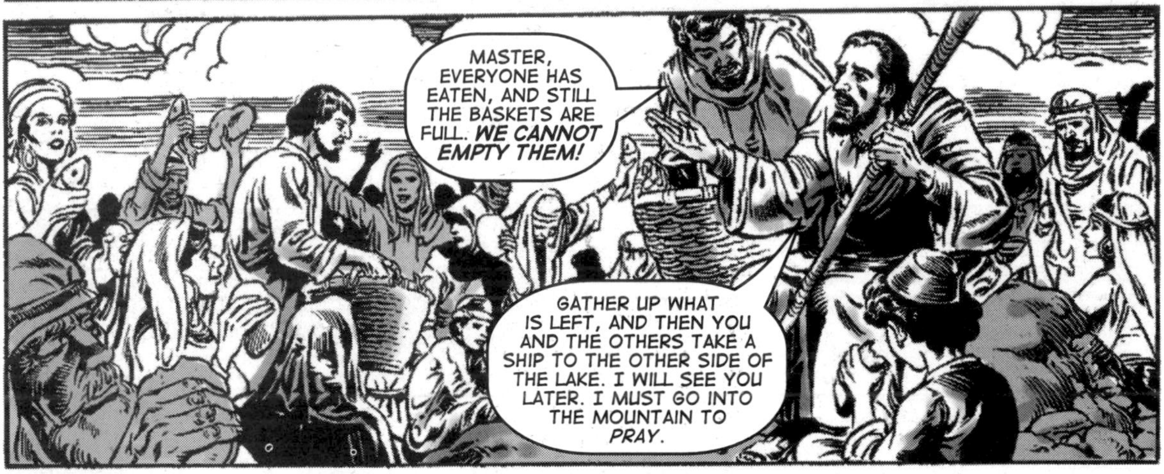
MASTER, EVERYONE HAS EATEN, AND STILL THE BASKETS ARE FULL. **WE CANNOT EMPTY THEM!**
GATHER UP WHAT IS LEFT, AND THEN YOU AND THE OTHERS TAKE A SHIP TO THE OTHER SIDE OF THE LAKE. I WILL SEE YOU LATER. I MUST GO INTO THE MOUNTAIN TO *PRAY*.

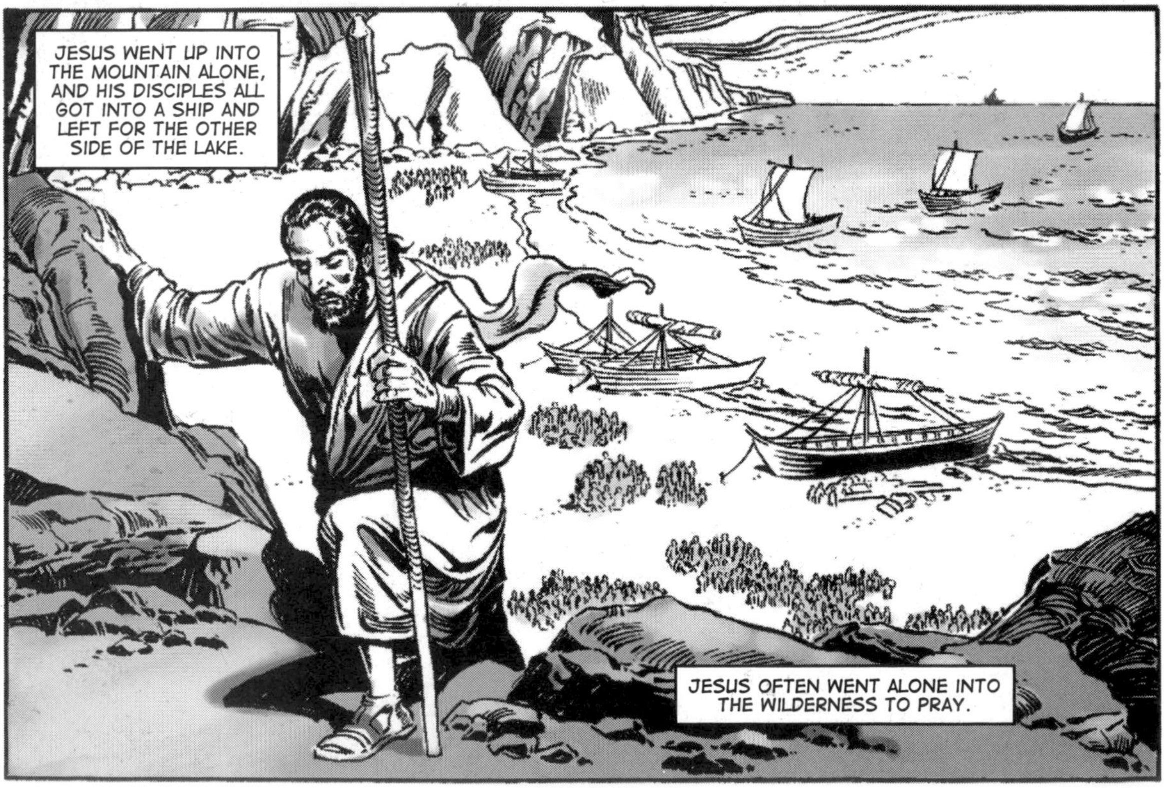
JESUS WENT UP INTO THE MOUNTAIN ALONE, AND HIS DISCIPLES ALL GOT INTO A SHIP AND LEFT FOR THE OTHER SIDE OF THE LAKE.
JESUS OFTEN WENT ALONE INTO THE WILDERNESS TO PRAY.

MATTHEW 14:20-23

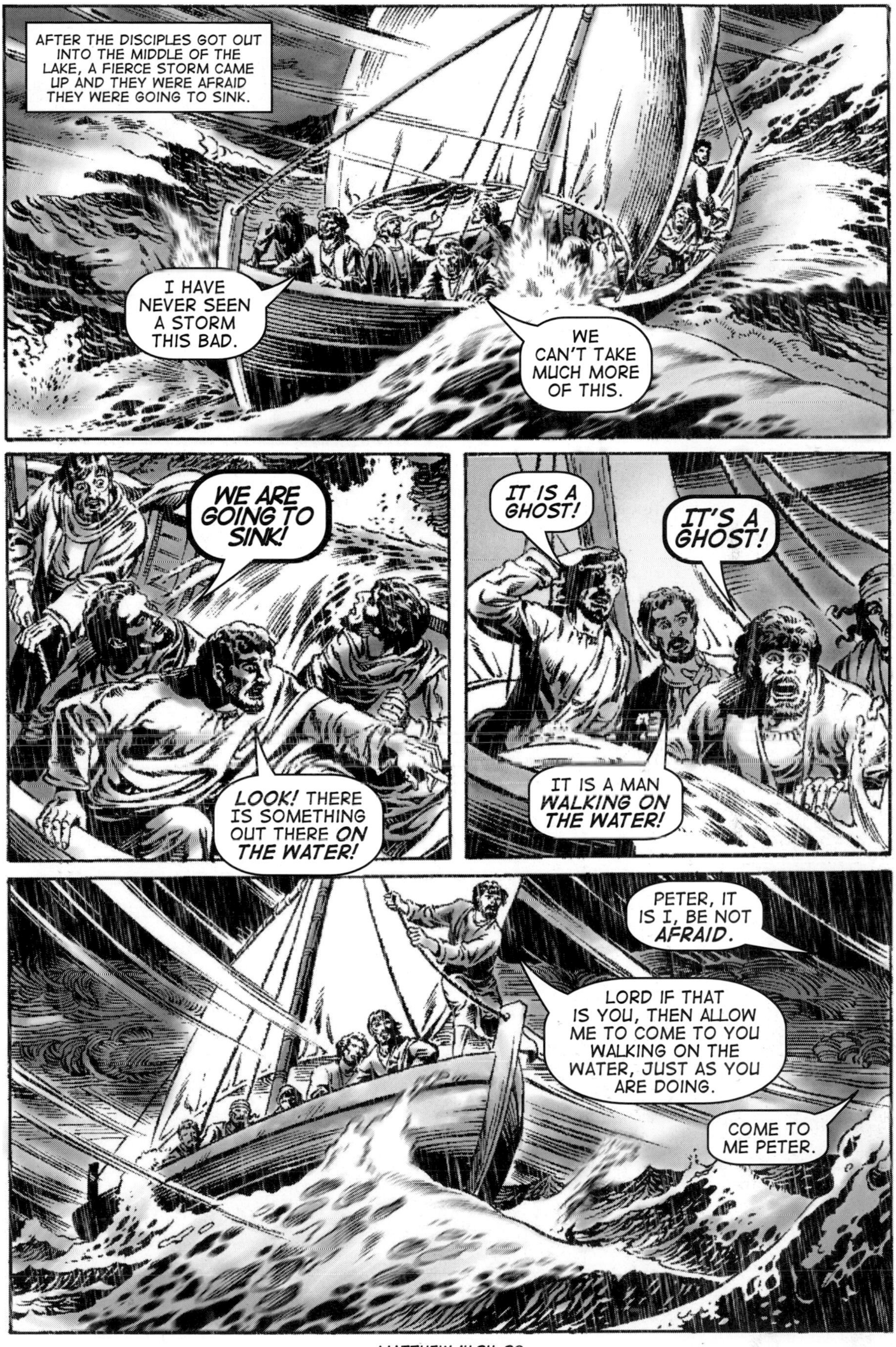
AFTER THE DISCIPLES GOT OUT INTO THE MIDDLE OF THE LAKE, A FIERCE STORM CAME UP AND THEY WERE AFRAID THEY WERE GOING TO SINK.
I HAVE NEVER SEEN A STORM THIS BAD.
WE CAN'T TAKE MUCH MORE OF THIS.
WE ARE GOING TO SINK!
LOOK! THERE IS SOMETHING OUT THERE ON THE WATER!
IT IS A GHOST!
IT'S A GHOST!
IT IS A MAN WALKING ON THE WATER!
PETER, IT IS I, BE NOT AFRAID.
LORD IF THAT IS YOU, THEN ALLOW ME TO COME TO YOU WALKING ON THE WATER, JUST AS YOU ARE DOING.
COME TO ME PETER.

MATTHEW 14:24-29

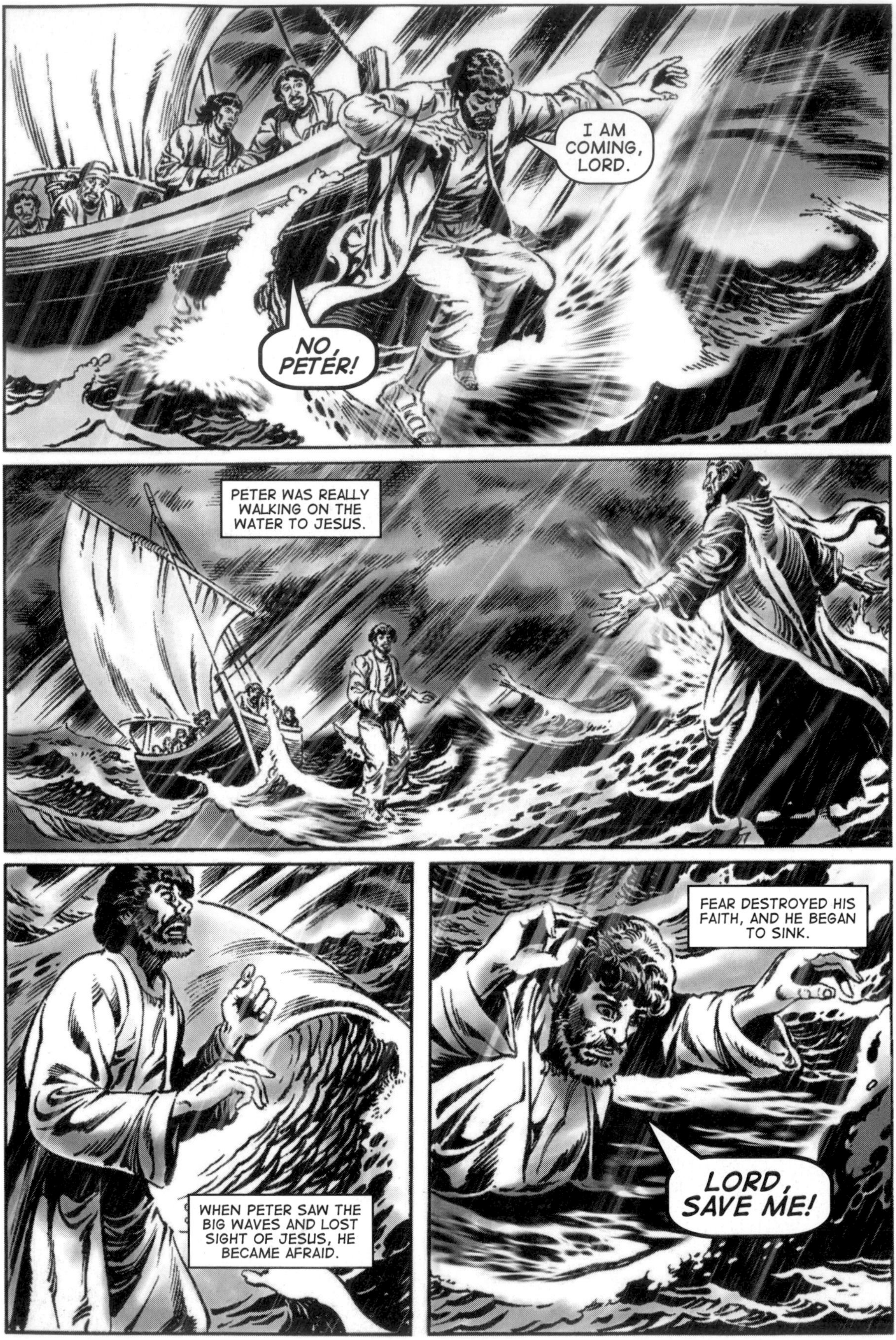
I AM COMING, LORD.
NO, PETER!
PETER WAS REALLY WALKING ON THE WATER TO JESUS.
WHEN PETER SAW THE BIG WAVES AND LOST SIGHT OF JESUS, HE BECAME AFRAID.
FEAR DESTROYED HIS FAITH, AND HE BEGAN TO SINK.
LORD, SAVE ME!

MATTHEW 14:29–30

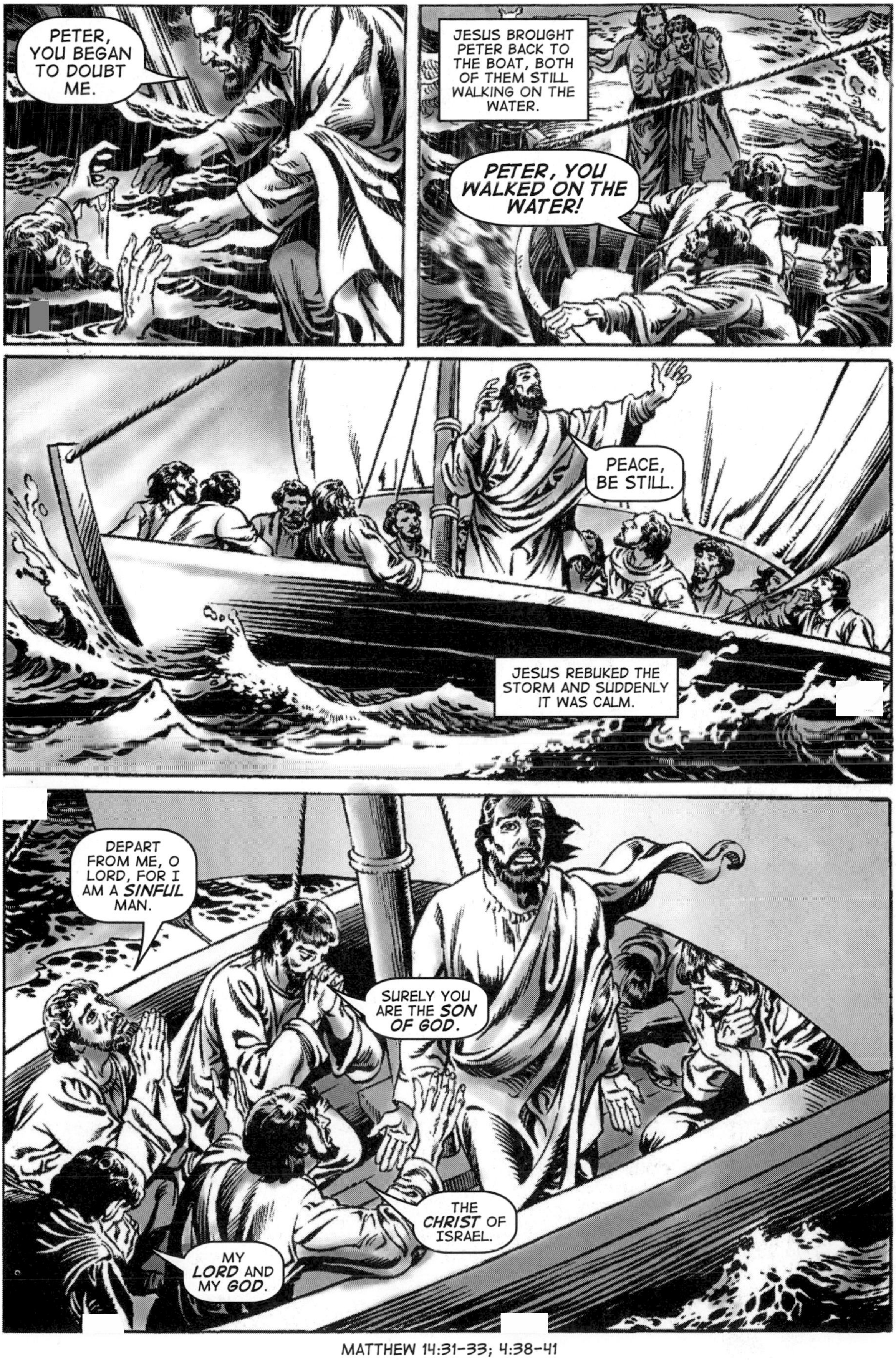
PETER, YOU BEGAN TO DOUBT ME.
JESUS BROUGHT PETER BACK TO THE BOAT, BOTH OF THEM STILL WALKING ON THE WATER.
PETER, YOU WALKED ON THE WATER!
PEACE, BE STILL.
JESUS REBUKED THE STORM AND SUDDENLY IT WAS CALM.
DEPART FROM ME, O LORD, FOR I AM A SINFUL MAN.
SURELY YOU ARE THE SON OF GOD.
THE CHRIST OF ISRAEL.
MY LORD AND MY GOD.

MATTHEW 14:31-33; 4:38-41

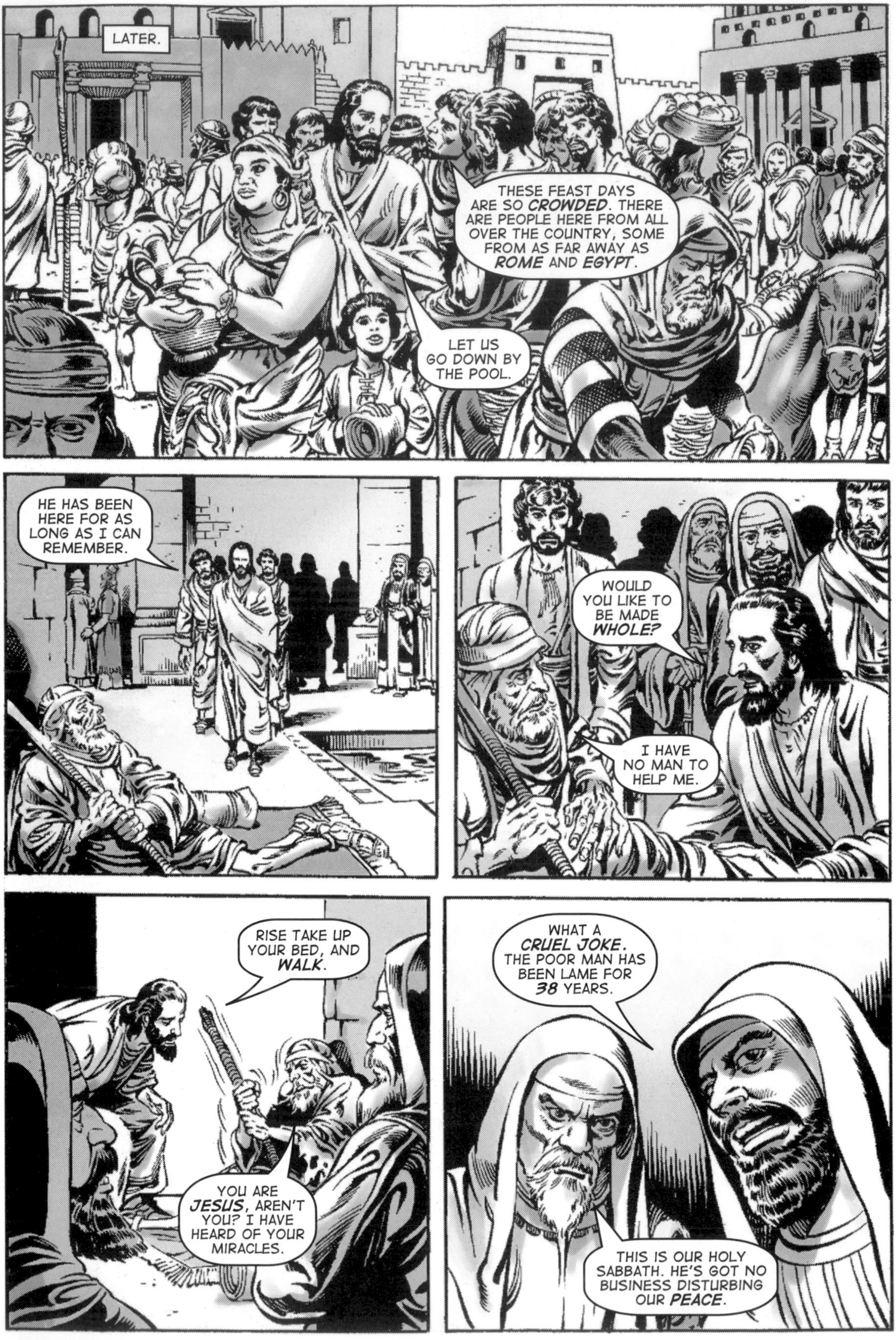
LATER.
THESE FEAST DAYS ARE SO CROWDED. THERE ARE PEOPLE HERE FROM ALL OVER THE COUNTRY, SOME FROM AS FAR AWAY AS ROME AND EGYPT.
LET US GO DOWN BY THE POOL.
HE HAS BEEN HERE FOR AS LONG AS I CAN REMEMBER.
WOULD YOU LIKE TO BE MADE WHOLE?
I HAVE NO MAN TO HELP ME.
RISE TAKE UP YOUR BED, AND WALK.
YOU ARE JESUS, AREN'T YOU? I HAVE HEARD OF YOUR MIRACLES.
WHAT A CRUEL JOKE. THE POOR MAN HAS BEEN LAME FOR 38 YEARS.
THIS IS OUR HOLY SABBATH. HE'S GOT NO BUSINESS DISTURBING OUR PEACE.

JOHN 5:1–8

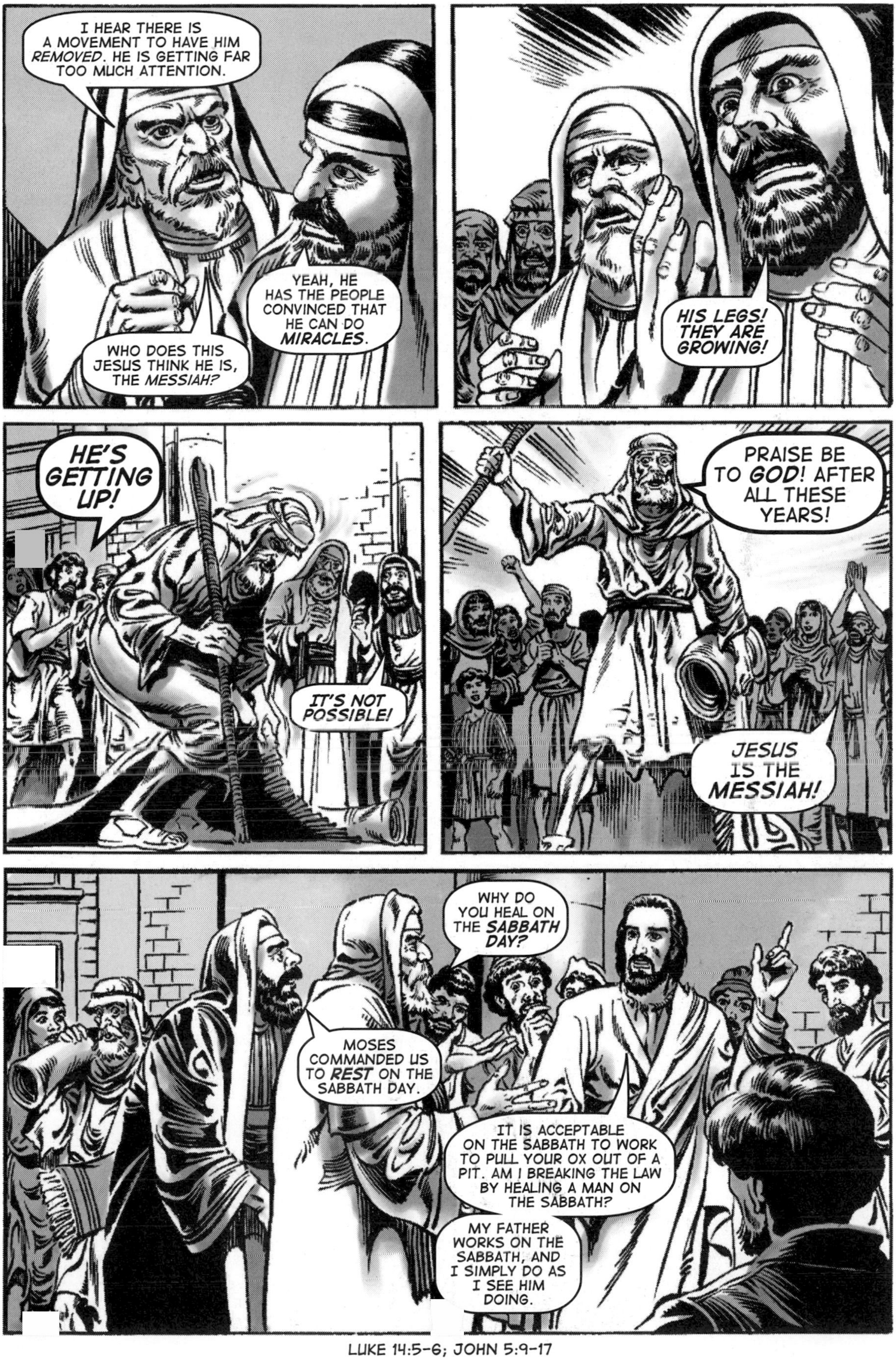
I HEAR THERE IS A MOVEMENT TO HAVE HIM *REMOVED*. HE IS GETTING FAR TOO MUCH ATTENTION.
YEAH, HE HAS THE PEOPLE CONVINCED THAT HE CAN DO ***MIRACLES***.
WHO DOES THIS JESUS THINK HE IS, THE *MESSIAH?*
HIS LEGS! THEY ARE GROWING!
HE'S GETTING UP!
IT'S NOT POSSIBLE!
PRAISE BE TO ***GOD***! AFTER ALL THESE YEARS!
JESUS IS THE ***MESSIAH!***
WHY DO YOU HEAL ON THE ***SABBATH DAY?***
MOSES COMMANDED US TO ***REST*** ON THE SABBATH DAY.
IT IS ACCEPTABLE ON THE SABBATH TO WORK TO PULL YOUR OX OUT OF A PIT. AM I BREAKING THE LAW BY HEALING A MAN ON THE SABBATH?
MY FATHER WORKS ON THE SABBATH, AND I SIMPLY DO AS I SEE HIM DOING.

LUKE 14:5-6; JOHN 5:9-17

JOHN 5:18-29

MATTHEW 5:6, 9; JOHN 4:14, 7:45-52

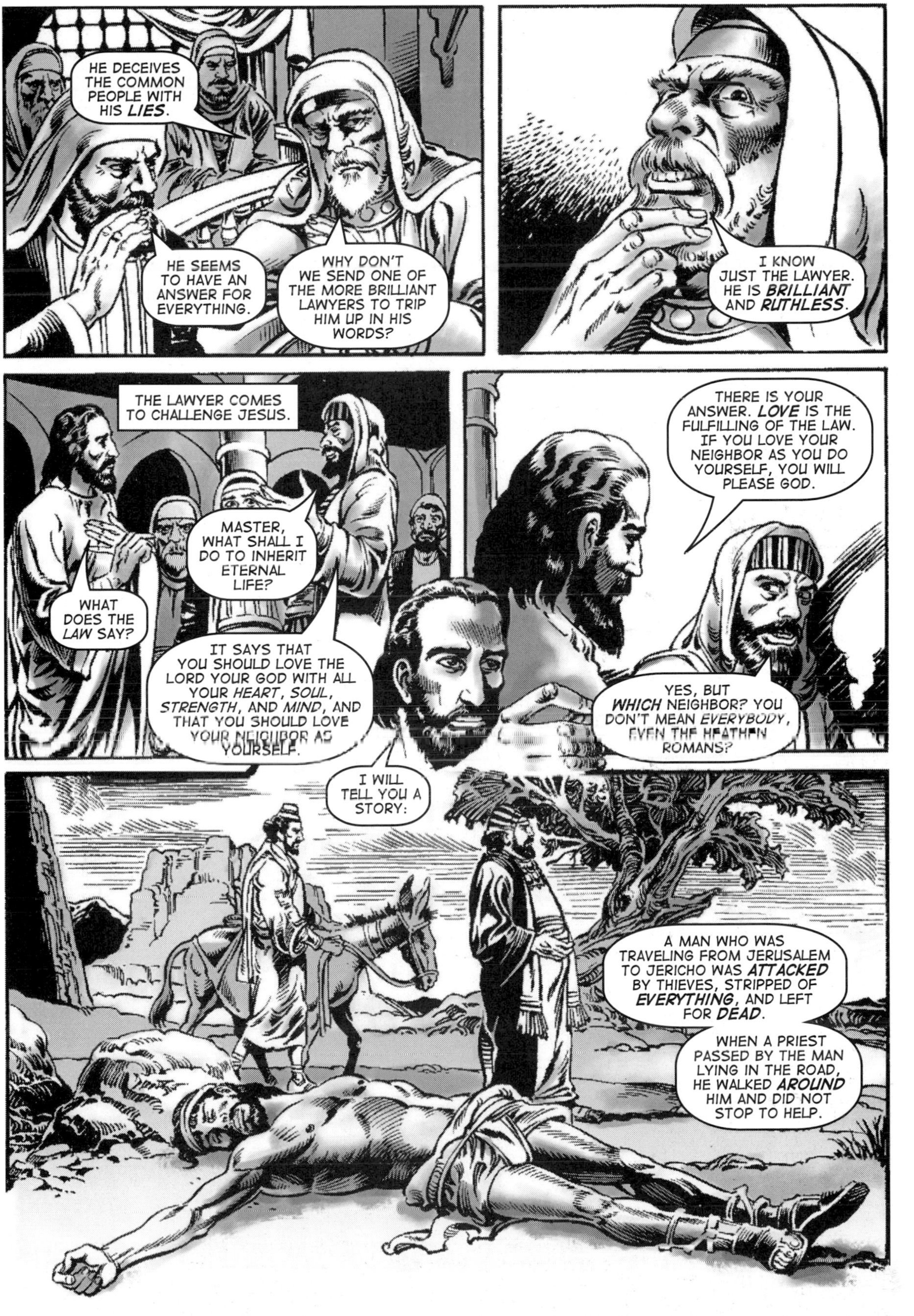
HE DECEIVES THE COMMON PEOPLE WITH HIS LIES.
HE SEEMS TO HAVE AN ANSWER FOR EVERYTHING.
WHY DON'T WE SEND ONE OF THE MORE BRILLIANT LAWYERS TO TRIP HIM UP IN HIS WORDS?
I KNOW JUST THE LAWYER. HE IS BRILLIANT AND RUTHLESS.
THE LAWYER COMES TO CHALLENGE JESUS.
MASTER, WHAT SHALL I DO TO INHERIT ETERNAL LIFE?
WHAT DOES THE LAW SAY?
IT SAYS THAT YOU SHOULD LOVE THE LORD YOUR GOD WITH ALL YOUR HEART, SOUL, STRENGTH, AND MIND, AND THAT YOU SHOULD LOVE YOUR NEIGHBOR AS YOURSELF.
THERE IS YOUR ANSWER. LOVE IS THE FULFILLING OF THE LAW. IF YOU LOVE YOUR NEIGHBOR AS YOU DO YOURSELF, YOU WILL PLEASE GOD.
YES, BUT WHICH NEIGHBOR? YOU DON'T MEAN EVERYBODY, EVEN THE HEATHEN ROMANS?
I WILL TELL YOU A STORY:
A MAN WHO WAS TRAVELING FROM JERUSALEM TO JERICHO WAS ATTACKED BY THIEVES, STRIPPED OF EVERYTHING, AND LEFT FOR DEAD.
WHEN A PRIEST PASSED BY THE MAN LYING IN THE ROAD, HE WALKED AROUND HIM AND DID NOT STOP TO HELP.

LUKE 10:25–31

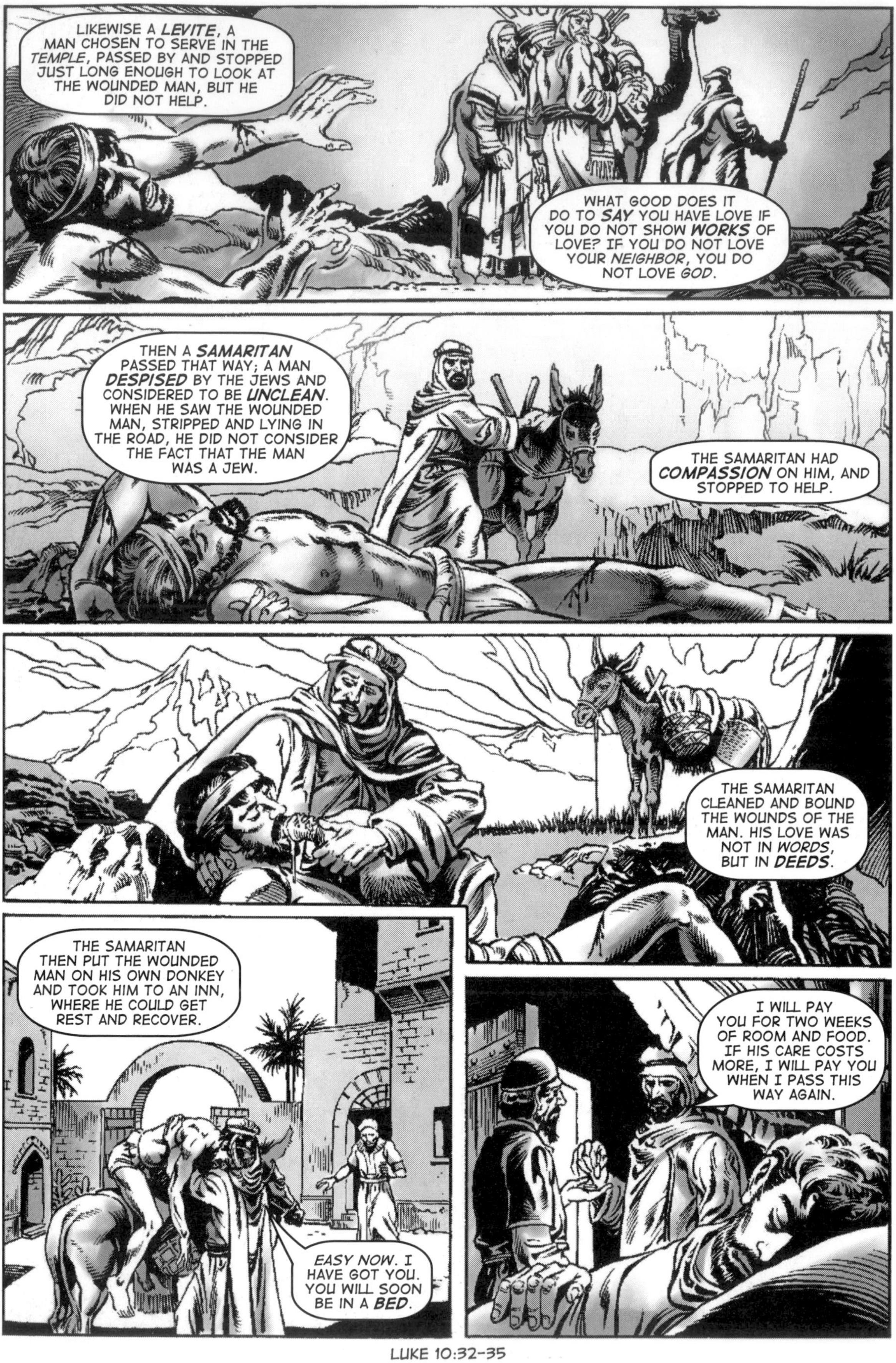
LIKEWISE A LEVITE, A MAN CHOSEN TO SERVE IN THE TEMPLE, PASSED BY AND STOPPED JUST LONG ENOUGH TO LOOK AT THE WOUNDED MAN, BUT HE DID NOT HELP.
WHAT GOOD DOES IT DO TO SAY YOU HAVE LOVE IF YOU DO NOT SHOW WORKS OF LOVE? IF YOU DO NOT LOVE YOUR NEIGHBOR, YOU DO NOT LOVE GOD.
THEN A SAMARITAN PASSED THAT WAY; A MAN DESPISED BY THE JEWS AND CONSIDERED TO BE UNCLEAN. WHEN HE SAW THE WOUNDED MAN, STRIPPED AND LYING IN THE ROAD, HE DID NOT CONSIDER THE FACT THAT THE MAN WAS A JEW.
THE SAMARITAN HAD COMPASSION ON HIM, AND STOPPED TO HELP.
THE SAMARITAN CLEANED AND BOUND THE WOUNDS OF THE MAN. HIS LOVE WAS NOT IN WORDS, BUT IN DEEDS.
THE SAMARITAN THEN PUT THE WOUNDED MAN ON HIS OWN DONKEY AND TOOK HIM TO AN INN, WHERE HE COULD GET REST AND RECOVER.
EASY NOW. I HAVE GOT YOU. YOU WILL SOON BE IN A BED.
I WILL PAY YOU FOR TWO WEEKS OF ROOM AND FOOD. IF HIS CARE COSTS MORE, I WILL PAY YOU WHEN I PASS THIS WAY AGAIN.

LUKE 10:32-35

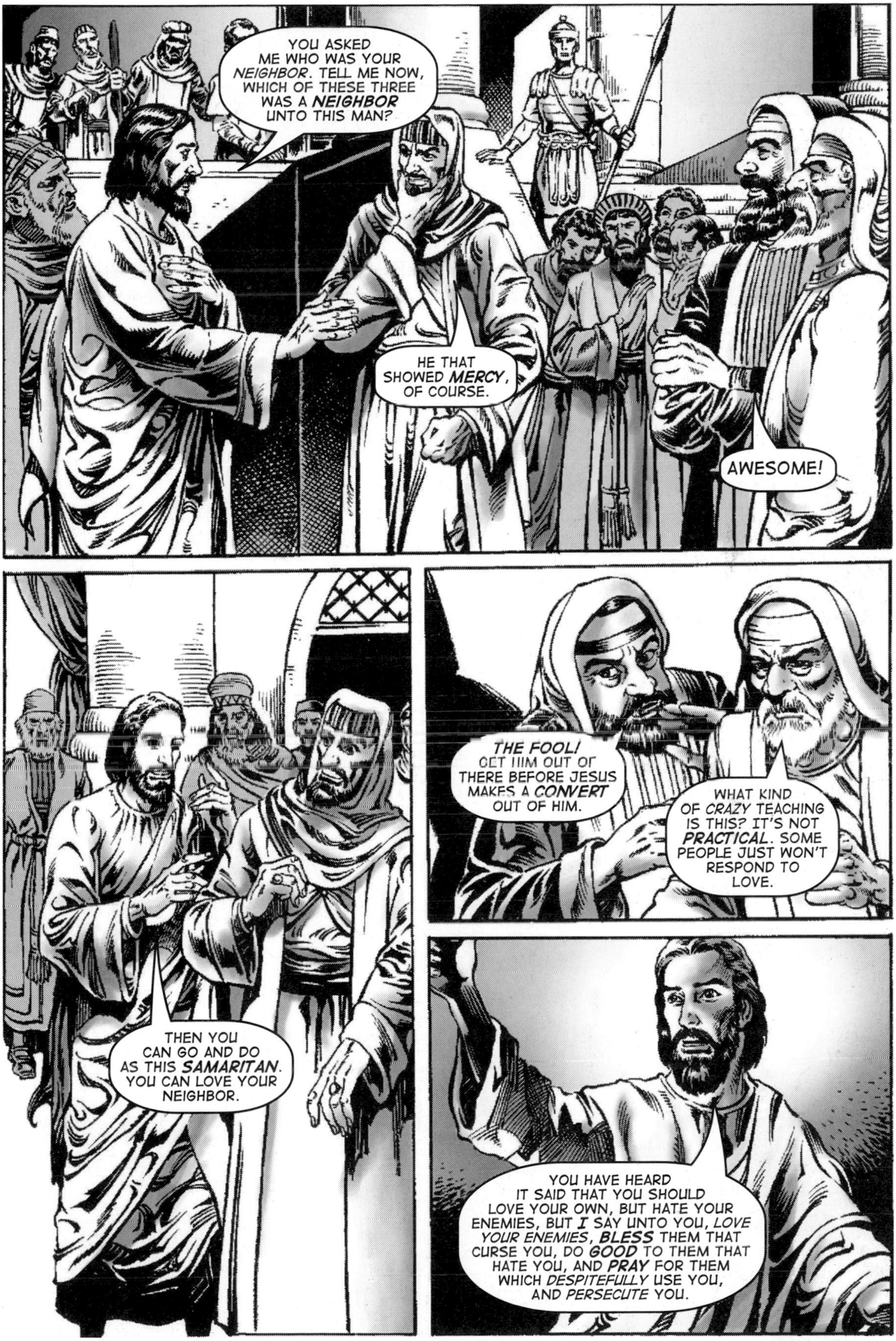
YOU ASKED ME WHO WAS YOUR *NEIGHBOR*. TELL ME NOW, WHICH OF THESE THREE WAS A **NEIGHBOR** UNTO THIS MAN?
HE THAT SHOWED **MERCY**, OF COURSE.
AWESOME!
THEN YOU CAN GO AND DO AS THIS **SAMARITAN**. YOU CAN LOVE YOUR NEIGHBOR.
THE FOOL! GET HIM OUT OF THERE BEFORE JESUS MAKES A **CONVERT** OUT OF HIM.
WHAT KIND OF *CRAZY* TEACHING IS THIS? IT'S NOT **PRACTICAL**. SOME PEOPLE JUST WON'T RESPOND TO LOVE.
YOU HAVE HEARD IT SAID THAT YOU SHOULD LOVE YOUR OWN, BUT HATE YOUR ENEMIES, BUT **I** SAY UNTO YOU, *LOVE YOUR ENEMIES*, **BLESS** THEM THAT CURSE YOU, DO **GOOD** TO THEM THAT HATE YOU, AND **PRAY** FOR THEM WHICH *DESPITEFULLY* USE YOU, AND *PERSECUTE* YOU.

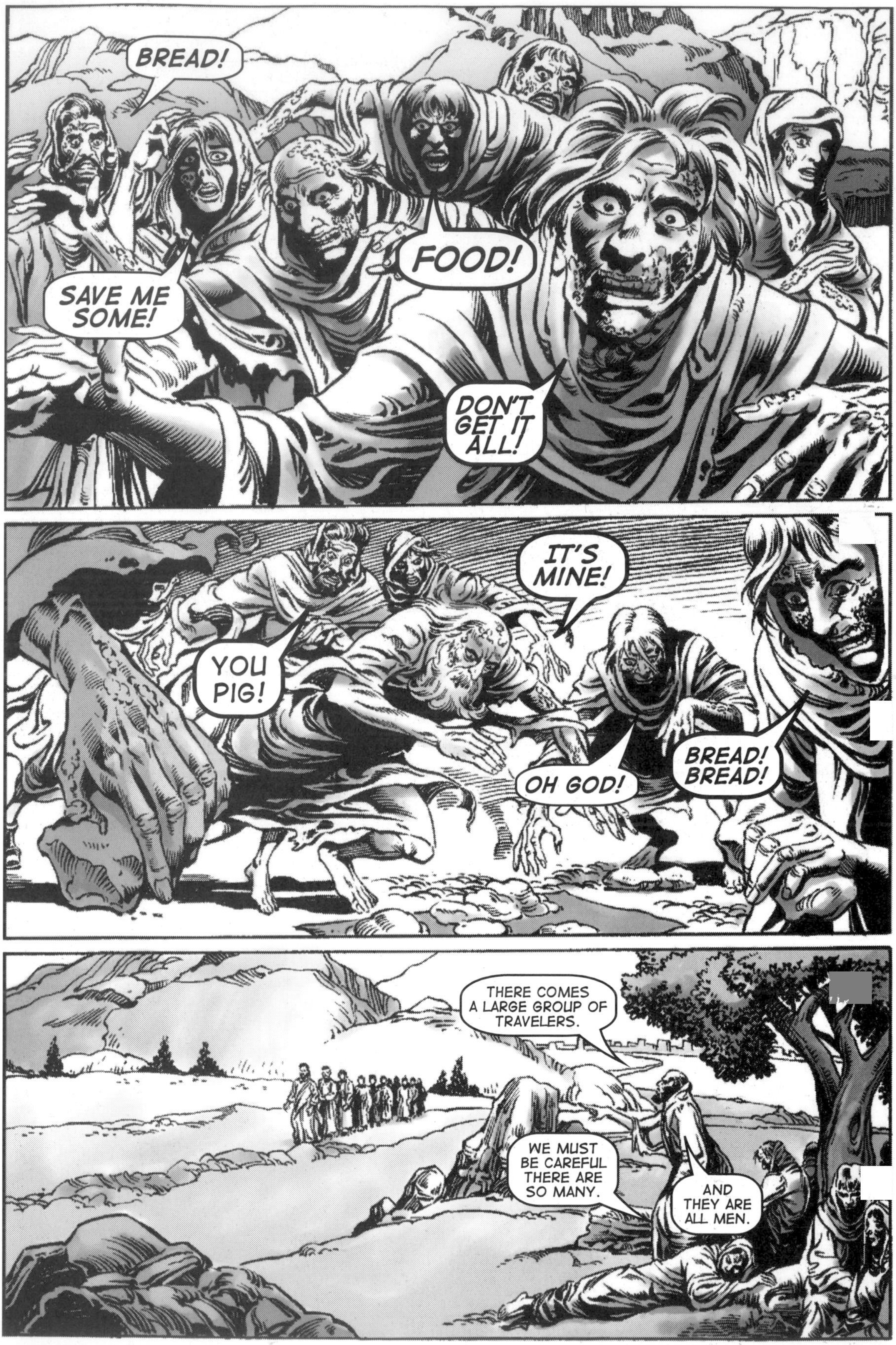
BREAD!
SAVE ME SOME!
FOOD!
DON'T GET IT ALL!
IT'S MINE!
YOU PIG!
OH GOD!
BREAD! BREAD!
THERE COMES A LARGE GROUP OF TRAVELERS.
WE MUST BE CAREFUL THERE ARE SO MANY.
AND THEY ARE ALL MEN.

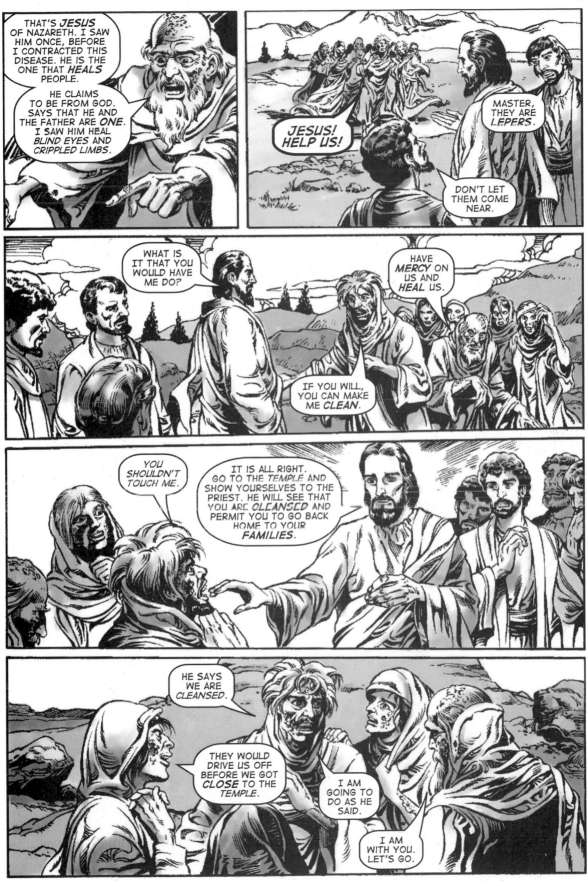

LUKE 17:11-14

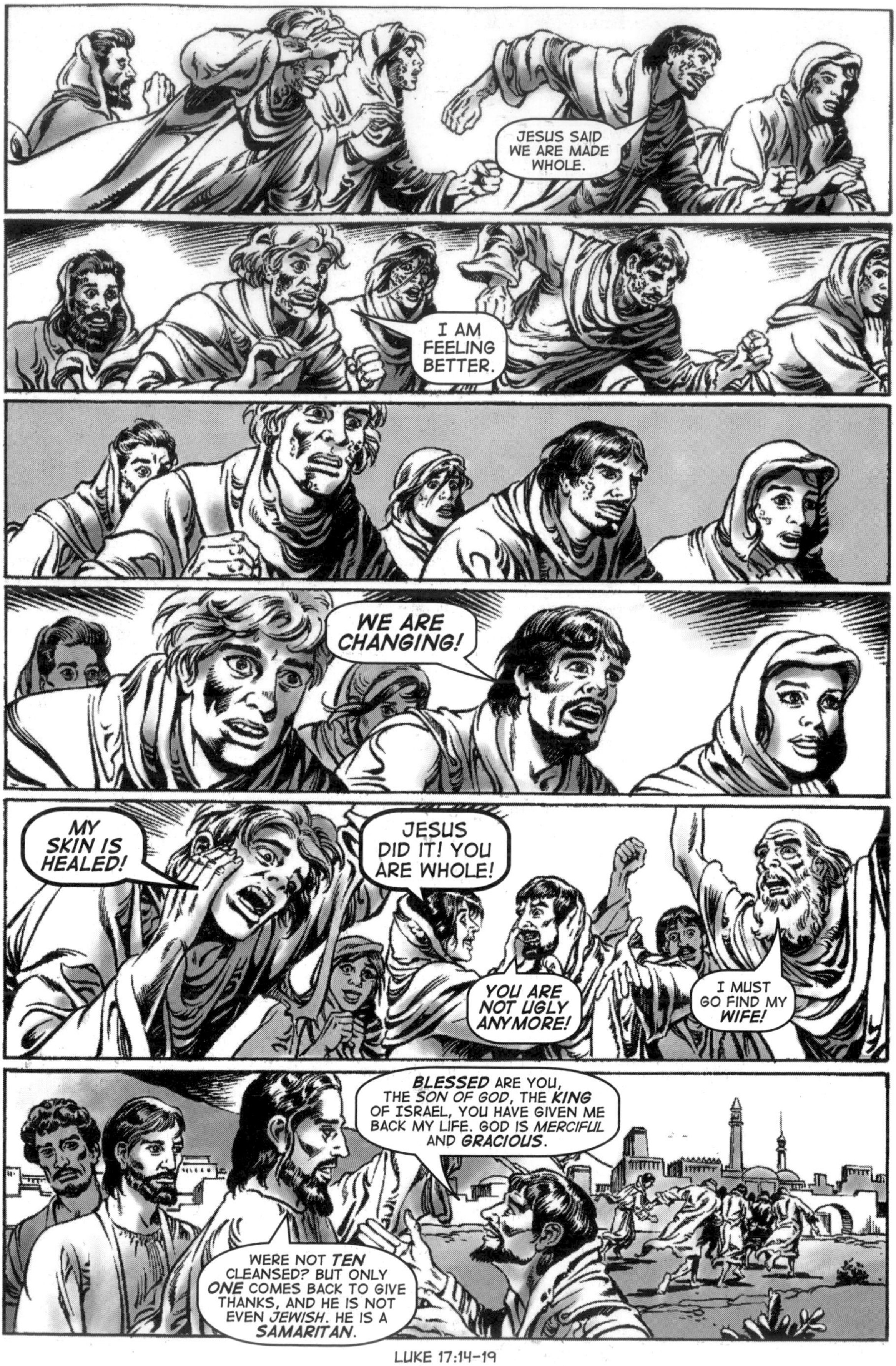
JESUS SAID WE ARE MADE WHOLE.
I AM FEELING BETTER.
WE ARE CHANGING!
MY SKIN IS HEALED!
JESUS DID IT! YOU ARE WHOLE!
YOU ARE NOT UGLY ANYMORE!
I MUST GO FIND MY WIFE!
BLESSED ARE YOU, THE SON OF GOD, THE KING OF ISRAEL, YOU HAVE GIVEN ME BACK MY LIFE. GOD IS MERCIFUL AND GRACIOUS.
WERE NOT TEN CLEANSED? BUT ONLY ONE COMES BACK TO GIVE THANKS, AND HE IS NOT EVEN JEWISH. HE IS A SAMARITAN.

LUKE 17:14–19

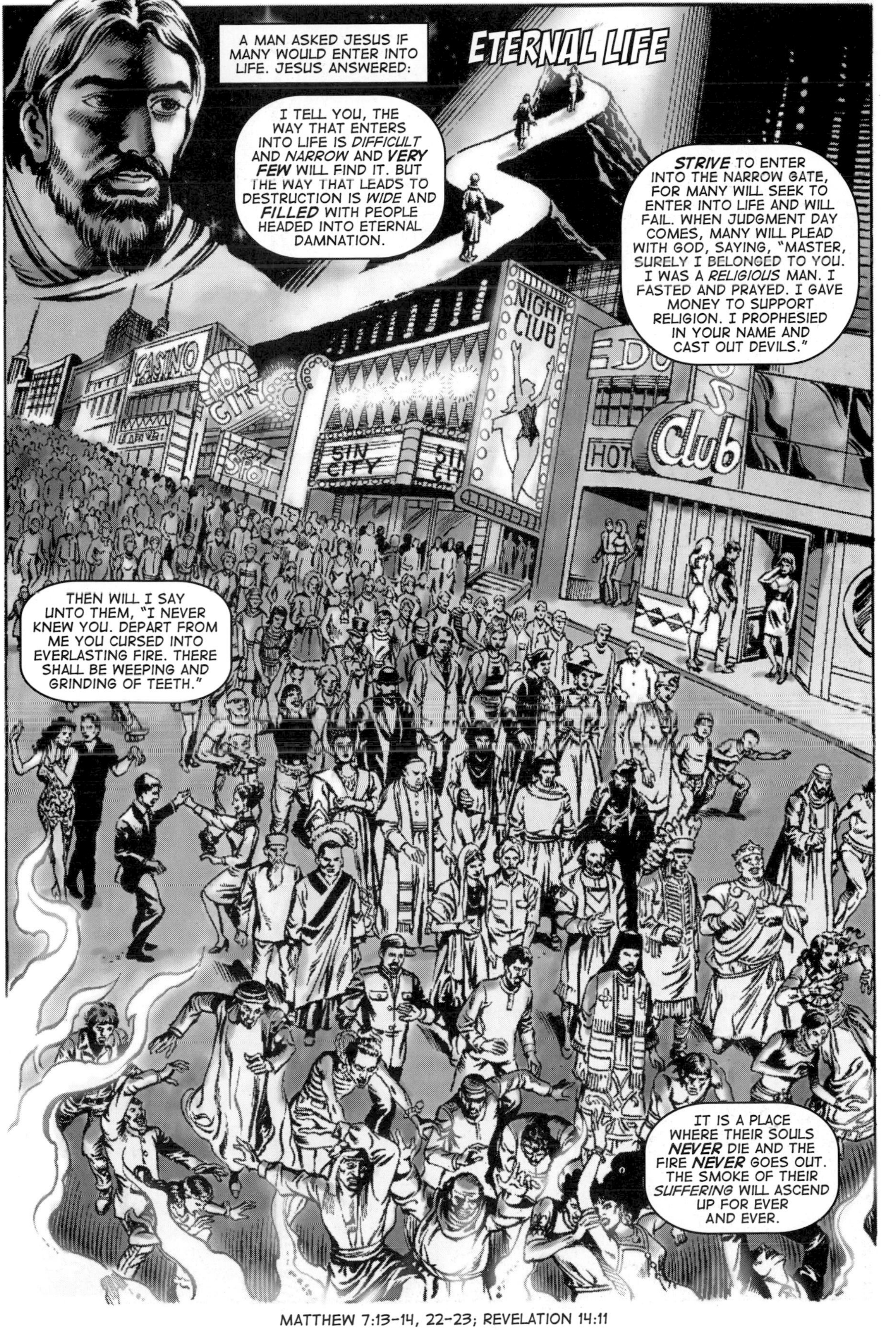
A MAN ASKED JESUS IF MANY WOULD ENTER INTO LIFE. JESUS ANSWERED:
ETERNAL LIFE
I TELL YOU, THE WAY THAT ENTERS INTO LIFE IS *DIFFICULT* AND *NARROW* AND ***VERY FEW*** WILL FIND IT. BUT THE WAY THAT LEADS TO DESTRUCTION IS *WIDE* AND ***FILLED*** WITH PEOPLE HEADED INTO ETERNAL DAMNATION.
STRIVE TO ENTER INTO THE NARROW GATE, FOR MANY WILL SEEK TO ENTER INTO LIFE AND WILL FAIL. WHEN JUDGMENT DAY COMES, MANY WILL PLEAD WITH GOD, SAYING, "MASTER, SURELY I BELONGED TO YOU. I WAS A *RELIGIOUS* MAN. I FASTED AND PRAYED. I GAVE MONEY TO SUPPORT RELIGION. I PROPHESIED IN YOUR NAME AND CAST OUT DEVILS."
CASINO
NIGHT CLUB
SIN CITY
Club
THEN WILL I SAY UNTO THEM, "I NEVER KNEW YOU. DEPART FROM ME YOU CURSED INTO EVERLASTING FIRE. THERE SHALL BE WEEPING AND GRINDING OF TEETH."
IT IS A PLACE WHERE THEIR SOULS ***NEVER*** DIE AND THE FIRE ***NEVER*** GOES OUT. THE SMOKE OF THEIR *SUFFERING* WILL ASCEND UP FOR EVER AND EVER.

MATTHEW 7:13–14, 22–23; REVELATION 14:11

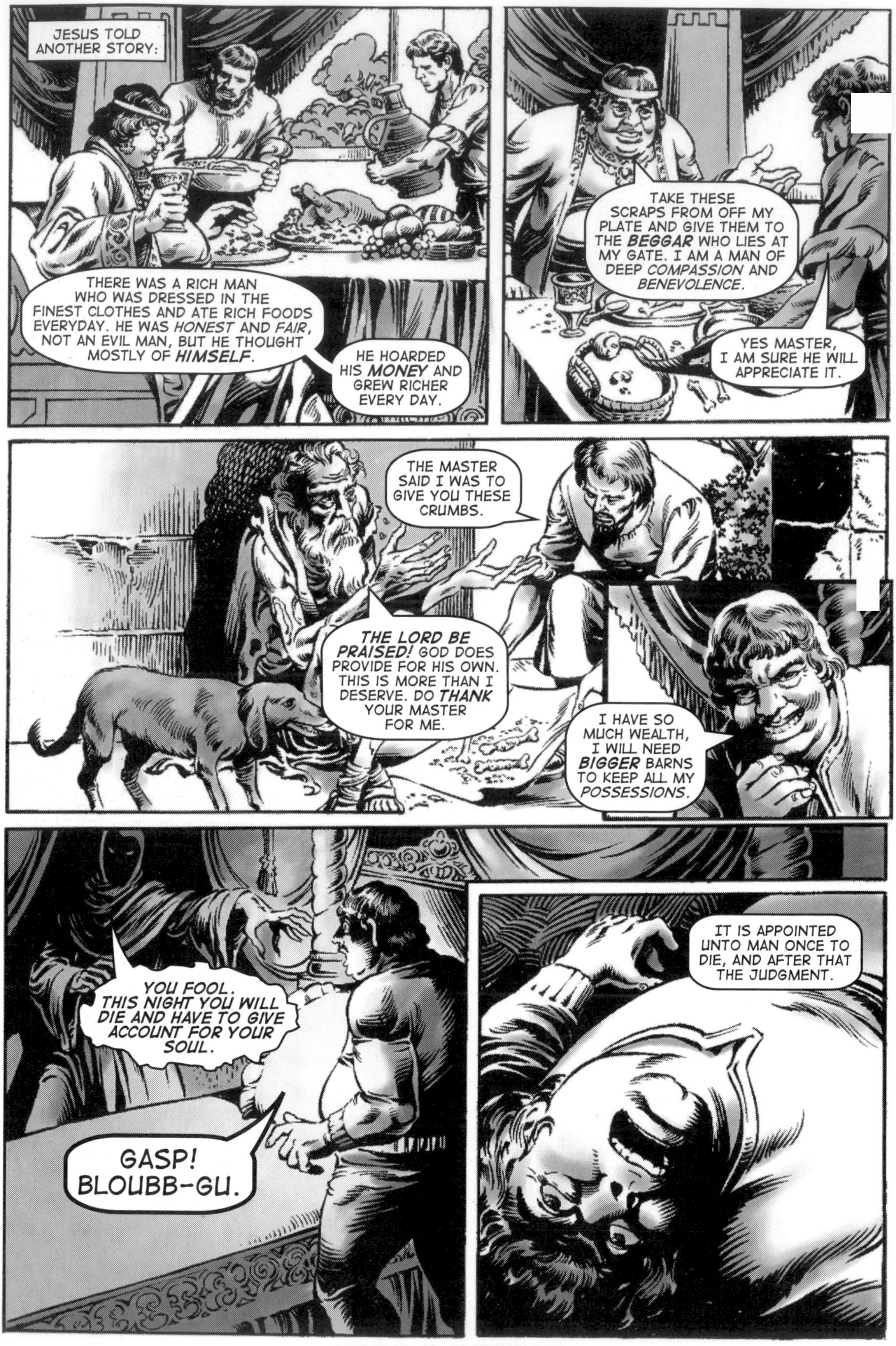
JESUS TOLD ANOTHER STORY:
THERE WAS A RICH MAN WHO WAS DRESSED IN THE FINEST CLOTHES AND ATE RICH FOODS EVERYDAY. HE WAS *HONEST* AND *FAIR*, NOT AN EVIL MAN, BUT HE THOUGHT MOSTLY OF ***HIMSELF***.
HE HOARDED HIS ***MONEY*** AND GREW RICHER EVERY DAY.
TAKE THESE SCRAPS FROM OFF MY PLATE AND GIVE THEM TO THE ***BEGGAR*** WHO LIES AT MY GATE. I AM A MAN OF DEEP *COMPASSION* AND *BENEVOLENCE*.
YES MASTER, I AM SURE HE WILL APPRECIATE IT.
THE MASTER SAID I WAS TO GIVE YOU THESE CRUMBS.
THE LORD BE PRAISED! GOD DOES PROVIDE FOR HIS OWN. THIS IS MORE THAN I DESERVE. DO ***THANK*** YOUR MASTER FOR ME.
I HAVE SO MUCH WEALTH, I WILL NEED ***BIGGER*** BARNS TO KEEP ALL MY *POSSESSIONS*.
YOU FOOL. THIS NIGHT YOU WILL DIE AND HAVE TO GIVE ACCOUNT FOR YOUR SOUL.
GASP! BLOUBB-GU.
IT IS APPOINTED UNTO MAN ONCE TO DIE, AND AFTER THAT THE JUDGMENT.

LUKE 16:19–22; HEBREWS 9:27

LUKE 16:22

EXODUS 20:14; LUKE 8:2; 1 JOHN 1:9

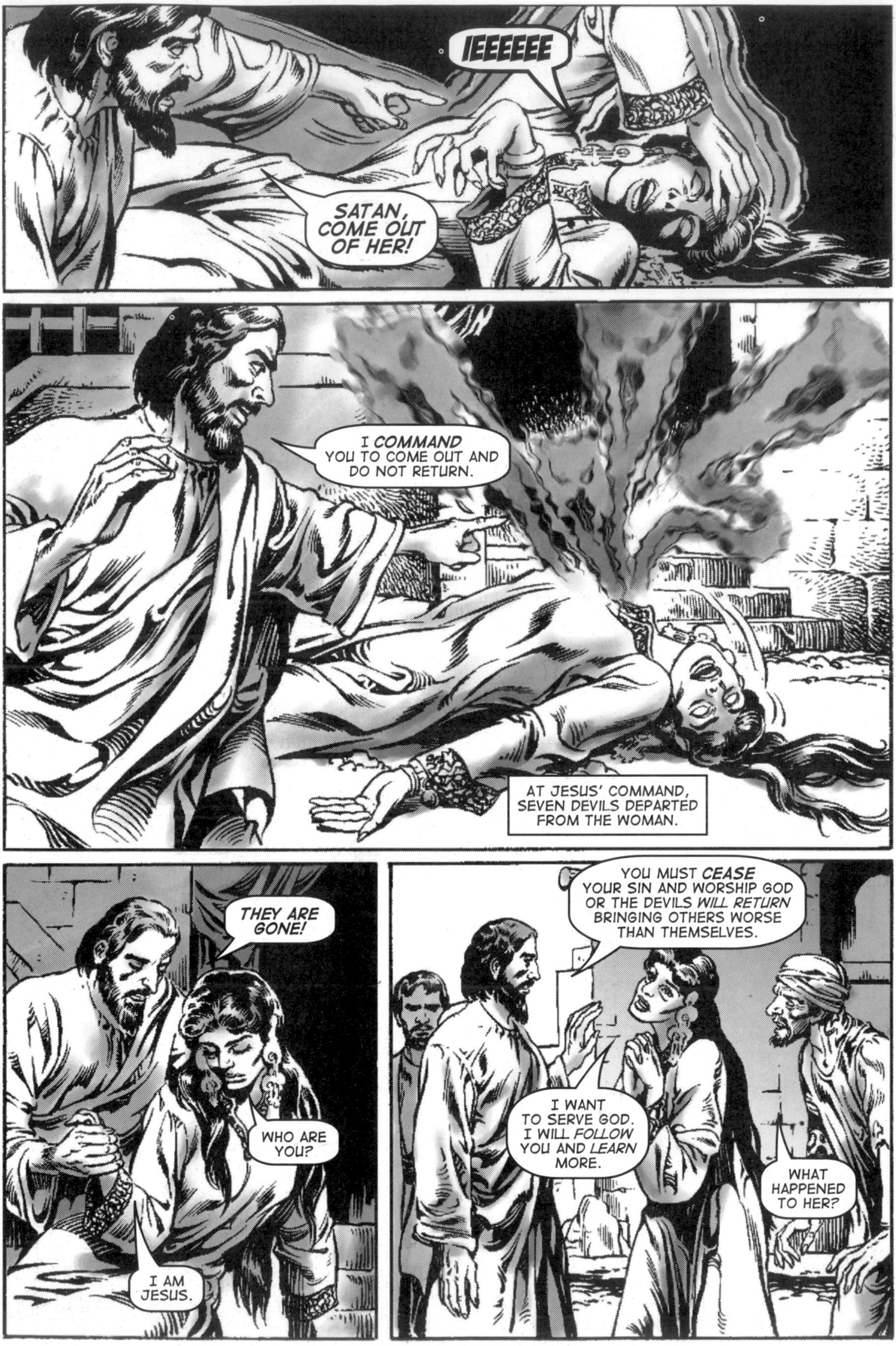
IEEEEEE
SATAN, COME OUT OF HER!
I COMMAND YOU TO COME OUT AND DO NOT RETURN.
AT JESUS' COMMAND, SEVEN DEVILS DEPARTED FROM THE WOMAN.
THEY ARE GONE!
WHO ARE YOU?
I AM JESUS.
YOU MUST CEASE YOUR SIN AND WORSHIP GOD OR THE DEVILS WILL RETURN BRINGING OTHERS WORSE THAN THEMSELVES.
I WANT TO SERVE GOD. I WILL FOLLOW YOU AND LEARN MORE.
WHAT HAPPENED TO HER?

LUKE 8:2, 11:24-26

ECCLESIASTES 12:14; MATTHEW 23:25, 6:19-21, 25, 28-30, 12:36; LUKE 15:1-3

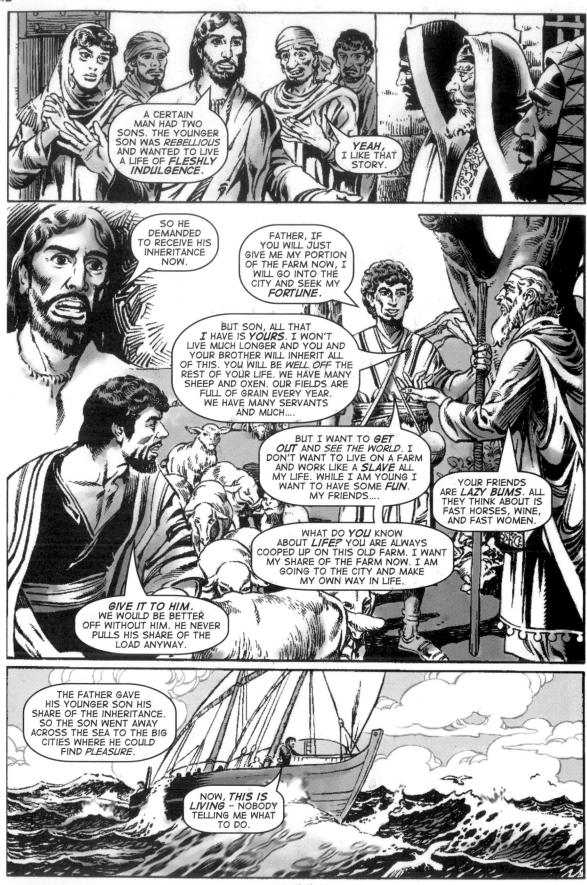

LUKE 15:11-13

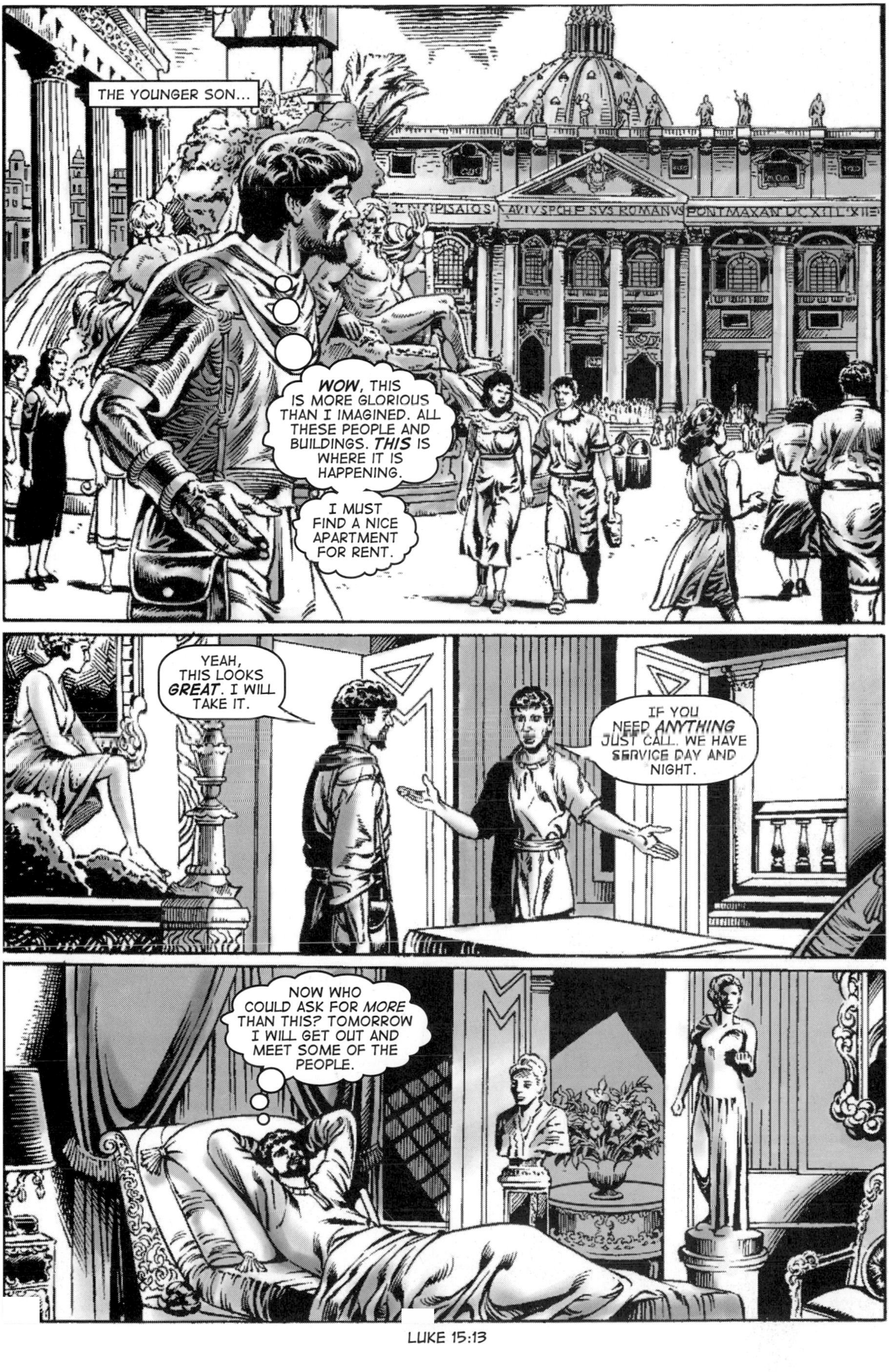
THE YOUNGER SON...
WOW, THIS IS MORE GLORIOUS THAN I IMAGINED. ALL THESE PEOPLE AND BUILDINGS. THIS IS WHERE IT IS HAPPENING.
I MUST FIND A NICE APARTMENT FOR RENT.
YEAH, THIS LOOKS GREAT. I WILL TAKE IT.
IF YOU NEED ANYTHING JUST CALL. WE HAVE SERVICE DAY AND NIGHT.
NOW WHO COULD ASK FOR MORE THAN THIS? TOMORROW I WILL GET OUT AND MEET SOME OF THE PEOPLE.

LUKE 15:13

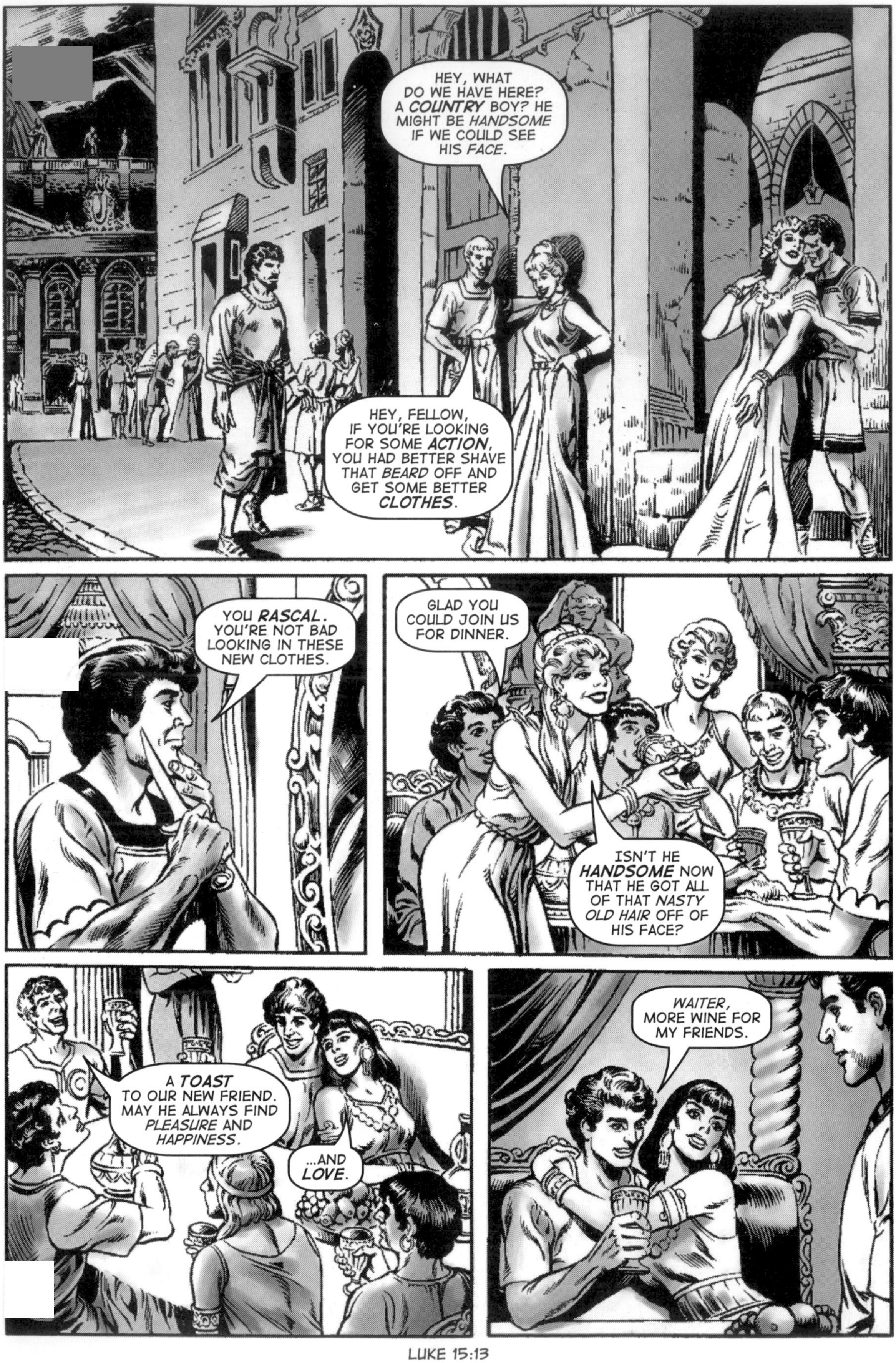
HEY, WHAT DO WE HAVE HERE? A COUNTRY BOY? HE MIGHT BE HANDSOME IF WE COULD SEE HIS FACE.
HEY, FELLOW, IF YOU'RE LOOKING FOR SOME ACTION, YOU HAD BETTER SHAVE THAT BEARD OFF AND GET SOME BETTER CLOTHES.
YOU RASCAL. YOU'RE NOT BAD LOOKING IN THESE NEW CLOTHES.
GLAD YOU COULD JOIN US FOR DINNER.
ISN'T HE HANDSOME NOW THAT HE GOT ALL OF THAT NASTY OLD HAIR OFF OF HIS FACE?
A TOAST TO OUR NEW FRIEND. MAY HE ALWAYS FIND PLEASURE AND HAPPINESS.
...AND LOVE.
WAITER, MORE WINE FOR MY FRIENDS.

LUKE 15:13

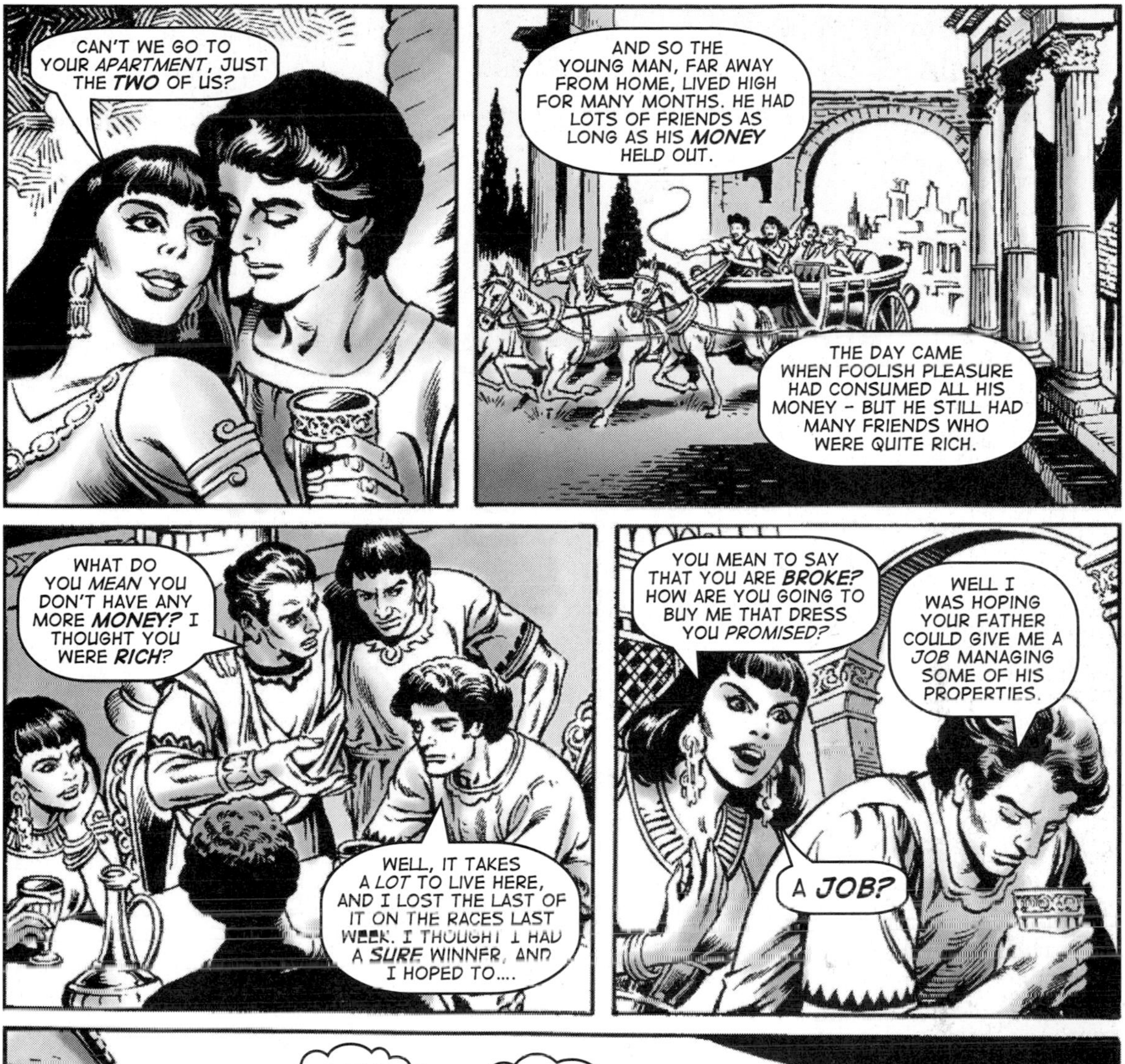
CAN'T WE GO TO YOUR APARTMENT, JUST THE TWO OF US?
AND SO THE YOUNG MAN, FAR AWAY FROM HOME, LIVED HIGH FOR MANY MONTHS. HE HAD LOTS OF FRIENDS AS LONG AS HIS MONEY HELD OUT.
THE DAY CAME WHEN FOOLISH PLEASURE HAD CONSUMED ALL HIS MONEY - BUT HE STILL HAD MANY FRIENDS WHO WERE QUITE RICH.
WHAT DO YOU MEAN YOU DON'T HAVE ANY MORE MONEY? I THOUGHT YOU WERE RICH?
WELL, IT TAKES A LOT TO LIVE HERE, AND I LOST THE LAST OF IT ON THE RACES LAST WEEK. I THOUGHT I HAD A SURE WINNER, AND I HOPED TO....
YOU MEAN TO SAY THAT YOU ARE BROKE? HOW ARE YOU GOING TO BUY ME THAT DRESS YOU PROMISED?
WELL I WAS HOPING YOUR FATHER COULD GIVE ME A JOB MANAGING SOME OF HIS PROPERTIES.
A JOB?
I CAN'T BELIEVE I'M FEEDING HOGS - THESE UNCLEAN, FILTHY ANIMALS.
I THOUGHT I HAD FRIENDS. THEY WON'T EVEN SPEAK TO ME NOW. BUT I WILL FIND A BETTER JOB AND GET BACK ON TOP.
OINK
SLUUUKK
GRUNT

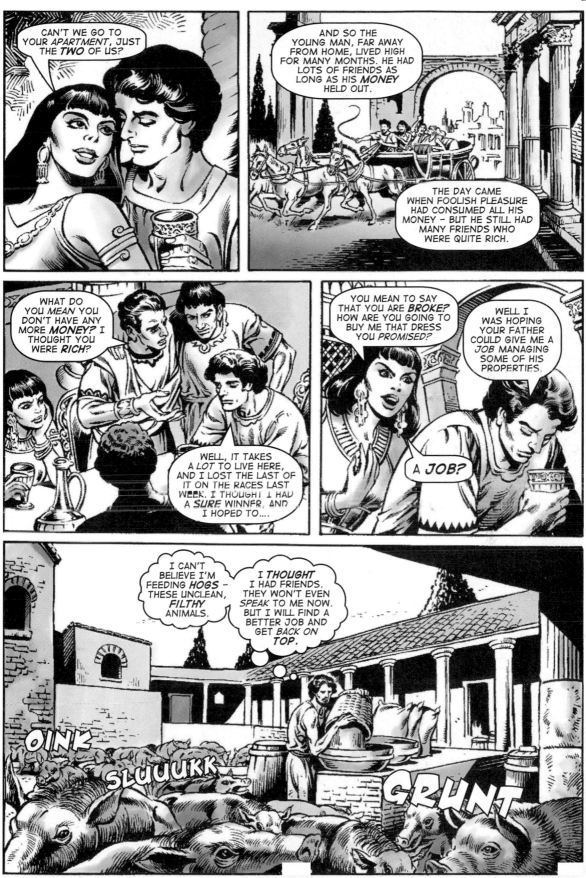

LUKE 15:13-15

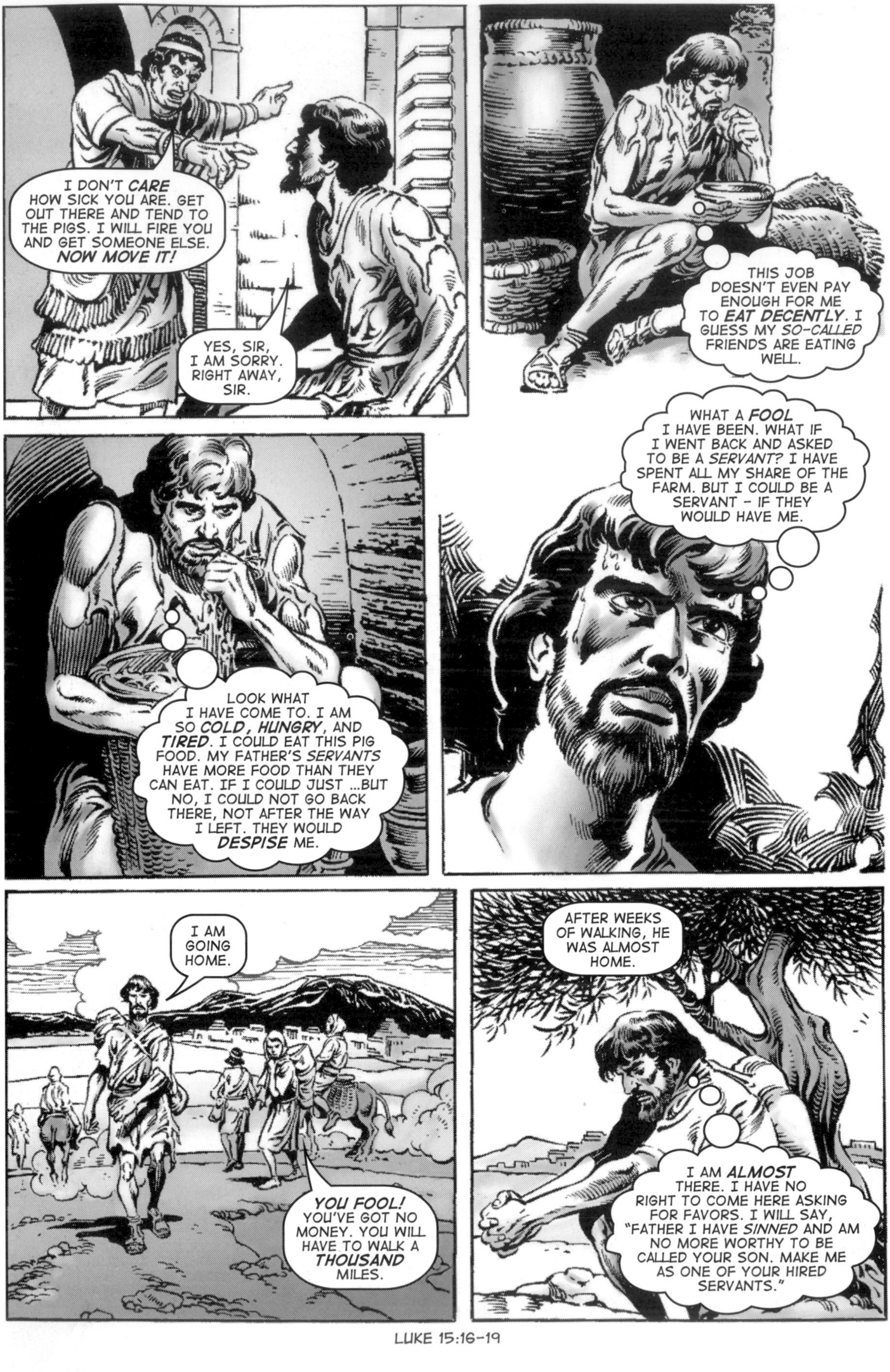
I DON'T CARE HOW SICK YOU ARE. GET OUT THERE AND TEND TO THE PIGS. I WILL FIRE YOU AND GET SOMEONE ELSE. NOW MOVE IT!
YES, SIR, I AM SORRY. RIGHT AWAY, SIR.
THIS JOB DOESN'T EVEN PAY ENOUGH FOR ME TO EAT DECENTLY. I GUESS MY SO-CALLED FRIENDS ARE EATING WELL.
LOOK WHAT I HAVE COME TO. I AM SO COLD, HUNGRY, AND TIRED. I COULD EAT THIS PIG FOOD. MY FATHER'S SERVANTS HAVE MORE FOOD THAN THEY CAN EAT. IF I COULD JUST ...BUT NO, I COULD NOT GO BACK THERE, NOT AFTER THE WAY I LEFT. THEY WOULD DESPISE ME.
WHAT A FOOL I HAVE BEEN. WHAT IF I WENT BACK AND ASKED TO BE A SERVANT? I HAVE SPENT ALL MY SHARE OF THE FARM. BUT I COULD BE A SERVANT - IF THEY WOULD HAVE ME.
I AM GOING HOME.
YOU FOOL! YOU'VE GOT NO MONEY. YOU WILL HAVE TO WALK A THOUSAND MILES.
AFTER WEEKS OF WALKING, HE WAS ALMOST HOME.
I AM ALMOST THERE. I HAVE NO RIGHT TO COME HERE ASKING FOR FAVORS. I WILL SAY, "FATHER I HAVE SINNED AND AM NO MORE WORTHY TO BE CALLED YOUR SON. MAKE ME AS ONE OF YOUR HIRED SERVANTS."

LUKE 15:16-19

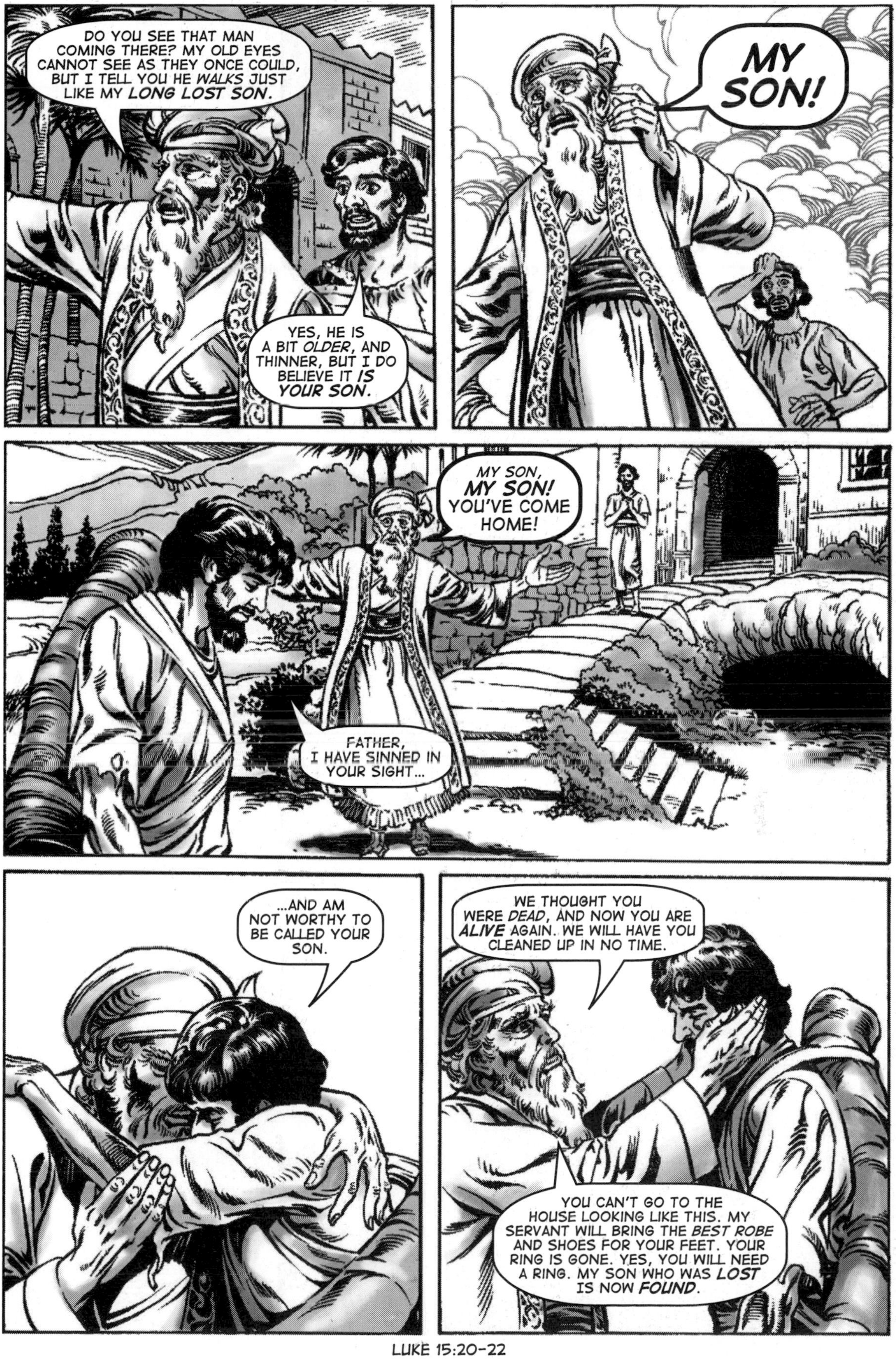
DO YOU SEE THAT MAN COMING THERE? MY OLD EYES CANNOT SEE AS THEY ONCE COULD, BUT I TELL YOU HE *WALKS* JUST LIKE MY ***LONG LOST SON***.
YES, HE IS A BIT *OLDER*, AND THINNER, BUT I DO BELIEVE IT ***IS YOUR SON***.
MY SON!
MY SON, ***MY SON!*** YOU'VE COME HOME!
FATHER, I HAVE SINNED IN YOUR SIGHT...
...AND AM NOT WORTHY TO BE CALLED YOUR SON.
WE THOUGHT YOU WERE *DEAD*, AND NOW YOU ARE ***ALIVE*** AGAIN. WE WILL HAVE YOU CLEANED UP IN NO TIME.
YOU CAN'T GO TO THE HOUSE LOOKING LIKE THIS. MY SERVANT WILL BRING THE *BEST ROBE* AND SHOES FOR YOUR FEET. YOUR RING IS GONE. YES, YOU WILL NEED A RING. MY SON WHO WAS ***LOST*** IS NOW ***FOUND***.

LUKE 15:20-22

LUKE 15:23-32

MATTHEW 20:17-20; JOHN 11:1-15

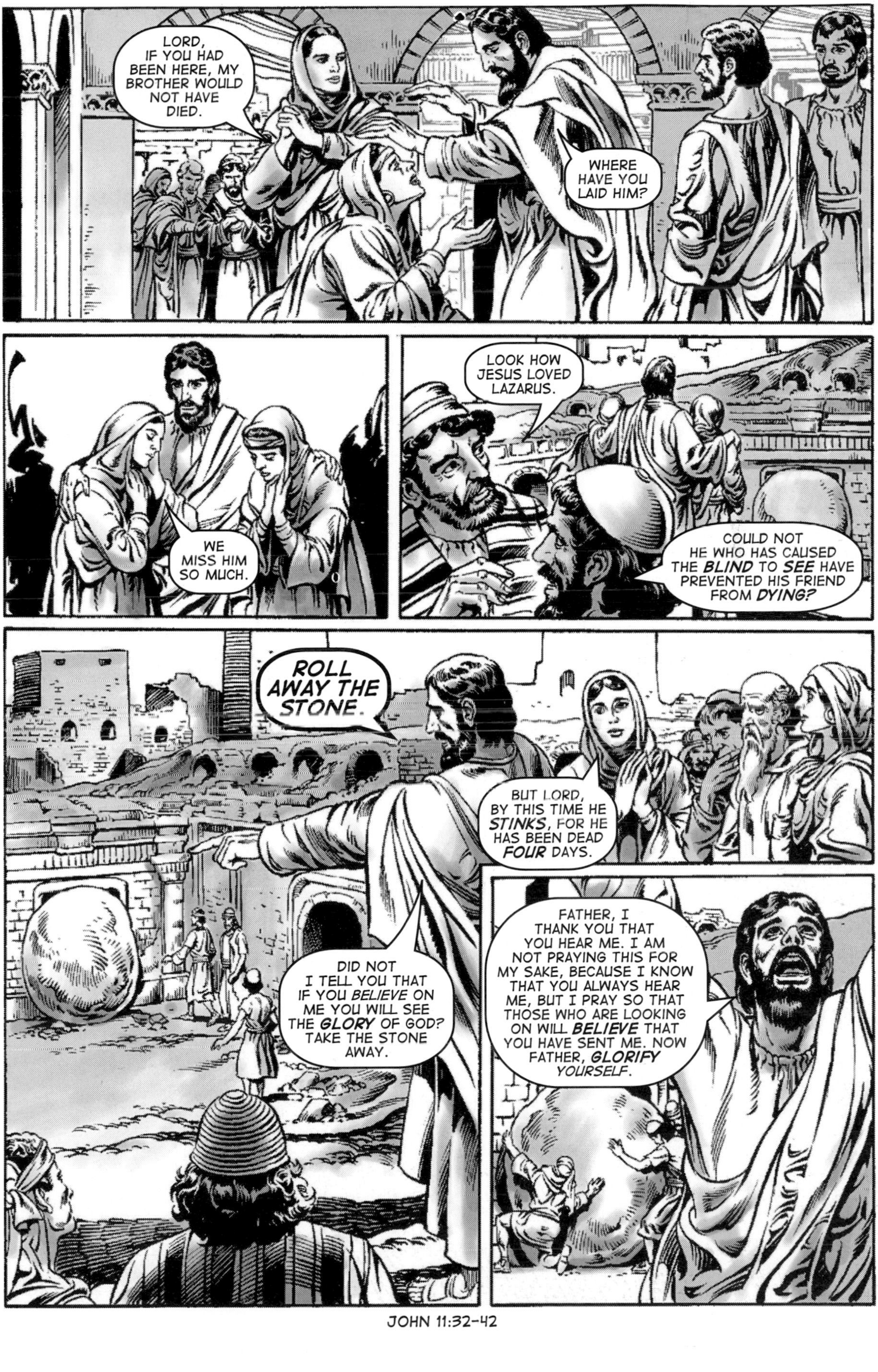
LORD, IF YOU HAD BEEN HERE, MY BROTHER WOULD NOT HAVE DIED.
WHERE HAVE YOU LAID HIM?
WE MISS HIM SO MUCH.
LOOK HOW JESUS LOVED LAZARUS.
COULD NOT HE WHO HAS CAUSED THE BLIND TO SEE HAVE PREVENTED HIS FRIEND FROM DYING?
ROLL AWAY THE STONE.
BUT LORD, BY THIS TIME HE STINKS, FOR HE HAS BEEN DEAD FOUR DAYS.
DID NOT I TELL YOU THAT IF YOU BELIEVE ON ME YOU WILL SEE THE GLORY OF GOD? TAKE THE STONE AWAY.
FATHER, I THANK YOU THAT YOU HEAR ME. I AM NOT PRAYING THIS FOR MY SAKE, BECAUSE I KNOW THAT YOU ALWAYS HEAR ME, BUT I PRAY SO THAT THOSE WHO ARE LOOKING ON WILL BELIEVE THAT YOU HAVE SENT ME. NOW FATHER, GLORIFY YOURSELF.

JOHN 11:32-42

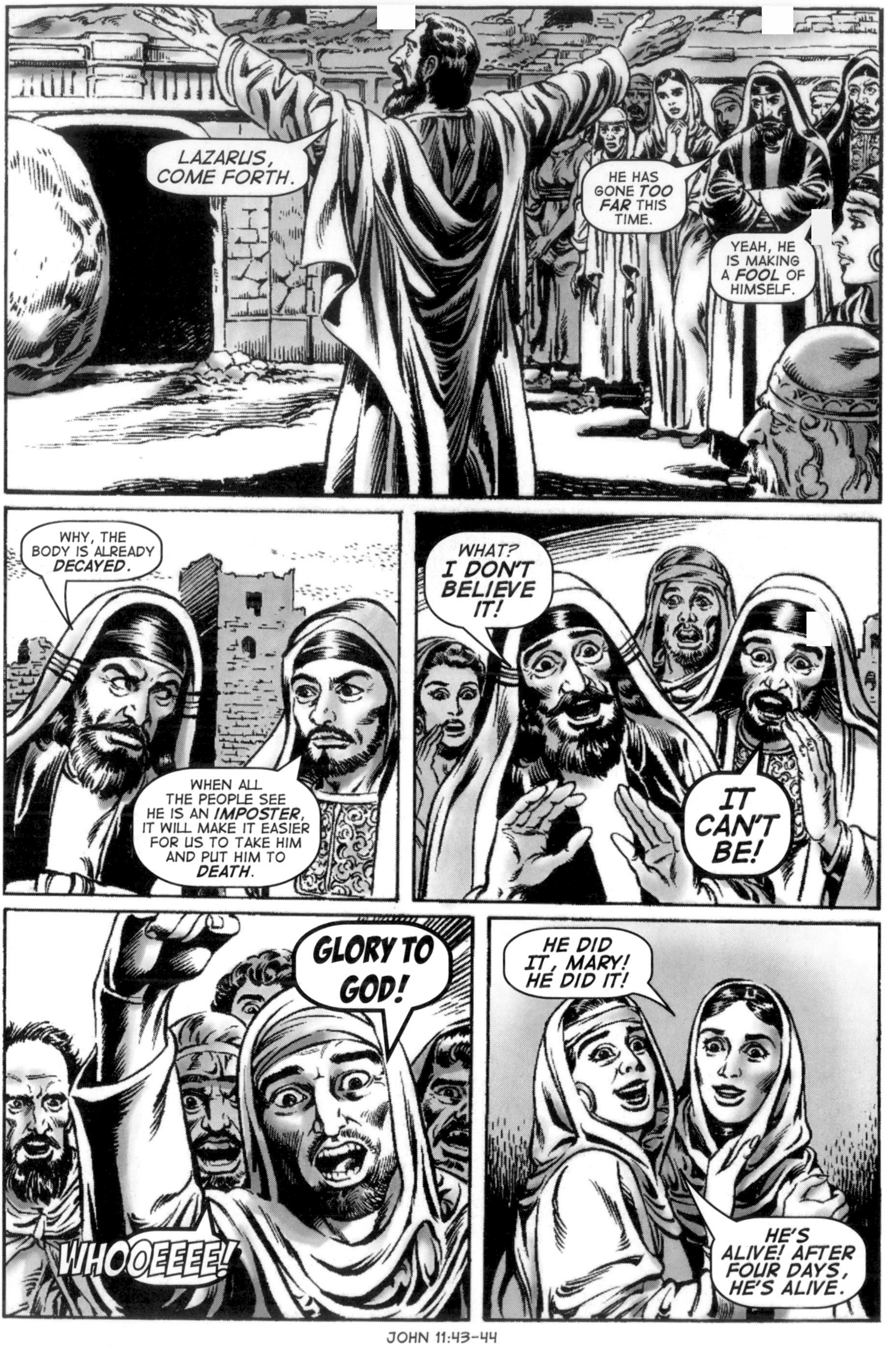
LAZARUS, COME FORTH.
HE HAS GONE TOO FAR THIS TIME.
YEAH, HE IS MAKING A FOOL OF HIMSELF.
WHY, THE BODY IS ALREADY DECAYED.
WHEN ALL THE PEOPLE SEE HE IS AN IMPOSTER, IT WILL MAKE IT EASIER FOR US TO TAKE HIM AND PUT HIM TO DEATH.
WHAT? I DON'T BELIEVE IT!
IT CAN'T BE!
GLORY TO GOD!
WHOOEEEE!
HE DID IT, MARY! HE DID IT!
HE'S ALIVE! AFTER FOUR DAYS, HE'S ALIVE.

JOHN 11:43–44

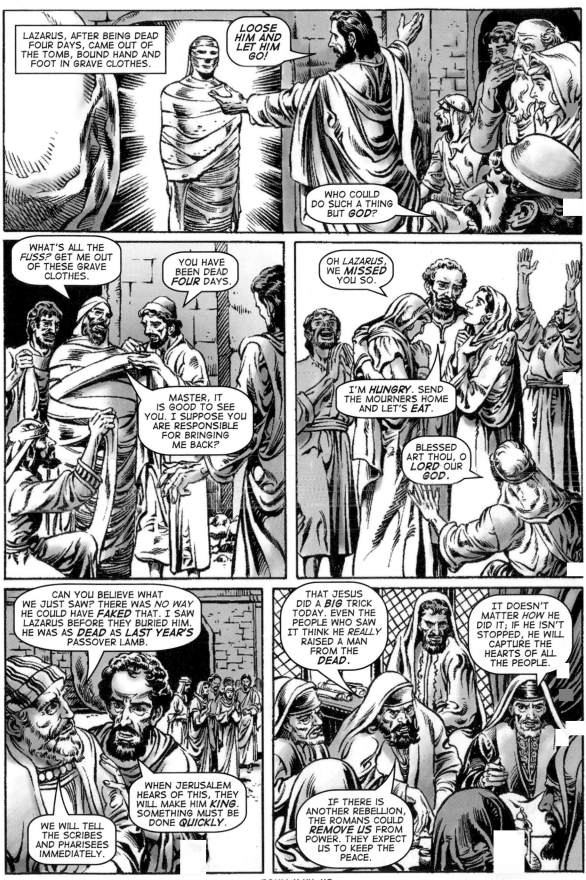

MATTHEW 10:22, 24:2, 5-9, 21, 27-31; LUKE 19:43-44, 21:8; JOHN 11:49-53; REVELATION 2:10

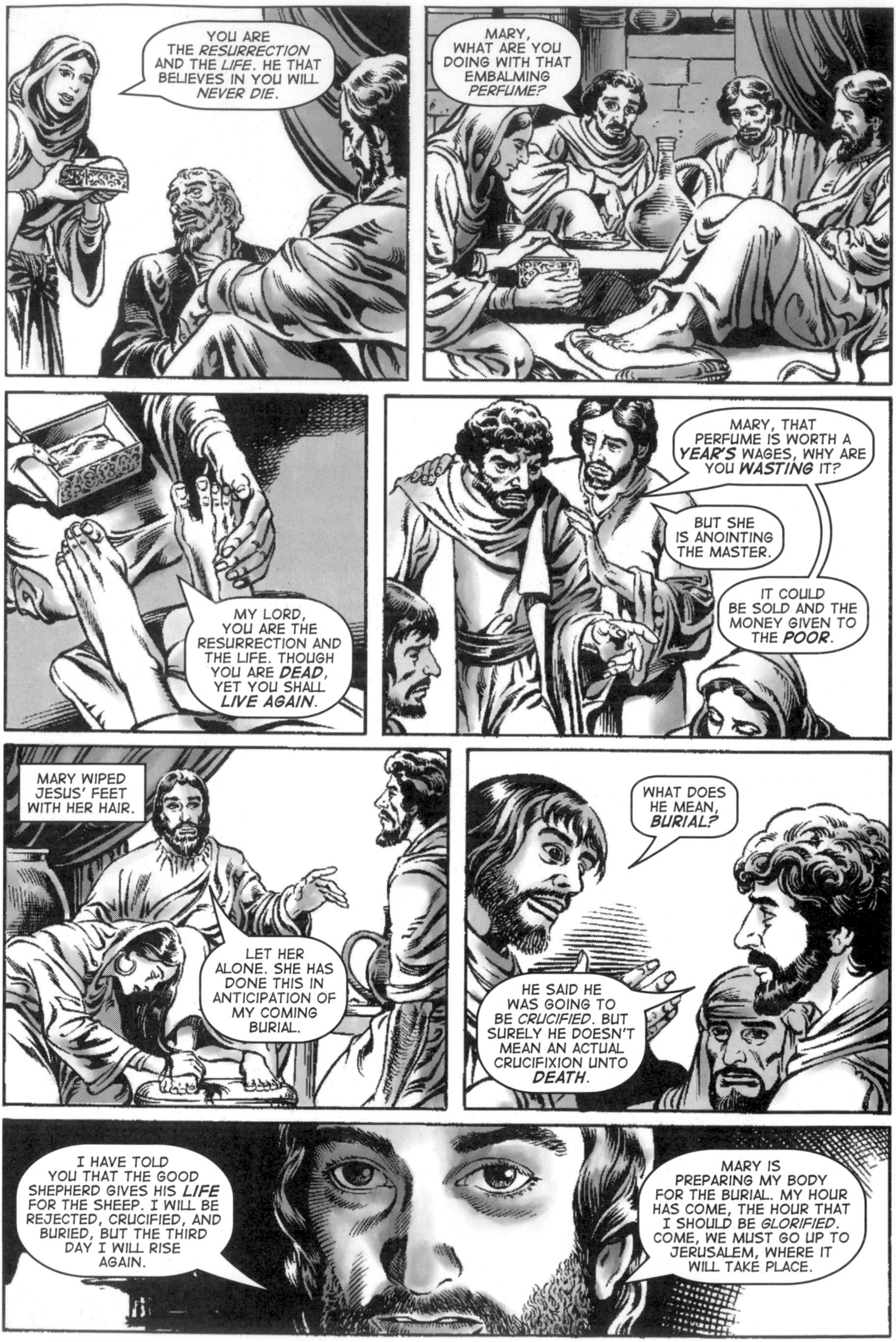
YOU ARE THE *RESURRECTION* AND THE *LIFE*. HE THAT BELIEVES IN YOU WILL *NEVER DIE*.
MARY, WHAT ARE YOU DOING WITH THAT EMBALMING *PERFUME?*
MY LORD, YOU ARE THE RESURRECTION AND THE LIFE. THOUGH YOU ARE *DEAD*, YET YOU SHALL *LIVE AGAIN*.
MARY, THAT PERFUME IS WORTH A ***YEAR'S*** WAGES, WHY ARE YOU ***WASTING*** IT?
BUT SHE IS ANOINTING THE MASTER.
IT COULD BE SOLD AND THE MONEY GIVEN TO THE ***POOR***.
MARY WIPED JESUS' FEET WITH HER HAIR.
LET HER ALONE. SHE HAS DONE THIS IN ANTICIPATION OF MY COMING BURIAL.
WHAT DOES HE MEAN, ***BURIAL?***
HE SAID HE WAS GOING TO BE *CRUCIFIED*. BUT SURELY HE DOESN'T MEAN AN ACTUAL CRUCIFIXION UNTO ***DEATH***.
I HAVE TOLD YOU THAT THE GOOD SHEPHERD GIVES HIS *LIFE* FOR THE SHEEP. I WILL BE REJECTED, CRUCIFIED, AND BURIED, BUT THE THIRD DAY I WILL RISE AGAIN.
MARY IS PREPARING MY BODY FOR THE BURIAL. MY HOUR HAS COME, THE HOUR THAT I SHOULD BE *GLORIFIED*. COME, WE MUST GO UP TO JERUSALEM, WHERE IT WILL TAKE PLACE.

MATTHEW 20:19; JOHN 12:3–8, 10:11

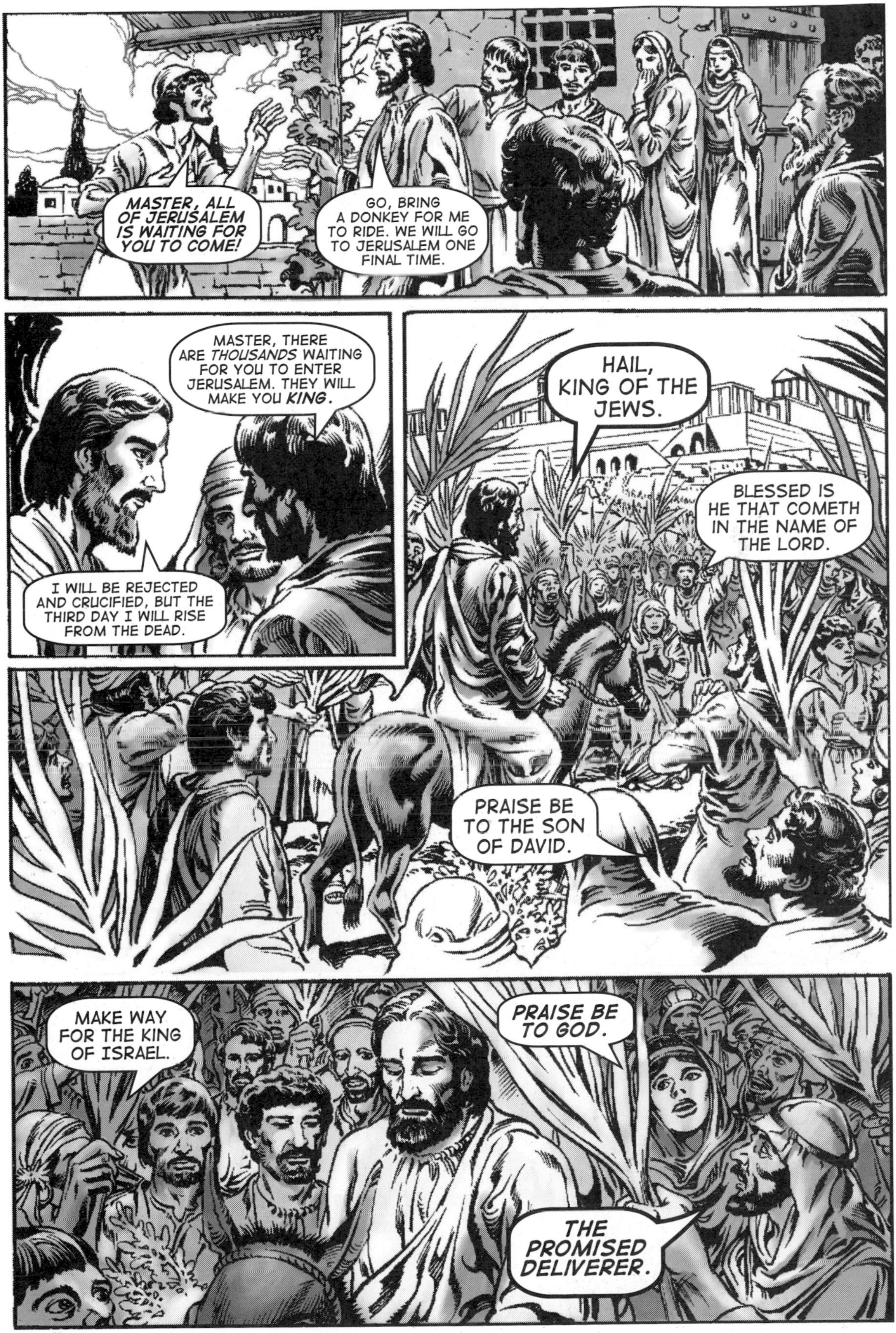
MASTER, ALL OF JERUSALEM IS WAITING FOR YOU TO COME!
GO, BRING A DONKEY FOR ME TO RIDE. WE WILL GO TO JERUSALEM ONE FINAL TIME.
MASTER, THERE ARE THOUSANDS WAITING FOR YOU TO ENTER JERUSALEM. THEY WILL MAKE YOU KING.
I WILL BE REJECTED AND CRUCIFIED, BUT THE THIRD DAY I WILL RISE FROM THE DEAD.
HAIL, KING OF THE JEWS.
BLESSED IS HE THAT COMETH IN THE NAME OF THE LORD.
PRAISE BE TO THE SON OF DAVID.
MAKE WAY FOR THE KING OF ISRAEL.
PRAISE BE TO GOD.
THE PROMISED DELIVERER.

JOHN 12:12–13

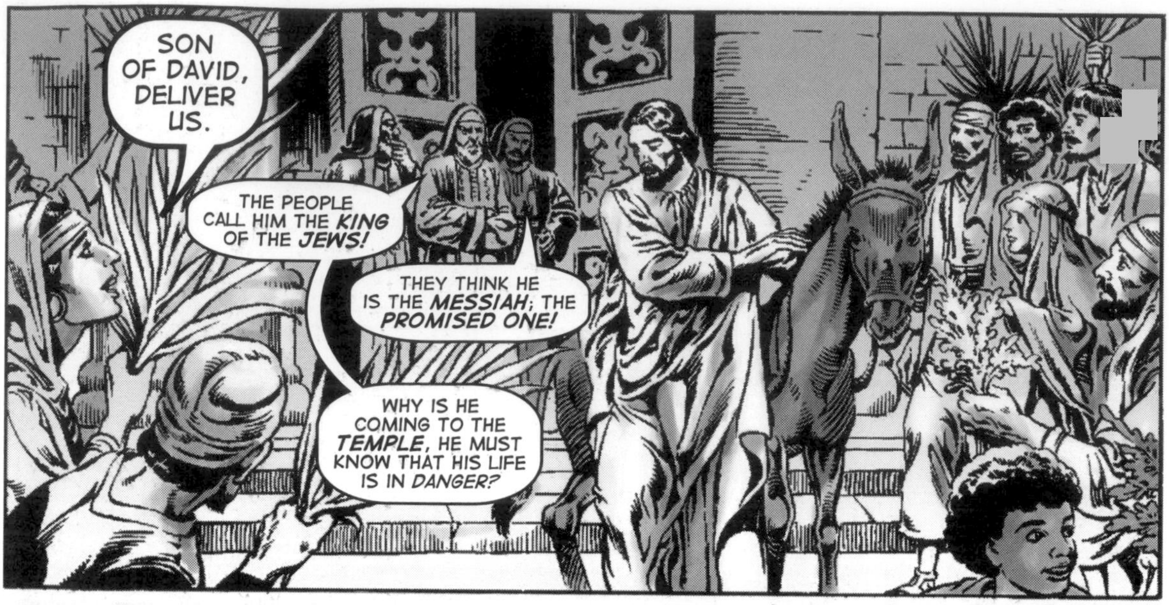
SON OF DAVID, DELIVER US.
THE PEOPLE CALL HIM THE KING OF THE JEWS!
THEY THINK HE IS THE MESSIAH; THE PROMISED ONE!
WHY IS HE COMING TO THE TEMPLE, HE MUST KNOW THAT HIS LIFE IS IN DANGER?

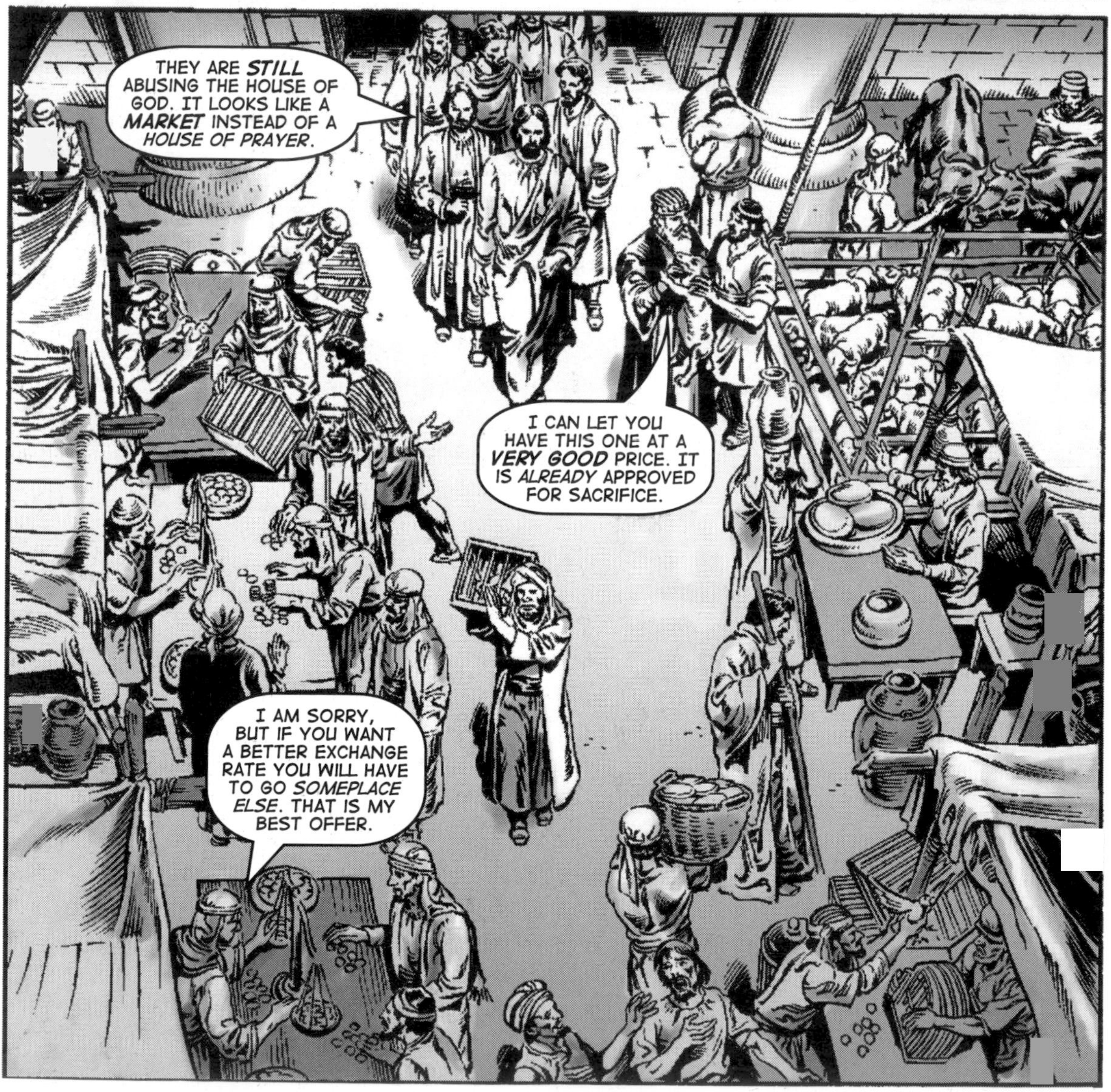
THEY ARE STILL ABUSING THE HOUSE OF GOD. IT LOOKS LIKE A MARKET INSTEAD OF A HOUSE OF PRAYER.
I CAN LET YOU HAVE THIS ONE AT A VERY GOOD PRICE. IT IS ALREADY APPROVED FOR SACRIFICE.
I AM SORRY, BUT IF YOU WANT A BETTER EXCHANGE RATE YOU WILL HAVE TO GO SOMEPLACE ELSE. THAT IS MY BEST OFFER.

MATTHEW 21:11–12

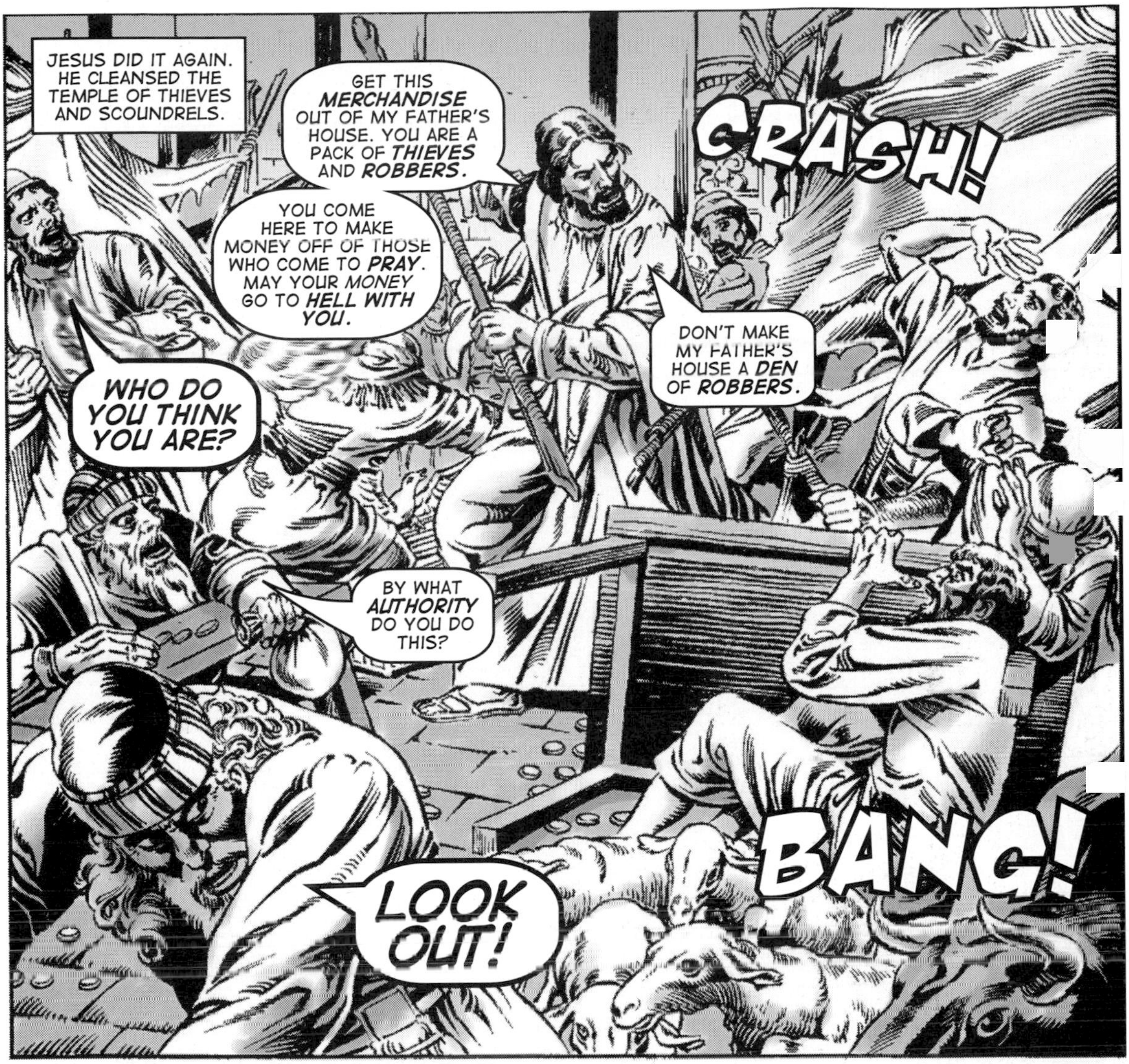
JESUS DID IT AGAIN. HE CLEANSED THE TEMPLE OF THIEVES AND SCOUNDRELS.
GET THIS MERCHANDISE OUT OF MY FATHER'S HOUSE. YOU ARE A PACK OF THIEVES AND ROBBERS.
CRASH!
YOU COME HERE TO MAKE MONEY OFF OF THOSE WHO COME TO PRAY. MAY YOUR MONEY GO TO HELL WITH YOU.
DON'T MAKE MY FATHER'S HOUSE A DEN OF ROBBERS.
WHO DO YOU THINK YOU ARE?
BY WHAT AUTHORITY DO YOU DO THIS?
BANG!
LOOK OUT!

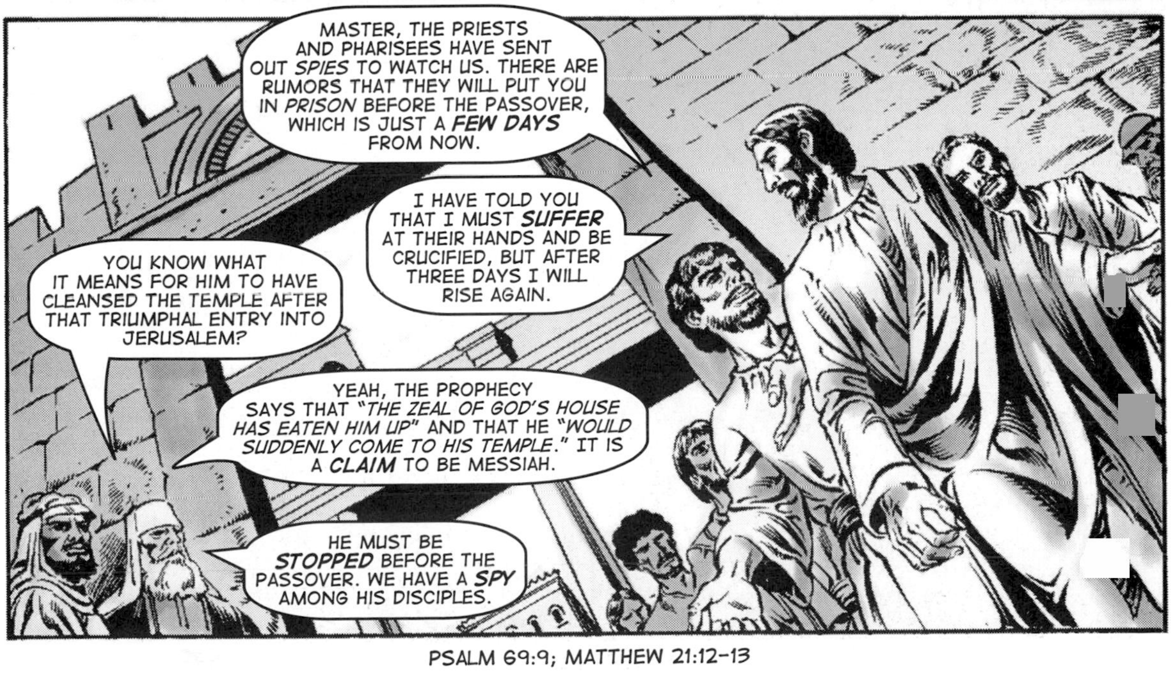
MASTER, THE PRIESTS AND PHARISEES HAVE SENT OUT SPIES TO WATCH US. THERE ARE RUMORS THAT THEY WILL PUT YOU IN PRISON BEFORE THE PASSOVER, WHICH IS JUST A FEW DAYS FROM NOW.
I HAVE TOLD YOU THAT I MUST SUFFER AT THEIR HANDS AND BE CRUCIFIED, BUT AFTER THREE DAYS I WILL RISE AGAIN.
YOU KNOW WHAT IT MEANS FOR HIM TO HAVE CLEANSED THE TEMPLE AFTER THAT TRIUMPHAL ENTRY INTO JERUSALEM?
YEAH, THE PROPHECY SAYS THAT "THE ZEAL OF GOD'S HOUSE HAS EATEN HIM UP" AND THAT HE "WOULD SUDDENLY COME TO HIS TEMPLE." IT IS A CLAIM TO BE MESSIAH.
HE MUST BE STOPPED BEFORE THE PASSOVER. WE HAVE A SPY AMONG HIS DISCIPLES.

PSALM 69:9; MATTHEW 21:12-13

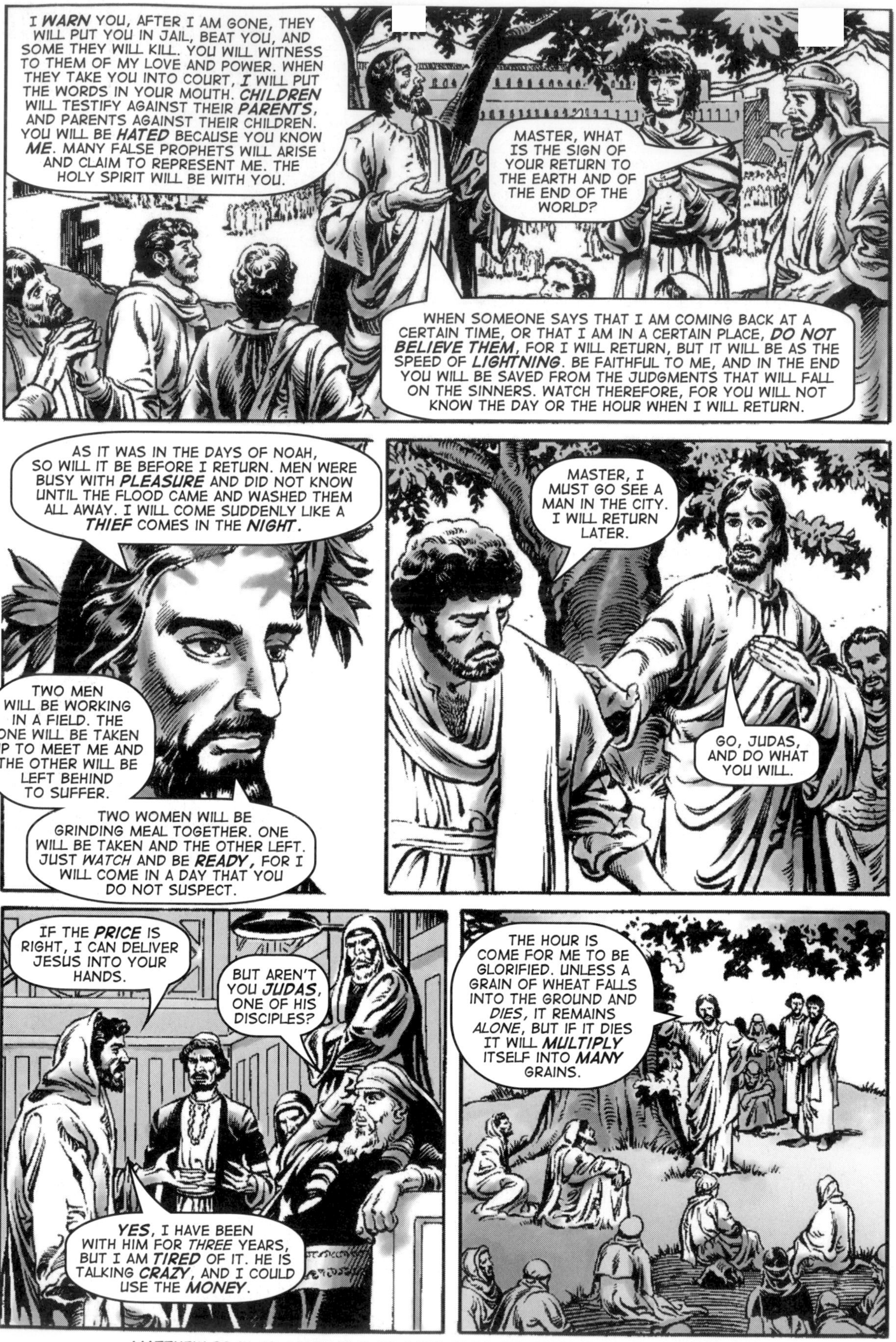
I WARN YOU, AFTER I AM GONE, THEY WILL PUT YOU IN JAIL, BEAT YOU, AND SOME THEY WILL KILL. YOU WILL WITNESS TO THEM OF MY LOVE AND POWER. WHEN THEY TAKE YOU INTO COURT, I WILL PUT THE WORDS IN YOUR MOUTH. CHILDREN WILL TESTIFY AGAINST THEIR PARENTS, AND PARENTS AGAINST THEIR CHILDREN. YOU WILL BE HATED BECAUSE YOU KNOW ME. MANY FALSE PROPHETS WILL ARISE AND CLAIM TO REPRESENT ME. THE HOLY SPIRIT WILL BE WITH YOU.
MASTER, WHAT IS THE SIGN OF YOUR RETURN TO THE EARTH AND OF THE END OF THE WORLD?
WHEN SOMEONE SAYS THAT I AM COMING BACK AT A CERTAIN TIME, OR THAT I AM IN A CERTAIN PLACE, DO NOT BELIEVE THEM, FOR I WILL RETURN, BUT IT WILL BE AS THE SPEED OF LIGHTNING. BE FAITHFUL TO ME, AND IN THE END YOU WILL BE SAVED FROM THE JUDGMENTS THAT WILL FALL ON THE SINNERS. WATCH THEREFORE, FOR YOU WILL NOT KNOW THE DAY OR THE HOUR WHEN I WILL RETURN.
AS IT WAS IN THE DAYS OF NOAH, SO WILL IT BE BEFORE I RETURN. MEN WERE BUSY WITH PLEASURE AND DID NOT KNOW UNTIL THE FLOOD CAME AND WASHED THEM ALL AWAY. I WILL COME SUDDENLY LIKE A THIEF COMES IN THE NIGHT.
TWO MEN WILL BE WORKING IN A FIELD. THE ONE WILL BE TAKEN UP TO MEET ME AND THE OTHER WILL BE LEFT BEHIND TO SUFFER.
TWO WOMEN WILL BE GRINDING MEAL TOGETHER. ONE WILL BE TAKEN AND THE OTHER LEFT. JUST WATCH AND BE READY, FOR I WILL COME IN A DAY THAT YOU DO NOT SUSPECT.
MASTER, I MUST GO SEE A MAN IN THE CITY. I WILL RETURN LATER.
GO, JUDAS, AND DO WHAT YOU WILL.
IF THE PRICE IS RIGHT, I CAN DELIVER JESUS INTO YOUR HANDS.
BUT AREN'T YOU JUDAS, ONE OF HIS DISCIPLES?
YES, I HAVE BEEN WITH HIM FOR THREE YEARS, BUT I AM TIRED OF IT. HE IS TALKING CRAZY, AND I COULD USE THE MONEY.
THE HOUR IS COME FOR ME TO BE GLORIFIED. UNLESS A GRAIN OF WHEAT FALLS INTO THE GROUND AND DIES, IT REMAINS ALONE, BUT IF IT DIES IT WILL MULTIPLY ITSELF INTO MANY GRAINS.

MATTHEW 26:14-16; MARK 13:5-13; LUKE 17:26-37; JOHN 12:23-24; 2 PETER 3:10

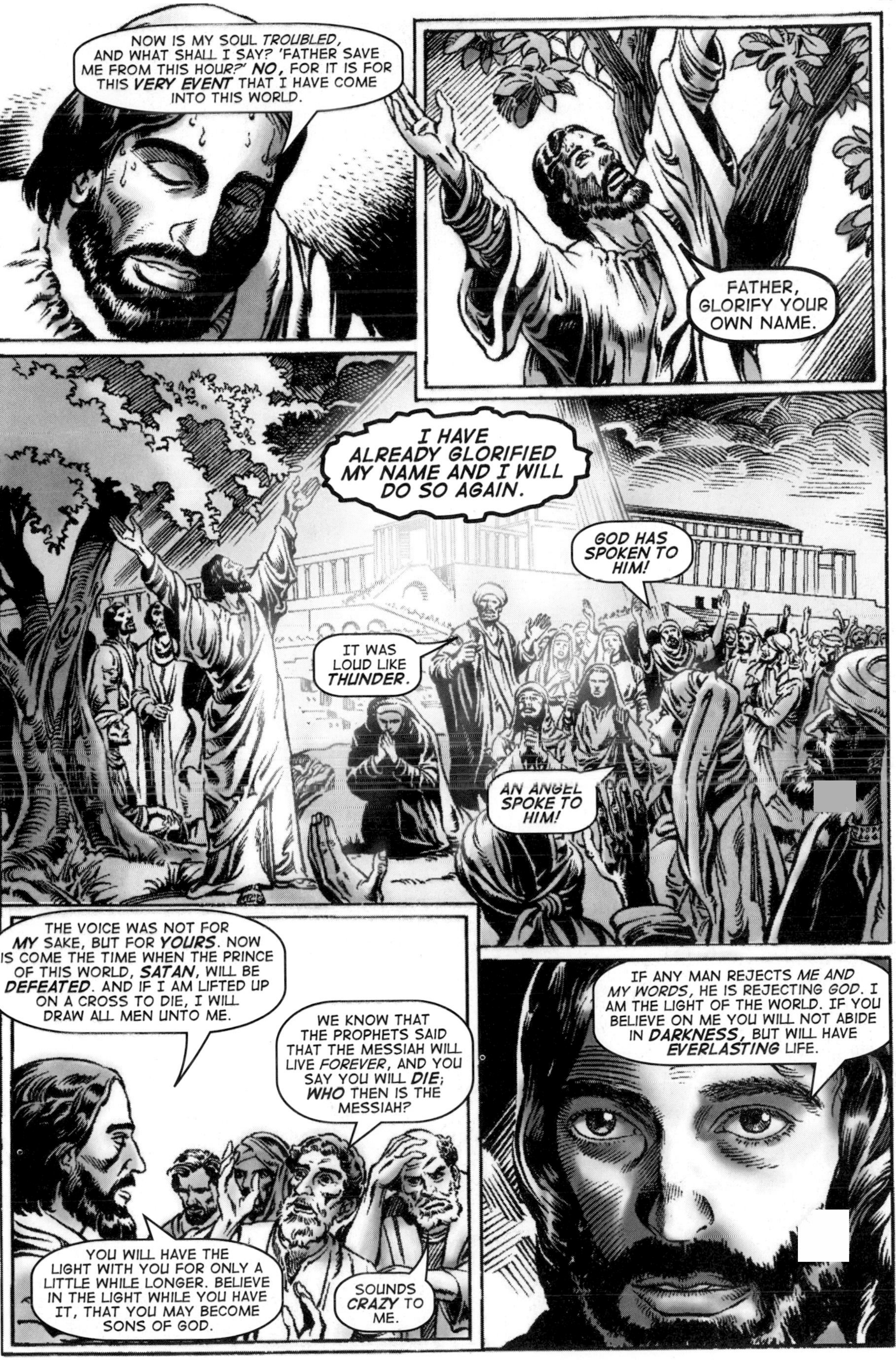
NOW IS MY SOUL TROUBLED, AND WHAT SHALL I SAY? 'FATHER SAVE ME FROM THIS HOUR?' NO, FOR IT IS FOR THIS VERY EVENT THAT I HAVE COME INTO THIS WORLD.
FATHER, GLORIFY YOUR OWN NAME.
I HAVE ALREADY GLORIFIED MY NAME AND I WILL DO SO AGAIN.
GOD HAS SPOKEN TO HIM!
IT WAS LOUD LIKE THUNDER.
AN ANGEL SPOKE TO HIM!
THE VOICE WAS NOT FOR MY SAKE, BUT FOR YOURS. NOW IS COME THE TIME WHEN THE PRINCE OF THIS WORLD, SATAN, WILL BE DEFEATED. AND IF I AM LIFTED UP ON A CROSS TO DIE, I WILL DRAW ALL MEN UNTO ME.
WE KNOW THAT THE PROPHETS SAID THAT THE MESSIAH WILL LIVE FOREVER, AND YOU SAY YOU WILL DIE; WHO THEN IS THE MESSIAH?
YOU WILL HAVE THE LIGHT WITH YOU FOR ONLY A LITTLE WHILE LONGER. BELIEVE IN THE LIGHT WHILE YOU HAVE IT, THAT YOU MAY BECOME SONS OF GOD.
SOUNDS CRAZY TO ME.
IF ANY MAN REJECTS ME AND MY WORDS, HE IS REJECTING GOD. I AM THE LIGHT OF THE WORLD. IF YOU BELIEVE ON ME YOU WILL NOT ABIDE IN DARKNESS, BUT WILL HAVE EVERLASTING LIFE.

JOHN 12:27-36

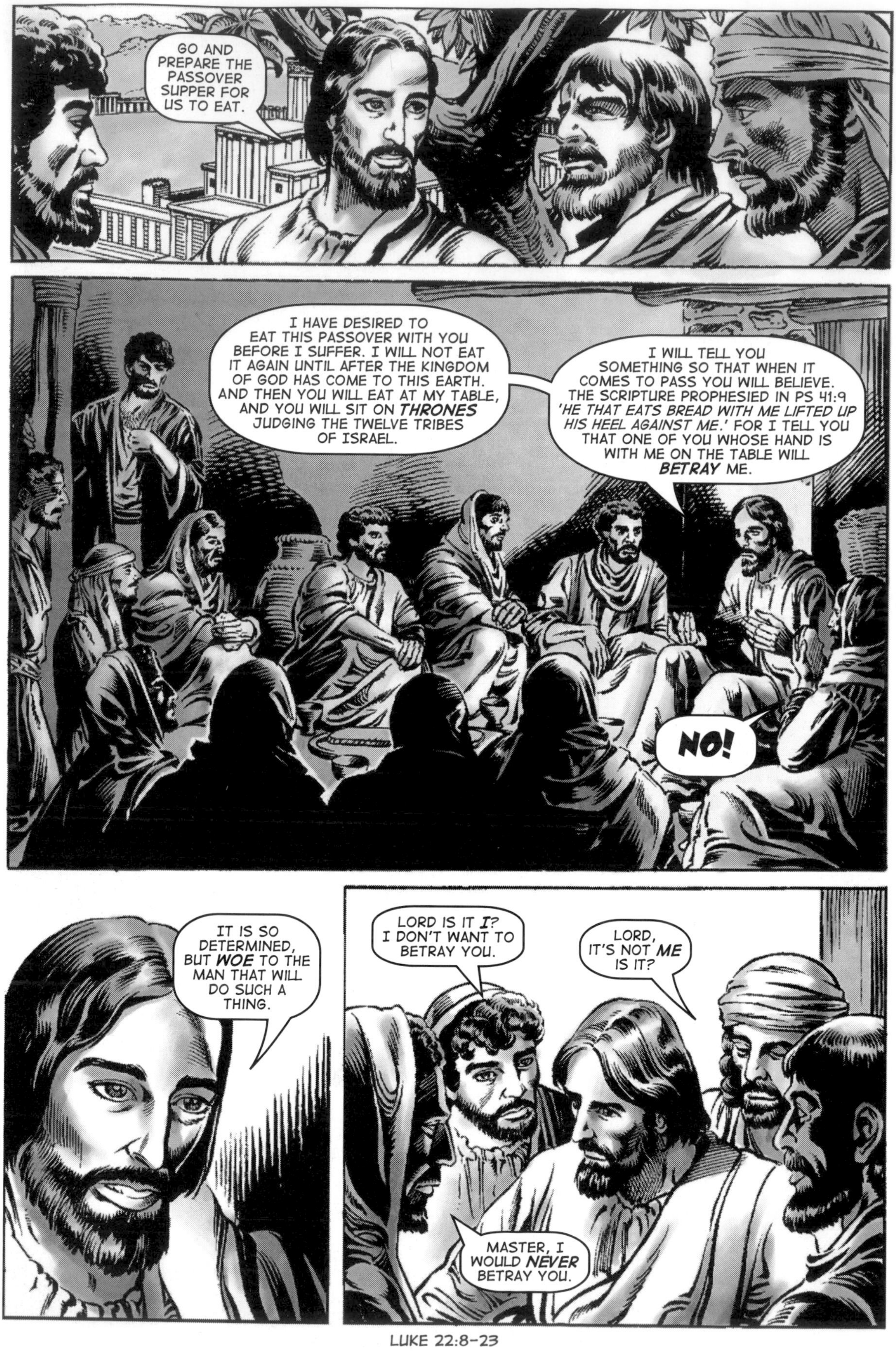
GO AND PREPARE THE PASSOVER SUPPER FOR US TO EAT.
I HAVE DESIRED TO EAT THIS PASSOVER WITH YOU BEFORE I SUFFER. I WILL NOT EAT IT AGAIN UNTIL AFTER THE KINGDOM OF GOD HAS COME TO THIS EARTH. AND THEN YOU WILL EAT AT MY TABLE, AND YOU WILL SIT ON **THRONES** JUDGING THE TWELVE TRIBES OF ISRAEL.
I WILL TELL YOU SOMETHING SO THAT WHEN IT COMES TO PASS YOU WILL BELIEVE. THE SCRIPTURE PROPHESIED IN PS 41:9 *'HE THAT EATS BREAD WITH ME LIFTED UP HIS HEEL AGAINST ME.'* FOR I TELL YOU THAT ONE OF YOU WHOSE HAND IS WITH ME ON THE TABLE WILL **BETRAY** ME.
NO!
IT IS SO DETERMINED, BUT **WOE** TO THE MAN THAT WILL DO SUCH A THING.
LORD IS IT ***I***? I DON'T WANT TO BETRAY YOU.
LORD, IT'S NOT ***ME*** IS IT?
MASTER, I WOULD ***NEVER*** BETRAY YOU.

LUKE 22:8-23

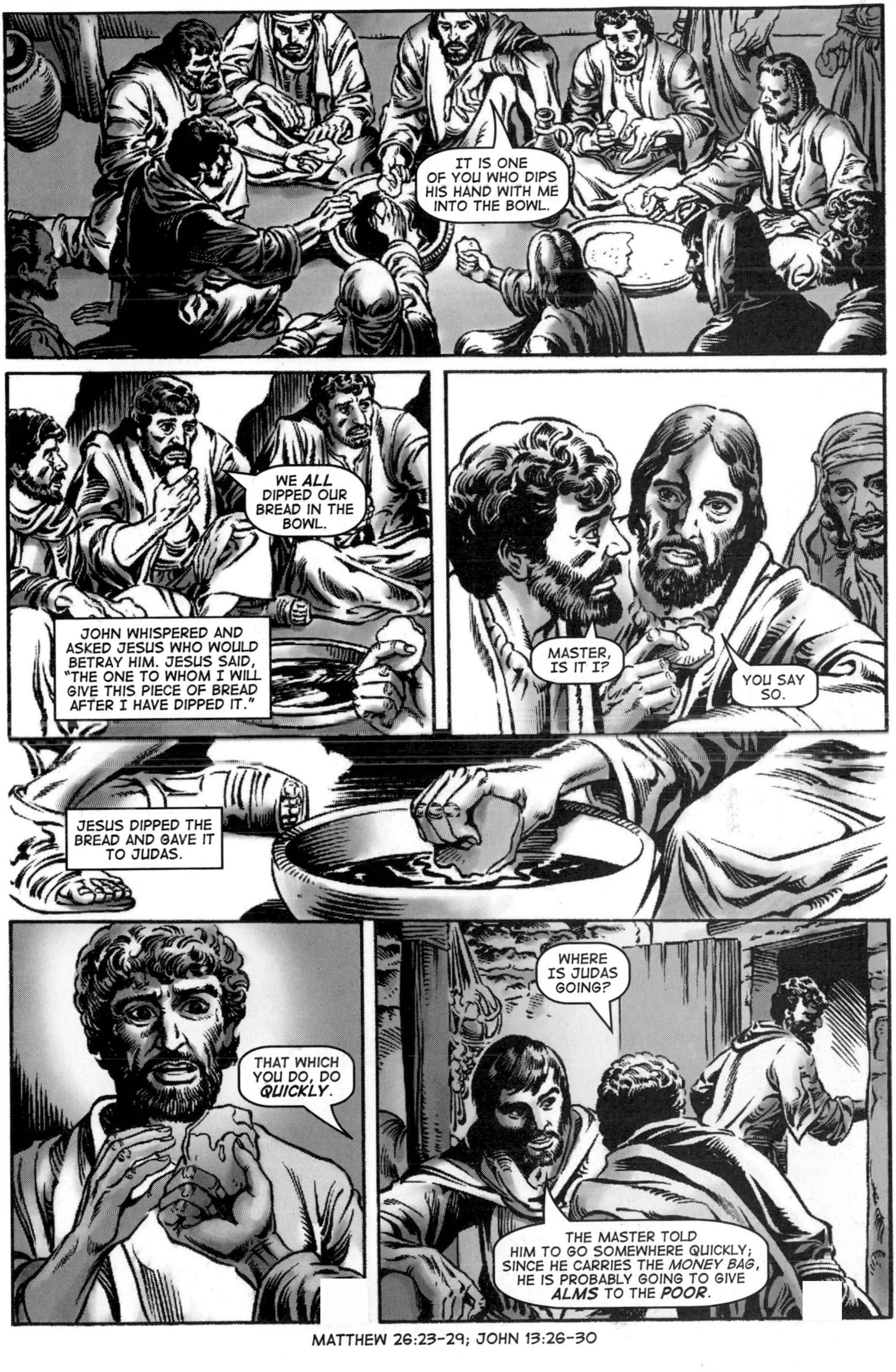
IT IS ONE OF YOU WHO DIPS HIS HAND WITH ME INTO THE BOWL.
WE ALL DIPPED OUR BREAD IN THE BOWL.
JOHN WHISPERED AND ASKED JESUS WHO WOULD BETRAY HIM. JESUS SAID, "THE ONE TO WHOM I WILL GIVE THIS PIECE OF BREAD AFTER I HAVE DIPPED IT."
MASTER, IS IT I?
YOU SAY SO.
JESUS DIPPED THE BREAD AND GAVE IT TO JUDAS.
THAT WHICH YOU DO, DO QUICKLY.
WHERE IS JUDAS GOING?
THE MASTER TOLD HIM TO GO SOMEWHERE QUICKLY; SINCE HE CARRIES THE MONEY BAG, HE IS PROBABLY GOING TO GIVE ALMS TO THE POOR.

MATTHEW 26:23-29; JOHN 13:26-30

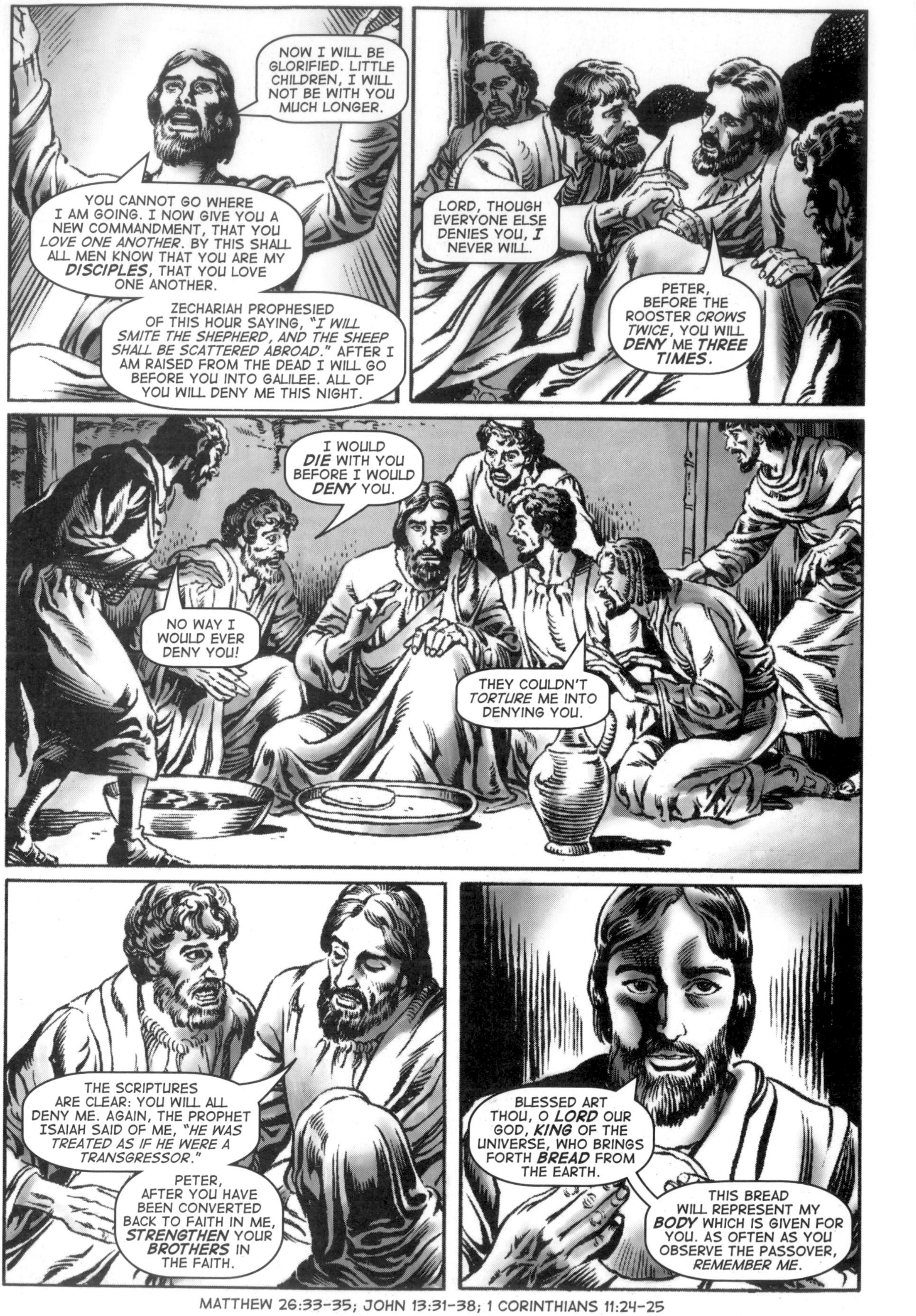
NOW I WILL BE GLORIFIED. LITTLE CHILDREN, I WILL NOT BE WITH YOU MUCH LONGER.
YOU CANNOT GO WHERE I AM GOING. I NOW GIVE YOU A NEW COMMANDMENT, THAT YOU *LOVE ONE ANOTHER*. BY THIS SHALL ALL MEN KNOW THAT YOU ARE MY ***DISCIPLES***, THAT YOU LOVE ONE ANOTHER.
ZECHARIAH PROPHESIED OF THIS HOUR SAYING, *"I WILL SMITE THE SHEPHERD, AND THE SHEEP SHALL BE SCATTERED ABROAD."* AFTER I AM RAISED FROM THE DEAD I WILL GO BEFORE YOU INTO GALILEE. ALL OF YOU WILL DENY ME THIS NIGHT.
LORD, THOUGH EVERYONE ELSE DENIES YOU, ***I*** NEVER WILL.
PETER, BEFORE THE ROOSTER *CROWS TWICE*, YOU WILL ***DENY*** ME ***THREE TIMES***.
I WOULD ***DIE*** WITH YOU BEFORE I WOULD ***DENY*** YOU.
NO WAY I WOULD EVER DENY YOU!
THEY COULDN'T *TORTURE* ME INTO DENYING YOU.
THE SCRIPTURES ARE CLEAR: YOU WILL ALL DENY ME. AGAIN, THE PROPHET ISAIAH SAID OF ME, *"HE WAS TREATED AS IF HE WERE A TRANSGRESSOR."*
PETER, AFTER YOU HAVE BEEN CONVERTED BACK TO FAITH IN ME, ***STRENGTHEN*** YOUR ***BROTHERS*** IN THE FAITH.
BLESSED ART THOU, O ***LORD*** OUR GOD, ***KING*** OF THE UNIVERSE, WHO BRINGS FORTH ***BREAD*** FROM THE EARTH.
THIS BREAD WILL REPRESENT MY ***BODY*** WHICH IS GIVEN FOR YOU. AS OFTEN AS YOU OBSERVE THE PASSOVER, *REMEMBER ME*.

MATTHEW 26:33-35; JOHN 13:31-38; 1 CORINTHIANS 11:24-25

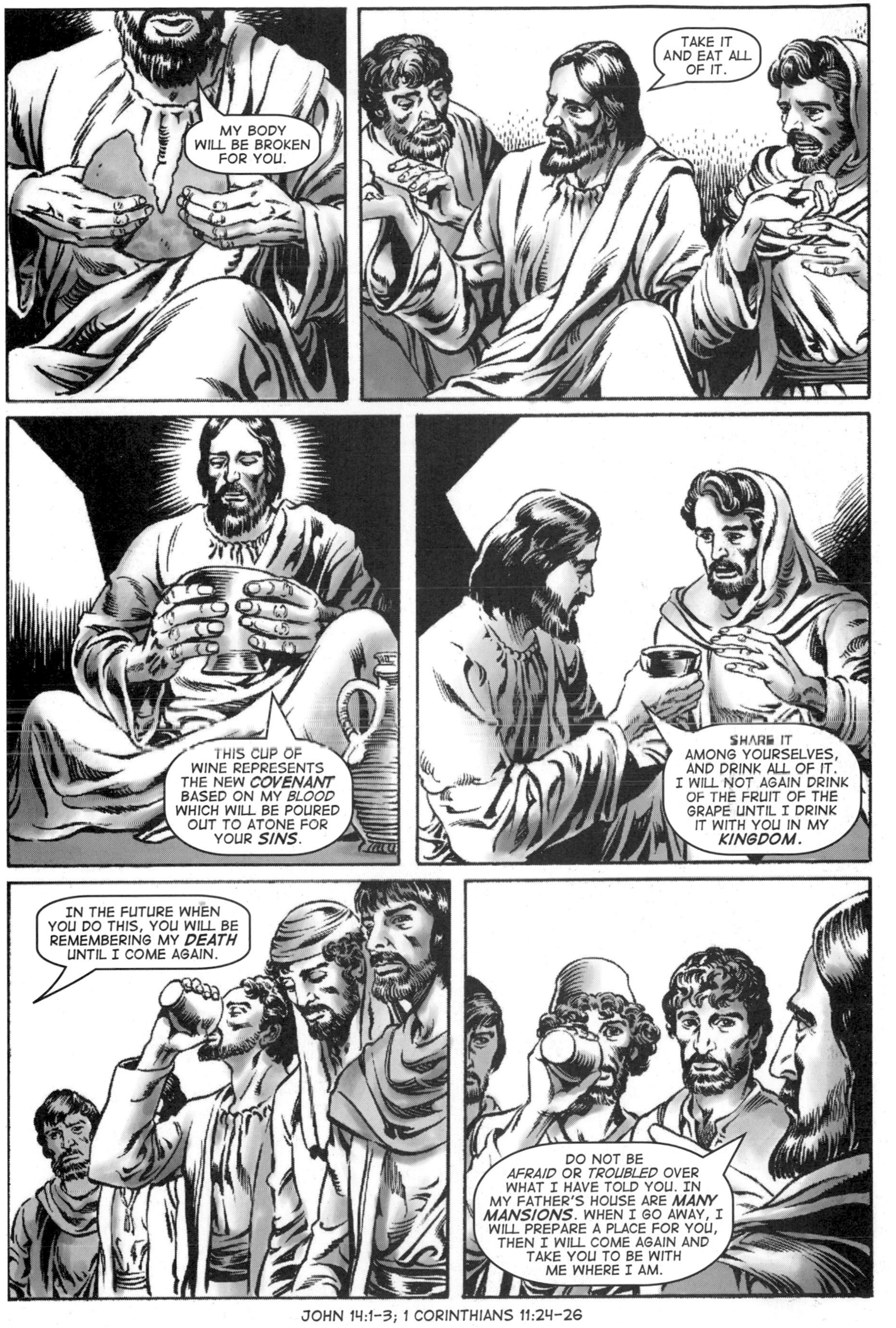
MY BODY WILL BE BROKEN FOR YOU.
TAKE IT AND EAT ALL OF IT.
THIS CUP OF WINE REPRESENTS THE NEW COVENANT BASED ON MY BLOOD WHICH WILL BE POURED OUT TO ATONE FOR YOUR SINS.
SHARE IT AMONG YOURSELVES, AND DRINK ALL OF IT. I WILL NOT AGAIN DRINK OF THE FRUIT OF THE GRAPE UNTIL I DRINK IT WITH YOU IN MY KINGDOM.
IN THE FUTURE WHEN YOU DO THIS, YOU WILL BE REMEMBERING MY DEATH UNTIL I COME AGAIN.
DO NOT BE AFRAID OR TROUBLED OVER WHAT I HAVE TOLD YOU. IN MY FATHER'S HOUSE ARE MANY MANSIONS. WHEN I GO AWAY, I WILL PREPARE A PLACE FOR YOU, THEN I WILL COME AGAIN AND TAKE YOU TO BE WITH ME WHERE I AM.

JOHN 14:1-3; 1 CORINTHIANS 11:24-26

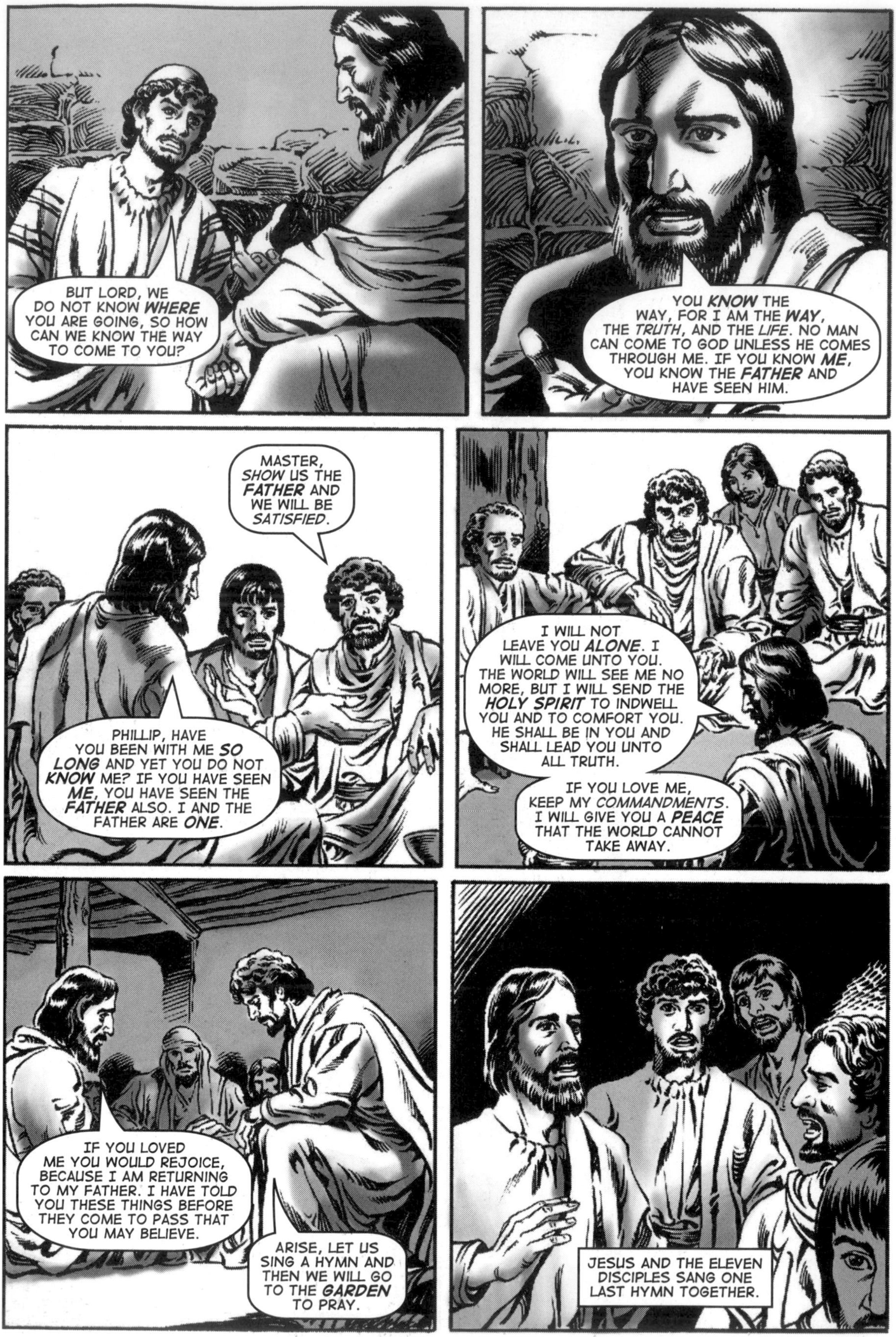
BUT LORD, WE DO NOT KNOW *WHERE* YOU ARE GOING, SO HOW CAN WE KNOW THE WAY TO COME TO YOU?
YOU *KNOW* THE WAY, FOR I AM THE *WAY*, THE *TRUTH*, AND THE *LIFE*. NO MAN CAN COME TO GOD UNLESS HE COMES THROUGH ME. IF YOU KNOW *ME*, YOU KNOW THE *FATHER* AND HAVE SEEN HIM.
MASTER, *SHOW* US THE *FATHER* AND WE WILL BE *SATISFIED*.
PHILLIP, HAVE YOU BEEN WITH ME *SO LONG* AND YET YOU DO NOT *KNOW* ME? IF YOU HAVE SEEN *ME*, YOU HAVE SEEN THE *FATHER* ALSO. I AND THE FATHER ARE *ONE*.
I WILL NOT LEAVE YOU *ALONE*. I WILL COME UNTO YOU. THE WORLD WILL SEE ME NO MORE, BUT I WILL SEND THE *HOLY SPIRIT* TO INDWELL YOU AND TO COMFORT YOU. HE SHALL BE IN YOU AND SHALL LEAD YOU UNTO ALL TRUTH.
IF YOU LOVE ME, KEEP MY *COMMANDMENTS*. I WILL GIVE YOU A *PEACE* THAT THE WORLD CANNOT TAKE AWAY.
IF YOU LOVED ME YOU WOULD REJOICE, BECAUSE I AM RETURNING TO MY FATHER. I HAVE TOLD YOU THESE THINGS BEFORE THEY COME TO PASS THAT YOU MAY BELIEVE.
ARISE, LET US SING A HYMN AND THEN WE WILL GO TO THE *GARDEN* TO PRAY.
JESUS AND THE ELEVEN DISCIPLES SANG ONE LAST HYMN TOGETHER.

MATTHEW 26:30; JOHN 14:5-10, 15, 25-30

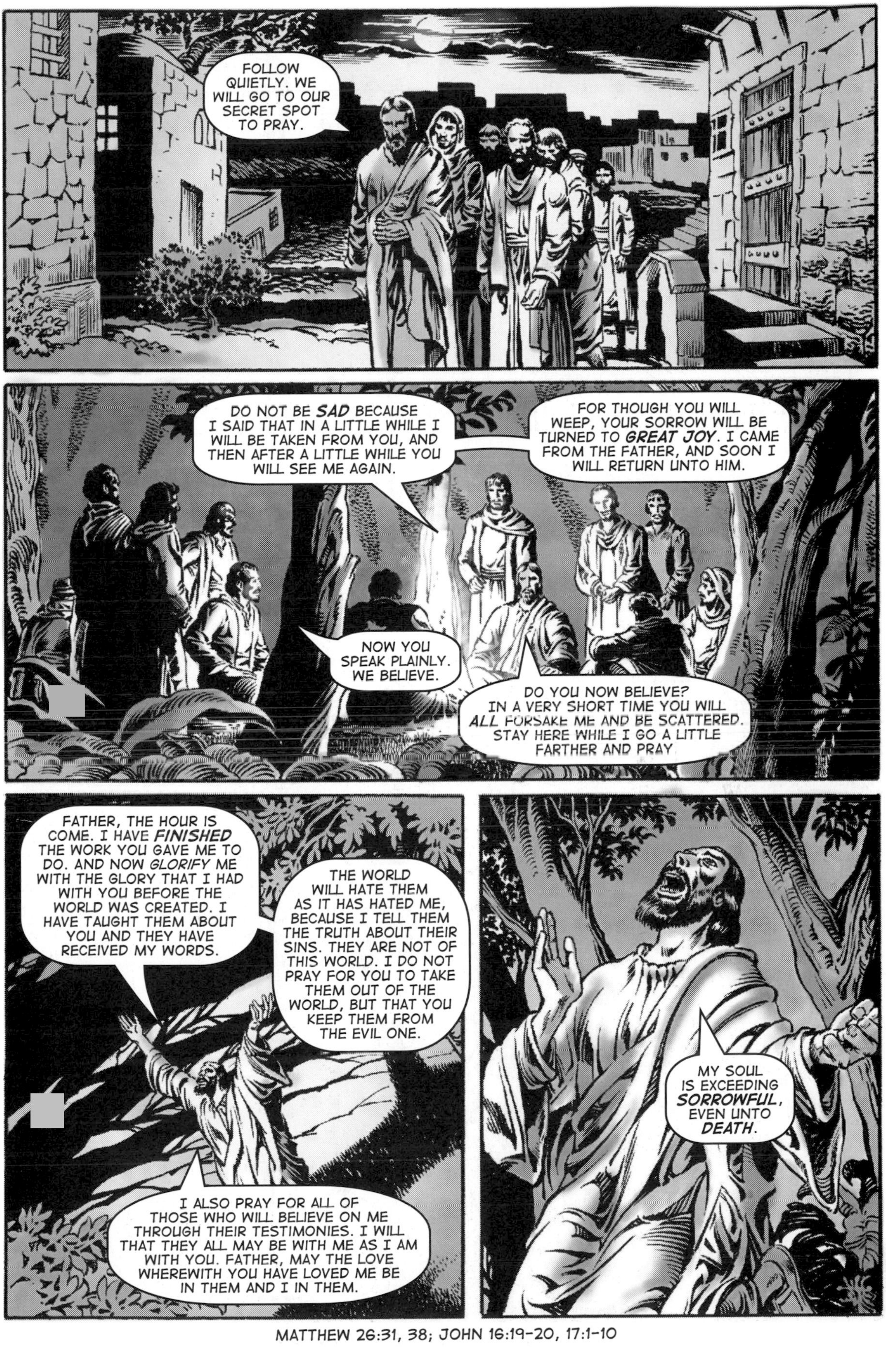
FOLLOW QUIETLY. WE WILL GO TO OUR SECRET SPOT TO PRAY.
DO NOT BE SAD BECAUSE I SAID THAT IN A LITTLE WHILE I WILL BE TAKEN FROM YOU, AND THEN AFTER A LITTLE WHILE YOU WILL SEE ME AGAIN.
FOR THOUGH YOU WILL WEEP, YOUR SORROW WILL BE TURNED TO GREAT JOY. I CAME FROM THE FATHER, AND SOON I WILL RETURN UNTO HIM.
NOW YOU SPEAK PLAINLY. WE BELIEVE.
DO YOU NOW BELIEVE? IN A VERY SHORT TIME YOU WILL ALL FORSAKE ME AND BE SCATTERED. STAY HERE WHILE I GO A LITTLE FARTHER AND PRAY
FATHER, THE HOUR IS COME. I HAVE FINISHED THE WORK YOU GAVE ME TO DO. AND NOW GLORIFY ME WITH THE GLORY THAT I HAD WITH YOU BEFORE THE WORLD WAS CREATED. I HAVE TAUGHT THEM ABOUT YOU AND THEY HAVE RECEIVED MY WORDS.
THE WORLD WILL HATE THEM AS IT HAS HATED ME, BECAUSE I TELL THEM THE TRUTH ABOUT THEIR SINS. THEY ARE NOT OF THIS WORLD. I DO NOT PRAY FOR YOU TO TAKE THEM OUT OF THE WORLD, BUT THAT YOU KEEP THEM FROM THE EVIL ONE.
I ALSO PRAY FOR ALL OF THOSE WHO WILL BELIEVE ON ME THROUGH THEIR TESTIMONIES. I WILL THAT THEY ALL MAY BE WITH ME AS I AM WITH YOU. FATHER, MAY THE LOVE WHEREWITH YOU HAVE LOVED ME BE IN THEM AND I IN THEM.
MY SOUL IS EXCEEDING SORROWFUL, EVEN UNTO DEATH.

MATTHEW 26:31, 38; JOHN 16:19-20, 17:1-10

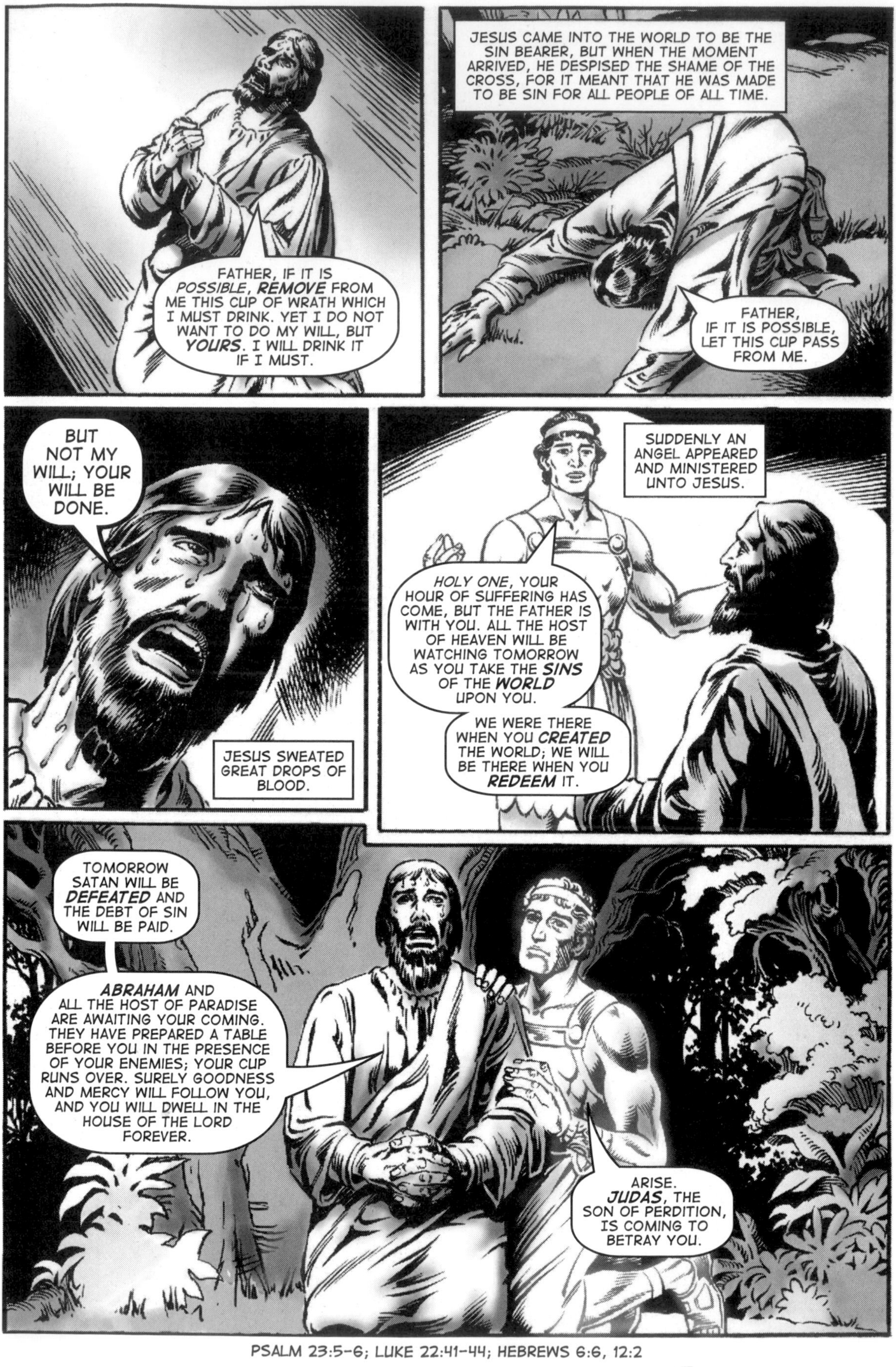
FATHER, IF IT IS *POSSIBLE*, **REMOVE** FROM ME THIS CUP OF WRATH WHICH I MUST DRINK. YET I DO NOT WANT TO DO MY WILL, BUT **YOURS**. I WILL DRINK IT IF I MUST.
JESUS CAME INTO THE WORLD TO BE THE SIN BEARER, BUT WHEN THE MOMENT ARRIVED, HE DESPISED THE SHAME OF THE CROSS, FOR IT MEANT THAT HE WAS MADE TO BE SIN FOR ALL PEOPLE OF ALL TIME.
FATHER, IF IT IS POSSIBLE, LET THIS CUP PASS FROM ME.
BUT NOT MY WILL; YOUR WILL BE DONE.
JESUS SWEATED GREAT DROPS OF BLOOD.
SUDDENLY AN ANGEL APPEARED AND MINISTERED UNTO JESUS.
HOLY ONE, YOUR HOUR OF SUFFERING HAS COME, BUT THE FATHER IS WITH YOU. ALL THE HOST OF HEAVEN WILL BE WATCHING TOMORROW AS YOU TAKE THE ***SINS*** OF THE ***WORLD*** UPON YOU.
WE WERE THERE WHEN YOU ***CREATED*** THE WORLD; WE WILL BE THERE WHEN YOU ***REDEEM*** IT.
TOMORROW SATAN WILL BE ***DEFEATED*** AND THE DEBT OF SIN WILL BE PAID.
ABRAHAM AND ALL THE HOST OF PARADISE ARE AWAITING YOUR COMING. THEY HAVE PREPARED A TABLE BEFORE YOU IN THE PRESENCE OF YOUR ENEMIES; YOUR CUP RUNS OVER. SURELY GOODNESS AND MERCY WILL FOLLOW YOU, AND YOU WILL DWELL IN THE HOUSE OF THE LORD FOREVER.
ARISE. ***JUDAS***, THE SON OF PERDITION, IS COMING TO BETRAY YOU.

PSALM 23:5-6; LUKE 22:41-44; HEBREWS 6:6, 12:2

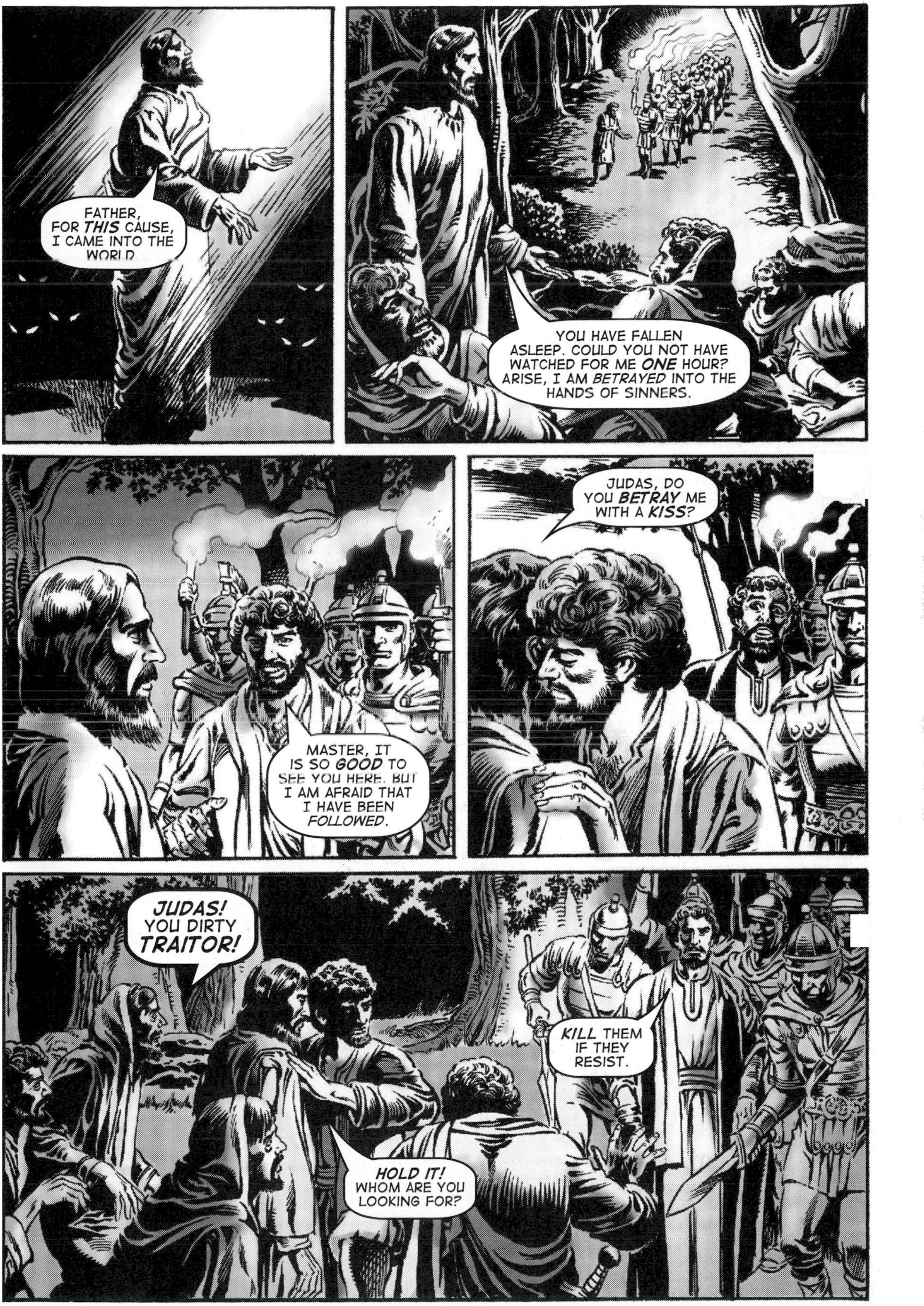
FATHER, FOR THIS CAUSE, I CAME INTO THE WORLD.
YOU HAVE FALLEN ASLEEP. COULD YOU NOT HAVE WATCHED FOR ME ONE HOUR? ARISE, I AM BETRAYED INTO THE HANDS OF SINNERS.
MASTER, IT IS SO GOOD TO SEE YOU HERE. BUT I AM AFRAID THAT I HAVE BEEN FOLLOWED.
JUDAS, DO YOU BETRAY ME WITH A KISS?
JUDAS! YOU DIRTY TRAITOR!
KILL THEM IF THEY RESIST.
HOLD IT! WHOM ARE YOU LOOKING FOR?

MATTHEW 26:40, 45-50; JOHN 12:27, 18:1-4

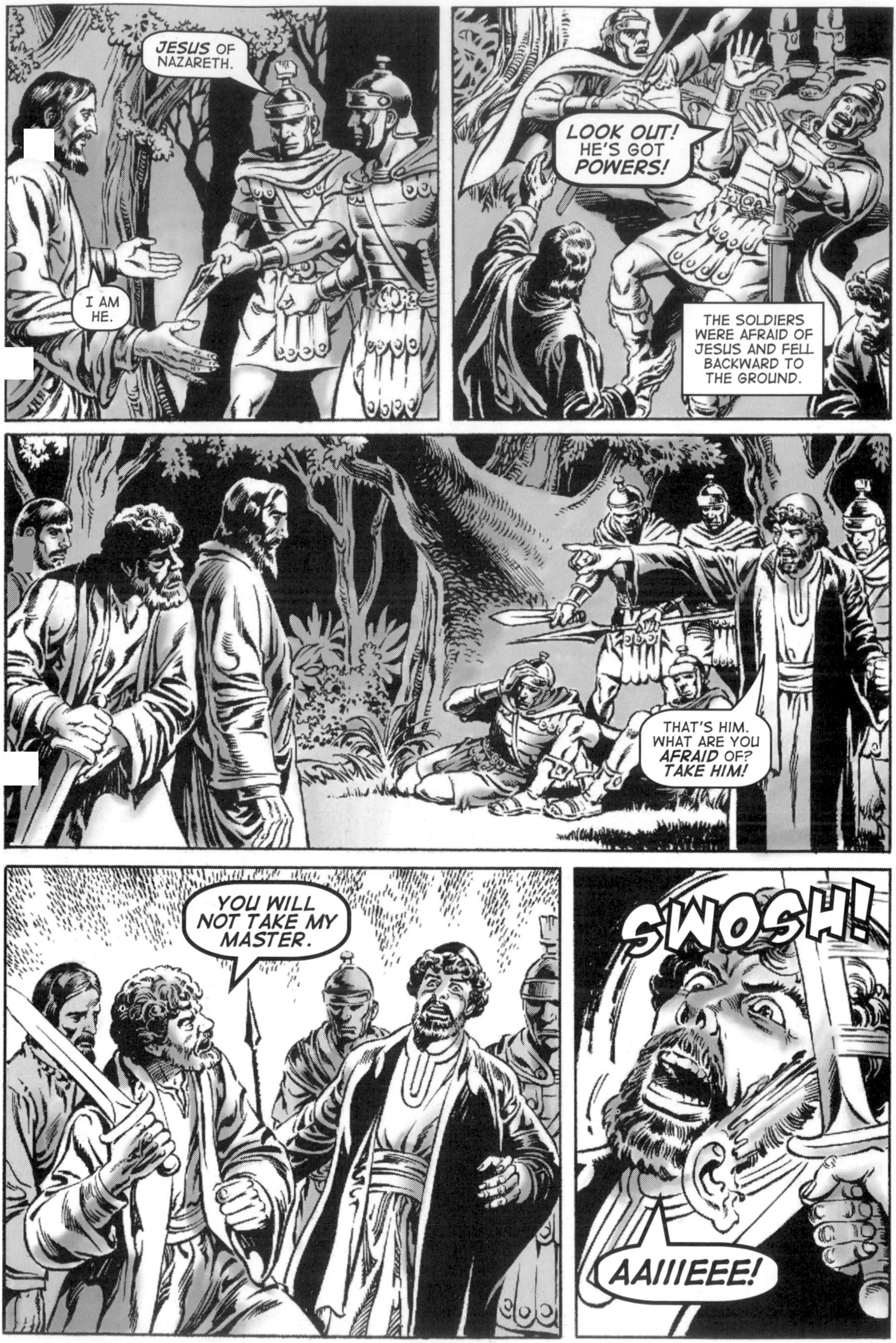
JESUS OF NAZARETH.
I AM HE.
LOOK OUT! HE'S GOT POWERS!
THE SOLDIERS WERE AFRAID OF JESUS AND FELL BACKWARD TO THE GROUND.
THAT'S HIM. WHAT ARE YOU AFRAID OF? TAKE HIM!
YOU WILL NOT TAKE MY MASTER.
SWOSH!
AAIIIEEE!

JOHN 18:4–6, 10

MATTHEW 26:52-57; MARK 14:51-52; LUKE 22:50-51

242

JOHN 18:19-23

MATTHEW 26:59-65

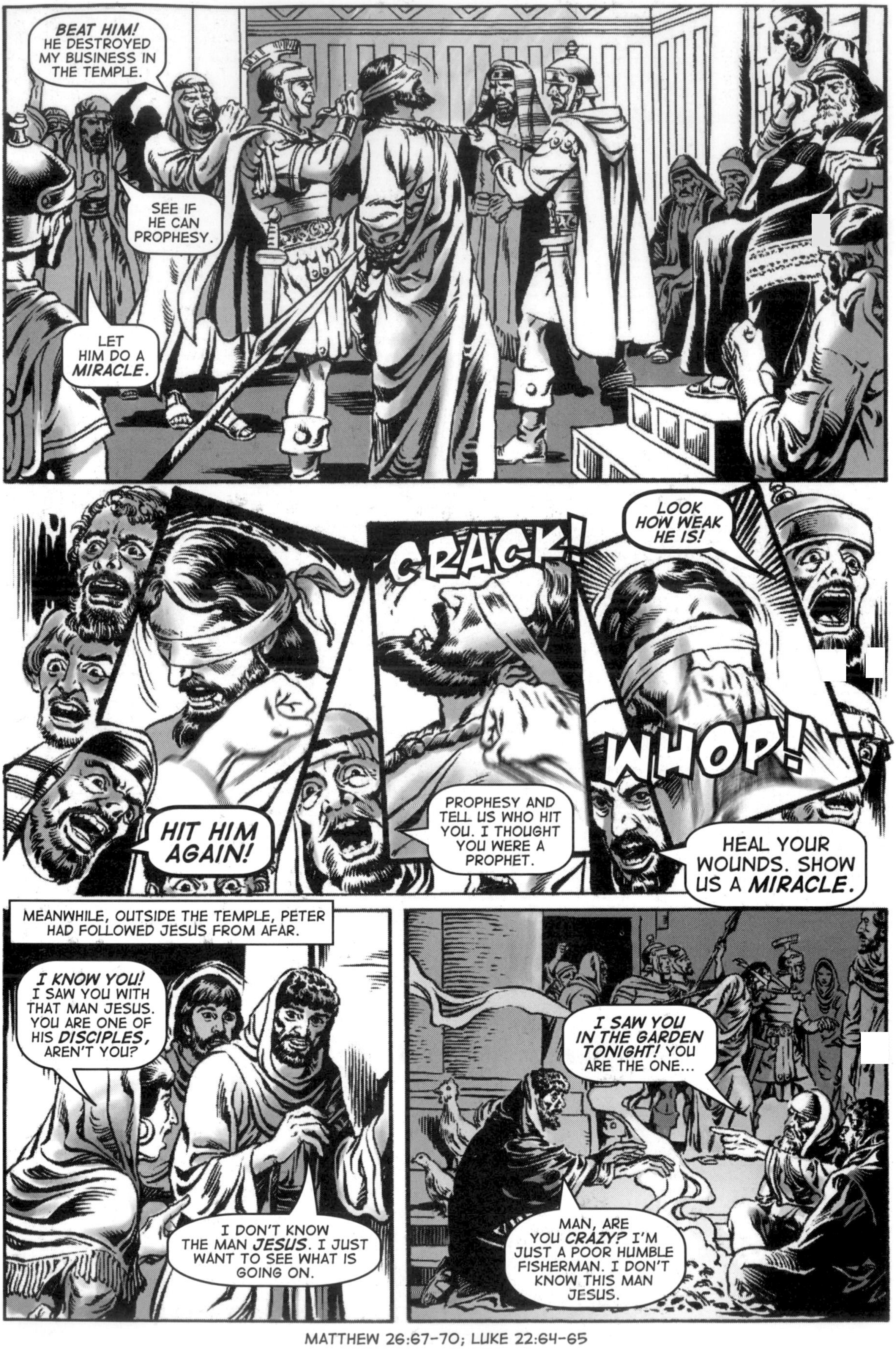
BEAT HIM! HE DESTROYED MY BUSINESS IN THE TEMPLE.
SEE IF HE CAN PROPHESY.
LET HIM DO A MIRACLE.
CRACK!
LOOK HOW WEAK HE IS!
WHOP!
HIT HIM AGAIN!
PROPHESY AND TELL US WHO HIT YOU. I THOUGHT YOU WERE A PROPHET.
HEAL YOUR WOUNDS. SHOW US A MIRACLE.
MEANWHILE, OUTSIDE THE TEMPLE, PETER HAD FOLLOWED JESUS FROM AFAR.
I KNOW YOU! I SAW YOU WITH THAT MAN JESUS. YOU ARE ONE OF HIS DISCIPLES, AREN'T YOU?
I DON'T KNOW THE MAN JESUS. I JUST WANT TO SEE WHAT IS GOING ON.
I SAW YOU IN THE GARDEN TONIGHT! YOU ARE THE ONE...
MAN, ARE YOU CRAZY? I'M JUST A POOR HUMBLE FISHERMAN. I DON'T KNOW THIS MAN JESUS.

MATTHEW 26:67–70; LUKE 22:64–65

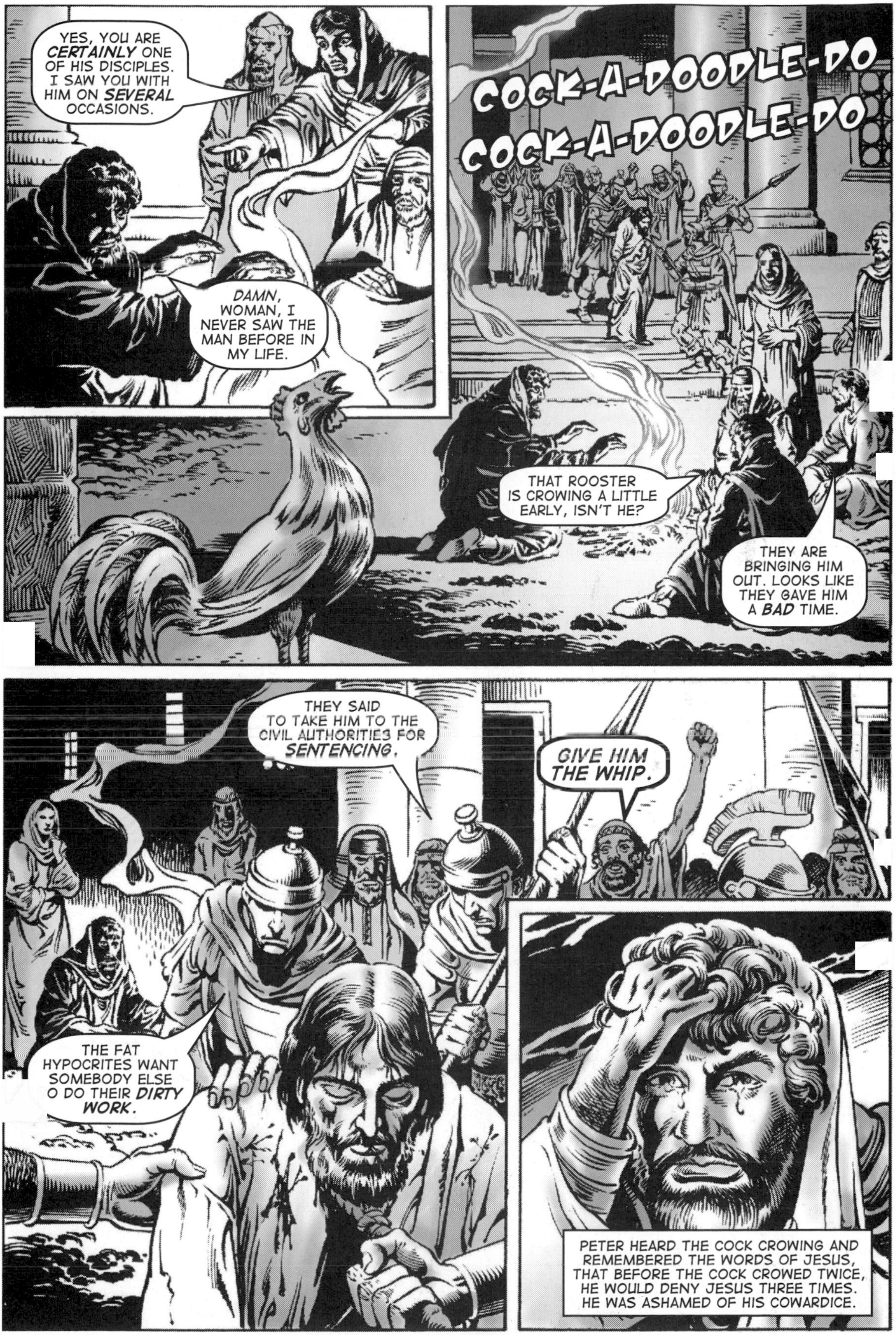
YES, YOU ARE CERTAINLY ONE OF HIS DISCIPLES. I SAW YOU WITH HIM ON SEVERAL OCCASIONS.
DAMN, WOMAN, I NEVER SAW THE MAN BEFORE IN MY LIFE.
COCK-A-DOODLE-DO
COCK-A-DOODLE-DO
THAT ROOSTER IS CROWING A LITTLE EARLY, ISN'T HE?
THEY ARE BRINGING HIM OUT. LOOKS LIKE THEY GAVE HIM A BAD TIME.
THEY SAID TO TAKE HIM TO THE CIVIL AUTHORITIES FOR SENTENCING.
GIVE HIM THE WHIP.
THE FAT HYPOCRITES WANT SOMEBODY ELSE O DO THEIR DIRTY WORK.
PETER HEARD THE COCK CROWING AND REMEMBERED THE WORDS OF JESUS, THAT BEFORE THE COCK CROWED TWICE, HE WOULD DENY JESUS THREE TIMES. HE WAS ASHAMED OF HIS COWARDICE.

MATTHEW 26:71-75, 27:1-2; LUKE 22:58-62, 23:1

MATTHEW 27:3-6

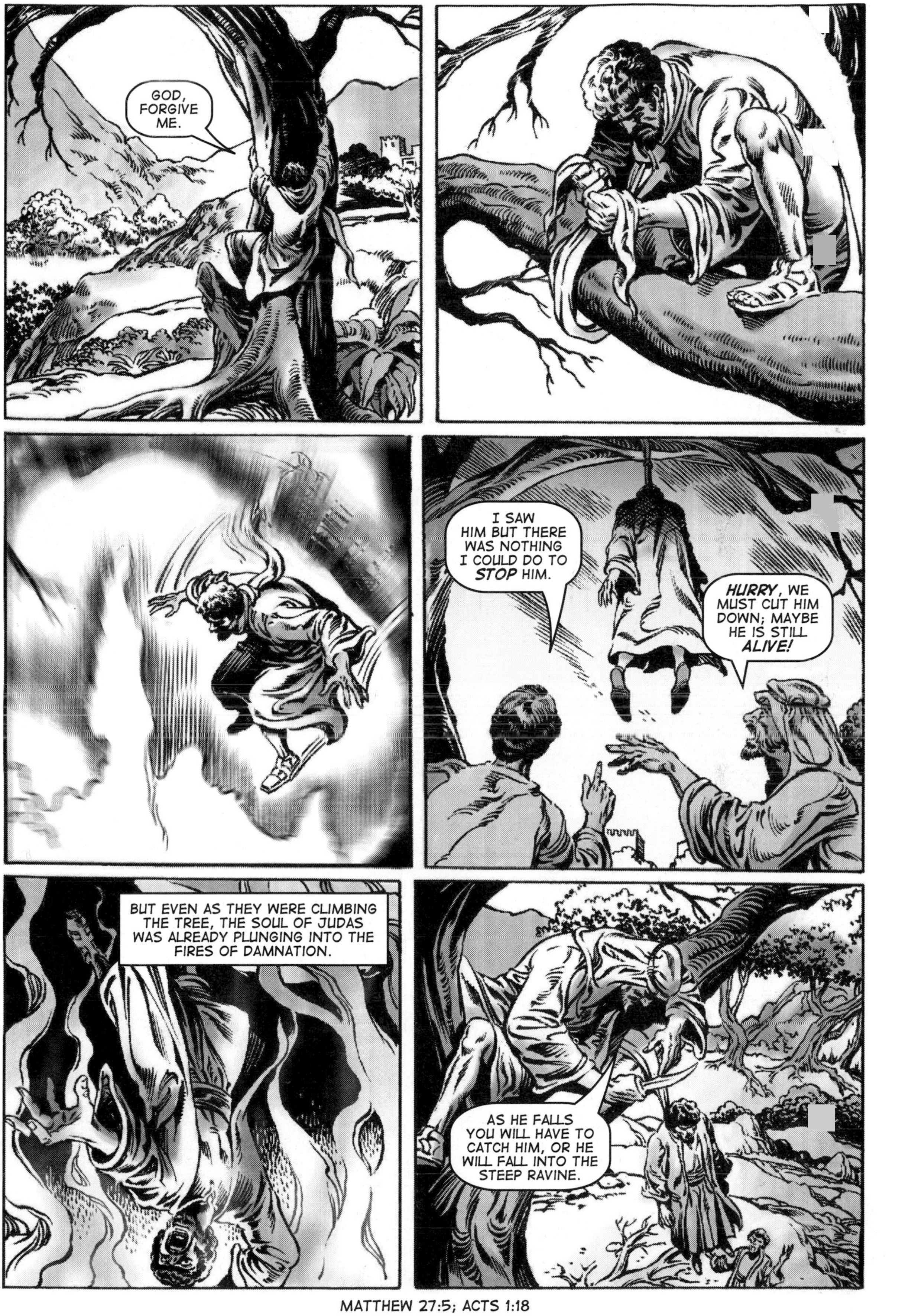
GOD, FORGIVE ME.
I SAW HIM BUT THERE WAS NOTHING I COULD DO TO **STOP** HIM.
HURRY, WE MUST CUT HIM DOWN; MAYBE HE IS STILL **ALIVE!**
BUT EVEN AS THEY WERE CLIMBING THE TREE, THE SOUL OF JUDAS WAS ALREADY PLUNGING INTO THE FIRES OF DAMNATION.
AS HE FALLS YOU WILL HAVE TO CATCH HIM, OR HE WILL FALL INTO THE STEEP RAVINE.

MATTHEW 27:5; ACTS 1:18

MATTHEW 27:8; MARK 15:14; LUKE 23:1-4; JOHN 18:29-38; ACTS 1:18

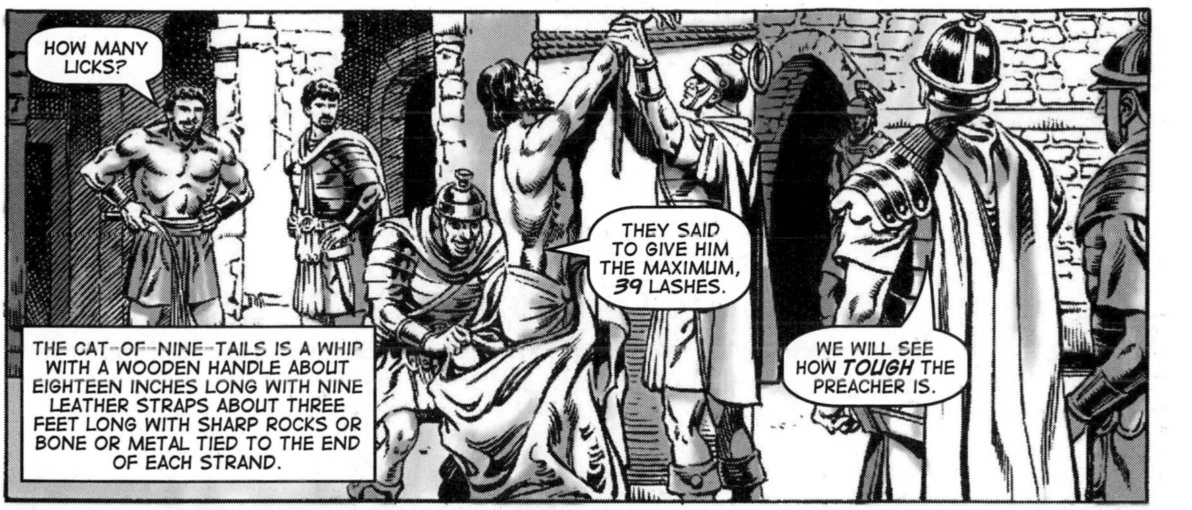
HOW MANY LICKS?
THEY SAID TO GIVE HIM THE MAXIMUM, 39 LASHES.
THE CAT-OF-NINE-TAILS IS A WHIP WITH A WOODEN HANDLE ABOUT EIGHTEEN INCHES LONG WITH NINE LEATHER STRAPS ABOUT THREE FEET LONG WITH SHARP ROCKS OR BONE OR METAL TIED TO THE END OF EACH STRAND.
WE WILL SEE HOW TOUGH THE PREACHER IS.

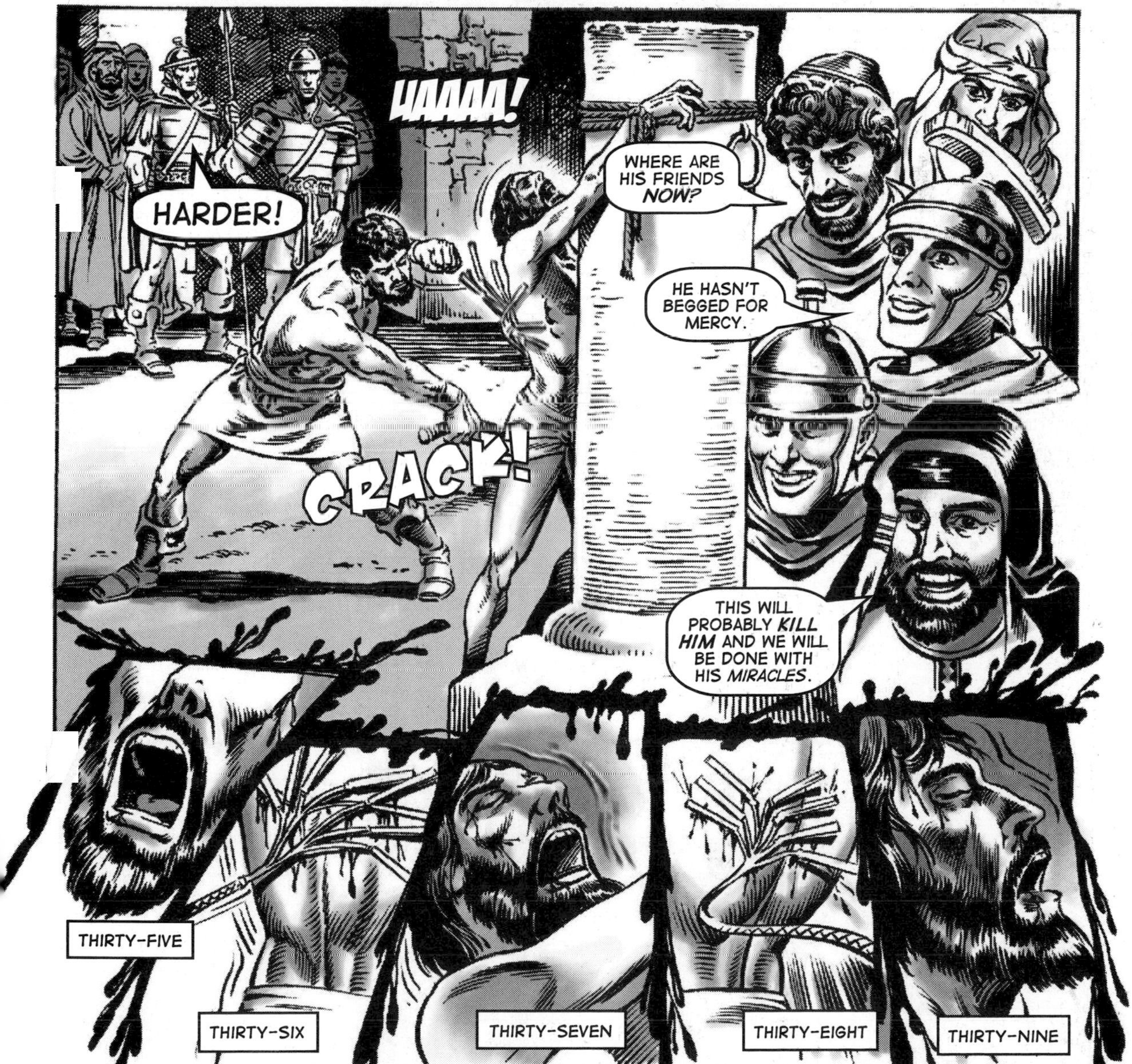
UAAAA!
HARDER!
WHERE ARE HIS FRIENDS NOW?
HE HASN'T BEGGED FOR MERCY.
CRACK!
THIS WILL PROBABLY KILL HIM AND WE WILL BE DONE WITH HIS MIRACLES.
THIRTY-FIVE
THIRTY-SIX
THIRTY-SEVEN
THIRTY-EIGHT
THIRTY-NINE

LUKE 23:11; JOHN 19:1-2

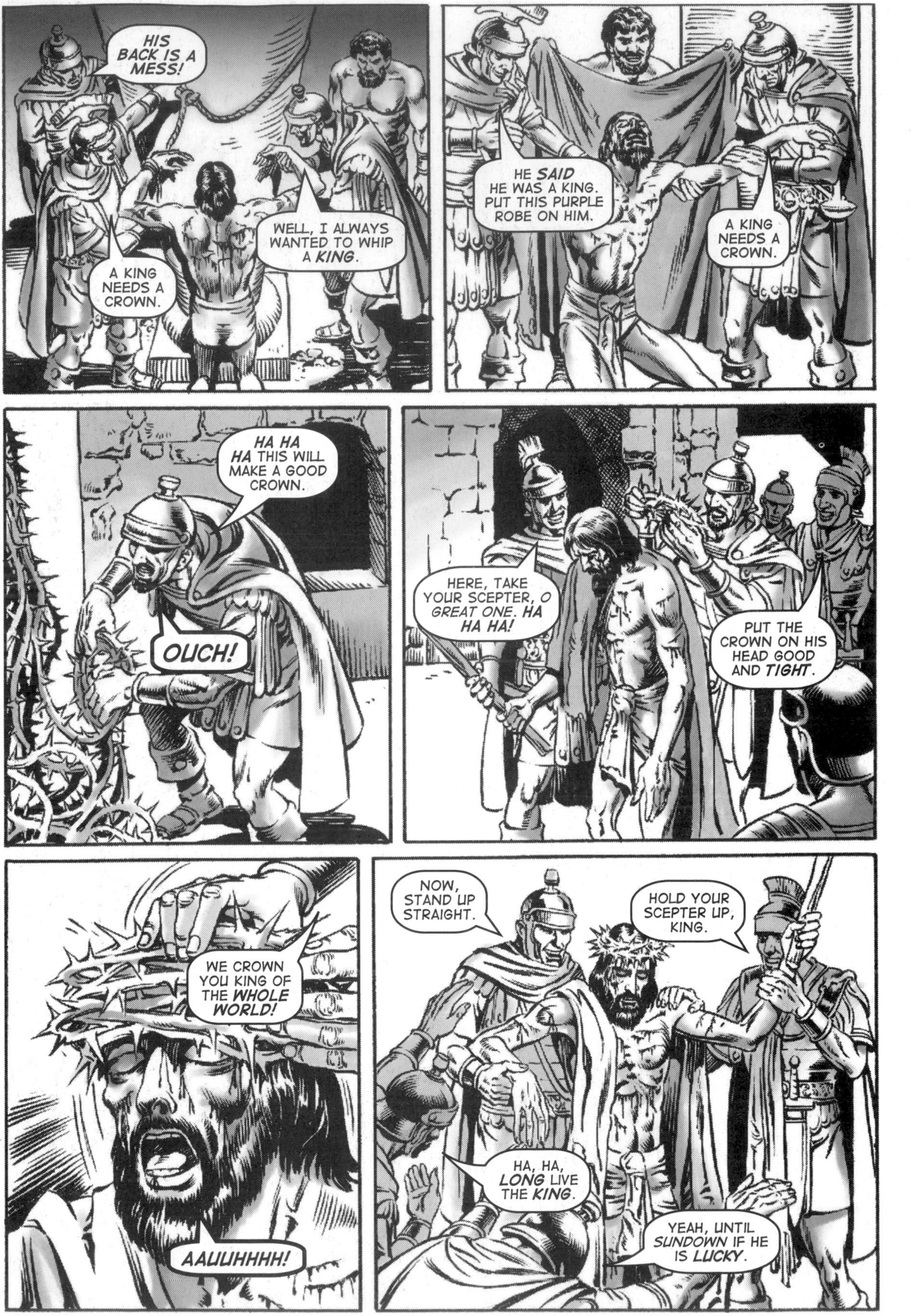
HIS BACK IS A MESS!
WELL, I ALWAYS WANTED TO WHIP A KING.
A KING NEEDS A CROWN.
HE SAID HE WAS A KING. PUT THIS PURPLE ROBE ON HIM.
A KING NEEDS A CROWN.
HA HA HA THIS WILL MAKE A GOOD CROWN.
OUCH!
HERE, TAKE YOUR SCEPTER, O GREAT ONE. HA HA HA!
PUT THE CROWN ON HIS HEAD GOOD AND TIGHT.
WE CROWN YOU KING OF THE WHOLE WORLD!
AAUUHHHH!
NOW, STAND UP STRAIGHT.
HOLD YOUR SCEPTER UP, KING.
HA, HA, LONG LIVE THE KING.
YEAH, UNTIL SUNDOWN IF HE IS LUCKY.

JOHN 19:1–3

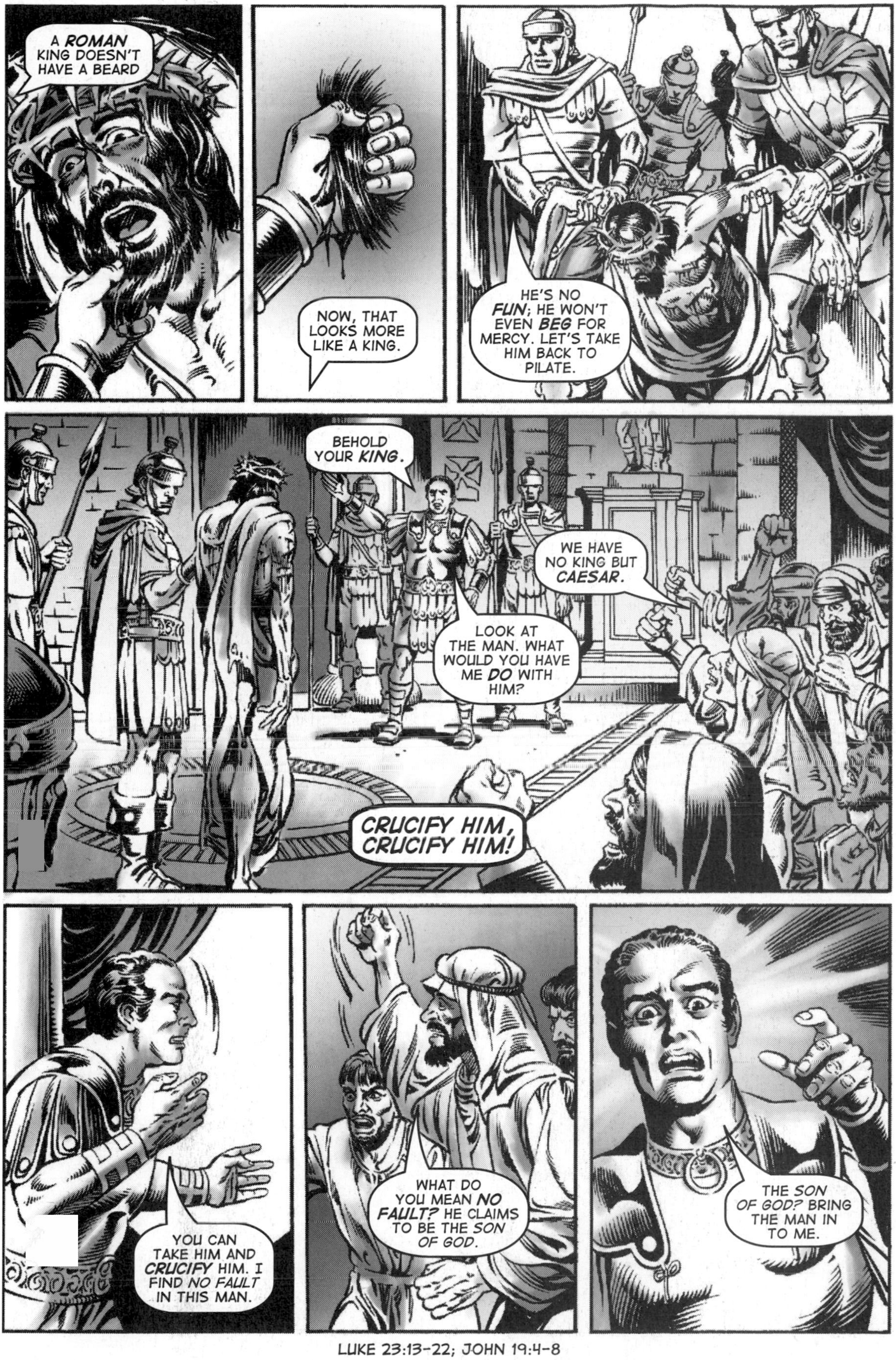
A ROMAN KING DOESN'T HAVE A BEARD
NOW, THAT LOOKS MORE LIKE A KING.
HE'S NO FUN; HE WON'T EVEN BEG FOR MERCY. LET'S TAKE HIM BACK TO PILATE.
BEHOLD YOUR KING.
LOOK AT THE MAN. WHAT WOULD YOU HAVE ME DO WITH HIM?
WE HAVE NO KING BUT CAESAR.
CRUCIFY HIM, CRUCIFY HIM!
YOU CAN TAKE HIM AND CRUCIFY HIM. I FIND NO FAULT IN THIS MAN.
WHAT DO YOU MEAN NO FAULT? HE CLAIMS TO BE THE SON OF GOD.
THE SON OF GOD? BRING THE MAN IN TO ME.

LUKE 23:13-22; JOHN 19:4-8

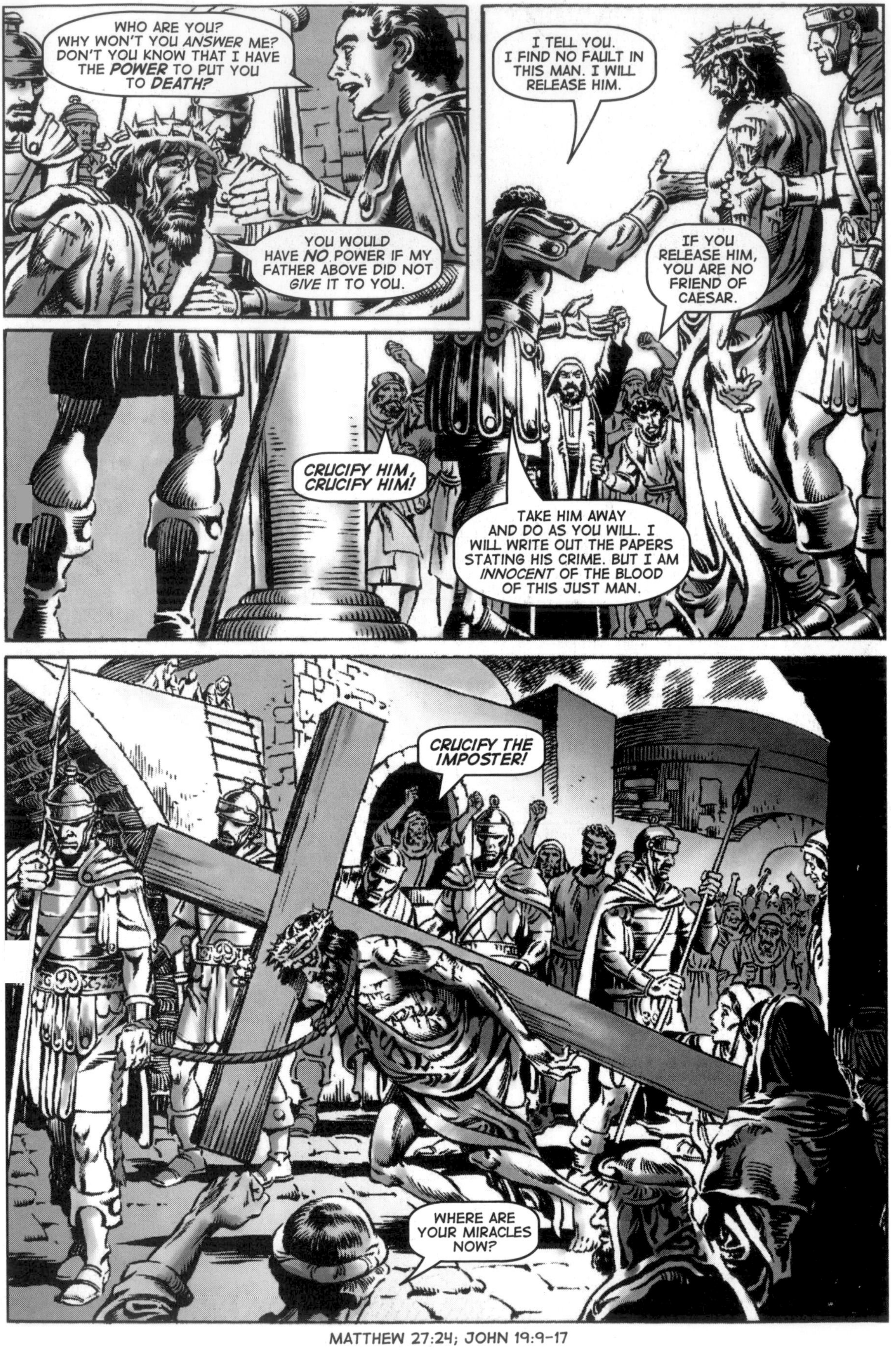
WHO ARE YOU? WHY WON'T YOU *ANSWER* ME? DON'T YOU KNOW THAT I HAVE THE **POWER** TO PUT YOU TO ***DEATH?***
YOU WOULD HAVE ***NO*** POWER IF MY FATHER ABOVE DID NOT *GIVE* IT TO YOU.
I TELL YOU. I FIND NO FAULT IN THIS MAN. I WILL RELEASE HIM.
IF YOU RELEASE HIM, YOU ARE NO FRIEND OF CAESAR.
CRUCIFY HIM, CRUCIFY HIM!
TAKE HIM AWAY AND DO AS YOU WILL. I WILL WRITE OUT THE PAPERS STATING HIS CRIME. BUT I AM *INNOCENT* OF THE BLOOD OF THIS JUST MAN.
CRUCIFY THE IMPOSTER!
WHERE ARE YOUR MIRACLES NOW?

MATTHEW 27:24; JOHN 19:9-17

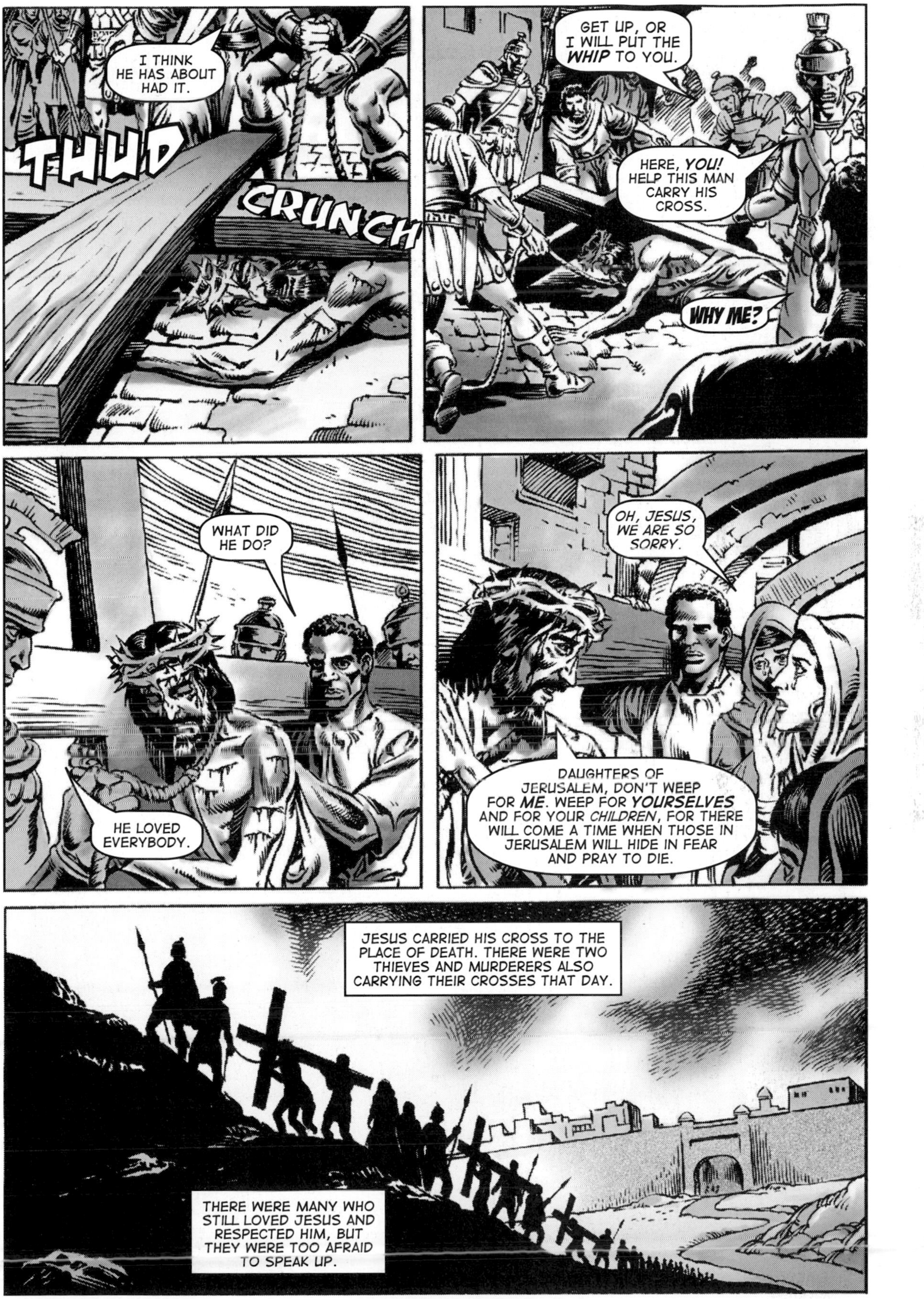
I THINK HE HAS ABOUT HAD IT.
THUD
CRUNCH
GET UP, OR I WILL PUT THE WHIP TO YOU.
HERE, YOU! HELP THIS MAN CARRY HIS CROSS.
WHY ME?
WHAT DID HE DO?
HE LOVED EVERYBODY.
OH, JESUS, WE ARE SO SORRY.
DAUGHTERS OF JERUSALEM, DON'T WEEP FOR ME. WEEP FOR YOURSELVES AND FOR YOUR CHILDREN, FOR THERE WILL COME A TIME WHEN THOSE IN JERUSALEM WILL HIDE IN FEAR AND PRAY TO DIE.
JESUS CARRIED HIS CROSS TO THE PLACE OF DEATH. THERE WERE TWO THIEVES AND MURDERERS ALSO CARRYING THEIR CROSSES THAT DAY.
THERE WERE MANY WHO STILL LOVED JESUS AND RESPECTED HIM, BUT THEY WERE TOO AFRAID TO SPEAK UP.

MATTHEW 27:32; LUKE 23:26-33

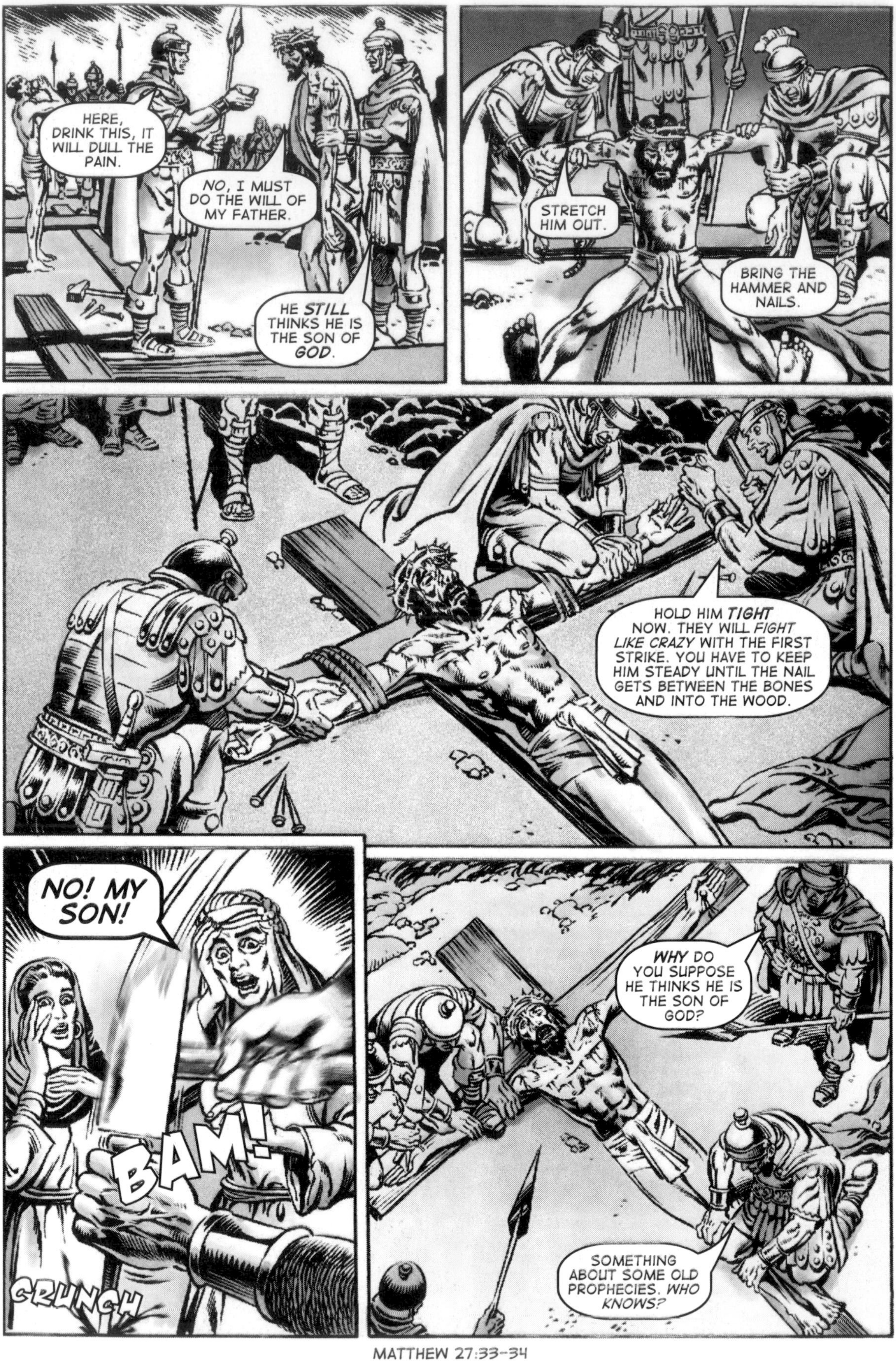
HERE, DRINK THIS, IT WILL DULL THE PAIN.
NO, I MUST DO THE WILL OF MY FATHER.
HE STILL THINKS HE IS THE SON OF GOD.
STRETCH HIM OUT.
BRING THE HAMMER AND NAILS.
HOLD HIM TIGHT NOW. THEY WILL FIGHT LIKE CRAZY WITH THE FIRST STRIKE. YOU HAVE TO KEEP HIM STEADY UNTIL THE NAIL GETS BETWEEN THE BONES AND INTO THE WOOD.
NO! MY SON!
BAM!
CRUNCH
WHY DO YOU SUPPOSE HE THINKS HE IS THE SON OF GOD?
SOMETHING ABOUT SOME OLD PROPHECIES. WHO KNOWS?

MATTHEW 27:33-34

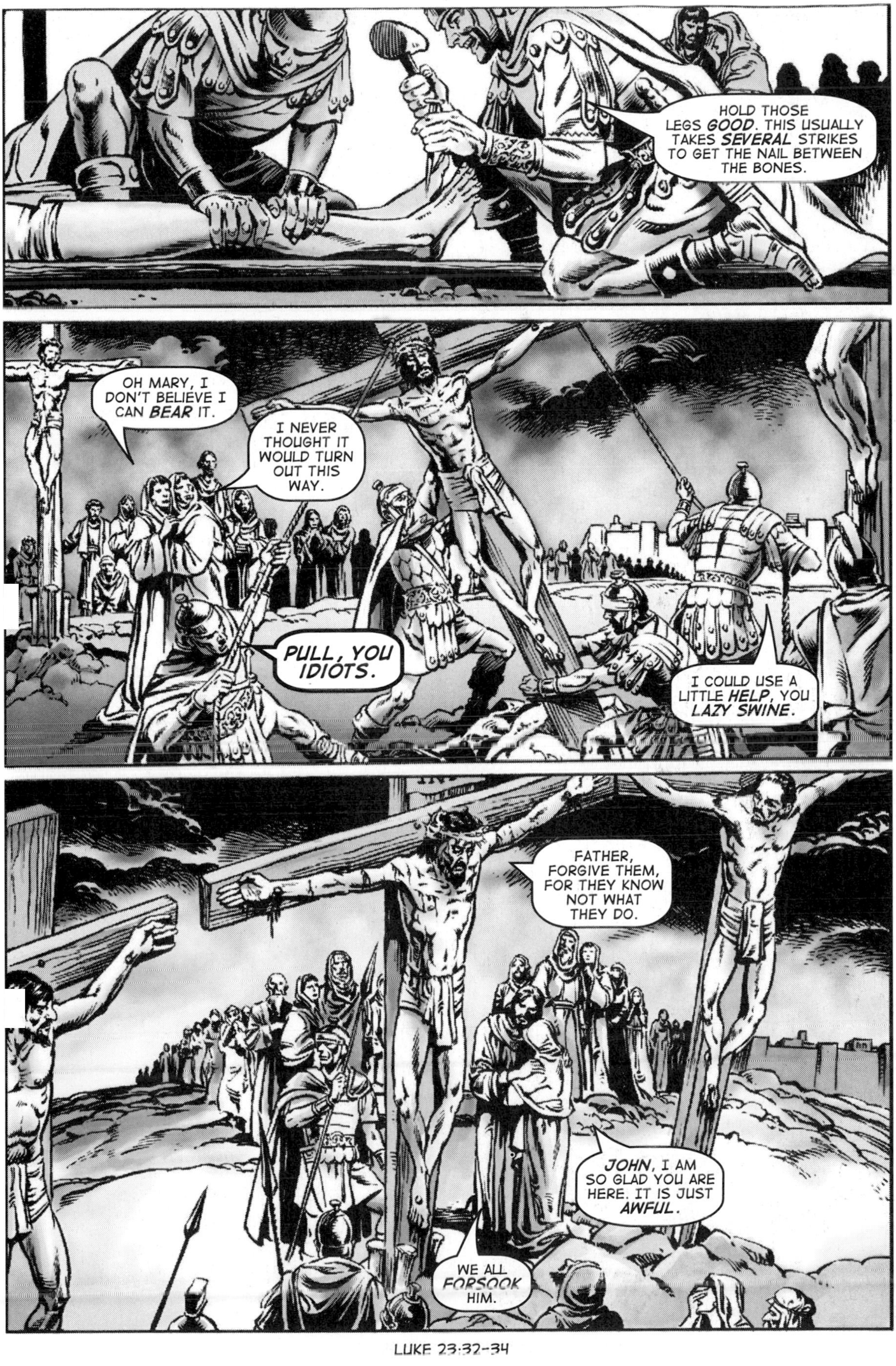
HOLD THOSE LEGS GOOD. THIS USUALLY TAKES SEVERAL STRIKES TO GET THE NAIL BETWEEN THE BONES.
OH MARY, I DON'T BELIEVE I CAN BEAR IT.
I NEVER THOUGHT IT WOULD TURN OUT THIS WAY.
PULL, YOU IDIOTS.
I COULD USE A LITTLE HELP, YOU LAZY SWINE.
FATHER, FORGIVE THEM, FOR THEY KNOW NOT WHAT THEY DO.
JOHN, I AM SO GLAD YOU ARE HERE. IT IS JUST AWFUL.
WE ALL FORSOOK HIM.

LUKE 23:32-34

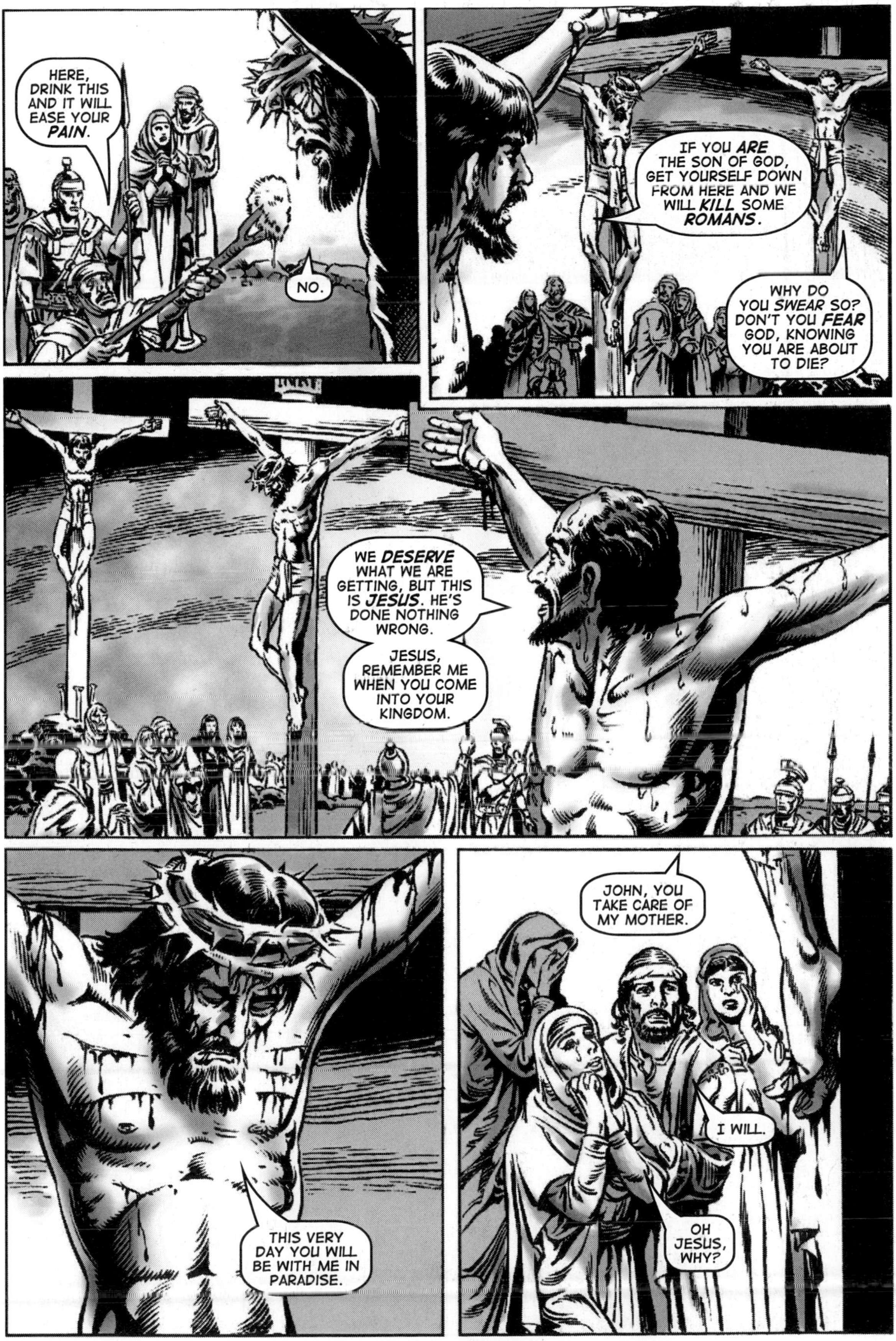
HERE, DRINK THIS AND IT WILL EASE YOUR PAIN.
NO.
IF YOU ARE THE SON OF GOD, GET YOURSELF DOWN FROM HERE AND WE WILL KILL SOME ROMANS.
WHY DO YOU SWEAR SO? DON'T YOU FEAR GOD, KNOWING YOU ARE ABOUT TO DIE?
WE DESERVE WHAT WE ARE GETTING, BUT THIS IS JESUS. HE'S DONE NOTHING WRONG.
JESUS, REMEMBER ME WHEN YOU COME INTO YOUR KINGDOM.
THIS VERY DAY YOU WILL BE WITH ME IN PARADISE.
JOHN, YOU TAKE CARE OF MY MOTHER.
I WILL.
OH JESUS, WHY?

LUKE 23:36-43; JOHN 19:25-27

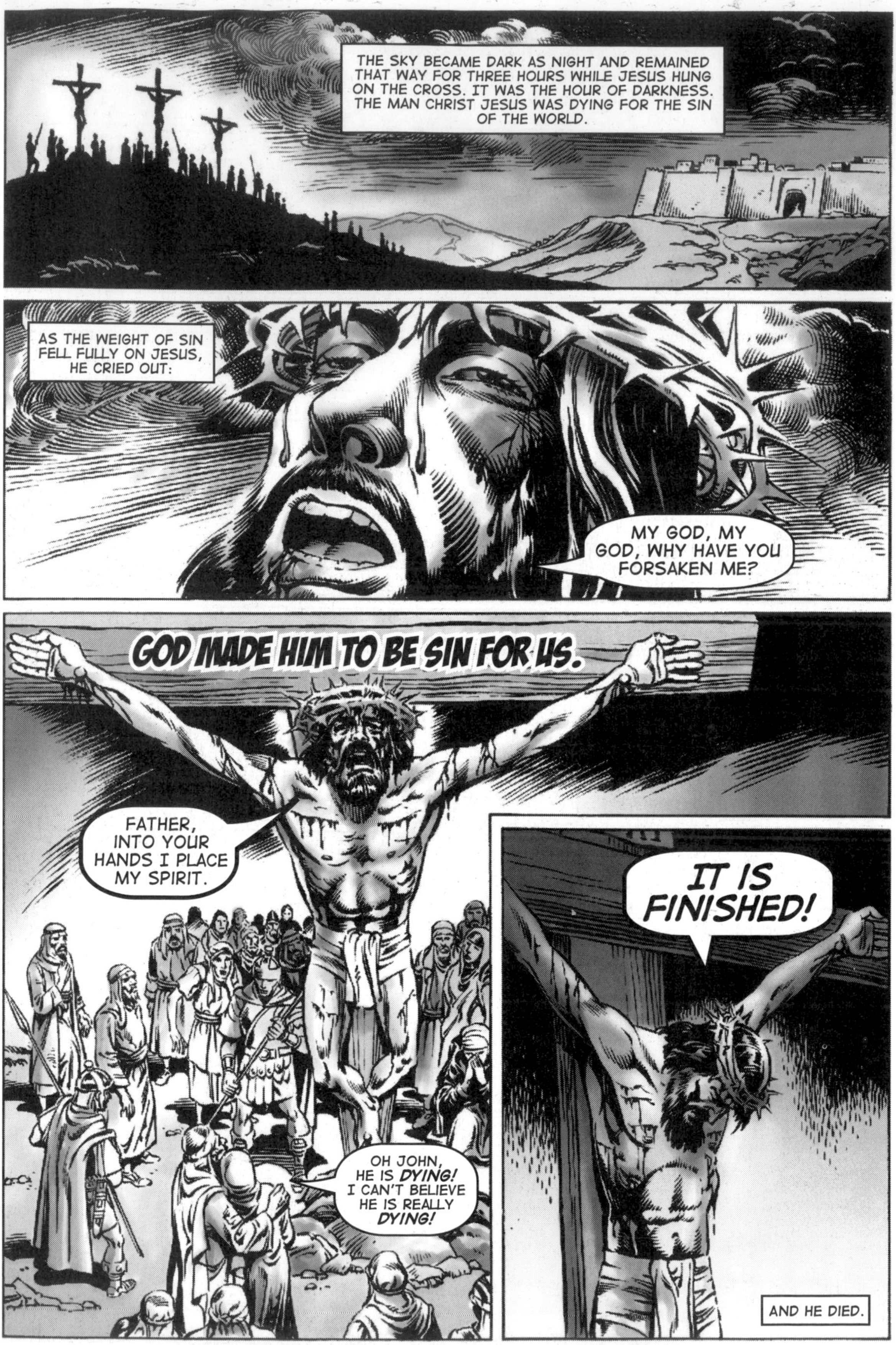
THE SKY BECAME DARK AS NIGHT AND REMAINED THAT WAY FOR THREE HOURS WHILE JESUS HUNG ON THE CROSS. IT WAS THE HOUR OF DARKNESS. THE MAN CHRIST JESUS WAS DYING FOR THE SIN OF THE WORLD.
AS THE WEIGHT OF SIN FELL FULLY ON JESUS, HE CRIED OUT:
MY GOD, MY GOD, WHY HAVE YOU FORSAKEN ME?
GOD MADE HIM TO BE SIN FOR US.
FATHER, INTO YOUR HANDS I PLACE MY SPIRIT.
OH JOHN, HE IS *DYING!* I CAN'T BELIEVE HE IS REALLY *DYING!*
IT IS FINISHED!
AND HE DIED.

MATTHEW 27:45-50; LUKE 23:44-46; JOHN 19:30; 2 CORINTHIANS 5:21

PSALM 34:20; ZECHARIAH 12:10; MATTHEW 27:54; JOHN 19:31-37

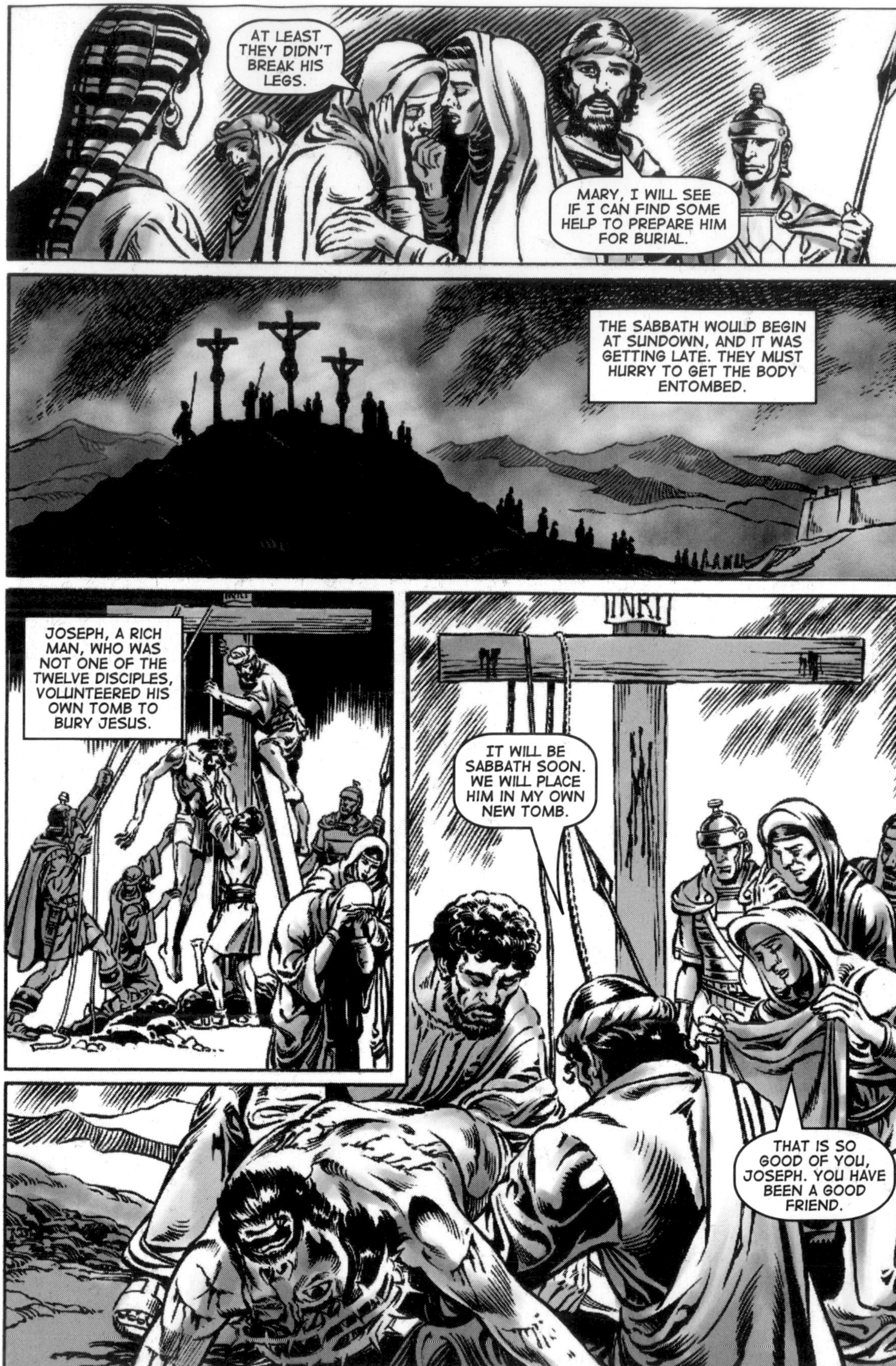
AT LEAST THEY DIDN'T BREAK HIS LEGS.
MARY, I WILL SEE IF I CAN FIND SOME HELP TO PREPARE HIM FOR BURIAL.
THE SABBATH WOULD BEGIN AT SUNDOWN, AND IT WAS GETTING LATE. THEY MUST HURRY TO GET THE BODY ENTOMBED.
JOSEPH, A RICH MAN, WHO WAS NOT ONE OF THE TWELVE DISCIPLES, VOLUNTEERED HIS OWN TOMB TO BURY JESUS.
INRI
IT WILL BE SABBATH SOON. WE WILL PLACE HIM IN MY OWN NEW TOMB.
THAT IS SO GOOD OF YOU, JOSEPH. YOU HAVE BEEN A GOOD FRIEND.

JOHN 19:31, 38

MATTHEW 27:59-66; JOHN 19:40

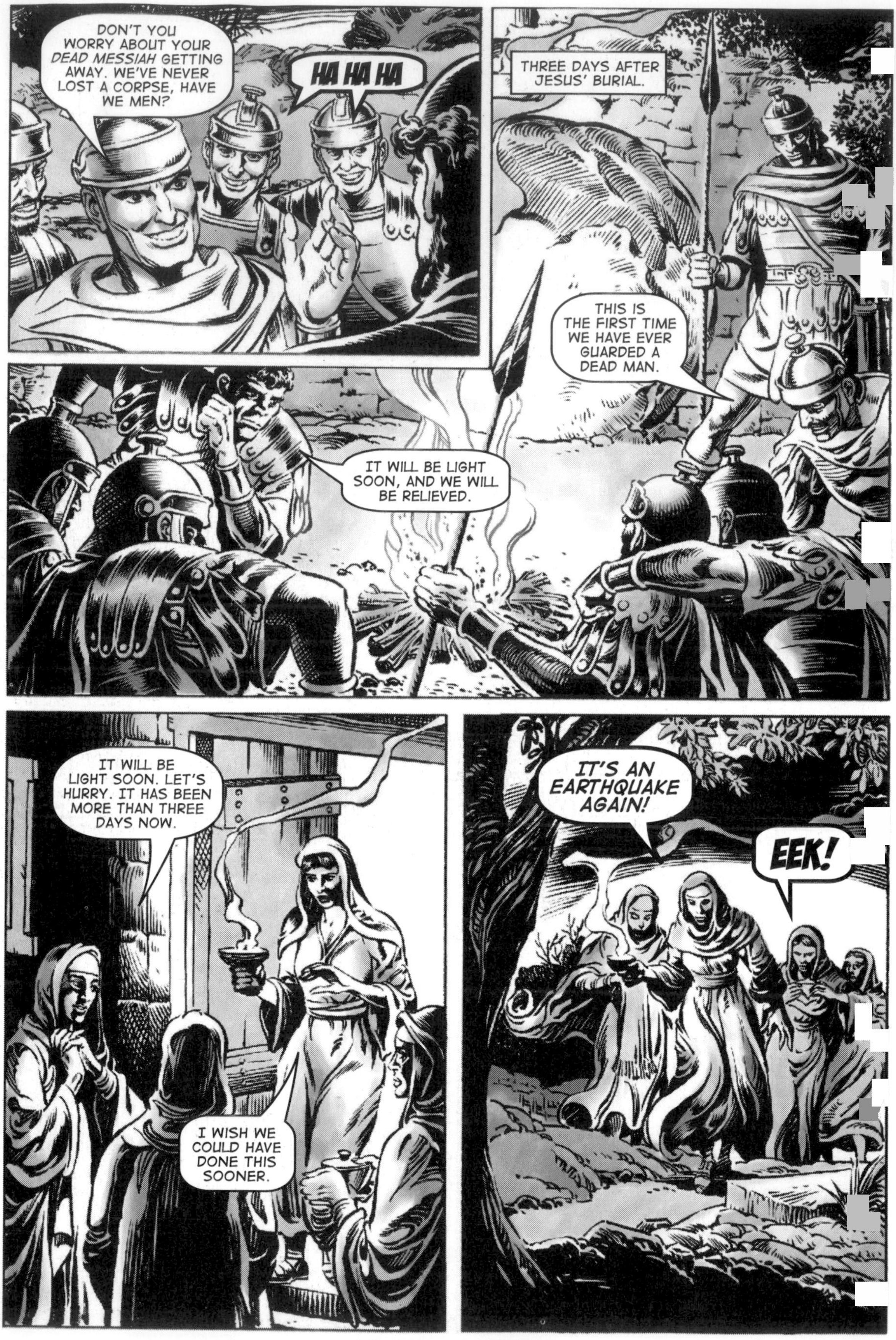
DON'T YOU WORRY ABOUT YOUR *DEAD MESSIAH* GETTING AWAY. WE'VE NEVER LOST A CORPSE, HAVE WE MEN?
HA HA HA
THREE DAYS AFTER JESUS' BURIAL.
THIS IS THE FIRST TIME WE HAVE EVER GUARDED A DEAD MAN.
IT WILL BE LIGHT SOON, AND WE WILL BE RELIEVED.
IT WILL BE LIGHT SOON. LET'S HURRY. IT HAS BEEN MORE THAN THREE DAYS NOW.
I WISH WE COULD HAVE DONE THIS SOONER.
IT'S AN EARTHQUAKE AGAIN!
EEK!

MATTHEW 28:1–2; LUKE 24:1

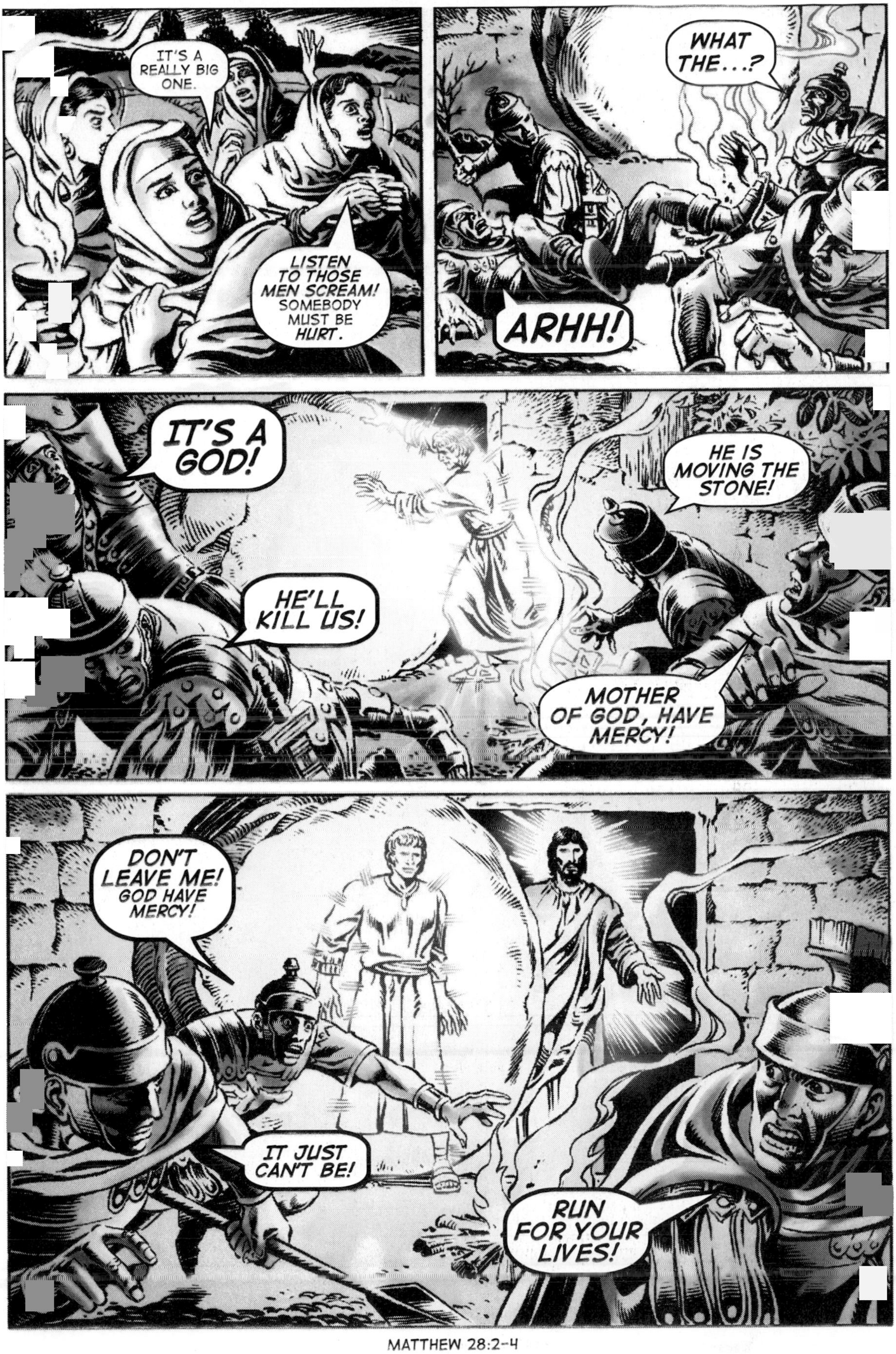
IT'S A REALLY BIG ONE.
LISTEN TO THOSE MEN SCREAM! SOMEBODY MUST BE HURT.
WHAT THE...?
ARHH!
IT'S A GOD!
HE IS MOVING THE STONE!
HE'LL KILL US!
MOTHER OF GOD, HAVE MERCY!
DON'T LEAVE ME! GOD HAVE MERCY!
IT JUST CAN'T BE!
RUN FOR YOUR LIVES!

MATTHEW 28:2-4

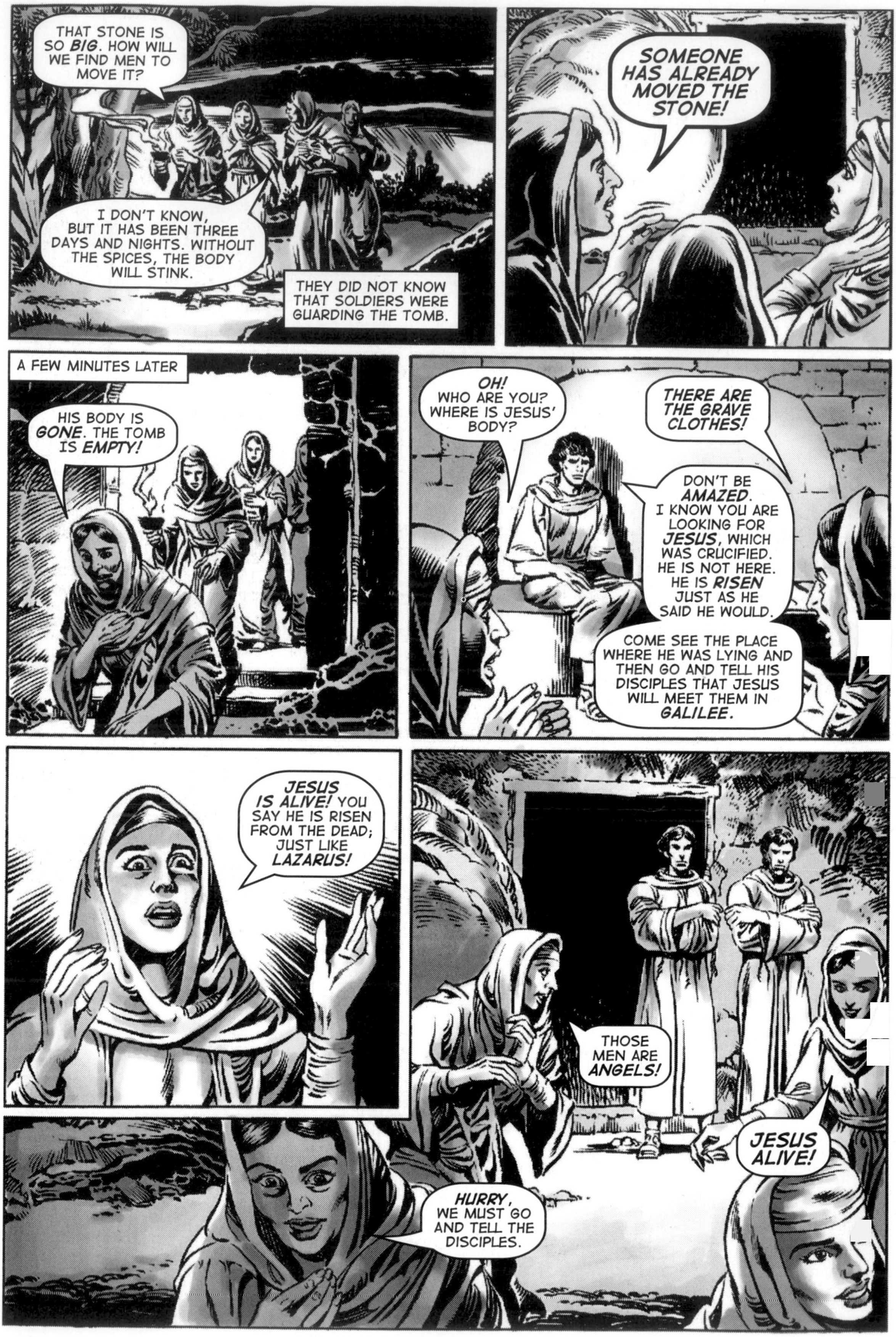
THAT STONE IS SO BIG. HOW WILL WE FIND MEN TO MOVE IT?
I DON'T KNOW, BUT IT HAS BEEN THREE DAYS AND NIGHTS. WITHOUT THE SPICES, THE BODY WILL STINK.
THEY DID NOT KNOW THAT SOLDIERS WERE GUARDING THE TOMB.
SOMEONE HAS ALREADY MOVED THE STONE!
A FEW MINUTES LATER
HIS BODY IS GONE. THE TOMB IS EMPTY!
OH! WHO ARE YOU? WHERE IS JESUS' BODY?
THERE ARE THE GRAVE CLOTHES!
DON'T BE AMAZED. I KNOW YOU ARE LOOKING FOR JESUS, WHICH WAS CRUCIFIED. HE IS NOT HERE. HE IS RISEN JUST AS HE SAID HE WOULD.
COME SEE THE PLACE WHERE HE WAS LYING AND THEN GO AND TELL HIS DISCIPLES THAT JESUS WILL MEET THEM IN GALILEE.
JESUS IS ALIVE! YOU SAY HE IS RISEN FROM THE DEAD; JUST LIKE LAZARUS!
THOSE MEN ARE ANGELS!
JESUS ALIVE!
HURRY, WE MUST GO AND TELL THE DISCIPLES.

MARK 16:3–8

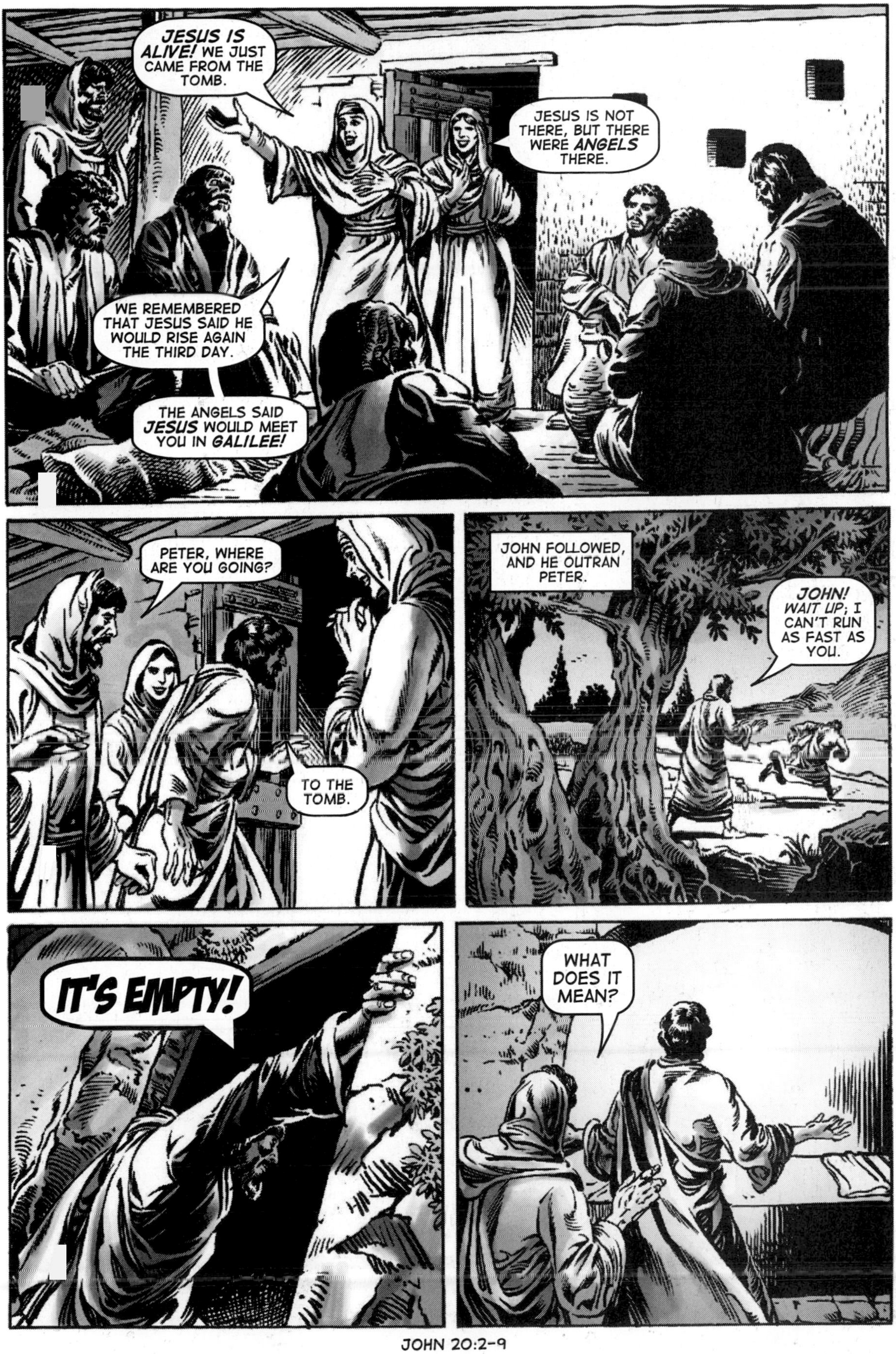
JESUS IS ALIVE! WE JUST CAME FROM THE TOMB.
JESUS IS NOT THERE, BUT THERE WERE ANGELS THERE.
WE REMEMBERED THAT JESUS SAID HE WOULD RISE AGAIN THE THIRD DAY.
THE ANGELS SAID JESUS WOULD MEET YOU IN GALILEE!
PETER, WHERE ARE YOU GOING?
TO THE TOMB.
JOHN FOLLOWED, AND HE OUTRAN PETER.
JOHN! WAIT UP; I CAN'T RUN AS FAST AS YOU.
IT'S EMPTY!
WHAT DOES IT MEAN?

JOHN 20:2-9

JOHN 20:7-17

LUKE 24:13-26

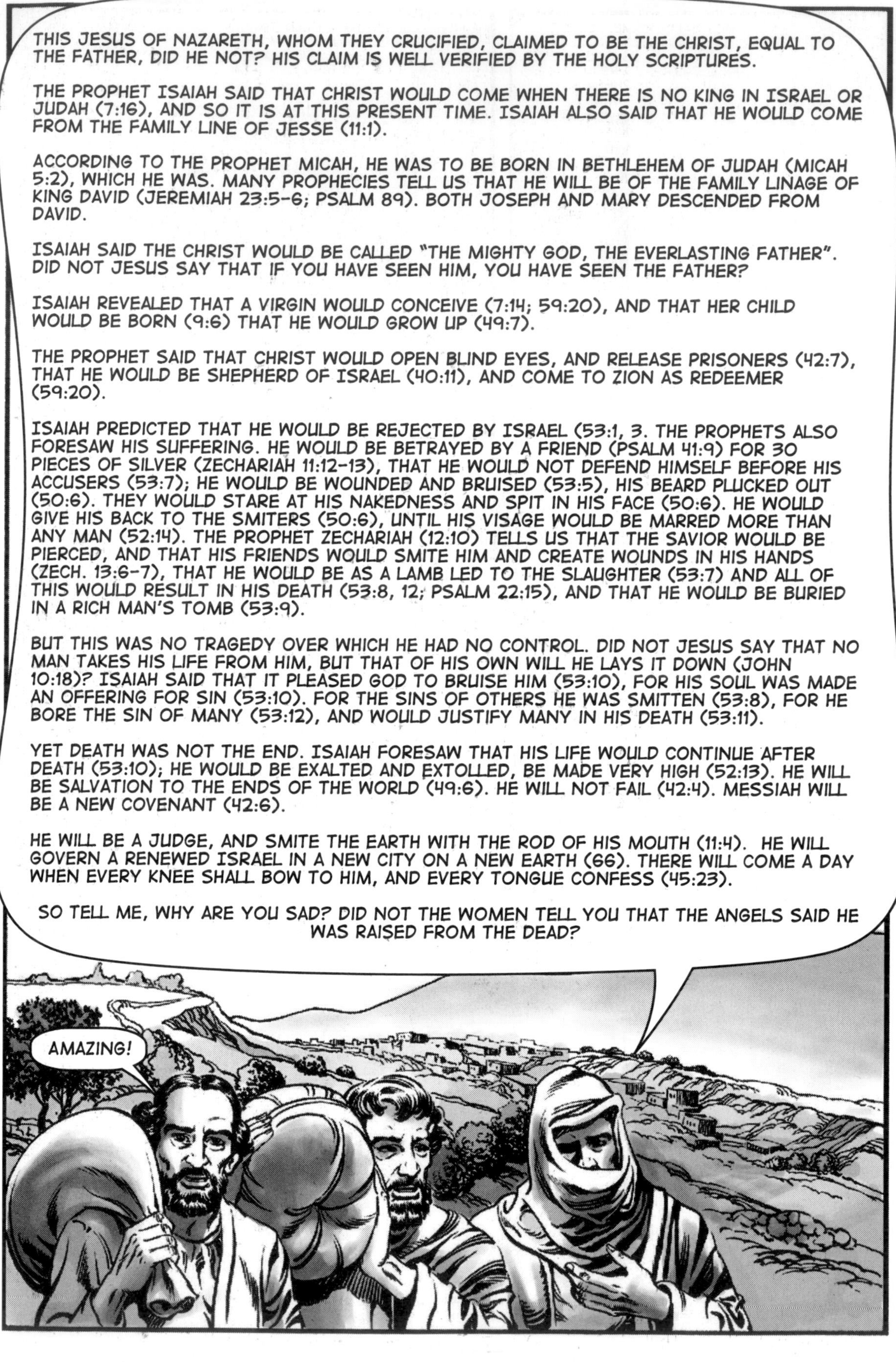
THIS JESUS OF NAZARETH, WHOM THEY CRUCIFIED, CLAIMED TO BE THE CHRIST, EQUAL TO THE FATHER, DID HE NOT? HIS CLAIM IS WELL VERIFIED BY THE HOLY SCRIPTURES.

THE PROPHET ISAIAH SAID THAT CHRIST WOULD COME WHEN THERE IS NO KING IN ISRAEL OR JUDAH (7:16), AND SO IT IS AT THIS PRESENT TIME. ISAIAH ALSO SAID THAT HE WOULD COME FROM THE FAMILY LINE OF JESSE (11:1).

ACCORDING TO THE PROPHET MICAH, HE WAS TO BE BORN IN BETHLEHEM OF JUDAH (MICAH 5:2), WHICH HE WAS. MANY PROPHECIES TELL US THAT HE WILL BE OF THE FAMILY LINAGE OF KING DAVID (JEREMIAH 23:5-6; PSALM 89). BOTH JOSEPH AND MARY DESCENDED FROM DAVID.

ISAIAH SAID THE CHRIST WOULD BE CALLED "THE MIGHTY GOD, THE EVERLASTING FATHER". DID NOT JESUS SAY THAT IF YOU HAVE SEEN HIM, YOU HAVE SEEN THE FATHER?

ISAIAH REVEALED THAT A VIRGIN WOULD CONCEIVE (7:14; 59:20), AND THAT HER CHILD WOULD BE BORN (9:6) THAT HE WOULD GROW UP (49:7).

THE PROPHET SAID THAT CHRIST WOULD OPEN BLIND EYES, AND RELEASE PRISONERS (42:7), THAT HE WOULD BE SHEPHERD OF ISRAEL (40:11), AND COME TO ZION AS REDEEMER (59:20).

ISAIAH PREDICTED THAT HE WOULD BE REJECTED BY ISRAEL (53:1, 3. THE PROPHETS ALSO FORESAW HIS SUFFERING. HE WOULD BE BETRAYED BY A FRIEND (PSALM 41:9) FOR 30 PIECES OF SILVER (ZECHARIAH 11:12-13), THAT HE WOULD NOT DEFEND HIMSELF BEFORE HIS ACCUSERS (53:7); HE WOULD BE WOUNDED AND BRUISED (53:5), HIS BEARD PLUCKED OUT (50:6). THEY WOULD STARE AT HIS NAKEDNESS AND SPIT IN HIS FACE (50:6). HE WOULD GIVE HIS BACK TO THE SMITERS (50:6), UNTIL HIS VISAGE WOULD BE MARRED MORE THAN ANY MAN (52:14). THE PROPHET ZECHARIAH (12:10) TELLS US THAT THE SAVIOR WOULD BE PIERCED, AND THAT HIS FRIENDS WOULD SMITE HIM AND CREATE WOUNDS IN HIS HANDS (ZECH. 13:6-7), THAT HE WOULD BE AS A LAMB LED TO THE SLAUGHTER (53:7) AND ALL OF THIS WOULD RESULT IN HIS DEATH (53:8, 12; PSALM 22:15), AND THAT HE WOULD BE BURIED IN A RICH MAN'S TOMB (53:9).

BUT THIS WAS NO TRAGEDY OVER WHICH HE HAD NO CONTROL. DID NOT JESUS SAY THAT NO MAN TAKES HIS LIFE FROM HIM, BUT THAT OF HIS OWN WILL HE LAYS IT DOWN (JOHN 10:18)? ISAIAH SAID THAT IT PLEASED GOD TO BRUISE HIM (53:10), FOR HIS SOUL WAS MADE AN OFFERING FOR SIN (53:10). FOR THE SINS OF OTHERS HE WAS SMITTEN (53:8), FOR HE BORE THE SIN OF MANY (53:12), AND WOULD JUSTIFY MANY IN HIS DEATH (53:11).

YET DEATH WAS NOT THE END. ISAIAH FORESAW THAT HIS LIFE WOULD CONTINUE AFTER DEATH (53:10); HE WOULD BE EXALTED AND EXTOLLED, BE MADE VERY HIGH (52:13). HE WILL BE SALVATION TO THE ENDS OF THE WORLD (49:6). HE WILL NOT FAIL (42:4). MESSIAH WILL BE A NEW COVENANT (42:6).

HE WILL BE A JUDGE, AND SMITE THE EARTH WITH THE ROD OF HIS MOUTH (11:4). HE WILL GOVERN A RENEWED ISRAEL IN A NEW CITY ON A NEW EARTH (66). THERE WILL COME A DAY WHEN EVERY KNEE SHALL BOW TO HIM, AND EVERY TONGUE CONFESS (45:23).

SO TELL ME, WHY ARE YOU SAD? DID NOT THE WOMEN TELL YOU THAT THE ANGELS SAID HE WAS RAISED FROM THE DEAD?
AMAZING!

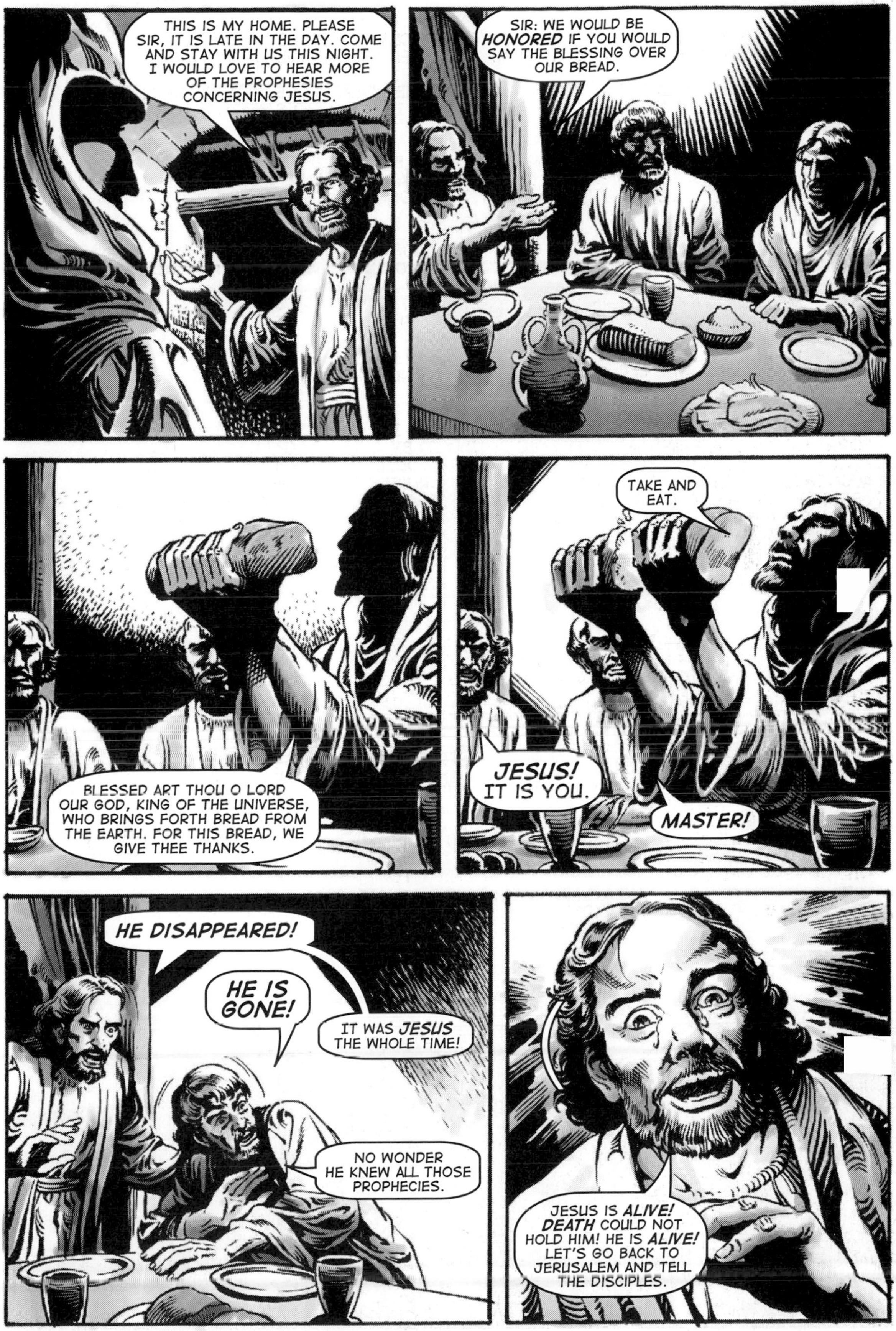
THIS IS MY HOME. PLEASE SIR, IT IS LATE IN THE DAY. COME AND STAY WITH US THIS NIGHT. I WOULD LOVE TO HEAR MORE OF THE PROPHESIES CONCERNING JESUS.
SIR: WE WOULD BE HONORED IF YOU WOULD SAY THE BLESSING OVER OUR BREAD.
BLESSED ART THOU O LORD OUR GOD, KING OF THE UNIVERSE, WHO BRINGS FORTH BREAD FROM THE EARTH. FOR THIS BREAD, WE GIVE THEE THANKS.
TAKE AND EAT.
JESUS! IT IS YOU.
MASTER!
HE DISAPPEARED!
HE IS GONE!
IT WAS JESUS THE WHOLE TIME!
NO WONDER HE KNEW ALL THOSE PROPHECIES.
JESUS IS ALIVE! DEATH COULD NOT HOLD HIM! HE IS ALIVE! LET'S GO BACK TO JERUSALEM AND TELL THE DISCIPLES.

LUKE 24:28-32

270

JOHN 20:26-31; LUKE 24:36-43

MATTHEW 28:18-20; LUKE 24:44-49; JOHN 14:2-4

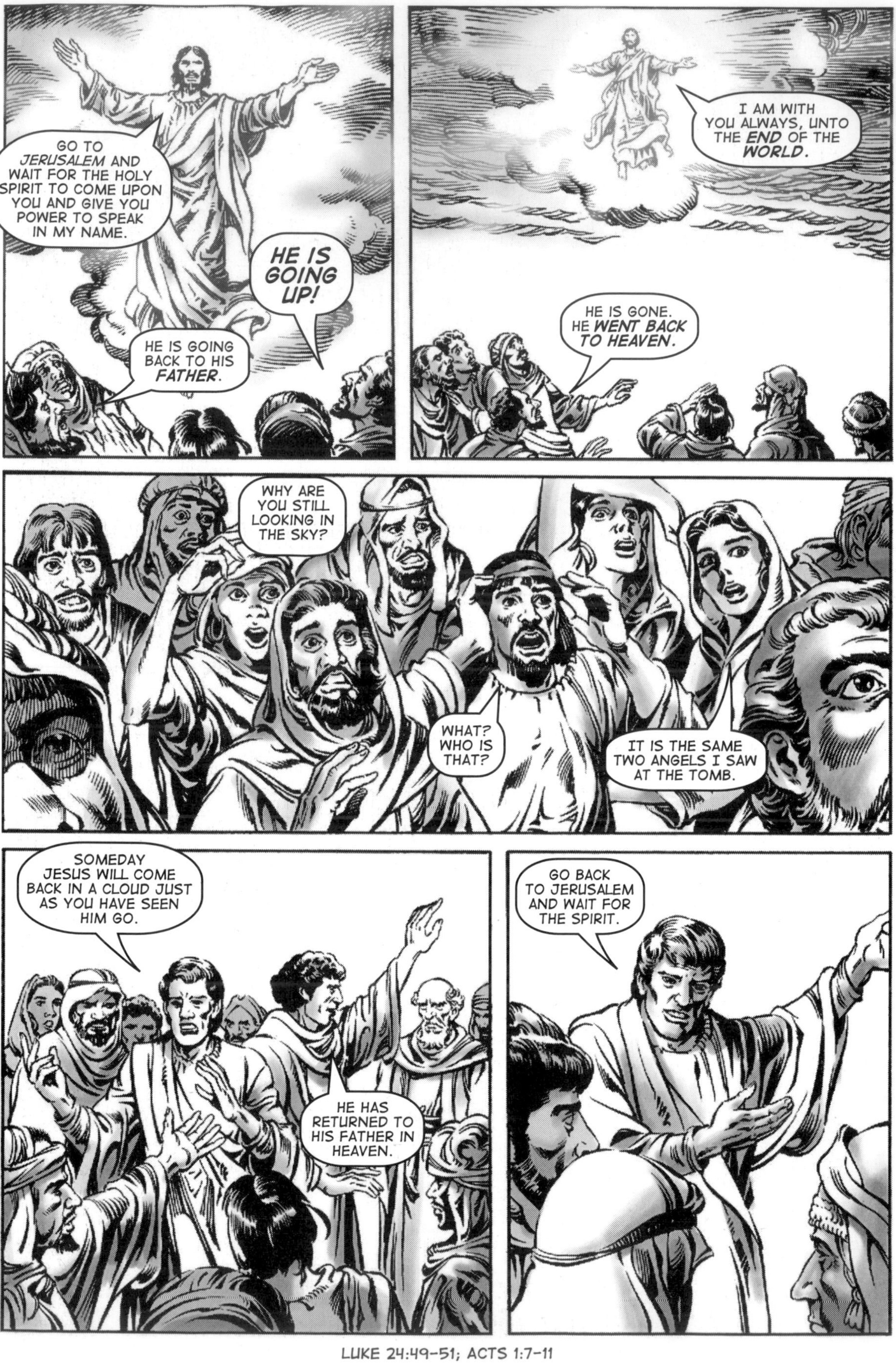
GO TO JERUSALEM AND WAIT FOR THE HOLY SPIRIT TO COME UPON YOU AND GIVE YOU POWER TO SPEAK IN MY NAME.
HE IS GOING UP!
HE IS GOING BACK TO HIS FATHER.
I AM WITH YOU ALWAYS, UNTO THE END OF THE WORLD.
HE IS GONE. HE WENT BACK TO HEAVEN.
WHY ARE YOU STILL LOOKING IN THE SKY?
WHAT? WHO IS THAT?
IT IS THE SAME TWO ANGELS I SAW AT THE TOMB.
SOMEDAY JESUS WILL COME BACK IN A CLOUD JUST AS YOU HAVE SEEN HIM GO.
HE HAS RETURNED TO HIS FATHER IN HEAVEN.
GO BACK TO JERUSALEM AND WAIT FOR THE SPIRIT.

LUKE 24:49-51; ACTS 1:7-11

ACTS 1:12-14, 2:1-13, 32, 36

ACTS 2:27, 37-41

ACTS 3:1-11

ACTS 3:12, 14-19, 4:1-3

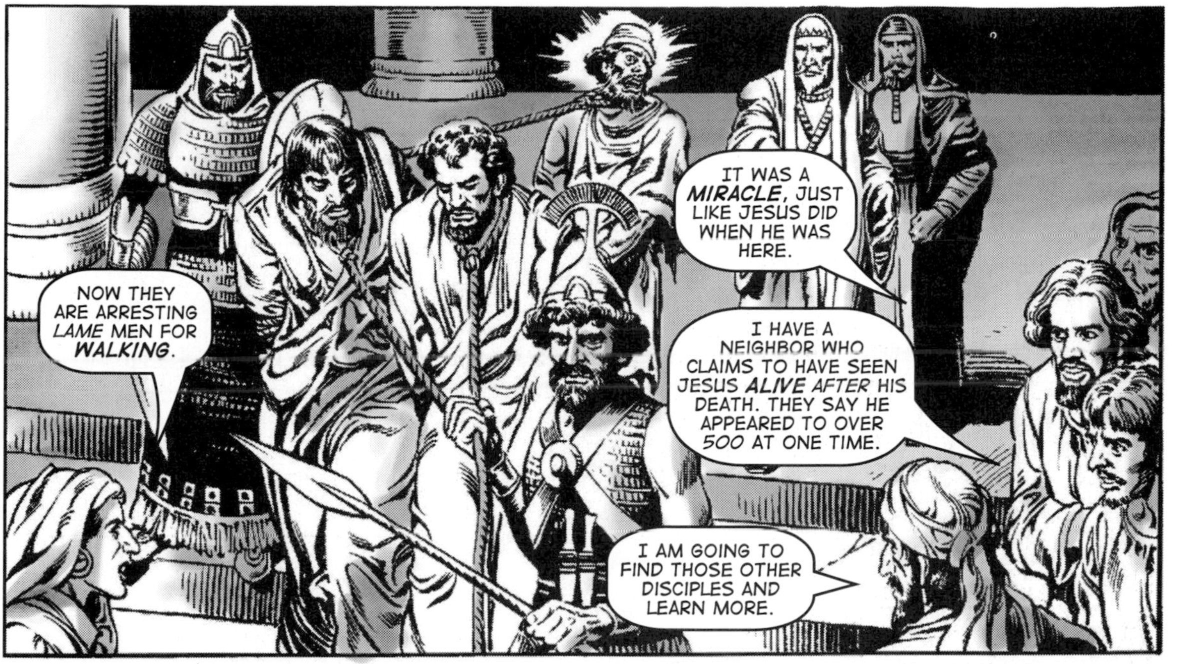
NOW THEY ARE ARRESTING *LAME* MEN FOR ***WALKING***.
IT WAS A ***MIRACLE***, JUST LIKE JESUS DID WHEN HE WAS HERE.
I HAVE A NEIGHBOR WHO CLAIMS TO HAVE SEEN JESUS *ALIVE AFTER* HIS DEATH. THEY SAY HE APPEARED TO OVER *500* AT ONE TIME.
I AM GOING TO FIND THOSE OTHER DISCIPLES AND LEARN MORE.

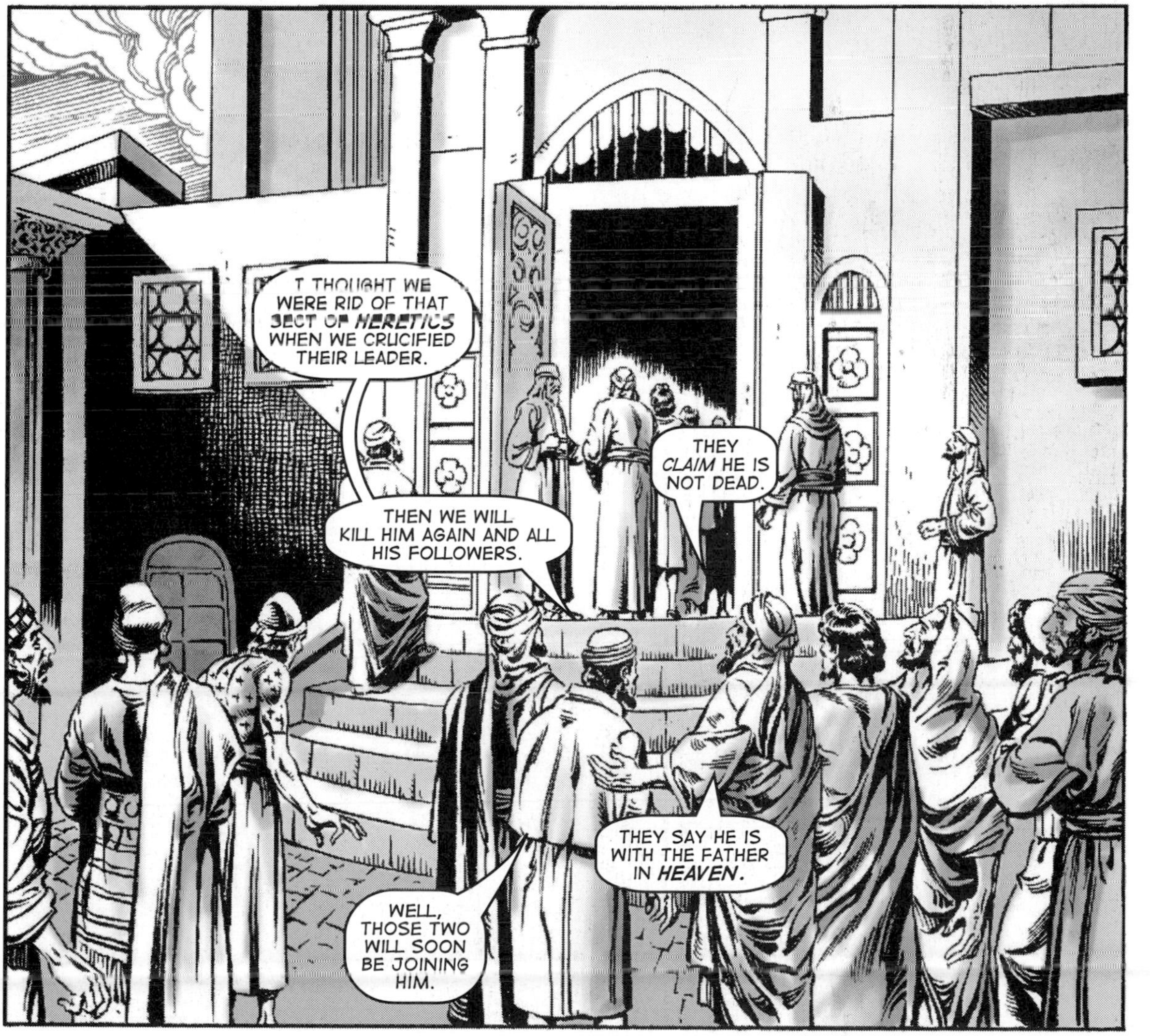
I THOUGHT WE WERE RID OF THAT SECT OF ***HERETICS*** WHEN WE CRUCIFIED THEIR LEADER.
THEY *CLAIM* HE IS NOT DEAD.
THEN WE WILL KILL HIM AGAIN AND ALL HIS FOLLOWERS.
THEY SAY HE IS WITH THE FATHER IN ***HEAVEN***.
WELL, THOSE TWO WILL SOON BE JOINING HIM.

ACTS 4:3-6

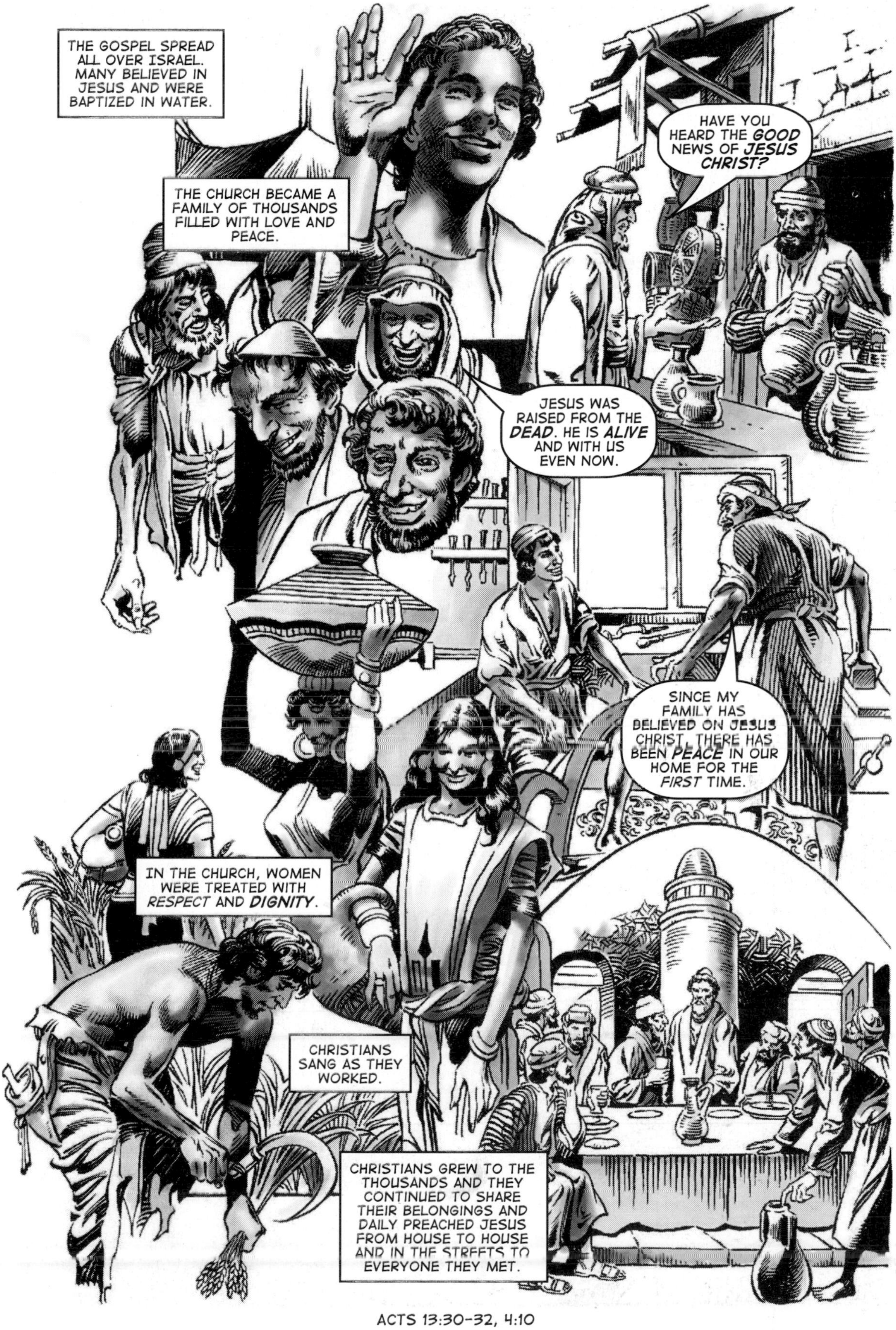
THE GOSPEL SPREAD ALL OVER ISRAEL. MANY BELIEVED IN JESUS AND WERE BAPTIZED IN WATER.
HAVE YOU HEARD THE ***GOOD*** NEWS OF ***JESUS CHRIST?***
THE CHURCH BECAME A FAMILY OF THOUSANDS FILLED WITH LOVE AND PEACE.
JESUS WAS RAISED FROM THE ***DEAD***. HE IS ***ALIVE*** AND WITH US EVEN NOW.
SINCE MY FAMILY HAS BELIEVED ON JESUS CHRIST, THERE HAS BEEN ***PEACE*** IN OUR HOME FOR THE *FIRST* TIME.
IN THE CHURCH, WOMEN WERE TREATED WITH *RESPECT* AND ***DIGNITY***.
CHRISTIANS SANG AS THEY WORKED.
CHRISTIANS GREW TO THE THOUSANDS AND THEY CONTINUED TO SHARE THEIR BELONGINGS AND DAILY PREACHED JESUS FROM HOUSE TO HOUSE AND IN THE STREETS TO EVERYONE THEY MET.

ACTS 13:30-32, 4:10

ACTS 7:1-57

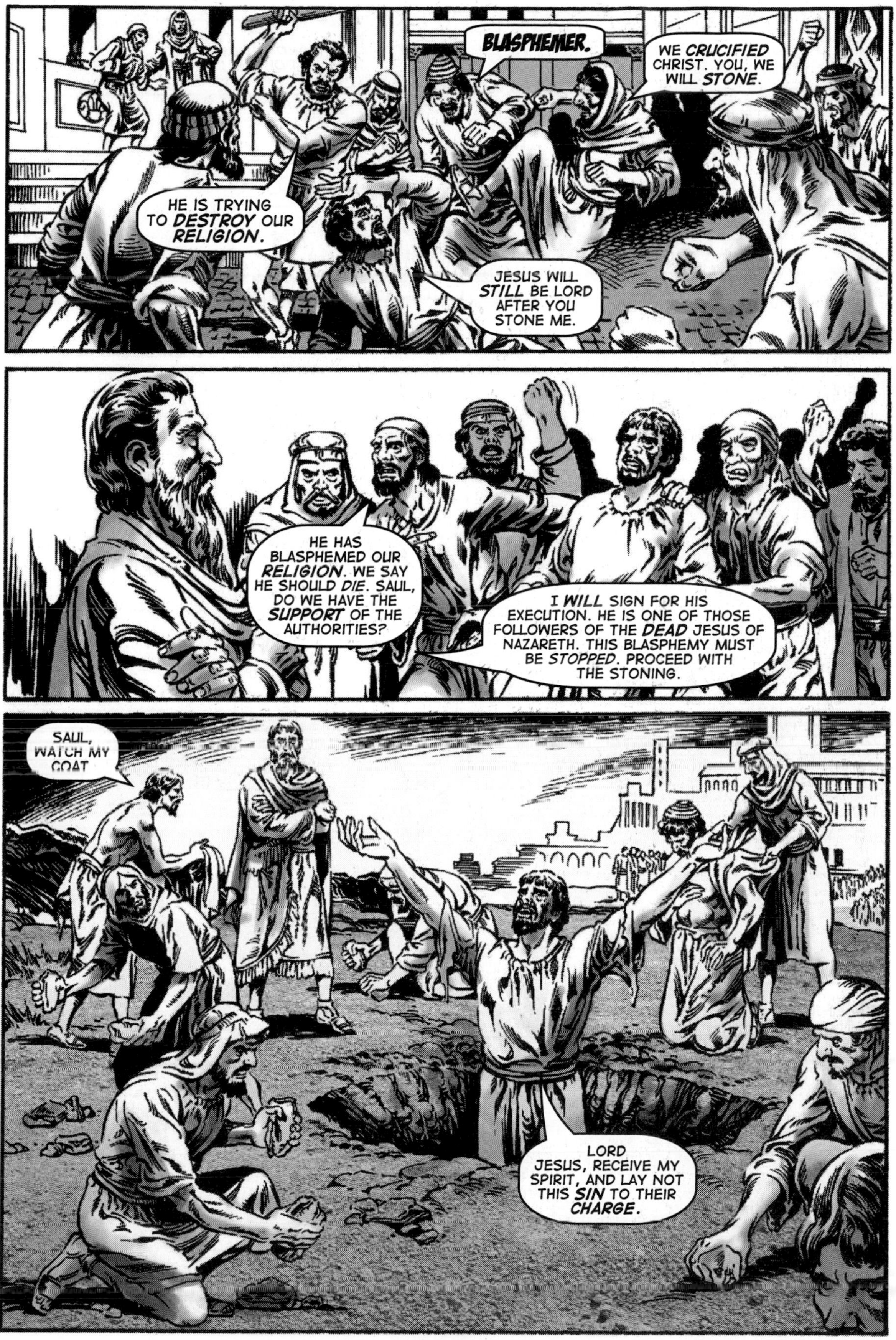
BLASPHEMER.
WE CRUCIFIED CHRIST. YOU, WE WILL STONE.
HE IS TRYING TO DESTROY OUR RELIGION.
JESUS WILL STILL BE LORD AFTER YOU STONE ME.
HE HAS BLASPHEMED OUR RELIGION. WE SAY HE SHOULD DIE. SAUL, DO WE HAVE THE SUPPORT OF THE AUTHORITIES?
I WILL SIGN FOR HIS EXECUTION. HE IS ONE OF THOSE FOLLOWERS OF THE DEAD JESUS OF NAZARETH. THIS BLASPHEMY MUST BE STOPPED. PROCEED WITH THE STONING.
SAUL, WATCH MY COAT
LORD JESUS, RECEIVE MY SPIRIT, AND LAY NOT THIS SIN TO THEIR CHARGE.

ACTS 7:58–59

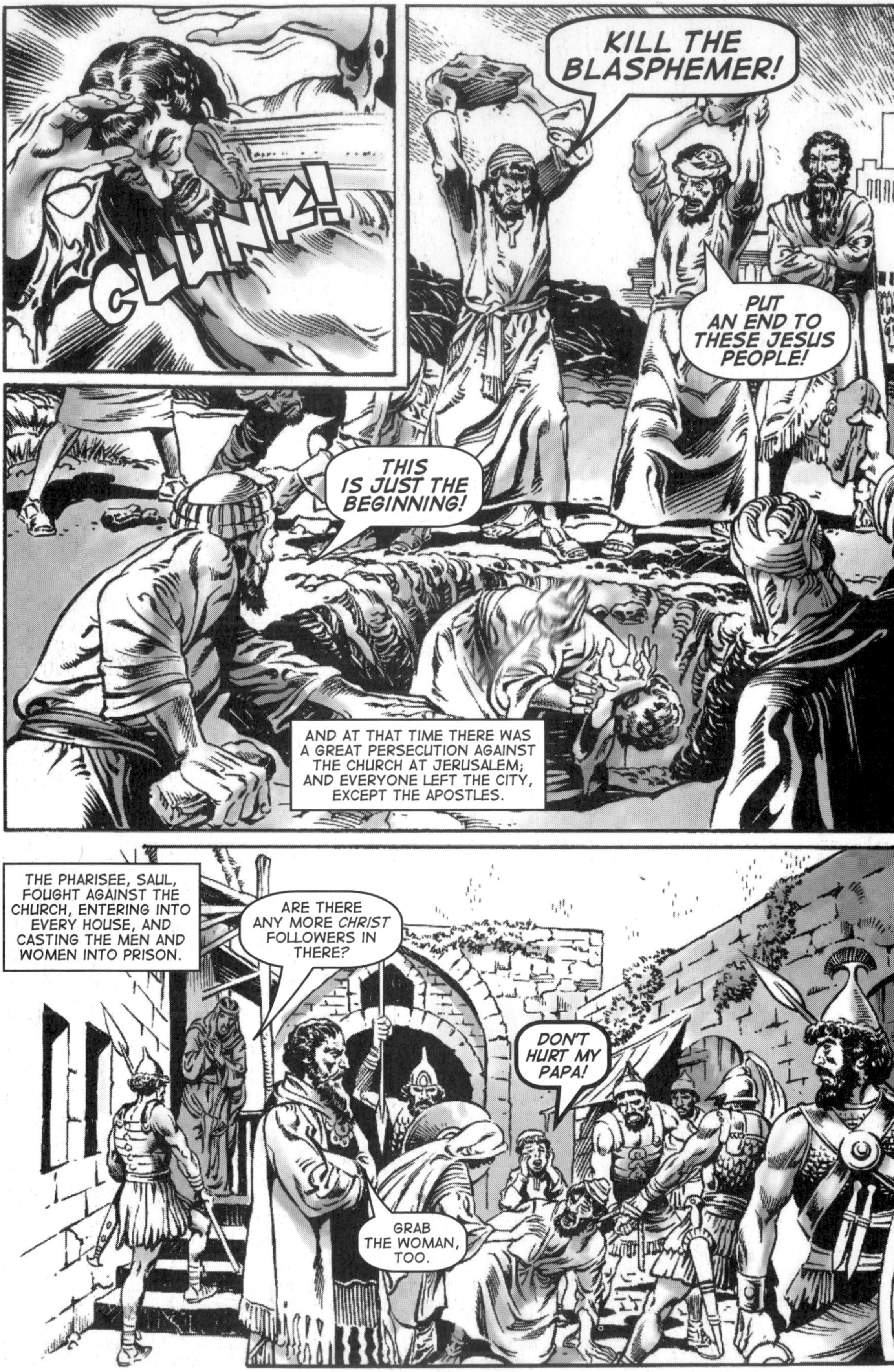
CLUNK!
KILL THE BLASPHEMER!
PUT AN END TO THESE JESUS PEOPLE!
THIS IS JUST THE BEGINNING!
AND AT THAT TIME THERE WAS A GREAT PERSECUTION AGAINST THE CHURCH AT JERUSALEM; AND EVERYONE LEFT THE CITY, EXCEPT THE APOSTLES.
THE PHARISEE, SAUL, FOUGHT AGAINST THE CHURCH, ENTERING INTO EVERY HOUSE, AND CASTING THE MEN AND WOMEN INTO PRISON.
ARE THERE ANY MORE *CHRIST* FOLLOWERS IN THERE?
DON'T HURT MY PAPA!
GRAB THE WOMAN, TOO.

ACTS 7:59–8:3

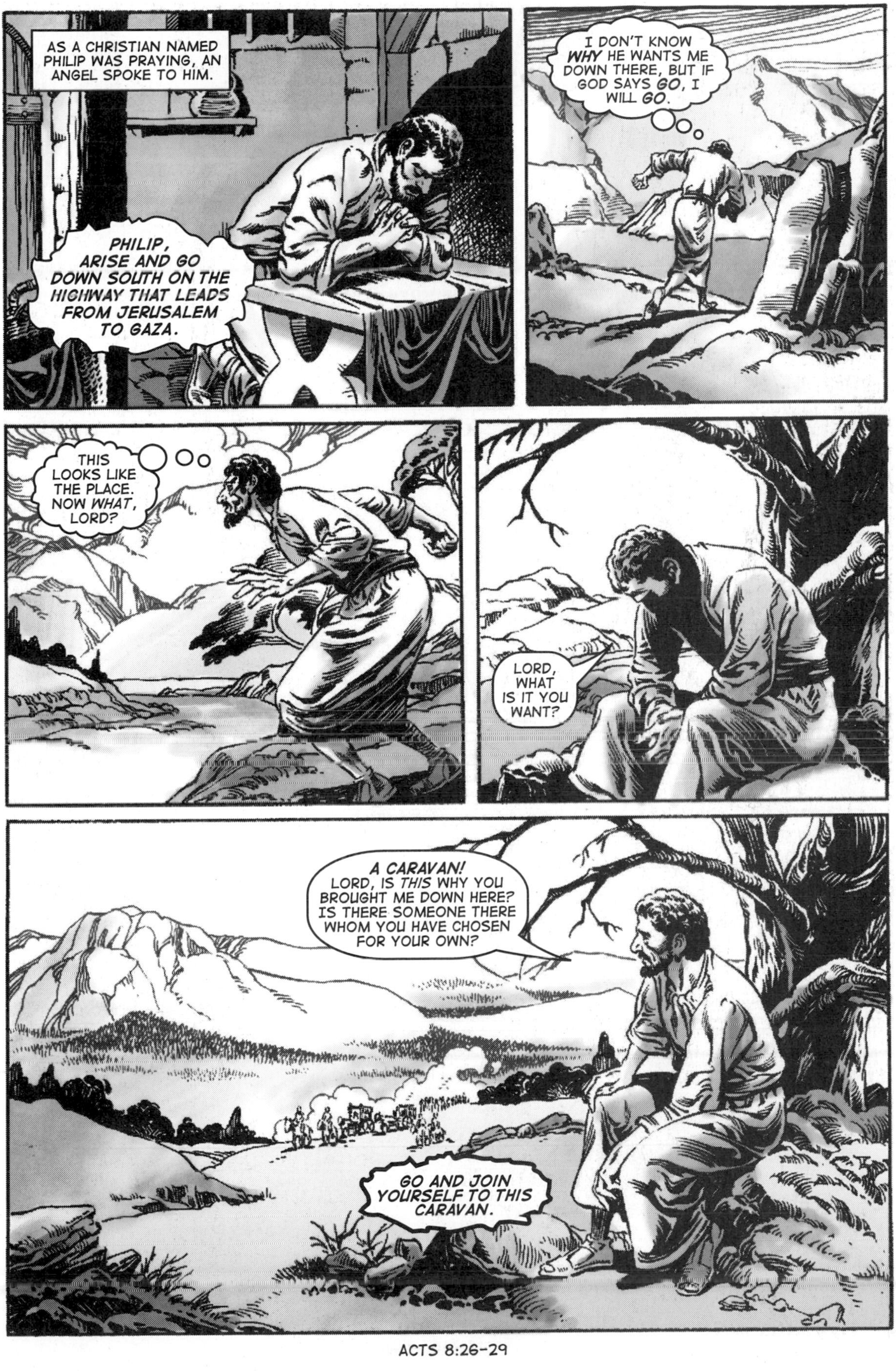
AS A CHRISTIAN NAMED PHILIP WAS PRAYING, AN ANGEL SPOKE TO HIM.
PHILIP, ARISE AND GO DOWN SOUTH ON THE HIGHWAY THAT LEADS FROM JERUSALEM TO GAZA.
I DON'T KNOW WHY HE WANTS ME DOWN THERE, BUT IF GOD SAYS GO, I WILL GO.
THIS LOOKS LIKE THE PLACE. NOW WHAT, LORD?
LORD, WHAT IS IT YOU WANT?
A CARAVAN! LORD, IS THIS WHY YOU BROUGHT ME DOWN HERE? IS THERE SOMEONE THERE WHOM YOU HAVE CHOSEN FOR YOUR OWN?
GO AND JOIN YOURSELF TO THIS CARAVAN.

ACTS 8:26-29

ACTS 8:27, 30-34

ISAIAH 53:3-10; ACTS 8:35; ROMANS 2:16

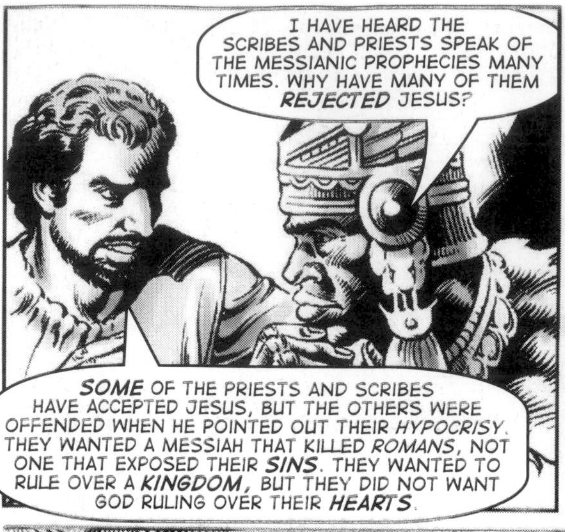
I HAVE HEARD THE SCRIBES AND PRIESTS SPEAK OF THE MESSIANIC PROPHECIES MANY TIMES. WHY HAVE MANY OF THEM *REJECTED* JESUS?
SOME OF THE PRIESTS AND SCRIBES HAVE ACCEPTED JESUS, BUT THE OTHERS WERE OFFENDED WHEN HE POINTED OUT THEIR *HYPOCRISY*. THEY WANTED A MESSIAH THAT KILLED *ROMANS*, NOT ONE THAT EXPOSED THEIR *SINS*. THEY WANTED TO RULE OVER A *KINGDOM*, BUT THEY DID NOT WANT GOD RULING OVER THEIR *HEARTS*.

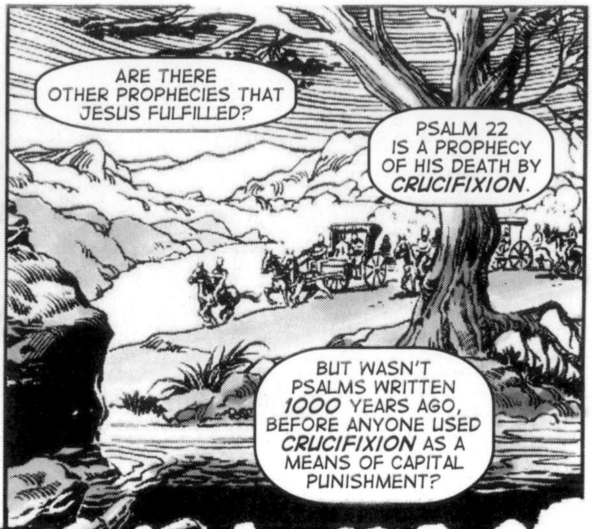
ARE THERE OTHER PROPHECIES THAT JESUS FULFILLED?
PSALM 22 IS A PROPHECY OF HIS DEATH BY *CRUCIFIXION*.
BUT WASN'T PSALMS WRITTEN *1000* YEARS AGO, BEFORE ANYONE USED *CRUCIFIXION* AS A MEANS OF CAPITAL PUNISHMENT?

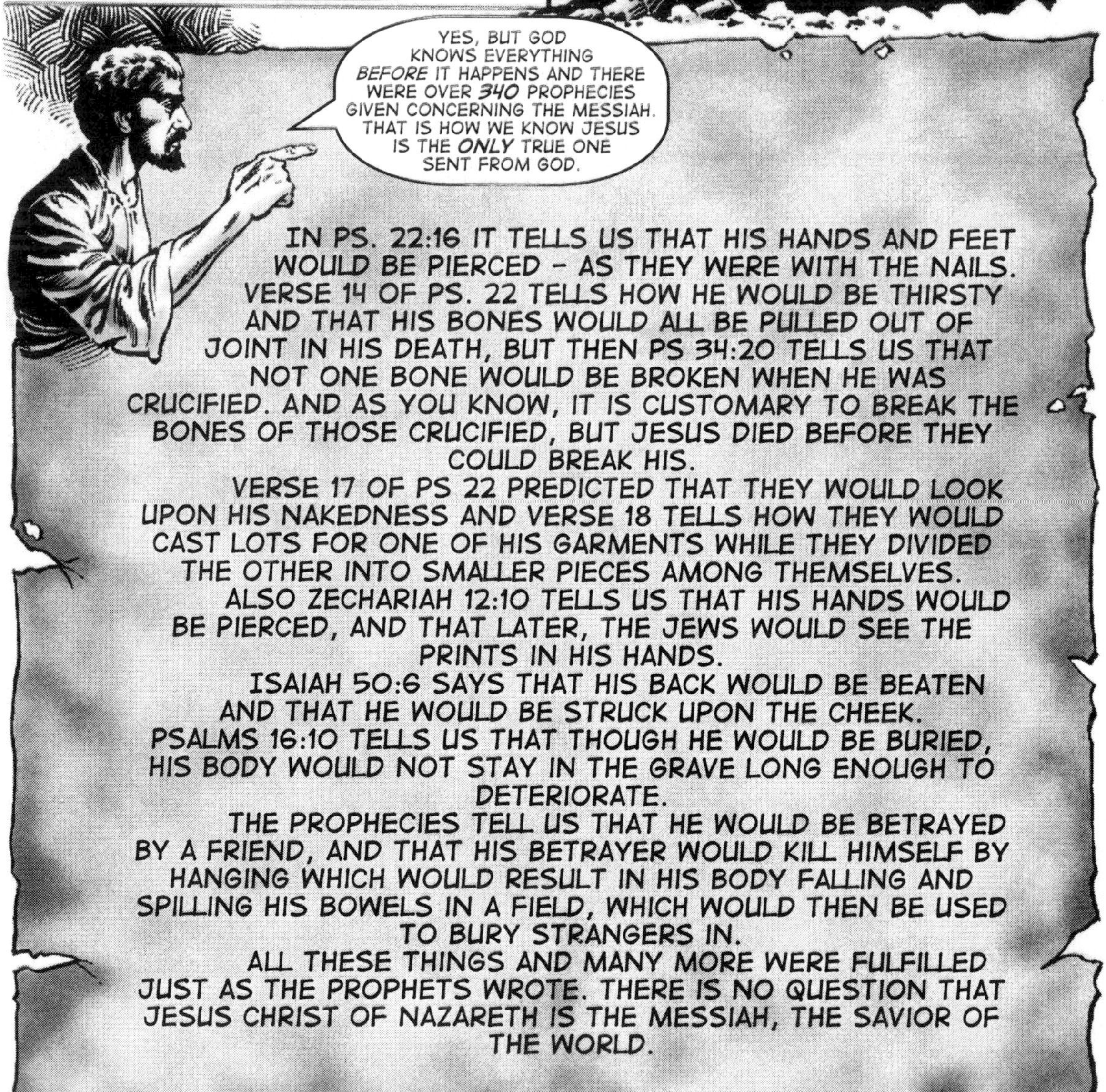
YES, BUT GOD KNOWS EVERYTHING *BEFORE* IT HAPPENS AND THERE WERE OVER *340* PROPHECIES GIVEN CONCERNING THE MESSIAH. THAT IS HOW WE KNOW JESUS IS THE *ONLY* TRUE ONE SENT FROM GOD.
IN PS. 22:16 IT TELLS US THAT HIS HANDS AND FEET WOULD BE PIERCED - AS THEY WERE WITH THE NAILS. VERSE 14 OF PS. 22 TELLS HOW HE WOULD BE THIRSTY AND THAT HIS BONES WOULD ALL BE PULLED OUT OF JOINT IN HIS DEATH, BUT THEN PS 34:20 TELLS US THAT NOT ONE BONE WOULD BE BROKEN WHEN HE WAS CRUCIFIED. AND AS YOU KNOW, IT IS CUSTOMARY TO BREAK THE BONES OF THOSE CRUCIFIED, BUT JESUS DIED BEFORE THEY COULD BREAK HIS.
VERSE 17 OF PS 22 PREDICTED THAT THEY WOULD LOOK UPON HIS NAKEDNESS AND VERSE 18 TELLS HOW THEY WOULD CAST LOTS FOR ONE OF HIS GARMENTS WHILE THEY DIVIDED THE OTHER INTO SMALLER PIECES AMONG THEMSELVES.
ALSO ZECHARIAH 12:10 TELLS US THAT HIS HANDS WOULD BE PIERCED, AND THAT LATER, THE JEWS WOULD SEE THE PRINTS IN HIS HANDS.
ISAIAH 50:6 SAYS THAT HIS BACK WOULD BE BEATEN AND THAT HE WOULD BE STRUCK UPON THE CHEEK. PSALMS 16:10 TELLS US THAT THOUGH HE WOULD BE BURIED, HIS BODY WOULD NOT STAY IN THE GRAVE LONG ENOUGH TO DETERIORATE.
THE PROPHECIES TELL US THAT HE WOULD BE BETRAYED BY A FRIEND, AND THAT HIS BETRAYER WOULD KILL HIMSELF BY HANGING WHICH WOULD RESULT IN HIS BODY FALLING AND SPILLING HIS BOWELS IN A FIELD, WHICH WOULD THEN BE USED TO BURY STRANGERS IN.
ALL THESE THINGS AND MANY MORE WERE FULFILLED JUST AS THE PROPHETS WROTE. THERE IS NO QUESTION THAT JESUS CHRIST OF NAZARETH IS THE MESSIAH, THE SAVIOR OF THE WORLD.

PSALM 22:6, 17-18, 16:10, 34:20; ISAIAH 50:6, ZECHARIAH 12:10

ACTS 8:36-39

288

MATTHEW 16:24; MARK 16:24; ACTS 9:1–2

ACTS 9:1-6

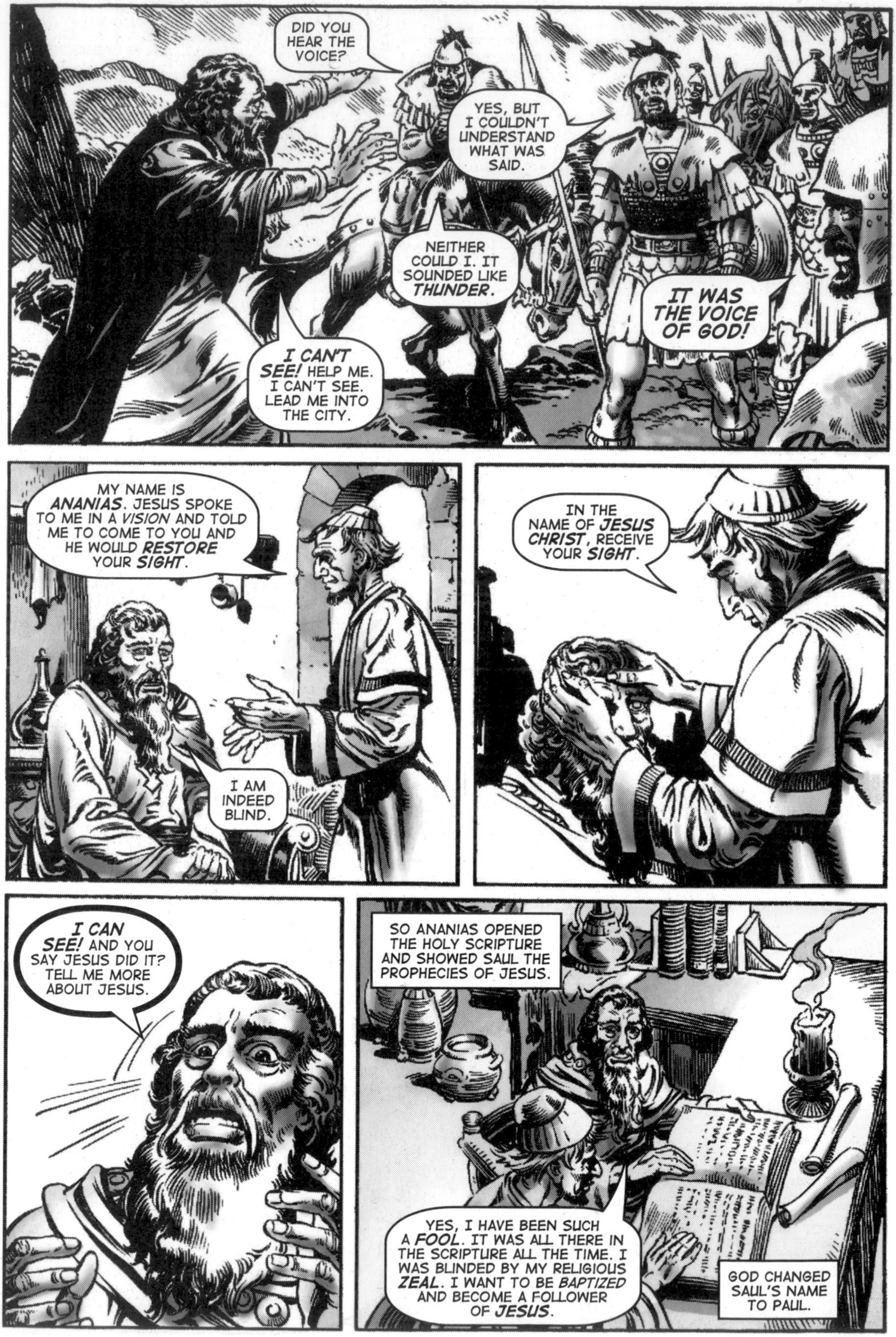
DID YOU HEAR THE VOICE?
YES, BUT I COULDN'T UNDERSTAND WHAT WAS SAID.
NEITHER COULD I. IT SOUNDED LIKE **THUNDER**.
IT WAS THE VOICE OF GOD!
I CAN'T SEE! HELP ME. I CAN'T SEE. LEAD ME INTO THE CITY.
MY NAME IS **ANANIAS**. JESUS SPOKE TO ME IN A *VISION* AND TOLD ME TO COME TO YOU AND HE WOULD **RESTORE** YOUR **SIGHT**.
I AM INDEED BLIND.
IN THE NAME OF **JESUS CHRIST**, RECEIVE YOUR **SIGHT**.
I CAN SEE! AND YOU SAY JESUS DID IT? TELL ME MORE ABOUT JESUS.
SO ANANIAS OPENED THE HOLY SCRIPTURE AND SHOWED SAUL THE PROPHECIES OF JESUS.
YES, I HAVE BEEN SUCH A **FOOL**. IT WAS ALL THERE IN THE SCRIPTURE ALL THE TIME. I WAS BLINDED BY MY RELIGIOUS **ZEAL**. I WANT TO BE *BAPTIZED* AND BECOME A FOLLOWER OF **JESUS**.
GOD CHANGED SAUL'S NAME TO PAUL.

ACTS 9:7-19

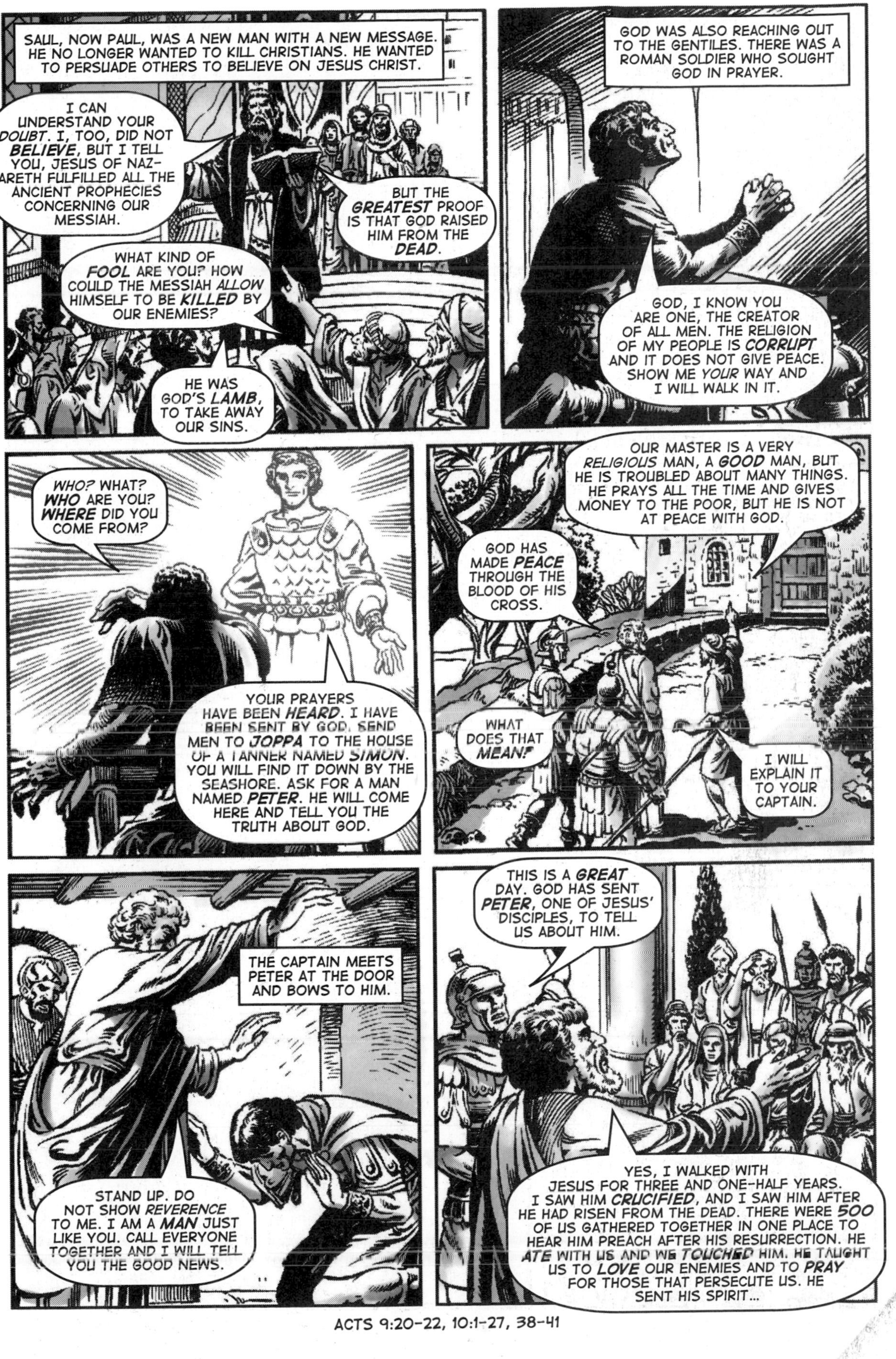
SAUL, NOW PAUL, WAS A NEW MAN WITH A NEW MESSAGE. HE NO LONGER WANTED TO KILL CHRISTIANS. HE WANTED TO PERSUADE OTHERS TO BELIEVE ON JESUS CHRIST.
I CAN UNDERSTAND YOUR *DOUBT*. I, TOO, DID NOT ***BELIEVE***, BUT I TELL YOU, JESUS OF NAZARETH FULFILLED ALL THE ANCIENT PROPHECIES CONCERNING OUR MESSIAH.
BUT THE ***GREATEST*** PROOF IS THAT GOD RAISED HIM FROM THE ***DEAD***.
WHAT KIND OF ***FOOL*** ARE YOU? HOW COULD THE MESSIAH *ALLOW* HIMSELF TO BE ***KILLED*** BY OUR ENEMIES?
HE WAS GOD'S ***LAMB***, TO TAKE AWAY OUR SINS.
GOD WAS ALSO REACHING OUT TO THE GENTILES. THERE WAS A ROMAN SOLDIER WHO SOUGHT GOD IN PRAYER.
GOD, I KNOW YOU ARE ONE, THE CREATOR OF ALL MEN. THE RELIGION OF MY PEOPLE IS ***CORRUPT*** AND IT DOES NOT GIVE PEACE. SHOW ME *YOUR* WAY AND I WILL WALK IN IT.
WHO? WHAT? ***WHO*** *ARE YOU?* ***WHERE*** *DID YOU COME FROM?*
YOUR PRAYERS HAVE BEEN ***HEARD***. I HAVE BEEN SENT BY GOD. SEND MEN TO ***JOPPA*** TO THE HOUSE OF A TANNER NAMED ***SIMON***. YOU WILL FIND IT DOWN BY THE SEASHORE. ASK FOR A MAN NAMED ***PETER***. HE WILL COME HERE AND TELL YOU THE TRUTH ABOUT GOD.
OUR MASTER IS A VERY *RELIGIOUS* MAN, A ***GOOD*** MAN, BUT HE IS TROUBLED ABOUT MANY THINGS. HE PRAYS ALL THE TIME AND GIVES MONEY TO THE POOR, BUT HE IS NOT AT PEACE WITH GOD.
GOD HAS MADE ***PEACE*** THROUGH THE BLOOD OF HIS CROSS.
WHAT DOES THAT ***MEAN?***
I WILL EXPLAIN IT TO YOUR CAPTAIN.
THE CAPTAIN MEETS PETER AT THE DOOR AND BOWS TO HIM.
STAND UP. DO NOT SHOW *REVERENCE* TO ME. I AM A ***MAN*** JUST LIKE YOU. CALL EVERYONE TOGETHER AND I WILL TELL YOU THE GOOD NEWS.
THIS IS A ***GREAT*** DAY. GOD HAS SENT ***PETER***, ONE OF JESUS' DISCIPLES, TO TELL US ABOUT HIM.
YES, I WALKED WITH JESUS FOR THREE AND ONE-HALF YEARS. I SAW HIM ***CRUCIFIED***, AND I SAW HIM AFTER HE HAD RISEN FROM THE DEAD. THERE WERE ***500*** OF US GATHERED TOGETHER IN ONE PLACE TO HEAR HIM PREACH AFTER HIS RESURRECTION. HE ***ATE*** WITH US AND WE ***TOUCHED*** HIM. HE TAUGHT US TO ***LOVE*** OUR ENEMIES AND TO ***PRAY*** FOR THOSE THAT PERSECUTE US. HE SENT HIS SPIRIT...

ACTS 9:20-22, 10:1-27, 38-41

292

ACTS 14:18–20

ACTS 14:19-20, 16:23-25; 2 CORINTHIANS 11:24-25

1 CORINTHIANS 10:14, 12:12–13, 18; 2 CORINTHIANS 11:25; GALATIANS 2:6; EPHESIANS 2:19

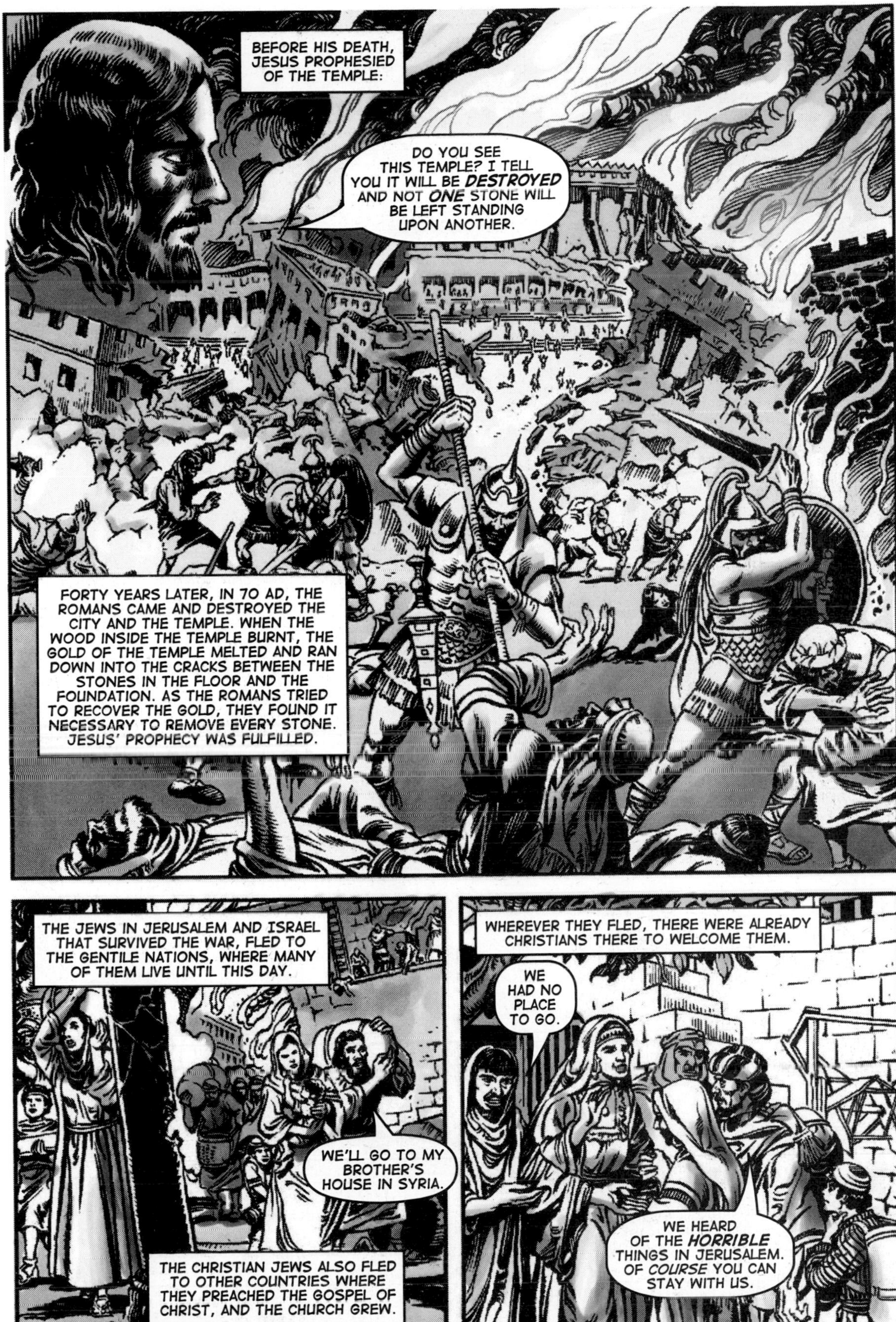
BEFORE HIS DEATH, JESUS PROPHESIED OF THE TEMPLE:
DO YOU SEE THIS TEMPLE? I TELL YOU IT WILL BE *DESTROYED* AND NOT *ONE* STONE WILL BE LEFT STANDING UPON ANOTHER.
FORTY YEARS LATER, IN 70 AD, THE ROMANS CAME AND DESTROYED THE CITY AND THE TEMPLE. WHEN THE WOOD INSIDE THE TEMPLE BURNT, THE GOLD OF THE TEMPLE MELTED AND RAN DOWN INTO THE CRACKS BETWEEN THE STONES IN THE FLOOR AND THE FOUNDATION. AS THE ROMANS TRIED TO RECOVER THE GOLD, THEY FOUND IT NECESSARY TO REMOVE EVERY STONE. JESUS' PROPHECY WAS FULFILLED.
THE JEWS IN JERUSALEM AND ISRAEL THAT SURVIVED THE WAR, FLED TO THE GENTILE NATIONS, WHERE MANY OF THEM LIVE UNTIL THIS DAY.
WE'LL GO TO MY BROTHER'S HOUSE IN SYRIA.
THE CHRISTIAN JEWS ALSO FLED TO OTHER COUNTRIES WHERE THEY PREACHED THE GOSPEL OF CHRIST, AND THE CHURCH GREW.
WHEREVER THEY FLED, THERE WERE ALREADY CHRISTIANS THERE TO WELCOME THEM.
WE HAD NO PLACE TO GO.
WE HEARD OF THE *HORRIBLE* THINGS IN JERUSALEM. OF *COURSE* YOU CAN STAY WITH US.

MATTHEW 24:2; LUKE 19:43-44

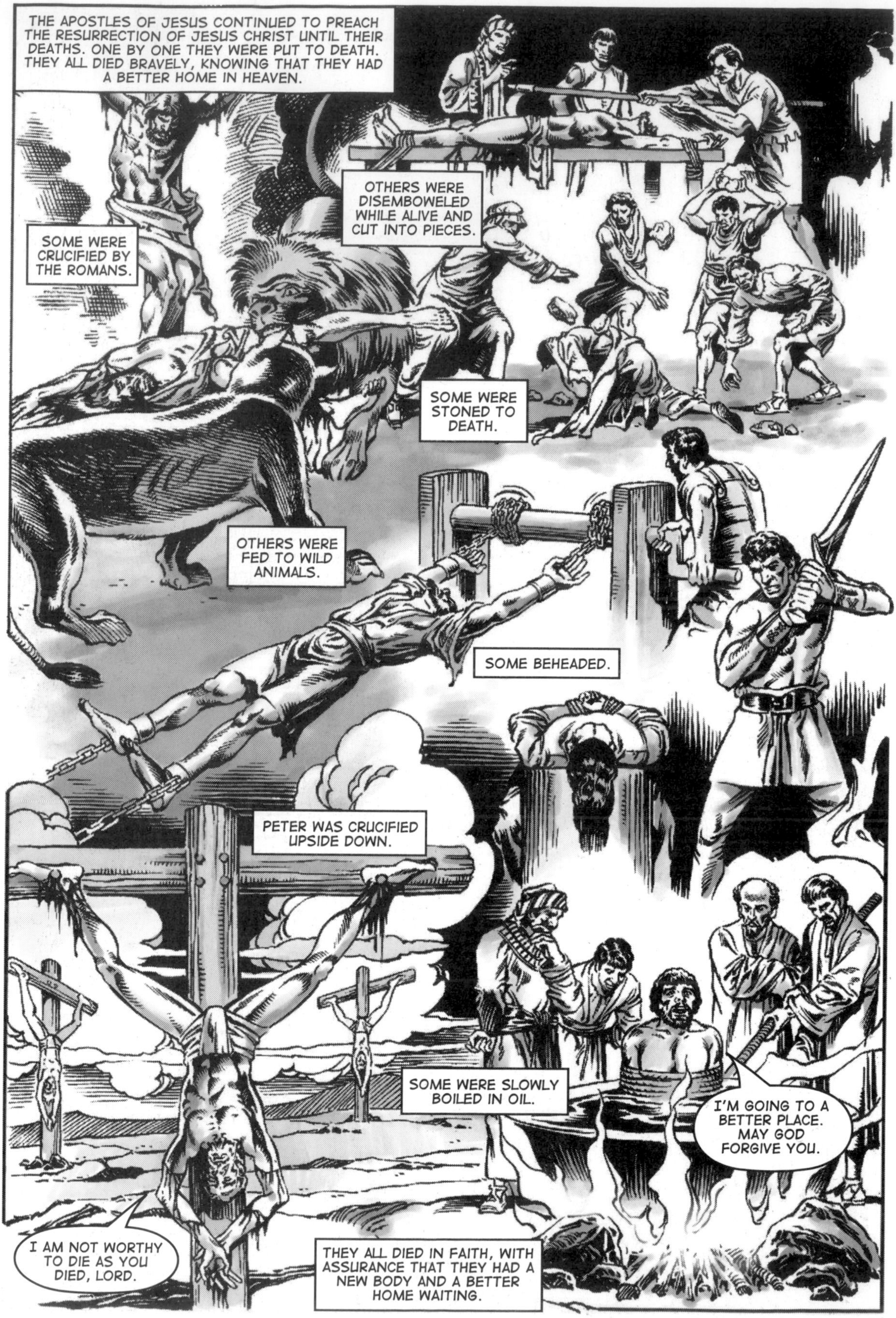
THE APOSTLES OF JESUS CONTINUED TO PREACH THE RESURRECTION OF JESUS CHRIST UNTIL THEIR DEATHS. ONE BY ONE THEY WERE PUT TO DEATH. THEY ALL DIED BRAVELY, KNOWING THAT THEY HAD A BETTER HOME IN HEAVEN.
SOME WERE CRUCIFIED BY THE ROMANS.
OTHERS WERE DISEMBOWELED WHILE ALIVE AND CUT INTO PIECES.
SOME WERE STONED TO DEATH.
OTHERS WERE FED TO WILD ANIMALS.
SOME BEHEADED.
PETER WAS CRUCIFIED UPSIDE DOWN.
SOME WERE SLOWLY BOILED IN OIL.
I'M GOING TO A BETTER PLACE. MAY GOD FORGIVE YOU.
I AM NOT WORTHY TO DIE AS YOU DIED, LORD.
THEY ALL DIED IN FAITH, WITH ASSURANCE THAT THEY HAD A NEW BODY AND A BETTER HOME WAITING.

MATTHEW 14:10; JOHN 21:18

1 THESSALONIANS 14:4, 4:16-17; 2 THESSALONIANS 2:3-4; REVELATION 1:9, 11, 8:1-13, 9:18, 13:16, 20:4

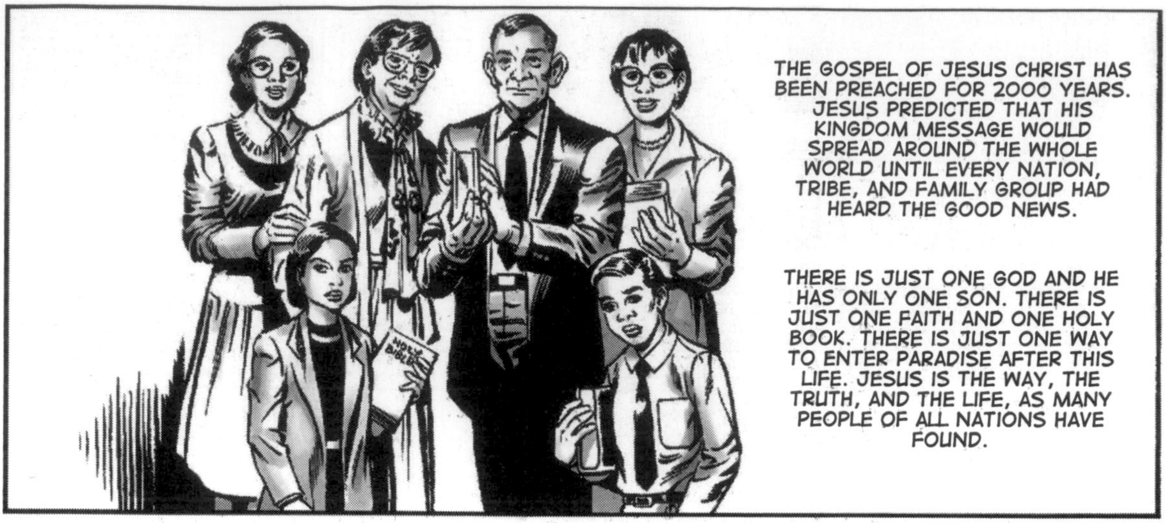
THE GOSPEL OF JESUS CHRIST HAS BEEN PREACHED FOR 2000 YEARS. JESUS PREDICTED THAT HIS KINGDOM MESSAGE WOULD SPREAD AROUND THE WHOLE WORLD UNTIL EVERY NATION, TRIBE, AND FAMILY GROUP HAD HEARD THE GOOD NEWS.
THERE IS JUST ONE GOD AND HE HAS ONLY ONE SON. THERE IS JUST ONE FAITH AND ONE HOLY BOOK. THERE IS JUST ONE WAY TO ENTER PARADISE AFTER THIS LIFE. JESUS IS THE WAY, THE TRUTH, AND THE LIFE, AS MANY PEOPLE OF ALL NATIONS HAVE FOUND.

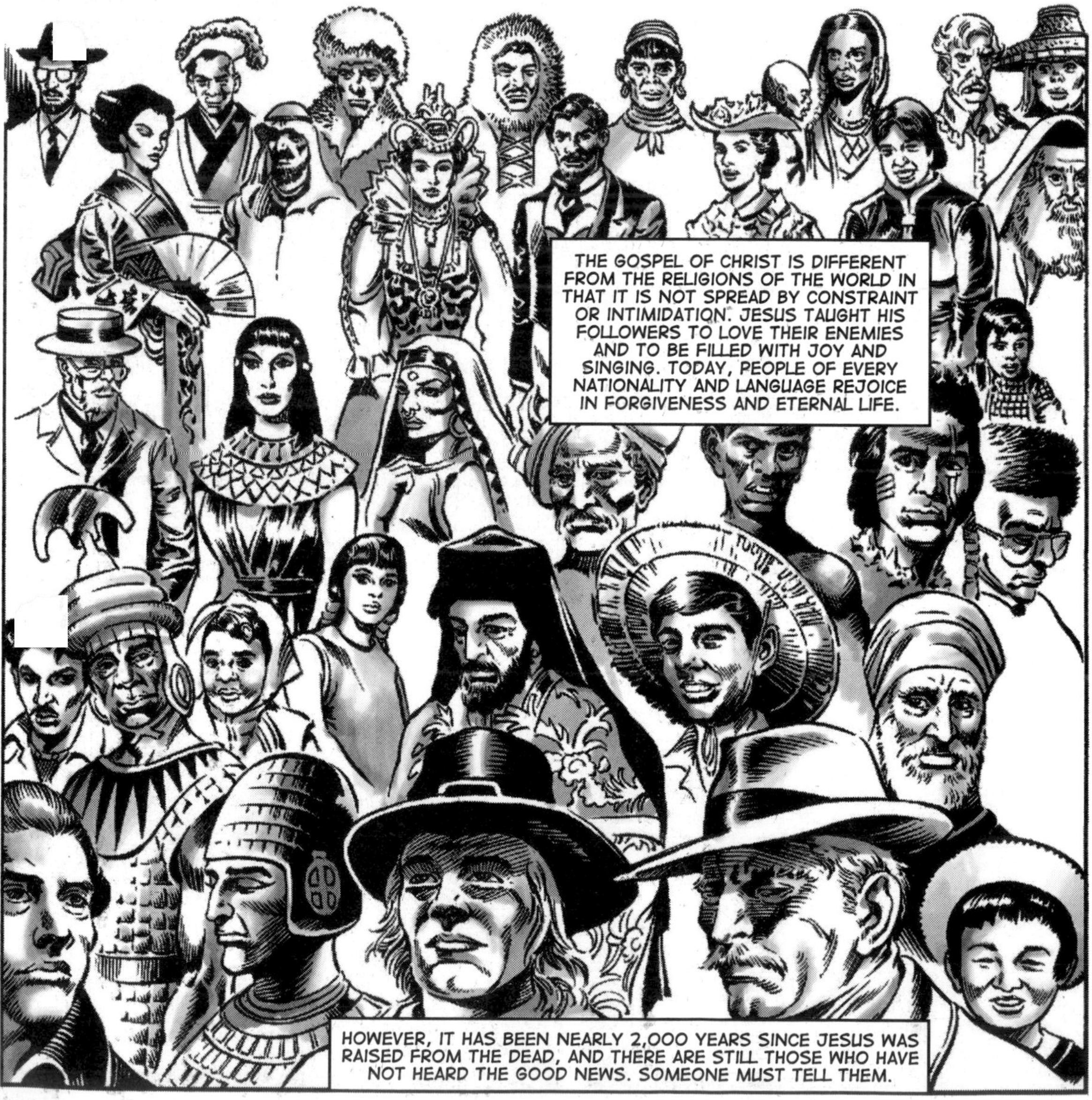
THE GOSPEL OF CHRIST IS DIFFERENT FROM THE RELIGIONS OF THE WORLD IN THAT IT IS NOT SPREAD BY CONSTRAINT OR INTIMIDATION. JESUS TAUGHT HIS FOLLOWERS TO LOVE THEIR ENEMIES AND TO BE FILLED WITH JOY AND SINGING. TODAY, PEOPLE OF EVERY NATIONALITY AND LANGUAGE REJOICE IN FORGIVENESS AND ETERNAL LIFE.
HOWEVER, IT HAS BEEN NEARLY 2,000 YEARS SINCE JESUS WAS RAISED FROM THE DEAD, AND THERE ARE STILL THOSE WHO HAVE NOT HEARD THE GOOD NEWS. SOMEONE MUST TELL THEM.

JOHN 3:16, 14:6

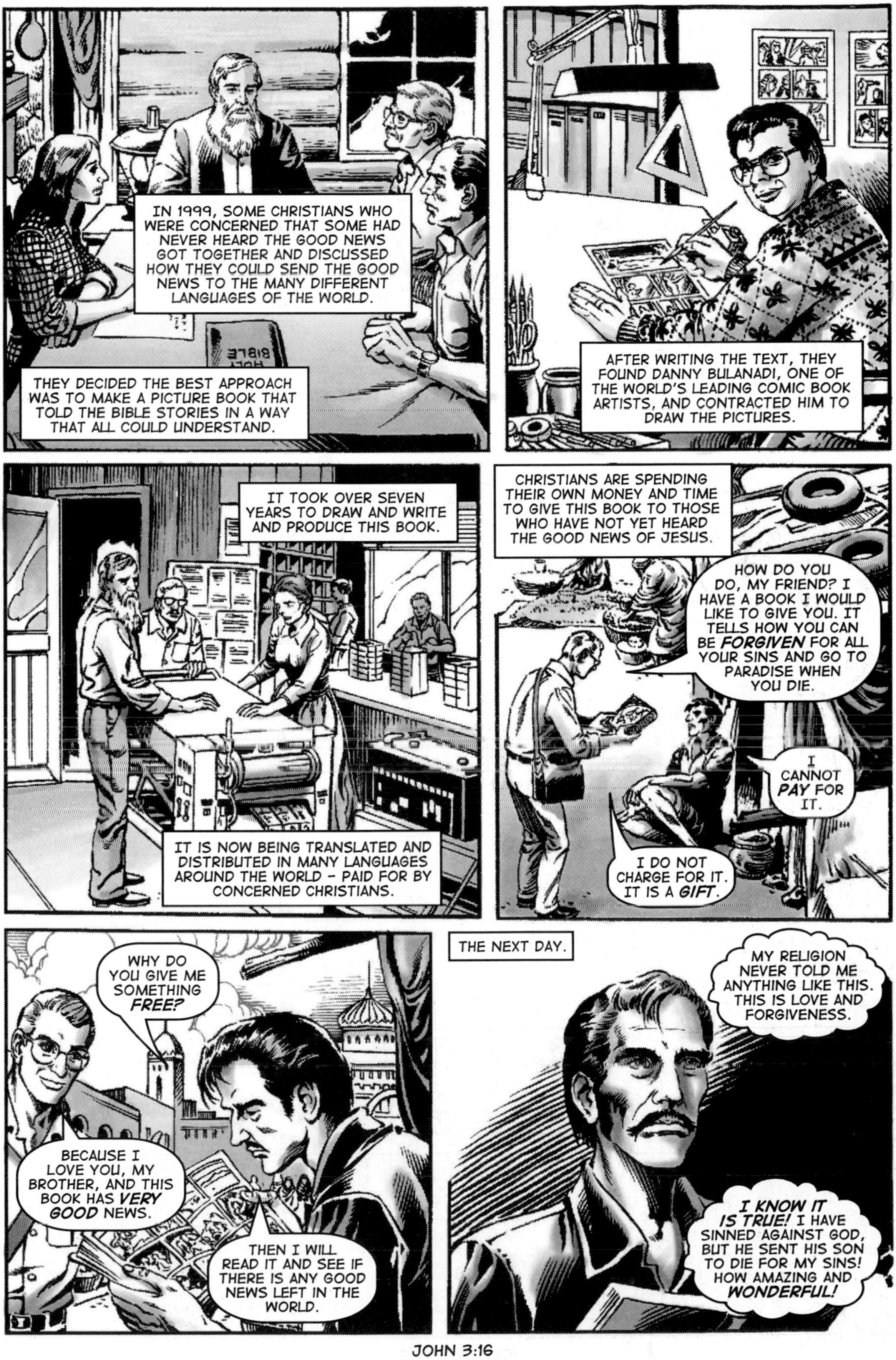
IN 1999, SOME CHRISTIANS WHO WERE CONCERNED THAT SOME HAD NEVER HEARD THE GOOD NEWS GOT TOGETHER AND DISCUSSED HOW THEY COULD SEND THE GOOD NEWS TO THE MANY DIFFERENT LANGUAGES OF THE WORLD.
HOLY BIBLE
THEY DECIDED THE BEST APPROACH WAS TO MAKE A PICTURE BOOK THAT TOLD THE BIBLE STORIES IN A WAY THAT ALL COULD UNDERSTAND.
AFTER WRITING THE TEXT, THEY FOUND DANNY BULANADI, ONE OF THE WORLD'S LEADING COMIC BOOK ARTISTS, AND CONTRACTED HIM TO DRAW THE PICTURES.
IT TOOK OVER SEVEN YEARS TO DRAW AND WRITE AND PRODUCE THIS BOOK.
IT IS NOW BEING TRANSLATED AND DISTRIBUTED IN MANY LANGUAGES AROUND THE WORLD - PAID FOR BY CONCERNED CHRISTIANS.
CHRISTIANS ARE SPENDING THEIR OWN MONEY AND TIME TO GIVE THIS BOOK TO THOSE WHO HAVE NOT YET HEARD THE GOOD NEWS OF JESUS.
HOW DO YOU DO, MY FRIEND? I HAVE A BOOK I WOULD LIKE TO GIVE YOU. IT TELLS HOW YOU CAN BE FORGIVEN FOR ALL YOUR SINS AND GO TO PARADISE WHEN YOU DIE.
I CANNOT PAY FOR IT.
I DO NOT CHARGE FOR IT. IT IS A GIFT.
WHY DO YOU GIVE ME SOMETHING FREE?
BECAUSE I LOVE YOU, MY BROTHER, AND THIS BOOK HAS VERY GOOD NEWS.
THEN I WILL READ IT AND SEE IF THERE IS ANY GOOD NEWS LEFT IN THE WORLD.
THE NEXT DAY.
MY RELIGION NEVER TOLD ME ANYTHING LIKE THIS. THIS IS LOVE AND FORGIVENESS.
I KNOW IT IS TRUE! I HAVE SINNED AGAINST GOD, BUT HE SENT HIS SON TO DIE FOR MY SINS! HOW AMAZING AND WONDERFUL!

JOHN 3:16

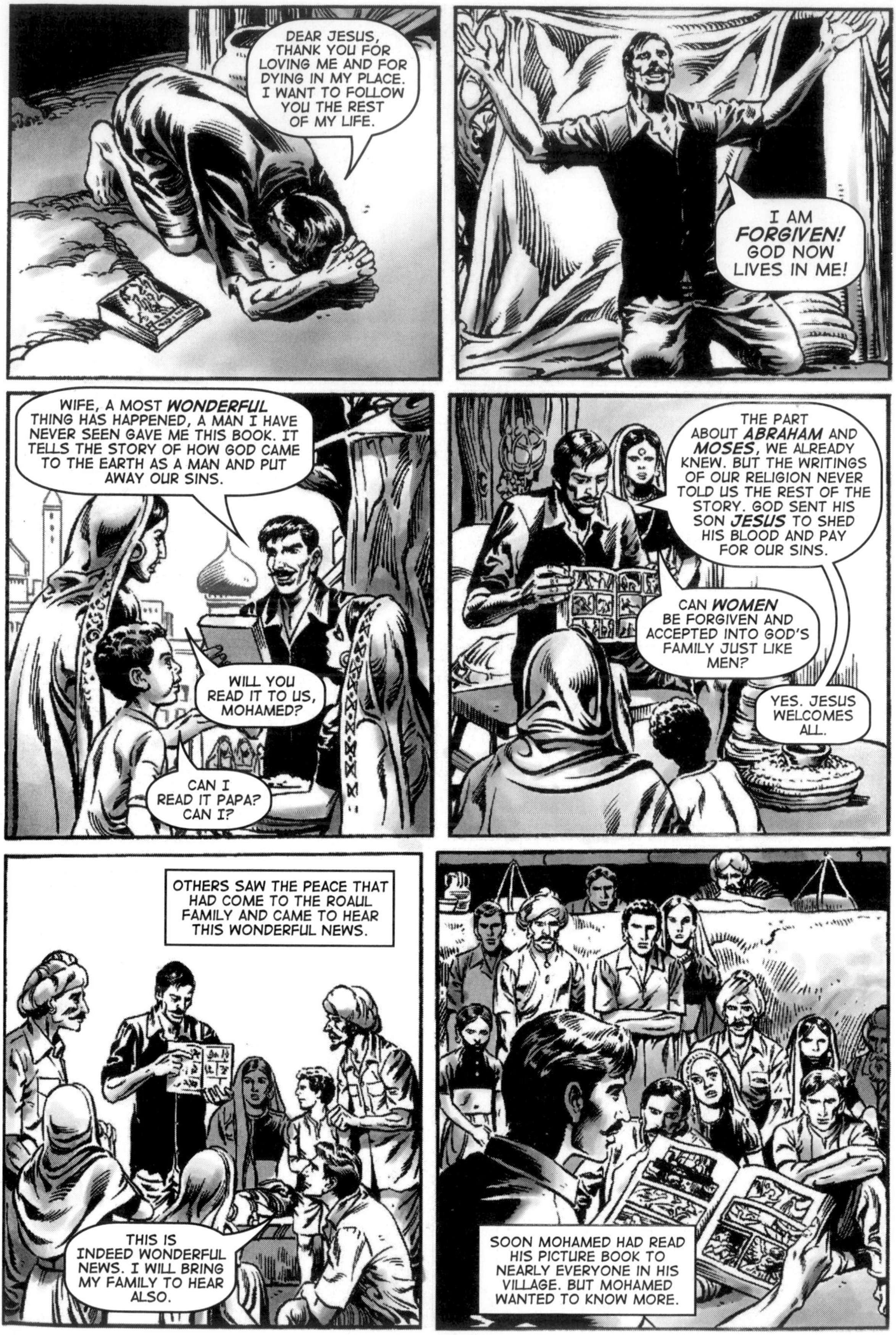
DEAR JESUS, THANK YOU FOR LOVING ME AND FOR DYING IN MY PLACE. I WANT TO FOLLOW YOU THE REST OF MY LIFE.
I AM FORGIVEN! GOD NOW LIVES IN ME!
WIFE, A MOST WONDERFUL THING HAS HAPPENED, A MAN I HAVE NEVER SEEN GAVE ME THIS BOOK. IT TELLS THE STORY OF HOW GOD CAME TO THE EARTH AS A MAN AND PUT AWAY OUR SINS.
WILL YOU READ IT TO US, MOHAMED?
CAN I READ IT PAPA? CAN I?
THE PART ABOUT ABRAHAM AND MOSES, WE ALREADY KNEW. BUT THE WRITINGS OF OUR RELIGION NEVER TOLD US THE REST OF THE STORY. GOD SENT HIS SON JESUS TO SHED HIS BLOOD AND PAY FOR OUR SINS.
CAN WOMEN BE FORGIVEN AND ACCEPTED INTO GOD'S FAMILY JUST LIKE MEN?
YES. JESUS WELCOMES ALL.
OTHERS SAW THE PEACE THAT HAD COME TO THE ROAUL FAMILY AND CAME TO HEAR THIS WONDERFUL NEWS.
THIS IS INDEED WONDERFUL NEWS. I WILL BRING MY FAMILY TO HEAR ALSO.
SOON MOHAMED HAD READ HIS PICTURE BOOK TO NEARLY EVERYONE IN HIS VILLAGE. BUT MOHAMED WANTED TO KNOW MORE.

ROMANS 3:23, 6:23, 10:9

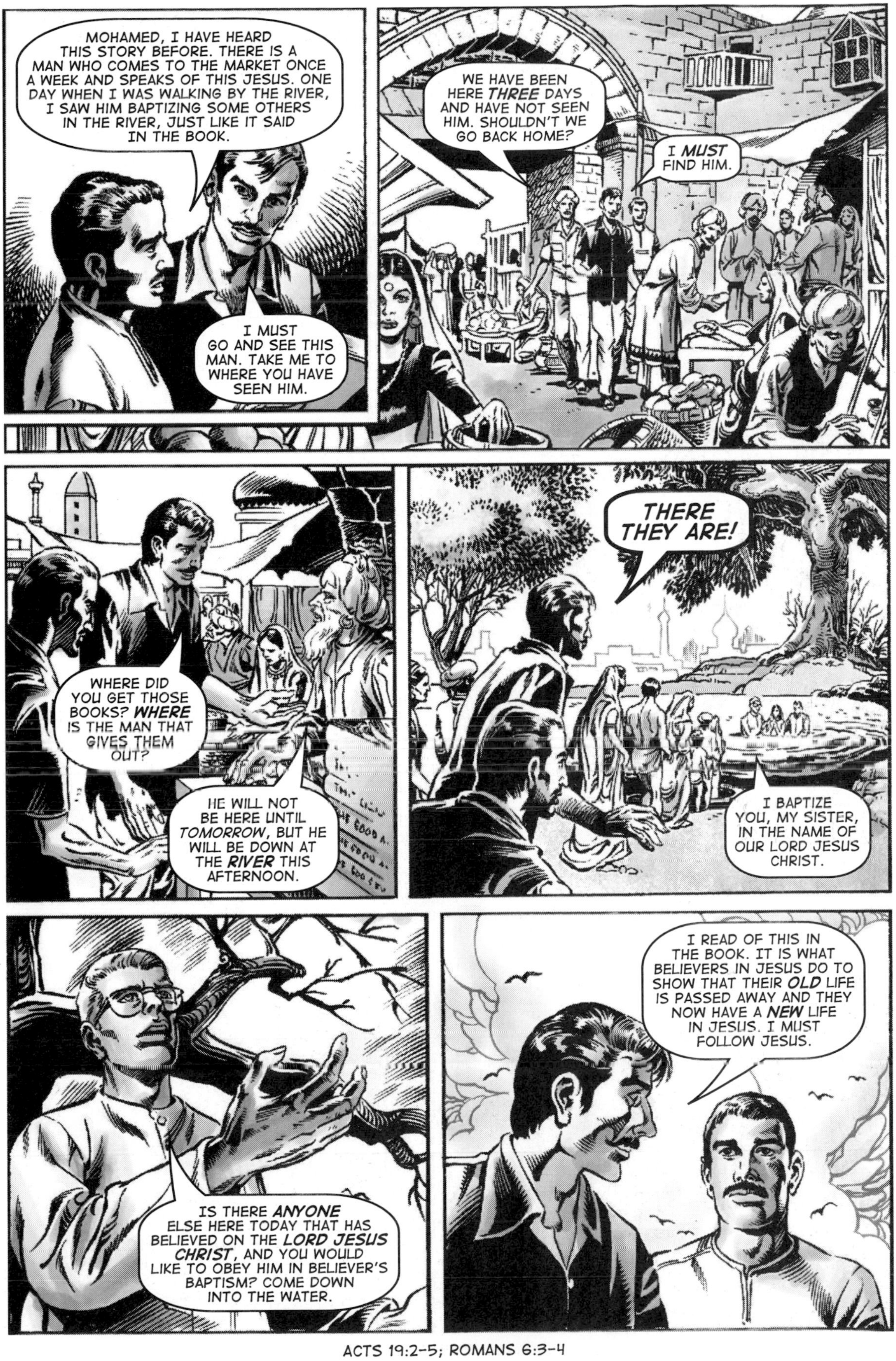
MOHAMED, I HAVE HEARD THIS STORY BEFORE. THERE IS A MAN WHO COMES TO THE MARKET ONCE A WEEK AND SPEAKS OF THIS JESUS. ONE DAY WHEN I WAS WALKING BY THE RIVER, I SAW HIM BAPTIZING SOME OTHERS IN THE RIVER, JUST LIKE IT SAID IN THE BOOK.
I MUST GO AND SEE THIS MAN. TAKE ME TO WHERE YOU HAVE SEEN HIM.
WE HAVE BEEN HERE THREE DAYS AND HAVE NOT SEEN HIM. SHOULDN'T WE GO BACK HOME?
I MUST FIND HIM.
WHERE DID YOU GET THOSE BOOKS? WHERE IS THE MAN THAT GIVES THEM OUT?
HE WILL NOT BE HERE UNTIL TOMORROW, BUT HE WILL BE DOWN AT THE RIVER THIS AFTERNOON.
THERE THEY ARE!
I BAPTIZE YOU, MY SISTER, IN THE NAME OF OUR LORD JESUS CHRIST.
IS THERE ANYONE ELSE HERE TODAY THAT HAS BELIEVED ON THE LORD JESUS CHRIST, AND YOU WOULD LIKE TO OBEY HIM IN BELIEVER'S BAPTISM? COME DOWN INTO THE WATER.
I READ OF THIS IN THE BOOK. IT IS WHAT BELIEVERS IN JESUS DO TO SHOW THAT THEIR OLD LIFE IS PASSED AWAY AND THEY NOW HAVE A NEW LIFE IN JESUS. I MUST FOLLOW JESUS.

ACTS 19:2-5; ROMANS 6:3-4

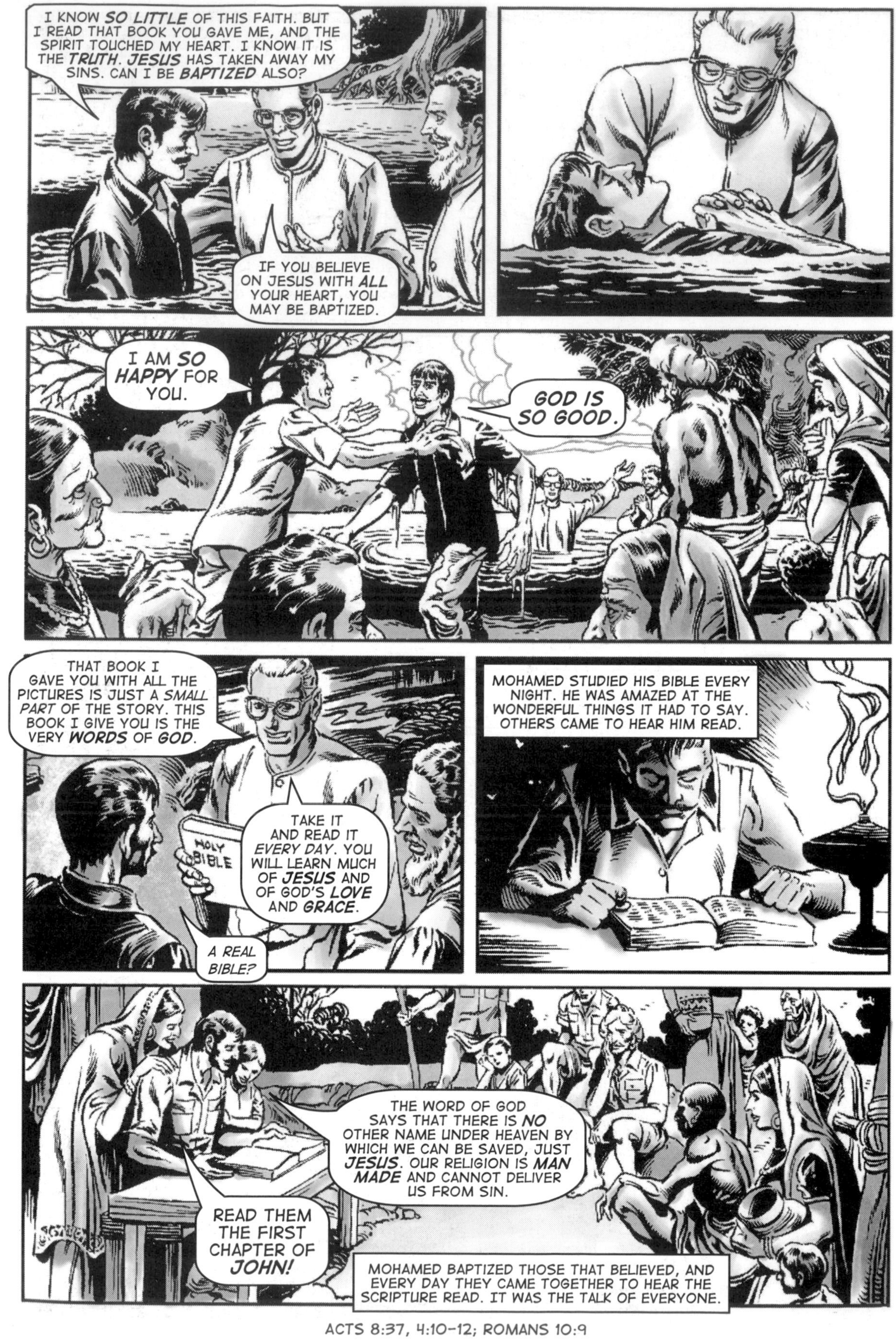
I KNOW SO LITTLE OF THIS FAITH. BUT I READ THAT BOOK YOU GAVE ME, AND THE SPIRIT TOUCHED MY HEART. I KNOW IT IS THE TRUTH. JESUS HAS TAKEN AWAY MY SINS. CAN I BE BAPTIZED ALSO?
IF YOU BELIEVE ON JESUS WITH ALL YOUR HEART, YOU MAY BE BAPTIZED.
I AM SO HAPPY FOR YOU.
GOD IS SO GOOD.
THAT BOOK I GAVE YOU WITH ALL THE PICTURES IS JUST A SMALL PART OF THE STORY. THIS BOOK I GIVE YOU IS THE VERY WORDS OF GOD.
HOLY BIBLE
TAKE IT AND READ IT EVERY DAY. YOU WILL LEARN MUCH OF JESUS AND OF GOD'S LOVE AND GRACE.
A REAL BIBLE?
MOHAMED STUDIED HIS BIBLE EVERY NIGHT. HE WAS AMAZED AT THE WONDERFUL THINGS IT HAD TO SAY. OTHERS CAME TO HEAR HIM READ.
THE WORD OF GOD SAYS THAT THERE IS NO OTHER NAME UNDER HEAVEN BY WHICH WE CAN BE SAVED, JUST JESUS. OUR RELIGION IS MAN MADE AND CANNOT DELIVER US FROM SIN.
READ THEM THE FIRST CHAPTER OF JOHN!
MOHAMED BAPTIZED THOSE THAT BELIEVED, AND EVERY DAY THEY CAME TOGETHER TO HEAR THE SCRIPTURE READ. IT WAS THE TALK OF EVERYONE.

ACTS 8:37, 4:10-12; ROMANS 10:9

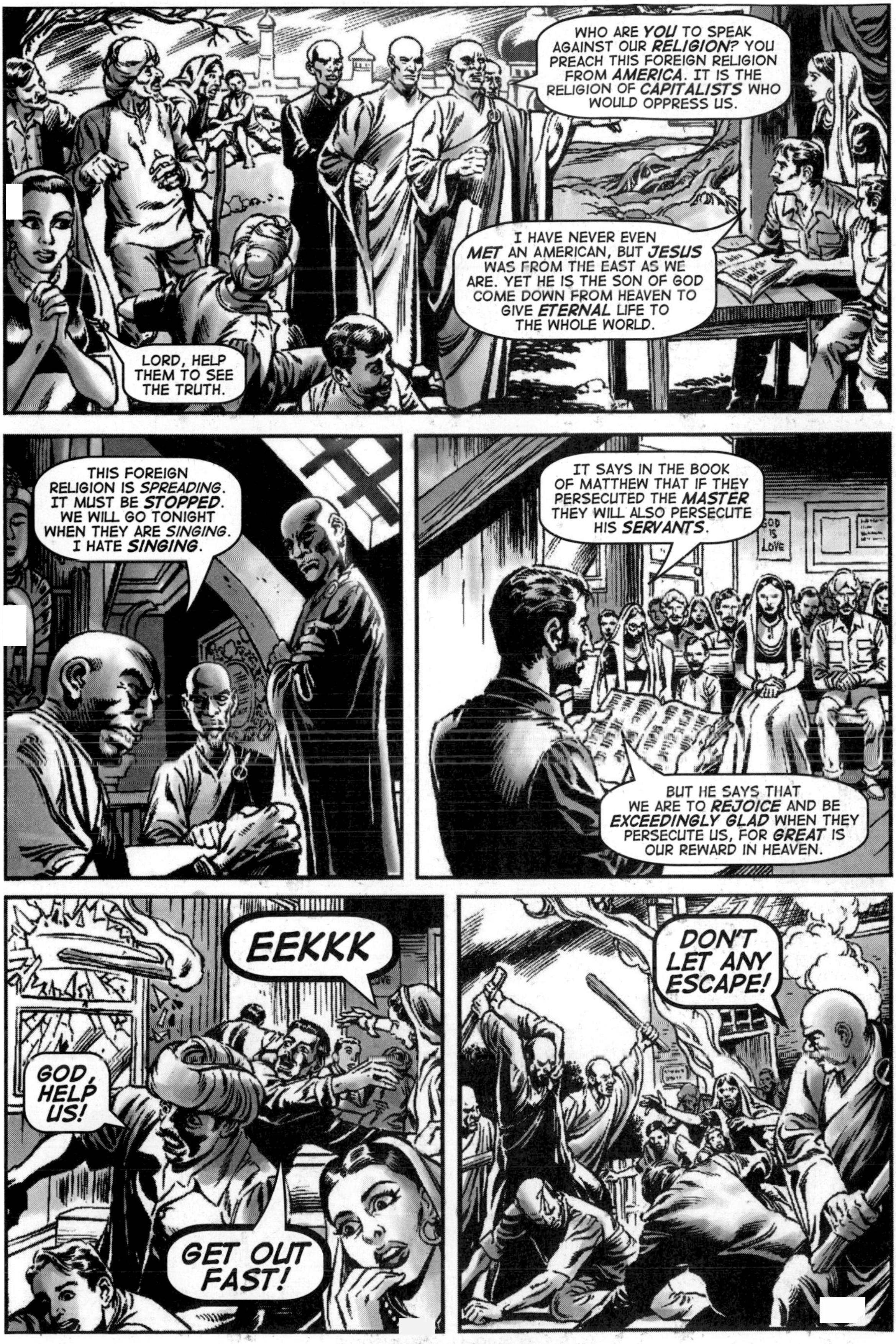
WHO ARE YOU TO SPEAK AGAINST OUR RELIGION? YOU PREACH THIS FOREIGN RELIGION FROM AMERICA. IT IS THE RELIGION OF CAPITALISTS WHO WOULD OPPRESS US.
I HAVE NEVER EVEN MET AN AMERICAN, BUT JESUS WAS FROM THE EAST AS WE ARE. YET HE IS THE SON OF GOD COME DOWN FROM HEAVEN TO GIVE ETERNAL LIFE TO THE WHOLE WORLD.
LORD, HELP THEM TO SEE THE TRUTH.
THIS FOREIGN RELIGION IS SPREADING. IT MUST BE STOPPED. WE WILL GO TONIGHT WHEN THEY ARE SINGING. I HATE SINGING.
IT SAYS IN THE BOOK OF MATTHEW THAT IF THEY PERSECUTED THE MASTER THEY WILL ALSO PERSECUTE HIS SERVANTS.
GOD IS LOVE
BUT HE SAYS THAT WE ARE TO REJOICE AND BE EXCEEDINGLY GLAD WHEN THEY PERSECUTE US, FOR GREAT IS OUR REWARD IN HEAVEN.
EEKKK
GOD, HELP US!
GET OUT FAST!
DON'T LET ANY ESCAPE!

JOHN 15:20; MATTHEW 5:11-12

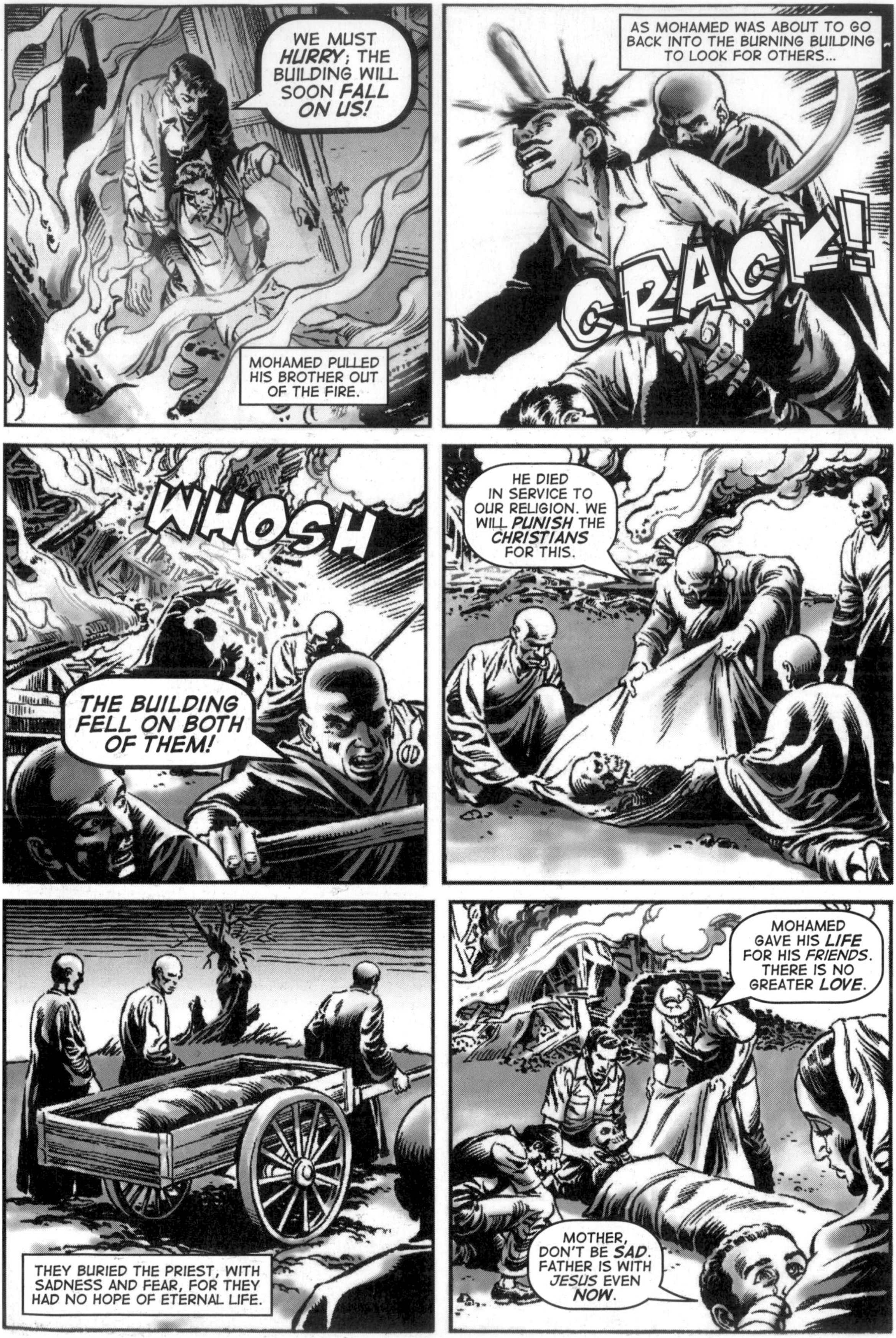
WE MUST HURRY; THE BUILDING WILL SOON FALL ON US!
MOHAMED PULLED HIS BROTHER OUT OF THE FIRE.
AS MOHAMED WAS ABOUT TO GO BACK INTO THE BURNING BUILDING TO LOOK FOR OTHERS...
CRACK!
WHOSH
THE BUILDING FELL ON BOTH OF THEM!
HE DIED IN SERVICE TO OUR RELIGION. WE WILL PUNISH THE CHRISTIANS FOR THIS.
THEY BURIED THE PRIEST, WITH SADNESS AND FEAR, FOR THEY HAD NO HOPE OF ETERNAL LIFE.
MOHAMED GAVE HIS LIFE FOR HIS FRIENDS. THERE IS NO GREATER LOVE.
MOTHER, DON'T BE SAD. FATHER IS WITH JESUS EVEN NOW.

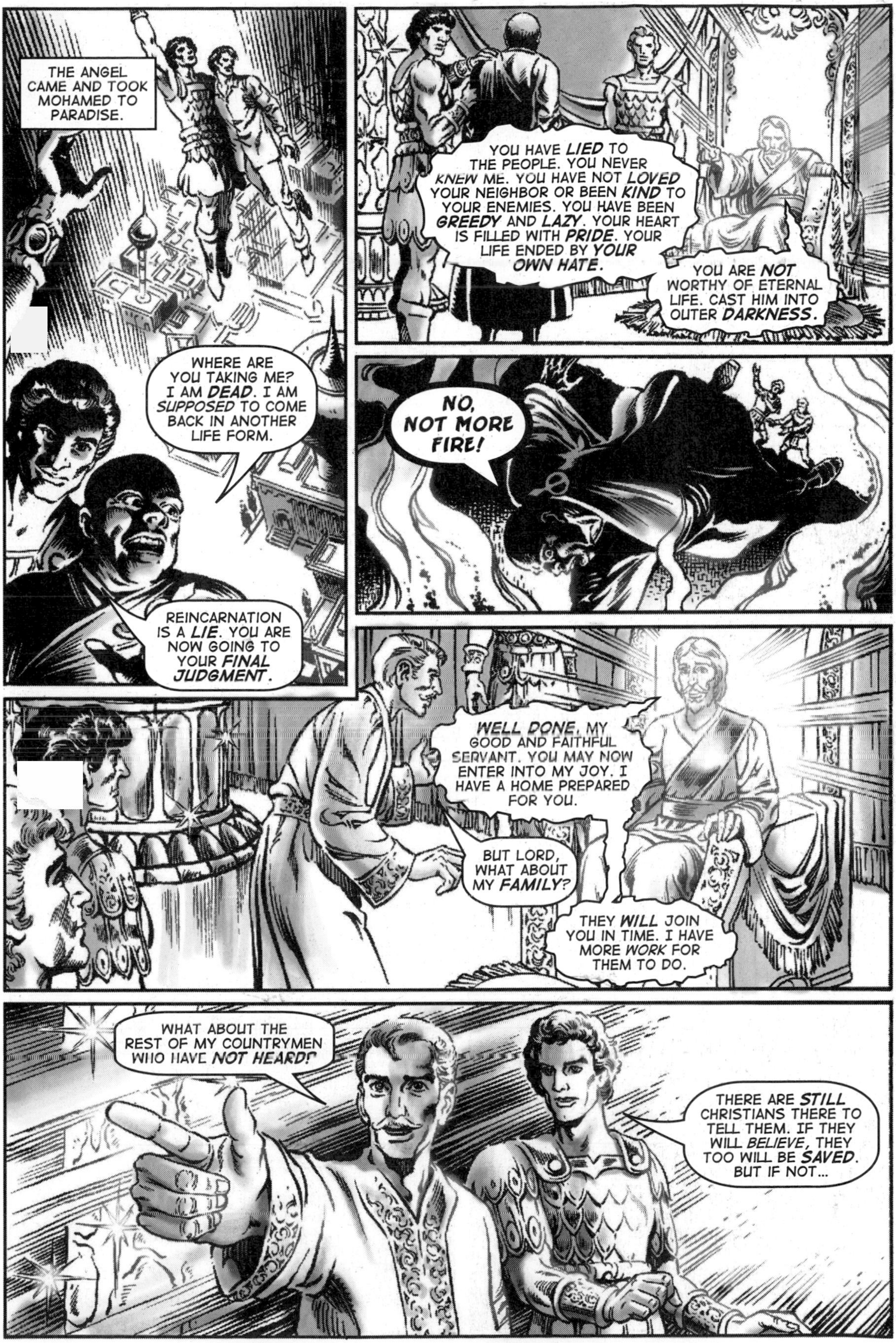
THE ANGEL CAME AND TOOK MOHAMED TO PARADISE.
WHERE ARE YOU TAKING ME? I AM DEAD. I AM SUPPOSED TO COME BACK IN ANOTHER LIFE FORM.
REINCARNATION IS A LIE. YOU ARE NOW GOING TO YOUR FINAL JUDGMENT.
YOU HAVE LIED TO THE PEOPLE. YOU NEVER KNEW ME. YOU HAVE NOT LOVED YOUR NEIGHBOR OR BEEN KIND TO YOUR ENEMIES. YOU HAVE BEEN GREEDY AND LAZY. YOUR HEART IS FILLED WITH PRIDE. YOUR LIFE ENDED BY YOUR OWN HATE.
YOU ARE NOT WORTHY OF ETERNAL LIFE. CAST HIM INTO OUTER DARKNESS.
NO, NOT MORE FIRE!
WELL DONE, MY GOOD AND FAITHFUL SERVANT. YOU MAY NOW ENTER INTO MY JOY. I HAVE A HOME PREPARED FOR YOU.
BUT LORD, WHAT ABOUT MY FAMILY?
THEY WILL JOIN YOU IN TIME. I HAVE MORE WORK FOR THEM TO DO.
WHAT ABOUT THE REST OF MY COUNTRYMEN WHO HAVE NOT HEARD?
THERE ARE STILL CHRISTIANS THERE TO TELL THEM. IF THEY WILL BELIEVE, THEY TOO WILL BE SAVED. BUT IF NOT...

MATTHEW 7:21-27, 25:21, 25:30; 1 CORINTHIANS 6:9-11; JAMES 4:11-17

THE VISION

At No Greater Joy Ministries, it is our goal to see this illustrated chronological gospel book translated and distributed into every language on the earth. That would be an impossible task for us to attempt alone. If you are a concerned Christian in a position to have this book translated into any foreign language, we are prepared to make it available to you, free of charge. We maintain the copyright in any and all languages, and are the sole distributorship in English, but for those who qualify doctrinally, we stand ready to make available to you all that you need to proceed with translation and formatting. Once it is translated into a given language, we maintain the right to make that translation available to other missionaries who are willing to print and distribute it. If you are interested in translating, contact us and we will send additional information.

As we go to print in English, Good and Evil is now being translated into the language of these countries: Cambodia, Thailand, Mongolia, Philippines, South Africa, China/Myanmar (Burma), Sweden, Peru, India, Ukraine and Suriname.

No Greater Joy Ministries
1000 Pearl Road
Pleasantville TN 37033

www.nogreaterjoy.org

If you enjoyed this book, consider these and other products by Michael and Debi Pearl that can purchased through www.nogreaterjoy.org or write to us at NGJ, 1000 Pearl Road, Pleasantville, TN 37033 for our free magazine with ordering information.

Romans - audio teaching

ROMANS

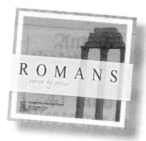

Verse by verse, word by word, this is a commentary on the book of Romans. We continually receive testimonies of lives changed and souls saved through listening to this greatest of all New Testament books. Until you know the book of Romans you don't know the Bible. If you have never listened to any Bible teaching by Michael Pearl, this is the place to start.

Available in: 20 CD set, 17 Cassette set or 1 MP3 CD

To Train Up a Child

- 500,000 In Print! -

To Train Up
A Child
Michael & Debi Pearl

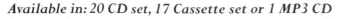

From successful parents, learn how to train up your children rather than discipline them up. With humor and real-life examples, this book shows you how to train your children before the need to discipline arises. Be done with corrective discipline; make them allies rather than adversaries. The stress will be gone and your obedient children will praise you.

122pg Book

Created to be His Help Meet

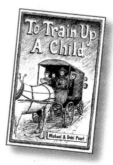

Somewhere over the passing years and changing culture, women have lost their way. This book is written to lead them back home. Regardless of how you began your marriage or how dark and lonely the path that has brought you to where you are now, I want you to know that it is possible today to have a marriage so good and so fulfilling that it can only be explained as a miracle.

What God is doing through this book is incredible! We constantly receive testimonies from women who's marriages have been renewed or restored from reading this book.

Available in: single volumes, cases of 24 (40% discount) and MP3 audio reading

By Divine Design

BY
DIVINE
DESIGN

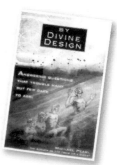

If you are philosophically minded, this book will appeal to you. Michael discusses difficult questions that trouble many: How can I believe and trust a "sovereign God" who allows so much evil? Why did God even make us capable of sinning? Why would the Creator let souls live forever in Hell and not just destroy them so they would not have to continue to suffer?

85pg Book

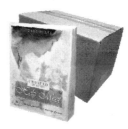

Sin No More

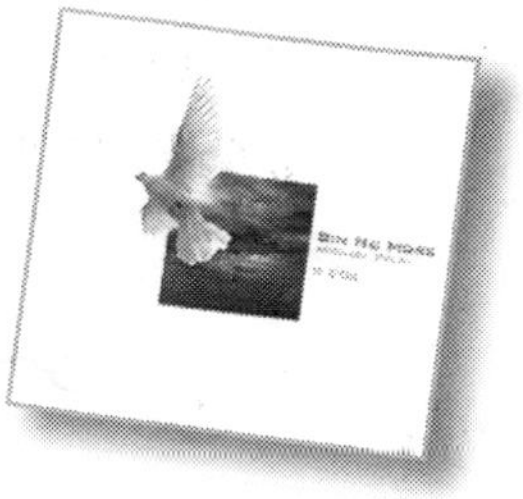

The big question is: "So how do I stop sinning?" You have confessed your sins, received the baptism of the Holy Ghost with evidence of everything but ceasing to sin; yet you are still a Romans 7 defeated Christian. I assure you, God not only saves his children from the penalty of sin but he saves them from its power as well.

You can stop sinning.

Available in 7 Cassette set or 9 CD set

Righteousness

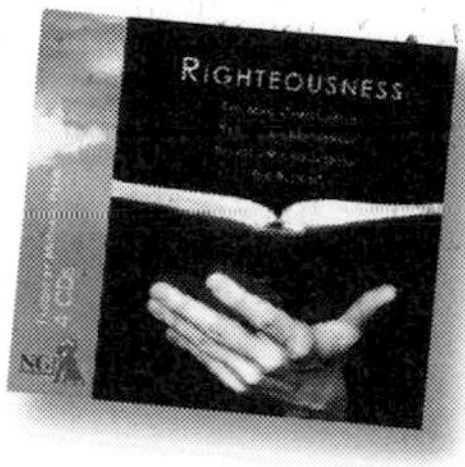
RIGHTEOUSNESS

This set contains four messages on salvation and righteousness: The Man Christ Jesus, Saving Righteousness, Imputed Righteousness and The Blood. The messages explore intriguing topics such as the humanity of Christ and why he refered to himself as "The Son of Man", why man's blood is required when he spills the blood of another man, God's clearly defined method of making a person righteous enough to get to heaven and how the blood of Jesus washes away our sins.

Available in a 3 Cassette set or a 4 CD set

Free Online Resources

There is a wealth of free resources and materials on our website, www.nogreaterjoy.org. The entire teaching of Romans is available for free download as well as the Am I Saved? series and a new weekly Bible teaching every Saturday. Read or listen to excerpts of many of our products or browse our topical archive of over 240 past NGJ magazine articles on subjects from child training to homemade herbal tinctures.

The store also offers several free products for ministry use, just tell us how many you want and we'll send it to you.

www. NoGreaterJoy.org

Free Magazine Subscription

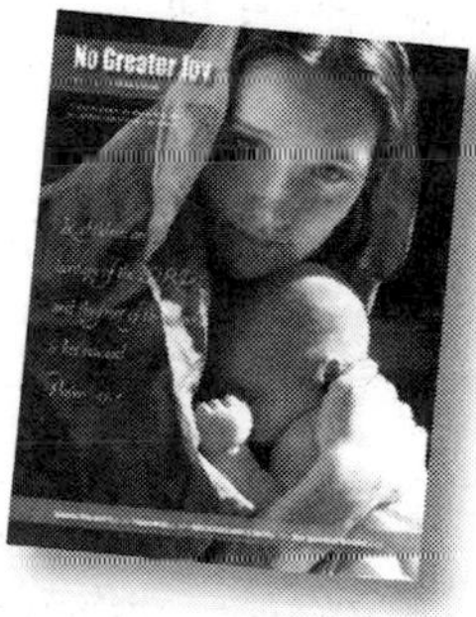
No Greater Joy

No Greater Joy Ministries Inc. publishes a bimonthly magazine with answers to questions received in the mail. The 24-page magazine covers topics such as child training, family relationships, homeschooling and Bible teaching.

Send your name and mailing address to NGJ, 1000 Pearl Road, Pleasantville TN 37033, and we will put you on our mailing list. Your information is confidential and will not be shared with anyone. If you are on our mailing list, you will also receive notification of when the Pearls are speaking in your area.

You can also read additional material on our website www.nogreaterjoy.org or you can sign up on our website to receive No Greater Joy.